HANDBOOK
OF
EQUIPMENT
LEASING
Second Edition

HANDBOOK OF EQUIPMENT LEASING
A Deal Maker's Guide
Second Edition

Richard M. Contino

amacom

American Management Association

New York • Atlanta • Boston • Chicago • Kansas City San Francisco • Washington, D.C.
Brussels • Mexico City • Tokyo • Toronto

Library of Congress Cataloging-in-Publication Data

Contino, Richard M., 1941–
    Handbook of equipment leasing : a deal maker's guide /
Richard M. Contino.—2nd ed.
      p.   cm.
    Includes index.
    ISBN 0-8144-0317-4 (hardcover)
    1. Industrial equipment leases—United States—Handbooks,
manuals, etc.   2. Lease or buy decisions—Handbooks, manuals,
etc.
    I. Title.
    HD39.4.C66   1996.
    658.15'242—dc20

                                          96-15977
                                                CIP

10 9 8 7 6 5 4

To May-Lynne and my father
In the future there is no past

Table of Contents

Chapter 5   Depreciation Advantages in Lease Transactions   107

Introduction
PART I: DEPRECIATION AFTER 1986

PART II: ACRS DEDUCTIONS

PART III: PRE-1981 DEPRECIATION

Chapter 6   The Minimum Tax's Role in Leasing   130

Introduction
PART I: THE CORPORATE AMT

Chapter 1

The Fundamentals of Equipment Leasing

A. Overview

The concept of the lease as a property right, as well as the rights and duties of lessors and lessees, has been part of our legal tradition for centuries, particularly with respect to real estate. During the 1950s, leasing began to emerge as a viable alternative to purchasing for acquiring equipment. Today, the equipment leasing industry plays a major role in the financial community: A user can lease virtually any type of equipment on a variety of terms. There is, however, a drawback: The legal requirements and financial considerations are, at times, extremely complex. In fact, many transactions involve concepts so sophisticated that even the most experienced people sometimes make mistakes that could cost them or their customers thousands of dollars.

The interest in leasing as an alternative means of acquiring equipment continues to prompt a deluge of questions not only from equipment users but also from the legal and financial community. For example:

- What are the tax advantages and disadvantages to the lessee?
- What are the tax benefits available to the lessor?
- What is the best business structure for a lease?
- How should a lease transaction be analyzed from a financial viewpoint?
- How are leases treated for accounting purposes?
- What are the leasing risks?

For these, and many other questions, there are no easy answers.

The 1986 Tax Reform Act (1986 TRA) took away the investment tax credit (ITC) and expanded the alternative minimum tax (AMT). The economic downturn of the late 1980s and early 1990s has sparked suggestions of new tax law changes to stimulate business, changes that could have a significant impact on leasing, and that could create new questions, issues, and business challenges. For the lessor and the prospective lessee, the tax aspects of leasing can be frustrating and can create uncertainties.

Unfortunately, because of the many variables involved in a lease decision, no book can presume to answer all the questions concerning the criteria for, and desirability of, entering into every conceivable transaction. In addition, the desirability of leasing and the lease evaluation criteria used by one company may be totally inappropriate for another company. This book will, however, provide the reader with a comprehensive working knowledge of the fundamental tools necessary to handle competently any lease situation from start to finish. The relevant issues that must be taken into account in developing a solid financing approach will be identified, described, and explained.

This chapter sets the stage for the following chapters. After briefly reviewing the tax motivations behind leasing transactions, it describes the major players (the typical lessees and lessors), explains the types of leases commonly offered, and then sets out what equipment users should consider when deciding to enter the leasing arena.

B. Tax Motivations of Leasing

1. The General Tax Picture

Although any type of equipment can be leased, the critical question for the prospective lessee is—at what cost? While the answer is complex, as a threshold matter leasing often is not an economical way to acquire equipment unless the lessor can take advantage of certain tax benefits and indirectly pass them on, at least in part, in the form of relatively lower lease rents. Consider the following hypothetical example.

> **Illustrative Example**—*The Tax Advantage:* Company Able wants to acquire the use of a $20,000 truck. It can borrow funds from its bank for five years at the prime rate, assumed for this example to be 10% a year. If Company Able were able to borrow 100% of the funds required, its cost to finance the truck would be the cost of the $20,000 loan.
>
> As an alternative, Company Able could lease the truck from Company Baker. Assume Company Baker also borrowed "at prime" from the same bank and that it would fund the truck purchase entirely from its bank borrowing. If there were no truck ownership tax advantages, the only way it could make a profit would be to charge a lease rate greater than its cost of funds. Thus, Company Able would have to pay something over prime rate to Company Baker, a not very attractive arrangement.

Although the above example is admittedly oversimplified and not completely realistic, it makes the point—leasing may not make any economic sense for a lessee unless the lessor is able to use available ownership tax benefits.

2. The Lessor's Tax Benefit

What tax benefits are available to the lessor? For equipment placed in service before 1986, the lessor could obtain both ITC and depreciation deductions as an equipment owner. With limited exceptions, the 1986 TRA did away with the ITC for equipment placed in service after 1985. Thus, the tax benefits for the lessor today are the depreciation deductions available under the Modified Accelerated Cost Recovery System (MACRS), introduced by the 1986 TRA.

Under MACRS, a lessor generally can write off its equipment's cost over a period significantly shorter than the equipment's useful life and at an accelerated rate. For example, a lessor can deduct the cost of leased computer equipment over a six-year period with the percentages for each year as 20%, 32%, 19.2%, 11.52%, 11.52%, and 5.76%. In a typical lease, the lessor's deductions in the early years will exceed the rental income, permitting the lessor to offset other income with those excess deductions.

▶ **Word of Warning:** As explained in Chapter 6, if the lessor is subject to the revised corporate and individual AMTs, its depreciation deductions will be deferred significantly. This in turn could have a major impact on what rents should be charged. Therefore, potential lessors must review their AMT exposure when pricing a leasing transaction.

3. The Lessee's Tax Consequences

Basically, an equipment user decreases its tax benefits by becoming a lessee rather than an owner. As lessee, the user can deduct its rental payments, but those will be less than the depreciation it could have deducted in earlier years if it *had* purchased the equipment. Then why should leasing be considered? As explained below, there are numerous financial and business reasons for a prospective lessee to lease rather than buy. Also, leasing is particularly attractive to equipment users who cannot take timely advantage of the depreciation deductions. Two types of users basically fall into this category. First are those who have negative taxable income or carryover losses, so that they have no taxable income to offset; and second, to a lesser extent, those subject to the AMT, because the AMT would reduce the value of an equipment owner's tax benefits, but will not in most cases affect deductions for rent. For those users, the rental payments charged by a lessor who is taking ownership tax benefits into account in setting its lease rate can be worth more than the ownership tax benefits.

4. The Importance of Lease Structuring

When the lessor anticipates tax benefits, it will suffer an economic loss if those benefits are unavailable. Those benefits will be available only if the lessor remains the equipment owner for tax purposes. The lessor will be treated as the tax owner only if the lease is a true lease. To qualify as a true lease for tax purposes certain tax guidelines must be met. These guidelines are explained in Chapter 8. Although, as explained in that chapter, there is the possibility of some variation from the guidelines, it is advisable to comply with the following:

- The lessor must make an economic profit, apart from the tax benefits, on the lease.

- The lessor's equity investment must be at least 20% of the equipment's cost throughout the lease term.
- The lessee cannot, with limited exceptions, make any investment in the property, or make any loan to the lessor.
- Lessee purchase options must be at the equipment's fair market value at the time of purchase.
- The property must be usable by a party other than the lessee after the lease term's end.

Poor lease structuring can lead to disaster. If the transaction does not qualify as a true lease, the lessee will not be able to deduct the rental payments and the lessor cannot use the ownership tax benefits. For example, if the lease is classified as a loan, the lessee is deemed the equipment owner and the lessor deemed the lender. Then, if the lessee cannot use any tax benefits and the lessor must have them for the transaction to make economic sense, everyone loses.

▶ **Observation:**   While all leases must be true leases for the lessor to obtain tax benefits, for leases where the lease term is significantly shorter than the equipment's useful life, there will be little risk that the lease will not be treated as a true lease, because the lessor's ownership status will be clear. Generally, the closer the lease term comes to matching the equipment's useful life, the more attention that must be paid to the true lease rules.

C.   Who Are the Prospective Lessees?

Any equipment user is a prospective lessee. The users can range from multinational corporations, to sole proprietorships, to individuals using equipment for personal reasons. Whether or not the user should lease is another, more complicated question, and depends on a variety of factors that vary with each situation. These factors are reviewed in Section F of this chapter.

D.   Who Are the Potential Lessors?

In theory, any company in the financing business can be a potential lessor of equipment. However, because of the competitive nature of equipment leasing and the expertise required, only certain types of organizations are actively in the leasing market.

For discussion purposes, it is useful to separate the potential lessors into five categories: individuals, independent leasing companies, lease brokers, captive leasing companies, and banks. Prospective lessees will find the categories helpful in narrowing the field of potential lessors. And prospective lessors may find the categories helpful in determining their potential competition.

1. Individuals

Prior to the 1986 TRA, the role of the individual as lessor was limited because of the rules restricting an individual from claiming ITCs on leased property. Now that the ITC is no longer available to lessors, wealthy individuals can be more rate competitive. This coupled with the fact that they often will take greater business risks than a traditional leasing company can make them a good choice in difficult financing situations. A few innovative equipment leasing companies and investment bankers have begun to develop interesting investment programs for individuals that will make them an increasing part of the equipment financing business. For example, some railcar lessors have set up individual investor programs that provide individuals with opportunities to invest in short-term railcar leases.

An individual considering becoming an equipment lessor must, however, now contend with the passive loss rules. An explanation of those rules is outside the scope of this book, and the reader is generally referred to Internal Revenue Code Section 469 for further information. A prospective lessee receiving a lease proposal from an individual lessor, however, need not be concerned with the passive loss rules, except to be sure that any indemnities do not require the lessee to reimburse the lessor for deductions lost under those rules.

▶ **A Word of Caution:** A prospective lessee considering leasing from an individual must look at more than the rent advantage. For example, because individuals often take aggressive tax positions, they may run afoul of the income tax laws. The IRS may then put a lien on all the individual's property, including the leased equipment. Also, individuals can be somewhat more arbitrary to deal with when variances from the lease terms are required.

2. Independent Leasing Companies

Independent leasing companies provide a major source of equipment lease financing. Because leasing is their principal source of revenue, they have to be extremely aggressive and, in some cases, are willing to bend the rules for the lessee's benefit to win a transaction. For example, some will give a lessee the right to buy the equipment at a low predetermined fixed price when the lease ends—a practice that can run the risk of adverse tax consequences. (See Chapter 8,C,6.)

There are two types of independent leasing companies: those that merely buy and lease equipment to the user ("finance leasing companies"); and those that also offer other services, such as maintenance and repair of the equipment ("service leasing companies").

a. Finance Leasing Companies

Finance leasing companies—lessors of millions of dollars worth of equipment each year—operate in much the same manner as banks or other financing companies. They do not maintain an equipment inventory, but rather, after agreeing on a lease with a lessee, buy the specific equipment needed for the lease. The lessee orders and receives the equipment from the vendor. When it arrives, the finance leasing company pays for it, takes title, and leases it to the equipment user.

Finance leasing companies typically write leases—referred to as finance leases—that run from 70 to 80% of the equipment's useful life. The total amounts received under these leases, including the rents payable and the equipment residual value proceeds, are usually sufficient to provide the lessor with a full return of his equipment investment and a profit. If the equipment purchase is leveraged with third-party debt, the rents will also be generally enough to cover the full repayment of the debt. This type of long-term lease is generally net to the lessee. That is, the lessee must assume substantially all the equipment ownership responsibilities, such as maintenance, taxes, and insurance.

b.   Service Leasing Companies

Service leasing companies provide nonfinancial services to lessees in addition to the equipment financing. Services may include equipment maintenance and repair or advice on the equipment's operation and design.

Service lessors typically limit their activity to a single type of equipment, such as computers, or to a single type of industry, such as the mining industry. The intense experience gained through the specialization enables them to reduce many leasing risks. For example, because they frequently handle used equipment, they know how to deal efficiently with equipment when it comes off lease, which, in turn, reduces their re-leasing or sale risk. Because of that reduced risk, they can offer attractive lease termination or equipment exchange privileges.

▶ **Observation:**   Many industry participants believe that product specialization is less risky for a lessor than industry specialization. *Reason:* There is a greater likelihood that an industry specialized lessor would suffer more if its industry hit hard times than an equipment specialized lessor would if one of the industries in which its equipment was used hit hard times.

Service lessors typically write leases with much shorter lease terms than finance leases. Nonpayout in nature, those leases do not permit the lessor to recoup its entire equipment investment during the first lease term. Thus, to recover its investment and make a profit, the service lessor must continue to re-lease the equipment. If the equipment becomes obsolete sooner than expected, the lessor may incur a loss. To be compensated for taking that high risk, and for providing other services, service lessors will generally charge higher rents than finance lessors.

When should a prospective lessee consider using a service leasing company? Basically, when the lessee needs the specialized services offered by the service lessor or wants a shorter lease term or early termination rights. A user may want the shorter term, when, for example, there is a high risk of equipment obsolescence or where the user's industry is in a down cycle.

▶ **Recommendation:**   A prospective lessee considering leasing equipment that it may want to return early should compare the higher rents typically payable under a shorter-term lease offered by service lessors against the lower rents, and early termination penalty, typically payable under a longer-term finance lease offered by financial lessors. Frequently, the short-term lease is economically preferable, because finance lease termination penalties are often substantial. *Reason:*

Financial lessors do not have as strong a remarketing capability as the service lessors.

3. Lease Brokers

Also referred to as "lease underwriters" or "syndicators," lease brokers package lease transactions for the account of third parties. Put simply, they match up prospective lessees with prospective lessor-investors. They charge a fee for their service—usually ranging from 0.75 to 8% of the leased equipment's cost—that is typically paid for by the lessor-investors.

To put the lease broker's role into perspective, it is helpful to understand how a broker normally operates. Generally, a lease broker begins by contacting all types of equipment users and vendors to determine whether they have any leasing needs. In the case of a prospective lessee, the lease broker will define the rough parameters through discussions with the prospective lessee. At this juncture, the broker may perform a credit check on the prospective lessee to make sure the credit is marketable. If there are not any problems, the broker will formulate a concise lease structure, including rental rate, and offer it to the equipment user, generally through a formal proposal letter.

If the user finds the proposed arrangement acceptable, the broker then proceeds to find prospective lessor-investors, commonly referred to as equity participants, or, in the case of smaller transactions, a leasing company. If the transaction is to be leveraged with third-party debt, a leverage lease, it may also put out feelers for prospective lenders, commonly referred to as debt participants, although usually the debt side is handled by an investment banker. Having located the equity and debt participants, the broker proceeds to shepherd the transaction through documentation to completion.

Although generally acting exclusively as a broker, a lease underwriter may, on occasion, invest some of its own funds in the equipment along with other third-party lessor-investors and, thereby, become a part owner. By doing so, the lease underwriter can add credibility to the investment and thus be able to sell the lease transaction to potential investors more readily.

One of a lease broker's major assets is its knowledge of the leasing industry. Because the broker is continually in the market, it will know where to find competitive, cooperative, and realistic equity participants. And it will know how to get those equity participants to agree to what meets the lessee's needs, including, for example, lease rates, overall transaction structure, and documentation.

▶ **Recommendations:**

- A prospective lessee considering a finance lease arrangement should invite a cross section of brokers to quote, in addition to regular lessors. Because of their ability to find aggressive equity participants, lease brokers will add a new dimension to the bidding environment.
- There is a risk in dealing with brokers for a prospective lessee. If they can not find the funding participants, the prospective lessee must start over looking for financing. A prospective lessee, therefore, should put some realistic performance time limits on any broker arranging the funding, and

plan for any nonperformance possibilities by, for example, having a backup leasing company ready in the event there is a funding problem.

4. *Captive Leasing Companies*

In increasing numbers, equipment vendors are setting up their own leasing companies, generally referred to as captive leasing companies, to service their customers. Although the purpose is usually to offer lease financing on equipment sold by an affiliated company, some captive leasing companies also may be willing to buy and lease equipment sold by a nonaffiliated company.

A captive leasing company marketing its affiliated company's equipment can often offer attractive rates. *Reason:* When it markets its affiliated company's equipment, that company makes a sale profit, and the captive lessor can then work with a lower financing profit than other types of lessors. Coupled with its knowledge of the equipment's potential residual value, this can result in attractive rents for a lessee.

▶ **Recommendation:**   When considering a certain vendor's equipment, a prospective lessee should always find out if the vendor has a captive leasing company. If so, the vendor's captive leasing company should be asked to submit a lease quotation.

▶ **Observation:**   Although captive leasing companies have a theoretical advantage over other types of lessors because of their connection with the vendor, in practice they often do not know how to take advantage of that position effectively. Perhaps this is because the equipment vendors do not have extensive experience in using leasing as a marketing tool and may not support the leasing operation as fully as they should.

5. *Banks*

Many banks, particularly national banks, are actively involved in equipment leasing. They usually are lessors in net finance leases because of regulatory requirements and because those leases provide the least risk and most similarity to their lending activity. (Finance leases are explained later in this chapter at Section E,1.)

Banks are not generally inclined to take aggressive equipment residual value positions, thus resulting in potentially higher market lease rates. However, in many cases, their cost of funds is lower than that of nonbank lessors, often offsetting their conservative residual value positions.

The terms and rates offered by bank lessors often vary significantly from one transaction to the next. Internal bank policies may contribute to that variation. Banks are not as dependent as most nonbank lessors on their leasing activities for revenues and so can afford to miss out on many deals. Periodically, however, they can go on major drives for lease business and, at those times, can be extremely rate aggressive.

There is a hidden risk in dealing with banks. Since leasing is not considered their main line of business, if they experience general financial difficulties, as they did in the late 1980s and early 1990s, their leasing department is usually one of the first to go. Management's rationale is they must go back to basics to get their financial house in order. Chase Manhattan Bank's sale of their profitable leasing subsidiaries in 1991 is a good example of what can happen when a bank experiences general financial problems.

▶ **Recommendation:** Given the unpredictability of bank lessors' responses to potential lease transactions and their commitment to the business, a prospective lessee is well advised to avoid relying exclusively on one to service all its financing needs.

Many bank lessors typically operate with a limited lease marketing staff. As a result, the transactions they see are fundamentally limited to those coming in through existing customers or lease brokers. Today, however, an increasing number of bank lessors are establishing strong marketing organizations and, as a group, are becoming more of a factor in the marketplace.

It is worth mentioning that banks directly participate in the leasing market in a another major way: They frequently act as lenders in leveraged lease transactions.

E.   Types of Leases

Significant differences exist among the various types of leases. Unfortunately, the industry jargon used to label the different types is sometimes less than precise. Further compounding the problem is the fact that many hybrid arrangements have surfaced that cross over the lines of the standard descriptive terminology. Once the fundamental characteristics of different leases are identified and understood, however, the confusion can be eliminated.

For explanation purposes, it will be helpful to separate all equipment leases into two main categories: financial leases and operating leases. The financial, or finance, lease typically represents a long-term lease commitment in which the sum of the rents due will approximate the equipment's purchase cost. Decisions to enter into a financial lease should be part of a company's financial, as opposed to operating, policy considerations. All equipment leases not fitting within the financial lease category can be put into the operating lease category. Because operating leases involve shorter-term financial commitments, decisions as to their use typically come within the scope of a company's operating policy.

Within those two broad categories, there are a number of basic variations: leveraged leases, nonleveraged leases, and service leases. These variations are sometimes incorrectly considered to be separate types of leases rather than what they are, descriptive forms of the basic types. For example, finance leases can be leveraged leases or nonleveraged leases, and service leases can be financial or operating in nature. However, they will be explained individually to give the reader a working perspective.

Table 1-1 sets out a general overview of some fundamental lease characteristics.

Table 1-1. Lease characteristics.

Type of Lease	Lease Term	Typical Type of Transaction	Comments
Finance lease	Substantial portion of asset's economic life	Underwritten and direct lessor	Payout-type lease
Net finance lease	Substantial portion of asset's economic life	Underwritten and direct lessor	Payout-type lease. Lessee has basically all ownership responsibilities.
Leveraged lease	Usually, substantial portion of asset's economic life	Underwritten	Usually net finance lease
Nonleveraged lease	Hours to substantial portion of asset's economic life	Direct lessor	Any lease where no third-party debt is involved
Operating lease	Hours to years	Direct lessor	Usually nonpayout

1. The Finance Lease

A common type of equipment lease, finance leases are considered long-term leases because the primary lease terms usually run for most of the equipment's useful life. Typically, the total cash flow over the term—from rents, tax savings, and equipment residual value—will be sufficient to pay back the lessor's investment, take care of his administrative expenses, pay off any equipment-related debt obligations and commissions, and provide a profit. Because they are entered into by lessors as long-term financial commitments, finance lessors usually impose a substantial repayment penalty for a lessee's early lease termination in an amount that will assure the lessor of a return of its investment and a profit, at least up to the date of termination.

Consistent with its financial nature, a finance lease is usually a net lease. A net lease means that the fundamental ownership responsibilities, such as maintaining and repairing the equipment, paying for the necessary insurance, and taking care of property, use, and sales taxes, are placed on the lessee. A net finance lease can be compared to an equipment loan in that the lessor, like a lender, is involved only in asset funding. The lessor's only basic responsibilities are to pay for the equipment, lease it to the lessee for the agreed-on term, and not interfere with its use.

Because a finance lease's term runs for most of the equipment's useful life, the lessee bears most of the risk of the equipment becoming obsolete. The degree of obsolescence risk that the finance lessor assumes depends on the equipment's anticipated residual value. If, for example, a lessor computes the rent based on a zero equipment residual value at the lease term's end, the lessor has no residual value risk and, thus, no obsolescence risk. This, of course, presumes there is no risk of premature equipment return as a result, for instance, of a lessee default. As a practical matter, however, a lessor must generally use a residual value greater than zero to be price competitive. The risk of obsolescence would then be on the lessor to the extent of the value estimated. If its profit is in part dependent on the anticipated residual value, the greater the risk of obsolescence, the greater the chance the transaction will not turn out to be as profitable as anticipated.

One of a financial lessor's principal concerns is the protection of his investment in the event of a lease default or an equipment casualty. Toward this end, finance leases usually include provisions to make the lessor whole if any of these events occur. From a casualty loss standpoint, the lease may include stipulated loss value provisions. Those provisions set out the amount the lessee must pay the lessor if an equipment casualty occurs, depending on when it occurs. The amount of the stipulated loss value is intended to guarantee the lessor a return of its investment, reimburse it for any tax benefit losses, and assure it of at least some of its profit. These stipulated loss values are also sometimes used as a measure of lease default damages, although there are other methods.

Finance leases frequently contain a "hell-or-high-water" rent commitment. Under this type of obligation, a lessee must pay the full rent unconditionally when it is due and cannot reduce the amount paid even though it has a legitimate claim against the lessor for money owed. This is not as bad as it sounds for a lessee, because it can still bring a lawsuit against the lessor for any claims.

The hell-or-high-water rent provision is critical for a finance lessor to have in a leverage lease transaction, when it wants to borrow money to purchase the equipment on a nonrecourse loan basis. *Reason:* In a nonrecourse loan, the lender agrees to look only to the lessee's rent payments and the equipment for a return of its investment. With a hell-or-high-water provision, the lender need not be concerned that a dispute between the lessor and the lessee will result in the lessee's withholding rent, and so the lender is more willing to offer an attractive loan arrangement.

2. The Operating Lease

If a lease's primary term is significantly shorter than the equipment's useful life, the lease is referred to as an operating lease. Operating leases typically run anywhere from a few months to a few years, although some are as short as a few hours.

Because the lease terms are relatively short, an operating lessor usually cannot earn much of its equipment investment back through the rents from one lease transaction. Thus, it must either sell or re-lease the equipment on attractive terms to come out ahead. The danger to an operating lessor, of course, is that the equipment's market value will be inadequate to allow it to sell or re-lease this equipment on economically favorable terms. In other words, it has the risk of equipment obsolescence. As a result, such a lessor will attempt to earn its money back faster to lessen its investment exposure by charging higher rent than a finance lessor.

The short lease terms and easy cancellation provisions of operating leases make them attractive to users in several situations. One is where the user anticipates using the equipment only for a short time, such as with certain types of railcars or aircraft. Another is where the user wants to be able to change equipment if something better comes out. For this reason, users often lease computer equipment under operating leases because of constant technological improvements.

3.   The Leveraged Lease

A leveraged lease is one where a percentage of the funds to buy the equipment, usually 60 to 80%, is loaned by a bank or other lender. Because the lessor has put up only a small percentage of the equipment's cost, its investment is said to be leveraged because its return is based on 100% of the cost. Leveraging generally enables a lessor to provide a lessee with relatively lower rents while at the same time maintaining its return. Frequently, net finance leases are structured as leveraged leases.

The debt used to leverage a lease transaction is usually nonrecourse debt. Where debt is nonrecourse, the lender has no recourse against the lessor for nonpayment of the loan, but rather must look only to the rental stream, the lessee, and the value of the equipment for its repayment. In such an arrangement, the lessor must assign to the lender its rights under the lease, including the right to the rental payments.

▶ **Observation:**   While a lessor has no repayment obligations to a nonrecourse lender if the lessee defaults, it does bear some risk because its rights against the lessee and the equipment are subordinated to the lender's repayment rights.

4.   The Nonleveraged Lease

Also referred to as an unleveraged or straight lease, a nonleveraged lease is one in which the lessor pays for the equipment from its own funds. Leasing companies often enter into nonleveraged leases.

A distinct advantage in using a nonleveraged lease structure is that there are usually only two principals involved, the lessee and the lessor. Because of the limited number of parties, the mechanics of putting together a transaction are simpler, saving time and documentation costs, such as legal fees. However, one disadvantage for a lessee is that the rent is usually higher than it would be if the lease were leveraged.

5.   The Service Lease

Leases in which the lessor assumes equipment ownership responsibilities, such as maintenance, repair, insurance, record keeping, or payment of property taxes, in addition to providing the asset financing, are usually called service leases. Service leases generally have relatively short lease terms.

F. The Pros and Cons of Leasing

Leasing is not always the best way for every user to acquire equipment. In some circumstances, it is advisable; in others, buying equipment is the right decision. Whether or not to lease certain equipment is not always an easy decision, and in each situation the user must weigh all the advantages and disadvantages. This section will provide the reader with the basic considerations essential to a comprehensive evaluation.

▶ **Observation:** Putting together a lease financing can require less red tape and time than in a loan transaction. As a result, there are situations in which the documentation time and expense that can be saved can offset an equipment lease interest rate that is higher than a loan interest rate. This is particularly true when the cost of the equipment involved is relatively small.

1. The Advantages of Leasing

a. Minimizes Obsolescence Concerns

When a user is concerned that equipment may become obsolete before the end of its useful life, and, therefore, have little or no resale value, leasing can reduce that concern if the lessor assumes an obsolescence risk by basing part of its investment return on a significant end-of-lease equipment sale or re-lease value. [The greater the residual value assumed by the lessor, the less rent a lessee pays over the lease term.] Typically, computer and other high-tech equipment users are faced with the obsolescence issue, because, in these fields, new, more efficient models quickly outdate their predecessors.

As a practical matter, as long as the equipment does its job, does it really matter whether there is better equipment available? In some situations it does. For example, a more efficient item of manufacturing equipment can lower production costs by a sufficient amount so that the user would have to acquire a new model before the old model has been written off to ensure its price-competitive position in the market. If a user had bought rather than leased the equipment, the overall cost of replacing it would be expensive. And if the old equipment's market value was significantly less than its book value at the time of replacement, the user could be confronted with a potentially undesirable book loss in addition to the replacement cash outlay.

▶ **Observation:** A lessor also runs the risk of financial loss through equipment obsolescence. Thus, to protect itself, it will undoubtedly build a premium into its lease rate to compensate for the risk. A prospective lessee may be willing to pay the premium as a form of insurance against a loss through obsolescence. Of course, if the equipment does not become obsolete the increased rental rate will have reduced the profits the lessee could have made had it owned the equipment.

► **Recommendation:** Because it is impossible to determine absolutely whether equipment will become obsolete, the obsolescence risk issue can cause a real dilemma. Evaluating the past history of the type of equipment under consideration can be helpful in predicting trends. Also, the user can estimate the impact on profits of continuing to use the older, technologically obsolete equipment.

b. Ideal When There Are Limited Use Needs

If equipment is needed only for a limited period of time, leasing can be an effective way of acquiring its use. It eliminates the remarketing risks an owner would have at the end of a short use period, and it also permits a more defined estimate of the effective cost of using the equipment. For example, a public utility building its own plant often must acquire certain specialized construction equipment to do the job. Once the plant is finished, the equipment may be of no further use to the utility, but it may still have many years of useful life left. If it cannot be sold for a reasonable price, the overall cost of its use can be high. Leasing removes the resale risk and allows the utility to determine in advance the total effective usage cost.

c. Preserves Capital

An advantage of leasing to some users is that it helps preserve their existing funds or bank lines for other uses. The absence of a down payment—in effect 100% financing—can assist high growth rate companies in maximizing their use of funds. That can be particularly attractive in periods of tight money.

► **Observation:** When evaluating whether to lease or to buy equipment, a user must carefully consider the real cost of borrowed funds. For example, a high compensating balance requirement can easily increase the effective cost of a bank loan. As this type of collateral loan cost increases, the attractiveness of leasing usually increases.

d. Obtain Value-Added Technical or Administrative Services

Users lacking the staff or expertise to attend to specialized equipment needs can lease equipment as a way to acquire those necessary technical or administrative services. Through service leases, users can avoid tying up time and manpower in activities that are outside of their normal operations. There is, of course, generally a charge built into the rent for the nonfinancial services supplied. Typically, lessors of office equipment, trucks, automobiles, and railcars offer some form of nonfinancial service as a supplement to their financing. For example, railcar lessors frequently offer maintenance services.

e. A Way Around Certain Borrowing Problems

Users with credit or borrowing problems may have an easier time getting leasing companies to fund their equipment needs since leasing companies often impose less stringent financial requirements than traditional lenders. *Reason:* They are willing to take greater risks because (1) they actually own the equipment and (2) they can more readily handle used equipment than can traditional lenders, if they must take possession from a defaulting lessee.

This is not to say that leasing companies will provide equipment financing to a user regardless of its financial condition. There still must be a reasonable assurance that the user will be able to meet the lease payments.

f. A Way to Trade Tax Benefits for Lower Rent

It is common for a user to be in a situation in which it cannot use the tax benefits—currently depreciation deductions—that would result from equipment ownership. For example, it may have an excess of accumulated tax benefits or insufficient earnings, either due to poor performance or to major acquisitions, that have used up its tax bill, or the user may be subject to the minimum tax and find the tax benefits deferred (explained in Chapter 6, Part III). Such a company can indirectly take advantage of most of the ownership tax benefits through leasing from a tax-sensitive lessor. Because such a lessor takes these tax benefits into account when calculating the transaction's economic return, it, in effect, passes these benefits through in the form of a relatively lower rent.

▶ **Observation:** A lessor will not pass 100% of the equipment ownership tax benefits on to a lessee through a reduced rental charge. It will make a profit on those benefits by adjusting the rent to reflect only a partial recognition. The rent adjustments vary with each lessor and each situation.

g. Bypasses Capital Budget Restrictions

Decisions to lease equipment are sometimes made to avoid a user's internal capital budget restrictions. For capital equipment purchases above a certain amount, a manager may be required to obtain prior approval, and that approval may be difficult or impossible to obtain. If the equipment is leased, it may be able to account for the rental payments as an operating expense—even though the lease represents a long-term financing similar to a capital expenditure—to get around the approval problem. In this way, it may also be able to maximize its capital budget.

▶ **Observation:** Top management in an increasing number of companies has prescribed rules in this area to avoid budget end-running, particularly with finance leases. For example, since long-term equipment leases can have a significant negative future impact on a company's earnings, particularly when cutbacks are necessary, very often these transactions require senior management or board of director approval.

h.   Inflation Hedge

Leasing equipment can provide a hedge against inflation. In effect, an equipment lease gives the equipment user the ability to acquire the equipment it needs at today's prices, and then pay for it from tomorrow's earnings.

i.   Possible Increased Cash Flow

Leasing equipment may be more cost-effective than purchasing it either entirely with internal funds or through the use of an equipment loan. Accordingly, the less the user has to pay to acquire necessary equipment, the more cash it has available—for example, its cash flow is increased.

j.   Possible Off-Balance Sheet Benefit

Although it is no longer a general leasing benefit, there is an old advantage that may, to a limited extent, still be available in some long-term lease situations. In the early days of leasing, many users leased equipment, instead of taking out long-term loans to buy equipment, to avoid burdening their balance sheet with long-term debt liabilities. The lease, regardless of its duration, was basically treated in such a manner that its rent payments were deemed to be an operating expense. As a result, a company's profit-to-fixed-asset ratios were improved, which, in turn, generally permitted a greater bank borrowing capability. Today, the circumstances have changed. Regardless of whether significant lease obligations have to be recorded on the balance sheet or not, many sophisticated lenders factor them into their evaluation of a company's financial condition. Also, and certainly most important, the accounting rules now effectively eliminate the traditional "off-balance sheet" benefit. In some situations, however, it is still possible to structure a long-term lease so that, for financial reporting purposes, the rent payments due will not have to be reported as a long-term liability, but rather can be reported as incurred as an operating expense.

2.   *Disadvantages of Leasing*

a.   Residual Upside Is Lost

When a user leases equipment, it forgoes the possibility of realizing a gain if the equipment appreciates in value during the lease term. Any such gain instead goes to the lessor. This is a common occurrence. For example, through inflation or buyer demand, a 10-year-old river barge may be worth more than it originally cost.

Many leases give lessees the option to buy the leased equipment at the lease term's end for its fair market value at that time. If the fair market value turns out to be high, the purchase price, coupled with the rent paid, can result in a very expensive transaction. In such a situation, the lessee would undoubtedly have been better off if it had originally bought the equipment. The problem is that there is no way of telling what the future value is going to be.

There is, however, one way for a prospective lessee to limit its cost exposure if it believes it is likely it will want to buy the equipment at the end of the term and, also, share in any residual upside—a fixed price purchase option. Under this option, a lessee has the right to buy the equipment at the end of a lease at a fixed price, say 25% of original cost, that was agreed on at the time the parties entered into the lease. If the equipment's market value at the lease term's end is high, say 75% of cost, the lessee has the option of taking advantage of the favorable market by buying it for 25% of cost and selling it for 75% of cost. However, there are two problems with fixed price purchase options: (1) not all lessors are willing to grant them and give up their residual upside, and (2) fixed price purchase options can jeopardize a lease's true lease status for tax purposes.

▶ **Recommendation:** If a prospective lessor is willing to grant a fixed price purchase right at, for example, 35% of cost, the prospective lessee should request that it be at 35% of cost or at the equipment's fair market value, whichever is less. This way, if the equipment's market value at the time of the option's exercise is lower than the fixed price, the lessee will not have to pay more than the equipment is worth if a purchase is necessary.

Frequently, a prospective lessee's concern over the loss of residual value upside is more emotional than practical. The potential loss must always be kept in the proper economic perspective. This can be done by attempting to put a realistic value on it by, for example, bringing in a qualified appraiser to give an opinion as to what the equipment is likely to be worth in the future and discounting the value to its present worth.

Illustrative Example—*A Residual Perspective:* Company Able is considering whether to lease or buy a heavy duty crane. Company Able's financial vice president recommends that it be leased; however, the operational vice president believes that it should be bought because of its favorable market value at the end of the period of use. The facts are as follows:

Crane cost:	$3 million
Lease term:	20 years
Depreciated book value at end of 20 years:	$300,000

If the market value of the crane is estimated to be $500,000 at the end of the lease term, Company Able would lose the chance at a $200,000 upside gain ($500,000 − $300,000) if it leased the equipment.

However, what if the potential loss is considered in terms of current dollars? The present value of such a loss 20 years out, computed using an annual discount rate of 10%, is approximately $30,000. Compared to the original cost of $3 million and considering the fact that the upside gain may not materialize, the residual concern may be overstated, particularly if any down payment that would have been required in a purchase was put to productive use.

b.   Equipment Control May Be Limited

When a lease ends, so does a lessee's right to use the equipment. This can create problems for an equipment user if suitable replacement equipment is not readily available and the lessor refuses to re-lease or sell it to the lessee. While purchase or renewal options theoretically eliminate this risk, from a practical standpoint, when a third party owns the equipment, there is no guarantee it will abide by the terms of the options voluntarily. Also, there is always the possibility, although remote, that a lessor will interfere with the lessee's right to use the equipment during the lease term, even though it may have no legal right to do so. Having the legal right of continued use may be of little consequence to a lessee when equipment essential to its continued operations becomes unavailable.

3.   *Key Situations: When to Consider Leasing*

In summary, there are certain indicators that suggest an equipment user should seriously consider leasing:

- If an equipment user must pay high interest rates for money borrowed, leasing can be an economically attractive equipment funding alternative. Users whose credit dictates high interest rates, however, may also dictate high leasing rates. *Reason:* The lessor must offset the increased credit risks by increased returns. The cost of leasing, however, will probably not increase proportionately as high as the cost of borrowing.
- An equipment user who cannot use a significant part or all of the equipment ownership tax benefits may come out ahead by leasing. This, of course, assumes the tax benefits can be used by the leasing company, and the benefits are passed through in the form of a relatively lower rental rate.
- Leasing is desirable when the equipment involved has unusual service problems that cannot be handled by a company internally, for example, because of the technical nature of the equipment or the company's inadequate staffing.
- If implicit lease interest rates are about the same as debt interest rates and there are significant ancillary costs to borrowing, such as high compensating balances or commitment fees, leasing should be considered.

G.   When-to-Lease Checklist

An equipment user should consider leasing when one or more of the following factors are present:

- There is a high risk that equipment will become obsolete before the end of its useful life.
- The equipment will be needed only for a short period of time.

- It is desirable to maximize available capital resources.
- Technical, administrative, or other nonfinancial equipment related services that are not internally available can be easily secured from a leasing company.
- High interest rates must be paid for borrowed money.
- The tax benefits resulting from the equipment ownership cannot be used.
- The equipment will have a poor market value at the end of its term of use.

H. Checklist for Prospective Lessees Approaching Potential Lessors

As the preliminary step in considering a lease transaction, an equipment user should review the following:

What basic type of lease arrangement is to be considered?

☐ Nonleveraged finance lease [*If you want a long-term lease and you need to get your lease in place in a hurry, this may be the best choice.*]

    1. Net lease [*If you don't need the lessor to provide any equipment services, such as maintenance, a net lease is the lease of choice.*]

☐ Leveraged finance lease [*This may provide the lowest long-term lease rate, but can take the longest to document because of third-party lender involvement.*]

    1. Net lease [*See same category comment for the nonleveraged lease.*]

☐ Operating lease [*This is the lease to use when you only want equipment for a short period of time, or you want lessor-supplied services, such as equipment repair.*]

    1. Long-term
    2. Short-term
    3. Nonfinancial services required

What potential sources of lease financing will be invited to submit lease quotations?

☐ Individuals [*This is a good choice if you need an aggressive lessor.*]

☐ Independent nonbank lease companies [*They should always be invited to bid. They are often the most innovative.*]

    1. Finance lessors
    2. Service lessors

☐ Banks or other financial institutions [*They typically offer fair lease documentation, but lease interest rates may vary depending on their internal needs.*]

☐ Captive leasing companies [*If your equipment supplier has one, ask its captive lessor to bid on your lease transaction. Although they have the capability to offer the lowest lease rate, they rarely do. But it never hurts to ask.*]

☐ Lease brokers [*The good ones can bring solid value-added benefits to your lease situation. Know, however, who you are dealing with; some are not as ethical as they should be.*]

If an individual is under consideration:

☐ Has the individual been involved in lease transactions before?
☐ Does the individual have experienced lease advisors and management representatives to assist him or her if transactions issues arise in the future?

If an independent nonbank leasing company is under consideration:

☐ Does it have a good reputation in the financial community?
☐ Have other existing lessees been contacted to determine how difficult it may be to deal with?
☐ Is its financial condition sufficient to ensure adequate and timely funding?
☐ Will the equipment be funded entirely from the lessor's own funds?
☐ If equipment related nonfinancial services will be supplied, does it have an adequate staff and facilities to supply these services on a timely basis?
☐ How tough is the lessor's lease documentation? [*A form of the lessor's lease should be reviewed.*]

If the prospective lessee's regular bank will be involved, will the lease restrict its future loan availability?

If a lease broker is under consideration:

☐ How many similar transactions has it completed in the last three years?
☐ What do other companies that have used its service say about its method of operation and its ability to follow through on a proposed transaction?
☐ Are there any banks or other prospective lessor-investors that should not be approached by the broker?

Chapter 2

The Proposal Stage: Where the Leasing Deal Is Made

A. Overview

Chapter 1 discusses a variety of lessor and lease alternatives open to a prospective lessee in considering a lease financing. All too often, prospective lessees approach these alternatives in an inefficient and disorganized manner. As a result, many pay too much and miss out on benefits they could receive. And some prospective lessors, failing to consider the many financing approaches, lose lessee financing opportunities.

This chapter provides guidelines to prospective lessees and lessors on how to efficiently set up a lease financing in an organized manner. The objective for both parties, during what is referred to as the "proposal stage," is to enter into a comprehensive outline of the leasing deal the parties intend to enter into—through the use of a lease proposal letter. By following the chapter guidelines, a prospective lessee and lessor can achieve maximum results.

B. Obtaining Bids: The Request-for-Bids Letter

Assume we have an equipment user considering leasing some equipment. How does this prospective lessee get the best lease deal? First, it must shop the lease market to determine what options are available. And that requires the prospective lessee to secure a meaningful number of specific proposals from potential lessors and lease underwriters. There are a number of ways to do this. Typically, however, a prospective lessee will get the best results by preparing and circulating a well thought out and comprehensive written request-for-bids letter, commonly referred to as a bid letter.

While preparing a bid letter may be somewhat time-consuming, it is an investment that will more than pay off. Such a letter will avoid time lost handling telephone calls or other inquiries from lessors and underwriters asking for additional information or clarification of the proposed deal's basic facts. It ensures that the responses will be on a uniform and thus comparable basis, making it easy to select the best offer. There is nothing more frustrating than receiving, for example, five proposals, each with a different rental payment mode—quarterly, in advance; semiannually, in arrears; semiannually, in advance; monthly, in arrears; and monthly, in advance. Not only is valuable time lost in making comparisons, but, even worse, there is a risk that re-quotes will be necessary because making valid comparisons may be impossible.

Another advantage to using a bid letter is that it will cause everyone concerned on the lessee's side to focus on what they need or would like to obtain from the leasing transaction. Generally, if a prospective lessee does not request a particular benefit, it will not be offered.

1. *Key Elements That Should Be Addressed*

What issues should be covered in a comprehensive bid letter? Because the bid letter's purpose is to yield proposals, it should address every subject necessary to make a comprehensive lease financing assessment. At a bare minimum, a prospective lessee should consider the following issues in putting together a bid letter:

- The equipment type and the manufacturer
- The number of equipment units that will be involved
- The equipment's aggregate and per unit cost
- When the equipment delivery is anticipated
- The lease type desired, that is, net financial lease or service lease
- The lease term and any renewal periods desired
- The rental payment mode, that is, monthly, quarterly, semiannually, or annually—in advance or in arrears
- The extent of any acceptable tax indemnifications
- Whether the equipment will be self-insured
- What options are required
- A request for appropriate casualty and termination values
- Who will have the responsibility for the transaction's fees and expenses
- Whether a tax ruling is necessary or desirable
- Whether it is acceptable for a favorable tax ruling to be a prerequisite to execute the lease documents
- Whether a favorable tax ruling should relieve any tax indemnification obligations assumed
- The deadline for the submission of lease quotations
- When the transaction will be awarded
- Whether underwriting bids are acceptable
- If underwriting proposals are permitted, whether the bids may be on a "firm" or "best efforts" basis
- Potential equity participants and lenders who may be unacceptable if the transaction is to be underwritten

These points are explained below in the context of describing the proposal letter.

► **Additional Sources:** The following are included to assist the prospective lessee in drafting the bid letter:

- Section H of this chapter sets out a proposal stage checklist for the lessee.
- The Appendix includes a sample request-for-bids letter.

C. What Is the Proposal Letter?

After receiving and reviewing the bid letter, interested prospective lessors or underwriters will make their proposal responding to the bid letter's terms. Their response should be written and is referred to as a proposal letter. The proposal letter is significant for several reasons. First, the letter will be the lessee's first opportunity to make preliminary selections from among the respondents to its bid letter. Second, after reviewing the proposal letters received, the lessee may request changes or additions, and the letter forms the focal point for those negotiations. And third, after successful negotiations, the lessee will accept one of the letter offers, and the letter will become the basis for the later deal documentation. It is important that the proposal letter cover all major business and legal points.

1. The Proposal Letter's Legal Status

Before reviewing the substance of a typical proposal letter, it is important to understand legally what the proposal letter does and does not do. After the prospective lessee has signed the letter, do the parties have a contract? Yes and no. While they have a contract—usually the offer, and sometimes the acceptance, is qualified—conditions are imposed that must be satisfied after all parties have signed the lease proposal. Typical conditions, for example, are

- Necessary governmental or regulatory approvals, licenses, or authorizations
- Favorable opinions of counsel
- The effective placement of the debt, in the case of a leveraged lease
- Acceptable financial covenants, such as a minimum debt-to-equity ratio
- Satisfactory audited financial statements
- Mutually satisfactory documentation
- Formal transaction approvals by the prospective equity participants and lenders
- A minimum dollar participation of equity and debt participants
- A detailed equipment list
- Favorable equipment appraisals justifying the equipment residual value

The "satisfactory documentation" condition gives the transaction's participants the most latitude to find justification to back out if they so desire. *Reason:*

Unless the parties can reach agreement on each term and condition contained in the lease documents, they don't have to go through with the transaction. This condition leaves room for some wide-open discussions on issues not even anticipated in the proposal stage, such as whether the lessee should pay for the equipment's return to any location designated by the lessor.

While the accepted proposal letter is usually not legally enforceable because of these conditions, it is important that it be comprehensive, detailed, and in writing for several reasons:

- While the proposal letter may not be legally enforceable, the parties will almost always make significant efforts to complete the deal once it has been accepted.
- The proposal letter serves as the guideline and reminder for the parties and their lawyers when they draft the documents.
- While unlikely, it is possible that if a party unreasonably backs out of the deal after the proposal letter has been accepted, the letter might form the basis of a legal action. This is particularly so if financial obligations have been incurred on the other side.

Thus, a comprehensive and formal proposal letter is beneficial to both parties, and should be used in every transaction.

2. *Proposal Stage Negotiating Strategies*

Because the major terms are decided and the lessor or underwriter is selected during the proposal stage, that stage is often determinative of the transaction. Besides focusing on specific terms and conditions, the prospective lessee should keep in mind that during the bidding stage, it has a considerable amount of negotiating leverage, particularly if more than one bidder is involved. One bidder's loss will not jeopardize the transaction, and the bidders know it. Thus, the time for the lessee to press for the tough concessions is before awarding the transaction. Prospective lessors are sometimes willing to concede points just to win the deal. Once the transaction has been awarded, the winning bidder is in a stronger negotiating position merely by virtue of the fact that the other bidders are no longer involved.

A prospective lessee's negotiating position will also be improved if it plans adequate lead time between a lease award and the equipment delivery. In this way, if problems develop after the award, there may still be time to go elsewhere for the financing. If this is not possible, and the prospective lessor starts to "get tough," some balance can be put back into the negotiations by letting it be known that because of the problems, the lessee is considering buying rather than leasing.

From the potential lessor's perspective, the negotiating strategy in the bidding stage is the reverse—the faster it can get a prospective lessee to "sign off" on a proposal letter, the less likely that the lessee will make a problem request. Once the lease documentation has begun, particularly if there are near-term equipment deliveries, a prospective lessor's negotiating position is improved. Psychologically, a prospective lessee is more reluctant to start over with new people once the document negotiations have started.

D. What Issues Should the Proposal Letter Address?

Stated simply, the proposal letter should outline the lease "deal." The letter does not have to cover every detail, but it should set the framework for the overall lease arrangement. To do this, however, the parties must know what points should be covered.

▶ **Recommendation:** If an important point comes up after a proposal letter has been accepted by a prospective lessee, but before the lease documentation has begun, the parties should consider amending the letter to include the point. This helps eliminate deal point "misunderstandings" from arising during documentation.

Typically, although an underwritten leveraged lease situation will be more complex than nonunderwritten transactions, they usually contain most of the same basic elements. By understanding the more complex transaction format, the others will fall into place and, thus, the following explanation will center on issues that should be addressed in an underwritten leveraged lease proposal.

The Appendix includes several proposal letters. The first is typical of that used by a leasing company acting on its own behalf, a nonunderwritten transaction, and the second is typical of that used by an underwriter acting on behalf of prospective third-party lessors. Both cover the major topics that should be identified and can be used as guidelines when drafting or reviewing a lease proposal. Because there can be many variables in a particular transaction, however, they should be used only for reference purposes. It may be helpful to review them before reading further, to put the following explanation into an overall perspective.

1. Defining the Offer

While all proposals will offer to provide equipment financing, proposals from different types of bidders have different consequences to the lessee. One type of proposal is a direct offer by a prospective lessor to lease the equipment to the prospective lessee, and another is an offer by an underwriter to arrange the lease financing of the equipment for the prospective lessee. In the latter case, the underwriter may or may not have a specific third-party lessor in mind. Even if the underwriter does, the name usually will not be disclosed in the proposal to protect its position as a broker.

> **Illustrative Language**—*Lessor Designation:* An unknown or undisclosed lessor may be described by an underwriter in the following manner: The lessor will be a trustee acting as owner trustee pursuant to an owner's trust for the benefit of one or more corporate investors.
>
> In a nonunderwritten transaction, the prospective lessor will make an offer directly as principal to lease the equipment to the prospective lessee. For example: ABC Leasing Company will purchase

and lease to XYZ Company the equipment designated in this proposal under the terms and conditions specified herein.

► **Recommendations:**

- In an underwriting situation, a prospective lessee is in a better position if it does not make an award to a particular underwriter until the underwriter has disclosed the prospective lessor, and someone with authority to represent the lessor has been contacted by the prospective lessee to confirm their interest. If there is going to be a problem, the time to find out is when the remaining bidders are still in the picture.
- An underwriter should make sure its proposal is only an offer to arrange the proposed financing, unless it is fully prepared to step in as lessor in the event a third-party investor cannot be found.

There are many types of offer combinations. For example, a direct lessor could offer to purchase and lease equipment using in part its own funds and in part funds from a nonrecourse loan, a simple form of leveraged lease. Or, an underwriter may offer to put together a leveraged lease using one or more lessor-investors and one or more third-party lenders. Another alternative is that the underwriter may propose to bring in a "single source" investor to act as lessor, such as a regional bank, which would pay for the equipment entirely from its own funds.

To the prospective lessee, the choice among the different variations represents a trade-off between delivery and price. A prospective lessee seeking a near-term equipment delivery situation may be well advised to limit its consideration to a direct lessor transaction, because dealing with one party directly will lessen the risk that the financing cannot be done within the short time frame. If there is plenty of time, the best approach may be to pursue a syndicated leveraged lease transaction. This type of transaction will certainly be more involved, but it can provide the best rental rate for a prospective lessee.

Because the amount of lead time available before the equipment will be delivered may dictate the type of transaction that can be considered, it is essential that all parties keep this aspect in mind. Table 2-1 can be used as a general guide for planning the timing of a proposed lease financing.

2. *"Best Efforts" or Firm Offer*

Typically, a lease underwriter will state in its proposal whether the offer is made on a "best efforts" or on a "firm" basis. A best efforts proposal is nothing more than an offer to try to arrange the lease financing on the stated terms and conditions. There are no performance guarantees, and the underwriter is generally not liable to the prospective lessee if it cannot perform.

> **Illustrative Language**—*"Best Efforts" Commitment:* ABC Leasing Company proposes to use its best efforts to arrange an equipment lease according to the terms and conditions set forth in this proposal.

Table 2-1. Recommended transaction lead time.

Type of Transaction	Anticipated Number of Lessor-Investors	Anticipated Number of Lenders	Recommended Lead Time[1] (Months)
Underwritten leveraged lease	Two or more	Two or more	Six
Underwritten leveraged lease	Two or more	One	Six
Underwritten leveraged lease	One	Two or more	Five
Underwritten leveraged lease	One	One	Four
Underwritten single investor[2]	One	Zero	Three
Direct lease[3]	One	One or more	Three
Direct lease	One	Zero	Two

[1]*Lead time* is defined as the time between the proposal's due date and the first equipment delivery. The estimates assume an allowable proposal analysis time of one month.
[2]An *underwritten single investor* transaction is defined as one in which the underwriter brings in only one lessor-investor, who puts up 100% of the funds required.
[3]A *direct lease* transaction is defined as one in which the prospective lessee will deal directly with the prospective lessor.

A firm underwriting bid is simply just that. The underwriter states that it can deliver the financing under the proposed terms and conditions.

> **Illustrative Language**—*Firm Commitment:* ABC Leasing Company proposes to arrange on a firm commitment basis an equipment lease for XYZ Inc., according to the terms and conditions set forth in this proposal.

From the prospective lessee's viewpoint, whether to go with a best efforts or firm offer is like the choice among bidders—a trade-off between delivery time and price. Underwriters will often offer a better price on a best efforts bid because that way they do not have to market the transaction to potential lessors until it has been awarded to them. Marketing an awarded deal saves the underwriter time, and also may make the potential lessors more willing to offer a better price—they will know the transaction is theirs if they accept the underwriter's bid, and so are more willing to invest time evaluating the transaction than if the transaction has not been awarded.

The best efforts offer, however, has a downside to the lessee—time. If the underwriter cannot rapidly find a lessor after having been awarded the deal, valuable documentation time is lost. In fact, if the underwriter takes an extended period to market the deal, the possibility becomes greater that no lessor will accept the deal. *Reason:* Prospective lessor-investors become suspicious when a transaction has been around the marketplace for a while and may refuse to consider it for that reason alone.

▶ **Recommendation:**   If a prospective lessee has adequate lead time, a best efforts underwriting should be permitted. If the winning underwriter cannot perform quickly, the prospective lessee can move on to the underwriter in second place without creating a timing problem.

As described previously, even an accepted firm offer will not usually be a binding agreement because of the various conditions—such as satisfactory documentation of the proposal letter terms. However, as a practical matter, some firm offers may be more likely to go ahead to a completed transaction than others. For example, there are situations when an underwriter will firmly commit to do the transaction, even though it does not have a commitment from any lessor prospects, and agree to buy and lease the equipment itself if it cannot broker it. This type of arrangement can be risky for a prospective lessee because if the underwriter cannot sell the deal, it may not want to go ahead and may seek an excuse to justify a way out. For example, offers conditioned on mutually satisfactory lease documentation can provide an underwriter with an opportunity to create a document "disagreement" and, thereby, a basis to refuse to go forward.

▶ **Recommendation:**   A prospective lessee should carefully investigate the financial situation of a lease underwriter offering a firm underwriting bid. If the underwriter does not have the financial resources to stand behind the transaction in the event it cannot deliver a lessor-investor, the fact that the offer is firm may be worth nothing.

If the offer is made directly by a prospective lessor instead of an underwriter, the situation will be different. Because the prospective lessor will use its own money to fund the transaction, the chances of the lessor looking for an excuse to back out are greatly reduced.

> **Illustrative Language**—*Direct Commitment:* ABC Leasing Company, as lessor, offers to purchase and lease to XYZ Inc. the equipment described below under the stated terms and conditions.

3.   *Specifying the Exact Cost*

The proposal letter should identify total equipment cost. Frequently, a prospective lessor will put a limit on, or "cap," the amount of money it is willing to commit to a transaction. For example, the prospective lessor may agree to buy and lease an oil tanker at a cost not to exceed $40 million. Without a cap, there is the risk that unexpected cost escalations will cause the lessor to invest more than it is comfortable with. An unanticipated cost increase thus may give a prospective lessor who no longer finds the transaction desirable an excuse to back out.

▶ **Recommendation:** A prospective lessee entering into a lease agreement covering equipment to be delivered in the future must make sure the lessor's cost commitment is adequate. For example, will it cover any allowable manufacturer price escalations? If there is a problem with determining an exact price, a dollar cushion can be built into the estimate. A word of caution, however, if a fee has been imposed by the prospective lessor for the failure to use all the committed funds (commonly referred to as a nonutilization fee): A prospective lessee should be careful not to build in an excessive cushion because any fee paid on the excess over the amount used will increase the effective cost of the financing.

4. Identifying the Real Lessee

While the proposal letter will identify the lessee responsible for the rent, sometimes the real lessee is not identified. For example, the proposal letter may name XYZ Inc. as lessee while XYZ Inc. plans to have a subsidiary be the lessee. The lessor will do a credit review and approval based on XYZ Inc.'s statements. If the subsidiary is the lessee, the check on the parent company will not be sufficient, and there may not be enough time to make any necessary adjustments. Getting the parent company's guarantee may be enough, but it may be difficult to obtain at the last minute.

5. Rent Payments: Rental Adjustment Clauses

The proposal should specify how often, how much, and for how long rent will be paid. For example, a five-year lease may provide for 20 consecutive, level, quarterly payments, in arrears, each payment to equal 3.000% of the equipment cost, beginning as of the start of the primary term.

When a leveraged lease is involved, the rent calculation becomes more complicated. The amount of rent a lessor charges is, in part, determined by the debt interest rate. However, the lessor generally will not secure the debt until after the award. *Reason:* It wouldn't be practical to spend the time and money necessary until there is a deal. Thus, to calculate the rent, the lessor will use an assumed debt interest rate and calculate the rent accordingly. Then, to protect its return in case the actual interest rate varies from the assumed rate, the lessor will often want a rental adjustment clause.

> **Illustrative Example**—*The Need for a Rent Adjustment Clause:* Company B proposes to lease to Company A a $10,000 item of mining equipment. The transaction will be leveraged with 80% debt at an assumed interest rate of 6% per annum. The terms are as follows:
>
> | | |
> |---|---|
> | Lease term: | 10 years |
> | Loan term: | 10 years |
> | Annual rent: | $1,200 |
> | Annual debt service (level, in arrears): | |
> | ($8,000 @ 6%) | $1,087 |

The annual rent will cover the annual debt service by $113 ($1,200 − $1,087). Assume that when Company B goes into the debt market the best available annual interest rate is 10%. The annual debt service, assuming level payments, will be approximately $1,302. In this case not only will the increased debt service expense erode the lessor's return, but the lessor will have to invest an additional $102 a year ($1,302 − $1,200) to make up for the shortfall.

The rental adjustment clause enables the lessor to be protected against an increased interest rate, and this provision should be stated in the proposal letter.

Illustrative Language—*Proposal Rent Adjustment:* Lessee shall make 20 consecutive, level, quarterly payments, in arrears, each equal to 3.000% of equipment cost, commencing on January 1, 19–. The rental percentage factor is based on the assumption that the interest rate on the leveraged debt will be 9.5% per annum. If the interest rate is other than 9.5%, the rental factor will be adjusted, upward or downward, accordingly so that lessor's economic return shall be maintained.

► **Recommendations:**

- If a prospective lessor has the right to protect its return by adjustments upward if the actual debt interest rate is higher than assumed, a prospective lessee should require a downward rent adjustment if the debt comes in lower than assumed.
- A prospective lessee should determine what criteria the prospective lessor will use to make any rent adjustment so the accuracy of the calculation can be independently confirmed.
- Any time a rental adjustment is permitted, the parties should also provide for appropriate adjustments in values that relate to the rent, such as casualty and termination values.

6. *Primary and Interim Lease Terms*

The proposal letter must specify the equipment's lease term and, if more than one item of equipment is to be leased, identify each item's lease period.

Also, where numerous items of equipment are involved, using an interim term in addition to the main or primary lease term will simplify rental payment mechanics. The interim term covers the period from the time the equipment is accepted for lease to the start of the primary term. The interim term concept is commonly used when many items of equipment are involved and deliveries are scattered over many months. By consolidating the start of the primary lease terms to, for example, calendar quarters, the rent payment and processing mechanics are simplified.

Illustrative   Example—*The Interim Technique for Rent Consolidation:* Company B wants to lease 120 trucks from Company A. The trucks will be delivered over a 12-month period at a rate of 10 trucks a month. Company B wants to pay the lease rent in quarterly, in arrears, payments. Company A proposes this solution:

1. There shall be four primary lease terms starting as follows:

    a. First primary term – April 1, 19__
    b. Second primary term – July 1, 19__
    c. Third primary term – October 1, 19__
    d. Fourth primary term – January 1, 19__

2. All trucks delivered and accepted for lease in the calendar quarter preceding the nearest primary term start date shall be on interim lease until the start date, at which time the primary term shall begin for such trucks.

Without the interim arrangement, Company A could end up with as many as 120 different primary lease term start dates and, thus, 120 different rental payment dates.

7. Credit Support for Lease Obligations

The prospective lessor should evaluate the prospective lessee's financial strength, and if the prospective lessee is not financially strong enough to support a particular leasing financing, the prospective lessor should require, in the proposal letter, some form of credit support. In that event, prospective lessors prefer to get a full and unconditional guarantee of all the lease obligations from a creditworthy entity, such as a parent company, a bank, or, possibly, an underwriter. Other acceptable forms of credit support include a manufacturer's deficiency guarantee or a "take or pay" contract assignment. Different forms may be acceptable in different situations. An experienced leasing company or underwriter should be able to offer some viable alternatives to meet the needs of a particular transaction.

▶ **Recommendation:** If the proposed lessee is a corporate subsidiary and credit support is required, the parent company should pursue a structure that will have the least impact on its future borrowing capabilities. For example, an assignment of a "take or pay" contract between the subsidiary and an outside entity may have little impact on the parent company. However, a full, unconditional guarantee could have a substantial impact.

8. Structure of Owning Entity

In structuring a typical underwritten leveraged lease transaction, an underwriter may propose one of a number of different alternative entities to own the equipment—a trust, partnership, or corporation. The underwriter's choice of entity should be decided in the proposal stage.

Tax issues and limited liability issues will be of greatest concern to a prospective lessor. This is particularly true when two or more entities are brought together to act as the lessor. On the tax side, the chosen structure should permit a direct flow-through of all the available tax benefits. As to limited liability, the lessors may want protection against direct liability on a specific transaction in the event of a lawsuit.

▶ **Recommendation:**   Trust arrangements can be a useful equipment owner-ship structure for prospective lessor-investors. If set up properly, it is generally agreed that they will be treated, for tax purposes, as a partnership and, for liabil-ity purposes, as a corporation.

The ownership vehicle form can also be important to a prospective lessee. For example, if the equipment ownership is not centralized in a multiple lessor-investor situation, the lessee may have to deal individually with each investor throughout the lease. The lessee may then have to issue separate prorated rent checks and, if a lease variance is necessary, obtain separate consents—a substan-tial inconvenience.

▶ **Recommendation:**   In a multiple lessor-investor situation, a prospective les-see should insist that there be a single representative with the authority to handle the day-to-day issues.

9.   The Debt Arrangement

If the lessor proposes a leveraged lease, the debt arrangement mechanics and terms should be outlined in the proposal letter. Points to consider concerning the debt are

- Who will fund the debt
- The debt repayment schedule
- The anticipated per annum interest charge
- The anticipated principal amount as a percentage of equipment cost
- The form of lender representative
- Whether the debt will be recourse or nonrecourse to the lessor

While the proposal should cover these points, the lessor may need the ability to make changes if the debt structure eventually obtained varies from that stated in the proposal.

> **Illustrative Language**—*Debt Structure:* ABC Leasing Company (ABC), or an investment banker acceptable to the lessee and to ABC, shall arrange for the private placement of a note ("Indebtedness") to be issued by the lessor for a principal amount of approximately 80% of the total cost of the equipment to certain institutional investors (Lenders). The Lenders may be represented by an indenture trustee or agent bank.
>   This proposal assumes that the Indebtedness shall be amortized in 20 payments of principal and interest at 9.5% per annum, payable quarterly, in arrears, over five years. The Indebtedness shall be secured

by a lease assignment and a security interest in the equipment, but otherwise shall be without recourse to the lessor. Any variance from the debt assumptions, other than interest rate, which is provided for in the rent adjustment clause, will relieve the offeror from its commitment thereunder, if so elected.

The proposal letter should address which party will handle the debt placement and pay the placement fees. Typically, the underwriter or lessor will pay those costs. If the lessor or underwriter places the debt, it will save the debt placement fee and, thereby, increase its profit. Keep in mind that if the underwriter or lessor handles the debt placement and there is a rent adjustment provision, the lessor may have little incentive to make sure a truly rock-bottom rate has been found.

▶ **Recommendations:**

- If the prospective underwriter or lessor is arranging the debt, the lessee should require the right to exclude any potential lender, for a number of reasons. First, the lessee should be able to protect itself against a lessor obtaining an unreasonably high interest rate and passing it along through the rental adjustment clause. Second, a lessee may not want any of its "line" banks to become involved because of potential future borrowing restrictions. Also, some lenders are difficult to deal with, and they should be brought in only as a last resort.
- If a prospective lessor or underwriter must pay the debt placement fee, it should have an equal say in the selection of the party that will place the debt. This will prevent the lessor from being stuck with an inappropriately high placement fee.

▶ **Documentation Suggestion:** Many documents used in a leveraged transaction will be subject to lender approval. Some lenders can be difficult to negotiate with and slow in responding. To avoid last-minute problems, the relevant papers should be sent to them as soon as possible and monitored carefully as to their review progress.

10. Tax or Business Reasons Requiring a Narrow Equipment Delivery Time Frame

In some instances, the equipment's delivery date may significantly affect the economic benefits to the lessor. Most lessors will be taking depreciation deductions on the equipment, and when the equipment is placed in service determines the first-year deduction. Different dates can substantially affect the lessor's deduction. For example, a lessor may want the deduction in a current year because it has substantial income to offset. Or the lessor may want the deduction in its next tax year because it cannot use the benefits in the current year. Or the lessor may want the deduction before or after its last quarter to avoid the mid-quarter depreciation convention treatment. (See Chapter 5, Part I,C,4.)

Business concerns can similarly dictate a narrow delivery time. For example, the lessor may not want to be obligated to provide lease financing at a particular fixed economic return beyond a certain date. Also, the prospective lessor may need to anticipate its cash needs for funding equipment purchases. Late deliveries can particularly be a problem when a long-term lease commitment involves many equipment items and the likelihood of delays is increased.

A solution to that problem is to use a commitment period. This limits the lessor's obligation to fund to a designated period, six months, for example, after the last expected delivery date. From a lessee's viewpoint, however, this may have a cost. The longer the commitment period, the more likely it is that a prospective lessor will impose a fee for holding the funds available. Such a fee, commonly referred to as a commitment fee, is usually based upon a percentage of equipment cost. For example, a lessor may charge a fee equal to 0.5% of the total funds committed.

▶ **Observation:**   Lessors are often willing to hold funds available for up to six months without charging a commitment fee.

▶ **Recommendation:**   A commitment fee should be included in a prospective lessee's cost-to-lease computation. A transaction with a lower rent and a commitment fee may be less attractive than one with a higher rent and no fee. This is not, however, always the case. Therefore, a prospective lessee should not automatically exclude a proposal just because it involves a commitment fee.

11. *Equipment Location*

The proposal letter should specify where the lessee intends to use the leased equipment. The lessor may want to make security interest filings to protect its ownership interest against a lessee's creditors. To do so, the lessor must know the equipment's location. Also, the lessor's potential tax benefits may depend on the equipment's location. For example, if the equipment is used outside the United States, the lessor will generally have less attractive depreciation deductions.

Another consideration is that the equipment's location may have psychological benefits that affect a lease underwriter's marketing effort. Certain lessor-investors or lenders may be more willing to participate in situations involving equipment used in their local area. For example, if the equipment is to be used in Maryland by a division of a California corporation, Maryland regional banks may be interested because of the possibility of doing future business with a company they normally may not be involved with.

12. *Purchase or Renewal Options*

To have the option to continue to use the equipment, a lessee may want the right to buy the equipment or renew the lease, under certain conditions, at the primary lease term's end. To do that, the lessee must have purchase or renewal options.

Illustrative Language—*Purchase and Renewal Options:*   At the end of the primary lease term, the lessee may (with 180 days' written notice prior to the end of such term):

1. Renew the lease with respect to the equipment for an amount equal to its then fair market rental value, or
2. Purchase the equipment for a price equal to its then fair market value.

▶ **Recommendation:** From a lessee's viewpoint a purchase option should be exercisable not only at the end of the main lease term, but also at the end of each renewal term. Also, the renewal term rights should adequately cover potential periods of extended use.

An alternative is a "right of first refusal" option. Basically, a first refusal option gives the lessee the right to buy or renew the equipment under the same terms as offered to the lessor by an unrelated third party.

Illustrative Language—*Right of First Refusal:* At the end of the primary lease term, the lessee will have a right of first refusal as to any sale or re-lease of the equipment.

▶ **Observation:** A right of first refusal can create a potential problem for a lessee. It is conceivable that a competitor would bid for equipment essential to a lessee's operations merely to attempt to interfere with its business.

In some situations prospective lessors want the right to require a lessee to buy the equipment at the lease's end. This type of right is commonly referred to as a "put" and should, as with the other options, be identified in the proposal. However, because of potential tax problems, puts are not generally used.

In recent years, a new purchase option has surfaced—called an early buyout option. There are certain tax risks in incorporating such an option into a lease arrangement, but, if they are carefully structured, some lessors are willing to grant them. Typically, the lessor requires the lessee to pay a premium at the time the purchase option is exercised.

▶ **Recommendation:** Lessors and lessees should seek the advice of experienced tax counsel before incorporating an early buyout option in a lease agreement. The wrong structure can result in adverse tax consequences for both the lessor and the lessee.

13. Early Termination Right

A prospective lessee may want what is called an early termination option—the right to end the lease prematurely as to any equipment that becomes obsolete or surplus to its needs. Some lessors do not like to grant termination options because they cut off future earnings. Thus, when they are granted, the lessee usually must pay a substantial premium to exercise the option, a premium referred to as a termination value payment.

Illustrative Language—*Termination Right:* At the expiration of each year during the primary lease term, the lessee shall have the right to terminate the lease at its option. The lessee will be required to give the lessor 90 days' prior written notice of its intention to terminate, and during the period from giving notice until the termination date, the lessee shall use its best efforts to obtain bids from unaffiliated third parties for the equipment's purchase. On the termination date, the lessor shall sell the equipment for cash for the highest bid received. The total proceeds of such sale shall be retained by the lessor, and the lessee will pay to the lessor the difference, if any, by which the sale proceeds are less than the appropriate termination value indicated on the attached schedule.

▶ **Recommendation:** If a prospective lessor is willing to grant a termination right, the prospective lessee should make sure that the termination values along with the right are incorporated into the lease proposal. These values are not standard and can vary significantly depending on the competition and the lessors. Too many times, the values are not seen until after the award, and sometimes only a few days before the anticipated lease document closing. If they turn out to be excessive, it may be too late to go elsewhere for the financing.

14. Upgrade Financing Right

There may be situations in which a prospective lessee will want the ability to have a lessor finance additions or changes, commonly referred to as upgrades, to equipment on lease with a lessor during the lease term. If the upgrade has no stand-alone value or utility, such as an internal modification to an existing computer system to enhance its performance, there would be only one lessor the lessee can turn to for the financing—the incumbent lessor. If the lessor is not willing to provide the financing, a lessee would have two alternatives—to pay for the upgrade itself, a cost which it typically cannot recover when it returns the leased equipment, or to forgo the upgrade. To avoid this problem, some prospective lessees negotiate an upgrade financing right—the right to require an incumbent lessor to finance all equipment upgrades to its leased equipment during the lease term at a pre-determined lease financing rate, or a rate which is to be determined by a set of guidelines that will be fair to both parties.

▶ **Recommendation:** Prospective lessees contemplating equipment upgrades should always require an upgrade financing right. This right should incorporate a formula for determining the upgrade financing interest rate—to avoid the lessee being forced into accepting an arbitrarily high rate offer from the incumbent lessor.

15. Equipment Damage or Loss

The proposal letter should identify the lessee's basic financial responsibilities in the event of a casualty loss. Typically, to protect its equipment investment, the lessor requires the lessee to pay a defined casualty value. How the casualty value amount will be determined should be set out in the proposal letter.

▶ **Recommendation:** Lessees required to insure equipment against casualty losses for the lessor's benefit should make sure any insurance proceeds received by the lessor will be credited against any casualty value due.

16. Tax Assumptions and Indemnification

A prospective lessor generally anticipates receiving certain tax benefits, such as depreciation, as a result of owning the leased equipment, and incorporates the assumed tax benefits into the rental computation. Those benefits, thus, become critical to the lessor's transaction economic return. When that is the case, the prospective lessor's lease proposal should spell out exactly what tax benefits are expected, as well as any responsibility a prospective lessee may have if benefits are lost.

Because of the adverse impact the loss of anticipated tax benefits can have for tax-oriented lessors, prospective lessees are frequently asked to provide indemnifications against any loss of expected tax benefits. Lessees, for their part, will usually agree to some indemnification, but will want to limit the circumstances triggering the indemnity as much as possible. While the precise terms of the indemnification will be negotiated during the documentation, the basic terms should be determined at the proposal stage.

17. Tax Law Changes

Where a lessor is anticipating tax benefits, a change in tax laws can affect the lessor's economic return. For example, changes in the tax laws affecting the equipment's depreciation life, the equipment depreciation method, or the federal tax rate on corporate income can have a substantial positive or negative impact.

▶ **Observation:** Because of the intense ongoing governmental focus on the federal tax laws in the equipment and the corporate tax rate areas, lessors and lessees should pay particular attention to the implications of anticipated changes.

One way to handle this risk is to quote the rent subject to an appropriate adjustment to reflect any tax law change affecting the lessor's expected economic return. The parties may agree, for example, that the rent will be adjusted to maintain the lessor's net return.

▶ **Recommendation:** The particular parameter that will serve as a guide for any rent adjustment should be defined precisely to prevent a calculation disagreement. "Net return," for example, can mean different things to different people. If a lessee does not know how to check a tax law change adjustment, it may pay more than necessary if the lessor tries to squeeze a little higher return. By the same token, a lessee may incorrectly object to a legitimate adjustment.

18. Tax Rulings

In response to a taxpayer's request, the IRS will rule on a transaction's tax conse-quences by delivering a tax letter ruling. If the taxpayer's request is complete and accurate, the IRS letter (called a private letter ruling) will be dispositive of the tax consequences. (See Chapter 8,B,1.) If a leasing transaction is particularly complex or involves uncertain tax law issues, a lessor may require a private letter ruling on a transaction's tax consequences before entering into it. Or, if the lease is signed before a ruling is made, a lessor may agree to release a lessee from required indemnifications on issues addressed favorably in a requested ruling. If such a ruling is considered necessary, the prospective lessor must make that a condition of its offer.

> **Illustrative Language**—*The Use of a Private Letter Ruling:*   The lessor plans to obtain a private IRS ruling with respect to the assumptions stated in this proposal letter. The lessee shall agree to indemnify the lessor for the tax assumptions that are the subject of the ruling request. Such indemnity shall remain in effect until a favorable ruling has been obtained on each of these points.

19. Transaction Expenses

The proposal letter should address who will pay what transaction expenses, par-ticularly in deals involving an underwritten leveraged lease. Where the lease is not an underwritten leveraged lease, the primary expense is legal fees, and the party incurring the expense usually pays for it. The matter is more complex in underwritten transactions. These types of transactions can involve many par-ties—equity participants, lenders, trustees, and an underwriter—and, possibly, a variety of substantial expenses, for example:

- Fees and disbursements of special counsel for the lenders and their repre-sentative
- Acceptance and annual fees of the lenders' representative—usually found in a trust arrangement
- Special counsel fees and disbursements for the equity participants and their representative
- Acceptance and annual fees of the equity participants' representative—usually found in a trust arrangement
- Fees and disbursements related to the filing for a private letter ruling
- Documentation expenses, such as reproduction and printing expenses
- Fees related to the placement of the debt

In practice, the expense allocation is not as great a problem as it may appear. *Reason:* Very often, the underwriter agrees to pay substantially all the expenses. An underwriter can, however, cap these expenses by agreeing to pay only up to a specified percentage, usually around 0.75 to 1.25% of the equipment cost, and the lessee must, then, pay the excess. Because an underwriter makes its money by charging the lessor-investors a set fee for bringing them the transaction, the more its expense responsibility is limited, the less it has to worry about fees and expenses eroding its profit. In a competitive market, however, many underwriters are willing, particularly if pushed a little, to assume the entire expense responsibility.

> **Illustrative Example**—*The Underwriter Expense Problem:* Company A, an underwriter, arranged for Company C and Company D to participate as the equity investors in the leveraged lease financing of one oceangoing tugboat to be leased to Company B. Companies C and D agreed to pay Company A a brokerage fee equal to 2% of the equipment's cost for bringing in the transaction. As a condition of the transaction award, Company A had to commit to Company B that Company B would not have to pay any expenses, except its own counsel fees. At the closing, the following costs were incurred:
>
> | | |
> |---|---|
> | Tugboat cost: | $6 million |
> | Fees for the lender's counsel: | $20,000 |
> | Counsel fees for Companies C & D: | $50,000 |
> | Counsel fees for Company A: | $2,000 |
> | Counsel fees for Company B: | $35,000 |
> | Printing expenses: | $21,000 |

What does Company A's profit picture look like? Company A's "gross" fee from the transaction is $120,000 (2% × $6 million). All fees and expenses, excluding Company B's counsel fees, total $93,000 ($20,000 + $50,000 + $2,000 + $21,000). Therefore, Company A "nets" $27,000 ($120,000 − $93,000). If Company A had a 1% "cap," its expense responsibility would have been limited to $60,000 (1% × $6 million) and it would have made $60,000 ($120,000 − $60,000) instead of $27,000.

a. What If the Deal Collapses?

The difficult expense question is who must pay what expenses if a proposed underwritten transaction collapses. The lenders and the prospective lessor-investors will refuse to have any responsibility if the transaction does not go through, so that leaves the underwriter and the prospective lessee. Some underwriters attempt to put the responsibility for all expenses incurred in such a situation on the prospective lessee by inserting an appropriate clause in the proposal letter. Typically, the clause provides that the prospective lessee must pay all expenses if the transaction is not consummated for any reason whatsoever. This can be a dangerous position for a prospective lessee, particularly when the underwriter's poor performance may be the reason the transaction failed.

▶ **Recommendation:** In a major underwritten lease financing, the expenses can be substantial. For example, it is not unheard of for the legal fees and other expenses in a complicated $10 million leveraged lease financing to run anywhere from $200,000 to $400,000. Thus, underwriters and prospective lessees should each carefully evaluate their potential expense exposure and clearly define the responsibilities in all events.

20. The Lease Type

As described in Chapter 1, there are a variety of different lease types, each imposing different responsibilities for the lessor and lessee. Care must be taken to ensure that the cost responsibilities are fully defined and understood. A typical net finance lease requires the lessee to pay all fixed expenses relating to the equipment during the lease term, such as maintenance, insurance, and certain taxes. For example, without a lessee fully understanding what the equipment-related expense obligations will be, the overall costs cannot be properly assessed. It can be an expensive surprise for a lessee to discover after the equipment is on lease that a substantial sales tax is owed.

E.   Agreement to the Proposal Letter

Following any proposal letter negotiations, a prospective lessee accepts the proposal offer by acknowledging its willingness to proceed on the basis of the terms presented. If the proposal is written it can be accepted by an appropriate officer signing the acceptance directly on the letter or in a separate writing properly referencing the proposal letter. Any acceptance condition should be clearly a part of the acceptance and identified as such. For example, if the acceptance is made by signing in a designated space on a proposal letter, the condition should precede the signature.

▶ **Recommendation:**   If a proposal letter is used, a prospective lessee should "accept" directly on the proposal letter, not in a separate writing, particularly if the acceptance is conditioned. Separate papers can easily be lost or misplaced.

F.   The Prospective Lessee's Obligations
After a Proposal Is Accepted

Because a proposal letter is generally not a contract, it may have no more than a psychological hold on the transaction because of various stated conditions, such as mutually satisfactory documentation, that are usually imposed. Thus, except for any obligation to pick up a collapsed transaction's expenses, the prospective lessee's obligations may be minimal or nonexistent at the time of the proposal acceptance. As a result, prospective lessors may be unable to require a prospective lessee to go through with a transaction or recover damages for its failure to proceed.

▶ **Recommendation:**   Inasmuch as a prospective lessee's obligations to go forward may be nonexistent after the acceptance of the offer, prospective lessors and underwriters must make sure transactions are quickly and efficiently completed.

G.   The Prospective Lessor's Obligations After a Proposal Is Accepted

Because the lease proposal is conditioned, the offeror's obligations after the prospective lessee accepts the proposal will probably be limited. For example, if the offer is conditioned on acceptable documentation, a prospective lessor may have no trouble finding "unacceptable" points and walking away from the transaction. Of course, there may be an ethical obligation to go forward, but this will be of little value to a prospective lessee when left standing at the last minute without the essential financing.

▶ **Recommendation:**   If a proposal is conditioned on certain lessor committee approvals, a prospective lessee should request written verification once the approvals have been given. Psychologically, this will bring the prospective lessor further into the transaction.

H.   A Proposal Stage Checklist for the Lessee

Following is a checklist of the issues that a prospective lessee must address during the proposal stage. The prospective lessee will want to review the list in preparing its bid letter and again to make sure the issues are addressed in the proposal letter.

Equipment Description

☐   What type will be involved?
☐   Who is the manufacturer?
☐   What is the model?
☐   How many units will be involved?

Equipment Cost

☐   What is the total cost involved?
☐   What is the cost per item?
☐   Is the cost per item fixed?

   1. If not, what is the probable cost escalation?

Equipment Payment

☐   When must the equipment be paid for?
☐   Must the entire purchase price be paid at once?

Equipment Delivery

☐ What is the anticipated delivery date?
☐ How long should the lease commitment run past the last anticipated delivery date?

Equipment Location

☐ Where will the equipment be located?

  1. At the lease inception
  2. During the lease term

Equipment Lease

☐ What type of lease is desired?

  1. Net finance lease
  2. Service lease
  3. Other

Lease Period

☐ How long must the lease run?
☐ Will an interim lease period be acceptable?

  1. If so, what is the latest date on which the primary term can begin?

☐ How long a renewal period is desired?
☐ How will the renewal right be structured? For example, five one-year periods, one five-year period, etc.

Rent Program

☐ When should the rent be payable?

  1. Annually
  2. Semiannually
  3. Quarterly
  4. Monthly
  5. Other

☐ Should the payments be "in advance" or "in arrears"?
☐ If there is an interim period, how should the interim rent be structured?

  1. Based on the primary rent (for example, the daily equivalent of the primary rent)
  2. Based on the long-term debt interest rate
  3. Other

☐ If there will be a renewal period, how should the renewal rent be structured?

  1. Fixed
  2. Fair rental value options

☐ What type of options are desired?
   1. Fair market value purchase right
   2. Fixed price purchase right
   3. Fair market rental value renewal right
   4. Fixed price renewal right
   5. Right of first refusal
   6. Termination right
   7. Upgrade right
   8. Other
☐ Is a right of first refusal specifically unacceptable?

Casualty and Termination Values

☐ If a termination right is required, will the termination values be a primary factor in the lease decision?
☐ Must the termination and casualty values be submitted at the time of the proposal?

Maintenance and Repair

☐ Who will have the equipment maintenance and repair obligations?

Tax Indemnifications

☐ What tax indemnifications will be acceptable, if any?

Insurance

☐ Is the right of self-insurance desired?

Taxes

☐ What taxes will be assumed?
   1. Sales
   2. Rental
   3. Other

Transaction Expenses (usually only a concern in underwritten transactions)

☐ What expenses other than lessee's legal fees, if any, will be assumed if the transaction is completed?
   1. Counsel fees for any lenders and their representative
   2. Acceptance and annual fees of any lender's representative (trust arrangement)
   3. Counsel fees for the lessor-investors and any representative
   4. Acceptance and annual fees of any lessor-investor's representative (trust arrangement)
   5. IRS private ruling letter fees

    6. Documentation expenses
    7. Debt placement fee
    8. Other

☐ What expenses, if any, will be assumed if the transaction collapses?

Tax Ruling

☐ Is an IRS private letter ruling necessary or desirable?
☐ Can a favorable letter ruling be a prerequisite to any of lessor's obligations?
☐ Should a private letter ruling relieve any tax indemnification obligations?

Submission Date

☐ What is the latest date on which the proposal can be submitted?

Award Date

☐ On what date will the transaction be awarded?

Type of Proposals

☐ Is an underwritten transaction acceptable? If so,

    1. Will "best efforts" or "firm" proposals be accepted?
    2. Is a leveraged or single-source transaction preferred?

☐ If "best efforts" proposals are acceptable, how long after the award will the underwriter have to firm up the prospective lessor-investors and any lenders?

Prospective Lessors—Underwritten Transaction

☐ Are any prospective lessors-investors not to be approached?

I. A Proposal Stage Checklist for the Lessor

The following checklist will serve as a guide to the prospective lessor in identifying issues, and in preparing and negotiating a proposal letter.

The Offer

☐ Will an underwritten or direct lessor proposal be involved?

☐ If an underwritten offer is involved,

    1. Will it be on a "best efforts" or "firm" basis?
    2. Must there be more than one equity participant?
    3. If it can be on a "best efforts" basis, is there any deadline when the equity participants must give their formal commitment?
    4. Will the transaction be leveraged with third-party debt?

The Lessee

☐ Has the lessee been accurately identified?
☐ Has the lessee's financial condition been reviewed?

Credit Support

☐ Can the lessee's financial condition support the entire lease obligation?
☐ If the lessee's "credit" is not sufficient, are there additional credit support alternatives available?

1. Parent company guarantee
2. Affiliated company guarantee
3. Unrelated third-party guarantee
4. Deficiency guarantee
5. Bank support
6. Other

☐ If credit support is necessary, has the financial condition of the entity giving the support been reviewed?

The Equipment Description

☐ What type will be involved?
☐ Who is the manufacturer?
☐ What is the model?
☐ How many units will be involved?

The Equipment Cost

☐ What is the total cost involved?
☐ What is the cost per item?
☐ Is the cost per item fixed?

1. If not, what is the probable cost escalation?

The Equipment Delivery

☐ What is the anticipated delivery date?
☐ Must the lease commitment run past the anticipated delivery date? If so, for how long?

1. Will a fee be charged for the commitment to lease future delivered equipment?

The Equipment Location

☐ Where will the equipment be located?

1. At the lease inception?
2. During the lease term?

The Rent Program

☐ What is the primary rent payment program structure?

1. Will the rent be payable "in advance" or "in arrears"?
2. Will the rent be payable annually, semiannually, quarterly, monthly, or other?

☐ Will interim rent be involved? If so,

1. Will it be based upon the primary rent, the long-term debt interest rate if leveraged, or other?
2. When will the payments be due?

The Term of the Lease

☐ How long will the lease run?

1. Primary lease term
2. Renewal period

☐ Will an interim lease term be involved? If so,

1. When will the interim lease term start?
2. When will the primary lease term start?

The Lessor

☐ How will the equipment be owned?

1. Directly
2. Indirectly through a partnership, trust, or corporation

☐ Will the ownership structure satisfy any tax and liability criteria?

1. Flow-through of tax benefits
2. Corporatelike liability protection
3. Other

The Debt—If the Transaction Is Leveraged

☐ What is the loan repayment program?

1. "In advance" or "in arrears"
2. Debt service to be payable annually, semiannually, quarterly, monthly, or other

☐ Who will be responsible for arranging for the placement of the debt?
☐ Will the rent be quoted on the basis of an assumed debt principal amount, per annum interest charge, etc.?

1. If so, will the rent quoted be subject to adjustment if other than assumed?

☐ If the rent is subject to a debt assumption adjustment, what adjustment criteria will be used?

1. After-tax yield
2. Cash flow

☐ 3. Net return
4. Other

☐ Who will be responsible for fees related to the debt?

1. Placement fee
2. Lender's commitment fee
3. Other

Options

☐ What special rights will the lessee have?

1. Fixed price purchase right
2. Fair market value purchase right
3. Fixed price renewal right
4. Fair market rental value renewal right
5. Right of first refusal
6. Termination right
7. Upgrade right
8. Other

☐ What special rights will the lessor have?

1. Fixed price sale right
2. Fixed price renewal right
3. Termination right
4. Other

Casualty Loss

☐ What financial responsibilities will the lessee have in the event of a casualty loss?

Casualty and Termination Values

☐ What amounts are to be used?

Tax Aspects

☐ What are the relevant tax assumptions?
☐ What tax assumptions, if any, will the lessee have to indemnify the lessor for in the event of loss or inability to claim?
☐ If there are lessee tax indemnifications, what events that result in tax benefit unavailability will trigger an indemnification payment?

1. Any reason
2. Acts or omissions of lessee
3. Acts or omissions of lessor
4. Change in law
5. Other

Tax Ruling

☐ Will a tax ruling be involved?
☐ If so, will a *favorable* ruling
    1. Relieve the lessee from any tax indemnifications?
    2. Be a prerequisite to the lessor's obligation to lease the equipment?

Transaction Expenses

☐ Who must pay for the expenses if
    1. The transaction goes through without problems?
    2. The transaction collapses before the lease documents are executed?
    3. The transaction collapses after the lease documents are executed but before the equipment is delivered?

Type of Lease

☐ What type of lease will be involved?
    1. Net finance lease
    2. Service lease
    3. Other

Conditions

☐ What conditions must be satisfied before the lessor is committed?
    1. Governmental or regulatory approvals
    2. Licenses or authorizations
    3. Favorable opinions of counsel
    4. Maintenance or achievement of certain financial tests
    5. Satisfactory audited financial statements
    6. Acceptable documentation
    7. Approvals by prospective lessor or equity participants
    8. Minimum dollar participation by equity and debt participants
    9. Favorable equipment appraisals justifying equipment residual value
   10. Other

Form of Proposal

☐ Will a written proposal be used? If so,
    1. How should acceptance be acknowledged?

Submission and Award Dates

☐ When is the latest date on which the proposal can be submitted?
☐ What is the anticipated transaction award date?
    1. Is there adequate time to do the deal?

Offer Termination Date

☐ How long will the prospective lessee have to accept the offer?

Chapter 3

Negotiating the Lease Document

A. What Is the Lease's Central Purpose?

Although a lease agreement can involve many complex, highly technical, and sometimes overwhelming concepts, its central purpose is very simple—it's a contract in which a property owner—the lessor—transfers the right to use the property to another—the lessee—for a period of time. The lessor retains title.

A lease differs from a conditional sale, an outright sale, or a mortgage type of transaction. Under a conditional sale, the property owner sells the property, not merely its use, to the buyer. At the time the agreement is reached, the seller transfers the property to the buyer, but retains title until the buyer performs certain conditions, usually the payment of the purchase price in installments. Following satisfaction of the conditions, the seller transfers title to the buyer.

In an outright sale, the property owner unconditionally transfers the property, including title, to the buyer and, at the same time, the buyer pays the seller the full purchase price. In a mortgage situation, a buyer of property borrows from a third-party lender some or all of the money necessary to buy the property. The lender, or mortgagee, as security for the repayment of its loan, requires the borrower, or mortgagor, to give it a security interest in the property. The borrower has possession of, and title to, the property subject to the lender's right to foreclose on the property in the event of a loan default.

B. The Common Lease Forms

Leases fall into one of two basic formats—the single transaction lease format and the master lease format. Although both follow the same fundamental structure, the lessor's format choice is dictated by the type of financing transaction, the relationship the lessor anticipates, and its document negotiation strategy. If the lessee has its own lease forms, the format choice is typically dictated by which is more cost-effective for a given relationship or transaction.

1.   *The Single Transaction Lease*

Lessors, particularly in small transactions and "vendor" programs, frequently use a "standard" preprinted single transaction lease. The standard lease form has fill-in blanks for those aspects, such as rent, that typically vary with each transaction. Although this type of lease format can be tailored to meet certain required variations, too many changes squeezed into the document margins, or attached as riders, can result in an unreadable document. Traditionally, preprinted single transaction leases are used in small ticket lease financings.

The preprinted lease format, whether it's the lessor's or the lessee's, is particularly attractive in small dollar lease transactions because it cuts down on drafting and negotiation, and thus helps to keep documentation costs, such as legal fees, at a minimum. That can help both parties because the greater the expenses, the less the profit to a lessor, and the greater the overall cost to the lessee. However, using a lessor's preprinted form lease can be risky for a lessee. They're often one-sided, giving few benefits to the lessee and containing many traps hidden in the fine print. Lessors use preprinted leases to create the impression that their document is standard in the industry and one that all lessees sign. Unfortunately, that is not true. Preprinted lease terms and conditions vary widely among lessors.

A few sophisticated lessees have recently begun to use lessor document strategies, developing and requiring the use of *their* preprinted standard form lease as a condition of a lease award. This approach not only saves documentation costs, but eliminates the potential for falling into lessor document traps.

▶ **Recommendation:**   The parties should always consider the estimated costs involved in documenting a lease in determining the transaction's economic attractiveness. Documentation expenses can be the same regardless of the dollar amount of equipment involved. A $10,000 legal fee may be reasonable for a $500,000 transaction, but it will not be for a $20,000 transaction.

2.   *The Master Lease*

A lease format set up to easily allow the addition of equipment to be delivered at a future date is commonly referred to as a master lease. It may be in a pre-printed form or specifically prepared—typed—for a particular transaction (a custom lease approach). Traditionally, master lease formats are used in medium-sized (middle market) and large ticket lease transactions.

A master lease has two parts: The main, or "boilerplate," portion contains the provisions that will remain the same from transaction to transaction (such as basic representations, warranties, tax obligations, and maintenance responsibilities); and the second part, sometimes called the "schedule," contains the items that will vary among transactions (such as equipment type, rent, and options). Typically, the schedule will be short—often only one or two pages—while the main portion may be 40 to 50 pages. The advantage to using a master lease format is that the parties can document future transactions with a minimum amount of time and expense by merely adding a schedule containing the information pertaining to the specific transaction. A master lease has been included in the Appendix.

▶ **Observations:**

- Strategically, a lessor with a master lease in place with a particular lessee has a competitive advantage over other prospective lessors in any new bidding situation. Because documenting new equipment additions on an existing master lease is simpler than negotiating an entirely new lease, companies having master leases frequently go out of their way to let an existing lessor win by, for example, giving the lessor the last opportunity to match a lower offer.
- An increasing number of companies that frequently lease large ticket items of equipment have developed their own master lease format and require that a prospective lessor agree to use it as a condition of a lease award. Where multimillion dollar financings are concerned, this can substantially reduce legal fees and other documentation and negotiation costs.

C. Subjects to Address in Negotiating the Lease

Before starting—and throughout the lease negotiations—the parties must understand the legal, financial, and practical aspects of a lease. Without that understanding, a party may inadvertently give up on an issue that is important, be too adamant about a point of little consequence, or miss an issue altogether. The following explanation identifies and describes issues that can arise in a major equipment lease, and suggests ways that the parties may resolve them. In preparing for the negotiations, the parties must weigh the relative values of different alternative approaches so that they will be able effectively to make necessary trade-offs.

▶ **Reminder:** In addition to the transaction's participants, another party must be considered in negotiating a tax-oriented lease—the IRS. Although the parties may find that one particular approach is in their business interests, that approach may jeopardize the lease's status as a true tax lease. The tax lease rules are explained in Chapter 8, and particular issues that may give rise to tax problems are noted below.

The following explanation uses a net finance lease as an example because it is generally the most comprehensive and complex form. Generally, understanding the issues arising in a net finance lease will enable an individual to deal with virtually any kind of equipment lease.

▶ **Note:** The Appendix includes a sample net finance lease. The reader is urged to read it in conjunction with the following explanation.

▶ **Recommendation:** In drafting a lengthy lease document, the parties should compile an index containing all the topic headings and page numbers to help the participants in the negotiation process locate relevant provisions.

1. *Identifying the Parties to the Lease*

The lease should begin by clearly stating each party's full legal name, the jurisdiction in which each is organized, and the mailing address of their principal places of business. This will prevent disputes as to who is intended to be bound by the contract.

> **Illustrative Language**—*The Proper Name Designations:* This Lease made as of the 25th day of February, 19××, by and between ARROW CORPORATION, a Delaware corporation, having its principal place of business at 200 Curtis Street, New York, New York (hereinafter called "Lessor") and THE HARRIS CORPORATION, a Missouri corporation, having its principal place of business at 100 Barkley Street, St. Louis, Missouri (hereinafter called "Lessee").

▶ **Recommendation:** Sometimes a corporation leases equipment to be used exclusively by one of its divisions. When such a division has been organized as a "profit center," the corporation frequently wants it to be the named "Lessee." However, if the division is not a separate legal entity, it cannot be bound by a contract. If the "division" is a corporate subsidiary, however, this problem will not be present because it will have a separate legal existence. A prospective lessor should, therefore, make sure that the lessee entity has been properly identified and is capable of being legally bound in the capacity indicated in the lease.

2. *Writing the Factual Summary*

When the lease document is typed specifically for the transaction, and is not a preprinted form, it is always a good idea for it to summarize the basic facts surrounding the transaction at the outset. Writing the summary helps each party focus on the overall transaction. And the summary provides a valuable future reference for individuals not involved at the time the lease was negotiated. For example, the summary might describe the equipment purchase contract the lessee entered into prior to the lease transaction and state that it has been assigned to the lessor as part of the transaction.

Typically, the factual summary is incorporated into what are referred to as "whereas" clauses. The factual summary is often followed by a statement of the consideration for the lease, generally stated as the mutual obligations of the lessor and the lessee under the agreement. This is usually done in a "Now, therefore" clause following the "Whereas" section. Stating the consideration for the transaction in this manner is not legally necessary, but many lawyers consider it good form to do so.

> **Illustrative Language**—*A Factual Summary:* Whereas, pursuant to a purchase agreement (the "Purchase Agreement") dated January 2, 19××, between White Aircraft Corporation (the "Manufacturer"), a Delaware corporation, and the Lessee identified above, the Manufacturer has agreed to manufacture and sell to the Lessee, and the Lessee

has agreed to purchase from the Manufacturer, one White Model A-14 aircraft, which is to be financed pursuant to this Lease; and

Whereas, the Lessee and the Lessor will enter into an assignment of the Purchase Agreement simultaneously with the execution of this Lease whereby the Lessee assigns to the Lessor all the Lessee's rights and interests under the Purchase Agreement, except to the extent reserved therein;

Now, therefore, in consideration of the mutual agreements contained in this Lease, the parties hereto agree as follows:

3. Defining the Key Terms

The lease should define the fundamental terms used repeatedly in the lease agreement that have special meaning in a separate section, preferably at the document's beginning. For example, terms such as "fair market purchase value," "fair market rental value," "manufacturer," "purchase contract," "stipulated loss value," and "termination value" will usually have certain meanings in a particular transaction, and the parties must agree on their meaning to prevent future ambiguities. Using such a definition section makes the text clearer, permits the parties to locate definitions more readily, and lessens the risk that an important term will accidentally be left undefined.

▶ **Recommendation:**   If a preprinted lease does not have such a section incorporated and the definitions are scattered throughout the text, it may be advisable to include a rider that lists all key terms and the page number and lease section where they were first defined.

4. Dealing With Future Delivered Equipment

Often the parties will want to enter into the lease well before the equipment's delivery date. Coming to terms on the lease in advance of the equipment's delivery can often benefit both parties: the prospective lessee can then be sure that no insurmountable problems will arise before it is too late to find another lessor; and an equally anxious prospective lessor may want to make sure that the lessee does not change its mind.

a.   Putting the Equipment Under the Lease

When a lease transaction is documented before the equipment's delivery, the parties must prescribe a method for putting the equipment under lease when it arrives. Usually the arrangement is for the lessee to notify the lessor in writing of the equipment's delivery and its acceptability for lease. The notification is usually in what is referred to as an "acceptance supplement," a written statement that lists the equipment delivered and states that the lessee accepted it for lease as of a specified date. If the equipment conforms to the agreement, the lessor automatically puts it on lease.

When the lease relates to equipment to be delivered in the future, the lessee's obligation to lease the equipment must be clearly spelled out. For example, the lessee may want the option to accept or reject the equipment when delivered. And the lessor should clearly be aware of the lessee's obligation. An ambiguous phrase such as "the lessee may accept the equipment when delivered by executing the appropriate acceptance supplement," can cause problems—the lessor may anticipate that the lessee is bound to accept the equipment, while the lessee may not believe it is bound.

b. Nonutilization and Commitment Fees

If the lessee wants the right to reject equipment to be delivered in the future, there are two ways a lessor can have some protection: a nonutilization fee and a commitment fee.

A nonutilization fee compensates a lessor for funds committed to future delivered equipment that remain unused at the end of the commitment period. Usually, the fee is expressed as a percentage of the originally estimated equipment cost and is payable in a lump sum at the end of the commitment period. If all or an agreed-on portion of the funds are used, the lessee owes nothing.

> **Illustrative Example**—*The Nonutilization Fee:*   Company Able, a leasing company, has agreed to give Company Baker a lease line of credit for 10 river barges. The barges' total cost will be $1 million, and they will be delivered over a 12-month period. Company Able, however, has a limited amount of funds available and wants to be sure it will be protected from an opportunity loss if the barges are not delivered or Company Baker decides not to lease them. Therefore, it imposes a 1% nonutilization fee. If only $400,000 worth of barges are delivered during the commitment period, how much of a fee is due?
>
> Company Baker would owe Company Able $6,000: 1% of the funds remaining unused ($600,000). If none of the equipment was put on lease, Company Baker would owe $10,000 (1% × $1 million). If $1 million worth of equipment was leased, Company Baker would owe nothing.

A nonutilization fee arrangement has risks for the lessee. An unexpectedly high equipment purchase cost (whether from a mistaken estimate or a price escalation) or a delivery delay may give the lessor the right to exclude equipment from the lease. If this happens, a lessee can end up paying a nonutilization fee based on the unused funds remaining at the end of the commitment period. It is not, however, generally considered unreasonable for the lessee to bear this type of risk in cases other than where a lessor could arbitrarily choose not to lease certain agreed-on equipment when it arrives.

▶ **Recommendation:**   If confronted with a nonutilization fee arrangement, a prospective lessee can lessen the payment impact resulting from equipment exclusions by negotiating a commitment percentage leeway. For example, the lease can provide for the fee to be payable only to the extent that greater than 10% of the committed funds are not used.

The other approach, a commitment fee, is more commonly used. Under this arrangement, a lessee pays a flat fee at the time the lease is entered based on the total equipment cost involved for the lease funding commitment. Generally, the fee is expressed as a percentage of total cost, commonly ranging from 0.375 to 1%. Because the commitment fee pays a lessor for holding funds available, the lessee can freely elect not to put equipment on lease.

▶ **Observation:** In a competitive lease market, lessors may find it difficult to make a lessee accept nonutilization and commitment fees because many other lessors may be willing to hold funds available without a fee to win business.

c. Minimum Grouping Requirements

When a lease involves many less expensive equipment items to be delivered over a long period of time, a lessor can require a minimum equipment acceptance grouping to reduce its administrative handling expenses. For example, a lessee may not be able to accept equipment for lease in aggregate cost groups of less than $100,000.

An equipment grouping requirement can cause serious problems for a lessee. For example, if the dollar minimum was set high, the lessee may have to manipulate deliveries to avoid having to pay for equipment for which it does not yet have lease funding until the specified amount is accumulated.

▶ **Recommendation:** When confronted with a minimum dollar amount equipment grouping requirement, the prospective lessee should seek a "best efforts" qualification. Under this provision, if it becomes impractical to do so, after using its best efforts to assemble the required minimum, the lessee will be permitted to have a smaller amount accepted.

5. *The Lease Terms*

The parties must clearly define the period of permitted use—the term of lease. Generally, there are two basic periods: (1) a main lease term, referred to as the "base lease term," the "primary lease term," or the "initial lease term"; and (2) a renewal term. Some transactions also call for an "interim lease term," beginning when the equipment becomes subject to lease until the start of a predetermined base term. The interim term concept is frequently used if many equipment items will go on lease at various times. For example, the base term may start on January 1, 19✕✕, for all equipment delivered during the prior three-month period. By consolidating the start of the primary lease term into one date after which all equipment will be delivered, administrative work and rent payment mechanics are simplified.

In setting up the renewal term options, generally, from the lessee's viewpoint, the more alternatives there are, the better. For example, one four-year renewal term is less preferable than four one-year terms because the lessee can compare market prices at more intervals. For the lessor, a longer renewal period will generally be preferable because it will want to have a longer period where its rents are predictable and it does not have to undertake remarketing the equipment.

6. The Rent Payment Structure

Because when the rent payments are due and how much the lessee must pay are key elements of every lease transaction, the lease must precisely set out those terms in detail. For example, a 10-year lease may call for rent to be payable in 20 consecutive, level, semiannual, in arrears payments, each payment to be equal to 2% of the total cost of the equipment.

a. Payment Mechanism

To avoid problems, the lease should specify (1) where the rent is payable, such as at the lessor's place of business; (2) the form of payment, such as in immediately available funds; and (3) when it is to be deemed received by the lessor, such as when deposited in a U.S. mailbox. Unless the lease specifies those terms, a lessee runs the risk of a lessor claiming a technical default based on what the lessor deems to be an incorrect or late payment, and a lessor runs the risk of losing interest it could have earned had the rent been paid in a manner that would have permitted an earlier use of the money. For example, a lessor will lose interest if payment is made by regular check, which would take time to clear, as opposed to immediately available funds through, for example, an electronic wire funds transfer.

▶ **Recommendation:** Lessees should establish appropriate internal rent payment procedures to avoid technical defaults through, for example, accidental late payments. If the rent must be sent to a special P.O. box number, all individuals responsible for handling the payments should be separately advised so that the rent does not instead get sent to the lessor's regular business address.

b. Fixing the Rental Amount

Besides using fixed dollar amounts, the lease may express the rent in different ways. One way is as a percentage of equipment cost. The parties frequently use this method when equipment is to be delivered after the lease is signed, because then the rent does not have to be recalculated if the purchase price varies from that anticipated. For example, if the annual rent is expressed as 2% of equipment cost, changes in cost will not require a lease adjustment. If, on the other hand, the lease sets rent at $2,000 a year based on a $100,000 item of equipment and the price later turns out to be $105,000, a lease amendment is needed to incorporate the proper rent.

When the rent is based on a percentage of equipment cost, the lease should define what expenses may be included, or "capitalized," in the "cost" term. If a prospective lessor has ample funds available, it may be eager to include more expenses into the rent computation cost base. For example, it may readily pay for sales taxes, freight charges, and installation costs and thereby increase the rent. If, however, its money supply is limited, it will probably want to exclude the extras. Also, when "soft" costs, such as installation costs, are substantial in relation to the raw equipment purchase price, a prospective lessor may not be willing to exceed a certain dollar amount on such costs because to do so would lessen its collateral value protection. For example, if a lessor financed the installation costs, and they ran 25% of the raw equipment cost, the lessor's collateral position would be diluted. In other words, 25% of the total amount financed would relate to installation charges that would have no remarketing value.

▶ **Recommendation:** The equipment related cost items that a prospective lessor is willing to finance can vary with each transaction. A prospective lessee should, therefore, define the ground rules in the proposal letter stage to eliminate potential misunderstandings or misconceptions.

c. Tax Law Rental Adjustment

When a prospective lessor's economic return depends in part on anticipated equipment ownership tax benefits, it may want to be able to make rent adjustments if unexpected tax law changes occur that adversely affect its return. For example, the lease can incorporate a provision that would allow the lessor to adjust the rent to maintain its "yield and after-tax cash flow." Instead of a yield and after-tax cash flow, leases sometimes use a maintenance of earnings or net return standard.

▶ **Recommendations:**

- A prospective lessor with the right to make rent adjustments in the event of adverse tax law changes should also have the ability to make appropriate adjustments to values that are based on the rent, such as termination or stipulated loss values. Without being able to adjust these rent-related values, the financial integrity of the transaction may not be maintained in the event, for example, of an early termination or a casualty loss.
- A prospective lessee should always make sure that the lease clearly defines any lessor rent adjustment criterion. Terms such as "yield" or "earnings," for example, do not have standard meanings and can be subject to many interpretations. The lease must set out the exact formula to be used in making any adjustment to enable an independent verification of any of the lessor's computations.
- If a lessor has the right to adjust the rent up in the event of an adverse change in the tax laws to compensate for any loss, a lessee should request the right to have the rent adjusted downward if there is a tax law change that is economically favorable to the lessor.
- If a specific tax law change looks likely during lease negotiations, it may be advisable to determine in advance what the rents and rent-related values will be should the change occur and incorporate them into the lease

agreement. This way everyone knows exactly what to expect before a final commitment is made.

d.   Conditions on Payment

In many equipment leases, particularly finance leases, the lessee's rent obligation is absolute and unconditional. That is, the lessee must pay the rent in full and on time regardless of any claim the lessee may have against the lessor. Commonly referred to as a "hell or high water" obligation, the provision at first sight shocks many new prospective lessees. The provision, however, is not as troublesome as it seems initially because it does not prevent a lessee from independently bringing a lawsuit against the lessor on any claim.

▶ **Recommendation:**   Although not technically necessary, a prospective lessee may want to insert a statement in a hell-or-high-water provision to the effect that any rights of action it may have for damages caused by the lessor will exist regardless of the hell-or-high-water rent commitment.

Typically, a lessor will want a hell-or-high-water provision when he is leveraging his investment through a nonrecourse loan. With this provision, a lender is more likely to lend on a nonrecourse-to-lessor basis because potential claims against the lessor would not affect the rental stream that is being relied on for the loan repayment.

▶ **Observations:**

- Using nonrecourse debt as opposed to recourse debt is the most desirable way for a lessor to leverage a lease transaction. For financial reporting purposes, the nonrecourse nature permits a lessor to disregard the loan obligation on its financial books because the lender may look only to the lessee and the collateral for repayment, not to the lessor's general funds.
- Sometimes a lessor's general lending bank requires a lessor to include hell-or-high-water lease provisions in all leases. If so, the obligation is included in the lending agreement and is usually coupled with a right to require an assignment of all the lessor's rights under each lease, including the right to the rent payments, as an additional form of security for the loans.

7.   *The Lessor's Right to Receive Reports*

To monitor the transaction, the lessor may want the right to receive certain reports from the lessee. The utility of the various possible lessee reports depends on each transaction. It is usually advisable, however, for a prospective lessor to at least require financial reports, accident reports, lease conformity reports, equipment location reports, and third-party claim reports. These will enable it to stay on top of a transaction.

a. Financial Reports

One of the best methods for a lessor to monitor a lessee's financial condition during the lease term is to require the lessee periodically to submit financial reports, such as current balance sheets and profit and loss statements. With these, a lessor will be in a good position to spot potential financial problems and take whatever early action may be necessary to protect its investment.

► **Recommendations:**

- A prospective lessor should require quarterly, as well as annual, balance sheets and profit and loss statements. And each should be certified by an independent public accounting firm.
- A prospective lessee should ensure that the time between the period when the information is gathered and when a financial report is due is adequate for its preparation and submission to avoid a potential default situation.

b. Accident Reports

A lessor should receive immediate notification of every significant or potentially significant accident involving the leased equipment, whether the damage is to the equipment or to persons or other property. Because it is not uncommon for a lessor to be sued solely on the basis of its ownership interest, lessee accident reports are a must. The reports should be in writing and contain a summary of the incident, including the time, place, and nature of the accident, and the persons and property involved. Reviewing all incidents may be a tedious job, particularly when many items of equipment are on lease, but it can prevent some costly surprises.

► **Recommendations:**

- When an accident could involve major dollar liability, the lease should require the lessee to notify the lessor by telephone immediately in addition to submitting a written report. A lessor's early arrival on the scene can produce facts that would otherwise be lost.
- A prospective lessee should limit accident notification responsibility only to incidents involving serious accidents. Minor accidents can create an unnecessary volume of paperwork. One approach is to set an estimated damage dollar amount below which notification is not required. If there is such a cutoff, the lessor should make the lessee responsible for inaccurate estimates because the lessor may not hear about a major claim until it has received notice of litigation.

c. Lease Conformity Reports

Lessors sometimes require lessees to submit annually an officer's certificate stating whether any events of default under the lease have occurred during the reporting year, and whether there are any existing conditions that could eventually result in an event of default. If there are any, an appropriate factual summary must accompany the certificate. From a lessor's viewpoint, this type of report can be a good early warning technique. Although the reports are somewhat of a burden from a lessee's viewpoint, they are useful in avoiding inadvertent lease default situations. For example, it is not unusual, particularly in larger companies, to discover at the end of the lease that the equipment has been misplaced— sometimes too late to locate it before delinquent return penalties are incurred.

d.   Equipment Location Reports

Requiring a lessee to prepare and submit equipment location reports is frequently advisable and sometimes necessary. If practical, a lessor should periodically inspect the leased equipment, particularly when the lessee has an obligation to maintain it. If the location is known, it is easy for the lessor to "drop in" to check up on its condition. Location reports may be essential if a lessor intends to keep any security interest or other collateral protection filings up-to-date, as a location change sometimes necessitates a new filing.

▶ **Recommendation:**   When the lessor has filed or intends to file security interests, the lease should require the lessee to notify the lessor at least 45 days before a change of equipment location occurs to give the lessor enough time to make any additional filings or amendments to existing filings.

e.   Third-Party Claim Reports

Generally, a lessor has a measure of security because it can take its equipment back if the lessee defaults. However, tax liens or other third-party claims imposed on the equipment, viable or not, can seriously jeopardize this protected position. Thus, the lease should require that the lessee notify the lessor of any events that result, or could result, in such an imposition so that it will have the opportunity to protect its position and equipment.

f.   Other Reports

The lessor should request the right to have the lessee submit reports that may be determined to be necessary in the future because unforeseeable events may require that the lessor receive certain additional information concerning the equipment. However, the lessee should seek to qualify any general reporting obligation so that only reasonable information relevant to the lease transaction can be requested.

8. *Equipment Maintenance and Alterations*

a.   Equipment Maintenance

The lease must specify which party has the obligation for maintenance and what will be acceptable maintenance. Many types of leases, such as net finance leases, put the normal maintenance responsibilities on the lessee. Regardless of the arrangement, however, the maintenance issue should be specifically addressed in the lease.

Usually, the lease will describe the maintenance requirements in terms of the condition in which the equipment will have to be maintained. A common provision requires the lessee to keep the equipment in "good working order, ordinary wear and tear excepted." Unfortunately, such a general requirement may be difficult to apply because it is somewhat vague, and more specific guidelines are difficult to come up with. Two ways to minimize the difficulties:

- If the lessee will use the equipment in a manner that may cause extra wear and tear, the maintenance provision can exclude ordinary wear and tear resulting from the lessee's intended use.
- If the equipment's manufacturer provides maintenance instructions, the lessee should follow them exactly.

Some types of equipment must be specially maintained. A leased aircraft, for example, must be maintained under standards put out by the Federal Aviation Administration. Failing to meet those standards may mean that the aircraft cannot be flown, or, even worse, could result in lawsuits.

▶ **Recommendations:**

- The parties should seek expert advice in specialized maintenance situations. Parties negotiating lease agreements frequently do not fully appreciate the cost effect of a proposed maintenance arrangement and, as a result, fail to protect themselves adequately.
- A lessee responsible for maintenance should also be required to keep maintenance records and to make them available to the lessor. Keeping records helps both parties; the lessor can determine whether the equipment is being properly serviced, and the lessee has greater protection should the lessor raise a claim of inadequate maintenance.
- If the lease permits the lessor access to the lessee's maintenance records, the lessee should limit access to normal business hours.

b. Equipment Alterations

A lessor should have the right to prohibit the lessee from making equipment alterations not related to normal maintenance. A lessee making alterations can affect the true lease status of the lease for tax purposes, thereby jeopardizing the lessor's tax benefits. These are explained in Chapter 8. In addition to the tax considerations, an alteration could affect the equipment's market value and impair its value to the lessor following the end of the lease term. Generally, this is handled by a lease provision requiring the lessee to get the lessor's prior written consent to a proposed change.

9. Specific Protection of Lessor's Ownership

There are certain basic possession, use, and operational conditions that may be necessary for a lessor to impose to protect its ownership interest in the leased equipment. This section will be devoted to a description of the most essential considerations.

a. Filings Must Be Made

In many cases, it will be necessary that filings be made to protect the lessor's ownership status. The lessor may want to file security interests under a state's Uniform Commercial Code laws to ensure priority over other creditors—typically referred to as "UCC filings." Certain types of equipment require special filings. An aircraft lessor, for example, must make certain filings with the Federal Aviation Administration to protect its ownership interest.

Who should be responsible to make the required filings? It is a matter of negotiation between the parties. If the lessee has that obligation, the lessor must require the lessee to confirm promptly that the designated action was taken. And, the lease should obligate the lessee to pay for any out-of-pocket losses incurred as a result of an improper filing.

b. An Equipment Marking Requirement

The lease should require the lessee to mark the leased equipment with the lessor's name and its principal place of business. Marking the equipment has two basic benefits for a lessor: A marking will help fend off a creditor of the lessee trying to claim the equipment for the lessee's unpaid debts, and it will enable a lessor to identify his equipment more readily during an inspection trip or if a reclaiming action is necessary.

> **Illustrative Language**—*Ownership Marking:* White Leasing Corporation, Owner-Lessor, San Francisco, California.

c. Certain Broad Use Prohibitions

The lease should prohibit the lessee from "using, operating, maintaining, or storing the leased equipment carelessly, improperly, in violation of law, or in a manner other than contemplated by the manufacturer." If, for example, improper handling or storing damages the leased equipment, and the lessor becomes responsible to a third party for damages caused through any of these actions, the lessor may have a basis for making a claim against the lessee.

▶ **Recommendations:**

- Because of the scope of some general usage prohibitions, a lessee can easily find itself in technical default for relatively minor violations. A prospective lessee should, therefore, attempt to define the parameters more specifically, such as pinpointing the exact laws with which it must comply.

- Lessees prohibited from using equipment other than in conformity with the manner contemplated by the manufacturer can unknowingly run into trouble. Frequently, equipment is acquired for a use different from that it was originally built to meet because, for example, nothing else is available. In such a case, a prospective lessee should attempt to get a use exception, a specific authorization to use the equipment as necessary.

10. Certain Key Assurances Required by the Lessor

The lease should require the lessee to make certain key representations on matters related to a lease transaction. The representations should be given as true on the date of the lease document's execution and, where relevant, should also be ongoing during the lease period. The lease should provide that the remedy for the lessee's failure to maintain the representations is that the lessor may declare an event of default and get out of its commitments.

a. That the Lessee Is Legally in Existence

The prospective lessor must assure itself through an appropriate lessee representation that the prospective lessee is a legal entity authorized to do business where the equipment will be used. A corporate lessee should, for example, be required to represent that it is properly organized, validly existing, and in good standing under the laws of its state of incorporation and that it is duly authorized to do business in those states where the equipment will be used. If the lessee is not, the lessor may have a difficult time suing the lessee, should it become necessary to do so. Also, any lack of proper legal standing can result in a seizure of the equipment by state authorities. The lessor's secured position could be jeopardized.

b. That the Lessee Has the Transactional Authority to Enter Into the Lease

A lessor must have the lessee represent that it is authorized to enter into the lease transaction and that the persons executing the lease, by name or official title, are fully authorized to sign on the lessee's behalf. For example, if the lessee is a corporation and it had not been properly empowered by its board of directors to make the lease commitment, a lessor may be unable to enforce the agreement against the corporation.

The lessor's only recourse may be against the individual executing the lease "on behalf of the corporation." Because it is unlikely that the signing party, in his individual capacity, would have enough personal wealth to satisfy any substantive claim, the lessor would be in a precarious position.

▶ **Observation:** Merely because a lessee represents a particular point does not mean it is necessarily true as stated. If, however, a falsehood is deemed an event of default, the lessor would have the ability to reclaim the equipment.

c. That There Are No Conflicting Agreements

Existing agreements may restrict a prospective lessee's ability to enter into a lease transaction. A bank credit agreement, for example, could prevent the borrower from taking out additional loans without the lender's consent. If "loans" are defined to include lease obligations, the failure to secure the lender's consent would most likely be treated as a loan default. Typically, if there is a loan default, the lender would have the right to demand an immediate repayment of the outstanding money, which, in turn, could adversely affect a lessee's financial condition. Any lessening of the lessee's financial strength can jeopardize its ability to meet its lease obligations. The lease should include a provision that by entering into the lease agreement the lessee is not violating any existing credit or other agreements.

d. That All Necessary Regulatory Approvals Have Been Obtained

In some situations, a prospective lessee may be required to secure regulatory approval for certain aspects of a lease transaction. For example, a public utility may be required to clear certain lease commitments with the appropriate utility regulatory authority. If they are not cleared, the lease commitments may be unenforceable. It is essential, therefore, that a lessor get a representation from the lessee that all necessary regulatory approvals have been obtained or, if none are needed, a representation to that effect.

► **Recommendations:**

- Because of the regulatory complexities existing in certain industries, such as public utilities, it may be wise for a prospective lessor to verify independently that the lessee has complied with all necessary regulatory aspects, rather than relying on the lessee's representation or its counsel's opinion. Failure to comply can result in a major problem. Although the lessor can reclaim the equipment if a misrepresentation is deemed an event of default, the expense and time involved in getting the equipment back, combined with the problem of having to dispose of, for example, 100 heavy-duty used trucks at a reasonable price, can present serious practical problems. Securing a favorable opinion from independent counsel expert in the area is advisable, but it is not an "ironclad" solution. The safest course of action, if possible, is to get the appropriate regulatory authority to issue a favorable written opinion on the relevant issues.
- Regulatory approval processes frequently take time. To avoid major delays, a prospective lessee should start the process as soon as possible so that, if necessary, it will be in a position to deliver the necessary assurances at the lease closing, such as supplying certified copies of any approvals obtained.

e. That There Are No Adverse Proceedings

A lessor must require the lessee to represent that there are no pending or threatened legal or administrative proceedings that could adversely affect the lessee's operations or financial condition. If there are such proceedings, the lessee should indicate what they are, and the lease (or another document) should expressly describe them. For example, it is not inconceivable for an impending lawsuit to be potentially serious enough to bankrupt a company. If it comes to a lessor's attention after the lease is signed, a no adverse proceeding representation would allow a lessor to terminate the transaction.

▶ **Recommendations:**

- It is sometimes impossible for a prospective lessee to be aware of all threatened lawsuits or similar proceedings, particularly those involving minor incidents. Thus, the proceeding representation should be qualified to the effect that there are no proceedings that would have a material adverse impact on the lessee's operations or financial condition of which it is aware.
- From a lessor's viewpoint, a no adverse proceeding representation should be broad enough to cover not only the lessee, but also its subsidiaries and affiliated companies, because a proceeding against a related company could jeopardize the lessee's financial condition.

f. That the Lessee's Financial Statements Are Accurate

Because the lessee's financial condition is a critical consideration in a lessor's credit analysis, the lessee should represent that all financial statements delivered to the lessor, including those prepared by the lessee's outside accountants, accurately represent its financial condition. Such a representation should be requested whether or not the statements have been certified by the lessee's independent accountants. For example, if a mistake were made, the lessor could reassess its willingness to continue with the transaction when the mistake is discovered.

11. *Certain Key Assurances Required by the Lessee*

The lessee should also require that the lessor make certain representations—a point often overlooked by prospective lessees.

a. That the Lessor Has the Transactional Authority to Lease the Equipment

Even though a prospective lessor presents itself to the public as being in the leasing business, there may be restrictions, such as in a credit agreement, prohibiting the lessor from entering into particular types of transactions. Also, a prospective lessor may have to go through prescribed internal procedures before a lease is in fact an authorized transaction. Violating any restrictions or procedures could jeopardize the lessee's right to continue using the equipment. Of course, an appropriate representation from a lessor will not guarantee there will be no use interference, but it will provide the lessee with another ground on which to base a claim in the event of a problem.

In underwritten transactions, the lessor-investors, "equity participants," are frequently not in the leasing business per se. Many corporations, for example, invest in leases on an irregular basis as equity participants, and if the lessor corporation has not obtained all the appropriate internal approvals for the transaction, a lessee may have some enforceability problems. In such a case, if a lessor backs out, a lessee may try to sue for performance on the basis that the lessor should be held to the contract based on its apparent authority to enter into the lease. If a lessor-investor is involved who is not regularly in the leasing market, this possible ground may be unavailable. Thus, it is important in underwritten transactions for a lessee to secure a representation that the transaction has been duly authorized by the lessor-investor.

b. That the Equipment Will Be Paid For

The lease must include a statement by the lessor that it will pay for and lease the equipment to the lessee, particularly when the lease is executed in advance of equipment deliveries. While a firm commitment will not guarantee that funds will be available, it will assist in a legal action for damages in the event the lessor does not follow through. The lessor, in turn, will want the commitment to be subject to the lessee's fulfilling certain obligations, such as equipment inspection and acceptance. As long as those conditions are within the lessee's capability, they should not be of concern.

▶ **Recommendations:**

- A lessor payment commitment representation is particularly important when a prospective lessee is dealing with smaller, less well financed leasing companies. It cannot, however, be relied on exclusively if the dollar amount of the equipment involved is significant, or last minute funding problems could cause a budgeting disruption. Thus, the reputation and financial background of a prospective lessor should be investigated to ensure that funding risk is at a minimum. A cheaper rental rate from a lesser-known leasing company, or equity participant in the case of an underwritten transaction, will quickly lose its appeal if the funds are not available when needed.
- The lessor should represent that the equipment will be, and will remain, free of all liens and encumbrances, except those of which the lessee is aware, such as the debt in a leveraged lease. That representation will help ensure that there will not be any interference with the lessee's equipment use from the lessor's third-party creditors.

c. That There Will Be No Interference With the Equipment's Use

A lessee's right to the quiet enjoyment and peaceful possession of the equipment during the lease period is fundamental, provided, of course, the lessee is not in default under the lease. A prospective lessee should require a representation to that effect.

▶ **Recommendation:** A prospective lessor should limit its representation of enjoyment to its own actions, as opposed to guaranteeing that the lessee will be entitled to quiet enjoyment in all events. If the representation is not so qualified, a lessor can be liable for damages if an unrelated third party, not claiming directly or indirectly through the lessor, interferes with the lessee's use of the equipment.

12. The Lessor Should Disclaim Certain Product Responsibility

If the lessor is not the equipment vendor, he will not typically be responsible to the lessee for anything that goes wrong with the equipment. However, to be on the safe side, a lessor should make an appropriate product warranty disclaimer to prevent any possible exposure to a lessee for defects in the equipment's design, suitability, operation, fitness for use, or merchantability. The lessee should be able to accept such a disclaimer because it can rely on the usual manufacturer's, subcontractor's, or supplier's product warranties.

13. It Is Advisable for the Lessee to Get an Assignment of Product Warranties

Where equipment is supplied by a manufacturer, subcontractor, or supplier, the lessee may be responsible for defects during or at the end of the lease term even though they were caused by the manufacturer, subcontractor, or supplier. To prevent that, a prospective lessee should obtain an assignment of any rights that the prospective lessor would have as equipment owner against any manufacturer, subcontractor, or supplier during the lease term. If these rights are not assignable because, for example, of a warranty restriction, a lessee should have the power to obligate the lessor to sue on its behalf if the lessee deems it necessary.

► **Recommendations:**

- If a prospective lessee finds it necessary to have the right to require the prospective lessor to sue in the name of the lessor because, for example, the product warranty rights cannot be assigned, that right should be coupled with the right to control the action, including the selection of counsel and the grounds of the lawsuit.
- If a prospective lessor agrees to allow the prospective lessee to be able to require it to sue on the lessee's behalf, it should also specify the extent of the lessee's obligation to pay the legal expenses. Generally, these will be the lessee's responsibility.

14. The Party With the Risk of Loss Should Be Specified

Generally, the lessee will bear the risk of equipment loss, whether due to damage, theft, requisition, or confiscation, because the lessee possesses the equipment. Net finance leases, for example, frequently require the lessee to guarantee that the lessor will receive a minimum amount of money, usually referred to as the "stipulated loss value" or "casualty value," if there is an equipment loss. The stipulated loss value, which decreases as the lease term runs, is calculated so that the lessor will not have to report a loss on its books. That obligation basically puts the lessee in the position of being the equipment's ultimate insurer.

▶ **Recommendations:**   If the lease imposes a stipulated loss obligation, a prospective lessee should

- Request an offset for any insurance proceeds or other awards resulting from the loss, and
- Make sure its obligations, including rent, under the lease as to the affected equipment terminate as of the loss date.

When a stipulated loss provision is incorporated, a prospective lessee should insist on a clear definition of the term "loss," because it can be susceptible of various interpretations. Generally, unless a defined loss has occurred, the rent must continue with the possible result that the lessee would be paying on unusable equipment. Typically, "loss" means destruction to the extent the equipment is no longer usable to the lessee. It is also worth noting that loss for the use intended may be somewhat less than actual total destruction. Thus, a prospective lessee should be careful in agreeing to the ground rules.

If a prospective lessee must repair equipment damaged by a third party at its own expense, it should insist on the right to claim any money received, at least up to the cost incurred, from the party causing the damage.

15. *Responsibility for Certain General Taxes*

In a typical net financial lease, the lessee is responsible for paying taxes imposed by any local, state, or federal taxing authority. A prospective lessee should take into account any tax payment obligations when determining its effective leasing cost. *Note:* Some taxes can be significant.

▶ **Recommendations:**

- Frequently, lease agreements require a lessee to pay equipment related taxes that, by law, the lessor must pay. If a lessor is improperly assessed by a taxing authority and refuses to institute a proceeding to correct the problem, the lessee may have to pay an incorrect assessment. Thus, a prospective lessee should require the right to be able to have any tax assessment contested or reviewed.
- If the lessee wants to contest a tax imposed on the lessor, the lessor should require that the lessee deliver an opinion from its counsel setting out that there is a legitimate basis for the action and should require the lessee to put up a reasonable amount of money in advance to cover the expenses.
- The lease should require each party to timely notify the other party of potential or actual imposition of any taxes or similar assessments on the equipment. This will allow the interested party to participate at the earliest possible time.

16. *Protecting the Lessor's Tax Benefits*

Generally, the parties to a lease will want the transaction to be classified as a "true" lease for federal income tax purposes (see Chapter 8). It is absolutely essential, therefore, that the parties draft the lease to ensure that the desired tax treatment will not be endangered.

If a lease does not qualify as a true tax lease, the lessor would undoubtedly lose ownership tax benefits, such as depreciation. Because such a loss can turn a favorable transaction into a highly unfavorable one, sophisticated tax lessors try to build protections into the lease documentation in two basic ways—prohibiting inconsistent actions and filings and requiring tax indemnifications.

a. Inconsistent Actions and Filings Should Be Prohibited

The lease should prohibit the lessee from taking any action or filing any documents, including income tax returns, that would be inconsistent with the true lease intent. Normally, this does not present a problem for lessees because by doing so they could lose their right to deduct the rent charges as an expense—often the reason the transaction was structured as a lease.

b. Tax Indemnifications: A Way to Protect a Lessor's Economics

The second way that lessors can attempt to protect themselves against tax benefit losses is through tax indemnification provisions. Typically, these provisions require the lessee to pay the lessor an amount of money that, after taxes, will put it in the same economic position as before the loss.

Tax indemnification provisions can be extremely complex, and to assess properly their effect and workability, one must understand how the ownership tax benefits can be lost. Basically, there are three ways: through acts or omissions of the lessor; through acts or omissions of the lessee; or through a change in law. For obvious reasons, lessors would like to put the economic burden of a loss or inability to claim all of the expected tax benefits on the lessees, regardless of the cause. Lessees, however, object to assuming the entire burden, and, as a result, a compromise is usually reached.

It is fairly standard in true leases to include a tax indemnity based on the lessee's acts or omissions. An indemnity based on the lessor's acts or omissions is rare, and a lessee should agree to such an indemnity only if the transaction provides significant other benefits. The third situation giving rise to potential tax problems, a change in law, can go either way, usually depending on the overall bargaining position of the parties.

c. Tax Law Changes

How significant is assuming the risk of tax benefit losses resulting from changes in tax law? To begin with, it should be recognized that the "risk" breaks down into a retroactive risk and a prospective risk, that is, changes that affect equipment already delivered and those that affect equipment to be delivered in the future.

▶ **Observation:**   A prospective lessee sometimes successfully shifts the burden of a retroactive change in tax laws to a prospective lessor by arguing that it is a "normal" leasing business risk that a lessor should assume. There is some logic to this position.

What about prospective changes in tax law, those affecting equipment that a lessor has made a commitment to lease, but that has not yet been delivered? In this case, the risk does not really have to be assumed by either party. For example, the lessor could be given the right to adjust the rent upward an appropriate amount if there is adverse change in the tax benefits before the equipment arrives or have the right to exclude affected equipment. The lessee, in turn, could exclude the equipment if the adjusted rent is too high. Alert prospective lessees usually make sure when a rent adjustment right is given that the lessor will have to make a downward adjustment if there is an increase in the available tax benefits.

▶ **Recommendations:**
- Before a prospective lessor agrees to adjust the rents downward if there is an increase in tax benefits affecting future delivered equipment, it should carefully determine whether it can use the increased tax benefits. If not, a downward rent adjustment will merely erode its economic return.
- As explained in the above section, if the parties agree to provide for a rent adjustment and couple it with a mutual exclusionary right if the adjustment is unfavorable, certain disadvantages must be considered. A lessor can lose alternative investment opportunities if a lessee excludes equipment at the last minute, and a lessee may not have enough time to find substitute lease financing if the lessor exercises its rights.
- If a prospective lessor excludes equipment based on a tax law change, it is possible that a nonutilization fee may be triggered. Thus, a prospective lessee should ensure that any nonutilization fee excludes the cost of equipment not leased as a result of a lessor's change-in-law exclusion right. If this is not provided for, a lessee will have to pay a fee on funds that remain unused as a result of the lessor's exclusion election.

d.   Tax Loss Payment Formula

When the lease includes a tax indemnification provision, the provision must set out a precise formula for determining the amount the lessee must pay. Because the indemnity formula's purpose is to make the indemnified party "whole," the formulas are typically broad in scope and provide for a payment that, after deduction of all fees, taxes, and other changes payable as a result of the indemnification payment, will put the indemnified party in the same economic position as before the loss.

Frequently, this will be expressed as paying the lessor enough money to maintain the lessor's "net return." Unfortunately, that term can have many meanings, for example, total earnings, discounted rate of return, or after-tax cash flow. Thus, the lease should define such terms and provide a precise formula for determining the amount of the loss.

The formula can become complicated, particularly if the lessor or equity participant is a large multinational corporation, because the payment may affect other aspects of the corporation's tax picture. As a result, if there are significant sums involved, it is usually necessary to retain experienced tax lawyers to work out the formulas.

In terms of the payment timing, there are two basic alternatives: a lump sum or a rent readjustment. Lessors often prefer the lump-sum payment so they can recoup their entire loss as quickly as possible.

e. The Tax Loss Date

The lease must identify the time when the lessee becomes obligated to pay the indemnity. For example, would the lessee become responsible to pay for a tax benefit loss when the lessor discovers the problem or when a court rules on it? In many situations the "loss date" is defined as the time when the tax benefit loss has been established by the final judgment of a court or administrative agency having jurisdiction over the matter.

▶ **Recommendations:**

- A prospective lessee should not agree to any provision that obligates it to make any tax indemnification payment until the lessor has actually incurred, or is about to incur, an out-of-pocket expense.
- A lessor should have the right under a tax indemnification clause to make justifiable tax adjustments without prompting from the IRS and call on the lessee to pay if it realizes that it may not properly claim a tax benefit. However, it may not always be clear what is a justifiable adjustment, and without some means of making that interpretation, the lessee could be required to pay an indemnity solely at the lessor's discretion. To avoid that problem, the indemnity provision should provide that the lessor will claim a benefit only after receiving the opinion of a jointly chosen lawyer, or under some other similar arrangement where each party will have some control.
- The lessee should have the right to require a lessor to contest any tax claim that will trigger an indemnification payment. Without it, a lessor could decide not to defend against a claim because he will not ultimately have to pay it.

f. Reimbursement for Erroneous Tax Loss Payments

The right to be reimbursed for any money incorrectly paid under a tax indemnification provision is an important concept to include within this arrangement. If the tax loss is determined not to exist, the indemnified party should be required to return promptly any money paid.

▶ **Recommendation:** When a lessee has the right to force a lessor to contest a tax claim, it should also have a right to the return of any amount that it has had to pay before a final resolution if the lessor later, without justification or consent, settles or discontinues the action. The purpose, of course, is to make sure the claim will be fully contested.

17. Equipment Return

The condition in which and the place where the leased equipment must be returned to the lessor are important considerations. Overlooking either can result in a costly omission for either the lessor or the lessee.

When the equipment is returned, a dispute can arise concerning whether the equipment's condition meets the standards required in the lease. If a lessor determines that the lessee did not properly maintain the equipment, it can insist that the lessee pay for any repairs necessary to restore the equipment. And even if the lessor's claim for repairs is legitimate, a lessee may believe that the maintenance standards in the lease were met and dispute payment. Thus, the lease should provide a means to determine whether the lessee has met the standard of care criteria defined in the lease.

The best approach is to set an objective, easy-to-measure "outside" standard, for example, agreeing that an aircraft under lease will be returned with no less than 50% of remaining engine operation time before the next major overhaul. Where an easily measurable objective criterion is not available, the parties might agree to use an independent equipment appraiser to assess the equipment's condition. The lease can either identify the equipment appraiser or set out a method to select appraisers if their services become necessary. A selection method can call for each party to pick an appraiser at the appropriate time, and, if the two selected appraisers cannot reach an agreement, the parties will then jointly select a third independent appraiser, whose opinion will be final and binding.

The lease should specify where the equipment is to be returned and who will bear the delivery expense. For example, if, at the lease's end, a lessor unexpectedly had to pay for the transportation of 200 trucks from 10 of a lessee's plants scattered up and down the East Coast to a central sale point in the Midwest, its profit margin could be noticeably affected. Although who pays for shipping expenses varies with each transaction, it is not unusual for a lessee to pay only for shipping charges to a general transportation shipping point near where the equipment is used.

▶ **Recommendations:**

- Prospective lessors without access to inexpensive equipment storage facilities should consider negotiating the right to store equipment on the prospective lessee's premises at the end of a lease until a buyer or new lessee can be found.
- Prospective lessees should be cautious about giving a lessor the right to store equipment on their company premises at the end of a lease until a buyer or new lessee can be found, unless they can do so without, or with minimal, cost. If you, as a prospective lessee, must agree to do so, put a

time limit on how long it may be so stored, and make sure you have no responsibility for insurance or loss while in storage. And you may want to consider charging the lessor a storage rent.

- Prospective lessees must carefully consider the potential expense exposure in agreeing to return equipment to a particular return point, particularly when many items are involved. For example, a trucking pickup location may be much closer and, therefore, less expensive than the nearest railhead. Having the right to choose between alternative return locations may also be advisable. Circumstances can change, and it may turn out to be more practical to transport the equipment to, for example, the nearest railhead instead of the nearest truck pickup point.

18. Events of Default

If a problem arises that would jeopardize a lessor's rights or interest in the lease or the equipment, the lessor should be in a position to end the lease and take other action as may be appropriate, such as reclaiming the equipment. The various "problem" situations that could give rise to this type of lessor right should be clearly specified in every lease agreement. Those situations are generally referred to as "events of default."

a.   If There Is a Nonpayment of Rent

The lessee's failure to pay the rent, when and in the amount due, should always be an event of default. Rent payment is a fundamental obligation, and a lessor should expect the fullest attention to it, perhaps allowing for a reasonable overdue payment grace period for unavoidable delays.

► **Recommendations:**

- Prospective lessees should seek both a reasonable overdue rent payment grace period and a lessor notice requirement. For example, the lease could provide that the failure to pay rent will not result in an event of default until a period of time, for example five days, after the lessee has received written notice from the lessor of the nonpayment.
- If a lessor agrees to an overdue rent notice provision as described in the above Recommendation, it should make sure the proper controls are instituted to monitor the timeliness of the rent payments.

b.   If There Is an Unauthorized Transfer

The lease should provide that if the lessee assigns or transfers the lease agreement or the equipment without the lessor's consent, there will be an event of default. *Reason:* The lessor enters into a lease transaction to a great extent relying on the quality and reputation of the lessee, so if assignments or transfers were freely permitted, the equipment could end up in the hands of an unacceptable third party. A sublease, for example, to someone who intended to use the equipment in a high-wear operation could seriously jeopardize the equipment's anticipated residual value. By controlling transfers and assignments, a lessor can protect its investment position.

c. If There Is a Failure to Perform an Obligation

It is in the lessor's interest to have an expansive definition of event of default, so it may seek to be able to declare a lease default if the lessee fails to observe or perform any condition or agreement in the lease. Whether or not a court would allow a lessor to actually terminate a lease agreement, no matter how minor the failure, may be open to discussion; however, the potential threat may keep a lessee in full compliance. Lawsuits are expensive, even for the winner.

▶ **Recommendations:**

- Many conditions and agreements in a lease may not be fundamental to the essence of the lease transaction, such as the correct marking of the equipment. Therefore, a prospective lessee should attempt to minimize the default risk by requiring that the breach be "material" before it gives rise to a default event.
- A good way for a lessee to avoid inadvertent lease defaults is to have the lessor obligated to give at least 30 days' prior written notice before a default can be declared. Lengthy notice requirements, however, could hinder a lessor's ability to move quickly to protect its equipment and should be carefully considered before being given.

d. If the Lessee Has Made a Material Misrepresentation

As explained above, a lessor will often require the lessee to represent certain facts that a lessor deems critical to its decision to enter into the lease. Any misrepresentation of a material nature could subject a lessor to a risk that it would not otherwise have assumed had it known the actual facts. In many cases a lessor will rely on the lessee's representation that there have been no adverse changes in the lessee's financial condition between the date of the latest financial statements and the transaction's closing date. If a lessor discovers the representation was not true after the lease is signed, it should be entitled to declare a default even if the misrepresentation was inadvertent.

e. If the Lessee Is Going Bankrupt

The following should also constitute events of default: a court order or decree declaring the lessee bankrupt or insolvent; the appointment of a receiver, liquidator, or trustee in bankruptcy for a lessee under any state or federal law; any similar action that would expose the leased equipment to a third-party claim or otherwise endanger the lessor's position; or any voluntary act by the lessee that would lead to any of these events.

19. Lessor's Remedies Following an Event of Default

The lease should set out what remedies a lessor can pursue if a lessee defaults under a lease. Although doing so will not necessarily guarantee a lessor that a particular action will be permitted if the parties end up in court, it will put a lessee on notice, and thus may weigh against any lessee objection.

Lease agreements incorporate many types of default remedies, usually representing nothing more than a commonsense approach to dealing with the default issue. The various remedies listed in a lease sometimes overlap, but from a lessor's viewpoint it is better to be somewhat redundant than to risk a claim that a certain course of action was waived by implication because it was omitted.

a.   Court Action

The most obvious default remedy that should be included is a right to bring a court action to require the lessee to perform any breached obligation or to get money damages for the failure to do so. This is the standard type of remedy available in a basic contract action.

b.   Termination of the Lease

The lessor's right to terminate a lessee's rights under the lease, including the lessee's right to use the equipment, is a basic default remedy. As a part of this right, a lessor usually has the ability to enter the lessee's premises immediately and take possession of the equipment. The reclaiming right is particularly useful when a lessee's creditors are trying to attach assets as security for their claims.

c.   Redelivery of the Equipment

Lessors commonly have the right to require a lessee to redeliver the equipment in an event of default. It usually imposes a greater burden than if the lease normally ran its course. For example, the lessee may have to redeliver the equipment at its own expense and risk to any location that the lessor designates rather than to the nearest general transportation pickup point. In an adversary proceeding, the expanded right may not have much more meaning than helping to measure damages, because a great deal of cooperation cannot be expected from the lessee.

d.   Storage of the Equipment

In a default situation, the lessor may not have a place to store the equipment readily. Thus, the lessor may want to obligate the lessee to store the equipment on its premises, free of charge, until the lessor can dispose of it following a default. Whether or not it is actually advisable to let a lessee retain control over the equipment is a separate issue that would have to be considered by the lessor when a default occurs. For example, a lessor may run the risk that other creditors would seize the equipment. Even though the creditors generally would not have a valid claim, the possible renting time lost and equipment deterioration could endanger the lessor's investment.

► **Recommendations:**

- To avoid a prolonged storage obligation, a prospective lessee should place a time limit on any lessor storage right. If a time cannot be negotiated, the lessor at least should be committed to proceed to sell, lease, or otherwise dispose of the property diligently.

- Any lessor right to have the lessee store the equipment should be accompanied by a right to enter the storage area for any reasonable purpose, including inspection by a prospective buyer or new lessee.
- When the lessee stores the equipment, there is the issue as to the responsibility for damage to the equipment. A prospective lessee, therefore, should specify that the risk of damage through third-party acts during any forced storage period is on the lessor.

e. Sale of the Equipment

A prospective lessor should insist that, after a lessee defaults, it can sell or otherwise dispose of the leased equipment, free and clear of any of the lessee's rights. However, the lessee should seek the right to have an offset of any proceeds received against any damages it otherwise owes.

▶ Recommendations:

- The more a lessor receives from an equipment disposition, the less default damages a lessee may owe if it has a right to an offset. To ensure that the lessor undertakes the maximum disposal effort, a lessee should insist on an accounting of the disposition proceeds.
- If a prospective lessor agrees to credit any sale or re-leasing proceeds received from third parties against any amounts that a defaulting lessee would owe, it should limit the credit obligation to the "net" proceeds actually received. The expenses that the lessor incurs, for example, to lease the equipment should be deducted from the amount that the lessee would be entitled to receive as a credit. Also, until the money is in fact in the lessor's hands, it should not have to recognize any credit.

f. Right to Hold or Re-Lease the Equipment

Besides being able to dispose of the equipment, a prospective lessor would want the right to "hold, use, operate, lease to others, or keep idle" any equipment that it has reacquired as a result of a lease default. Ideally, then, a lessor could take what action it deems to be in its best interest. Of course, if a court finds that the lessor did not act in a manner to minimize the damages suffered, it may limit any recovery that a lessor may be able to get.

g. Liquidated Damages

A "liquidated damage" provision should always be included as an alternative default remedy. Under this provision, the parties agree on a method for determining what damages the lessor is entitled to if a default occurs. Generally, courts will uphold a liquidated damage arrangement if it fairly anticipates the losses that may result from the lessee's nonperformance and is not a penalty.

Although there are no industry-standard formulas used to measure the damages that a lessor would suffer because of a lessee's default, two types frequently are used. One provides for the lessee to pay an amount equal to the present worth of the aggregate remaining rentals that the lessor would have received, but for the default, reduced by the equipment's fair market sales value or the present worth of the equipment's fair market rental value over the original remaining lease term. The other calls for the payment of an amount equal to the equipment's stipulated loss value as of the date of default, reduced by the equipment's fair market sales value or the present worth of the equipment's fair market rental value over the original remaining lease term. A prescribed per annum discount rate, such as the prime commercial lending rate in effect at the time of termination, is incorporated into the liquidated damage "formula" for present worth computation purposes.

▶ **Observation:** The discount rate agreed on to compute the present worth of the remaining rental stream can significantly affect what will be owed. Too often parties agree to arbitrary rates without considering the consequences. The higher the rate, the less the offsetting credit and the greater the damage amount payable.

Illustrative Example—*Liquidated Damage Formula Computation:* Company Able leased a $1 million aircraft to Company Baker for a 10-year term. As part of the agreement, the parties incorporated a liquidated damage formula that they considered to be a fair measure of the damages Company Able would suffer if Company Baker defaulted. The formula provided that Company Able would be entitled to an amount equal to the present worth of any remaining rents that would otherwise have been due but for the default, offset by the present worth of the aircraft's fair market rental value over the original remaining lease term. The per annum discount rate to be used to compute the present worth was specified as 10%, the current prime lending rate at Company Able's bank. At the end of the fifth year Company Baker defaulted. For simplicity we will assume that the rents are payable annually, in advance. The facts are:

Unexpired lease term:	5 years
Annual rent:	$120,000
Annual fair market rental value:	$100,000

The present worth of the remaining rents under the lease, calculated using a 10% discount rate, is $500,384. The present worth of the aggregate fair market rental value over a five-year period is $416,986. The amount that the lessee owes is $83,398, the difference between the present worth of the unpaid rents and the fair market value rents.

If the parties had agreed on a discount rate of 8% instead of 10%, the lessee would owe $86,242, instead of $83,392. On the other hand, if the discount rate were 12% instead of 10%, the lessee would owe $80,747. As the reader can see, the discount rate should not be treated lightly.

▶ **Recommendation:** Because the future fair market rental value is an estimate, the actual rentals may be higher or lower, resulting in either an underpayment or overpayment by the lessee. To solve this situation, both parties might consider the possibility of allowing for a future adjustment if the actual amounts vary from the appraisal.

20. *A Lessor May Want Certain Lease Assignment Rights*

Prospective lessors frequently ask for the right to assign their interest in a lease and the equipment at any time during the term. While a general assignment right sometimes makes prospective lessees uneasy, this should not cause concern if it is properly negotiated. To help protect its rights, a prospective lessee could insist that any assignment not adversely affect its lease rights.

a.   Assignment to a Lender

In many cases, a lessor's lenders will require as part of their credit arrangement that the lessor incorporate in all leases a provision giving the lenders a right to an assignment of the rights, including title to the equipment, if certain loan restrictions are violated. Generally, the purpose of the assignment provisions is to enable a lender to take over the leases as security if there is a loan default. If an assignment requirement exists in a lessor's loan agreement, it must be in each lease agreement, and it is not a negotiable point between the lessor and lessee. In certain situations, a lessor may want to have the ability to borrow a portion of the equipment purchase cost from a lender on a nonrecourse basis. To do that, the lessor usually must assign to the lender all the lessor's lease contract rights, such as the right to receive uninterrupted rentals.

▶ **Recommendation:** Any time a prospective lessee must agree to allow a lessor to be able to assign any or all of its interest in a lease to its lenders, the lessee should require that any such transfer be subject and subordinate to the terms of the lease. Thus, if there is an assignment, the lessee's rights, including the right to use the equipment, will not in any way be jeopardized by the lessor's assignment of its rights to the bank. The lease should provide that any transfer will not relieve the lessor from any of its obligations under the lease. This will give a prospective lessee the assurance that it will always have what it originally bargained for.

b.   Assignment to an Investor

A lessor will sometimes want the right to "sell" the lease, including title to the equipment, to a third party. Under this arrangement, the third-party buyer would become the equipment owner, would take subject to the terms and conditions of the lease agreement, and would, therefore, become the "lessor." The original lessor would no longer have any rights or duties under the lease.

A broad assignment right can expose a lessee to certain risks. A lease sold to a financially unstable lessor, for example, may endanger the lessee's right to the continued use of the equipment because of potential creditor actions against the new lessor. Also, an assignment to a lessor who is difficult to deal with can create problems, for example, where the lease must be modified.

▶ **Recommendations:**

- A prospective lessor seeking a lease assignment right should also seek the right to require the lessee to execute any documents necessary to effect the assignment. Without that right, a lessee could, intentionally or unintentionally, block the assignment.
- A lessee may want some control over a lease assignment. For example, if the lessor assigned the lease to any of the lessee's banks or lending institutions, that assignment could restrict the lessee's borrowing capability. To prevent that, the lessee could request the right to pass on any potential transferees, or, if a prospective lessor is unwilling to grant such a right, it could specifically define the limits of who would be acceptable.

21.   *A Lessee May Want Certain Equipment Sublease Rights*

A lessee with the right to sublease equipment is in the best position to lessen or eliminate the impact of having to pay rent on assets that become unproductive because of changes in use needs during the lease term. If there are no restrictions, such as those that would limit transfers to affiliated companies only, a lessee will have the maximum flexibility.

▶ **Recommendations:**

- Prospective lessors consenting to a subleasing right should insist that the lessee remain primarily liable under the lease agreement during the sublet period.
- Prospective lessees desiring subleasing rights should try to avoid agreeing to any exercise conditions, such as having to obtain the lessor's prior written consent. Time wasted waiting for a consent could result in lost revenue.
- From the lessor's perspective, however, it may not be advisable to give a prospective lessee an unrestricted right to sublease the equipment to any party, even though the original lessee will remain primarily liable under the lease. Having the right to pass judgment on any proposed sublessee will prevent knowing transfers to parties who may misuse the equipment or who are financially unstable. Regardless of the original lessee's primary responsibility, misuse can diminish the equipment's value, and a sublessee's bankruptcy could interfere with the equipment's return.

22.   *Lessor's Options to Renew, Sell, or Terminate*

There are a few situations when a prospective lessor will want certain rights that are not usually requested, such as a right to terminate the lease in a nondefault situation, a right to force a sale of the equipment to the lessee, a right to force the lessee to renew a lease, or a right to abandon the equipment. These rights can create substantial tax problems or be otherwise undesirable from a lessee's viewpoint. Thus, if proposed, their possible effect should be carefully reviewed.

a. The Right to Terminate the Lease

It is conceivable, although extremely unlikely, that a prospective lessor would want to be able to terminate a lease *for any reason it chooses* during its term without the lessee's consent. For example, if a prospective lessor believes the rental market will rise before the end of the negotiated lease term, it may want to have the ability to go after a better rate.

▶ **Recommendation:**   For obvious reasons, a prospective lessee should not put itself in a position where a lessor could prematurely terminate the lease without the lessee's prior consent and without reason.

b. The Right to Force a Sale of the Equipment to the Lessee

In certain situations a prospective lessor will insist on having the right (commonly referred to as a "put") to force a lessee to buy the equipment under lease at the end of the term. Generally, this right is expressed as a fixed percentage of the original equipment's cost rather than a defined dollar amount. For example, a lessor may have the right to sell the equipment to the lessee for an amount equal to 10% of cost. In effect, a put eliminates any risk that a lessor will not realize its assumed residual value, which, in turn, protects its anticipated profit. Transactions involving certain types of store fixtures or equipment that will be difficult or uneconomical to move, such as certain heavy storage tanks, sometimes incorporate a forced sale right.

▶ **Recommendations:**

- The use of a put may impair the tax status of a lease transaction. (See Chapter 8.) They should be incorporated only with the advice of tax counsel.
- If a prospective lessor insists on having a put, the prospective lessee should make sure it will not be required to indemnify the lessor for any loss of tax benefits a lessor can suffer if the put causes the lease not to qualify as a true tax lease.

c. The Right to Abandon the Equipment

In the past, equipment abandonment rights had been used in leases of equipment that would be difficult and costly, if not totally impractical, to reclaim if the lessee decided not to buy it at the end of the term. A good example of the type of leases that involved abandonment rights were those relating to certain kinds of commercial storage tanks that were so large that the only way to move them was to cut them into pieces and then reweld them at the new site. In these situations, the expenses involved could be so great that the lessor could not reasonably recoup them through a re-leasing or a sale.

Lessors sometimes attempt to solve an equipment removal expense problem by requiring the equipment to be delivered to them at the end of the term at the lessee's expense. If the lessee refuses to do so, however, the lessor's only recourse, without a right of abandonment, would be to bring a lawsuit to force the lessee to live up to its agreement or, possibly, pay for any resulting damages. If the lessee is in financial trouble, a lawsuit may be of little use. Having an abandonment right allows the lessor to drop the property in the lessee's lap and rid itself of any lingering responsibility or expense exposure.

▶ **Recommendation:**   The lessor's right to abandon the equipment is prohibited under the IRS Guidelines and can create serious tax lease treatment problems (See Chapter 8,C,7.) It should be used only on the advice of tax counsel.

d.   The Right to Require a Lease Renewal

In situations where an abandonment right or a put might be considered, a lessor may instead use a forced lease renewal right. Under this right, a lessor could make the lessee re-lease the equipment at a predetermined rental.

▶ **Recommendation:**   The right of a lessor to require a lessee to renew a lease could also run afoul of the IRS Guidelines and can create serious tax lease treatment problems. It should be used only on the advice of tax counsel.

23. *Lessee Options to Buy, Renew, Terminate, or Upgrade the Equipment*

Invariably, a prospective lessee will ask for certain rights, referred to as "options," that will enable it to maintain some form of control over the equipment's use, such as an equipment purchase right, a lease renewal right, or a lease termination right. Generally, these types of options are willingly granted by prospective lessors.

a.   The Right to Buy the Equipment at Fair Market Value

A prospective lessee typically wants to be able to buy the leased equipment at the lease's end. In many situations, this is done through a fair market value purchase option. Basically, the option gives the lessee the right to buy the equipment for whatever its fair market value is at the time it is exercised.

Although the term "fair market value" appears self-explanatory, the parties should agree on a method for its determination. Generally, the "fair market value" of a piece of equipment is the amount that a willing buyer under no compulsion to purchase would pay a willing seller under no compulsion to sell in the open market. As a practical matter, however, how is the value actually determined between a lessor and a lessee? Typically, it is done through an equipment appraisal. The parties can designate in the lease an independent appraiser who will evaluate the equipment at the appropriate time.

Alternatively, the parties can each select an independent appraiser to come in and make an assessment when necessary. If the two appraisers cannot agree on a satisfactory value, then they must jointly select a third appraiser, whose opinion will be binding.

▶ **Recommendation:**   A fair market value purchase option can be an expensive way for a lessee to acquire equipment with a typically strong resale value. A purchase price "cap" is sometimes negotiated to limit how much the lessee would have to pay. For example, the lessee would have the right to buy the equipment at fair market value or 30% of the equipment's original cost, whichever is less. However, a cap can present tax problems. (See Chapter 8,C,6.)

b.   The Right to Buy the Equipment at a Fixed Price

When equipment has traditionally maintained a favorable resale value, many companies refuse to lease because a fair market purchase option coupled with the lease rents could result in an economically unfavorable way of acquiring it. As a result, a fixed price purchase option is sometimes given to induce them to lease. Under a fixed price purchase option, commonly referred to as a "call," the lessee can buy the equipment at the end of the lease for a predetermined price. The price is usually expressed as a percentage of the equipment's original cost. For example, the lessee may have the right to buy designated equipment for 35% of cost. In this way, the lessee knows the maximum amount of money he will have to spend if he wants to buy the equipment when the lease is over.

▶ **Observation:**   A lessee fixed price purchase option can cause a lease to fail to be characterized as a lease for federal income tax purposes. If the exercise price is so low that the lessee may, in effect, have a bargain purchase right, the IRS may be able to challenge successfully its status as a true tax lease. Fixed price purchase options, therefore, should be granted with care, and only with the advice of tax counsel, if it is important that a lease qualify as a true tax lease.

c.   The Right to Renew the Lease at Fair Rental Value

Providing a lessee with the right to renew a lease at the equipment's fair market rental value at the time of renewal is acceptable, both from the standpoint of the IRS and, generally, a lessor. The parties can determine the fair rental in a manner similar to that of the determination of the fair market purchase value, through independent appraisal at the time of the intended renewal.

▶ **Recommendation:**   When equipment is vital to a prospective lessee's operations, it should make sure the lease renewal terms are adequate to cover any anticipated needs. For example, if a four-year renewal is desirable, an option that would allow a selection of two two-year periods, four one-year periods, one one-year period followed by a three-year period, or a four-year period would provide a great deal of flexibility as to term and as to rental rate. A structure such as this would give the lessee the ability to limit its renewal costs in a high rental market or to "lock in" for a longer period of time in a low rental market. From a lessor's viewpoint, of course, too much latitude on the lessee's side can lessen its chances of maximizing its renewal profits and, therefore, any such arrangement should be carefully thought out as to the possible future effects.

d. The Right to Renew the Lease at a Fixed Price

Prospective lessees sometimes request a fixed price renewal option. By knowing in advance the exact dollar amount of the renewal rents, they know where they would stand if they wanted to continue to use the equipment beyond the main lease term. This would, of course, not be possible with a fair market renewal option.

▶ **Observation:** A fixed price renewal right may result in adverse tax consequences. (See Chapter 8,C,1.) Thus, the amount of fixed renewal option must be carefully considered.

e. The Right to Terminate the Lease

It is not uncommon for a prospective lessee to have the ability to terminate a lease early, particularly when it believes the equipment could become technically obsolete or surplus to its needs before the lease would normally end. When this right is granted, the lessee frequently will be required to pay the lessor a predetermined amount of money, commonly referred to as the "termination value," on exercise. Because most lessors do not like to grant termination rights, the termination amount is usually high.

f. The Right of First Refusal

A purchase "right of first refusal" is sometimes used as an alternative to a fair market value purchase option. Under this option, a lessee is given the right to buy the leased equipment at the end of the lease term under the same terms and conditions as offered by an unaffiliated third party. The disadvantage to using it is that a lessee may run the risk that a competitor may bid for the equipment either to push the price up or to acquire it for its own operations.

> **Illustrative Language**—*Right of First Refusal:* Unless an Event of Default shall have occurred and be continuing at the end of the term of this lease, or any event or condition which, upon lapse of time or giving of notice, or both, would constitute such an Event of Default shall have occurred and be continuing at such time, the lessor shall not, at or following the end of the term of this lease, sell any item of equipment (including any sale prior to the end of such term for delivery of such equipment at or following the end of such term) unless
>
> 1. The lessor shall have received from a responsible purchaser a bona fide offer in writing to purchase such equipment;
> 2. The lessor shall have given the lessee notice (a) setting forth in detail the identity of such purchaser, the proposed purchase

price, the proposed date of purchase, and all other material terms and conditions of such purchase, and (b) offering to sell such equipment to the lessee upon the same terms and conditions as those set forth in such notice; and

3. The lessee shall not have notified the lessor, within 20 days following receipt of such notice, of its election to purchase such equipment upon such terms and conditions.

If the lessee shall not have so elected to purchase such equipment, the lessor may at any time sell such equipment to any party at a price and upon other terms and conditions no less favorable to the lessor than those specified in such notice.

g.   The Right to Upgrade Financing

At times, companies lease equipment, such as computer systems, that requires upgrading during the lease term to ensure maximum performance by adding additional equipment or modifying the original equipment. Typically, such an upgrade may not be done without the lessor's prior written consent. In some situations, the upgrade may be of such a nature that no one other than the original lessor would consider financing it—for example, internal equipment modifications that have no stand-alone value. In these situations the incumbent lessor has absolute negotiating control over the financing, and can charge the lessee more than the going market rate.

▶ **Recommendation:**   Prospective lessees, to avoid having to accept whatever rate an incumbent lessor offers for equipment upgrade financing when no other lessor may be willing to finance an upgrade, should insist on having an option to require equipment upgrade financing on reasonable terms. The upgrade financing right should be at a predetermined fixed lease rate, or at a rate which is to be determined in accordance with acceptable standards at the time of financing—such as the original lease rate adjusted for changes in the lessor's debt borrowing rate.

24.   A Defaulting Party Should Lose Certain Options

Generally, the lease should provide that the party holding an option forfeits its exercise right if it is in default under the lease. For example, a lessee should lose its right to buy the equipment under a purchase option if the lease is terminated because of default on its part.

25.   Designate the Law Governing the Lease

It is always advisable for the parties to specify what jurisdiction's law will apply to their rights and obligations under a lease agreement. For example, the parties can agree that all actions on lease issues will be decided under the laws of New York State, regardless of whether the proceedings are instituted in a New York court. By doing this, the attorneys are able to draft the documents under the law they believe will give the fairest known outcome.

26. Severability Clause

The lease should include a severability clause, providing that any lease provision determined to be legally unenforceable will be severed. Under this clause, the severed provision is treated as though it never existed. This may prevent the entire lease agreement from being held invalid if only certain provisions are unenforceable.

27. The Interest Penalty for Late Payments

A lease agreement should prescribe the interest rate that will be charged on any overdue payments, such as delinquent rent payments. This will eliminate disputes over late charges, and will assist in assessing damages if a lawsuit arises.

▶ **Recommendations:**

- When the lease specifies an overdue payment interest penalty, the prospective lessor should also incorporate a qualification that the rate will in no event be higher than the maximum enforceable legal rate to avoid any potential enforceability problems if the legal limit is inadvertently exceeded.
- Prospective lessors will want interest on overdue obligations to run from the date the money is due to the payment date. Prospective lessees, on the other hand, should attempt to get it to run from the date the lessee receives written notice of the overdue obligation from the lessor.

28. The Lease Should Identify Where and How to Send any Required Notifications and Payments

While leases usually provide that all required notifications and payments, such as loss notifications and rent payments, must be promptly made, they sometimes fail to identify exactly *where* they should be sent. As a result, payments or notifications could be misdirected and money or valuable time lost. The lease should, therefore, expressly state the appropriate mailing addresses.

In addition to specifying where payments and notifications must be sent, the lease should specify the notification and payment manner. For example, it may be agreed that a notice will be deemed given when it is deposited in a U.S. mail box, sent by prepaid telegraph, or sent by certified mail.

29. The Lease Should Be Correctly Signed

All parties to a lease should make sure it is signed in the proper capacities. Leases to be signed by an individual representing himself generally do not present any problems. Leases to be signed by an individual representing a firm, such as a partnership, corporation, or trust, sometimes do. If, in the latter case, the signature is not made in the correct representative capacity, the represented firm may not be bound. For example, if a vice president intends to sign on behalf of his corporation, the signature block should be set up as follows:

> XYZ Corporation
> by: _____
> R. Smith, Vice President

If the signature form is not correct, the signing individual may run the risk that he is personally liable on the contract—certainly, a less-than-desirable outcome for all parties concerned.

D.   A Checklist for Drafting and Negotiating a Lease Agreement

In preparing a well-drafted lease agreement, the parties should cover all the important issues involved in a transaction. The following checklist pinpoints the issues frequently encountered.

What form of lease is appropriate?

- ☐   A single transaction lease
- ☐   A master lease

Should a master lease be used?

Does the lease agreement cover the following issues?

- ☐   Has a page index of all topic headings been included?
- ☐   Have the parties been properly identified?
  1. Lessor
  2. Lessee
- ☐   Is the lessee a valid legal entity?
- ☐   Has a factual summary of the circumstances giving rise to the transaction been included?
- ☐   Has the consideration for the transaction been stated?
- ☐   Have the key terms been defined in a definition section? For example:
  1. Affiliate
  2. Business day
  3. Buyer-furnished equipment
  4. Equipment delivery date
  5. Equipment manufacturer
  6. Event of default
  7. Event of loss
  8. Fair market value
  9. Indenture

> 10. Interim rent
> 11. Lease
> 12. Lease period
> 13. Lease supplement
> 14. Lessor's cost
> 15. Lien
> 16. Loan certificates
> 17. Loan participant
> 18. Overdue interest rate
> 19. Primary rent
> 20. Casualty loss value

☐ If equipment will be delivered after the lease is signed, has a procedure for adding it been established?

1. Can the lessee decide not to lease future delivered equipment when it arrives? If so, will the lessee be obligated to pay

   a. A nonutilization fee?
   b. A commitment fee?

2. Can future delivered equipment be accepted for lease as it arrives or must the lessee aggregate a minimum dollar amount?

☐ The lease period should be defined.

1. Will there be an interim lease term? If so, when will it begin and end?
2. When will the primary term begin?
3. How long will the primary term run?
4. Will the lessee be permitted to renew the lease? If so, what is the renewal period arrangement?

☐ The rent structure must be defined.

1. Will a percentage rent factor be used? If so, what may be included in the equipment cost base?

   a. Sales tax
   b. Transportation charges
   c. Installation charges
   d. Other

2. How much rent must be paid?
3. When will the rent be due?
4. How must the rent be paid?

   a. Check
   b. Wire transfer
   c. Other

5. Where must the rent be paid?

   a. Has a post office box or other address been specified?

6. Can or must the lessor adjust the rent charge if there is a tax law change affecting, favorably or unfavorably, the lessor's economic return?

   a. If a rent adjustment is provided for, has the exact criterion for making it been clearly specified?

b. If the tax law change applies to future delivered equipment and a rent adjustment is not acceptable, can the party adversely affected elect to exclude the equipment?

7. Will the rent obligation be a hell- or- high-water obligation?

☐ What is the lessor's total dollar equipment cost commitment?

1. Will a percentage variance be permitted?

☐ Will the lessee be required to submit reports? For example:

1. Financial reports

   a. Profit and loss statements
   b. Balance sheets
   c. Other

2. Accident reports

   a. Has a minimum estimated accident dollar amount been agreed upon below which a report is not required?
   b. Will the lessee be obligated to immediately telephone if an accident occurs?

3. Lease conformity reports
4. Equipment location reports
5. Third-party claim reports

☐ Has a time been established for when lessee reports are due?
☐ Has a general lessee reporting requirement been imposed as to reports that may be deemed necessary by the lessor in the future?
☐ Equipment maintenance

1. Who has the responsibility for insuring proper maintenance?

   a. Lessor
   b. Lessee
   c. A third party

2. Who must bear the cost of the maintenance?

   a. Lessor
   b. Lessee

3. Will maintenance records be required?

   a. Will the lessor be permitted access to the maintenance records? If so, at what times?

      (1) Normal business hours
      (2) Any time requested

☐ Will equipment alterations be permitted? If so,

1. Will the lessor's consent be required before

   a. An addition that may impair the equipment's originally intended function or that cannot be removed without impairing such function?
   b. Any change?

2. Who will have title to any addition or other alteration?

   a. If it can be easily removed without equipment damage?
   b. If it cannot be removed without function impairment?
   c. What rights will the lessor have to buy the alteration?

☐ Will certain lessor ownership protection filings be advisable or necessary?

    1. Federal regulatory agencies, such as the Federal Aviation Administration
    2. Uniform Commercial Code
    3. Other

☐ If lessor ownership protection filings will be made, who has the responsibility for making them and who must bear the expense?

    1. Lessor
    2. Lessee

☐ If the lessee must make required filings for the lessor, will the lessee have to confirm they have been made?

☐ Will the equipment be marked with the lessor's name and address? If so, who will have the marking responsibility and expense?

    1. Lessor
    2. Lessee

☐ Has the lessee been specifically prohibited from using, operating, storing, or maintaining the equipment carelessly, improperly, in violation of the law, or in a manner not contemplated by the manufacturer?

    1. If the lessee must use the equipment for a purpose other than intended, an exception should be negotiated.

☐ The lessee must be required to provide certain key representations:

    1. That the lessee is properly organized, validly existing, and in good standing
    2. That it has proper authorization to do business in the state where the equipment will be located
    3. That the lessee has the transactional authority to enter into the lease

        a. That necessary board of director approvals have been obtained covering the transaction *and* the person signing the lease on behalf of the lessee
        b. That any other required approvals have been obtained

    4. That there are not conflicting agreements

        a. Bank credit agreements
        b. Other loan agreements
        c. Mortgages
        d. Other leases

    5. That all necessary regulatory approvals have been obtained
    6. That there are no pending or threatened adverse legal or administrative proceedings that would affect the lessee's operations or financial condition
    7. That there have been no adverse changes as of the lease closing in the lessee's financial condition since the latest available financial statements

☐ The lessor must be required to provide certain key representations:

    1. That the lessor has the transactional authority to lease the equipment

        a. That any necessary board of director approval has been obtained
        b. That any other approvals have been obtained or, if none are required, a statement that none are required

   2. That the lessor will pay for the equipment in full

   3. That the lessor will not interfere with the lessee's use of the equipment

      a. Has an exception when the lessee is in default been negotiated by the lessor?

☐ The lessee should require product warranties to be assigned if the lessor has no equipment defect responsibility.

   1. If the warranties are not assignable, the lessor should be required to act on the lessee's behalf.

☐ Who has the responsibility for equipment casualty losses?

   1. Lessor

   2. Lessee

☐ Do the casualty loss values give adequate financial protection to the lessor?

☐ Are the casualty loss values competitive from the lessee's viewpoint?

☐ As of what time will a casualty loss be deemed to have occurred—has a "loss date" been defined?

   1. What obligations change or come into effect on the loss date?

☐ When is the casualty loss value payable and when does interest on the amount payable begin to run?

☐ What taxes must be paid?

   1. Sales tax

   2. Property taxes

   3. Rental taxes

   4. Withholding taxes

   5. Income taxes

   6. Other

☐ Who must pay the taxes?

   1. The lessor

   2. The lessee

☐ For any taxes that a lessee must reimburse a lessor for payment, does the lessee have the right to have the taxes contested?

   1.What happens if the lessor does not fully pursue its contest remedies?

☐ Is each party required to immediately notify the other of any tax imposition for which they will be responsible?

☐ Do the parties intend a true tax lease? If so,

   1. Inconsistent actions and filings should be prohibited.

   2. Will tax loss indemnifications be required?

   3. Will any tax indemnity cover all lessor tax losses or only those resulting from the lessee's acts or omissions?

☐ Who has the economic risk of a change in tax law?

   1. For past delivered equipment

   2. For future delivered equipment

      a. Can either party elect not to lease if the economics are no longer favorable?

☐ Has a formula been agreed on for measuring the amount of any tax benefit loss and the amount of any required reimbursement?

1. Does the formula make the indemnified party whole?
2. Is the formula absolutely clear?

☐ Has the tax loss date been determined?
☐ Who has the expense responsibility for the equipment return and where must it be returned to

1. If the lease ends normally?
2. If the lease ends prematurely?

☐ May either party designate an alternative return location? If so, what is the expense responsibility?
☐ The lessor should be able to terminate the lease early or take other protective action in certain situations:

1. When the rent is not paid
2. When the lessee makes an unauthorized transfer of the equipment or any of its rights under the lease
3. When there is a general failure to perform the obligations under the lease
4. When the lessor discovers the lessee has made a material misrepresentation
5. When there is a bankruptcy or similar event that would jeopardize the lessor's position

☐ The actions that the lessor may take in the event of default must be specified:

1. Court action
2. Terminate the lease
3. Cause a redelivery of the equipment
4. Cause the lessee to store the equipment
5. Sell the equipment under its own terms
6. Be able to hold or re-lease the equipment
7. Be entitled to a predetermined amount of money as damages for a lease default

☐ Certain lessor assignment rights may be desirable or required:

1. To a lender as security
2. To an investor

☐ Will the lessee be able to sublease the equipment? If so,

1. Will the lessee remain primarily liable under the lease during the sublease period?
2. Will the lessor have any control over who the sublessee will be?

☐ Have all the lessor's options been included? For example:

1. Right to terminate the lease
2. Right to force a sale of the equipment to the lessee
3. Right to abandon the equipment
4. Right to force a lease renewal

☐ Have all the lessee's options been included? For example:

1. A purchase right
   a. Fair market purchase value
   b. Fixed purchase price
2. A renewal right
   a. Fair market purchase value
   b. Fixed price rental
3. A termination right
4. A right of first refusal
5. An upgrade financing right

☐ Will a defaulting party retain any of its option rights under the lease?
☐ Has the law of a jurisdiction been specified to control any issues that arise under the lease?
☐ Is there a severability clause?
☐ Is there any interest penalty for overdue payments?
☐ Has each side specified how and where any required notifications and payments will be made?

1. The address where notifications and payments must be sent
2. The manner in which the notifications and payments must be made
   a. U.S. mail
   b. Other

☐ Has the signature section been set up properly for

1. An individual?
2. A corporation?
3. A partnership?
4. A trust?
5. Other?

☐ Has the signature been made in the proper capacity?

Chapter 4

Closing the Lease Financing

A.   Overview

Once the terms and conditions of a lease agreement have been negotiated, it is time to put it in final form and to prepare for what is referred to as the lease "closing." At the closing, all parties will sign the lease agreement and, in addition, fulfill any closing conditions identified or requested in accordance with the lease or other governing papers, such as the lessee delivering to the lessor any specified "collateral" documents requested. These collateral, or supplemental, documents range from those that essentially provide comfort on specified issues, such as opinions of counsel, to those that define critical supportive arrangements, such as guarantee agreements. All the collateral documents are an integral part of the finance closing. For example, if the lessee is unable to provide any, the lessor has no obligation to provide the financing.

As explained in Chapter 1, the leveraged lease closing is the most complex because of the added participant—the third-party equipment lender. Even though the actual leveraged lease agreement does not differ radically from that of a nonleveraged lease, additional supplemental closing documents are usually involved, such as a security and loan agreement, to accommodate the loan arrangement requirements.

Although drafting the supplemental papers will be the responsibility of the transaction's lawyers, the businesspeople should understand the fundamental concepts involved so that the papers can be meaningfully reviewed to ensure they accurately reflect the agreements reached. Also, understanding the purpose of the collateral documents will enable the business participants to more readily negotiate compromises when the lawyers reach impasses. And that is the purpose of this chapter—to provide you with a closing document overview so that you know in advance what to expect and to enable you to facilitate a smooth closing.

One final point before we begin. While this chapter provides a general working knowledge of the typical collateral lease documents, keep in mind that most transactions have their own unique aspects that must also be taken into account.

B. Legal Opinions

1. *The Function of Legal Opinions*

In large ticket and, at times, middle market lease transactions, legal opinions are typically required by lessors and, in some cases, by sophisticated lessees. Before going into the various opinions possible and what they might address, let us take a moment to discuss what the practical value of such an opinion may be from a business point of view. To begin with, it is important to understand what a legal opinion does not do. It does not guarantee that the conclusions expressed in the opinion are correct. Regardless of the quality of the lawyer's work in preparing the opinion, a court or administrative agency may interpret the law or facts differently—and their decision, not the legal opinion, will be controlling. A legal opinion, however, does provide the recipient with value:

- It provides the participants with a significant degree of comfort, because the lawyer's opinion usually will be correct.
- In drafting the opinion, the lawyer will need access to relevant information; therefore, writing it may bring to light transaction trouble spots that can be corrected.
- If a court or agency disagrees with the opinion, having it may help show that the parties exercised due care in entering the transaction and may prevent the imposition of any penalties.

The problem with legal opinions is they are invariably qualified, for example, by stating a very specific set of facts on which they are based. To the extent that the relevant facts are not properly conveyed to the lawyer providing the opinion, therefore, the opinion may be of little value.

▶ **Recommendations:**

- Although legal opinions often make the recipient feel secure on the issues covered, there are times when more certainty is required. For example, a lessor or lessee concerned about whether a certain lease structure qualifies as a lease for federal income tax purposes is often well advised to consider getting an Internal Revenue Service ruling on the issue. (See Chapter 8.)
- The "expertness" of the lawyer providing an opinion is a critical consideration, particularly when complex legal issues are involved. Therefore, if you need a legal opinion in a lease transaction, choose a lawyer with solid leasing experience.

2. *Opinion From Lessee's Lawyer*

The lessor should ask the lessee to have its attorney deliver a legal opinion on relevant legal issues. The opinion's goal is to provide the lessor with assurances that no legal issues exist that will undermine the lease transaction. Thus, a lessor will typically want the lessee's lawyer to opine whether

- The lessee has been properly organized, is validly in existence, and is in good standing under the laws of its state of incorporation.
- The lessee has the authority to enter into the lease.
- The lessee has the ability to perform all of its lease obligations.
- All the lessee's lease commitments are legally binding.
- Any consents, such as those of the shareholders or lenders, are necessary and, if so, whether they have been obtained.
- Any regulatory approvals, such as that of a state public utility commission, are necessary and, if so, whether all the proper actions have been taken.
- There are any adverse pending or threatened court or administrative proceedings against the lessee and, if so, their probable outcome.
- The lessee would violate any law, rule, or provision of any of its existing agreements by entering into the lease arrangement or complying with any of its terms.

3. Opinions From Lessor's Lawyer

a. To the Lessee

In certain situations, particularly in large ticket underwritten leveraged lease transactions, the lessee should obtain an opinion from the lessor's lawyer concerning the lessor's legal ability to enter into and perform its obligations. That opinion should minimally confirm that the lessor is properly

- Incorporated or organized, as the case may be, at the time the lease is signed.
- Qualified to do business in the state where the equipment will be used. (There may be a risk that the equipment could be attached by the state authorities for the nonpayment of any taxes that the lessor may owe.)

b. To the Lender

An equipment lender should always request a written opinion from the lessor's lawyer on key issues relating to its loan arrangement with the lessor. This type of opinion generally covers the same issues as those covered in the opinion given to the lessee, for example, whether

- The lessor is duly organized, validly existing, and in good standing in its state of incorporation.
- All the necessary transaction authorizations have been secured.
- The lessor's obligations under the loan documents are fully enforceable.

Also, if the equipment loan is to be nonrecourse to the lessor, permitting the lender to look only to the lease payments and equipment for repayment, the lender will want an opinion stating that

- The lessor has good and marketable title to the equipment covered by the lease.

- The equipment is free and clear of any liens or encumbrances other than those of which the lender is aware.
- The lessor has not made any other lease assignments.
- The lender has a free and unencumbered right to receive all payments, such as rent, under the lease agreement.

▶ **Recommendation:** A prospective lessor should consider requiring an opinion from the prospective lender's lawyer confirming that all the necessary action in connection with the loan's authorization has been taken. Many prospective lessors are so grateful to get the loan that they sometimes neglect to determine whether it was properly authorized. A loan without proper authorization may be withdrawn.

4. Opinion From the Guarantor's Lawyer

In many situations, a third party will guarantee the lessee's lease obligations. For example, the parent company of a financially weak corporate lessee may be asked to guarantee the lease obligations as a condition to the lessor's lease commitment. In that case, the strength and viability of the guarantor's commitment is critical to the lessor and any nonrecourse equipment lender. To help confirm the guarantee's worth, a lessor should request a favorable opinion from the guarantor's lawyer on the applicable aspects.

Such an opinion should address legal issues that relate to the guarantor's ability to fulfill the guarantee. For example, the opinion may be required to state whether

- The guarantor is duly organized, validly existing, and in good standing.
- Anything exists that could adversely affect the guarantee's quality, such as material litigation.
- The guarantee has been fully and properly authorized.
- The guarantee is a legally enforceable obligation.

5. Opinion From the Vendor's Lawyer

Usually the leased equipment's vendor is not asked to provide any legal opinion because it has only to deliver clear title to the equipment. An adequate bill of sale containing proper seller representations and warranties typically gives the necessary comfort. In certain situations, particularly if a substantial dollar amount of equipment is involved, a prospective lessor might want to ask the equipment vendor for its lawyer to provide a legal opinion confirming that the vendor has, upon equipment payment, delivered clear title to the equipment.

C. Financial Reports

The financial strength of every party to the lease transaction—such as the lessor, the lessee, and any third-party guarantor—is a key factor in a lease financing, and therefore it is important that reliable and up-to-date financial information be obtained. The degree of information necessary depends on the transaction's size—a lease of a $900 office copier will not warrant the same degree of investigation that would be called for in the lease of a multimillion dollar printing press.

1. Why Financial Information Is Necessary

a. Of the Lessor

The financial condition of a lessor is an important lessee consideration—a solid lessor contractual commitment to lease is worthless if it does not have funds available when the equipment arrives for lease. All too often a prospective lessee fails to check the lessor's financial condition, apparently assuming that a lessor always has adequate funds and that, once the deal has been signed, there is nothing to be concerned about. This may not be true. A financially weak lessor may not have purchase funds available when the equipment is ready for lease. And, even if the equipment has been paid for and put on lease, there is a risk—although unlikely—that such a lessor's creditors may seize the leased equipment as security for an unpaid obligation.

The availability of adequate funds for equipment purchase is of particular concern if a lease line of credit is involved—that is, when the lessor has committed to buy and lease many items of equipment to be delivered over a long period of time. Any lack of available lessor financing when equipment arrives could be a serious problem for a would-be lessee.

b. Of the Lessee

Similarly, the lessee's financial condition is a critical element in the lessor's decision as to whether to enter into a particular lease financing, particularly if a multimillion dollar, long-term lease is involved. At all times, particularly at the lease closing and when it must advance funds, the lessor will want to be assured that the lessee has the financial capability to meet all of its contractual obligations, including payment of rent, for the full lease term.

c. Of a Controlling Corporation

If the lessee is owned by another company, very often a lessor will want to review the parent company's financial statements—even if the parent does not guarantee the lease obligations and regardless of the financial strength of the lessee. The weaker the financial condition of an owning company, the greater the possibility that it will drain the lessee's cash to solve any of its financial problems.

▶ **Recommendation:** When there is a risk that a controlling corporation could drain a perspective lessee's cash, a lessor must take precautions. One such precaution is to impose a restriction on the amount of dividends that the lessee can declare and distribute to the controlling corporation.

d. Of the Guarantor

If the lessee's financial condition is inadequate as a condition to going forward with the financing, the lessor may ask for a transaction guarantee from a financially solid entity, such as a parent company or equipment vendor. In this event, the guarantor's financial strength is of primary importance and relevant financial information will be included in the closing.

2. Type of Financial Information Needed

Typically, the financial condition of a company can be adequately assessed in a review of its past and present financial statements, including profit and loss statements and balance sheets. A lessor may also require bank and trade references to further verify the financial integrity of the company being reviewed. And it may check, particularly in the case of smaller companies, with credit reporting services, such as Dunn & Bradstreet and TRW, to see if there is any adverse information on file.

Often, the lessor's financial review is done prior to its issuing a lease proposal offer, but sometimes, not until shortly after the lease award. In any event, it is always well in advance of starting the documentation negotiation. As a result, the lessor will typically ask that the financially reviewed entity, particularly if there is a long time between the review and the lease signing, bring its financial information up to the closing date.

One of the most common ways a participant's financial picture is brought up to the transaction's closing date is to require the reviewed entity's financial officer to deliver a certificate at the closing presenting relevant financial information since the last published statements. For example, if the most current financial statements reflect a company's condition as of June 15, 19××, and the transaction does not close until September 25, 19××, the certificate must essentially provide that as of the closing date, September 25, 19××, there have been no materially adverse financial changes since the date of the latest financial statements, June 15, 19××. Of course, it would be more comforting to get the company's independent accountants to issue the certificate, but this is generally not practical.

▶ **Recommendation:** It is always wise for any other party concerned to request updates as of the lease signing from any party whose financial condition may affect the transaction's viability. So, for example, a lessee might consider requiring a financial update from a lessor whose financial condition the lessee thought it necessary to review before making an award. This may be done through a financial certificate from the lessor's financial officer.

D. Corporate Authorization Documents

When a corporation participates in a lease transaction, the other parties generally should require a copy of the corporation's board of directors' resolutions authorizing the transaction. The resolutions should be certified by the corporate secretary or assistant secretary and delivered at the closing. The typical lessee corporate resolution, for example, will state that the lessee has been duly authorized to enter into the transaction for the specified dollar amount and that a certain person has been authorized to execute the documents on behalf of the corporation.

► **Recommendations:**

- While lessors and lenders usually require lessees to deliver appropriate board of directors' resolutions at a lease closing, lessees rarely ask for authorizing resolutions from the other parties. However, they should seriously consider doing so, particularly from corporate lessors and lenders not regularly engaged in leasing or lending.
- If the participant is not a corporation, and, for example, is a limited partnership, your attorney should be consulted about what authorization assurances might be advisable.
- After the lease has been signed, if you discover, for example, that a key party failed to get the necessary corporate board of directors' transaction approval, you should immediately request that it deliver appropriate resolutions approving, ratifying, and confirming all actions that have been taken.
- While board of directors' resolutions should be reasonably broad in scope, corporate directors must be careful not to grant more than is necessary. For example, if a lease transaction is to involve a large conveyor system, its cost should be specified with leeway for reasonable changes. Without designating the cost, an individual representing the corporation may be able to bind it to a lease even if there were unexpected and significant cost increases.

E. Guarantees

When a prospective lessee wants to lease more equipment than its credit capability justifies, it will be asked for additional credit support. Very often, the lessor will suggest that a financially strong third party be brought in to guarantee the lessee's obligations. The guarantee request may vary anywhere from a full guarantee of all the lease obligations to something significantly less.

The most favorable guarantee for a lessor would be a full lessee guarantee, in which the guarantor unconditionally obligates itself to ensure the lessee's full and prompt performance of all the lease obligations, covenants, and conditions. For example, if the lessee fails to pay the rent, the lessor could go directly to the guarantor for payment.

Under a partial guarantee, the guarantor may, for example, only be responsible for the repayment of 15% of the total lease payments. Partial guarantees may be acceptable to a lessor when the proposed transaction is financially attractive.

F.   Proof of Insurance Documents

Frequently, the lease agreement will require that the lessee have personal injury and property damage insurance covering the leased equipment. In these cases, the lessor will want the lessee to confirm that the insurance will be in effect when the equipment is accepted for lease. That confirmation should be required to be delivered at the lease closing and will take the form of a certificate of insurance from the lessee's insurance company stating that the necessary coverage will be in effect.

▶ **Recommendations:**

- A certificate of insurance should be obtained and carefully reviewed well in advance of the lease closing to verify that the coverage outlined is proper and that it will be in effect when necessary. A lessor should pay particular attention to any coverage limitations, such as restricted equipment usage. A prospective lessee should clear the insurance coverage with a prospective lessor in advance of the closing. Finding out at the closing that the insurance certificate is inadequate will not only be embarrassing, but will delay the financing. The best approach is to send a draft certificate to the lessor weeks ahead of the closing for its review and acceptance.
- A lessor should insist that the required insurance coverage cannot be canceled without prior written notice to it, and only after an adequate grace period, to give it an opportunity to take out insurance if the lessee fails to keep it in force. Insurance companies are willing to make such a commitment when asked.

G.   Equipment Purchase Agreements

Unless the equipment has been built or is already owned by the lessee, the lessor has to purchase it from a third-party supplier. If the equipment is available at the time the lease is signed, and the equipment is ready for lease acceptance, the lessor simply buys it at that time. If not, an equipment purchase may have to be entered into for ordering the equipment.

At times, vendors ask the lessor to enter directly into the purchase agreement since they know that the equipment will be put on lease. For a variety of reasons that is rarely a good idea for the lessor or the lessee. If the lessee, with or without justification, refuses to accept the equipment for lease, the lessor may still be legally obligated to buy the equipment—something it will not want to do if it has no lessee for it. Thus, if a purchase agreement must be executed early, the prospective lessor should insist that the lessee be the signing party.

From a lessee's viewpoint, it is always advisable for it to enter into the purchase agreement directly with the equipment vendor and then assign only its right to purchase the equipment to the lessor, subject, of course, to the lessor fulfilling its lease commitment. This is typically done by using a purchase agreement assignment. Under such an assignment, the lessee has direct contract rights with the supplier on warranty or other equipment-related claims, and the lessor has what it needs—the right to purchase the equipment directly from the supplier.

Here's how a purchase agreement and assignment might work. The lessee and the equipment supplier enter into the necessary purchase agreement, and then the lessor and the lessee enter into an assignment of this agreement. Under the assignment, the lessor generally acquires the lessee's contract purchase right, but not its obligations. The assignment may also provide that the lessor will acquire additional rights, such as service or training, as well as all buyer warranties or indemnities, as of the time the lease ends and the equipment is returned to the lessor. Further, the assignment often states that the lessee shall remain liable on the purchase contract as if the assignment had not been made and requires the supplier's written consent to the assignment. The supplier is also often asked to specifically acknowledge that the lessor will not be liable for any of the purchase contract duties or obligations.

▶ **Recommendations:**

- If a prospective lessor enters into a purchase agreement assignment, it must be careful not to assume any of the buyer's duties or obligations under the purchase agreement. The assignment should specify that the prospective lessee will remain liable on the purchase contract as if the assignment had not been made.
- When a prospective lessor enters into an equipment purchase agreement assignment, it should, at the same time, get the supplier's written consent to the assignment. The consent should acknowledge the assignment and provide that any rights assigned (such as supplier warranties) will accrue to the lessor's benefit, just as though it had been originally named as the buyer. Also, the supplier should be asked to acknowledge that the prospective lessor will not be liable for any of the purchase contract duties or obligations.

H. An Equipment Bill of Sale

A prospective lessor generally requires that the equipment seller deliver a bill of sale when it pays for the equipment. Typically, the bill of sale is a warranty bill of sale in which the seller not only transfers equipment title, but also warrants that it has delivered to the purchaser full legal and beneficial ownership to the equipment, free and clear of any encumbrances, mortgages, or security interests. Such a bill of sale generally contains a seller representation that it has the lawful right and the appropriate authority to sell the equipment.

▶ **Recommendation:**   A prospective lessor should insist that the bill of sale, in addition to typical seller representations and warranties, contain a seller representation that it will defend the lessor's title to the equipment against any person or entity claiming an interest in the equipment.

I. Waivers From Landowners or Mortgagees

Very often, the leased equipment will be located on real property leased from a third party or on property that is subject to a mortgage. In this case, statutory lien rights may exist that, for example, permit a landlord to attach any equipment on its land, including leased equipment, if its rent is not paid. Similarly, the holder of a mortgage on a lessee's building may, under a general mortgage claim right, be able to go after leased equipment located in the building. In these situations, the prospective lessor should require, as a closing document, a waiver from the landlord or mortgagee of any claim to the leased equipment.

J. Security Interest Filings

Although not technically necessary in most lease situations, a lessor will generally want to file appropriate Uniform Commercial Code (UCC) financing statements to ensure priority over other parties who may claim an interest in the equipment, particularly the lessee's creditors. If the UCC statement is not correctly filed, the lessor's claim to the equipment will not be perfected as to third parties, such as the lessee's general creditors, and won't give the desired protection. Simple in form, the statement basically requires nothing more than a description of the parties and the equipment. The UCC filing will be a condition of the lease closing. The filing procedures are routine, and the expenses are nominal.

K. Participation Agreements

A participation agreement, a closing document setting out the lease financing's structural terms and conditions, is frequently used in underwritten lease transactions, particularly leveraged transactions. The parties to such an agreement may include the lessee, the equity participants, the debt participants, and any trust established for the debt or equity participants. The participation agreement states the terms under which the debt participants must make their loans and the equity participants must make their equity investments. It also generally incorporates a method for substituting any defaulting participants, and may include any prescribed tax indemnification provisions.

L. The Owner's Trust Agreement

It is not unusual for a trust to be established for equity participants in a leveraged lease transaction, particularly if more than one equity participant is involved. The trust arrangement, referred to as an owner's trust, provides the equity participants with corporatelike liability protection and partnershiplike income tax treatment and, thus, can be a desirable ownership vehicle.

To set up a trust, the equity participants enter into a trust agreement with an entity, such as a bank, that will act as the trustee, referred to as the "owner trustee." The agreement sets out in detail how, and to what extent, the trustee will act on behalf of the equity participants.

As a part of its trust obligations, the trustee will execute all relevant documents, including the lease, any participation agreement, the indenture, and any purchase agreement assignment, on behalf of each equity participant. The right, title, and interest in the equipment, the lease, any purchase agreement, and any purchase agreement assignment is collectively referred to as the trust estate, and legal title to it is held in the owner trustee's name. The owner trustee is, however, only a figurehead owner, the beneficial interest in the trust estate residing with the equity participants. The equity participants' interests are represented by certificates, referred to as owner certificates, issued by the owner trustee.

M. A Lender's Trust Agreement

If the financing is structured as a leveraged lease, the debt participants will typically act through a trust arrangement, which enables them to receive favorable tax treatment and liability protection. The arrangement is typically set up through a trust indenture and mortgage agreement entered into between the equity participants and debt participants. A trust indenture and mortgage agreement defines the basic debt financing parameters and provides for issuing loan certificates that set out the debt repayment obligations. The agreement also grants a security interest to the lenders in the equipment and the lease while the loan is outstanding. As with a participation agreement it will be one of the lease closing documents.

The debt trust structure is similar to the equity trust structure. The debt participants are represented by a trustee, referred to as the "loan trustee," and it stands in the same position to the debt participants as does the owner trustee to the equity participants. As the lender's "watchdog," the trustee can take any prescribed action that may be necessary to protect the debt participants' interests, such as foreclosing on the lease in case of default.

N. Using a Partnership Instead of a Trust Arrangement

At times, multiple equity or debt participants find it undesirable or impractical to act through a trust arrangement. In that case, they frequently use instead a partnership structure. Here, the "lessor" or "lender," as the case may be, is the partnership, with the equity or debt participants as partners in the partnership. It is usually advisable for a formal partnership agreement to be entered into that defines each partner's rights and obligations. The agreement will be a part of the lease closing.

O. The Underwriter's Fee Agreement

In underwritten transactions, the lease underwriter will be responsible for bringing together the equity participants, the lessee, and, if the transaction is leveraged, the debt participants. For its services, the underwriter will be entitled to a fee, typically varying with each transaction and each broker, and typically payable by the equity participants. To protect itself and prevent later misunderstandings as to the payment terms, the underwriter may ask that the equity participants enter into a formal fee agreement clearly defining the fee arrangement, which will also be included as a closing document.

P. A Supplemental Lease Document Closing Checklist

Although the type of additional closing documents required in a lease transaction will vary with each situation, the following checklist can be used as a general guideline.

Concerning the required legal opinions:

☐ Is the lawyer rendering the legal opinion thoroughly experienced in the area to be covered by the opinion? For example, if an opinion is required on complex tax issues, is he or she fully knowledgeable on all the relevant aspects?

☐ How much has the legal opinion been conditioned? In other words, has the lawyer left so many outs as to his or her position that he or she really has provided little comfort?

☐ To the extent that the legal opinion is based on facts supplied to the lawyer, are the facts accurate and complete?

Does the opinion of the lessee's lawyer, to be delivered to the lessor, address the following issues:

☐ Proper organization, valid existence, and good standing of the lessee?
☐ The lessee's full authority to enter into the lease?
☐ The lessee's complete and unrestricted ability to perform all obligations?
☐ Whether all the lessee's lease commitments are legally binding?
☐ Whether all necessary consents have been obtained?
☐ Whether all necessary regulatory approvals have been obtained?
☐ Whether there are any pending or threatened adverse court or administrative proceedings? If so, what the potential impact may be?
☐ Whether any law, rule, or collateral agreement will be violated by the lessee entering the lease transaction?

Does the opinion of the lessor's lawyer, to be delivered to the lessee, address the following issues:

☐ Whether the lessor is properly organized, validly existing, and in good standing?
☐ Whether the lessor is properly authorized to do business in the jurisdiction where the equipment will be located?

☐ Whether the transaction has been fully authorized by the lessor? For example, have all necessary committee and board of director approvals been secured?

☐ Whether all the lessor's commitments are binding?

☐ Whether the lessor's ability to perform its obligations is unrestricted?

☐ Whether any shareholder, lender, etc., consents are necessary? If so, have they been obtained?

☐ Whether the transaction will violate any law, rule, or collateral agreement as to the lessor?

Does the opinion of the lessor's lawyer, to be delivered to a third-party lender, address the following issues:

☐ Whether the lessor is properly organized, validly existing, and in good standing?

☐ Whether all necessary authorizations, both as to the lease financing and the loan financing, have been obtained?

☐ Whether the loan obligations are fully enforceable against the lessor?

☐ Whether the lessor has good and marketable title to the leased equipment?

☐ Whether the equipment has any liens or encumbrances on it?

☐ Whether the lessor's rights under the lease are unencumbered, including its right to receive the rent payments?

Does the opinion of the guarantor's lawyer, to be delivered to the lessor, address the following issues:

☐ Whether the guarantor is properly organized, validly existing, and in good standing?

☐ Whether all necessary authorizations as to the lease financing have been obtained?

☐ Whether the lease obligations are fully enforceable against the guarantor?

Does the opinion of the vendor's lawyer, to be delivered to the lessor, address the following issues:

☐ Whether the title of the equipment will be delivered free and clear to the lessor?

☐ Whether all necessary internal authorizations have been obtained?

Has the lessor been supplied with the required lessee, lessee controlling corporation, and guarantor financial statements? For example:

☐ Profit and loss statements
☐ Balance sheets
☐ Officer's certificate updating the prior financial statements to the closing

Have adequate lessor financial statements or information been obtained? For example:

☐ Profit and loss statements
☐ Balance sheets
☐ Officer's certificate updating the prior financial statements to the closing

Have all the critical financial statements been certified by an independent certified public accounting firm?

Has a certified copy of any relevant corporate board of director resolutions been delivered?

If the lease obligations will be guaranteed by a third party, will it be a full and unconditional guarantee? If not, is the limited extent of the guarantee understood?

If personal injury and property damage insurance is required, does the insurance company's certificate of insurance properly represent the required insurance?

If the lessor must enter into an equipment purchase agreement directly with the vendor, is it prepared to buy the equipment if the lessee backs away? If not, can a purchase agreement assignment be used?

☐ Does any equipment purchase agreement assignment specifically provide that only the rights, not the obligations, will be transferred to the lessor?
☐ Under an equipment purchase agreement assignment, will the lessor be entitled to all vendor supplied services, training, information, warranties, and indemnities?
☐ Has the vendor's consent been obtained as to the purchase agreement assignment? If so, does it
  1. Acknowledge the assignment?
  2. Acknowledge that the lessor will not have to buy the equipment if the lessee backs out before the lease is executed?

Has an equipment bill of sale been included? If so,

☐ Is it a warranty bill of sale?
☐ Does it contain a representation that the seller has the lawful right and authority to sell the equipment?

If the equipment will be located on leased or mortgaged property, has the landowner or mortgagee supplied a written waiver of any present or future claim to the leased equipment?

Have appropriate UCC financing statements (UCC-1's) been prepared for filing?

If the transaction is underwritten,

☐ Has a participation agreement been prepared?
☐ Will the lenders and the equity participants each act through
  1. A trust arrangement?
  2. A partnership arrangement?

Has a fee agreement been prepared to formalize the underwriter's fee arrangement?

Chapter 5

Depreciation Advantages in Lease Transactions

Introduction

A lessor's ability to write off, or depreciate, the cost of the leased equipment is crucial to the lease transaction's economic viability. The 1986 Tax Reform Act (TRA) magnified depreciation's importance by doing away with the investment tax credit and, correspondingly, enhancing depreciation deductions for most equipment. A prospective lessor, therefore, must have a thorough understanding of the depreciation rules to evaluate a leasing transaction. These rules are also important to a prospective lessee, for two reasons:

- Unless the benefits available are fully understood and evaluated, an intelligent lease-versus-purchase analysis cannot be made.
- If a prospective lessor requires depreciation indemnities, the lessee cannot properly assess the potential risks without a clear appreciation of the technical intricacies.

▶ **Note:** If a transaction that purports to be a lease in fact does not qualify as a true lease for federal income tax purposes, the lessor is not entitled to depreciate the leased asset. The reader is referred to Chapter 8 for an explanation of the guidelines that determine whether a transaction will qualify for true lease classification under the tax rules.

This chapter proceeds in three parts. First, it describes the Modified Accelerated Cost Recovery System (MACRS), the system that, because it determines the available depreciation deductions for most property placed in service after 1986, applies to most equipment leasing deals entered into today. The second part describes the Accelerated Cost Recovery System (ACRS), the system that applied to most property placed in service between 1981 and 1987 and that applies to certain transactions not covered by MACRS. The third part describes the depreciation methods in effect before 1981. Certain older completed lease transactions are subject to these rules. This chapter explains the rules concerning personal property only, and does not cover real property depreciation.

▶ **Caution:**   The depreciation rules explained in this chapter may be altered if the alternative minimum tax applies, so Chapter 6 must be read in conjunction with this chapter.

Part I: Depreciation After 1986
A.   An Overview

Among the wide-reaching changes introduced by the 1986 TRA was Section 168's Modified Accelerated Cost Recovery System (MACRS)—a revised depreciation system. Replacing the Accelerated Cost Recovery System (ACRS), the MACRS rules generally apply to property placed in service by a taxpayer on or after January 1, 1987, with certain exceptions.

Although MACRS incorporates some of the ACRS concepts, there are substantial and fundamental differences. MACRS, for example, retains the concept of property classes, but reclassifies certain assets into different property classes (also called recovery classes) and adds more classes. There were also changes in depreciation methods and in depreciation conventions.

Under MACRS, three depreciation methods, six recovery periods, and two averaging conventions apply to equipment, depending on a variety of factors.

B.   Property Eligible for MACRS

Besides meeting the MACRS requirements to be depreciable, equipment must pass muster under Section 167(a). Section 167 establishes the basic rule authorizing an equipment owner to a deduction, in computing federal income tax liability, for the exhaustion, wear, and tear of property used in a trade or business or held for the production of income. All depreciation deductions under MACRS and previous systems must fulfill those threshold requirements: The property must be depreciable (for example, land is considered not to wear out and so is not depreciable) and must be used in a business or income-producing activity.

Generally, property qualifying under Section 167(a) may be depreciated under MACRS. The following types of property, however, are excluded:

- Intangible property (for example, copyrights, licenses). This property also does not qualify for ACRS and is amortized under other rules.
- Property that is classified as public utility property (unless the taxpayer uses a normalization method of accounting).
- Certain property to which a lessor has elected to apply a depreciation method not expressed in terms of years (such as the unit of production method).
- Motion picture films, videotapes, sound recordings (such as music tapes).
- Property covered by MACRS antichurning or transition rules.

Where property is transferred in a nonrecognition transaction under Sections 332, 351, 361, 371(a), 374(a), 721, or 731, MACRS may be used for only a portion of the equipment's basis.

Also, certain property must be depreciated under an alternative MACRS method, described later on in this chapter.

C. MACRS Deduction Computations

Four steps determine the annual MACRS depreciation deduction amount for any leased equipment. First, determine the total amount to be depreciated; next, determine the applicable MACRS recovery class from among the six classes; third, apply the appropriate depreciation method; and fourth, incorporate the applicable convention.

1. Total Amount to Be Depreciated

The total amount a lessor can write off for acquired equipment, and thus the annual deduction amount, depends on the lessor's basis in the equipment. For MACRS purposes, basis is determined under general Internal Revenue Code rules for determining the gain or loss on the sale or other disposition of an asset, and includes not only what the lessor paid for the equipment, but also the costs incurred in acquiring the equipment.

However, a lessor must reduce the basis so calculated by any amount expensed under Section 179, and if the investment tax credit (ITC) is available, because of a grandfathering provision, account for that ITC. There is, however, no reduction for salvage value.

2. MACRS Recovery Classes

MACRS continues, with modifications, the recovery class concept instituted by ACRS. The recovery class concept represents the current solution to the long-standing tax question, Over how long a period should depreciation deductions be spread? Before 1971, the lessor took depreciation deductions over an estimate of the equipment's useful life—determined based on the facts and circumstances. While having the virtue of potential accuracy, the facts and circumstances method was cumbersome and difficult for both taxpayers and the IRS to administer.

In 1971, the IRS simplified matters by promulgating the Class Life Asset Depreciation Range System (ADR). ADR set out a list of prescribed asset classes. Generally, an asset's useful life was determined by referring to the list. (For an explanation of pre-ACRS property, see Part III of this chapter.)

In 1981, the Economic Recovery Tax Act (ERTA) introduced ACRS. ACRS grouped assets based on their ADR class lives into recovery classes. For example, property with an ADR class life of more than 4 years, but less than 10, was put into the 5-year class. Under ACRS, all personal property fell into one of four personal property recovery classes. ERTA also replaced the various optional depreciation methods with statutory write-off periods.

MACRS continues the recovery class concept, grouping equipment into one of six recovery classes. Like ACRS, the MACRS recovery class grouping is based on the equipment's class life, assigned by the ADR tables. The ADR class lives for

MACRS purposes from Revenue Procedure 87-57 [IRB 1987-42] are reproduced in the Appendix.

MACRS also assigns certain equipment to particular recovery classes notwithstanding their ADR classification. Property neither assigned to an ADR class life nor specifically assigned by MACRS falls within the 7-year class. The Treasury has, within certain restrictions, the authority to shift the property assigned by MACRS from one class to another.

The following are the six recovery classes applicable to equipment:

- *3-Year Property.* The 3-year MACRS class generally includes property with an ADR class life of four years or less (for example, special tools and devices for the manufacture of rubber products and special handling devices for the manufacture of food and beverages). Automobiles and light general purpose trucks that have ADR lives of less than four years have been expressly assigned to the 5-year class.

▶ **Note:**   There are certain depreciation restrictions and requirements placed on passenger automobiles used for business. The reader is referred to Internal Revenue Code Section 280F for details.

- *5-Year Property.* The 5-year property class generally includes equipment with an ADR class life of greater than 4 years and less than 10 years. Heavy general purpose trucks, computer equipment, trailers and trailer-mounted containers, duplicating equipment, and typewriters are examples of types of equipment that come within the 5-year classification. Certain equipment is assigned to the 5-year class notwithstanding its ADR classification: automobiles; light general purpose trucks; computer-based telephone central office switching equipment; semiconductor manufacturing equipment; qualified technological equipment; equipment used in connection with research and experimentation; certain specified biomass properties that qualify as small power production facilities under the Federal Power Act; and ocean thermal, geothermal, wind, and solar energy properties.
- *7-Year Property.* The 7-year MACRS class generally includes property with an ADR class life of 10 years or greater but less than 16 years, for example, office furniture, fixtures, and equipment, and equipment used in the manufacture of tobacco and food products (other than those listed in the 10-year class). Railroad track and single purpose agricultural and horticultural structures are specifically assigned by MACRS to the 7-year class.
- *10-Year Property.* The 10-year MACRS property class generally includes property with an ADR class life equal to 16 years or greater but less than 20 years. This class includes equipment used in the manufacture of grain and grain mill products, sugar and sugar mill products, and vegetable oils and vegetable oil products, and equipment used in petroleum refining.
- *15-Year Property.* The 15-year MACRS property class includes property with an ADR class life of 20 years or greater but less than 25 years. This class includes municipal sewage treatment plants, telephone distribution

plants, and comparable equipment that is used for two-way exchange of voice and data communications. Cable television equipment that is used primarily for one-way communication is not "comparable equipment" for the purposes of this asset classification.

- *20-Year Property.* The 20-year MACRS property class includes property with an ADR class life of 25 years and greater. Specifically included in this class by statute are municipal sewers.

3. Depreciation Methods

Under MACRS, the lessor recovers the equipment's cost over the number of years in the recovery class plus one, for example, 3-year property yields deductions over a 4-year period. For equipment in the 3-, 5-, 7-, or 10-year class, the lessor uses the 200% declining balance method of depreciation, with a switch to straight-line depreciation at the time that maximizes the deduction. For property in the 15- and 20-year classes, the lessor uses the 150% declining balance method with a switch to the straight-line method at a time that maximizes the deduction.

Under the declining balance method, the equipment owner calculates the depreciation deduction for any year by multiplying the asset's basis—reduced by any prior years' depreciation deductions—by the declining balance rate, and then multiplying by the percent available each year. Thus, for example, for an asset with a $100 basis and a 5-year recovery period, the first year's depreciation is $40 (ignoring the averaging conventions):

$$\textit{\$100 basis} \times 2 \times 20\% = \textit{\$40}$$

For the second year, the MACRS deduction would be $24:

$$\textit{\$100 basis} - \textit{\$40 first-year deduction} = \textit{\$60}$$

$$\textit{\$60} \times 2 \times 20\% = \textit{\$24}$$

And so on, for three more years.

At the point when the declining balance method yields smaller deductions than straight-line, the method switches to straight-line. (Depreciation methods are explained in more detail below at Part III, Section C.) The 200% balance method resulted in more accelerated deductions than had been available under ACRS. The IRS has calculated and published, in Revenue Procedure 87-57 [IRB 1987-42], the appropriate annual deductions applying the 200% and 150% methods for each MACRS recovery class (set out in the Appendix).

A lessor can elect to use the straight-line depreciation method instead of the prescribed MACRS accelerated method established for MACRS property classes. If the election is made, it is irrevocable and applies to all the MACRS eligible property within the same asset class that is placed in service during the relevant tax year. The assets within the class for which a straight-line method is elected are to be written off over the recovery period prescribed under the applicable regular recovery period.

▶ **Note:**   For certain depreciable computer software that has been acquired after August 10, 1993, and which is not an amortizable Section 197 intangible, the taxpayer may depreciate it using the straight-line method of depreciation over a 3-year period [see Internal Revenue Code Section 167(f)]. Prior to August 11, 1993, if the taxpayer received computer software with its computer and the cost of the software was "bundled" with the computer hardware cost (not separately stated), the taxpayer depreciated it along with the computer hardware under MACRS over the specified 5-year recovery period. If the software cost was separately stated ("unbundled"), its cost had to be amortized over a 5-year period on a straight-line basis. If the software had a useful life of less than one year, it was simply expensed.

4. MACRS Averaging Conventions

In determining how to handle depreciation deductions under any system, there is an issue of how to handle placements in, and retirements from, service that occurs during the year.

Generally, under MACRS, a lessor recovers equipment costs using the half-year convention. Under that convention, equipment is deemed to have been placed in service at the mid-point of the year in which it was placed in service, regardless of when during the year it was placed in service. Similarly, an asset is deemed to have been disposed of or retired from service at the mid-point of the year during which it was disposed of or retired, regardless of when in fact it was disposed of during the year. Thus, a lessor is entitled to one-half a full year's permitted depreciation in the year it places an eligible asset in service, and one-half a full year's depreciation in the year it disposes of or retires the asset from service. When there is a short tax year (a year less than 12 months), an asset is deemed to have been placed in service for a period of time equal to one-half the number of months in the short tax year.

To prevent taxpayers from abusing the half-year convention by bunching purchases at year's end, MACRS includes a mid-quarter convention. That convention kicks in if a taxpayer places in service, in the tax year's last quarter, over 40% of the aggregate bases of property placed in service during the tax year. Under the mid-quarter convention, all property placed in service (or disposed of) during a tax-year quarter is treated as though placed in service (or disposed of) in the middle of such quarter.

5. Applying MACRS

To summarize: Find the appropriate recovery class and check the averaging convention. Then refer to Revenue Procedure 87-57 to find the MACRS deduction's annual percentage. Set out in the Appendix are some tables from that Revenue Procedure. (Note: 3-, 5-, 7-, and 10-year classes are based on 200% declining method; 15- and 20-year classes use 150% method.)

D. The Alternative MACRS Depreciation Approach

The 1986 TRA established an alternative depreciation system (ADS) that the lessor must use in certain select cases and can elect in other situations. Under ADS, a taxpayer generally is to compute its permitted depreciation allowance by applying the straight-line method, without making a basis reduction for salvage value, over a recovery period typically longer than that specified under the other MACRS approaches. The applicable averaging conventions—the half-year or mid-quarter convention—apply in the same situations as under the regular MACRS.

1. When Must ADS Be Used?

A taxpayer must use ADS to depreciate the following:

- *Equipment used predominantly outside the United States.* This is equipment located for more than 50% of the time during a tax year outside the United States. To determine U.S. use, the rules relating to the ITC have been deemed to apply. Under the 1986 TRA rules, there is an additional special exception to the predominant use outside of the United States classification for property that qualifies as a satellite or other spacecraft or interest therein held by a U.S. person and that is launched within the United States.
- *Tax-exempt bond financed property.* This is equipment that has been financed out of the proceeds of tax-exempt bonds that were issued after March 1, 1986. It includes any property to the extent that it is financed directly or indirectly by an obligation if the interest from that obligation is tax exempt.
- *Tax-exempt use property.* This includes equipment that's leased to a tax-exempt entity under certain types of leases that do not fit specified Internal Revenue Code requirements (known as "disqualified" leases). A lease is considered to be a disqualified lease if, for example, its lease term exceeds 20 years.
- *Imported property.* This is equipment produced or manufactured in a foreign country and is the subject of an executive order issued by the U.S. president. It is considered made outside the United States if it is completed outside the United States or 50% or more of its basis is attributable to value added outside of the United States. The president has the authority to issue an executive order for property brought in from a foreign country that either maintains burdensome trade restrictions that are inconsistent with trade agreements or engages in discriminatory or other acts that unjustifiably restrict U.S. commerce.
- *For alternative minimum tax depreciation preference computation purposes.* [Section 56(g)(4).]
- *To figure the earnings and profits of a domestic corporation or a controlled foreign corporation.* [Section 31 2(k)(3).]
- *For "listed property,"* if the property's business use does not exceed 50% for the year.

2. When Can ADS Be Elected?

A lessor can elect to use ADS as to any MACRS property for any MACRS eligible tax year. The election, once made, is irrevocable and applies to all property in the class that the taxpayer has placed in service during the election year.

3. What Are the ADS Recovery Periods?

Under ADS, the lessor will generally depreciate the equipment over the ADR class life period. The following are assigned specific recovery periods notwithstanding their ADR class lives:

- *5 years.* Automobiles, light general purpose trucks, semiconductor manufacturing equipment, computer or peripheral equipment, any high technology telephone station equipment installed on the customer's premises, and any high technology medical equipment.
- *9.5 years.* Any computer-based telephone central office switching equipment.
- *10 years.* Any railroad track.
- *12 years.* Personal property with no class life.
- *15 years.* Single purpose agricultural or horticultural structures.
- *24 years.* Any municipal wastewater treatment plant and any telephone plant and comparable equipment used for two-way exchange of voice and data communications.

4. When Can ADS Be Applied?

Revenue Procedure 87-57 sets out tables to find the annual deduction percentage amount for equipment depreciated under ADS with a recovery period of 2.5 to 50 years. Table 8 prescribes the percentages for the half-year convention; Tables 9 through 12 set out the percentages for equipment subject to the mid-quarter convention. These tables are included in the Appendix.

E. Antiabuse Rules Under MACRS

Because MACRS generally permits more rapid deductions than prior systems, Congress was concerned that certain taxpayers might try to use MACRS on equipment previously placed in service through transfers not resulting in substantive ownership changes. To address this concern, MACRS incorporated antichurning provisions that precluded specified property from qualifying under MACRS rules. As a result, the 1986 TRA incorporated into the law special provisions to prevent the improper "churning" so as to obtain enhanced benefits under the MACRS method. If one of the antichurning provisions applies, the taxpayer cannot use MACRS. Thus, MACRS cannot be used if the equipment was any of the following:

- Owned or used at any time during 1986 by the taxpayer or a related person
- Acquired from a person who owned the property at any time during 1986 and, as part of the transaction, the property user remained the same
- Leased by the taxpayer to a person, or any person related to such person, who owned or used the property at any time during 1986
- Acquired in a transaction where the property user did not change, and it was not MACRS eligible property in the transferor's hands

▶ **Caveat:** These antichurning rules do not apply if, by using them, a taxpayer would receive a more generous write-off for the year the property was placed in service than under the MACRS method. These rules also do not apply to property, used for personal use before 1987, that first was used for business purposes after 1986, so that the property is deemed to have been placed in service when it is first used for business.

F. Special Depreciation Rules for Automobiles and Listed Property

Section 280F specially limits MACRS deductions available for automobiles and certain other equipment. MACRS deductions available for automobiles are limited to $2,560 for the first tax year, $4,100 for the second tax year, $2,450 for the third tax year, and $1,475 for each succeeding tax year. Also, a lessor must use ADS, rather than regular MACRS, for automobiles and other listed property costs, if the business use of the property fails to exceed 50% of its use. Listed property includes

- Any property used as a means of transportation
- Any property of a type generally used for purposes of entertainment, recreation, or amusement
- Any computer or peripheral equipment (unless used exclusively at a regular business establishment and owned or leased by the person operating that establishment)

If the business use exceeds 50% of annual usage, and then, in a later year, drops below 50%, the lessor must recapture the excess of accelerated depreciation over the straight-line amount claimed in earlier years.

G. Recapture

Generally, on disposition of MACRS equipment, the equipment owner must recapture, as ordinary income, the MACRS deduction—including any Section 179 deduction—up to the amount realized on the equipment disposition.

H. Expensing

Under Section 179, an equipment owner can currently elect to deduct up to $17,500 of MACRS property used in the active conduct of its business. (The $17,500 limit is the total per taxpayer, not for each equipment item.) However, if a taxpayer places in service over $200,000 of Section 179 property in a year, the amount that can be expensed is reduced dollar-for-dollar by the excess over $200,000. Expensing is available to noncorporate lessors only if they meet the requirements of Section 46(e)(3) (describing when a noncorporate lessor may be eligible for ITC).

I. MACRS Effective Dates

The 1986 TRA depreciation rules are generally effective for property placed in service on or after January 1, 1987, for tax years that end on or after that date. A lessor can elect to use the MACRS rules for property placed in service after July 31, 1986, and before January 1, 1987, if the property is not transition property. That election can be on an asset-by-asset basis and is irrevocable.

1. *Transition Rules*

The general effective dates do not apply to property subject to transitional rules. Under the general transitional rules, MACRS does not apply to property placed in service after December 31, 1986, and pre-MACRS rules apply if the property

- Was constructed or acquired by the taxpayer under a written contract binding on March 1, 1986;
- Was an equipped building (including equipment and machinery to be used in or incidental to the building), or a plant facility not housed in a building, on which construction began no later than March 1, 1986, under a specific written plan and greater than 50% of the cost was either incurred or committed no later than March 1, 1986; or
- Was self-constructed property (constructed or reconstructed by the taxpayer) where the construction or reconstruction started by, and at least the lesser of 5% of the property's cost or $1 million was incurred or committed by, March 1, 1986.

Transition property with an ADR class life of at least 7 years but less than 20 years must have been placed in service before January 1, 1989. Transition property with a class life of 20 years or greater must have been placed in service before January 1, 1991.

Special transition property rules apply to certain specified property. These include property that is an integral part of a qualified urban renewal project, certain projects that qualify under the 1978 Public Utility Regulatory Policies Act, property that is integral to carrying out certain supply or service contracts, and certain solid waste disposal facilities. The lessor writes off property that comes within the special transitional rules under pre-1987 depreciation rules.

2. The Sale-Leaseback Rule

Property that qualifies as transition property in a lessee's hands, or that was originally placed in service by the lessee before January 1, 1987, may come within the pre-1987 depreciation rules if it meets certain sale-leaseback date requirements. The lessee must (1) have placed the property in service by January 1, 1987, or the property must be covered by one of the transition rules described above, and (2) the property must be sold and leased back by the lessee no later than the earlier of the applicable transition dates or three months after it was placed in service.

Part II: ACRS Deductions
A. Overview

Generally, for property placed in service between January 1, 1981, and December 31, 1986, an equipment owner depreciated property using ACRS. Part of ERTA, ACRS both substantially simplified the previous depreciation methods and, by accelerating depreciation deductions, was designed to provide incentives to stimulate capital investment in an economic climate where inflation was eroding the value of existing depreciation allowances.

MACRS has replaced ACRS for most equipment placed in service after 1986. The ACRS rules, however, continue to apply to the numerous leasing deals entered into between 1981 and 1987. Also, ACRS applies to new leasing transactions where property is covered by a MACRS antichurning or transition rule.

B. Property Eligible for ACRS

Generally, ACRS applied to the same property as does MACRS. The following are specific exclusions:

- Certain public utility property
- Property covered by antichurning rules
- Property depreciated using a method not based on a term of years
- Certain property amortized under the tax rules, such as rehabilitated low-income housing
- Property that a taxpayer acquired in specified types of transactions where gain or loss was not recognized for tax purposes

C. Computing ACRS Deductions

Calculating an ACRS deduction was similar to the method described above for MACRS deductions. The same steps are involved: Calculate the basis and then determine the recovery class. The equipment owner then simply multiplies the applicable recovery property class percentage for the appropriate tax year times the equipment basis. In statutory tables, ACRS prescribed the applicable percentage deduction for each class, incorporating the following:

- The method used was the 150% declining balance method switching to straight-line at the time that maximizes the deduction. (Depreciation methods are explained below in Part III, Section C.)
- The averaging convention, like MACRS, was the half-year convention under which the equipment owner received a half-year deduction for all property placed in service during the year. Unlike MACRS, there was no deduction in the year the property was retired from service, and the deductions were spread out over the number of years in the recovery class (without the additional year as under MACRS).

ACRS recovery classes, based on ADR class lives—set out for ACRS purposes in Revenue Procedure 83-35, [1983-1 CB 745]—grouped personal property into the four classes: 3-year, 5-year, 10-year, and 15-year.

- *3-Year Recovery Property.* The 3-year recovery property class includes, generally, all Section 1245 property (essentially depreciable personal property) having an ADR class life of not greater than four years. Thus, 3-year property includes cars, light trucks (trucks with an unloaded weight of less than 13,000 pounds), over-the-road tractors, and certain specified manufacturing activity tools and handling devices. Also, the statute specifically includes equipment and machinery used in connection with research and experimentation.

The recovery property percentages applicable to 3-year property were

Year	Percentage
1	25%
2	38
3	37

- *5-Year Recovery Property.* The 5-year recovery property class included, in general, Section 1245 property that did not qualify as 3-year property, 10-year property, or 5-year public utility property. As a practical matter, most equipment was 5-year property.

The recovery percentages applicable to 5-year recovery property were

Year	Percentage
1	15%
2	22
3	21
4	21
5	21

- *10-Year Recovery Property.* The 10-year recovery property class included public utility personal property that had an ADR class life of greater than 18 years but not more than 25 years. Railroad tank cars and certain coal utilization property were also part of this ACRS property class.

The recovery percentages applicable to 10-year recovery property were

Year	Percentage
1	8%
2	14
3	12
4	10
5	10
6	10
7	9
8	9
9	9
10	9

- *15-Year Public Utility Recovery Property.* The 5-year public utility recovery property class included public utility personal property with an ADR class life of greater than 25 years. Public utility personal property used in connection with research and experimentation was deemed to be 3-year recovery property even though it might have qualified in another recovery property class.

The recovery percentages applicable to 15-year public utility recovery property were

Year	Percentage
1	5%
2	10
3	9
4	8
5	7
6	7
7	6
8	6
9	6
10	6
11	6
12	6
13	6
14	6
15	6

D. Straight-Line Election

Under ACRS, like MACRS, an equipment owner could elect to depreciate ACRS property more slowly, by using the straight-line method and a longer depreciation period. For each recovery class, two longer periods may be used in addition to the normal recovery period; for 3-year property, the alternative periods are 5 or 12 years; for 5-year property, 12 or 25 years; for 10-year property, 25 or 35 years; and for 15-year public utility property, 35 or 45 years. *Note:* If an equipment owner makes a straight-line election, the same election has to be made for all property in the same recovery class put into service in the election year.

E. Equipment Used Outside the United States

The ACRS recovery classes did not apply to equipment used predominantly outside the United States. Generally, a taxpayer had to recover the equipment's cost over the property's ADR class life. Where the equipment did not have a class life, a 12-year period was used.

F. ITC Adjustment

The 1982 Tax Equity and Fiscal Responsibility Act (TEFRA) amended ACRS to require an equipment owner intending to claim ITC on ACRS property placed in service after 1982 to either (1) reduce the asset's basis by 50% of the ITC claimed or (2) reduce the ITC amount claimed by 2%. For example, a taxpayer allowed to claim a 10% ITC on an item of computer equipment that cost $1 million could have claimed an $80,000 ITC [8% × $1 million = $80,000] and depreciated the computer in an amount equal to $1 million. As an alternative, the taxpayer could have claimed a $100,000 ITC [10% × $1 million = $100,000] and depreciated the computer in an amount equal to $950,000 [$1 million − $50,000 (5% × $1 million) = $950,000)].

▶ **Observation:** Generally speaking, equipment lessors who could use the ITC found it more advantageous to claim the full available ITC and take ACRS reductions, rather than take the reduced ITC.

G. Antichurning Rules

Like MACRS, ACRS incorporated antichurning provisions into the law that precluded specified property from qualifying under the ACRS rules. The antichurning provisions disqualified personal property from ACRS treatment that

- The taxpayer, or a related person, owned or used at any time during 1980
- Was acquired from a person who owned the property at any time during 1980 and, as a part of the transaction, the property user remained the same

- Was leased by the taxpayer to a person, or a person related to that person, who owned or used the property at any time during 1980
- Was acquired in a transaction where the property user did not change, and the property was not considered recovery property in the transferor's hands because it came within the scope of the second or third rule above

Of particular importance to lessors were the antichurning rules requiring the user to change because those rules precluded equipment lessors from exchanging equipment to fit within the ACRS recovery rules.

The term "related person" for these antichurning rule purposes casts a wide net. The related persons rule of Sections 267(b) [limiting losses between related parties] and 707(b)(1) [disallowing losses among certain partnerships] apply with 10% substituted for 50%. Also, persons engaged in trades or businesses under common control are related persons.

H.   The Short Tax Year Rule

If the taxpayer's tax year was less than 12 months long, the taxpayer had to reduce the full year's ACRS deduction by a fraction, the numerator of which was the number of months in the short tax year and the denominator of which was 12; the ACRS deductions for later years were also affected.

Part III: Pre-1981 Depreciation

As explained, ACRS made sweeping changes to the depreciation rules, generally effective for property placed in service after December 31, 1980. The pre-ACRS depreciation rules, however, continue to govern leasing transactions entered into before that date, many of which are ongoing. Also, those rules cover certain other limited transactions, such as those excluded from both ACRS and MACRS by antichurning rules. Thus, the pre-ACRS rules have some continuing importance and are explained below.

Governed by Section 167, calculating depreciation deductions before ACRS was more complex, but followed the same pattern:

- Over how long a period was that amount spread?
- What is the total amount that could be depreciated?
- What depreciation methods could be used?
- How were placements and retirements during the year treated?

This portion of the chapter first addresses these questions for pre-1981 depreciation, generally. Then, the Classified Asset Depreciation Range System (ADR), instituted in 1971, which provided additional depreciation options, is explained.

A. Useful Life

Under pre-ACRS rules, an equipment owner depreciated an asset over its "useful life." An asset's useful life was determined under the facts and circumstances method.

Under that method, an equipment owner determined an asset's useful life based on its experience with similar property. To do that, it had to take into account any current or anticipated future conditions that could affect its conclusion. For example, the equipment owner had to consider (1) wear and tear and decay or decline from natural causes; (2) normal progress of the state of the art; (3) economic changes, inventions, and current developments inside that taxpayer's industry and trade or business; (4) climatic and other relevant local conditions that could affect the taxpayer's trade or business; and (5) the taxpayer's repair, renewal, and replacement program. If it lacked enough experience with a particular asset to make a judgment, it could base its estimate on the general experience in its industry. Once the useful life determination had been made, it could not be varied unless the anticipated conditions forming the basis for its determination changed. If these conditions did change, the useful life had to be revised.

B. The Total Amount to Be Depreciated:
Salvage Value

Generally, in determining the total amount to be depreciated, an equipment owner started with the asset's basis, calculated under the general Internal Revenue Code principles. Next, an equipment owner had to determine the asset's salvage value.

What is an asset's salvage value? It is that amount that a taxpayer estimates, at the time the asset is acquired, that it will bring when the taxpayer retires it from service, whether through sale or other disposition. This value is sometimes referred to as the asset's "gross salvage value." In computing the depreciation allowance, the asset's "net salvage value" could be used instead of its gross value, provided the taxpayer's choice was consistent with its prior practice. The net value is nothing more than the gross value reduced by removal, disposition, or other similar costs.

Depending on the method chosen to depreciate an asset, that is, declining-balance, sum-of-the-years'-digits, or straight-line, the salvage value would either be deducted from the amount that was to be depreciated or act as a depreciation cutoff:

- Using the straight-line or sum-of-the-years'-digits method, salvage value had to be deducted from the asset's basis.
- Using the declining-balance method, the asset's basis did not have to be reduced by its salvage value before computing the annual deductions; however, the taxpayer no longer could depreciate the asset when it had been written down to its salvage value.

If the ADR was elected, the salvage value did not have to be deducted from an asset's basis before determining the depreciation allowance regardless of the way it was depreciated, that is, whether the declining-balance, sum-of-the-years'-digits, or straight-line method was used. The asset could not, however, be depreciated below its salvage value.

In computing the depreciation allowance for personal property having a useful life of at least three years, a taxpayer could, generally, have elected to reduce the property's expected salvage value by an additional amount up to 10% of its basis. This, in effect, increased the amount that could be written off.

C. Depreciation Methods

When depreciating equipment, an equipment owner could use the straight-line, the sum-of-the-years'-digits, or the declining-balance method. However, an equipment owner could basically use any consistent method it wanted to use to compute its annual equipment depreciation allowance, provided the sum of the annual allowance and all its prior allowances did not exceed the total amount that would have been permitted during the first two-thirds of the asset's useful life had the declining-balance method been used. The consistent method requirement was met if the treatment was consistent for a particular asset or group of assets. The requirement did not prevent other depreciation methods from being chosen for other assets or groups of assets, or the same asset or group of assets acquired in a later year.

Although there appeared to be reasonable leeway in the choice of depreciation rate methods, lessors typically selected one of three methods, or a combination thereof, specifically prescribed in Section 167(b). They were, as already mentioned, the straight-line method, the sum-of-the-years'-digits method, and the declining-balance method.

1. The Straight-Line Method

To use the straight-line method, the equipment owner simply divides the asset's basis, after subtracting its salvage value by its useful life. This method produces the smallest write-off in the early years of an asset's use. The straight-line method could be elected whether the asset was new or used.

2. The Declining-Balance Method

Under the declining-balance method, the equipment owner multiplied the asset's basis (reduced by any prior years' depreciation deductions) by the declining-balance rate. This method could be used only if the asset had a useful life of at least three years. This method could produce, for new assets, an initial deduction far greater than either of the other two methods. For new equipment, the user could use the 200% or double-declining method; for used equipment, the lessor was limited to the 150% method. When the declining-balance method was used, the asset's salvage value did not have to be deducted from its basis before calculating the annual depreciation allowance. The asset could not, however, be depreciated below its salvage value.

3.   The Sum-of-the-Years'-Digits Method

Under the sum-of-the-years'-digits method, the deduction for any year was determined by multiplying the basis of the asset (reduced by its salvage value) by a prescribed fraction that would vary for each year. The numerator of the fraction was the number of years remaining in its useful life as of the beginning of the computation year, and the denominator was an amount equal to the sum of the number of years of the asset's useful life. This method could be used only for new assets with a useful life of at least three years.

> **Illustrative Example**—*Depreciation Methods:*   In 1980 Able Company bought a new truck for $10,000. Able estimated the truck's useful life to be 10 years, and its salvage value at the end of the 10-year period to be $1,000. Under the various depreciation methods, how much could Able have written off each year?
>
> ● *Straight-line.* The annual straight-line deduction (($10,000 − $1,000) × 10%) would have been $900 for each of the 10 years.
> ● *Declining balance.* The 200% declining-balance rate is two times the straight-line rate, here 10%. Thus, the following deductions were available:
>
> > 1st year: $2,000 (2 × 10% × $10,000)
> > 2nd year: $1,600 (2 × 10% × $8,000)
> > 3rd year: $1,280 (2 × 10% × $6,400)
> > 4th year: $1,024 (2 × 10% × $5,120)
> > 5th year: $819 (2 × 10% × $4,096)
> > 6th year: $655 (2 × 10% × $3,277)
> > 7th year: $524 (2 × 10% × $2,621)
> > 8th year: $419 (2 × 10% × $2,097)
> > 9th year: $336 (2 × 10% × $1,678)
> > 10th year: $268 (2 × 10% × $1,342)
>
> ● *Sum-of-the-Years:* The denominator of the multiplying fraction is the sum of 10 + 9 + 8 + 7 + 6 + 5 + 4 + 3 + 2 + 1 = 55. Therefore, for each of the 10 years the depreciation deductions are calculated as follows:
>
> > 1st year: $1,636 (10/55 × ($10,000 − $1,000 = $9,000)
> > 2nd year: $1,473 (9/55 × $9,000)
> > 3rd year: $1,309 (8/55 × $9,000)
> > 4th year: $1,145 (7/55 × $9,000)
> > 5th year: $982 (6/55 × $9,000)

6th year:	$818	(5/55 × $9,000)
7th year:	$655	(4/55 × $9,000)
8th year:	$491	(3/55 × $9,000)
9th year:	$327	(2/55 × $9,000)
10th year:	$164	(1/55 × $9,000)

Comparing the three methods reveals that the 200% declining-balance method yielded the largest early year deductions, the sum-of-the-years'-digits the next largest, and the straight-line the smallest. For later years, of course, the result was the opposite. Thus, to maximize the available depreciation deductions, lessors initially using the declining-balance method sometimes switched to the straight-line method when it would produce a greater annual allowance. At the time the change was made, the original depreciable amount, reduced by the sum of the previous deductions, was to be straight-lined over the remaining useful life. If, in the preceding example, the switch to the straight-line method was made after the fifth year, the annual allowance would be computed on the remaining basis of $3,277 ($10,000 − $6,723). If an election had been made to reduce the salvage value by the permitted 10% of original basis and if the remaining basis were multiplied by the straight-line rate, 20% over the remaining five years, the depreciation deduction for the sixth year would be equal to $655 (20% × $3,277). Because for the seventh through tenth years the amount would also be equal to $655, it is easy to see what the increase in benefit would be by switching to the straight-line method.

D.   How to Account for Depreciation

An equipment owner could record equipment subject to depreciation in one of two ways—on an *item by item* basis or on a *group* basis. Under the group approach, the taxpayer would put two or more assets into a single depreciation account, referred to as *multiple asset accounting.*

The grouping into one account could be done in a number of ways. One method was to group those used in a particular business into one account. These accounts were referred to as composite accounts because no weight was given to the type or useful life of the asset. Another way—called group accounts—was to group them on the basis of similarity in kind and useful lives. Under a third way—called classified accounts—assets were grouped on the basis of similar use. And, finally, if the ADR method was elected, all ADR eligible assets had to be put into vintage accounts. A vintage account was essentially a grouping of assets based on the year the assets were first placed in service.

E.   Mid-Year Placements in Service and Retirements

The general rule is that an asset's depreciation begins when placed in service and ends when retired. Generally, if an asset was placed in service during the year, only a percentage of a year's depreciation could be taken for the first year. Similarly, only a portion was available for a year in which the asset was retired from use before the end of the taxpayer's full reporting year. In these situations, the depreciation percentage available was the percentage of the year the asset was held.

For multiple asset accounts, however, the treatment was different. The beginning and ending annual depreciation amounts were determined on the basis of certain averaging conventions that, in effect, created artificial beginning and ending depreciation dates. For example, under a certain convention, all equipment additions and retirements in the first half of a tax year were treated as having taken place on the first day of that year, and all those in the second half were treated as having taken place on the first day of the following year. In this case, for the year the assets were placed in service, a full year's depreciation was permitted on first-half assets and none was permitted on the second-half assets. Correspondingly, no depreciation could be claimed on assets retired in the first half of the year, and assets retired during the second half of the year were entitled to a full year's depreciation deduction.

How was the depreciation calculation handled for assets that were not placed in service on the first day of a month or retired on the last day of a month? There were a number of methods commonly used. One provided that an asset placed in service after the first day of a month, but on or before the 15th of that month, would be entitled to a full initial month's depreciation. If the asset was placed in service after the 15th day of the initial month, the taxpayer had to exclude the initial month in computing the available depreciation. For example, an asset placed in service on June 14 would have been entitled to a full seven months' depreciation for a calendar-year taxpayer. If the asset was placed in service on June 19, only six months could be claimed. Under this method, asset retirements had to be treated in a consistent manner. Another method often employed was for the initial month to be consistently excluded, and the retirement month consistently included. The specific acquisition or retirement date was ignored. A third alternative was for a taxpayer to claim the exact number of days an asset was held, and, thereby, not lose or gain any depreciation for the acquiring or retiring year. Generally speaking, however, this technique may not have been practical to use when many assets were involved.

F.   The ADR System

In 1971, to reduce potential factual disagreements concerning useful life, salvage value, and treatment of repairs, the IRS instituted the Class Life Asset Depreciation Range System (ADR). ADR grouped assets into classes, including either a range of years (asset depreciation range) or a specified year life (class life) from which an equipment owner would choose a useful life. Called the asset depreciation period, the ADR life provided an alternative to the facts and circumstances approach and, in many instances, resulted in shorter depreciation, and thus quicker write-offs.

Generally, ADR followed the facts and circumstances method for computing depreciation. However, ADR also entailed other requirements, highlighted below.

1. Eligible Property

To qualify for ADR treatment, equipment had to be

- Depreciable
- Tangible
- First placed in service by the taxpayer after 1970
- Subject to a taxpayer's ADR election
- Property for which a class and class life were in effect
- Property qualifying under Section 1245 (basically, depreciable personal property or certain other tangible property that is not a building or a building's structural component)
- Not subject to certain special depreciation or amortization deductions

2. Election Required

To use the ADR method for a particular tax year, an equipment owner had to elect ADR when it filed its federal income tax return. Generally, once the election was made, all ADR eligible property first placed in service during the electing year had to be included within the election. Any related ADR elections, such as the choice of the preferred first-year convention, also had to be made at that time.

A taxpayer generally could not revoke or modify an ADR election after the last day that was prescribed for filing for the election. Also, other modifications, such as changes in the vintage accounts, depreciation periods, or first-year conventions, generally could not be made after this time unless required by the rules. An example of a required change would be if an incorrect asset guideline class had been selected.

3. Selecting the ADR Depreciation Period

To determine the appropriate ADR asset depreciation period, certain terms—asset guideline class, asset guideline period, and asset depreciation range—which form the conceptual basis of the system, had to be understood.

Asset guideline class meant essentially a specified asset category for which a separate asset guideline period was provided. An asset guideline period was defined as the average class life that had been prescribed for a particular asset's class. Generally, the average class life, or mid-range ADR depreciation life, was referred to simply as the class life of an asset. Typically, a particular class of asset had a range of years above and below its class life. This range was referred to as the asset depreciation range of the asset's class. The range's lower limit was set at 80% of the *asset guideline period*, and its upper limit was set at 120% of the *asset guideline period*. If an *asset depreciation range* existed for a particular asset, a taxpayer could generally choose any number of years, plus a half year, within the established asset depreciation range. The period selected was the period over which the asset was depreciated and was referred to as the *asset depreciation period*. If an asset depreciation range was not in effect for an asset class, the asset depreciation period would be the prescribed asset guideline period. Assets used predominantly outside the United States, for example, did not have an asset depreciation range.

ADR included both *type* categories—such as trucks—and *activity* categories—such as mining. To make the asset guideline selection, an equipment owner would use an asset's type category, unless none existed, in which case it referred to the activity category. The asset's primary use during the election year determined the asset's appropriate activity class. The fact that a taxpayer used the asset in a different activity in a later year would not affect the initial choice.

For the most part, the asset depreciation period was treated as the asset's useful life for all federal income tax purposes, including the ITC computation. It was not used, however, for the purpose of determining salvage value, whether a true tax lease existed, or whether an expenditure added to an asset's useful life.

The ADR asset guideline periods, as well as asset guideline classes and asset depreciation ranges, for classified assets were embodied in Revenue Procedure 77-10 [1977-1 CB 548]. Generally, the periods, classes, and ranges in effect on the last day of an ADR election year were to be referred to for all vintage accounts established during an election year. A taxpayer could not make changes in its selection to incorporate modifications effective following the last day of the election year.

4. The ADR Vintage Account

To elect ADR treatment for a particular year, the equipment owner had to establish a "vintage account" for each eligible asset, or group of assets, covered by a single asset guideline class. An asset vintage account was a closed-end depreciation account that contained ADR eligible assets, or groups of assets, that had first been placed in service during the election year. The tax year during which the asset, or group of assets, was placed in service established the account's vintage. Each account could only contain ADR eligible property that came within a single asset guideline class and could have only one ADR depreciation period. The number of vintage accounts that could be established, however, was unlimited, and different assets within the same asset guideline class could be placed in separate vintage accounts.

A taxpayer had to set aside a certain amount of money as a "depreciation reserve" for each vintage account, and the reserve had to be included on each federal income tax return. Essentially, an account's depreciation reserve was the total accumulated depreciation on the assets in the account, adjusted for certain required increases and decreases.

5. ADR Depreciation Methods

An equipment owner using ADR generally faced the same options—the straight-line, declining-balance, and sum-of-the-years methods—as one using the facts and circumstances approach. Other ADR points included the following:

- An equipment owner had to select a depreciation method for each vintage account and depreciate all account assets under that method.
- The annual ADR depreciation allowance was computed without regard to

salvage value. The assets, however, could not be depreciated below salvage value. *Note:* Salvage value for these purposes is based on the asset's value at the end of its non-ADR useful life.

- When applying a depreciation method to vintage account assets, the account's *unadjusted* basis was used. An asset's unadjusted basis is, generally, its undepreciated, or unamortized, cost. The excess of an unadjusted basis over the allowable depreciation is called the adjusted basis of an asset.

- An equipment owner could, without IRS approval, switch (1) from the declining-balance depreciation method to the sum-of-the-years'-digits methods or (2) from the declining-balance or the sum-of-the-years'-digits method to the straight-line method. Most other changes required IRS approval.

6.   *First-Year Conventions*

An equipment owner could select either of the two specified conventions available under ADR—the *modified half-year* convention or the *half-year* convention. While an equipment owner had to apply the same convention to all vintage accounts established during an ADR electing year, it could, however, change its vintage account conventions in any other year.

a.   The Modified Half-Year Convention

Under the modified half-year convention, an equipment owner calculated the amount of first-year depreciation for a vintage account by considering all the account's assets placed in service during the first half of the tax year as having been placed in service on the year's first day. All assets placed in service during the year's second half were treated as having been placed in service on the first day of the following tax year. A taxpayer had to follow certain specific rules for assets subject to the modified half-year convention that were extraordinarily retired.

b.   The Half-Year Convention

Under the half-year convention, an equipment owner computed the depreciation allowance for the first tax year by treating assets placed in service anytime during the tax year as placed in service on the first day of the second half of the tax year. For example, for a calendar-year taxpayer, an asset placed in service in January and an asset placed in service in November of the same year would each be entitled to one-half year's depreciation. Extraordinary retirements under this convention were treated as all having taken place on the first day of the second half of the retirement year.

7.   *Leased ADR Equipment*

A lessor using the ADR approach determined the ADR asset depreciation range, and the asset depreciation period for leased equipment, without regard to the lease term. The asset guideline class that generally had to be used was the class the lessee would use if it had been the equipment owner, unless there was a class in effect for lessors covering the particular equipment.

Chapter 6

The Minimum Tax's Role in Leasing

Introduction

The 1986 Tax Reform Act (TRA) enacted a tax applicable to corporations, an alternative minimum tax (AMT), replacing the previous add-on minimum tax. The 1986 TRA also expanded the coverage of the AMT applicable to noncorporate taxpayers.

The key to understanding the AMT is to understand that it is an "alternative" tax system. Essentially, it sets up a separate system of taxation that runs parallel with the regular tax system, with its own rules for deductions, credits, and income inclusion.

In the leasing community, the revised AMT has given rise to questions for both the prospective lessee and lessor:

- For equipment users, the key question is what effect any potential AMT liability may have on their decision to lease or buy equipment.
- For prospective lessors, the question is how to take account of the AMT in making their lease pricing decisions.

To answer these questions, it is necessary to understand the overall AMT. This chapter discusses the AMT in three parts. The first part explains, in general, the corporate AMT. The second part summarizes the individual AMT. And the final part is devoted to the AMT implications for equipment leasing transactions.

Part I: The Corporate AMT

A.   Overview

Before the 1986 TRA, corporations had been subject to an add-on minimum tax—simply a tax that corporations had to pay in addition to their regular tax under certain conditions. A corporation became subject to that additional tax—computed at a 15% rate—if it reduced its tax liability through the use of certain tax preference items. For example, the amount by which accelerated depreciation claimed on real property the corporation owned exceeded straight-line depreciation could give rise to add-on tax liability.

The existing AMT alters the tax picture for many more corporations than did the prior add-on tax. Congress's intent in enacting the AMT was to stop profitable corporations from excessively reducing their tax liability through deductions, credits, and exclusions, in effect ensuring that corporations pay their "fair" share of federal income taxes.

This chapter will provide the reader with a general understanding of the AMT rules so that the leasing implications can be addressed.

B. The AMT's General Approach

The conceptual approach under the corporate income tax rules is straightforward. The corporation first computes its income tax liability under the regular method prescribed by the Internal Revenue Code. It then calculates its AMT "tentative" tax under the AMT rules (referred to as the tentative minimum tax or, simply, the TMT). If the TMT exceeds the "regular" income tax liability, the taxpayer must pay the TMT excess in addition to its regular tax liability. If there is no excess, only the regular tax is paid.

> **Illustrative Example:** White Corporation determines that its federal income tax liability computed under the prevailing "regular" rules is $120,000. Under the AMT tax system, White Corporation calculates that its TMT is $150,000. What is White Corporation's federal tax liability?
>
> Because the TMT is greater than the tax liability computed under the regular rules, White Corporation must pay its regular tax liability of $120,000 and, in addition, must pay another $30,000; the excess of the TMT ($150,000) over the regular tax liability ($120,000). If its TMT were $110,000, White Corporation would pay only $120,000, its tax liability computed under the regular tax rules.

To determine its AMT, a corporation first calculates its regular taxable income. To the taxable income, the corporation adds preferences, adds or subtracts adjustments, and subtracts the AMT net operating loss (NOL), resulting in its alternative minimum taxable income (AMTI). From that amount, the corporation subtracts an exemption, if available, up to $40,000. The corporation then multiplies the result by the AMT tax rate (currently 20%) and subtracts any allowed foreign tax credits (FTCs) and investment tax credits (ITCs). This total is the corporation's TMT. The excess over the regular tax liability is the corporation's AMT.

▶ **Observation:** At first glance it may seem that the TMT would always be lower than the regular corporate tax liability because the AMT tax rate (currently 20%) is much lower than the regular corporate income tax rate. This is often not the case because the AMT's income base, the AMTI, is significantly greater than the regular corporate tax income base.

The following sets out the steps involved in computing the AMT, explained further in the following pages:

AMT Road Map

Regular Taxable Income

+ AMT Tax Preferences
± AMT Adjustments *(other than ACE adjustment)*

= Tentative AMTI
± AMT ACE Adjustment
− *AMT NOL*

= AMTI
− AMT Exemption
− 20% AMT Rate
− *AMT FTCs and AMT ITCs*

= TMT
− *Regular tax liability (after allowable tax credits)*

= AMT

▶ **Note:** For tax years beginning after 1986 and before 1996, corporations are required to pay an environmental tax equal to $12 for every $10,000 of AMTI. The reader is referred to Internal Revenue Code Section 59A for more details on the environmental tax.

1. *The AMT Tax Preferences*

In determining whether it has any AMT liability, a corporation's first step is to calculate the amount of its AMT tax preferences. The tax preferences that must be added to taxable income include

a. Tax-Exempt Interest

Tax-exempt interest on certain "private activity bonds" issued after August 7, 1986, is an item of AMT tax preference. A "private activity bond" is essentially one issued by a state or local authority in which (1) more than 10% of the proceeds are to be used for private business use and (2) either (a) more than 10% of the bond proceeds are secured with private business activity property or (b) more than 10% of the principal or interest on the bond is to be repaid from private business activity revenue.

There are certain exceptions to the tax-exempt interest inclusion rule. For example, tax-exempt interest on certain bonds issued to benefit specified charitable organizations is not a preference.

b. Charitable Contributions

For contributions of appreciated capital gain tangible personal property in a tax year beginning after 1986 and before 1991, and contributions of appreciated other capital gain property after 1986 and before 1993, there is an AMT preference in the amount that the donated property's fair market value exceeds the property's adjusted basis. The preference does not apply to carryovers arising from charitable contributions made before August 16, 1986. There is no tax preference for contributions of appreciated tangible personal property in tax years beginning after 1990, nor for contributions of other appreciated capital gain property after 1992.

c. Percentage Depletion

Under the percentage depletion method of determining deductions for certain natural resource reserves, corporations can take percentage depletion deductions exceeding the property's basis. When a corporation does that, it gives rise to a preference in the amount by which percentage depletion deductions exceed the property's adjusted basis. This was also a tax preference item under the prior tax law.

d. Intangible Drilling Costs (IDCs)

IDCs were an item of tax preference for individuals under the prior tax law, and they are an AMT tax preference for corporations under the 1986 TRA. The portion treated as a preference item is the amount by which the excess of (1) deductions determined by expensing IDCs over (2) deductions that would result from 10-year straight-line amortization of such costs is greater than 65% of the net income from oil, gas, and geothermal properties for such year.

▶ **Note:** After 1992, independent producers are not subject to this tax preference, depending on certain restrictions.

e. Bad Debt Reserves for Financial Institutions

The amount by which reasonable bad debt reserve deductions exceeds the deductions that would be computed based on the prior year's actual bad debt loss of certain financial institutions is deemed to be an item of AMT tax preference. The bad debt reserve preference was an item of preference under the prior tax law.

f. Pre-1987 Real Property Depreciation

The amount by which the accelerated depreciation deductions on real property placed in service before 1987 exceeds the straight-line depreciation deductions on such property is an item of AMT tax preference. For personal holding companies, the same rule applies to leased personal property.

g. Pre-1987 Pollution Control Facilities

The excess of the allowable rapid amortization deductions (generally over 5 years) on certified pollution control facilities that were placed in service before

1987 over otherwise permitted depreciation deductions (usually 15 years) must be included as an item of tax preference.

2. *AMT Adjustments*

In determining a corporation's AMT liability certain specified adjustments must be made to its regular taxable income in computing its AMTI. The concept of adjustments evolved to address items that are really deferral preferences—items where the timing of the deduction or income, as opposed to its amount, is the basis for its being treated as a tax preference. For an equipment item that a taxpayer depreciates on an accelerated basis, for example, the adjustment will be positive (added to regular taxable income in computing AMTI) in early years and negative (subtracted from regular taxable income in computing AMTI) in later years. The aggregate of the adjustments made over the item of equipment's depreciable life will net to zero.

▶ **Further Explanation:** Before the 1986 TRA, the AMT (applicable only to individuals) did not fully address a tax preference resulting from a timing difference. For example, for a deferral preference resulting from the excess of accelerated over straight-line depreciation, the later years' AMT liability calculations did not take into account the fact that the regular tax deductions would be less than they would have been if the equipment had been depreciated on a straight-line basis over the equipment's depreciable life.

The corporate AMT includes numerous tax adjustments. The following briefly describes the most important ones and lists adjustments of more limited application.

a. Depreciation on Personal Property Placed in Service After 1986

A corporation must make an AMT adjustment for personal property placed in service after 1986, in the amount of the difference between the regular accelerated depreciation deduction and the AMT depreciation deduction. The AMT alternative depreciation deduction uses the 150% declining-balance method (switching to a straight-line at the time to maximize the allowance) over a specified AMT recovery period. The AMT recovery period for personal property is the period used for the Alternative Depreciation System: With certain exceptions, it is the ADR class life. (See Chapter 5,D,3.) The regular tax depreciation averaging conventions apply to AMT depreciation deductions. (See Chapter 5,C,4.)

The AMT depreciation deductions result in slower write-offs than the regular MACRS deduction. *Result:* There will be a positive adjustment in the earlier years of an item of equipment's depreciation, and a negative adjustment in the later years.

▶ **Note:** To determine gain or loss on an asset's disposition for AMT purposes, the asset's basis is adjusted using the AMT depreciation rules. As a result, the

AMT basis may often be higher than the regular tax basis, causing any gain for regular tax purposes to be larger than the gain for AMT purposes.

b. Post-1986 Real Property Depreciation

For real property placed in service after 1986, the Alternative Depreciation System deduction, generally computed by using the straight-line method of depreciation over a 40-year period, must be used instead of the more regular accelerated depreciation deduction.

c. Post-1986 Pollution Control Facility Depreciation

For certified pollution control facilities that are placed in service after 1986, a corporation must substitute, in calculating its AMTI, the straight-line method of depreciation over the facility's Alternative Depreciation System life for the 60-month amortization period permitted under the regular tax rules.

d. Mining Exploration and Development Costs

Mining exploration and development costs, which otherwise may be currently deducted, must be amortized over a 10-year period. Only costs that have been incurred or paid after 1986 come within this rule.

e. Long-Term Contracts

Long-term contracts that have been entered into by a corporation on or after March 1, 1986, can give rise to an AMT adjustment. A corporation must use the specified "percentage of completion" method of accounting for these contracts in computing its AMTI if any other accounting method, such as the completed contract or cash basis method, had been used.

f. Dealer Installment Sales

Generally, a corporation that sells property in the regular course of business must report for AMT purposes all gains on property sales in the year in which the property is actually sold. In other words, a dealer is not permitted to recognize profits on the sale of dealer property for AMT purposes on the installment method. Property that is disposed of on or after March 1, 1986, is subject to this rule.

g. Other Adjustments

Other adjustments pertaining in more limited circumstances are

- Merchant marine capital construction fund deposits and earnings
- Blue Cross/Blue Shield special deductions
- Passive activity losses (applicable to closely held corporations and personal service corporations only)

- Farm losses (applicable to personal service corporations only)
- Circulation expenses (applicable to personal holding companies only)

3. *The Book Income and ACE Adjustments*

The 1986 TRA prescribed that corporations make a book income adjustment, defined below, to AMTI for tax years beginning in 1987, 1988, and 1989. Basically, this adjustment required an addition to a tentative AMTI of 50% of the difference between a corporation's book profits or losses and its tentative AMTI.

The book income adjustment worked this way: All other preferences and adjustments were to be computed and added or subtracted from taxable income to arrive at the tentative AMTI. The tentative AMTI was to be compared to the corporation's "adjusted net book income," and if that book income was greater, then 50% of the excess was added to the tentative AMTI. (There was no required adjustment if the book income was less than the tentative AMTI.)

The "adjusted net book income" was defined as the corporation's income or loss reported on its "applicable financial statement," subject to adjustments. The first step, then, in determining the adjusted book net income, was identifying the corporation's applicable financial statement from which the book income was taken. As different corporations have different types of statements, the IRS had issued some priority rules that had to be followed. Financial statements filed with the Securities and Exchange Commission were given the highest priority. The tax regulations can be consulted for additional guidelines on the relative priorities of other statements.

Once the corporation had selected its applicable financial statement it had to make the required adjustments. Taxpayer guidance for these complex adjustments was found in the tax regulations. In summary, adjustments were required

- For certain taxes
- To prevent omission or duplication
- For footnote disclosure or other supplementary information
- To take account of related corporations

There were also special rules if the corporation's tax and financial years differed.

The book income adjustment applied to all regular corporations. S corporations, regulated investment companies (RICs), real estate investment trusts (REITs), and real estate mortgage investment companies (REMICs) were excluded. The book income adjustment presented corporations with numerous planning possibilities and raised other issues not directly affecting leasing. [A detailed explanation of those is outside this book's scope.]

For tax years starting in 1990, the book income adjustment has been replaced by an adjustment based on the corporation's earnings and profits, referred to as its "adjusted current earnings," or simply its "ACE." A corporation's ACE is basically its earnings and profits, adjusted by certain specified items. Determining the ACE involves complexities for many corporations. Generally, ACE is a concept used to determine the tax status of corporate distributions to shareholders.

This particular preference is not geared toward recapturing a tax *benefit* that a corporation derives from the use of a specific tax deduction or exclusion, such as that available through using the depletion deduction described in Section B,1,c of this chapter. Rather, the purpose of the ACE adjustment is to recapture some of the tax *savings* a corporation would enjoy in cases where large earnings are reported to its shareholders and creditors, but, because of the availability of tax benefits, it has to pay few or no taxes.

The ACE adjustment is an amount equal to 75% of the difference between the corporation's adjusted current earnings and its tentative AMTI. If the adjusted current earnings exceed the tentative AMTI amount, the corporation must add 75% of the excess to its tentative AMTI. If the tentative AMTI exceeds the adjusted current earnings, 75% of that excess is subtracted, within certain limitations—basically the corporation cannot decrease its AMTI over a period of years by an amount greater than the amount which the ACE increased its AMTI over that same period of time.

> **Illustrative Example:** White Corporation has a tentative AMTI equal to $200,000 before taking into account adjustments for its AMT NOL or ACE. White Corporation's ACE for its current tax year is $400,000. As a result, White Corporation has an ACE preference of $150,000 ($400,000 − $200,000 = $200,000 × 75% = $150,000), which increases its AMTI to $350,000.

▶ **Observation:** The AMT book income adjustment could not reduce the tentative AMTI. If the adjusted net book income was lower than the tentative AMTI, there was simply no change. By contrast, the ACE adjustment can, within certain limitations, either add to or reduce the tentative AMTI.

4. AMT Net Operating Losses (NOLs)

After taking into account its preferences and adjustments, the next step in computing the AMT is to subtract any AMT NOL. A corporation computes its AMT NOL in the same way it computes its regular tax NOL, with certain exceptions. To compute its AMT NOL, the corporation must add back its loss-year tax preferences and adjustments to its regular tax NOL. The AMT NOL may not be used to offset more than 90% of tentative AMTI (determined without taking into account the AMT NOL deduction).

> **Illustrative Example:** White Corporation's taxable income for its current tax year is $250,000. It had tax losses equal to $300,000, of which $40,000 were attributable to tax preference items. White Corporation's NOL for regular tax purposes is $50,000 ($250,000 − $300,000 = $50,000). In computing its AMTI, however, tax preference items cannot be used. As a result, only $260,000 of the losses can be used to offset

income ($300,000 − $40,000 = $260,000), leaving White Corporation with an AMT NOL equal to $10,000 ($250,000 − $260,000 = $10,000).

A special transition rule permitted corporations to carry forward for AMT purposes all pre-1987 law regular tax NOLs as AMT NOLs. While those NOLs had to be applied to the corporation's first tax year to which the AMT applied, they then could be carried forward until they were used up. If, however, the corporation had a pre-1987 deferral of add-on minimum tax liability, a reduction was required to be made to the loss amount that was carried forward to the first tax year beginning after 1986 for any preferences that gave rise to the deferred AMT liability. The reader is referred to the Internal Revenue Code and related regulations for greater detail on the carryforward and carryback rules.

▶ **Observation:**   The AMT NOL rules often keep a corporation's tax department busy because a corporation must keep track of its AMT NOLs separately from its regular tax NOLs.

5.   Corporate AMT Exemption

After a corporation subtracts its AMT NOL the next step is to subtract the exemption amount, if any. A corporation is permitted a $40,000 exemption.

6.   Applying AMT Rate

After subtracting any exemption from the AMTI, the corporation multiplies the result by the AMT tax rate (currently 20%).

7.   Foreign Tax Credits (FTCs) and Investment Tax Credits (ITCs)

A corporation then subtracts any AMT FTCs. Basically, the AMT FTC is computed by making AMT substitutions to the regular tax FTC calculation. The reader should consult the FTC rules in making the determination. To the extent that there are any available ITCs, generally limited after 1986 (see Chapter 7, Part III, D), they can be used, within certain restrictions, to reduce AMT.

8.   TMT

After the credits are subtracted, the result is the corporation's TMT. The corporation must pay the amount that the TMT exceeds its regular tax liability.

9.   AMT Credit

A corporation having to pay the AMT may be able to obtain a credit, called the AMT credit, for use in future years. Designed to prevent double taxation, the AMT credit is the amount of the TMT that exceeds the regular tax liability (reduced by certain nonrefundable credit). In tax years that began after 1989, the credit earned by corporate taxpayers is based upon their total AMT liability, not, as in the case of earlier tax years, upon deferral-type AMT adjustments and preferences.

The AMT credit can only be used to reduce a corporation's regular, not AMT, tax liability. It can be carried forward indefinitely, but cannot be carried back to earlier tax years.

Part II: The Individual AMT

A. Overview

The 1986 TRA expanded the prior version of the individual AMT. Because its format is the same as the corporate AMT, this section will only summarize its provisions.

B. Computing the Individual AMT

The individual AMT is calculated as follows: The taxpayer starts with taxable income. To that, preferences are added, adjustments added or subtracted, and the AMT NOL is subtracted, resulting in AMTI. The AMT exemption, if available, is then subtracted, and the result is multiplied by the AMT tax rate. AMT foreign tax credits are subtracted. The result is compared with the taxpayer's regular tax liability, and the taxpayer must add any AMT excess to his or her tax liability.

1. AMT Preferences

Many of the individual AMT preferences are the same as those for corporate AMT. Those include

- Charitable contributions of appreciated capital gain property
- Intangible drilling costs
- Interest on private-activity bonds
- Percentage depletion

There are two additional preferences:

- For most property placed in service prior to 1987, the excess of accelerated depreciation on leased personal property over its straight-line depreciation
- For most property placed in service prior to 1987, subject to certain guidelines, the excess of the ACRS deduction for lease recovery property over its straight-line depreciation deduction

2. AMT Adjustments

Many of the individual AMT adjustments are the same as those for the corporate AMT. They are

- Excess depreciation on personal property placed in service after 1986
- Excess depreciation on real property placed in service after 1986
- Long-term contracts
- Installment sales
- Mining exploration and development costs
- Passive activity losses
- Farm losses
- Circulation expenses

Additionally, there are individual AMT adjustments not applicable to corporations, as follows:

- Certain gains on incentive stock options.
- Research and experimentation expenses. For AMT purposes these expenses are amortized over 10 years.
- Certain itemized deductions. An individual must add back the standard deduction, consumer interest, and certain state, local, and foreign taxes. The deductions for medical expenses, investment interest, and qualified residence interest are subject to certain adjustments.

▶ **Note:** There was no book income adjustment, and there is no ACE adjustment, for noncorporate taxpayers, even if they are doing business as partnerships or in other forms.

After taking into account the preferences and adjustments, the AMT NOL is subtracted. The result is the taxpayer's AMTI.

3. AMT Exemption

The next step is to apply the AMT exemption. The exempt amounts are

- For married couples filing joint returns, $45,000. It begins to be phased out when AMTI exceeds $150,000 and is completely phased out at $330,000.
- For singles or heads of households, $33,750, phased out at AMTl between $112,500 and $247,500.
- For married taxpayers filing separately, $22,500, phased out at AMTI between $75,000 and $165,000.

After subtracting the applicable exemption, the result is multiplied by the AMT rate for noncorporate taxpayers, currently 26% for the first $175,000 of a taxpayer's AMTI over the exemption amount, and 28% for the AMTI in excess of $175,000 over the exemption amount.

4. AMT Foreign Tax Credit

The taxpayer then can subtract his or her AMT foreign tax credit. The result is the TMT liability. This is compared with the taxpayer's regular tax liability, and the taxpayer must pay the amount by which the TMT exceeds the regular tax liability, in addition to his or her regular tax liability.

5. AMT Credit

Taxpayers who have AMT liability may be able to use the AMT credit in later years. Basically, the AMT credit is the amount by which AMT exceeds regular tax (subject to certain specified adjustments) for a tax year. The AMT credit can offset regular tax liability in later years, but cannot reduce the AMT liability in later years.

Part III: The AMT Considerations for Leasing

A.   Working With the AMT

It is apparent that the AMT rules are complex. Corporate and noncorporate taxpayers must consider their entire tax and financial situations to assess their AMT liability and its implications. Because of their complexity, it has taken a long time to understand the ramifications for equipment leasing. In a nutshell, the AMT is a sneaky and punitive tax. It takes away the tax benefits that had been given by Congress. The only chance you have against what can result in a significant tax problem is, if you can see AMT coming, to use proper planning to avoid, or at least reduce, its impact.

Initially, there were many concerns by lessors and lessees—many unfounded and many founded. Companies and their advisors struggled frantically to get a handle on what the AMT law changes meant, how they actually worked, and how to deal with any vagueness or ambiguity. Even today, there are still questions—and difficulties—in working with the AMT rules. One aspect of the AMT rules, however, is clear: The AMT rules have made it more difficult to assess whether purchasing or leasing an item of equipment is the best choice.

▶ **Observation:**   The AMT for individuals was ostensibly aimed at wealthy people who were taking advantage of tax shelter-type benefits, such as accelerated depreciation, to reduce their taxable income below what was felt to be a politically acceptable amount. In fact, it has had an adverse impact on people not so wealthy. For example, in 1991, the most recently available statistical year at the time of this writing, 244,000 not-so-wealthy people had to pay an AMT, which cost them, in the aggregate, approximately $1 billion more in taxes than they would have otherwise had to pay.

B.   Overview

It should be apparent from the preceding material that the current corporate and individual AMT has an effect on equipment leasing for both lessors and lessees. From the prospective lessee's standpoint, the issue is whether the AMT makes leasing equipment more desirable than buying it. To the potential lessor, the question is how the AMT will alter the tax benefits that the lessor may receive by owning the leased equipment, and, thus, what lease rate it can profitably charge a lessee.

A taxpayer's first step in answering both those questions is to review the AMT steps described above, as applied to its overall tax position. If the taxpayer determines that it may be subject to the AMT, it must analyze the leasing deal taking that possibility into account.

There are no general guidelines that, if followed, provide all the answers for a particular lessee or lessor. The following discussion will assist lessees and lessors in putting a quick perspective on the impact the AMT has on equipment leasing transactions.

C.   The Deferral Effect

Keep in mind that, from an equipment leasing standpoint, the AMT generally defers, rather than eliminates, certain tax benefits. The deferral effect is achieved by means of the AMT credit. As described above, a credit in the amount of the AMT paid, within certain restrictions, may be used to offset regular tax liability in later years. Thus, the amount lost through the AMT, as described below, may be recouped through the use of the AMT credit.

While it may be recouped, there are two caveats. First, the AMT credit can be used only to offset regular tax liability. Thus, a taxpayer subject to the AMT in many or most years may not receive the AMT credit benefit for many years, or at all. Secondly, depending on how long it is before the taxpayer can use the credit, the taxpayer is losing the time value of money. The funds that the taxpayer does not have as a result of the deferral could be earning other money; if nothing else, interest could have been earned if the unavailable funds were invested in attractive investment instruments.

▶ **Important:**   Thus, in summary, in the following explanation, it is important to remember that when the AMT reduces a tax benefit, it is usually merely deferring it. The taxpayer's loss is, for the most part, the loss of the time value of money.

D.   The AMT and the Lessee

1.   *AMT's Impact on a Lessee*

When a lessee leases equipment and pays rentals, those payments are not preferences or adjustments under the AMT. Thus—assuming the lease is a true lease and the lessee is not the equipment owner—the lessee may deduct its lease payments without increasing its AMTI.

2.   *Purchasing Equipment*

If the lessee bought the equipment instead, there would be greater AMT consequences. For AMT computation purposes, a taxpayer must depreciate equipment it owns and placed in service after 1986 by using the prescribed 150% declining-balance method over a longer recovery period. As compared with the regular MACRS depreciation, generally, the AMT write-off period is longer, and the rate of depreciation is slower. *Reason:* The regular MACRS depreciation method is the 200% declining-balance method. Thus, for AMT calculation purposes, if (1) the depreciation rate is less than for regular tax purposes (150% rather than 200% declining-balance method) and (2) the required write-off period is longer than for regular tax purposes, the ownership of the equipment under consideration will result in a relative increase in a corporation's potential AMT as a result of the AMT depreciation preference adjustment.

Illustrative Example: Assume John Jones buys and places in service a $10,000 printing press for use in his company. For regular MACRS purposes, the press is 7-year property. He is, however, subject to the AMT. The press has an 11-year ADR class life. Assuming the mid-quarter convention did not apply, the depreciation deductions under the regular MACRS and AMT are as follows:

Year	Regular MACRS	AMT
1	$1,429	$662
2	$2,449	$1,271
3	$1,749	$1,097
4	$1,249	$948
5	$893	$818
6	$892	$798
7	$893	$797
8	$446	$798
9		$797
10		$798
11		$797
12		$399

E.   The Lessor and the AMT

The lessor's decision in considering its equipment lease rent pricing is to determine how any potential AMT liability will impact the lessor's lease economic return. Since the lease rate will be determined in large part by the transaction's tax benefits and when they will be fully available, the lessor must decide whether the tax benefits and their timing of receipt will be sufficient if the AMT applies, so that it can make an attractive offer to a prospective lessee.

Both corporate and noncorporate lessors will be affected by the adjustment on depreciation of personal property. As described above, this means the lessor must use the slower AMT depreciation method. It will thus have lower write-offs in earlier years and larger write-offs in later years for AMT computation purposes.

Chapter 7
Investment Tax Credit

Introduction

Before 1986, the investment tax credit (ITC) offered a taxpayer a big reward for buying new equipment—a 10% credit. Like other credits, the ITC did not merely reduce taxable income, but rather offset, dollar for dollar, the equipment owner's federal income tax liability. The 1986 Tax Reform Act (TRA) dramatically changed the ITC picture. Except for certain transition property—generally property in the works before 1986—the ITC is gone.

Gone perhaps, but not forgotten. Where the ITC was claimed on leased property before 1986, its rules may still come into play—for example, the equipment may be disposed of or damaged, or the IRS may contest the ITC claimed. Additionally, there is little doubt in the author's and most tax practitioners' minds that the ITC will reappear.

▶ **Observation:** Before the actual general ITC repeal, equipment lessors were extremely concerned over the adverse impact a general repeal would have on their business. Although equipment lessors have aggressively pursued new equipment financing opportunities, the ITC repeal did adversely affect the equipment leasing business. Today, however, innovative lessors are beginning to bounce back by pursuing creative lease structures and new areas of profit opportunity—such as consumer leasing.

The ITC's purpose was to encourage investment in new equipment to stimulate economic growth. The tax writers also used it to encourage the growth, development, and stabilization of a business area that the federal government sought to promote.

The ITC rules implemented that purpose by permitting an equipment owner to claim a tax credit in an amount equal to a specified percentage of the cost of equipment bought in a particular tax year against its potential tax liability for that same year. Generally, for equipment placed in service before January 1, 1986, a taxpayer could claim a maximum investment tax credit equal to 10% of the cost of equipment acquired during a tax year. Thus, for example, a taxpayer buying an equipment item in a particular tax year that cost $1 million could reduce its federal income tax liability by an amount equal to $100,000 (10% × $1 million =

$100,000) for that year. If a taxpayer had owed $250,000 in federal income taxes for the purchase year apart from the ITC, it would actually have had to pay only $150,000 ($250,000 − $100,000 = $150,000) after claiming the ITC.

Given that tax reduction, the ITC played a major role in equipment leasing. If the lease qualified as a true lease (explained in Chapter 8), the lessor was treated as owner and could claim the ITC. The ITC has numerous requirements, and the prospective lessor had to understand the ITC rules before entering a leasing transaction.

It was also important for prospective lessees, and their representatives, to have a solid appreciation of the ITC for two reasons:

- Prospective lessees could not evaluate whether to buy or lease equipment unless they knew how to work with those rules.
- Lessors frequently required lessees to indemnify them against an ITC loss that might arise in certain circumstances. Thus, the prospective lessee was not able to understand the indemnity risks unless it was fully aware of what it was asked to provide.

This chapter proceeds in three parts. Part I explains generally how the ITC worked before 1986. Part II covers how events in an ongoing leasing transaction could result in a retroactive loss of a previously claimed ITC. This part may be particularly useful to parties who entered leasing transactions before 1986. Part III explains what remains of the ITC for equipment placed in service after 1986.

Part I: ITC Before 1986

A. Computing the ITC

The amount of ITC that a taxpayer could claim for a tax year was calculated by multiplying the appropriate investment credit rate times its "qualified investment" in eligible property. Calculating a taxpayer's qualified investment took a little work. The basic determining rule provided that a taxpayer's qualified investment for any tax year was equal to the sum of

- The applicable percentage of the basis of each item of new Section 38 property that the taxpayer placed in service during that tax year plus
- The applicable percentage of the cost of each item of used Section 38 property that the taxpayer placed in service during that tax year

The resulting ITC amount was then subject to annual limitations. The steps to be taken to arrive at that amount were

- Determining what property was Section 38 property
- Calculating the basis of the new Section 38 property
- Calculating the cost of the used Section 38 property
- Determining the applicable percentage for the property

- Determining when the property was placed in service
- Deciding whether the property was new or used
- Applying the annual limitations on the amount that could be claimed

1. Section 38 Property

ITC was available only on Section 38 property. To be Section 38 property, the property had to be depreciable—that is, subject to wear and tear and used in the taxpayer's trade or business or held for the production of income—and had to be either tangible personal property or other tangible property. The other tangible property, property that generally would have been considered real property, had to meet *one of* the following tests. It had to be

- Used as an integral part of a manufacturing, production, or extraction activity, or be an integral part of the furnishing of transportation, communication, electrical energy, gas, water, or sewage disposal services
- A research facility used in connection with any of the activities specified above
- A facility used in connection with any of the activities specified above for the bulk storage of fungible commodities, including commodities in a liquid or gaseous state

Generally, most office equipment and machinery qualified under the tangible personal property test. Even equipment affixed to the ground generally qualified.

To satisfy the integral part test, the other tangible property had to be used directly in, and be essential to the completeness of, the qualifying activity. For example, docks, railroad tracks, or bridges may be considered to be an integral part of a manufacturing activity. (See Reg. Sec. 1.48-1(d) for additional examples.)

Generally, a building and its structural components do not qualify as Section 38 property. (These are defined in Reg. Sec. 1.48-1(e).)

2. Basis for ITC Purposes

Before 1983, basis for ITC purposes was determined under general Internal Revenue Code principles. For example, if a taxpayer bought new Section 38 property, its basis in the property was its cost. In making the computation, the taxpayer could include such items as freight, sales, and installation charges.

The 1982 Tax Equity and Fiscal Responsibility Act (TEFRA) introduced an ITC adjustment rule. For ITC eligible property placed in service after December 31, 1982, a taxpayer had to reduce its basis in that property for depreciation and disposition purposes by 50% of the ITC claimed. Alternatively, a taxpayer could elect to reduce the amount of available ITC by 2%, in which case the property's basis did not have to be reduced.

3. Applicable Percentage

As explained in Chapter 5, the 1981 Economic Recovery Tax Act (ERTA) introduced the Accelerated Cost Recovery System (ACRS). ACRS greatly simplified depreciation, including introducing recovery classes to determine the period over which an asset's cost was recovered. ERTA made corresponding changes to the way a taxpayer determined the applicable percentage for ITC purposes. For property placed in service after 1980, the applicable percentages were

- For property in the 5-, 10-, or 15-year public utility recovery class, 100% of the basis could be used to compute ITC.
- For property in the 3-year class, 60% of the property's basis was eligible for ITC. Certain property, assigned to the 3-year recovery class for ACRS purposes (for example, commuter highway vehicles), was assigned a 100% applicable percentage.

Determining the applicable percentage for property placed in service before 1981 was more complex. The percentages depended on the property's useful life as follows:

- For property with a useful life of at least three years, but less than five years, the applicable percentage was equal to 33 1/3%.
- For property with a useful life of at least five years, but less than seven, it was 66 2/3%.
- For property which had a useful life of at least seven years, the applicable percentage was 100%.
- Property with a useful life of less than three years was not eligible for the ITC.

Determining property's useful life was done under the facts and circumstances approach or using the Class Life Asset Depreciation Range System. These are explained in Chapter 5.

▶ **Observation:** A taxpayer's choice of useful life for depreciation purposes would "lock in" the useful life for ITC computation purposes. Thus, if a taxpayer depreciated an asset over a five-year-period useful life, the applicable percentage was 66 2/3% for qualified investment determination purposes.

4. *Placed in Service*

Except for qualified progress expenditures, a taxpayer could claim ITC generally only for the year the equipment was placed in service, regardless of when during the year it is so placed. For ITC purposes, property was deemed placed in service in the *earlier* of the following years:

- The year in which, under the taxpayer's depreciation practice, the taxpayer began to depreciate the property
- The year in which the property was placed in a condition or state of readiness and availability for a specifically assigned function, whether in a trade or business, in the production of income, in a tax-exempt activity, or in a personal activity

The second test was designed to prevent taxpayers from postponing the ITC by delaying the start of the property's depreciation. Determining whether property was in a condition or state of readiness could be a difficult judgment; the regulations [Reg. Sec. 1.46-3(d)(2)] provide guidelines by examples.

▶ **Leasing Pitfall:**   The condition or state of readiness for use test could wreak havoc on a leasing deal where the parties were not careful. If the lessee constructed and completed the equipment, or it was delivered to the lessee before the deal was completed, the equipment could have been deemed placed in service at that point by the lessee, not the lessor. Then, when the lessor bought the equipment and leased it to the lessee, the lessor generally could not claim the ITC. The best way to minimize this risk was for the lessee to pay close attention to construction or delivery schedules, and for the parties and their lawyers to complete the transaction before the equipment was constructed or delivered. Also, many lessors wanted to protect themselves against the risk that the property could inadvertently have been deemed placed in service before they bought it by using tax indemnification provisions, under which the lessee would indemnify the lessor for its lost tax benefits.

5.   New and Used Property

ITC was generally available on both new and used Section 38 property. However, only $125,000 of used Section 38 property could qualify for the credit in any one year. Also, ITC on used property could not be passed through to the lessee.

Equipment was considered new when its original use began with the taxpayer. "Original use" is considered to be the first use to which the property is put, regardless of whether the use corresponds to the taxpayer's use. Under this rule, the original use could not begin with a taxpayer if the property had been reconditioned or rebuilt before it was acquired. The fact that property had used parts, however, did not automatically disqualify it as new property unless there were so many used parts that it would fall within the rebuilt or reconditioned category.

Property initially qualifying as new Section 38 property would not lose its status if the owner sold the property and simultaneously leased it back. The rationale was that the property continued to be used by the person who used it before its sale. However, the lessor could then not claim the ITC. If a lessee leased equipment that was new Section 38 property in the lessor's hands at the time the lessee leased it, it would remain new to the lessor. *Reason:* By being used by the lessee, it is deemed used by the lessor. Also, if certain corporate, partner, or related taxpayer relationships existed between a seller and a buyer, new Section 38 property in the hands of the seller did not, on transfer, become used Section 38 property.

6.   Annual Limitations on ITC Claimed

While a taxpayer could earn an unlimited amount of ITC in any given year, the amount it could claim in a year was limited. In calculating the limitation, the taxpayer combined its available ITC energy credits, targeted jobs credit, alcohol fuels credit, and ESOP credit into a single, general business credit. If the taxpayer's federal tax liability for a year, apart from the credits, was $25,000 or less, it could use $25,000 of credits. If the taxpayer's tax liability exceeded $25,000, then the limit was $25,000, plus 85% (for years before 1986) of its tax liability apart from the credits. Unused business credits were first carried back 3 years, and then any remaining unused credits could be carried forward 10 years. The annual limitation applied to carryback and carryover amounts.

B.   ITC "Pass Through" to Lessee

Generally, a lessor of new Section 38 property could, under Section 48(d), elect to treat the lessee as the equipment's buyer for ITC purposes. In other words, the lessor could "pass through" the credit to the lessee so that the lessee could claim it directly.

The lessee's qualified investment in property on which a Section 48(d) election had been made was generally the property's fair market value on the transfer date. In the case of a lease between certain related corporations, however, the lessee's qualified investment was instead equal to the equipment's basis in the lessor's hands on the transfer date.

The determination of the property's "original use" as to a lessee was made within the same guidelines as if the lessee were the owner. In this regard, if the lessor or any third party had used the property before the lessee, or if it had been reconstructed, rebuilt, or reconditioned property, the lessee would not be able to claim any investment credit. *Reason:* The property's original use would not have begun with the lessee. The lessor's mere testing or storing of property was not considered prior use.

▶ **Observation:**   A lessee could elect to "pass through" to a sublessee the ITC that had been passed through to the lessee. The lessee's ITC "pass-through" was treated as if the original lessor had leased the property directly to the sublessee for the sublease term.

The "pass-through" election could be made either (1) on an item-by-item basis or (2) on a general basis as to all property that was leased by the electing lessor to the lessee. In either case, the lessor made the election by filing an appropriate statement with the lessee, on or before the lessee's federal income tax return was due for the tax year during which possession was transferred to the lessee. The election was irrevocable as of the time the statement was filed with the lessee.

C.   Limits on Noncorporate Lessors

Noncorporate lessors could claim ITC on property they leased to third parties only in two situations:

- The noncorporate lessor either manufactured or produced the leased property in the ordinary course of business.
- The lease term (including any renewal options) was less than 50% of the property's estimated useful life, and the lessor's total allowable Section 162 deductions during the initial 12-month period beginning on the date the property was transferred to the lessee exceeded 15% of the lease rental income.

▶ **Observation:**   The noncorporate lessor rule did not apply to corporate lessor-partners. Thus, each corporate partner could claim ITC on its proportionate investment in Section 38 property held by the partnership.

D.   Use Outside
the United States

An equipment owner could not claim ITC on property used predominantly out-side of the United States during a tax year. Property would be considered "predominantly" used outside the United States if it was physically located for more than 50% of the tax year outside the United States. In the event the property was placed in service during a tax year, the 50% test would be applied against the portion of the year beginning when it was so placed in service. If a lessor elected to "pass through" the ITC to the lessee under Section 48(d), the predominant use test would be based on the property's predominant use during the lessee's tax year.

Property that was used predominantly outside the United States during the tax year it was placed in service would not qualify as Section 38 property even though, in a later year, it was permanently returned to the United States. If the predominant use test was satisfied when the property was placed in service, but in a later year it was not satisfied, the property would cease to be Section 38 property regardless of who, in fact, used the property outside the United States during that year.

There are several exceptions to the predominant use test, including certain aircraft and vessels. (See Reg. Sec. 1.48-1(g)(2).)

E.   Qualified Progress
Expenditures

If Section 38 property had a construction period of over two years, it was possible to claim a portion of the ITC before the property was placed in service. Called qualified progress expenditures, these are costs incurred in constructing the property. To take qualified progress expenditures, it had to be reasonable to expect that the equipment would qualify for ITC when placed in service, and the equipment must have had a normal construction period of at least two years.

Part II: Losing ITC

A. ITC Recapture

While the ITC on an item of equipment was all earned in the year the taxpayer placed the property in service, some or all of it could be lost if the property ceased to qualify as Section 38 property or was disposed of in later years. This later ITC loss is referred to as ITC recapture.

For property placed in service after 1980, and subject to ACRS rules, the recapture rules are straightforward. For each year the property continued to be Section 38 property, 2% of the ITC vests. Put another way, for each year short of the end of the recapture period in which the recapture event occurs, 2% must be recaptured. The 2% rule applies whether the ITC claimed was 10% or 6%. The following chart illustrates the recapture amounts.

	Recapture	
If disposed of:	*3-year property*	*15-year, 10-year, and 5-year property*
Within 1 year	6%	10%
After 1 year	4	8
After 2 years	2	6
After 3 years	-0-	4
After 4 years	-0-	2
After 5 years	-0-	-0-

Illustrative Example: In 1983, Company Able bought a $10,000 drill press and claimed the $1,000 ITC. In 1987, it sold the drill press. As the press was in its fourth year of use, Company Able would have recapture of $2,000 (2% of the $10,000 investment). The $2,000 is added directly to Company Able's otherwise computed tax liability. It also cannot be offset by ITC or other business credits earned on other property in that year.

For ITC earned before 1981, where the ITC was determined under pre-ACRS rules, the recapture amount was based on a redetermination of the property's useful life. The amount that had to be recaptured was equal to the difference between the total credit originally claimed and an ITC computed on the basis of a useful life, computed from the time the property was placed in service by the taxpayer to the date of the disqualifying event. Thus, if a taxpayer disposed of property four years after the taxpayer bought it (on which it had initially claimed an ITC based on a useful life of nine years), its federal income tax liability for the year of disposition would have been increased by an amount equal to two-thirds of the credit initially claimed because the qualified investment applicable percentage for a four-year useful life is 33 1/3%, as opposed to 100%, for a nine-year useful life.

For the purpose of ITC recapture calculations, the determining useful life was the shortest life within the useful life category used to establish the appropriate qualified investment applicable percentage. That is, if the taxpayer claimed a credit when the property was placed in service based on a four-year useful life, but the property was disposed of or ceased to be Section 38 property in the third year, the property would not have been deemed to have been disposed of before the end of its useful life.

B. Events Triggering Recapture

Generally, a recapture event occurs when the taxpayer either disposes of the property or it ceases to be Section 38 property in the taxpayer's hands. There are certain exceptions, some of which are explained below. (See Reg. Secs. 1.47-2–1.47-6 for further explanation.)

1. Special Rules Concerning Leased Equipment

- If a taxpayer has placed Section 38 property in service, and later enters into a sale-leaseback of that property, there is no disposition for ITC purposes. This was true even though the taxpayer had to recognize a gain or loss on the property and could no longer depreciate it.
- If the lessor was entitled to claim ITC on property, but later the lessee stopped using it for a qualified use, the lessor was subject to ITC recapture.
- If the lessor had elected to pass through the ITC to the lessee, normally the lessor could dispose of the property without causing a disposition. However, if the new lessor was not eligible to make the pass-through election, the lessee was subject to ITC recapture.

2. Changes of Ownership Form

Generally, if a taxpayer changed the form of the trade or business in which Section 38 property was used, a "disposition" or "cessation" for ITC purposes was not deemed to have occurred. For example, if the taxpayer was initially a member of a partnership when it acquired ITC eligible equipment, a change to a corporate form would not result in ITC recapture. The rule, however, was subject to the following conditions:

- The property must have been retained as Section 38 property in the same trade or business.
- The transferor of the property must have retained a substantial interest in the trade or business.
- Substantially all the assets of the trade or business necessary for its operation must have been transferred to the transferee of the Section 38 property.
- The basis of the Section 38 property must have been carried over in part or in whole.

Whether a transferor had retained a "substantial interest" in a trade or business was sometimes a difficult issue. The criterion was satisfied if, after the change in form, its interest was substantial in relation to the remaining interests or was at least equal to its prior interest. For example, a taxpayer who formerly held a 5% interest in a partnership that was converted into a corporation and who, after the conversion, had a 5% interest in the corporation, retained a "substantial interest" in the trade or business.

3. S Corporations and Partnerships

If an S corporation or a partnership acquired Section 38 property, the shareholder or partner took the ITC individually. If the S corporation or partnership disposed of the property, the shareholder or partner had to take any recapture. Also, if a shareholder of an S corporation having ITC that had not completely vested sold its stock, it had made a disposition and might be subject to recapture. Similarly, if a partner's proportionate interest in the general partnership's profits was reduced, there might be recapture.

C. If Section 38 Property Lost Its Status, It Had to Be Regularly Reviewed

During the ITC vesting period, a taxpayer had to, at the end of each tax year following the year the ITC was claimed, determine whether any Section 38 property had ceased to be Section 38 property. If any of that property would no longer qualify as Section 38 property, the taxpayer had to recompute the amount of credit to which it was entitled and make the appropriate adjustment to its federal income tax liability.

▶ **Observation:** If property otherwise qualified as Section 38 property, the fact that it could no longer be depreciated under the taxpayer's depreciation practice would not cause it to lose Section 38 status if the taxpayer continued to use the property in its trade or business or in the production of income.

Part III: ITC After 1985

A. ITC Repeal

The 1986 TRA essentially wiped out the regular ITC for equipment placed in service after 1985, except for ITC transition property and qualified progress expenditures. The 1986 TRA also curtailed the use of many ITCs still available to taxpayers and increased the required basis adjustment for property on which ITC could still be claimed after 1985.

▶ **Note:** One investment credit still available has viable possibilities for lessors in a limited area—the energy investment credit. The current tax rules permit a taxpayer to claim a business energy investment credit equal to 10% of the basis of energy property, subject to certain limitations. Energy property includes equipment that uses solar energy to produce electricity to cool or heat a structure or that is used to generate solar process heat. Energy property also includes equipment that uses, produces, or distributes energy derived from geothermal deposits, within certain specified limitations.

B. ITC Transition Property

To assuage some of the harshness of the ITC repeal, the 1986 TRA allowed ITC to be claimed on transition property—basically, property to which the taxpayers had committed sufficient resources before 1986. Specifically, ITC transition property is property placed in service after 1985 with the following characteristics:

- It is self-constructed property (that the taxpayer constructed or reconstructed) on which the construction or reconstruction started by December 31, 1985, and at least the lesser of (1) 5% of the property's cost or (2) $1 million was incurred or committed by December 31, 1985;
- It is constructed, reconstructed, or acquired under a written contract binding on December 31, 1985;
- It is an equipped building (equipment and machinery to be used in or incidental to the building come within this rule), or a plant facility that is not housed in a building, on which construction began no later than December 31, 1985, under a specific written plan, and greater than 50% of the cost was either incurred or committed no later than December 31, 1985; or
- It is readily identifiable as belonging to, and necessary to be used in connection with performing, a written supply or service contract, or lease agreement, that was binding as of December 31, 1985.

A special sale-leaseback provision permits lessors to claim ITCs after 1985 under certain conditions. First, the property must have been placed in service by the lessee before 1986 or be ITC transitional property in the lessee's hands. Second, the property must be leased back by the lessor to the lessee by the earlier of (1) the placed in service date for the applicable property class (set out below) or (2) three months following the date when it was originally placed in service.

The 1986 TRA does set cutoff dates by which the transition property must have been placed in service. Those dates, set out below, are based on the property's ADR class life (explained in Chapter 5).

- Transitional property with an ADR midpoint of less than five years must have been placed in service before July 1, 1986.
- Property with an ADR midpoint of at least five years, but less than seven years (and computer-based telephone switching equipment) must have been placed in service before January 1, 1987.
- Property with an ADR midpoint of at least 7 years, but less than 20 years, must have been placed in service before January 1, 1989.

- Property with no ADR midpoint must have been placed in service before January 1, 1989.
- Property with an ADR midpoint of 20 years or more must have been placed in service before January 1, 1991.

In addition to the above rules, ITC transition property must comply with detailed guidelines. Parties involved in a lease of transition property must consult those guidelines (see Revenue Ruling 87-113, IRB 1987-45, p. 4).

C. Qualified Progress Expenditures

Before the 1986 TRA, taxpayers could claim a portion of the property's ITC in advance when the property's construction lasted over two years. Taxpayers could still claim those credits after 1986, but only as to property that it was reasonable to expect would be ITC transition property when placed in service. If the property was not transition property when placed in service—for example, it was not placed in service by its extended deadline—the credits had to be adjusted.

D. ITC Reductions

Not only did the 1986 TRA virtually eliminate the ITC, it cut down on the value of those ITCs that remained. Generally, a taxpayer claiming ITC after 1985 under an ITC transitional rule or an ITC carryforward provision from a tax year ending before July 1, 1987, must reduce the ITC amount by 35%. The reduction is effective for tax years beginning after June 30, 1987. For tax years that begin before and end after July 1, 1987, the 35% ITC amount reduction is prorated under a ratio based on the post-June 30, 1987, tax-year months over the total tax-year months. The ITC amount not available because of the 35% reduction could not be taken in a prior or succeeding year.

E. Basis Reductions

Before the 1986 TRA, taxpayers had to reduce their equipment's basis—for depreciation or disposition purposes—by 50% of the ITC claimed. After 1986, the equipment's basis is generally reduced by the full amount of the ITC claimed. Thus, if in 1988 a taxpayer were to claim a $100,000 ITC on $1 million of equipment, its basis would be $900,000. If the 35% ITC reduction applies, the basis reduction is limited to that reduced amount.

Chapter 8

How to Cope Successfully With the Tax Lease Rules

A.   The True Lease

When the parties sign a document entitled a "lease," and the document is a lease under state and local law, is it a lease for federal income tax purposes? Not necessarily. Under the federal tax laws, the financing transaction must be considered a "true" lease—a lease for federal income tax purposes—which means that the lessor must be deemed to be the lease asset's owner. Failure to so qualify as the tax owner will cause the lessor to lose the available ownership tax benefits (and even possibly to be subjected to penalties) and the lessee to forfeit rent deductions. *Result:* The leasing transaction will sink into a pool of red ink.

What, then, characterizes a "true lease"? The term is not specifically defined as such in the Internal Revenue Code or its underlying regulations. However, two U.S. Supreme Court cases have established basic definitional rules—*Helvering* v. *F. & R. Lazarus & Co.,* 308 U.S. 252 (1939), and *Frank Lyon Company* v. *United States,* 435 U.S. 561 (1978). *Helvering* is noted for setting down the substance-over-form rule: that the tax nature of what is purported to be a true lease depends on whether the lessor can be determined to have sufficient property ownership of the asset involved, taking into account all the surrounding facts and circumstances, to be accorded the tax attributes available to an asset owner, or whether the purported lessor is really a conditional seller, an option holder, a lender, or some other type of transaction participant. The *Helvering* decision, although very general in nature, was the basic guidance looked to until the advent of *Frank Lyon* in 1978, where, for the first time since the 1939 *Helvering* decision, the Court took another look at the leasing tax ownership issue. In considering tax ownership and therefore true lease status, as summarized by the U.S. Supreme Court, the bottom line of the *Frank Lyon* decision is that it is necessary to determine whether the lessor, rather than the lessee, is the equipment's tax owner, having "significant and genuine attributes of the traditional lessor status. . . . What those attributes are in any particular case will necessarily depend upon its facts."

While the ultimate "true" lease test is based on the facts and circumstances of the transaction, the IRS provided guidelines for leveraged lease transactions in 1975 which, if followed, will help ensure that a leasing transaction stays afloat. In four published Revenue Procedures (Revenue Procedure 75-21, Revenue Procedure 75-28, Revenue Procedure 76-30, and Revenue Procedure 79-48) collectively called the *Guidelines,* the IRS sets out the formal criteria that must be met if the parties to a transaction want to obtain a ruling (referred to as a private ruling) from the IRS that the transaction qualifies as a lease for federal income tax purposes. While nominally limited to ruling requests, the *Guidelines* provide helpful advice on achieving true lease status, even if the parties to the transaction do not request an IRS private ruling. Prior to the issuance of the *Guidelines,* the parties to a lease transaction found some guidance in Revenue Ruling 55-540 [1955-2 CB 39], discussed later in this chapter. Revenue Ruling 55-540, which still has guidance applicability, focuses primarily on describing aspects of a transaction that would cause it to fail to qualify as a true lease. It has applicability to *all* purported lease transactions, not just *leveraged* lease transactions.

B. Procedural Alternatives

How do the parties maximize their chances of obtaining true lease status? The two best alternatives: Obtain an IRS *private letter ruling* or proceed without one while following the *Guidelines* and Revenue Ruling 55-540.

1. A Private Letter Ruling

As a general matter, if a taxpayer submits a ruling request to the IRS concerning a transaction, the IRS will rule on some or all of the transaction's tax consequences after reviewing the request. Then, provided the information submitted is accurate and complete, the IRS's position on the issues on which it has ruled is considered final. In cases of leveraged leasing transactions, the *Guidelines* not only prescribe the criteria that must be met for a transaction to receive a favorable true lease ruling but set out the specific submission procedures that the submitting taxpayer must follow when making the request. If parties to the transaction receive a favorable ruling from the IRS, they can rest assured that the transaction's anticipated tax results will not be challenged.

While the safest route is to obtain a ruling, there are a number of reasons why it is not always the optimum alternative. First, it is costly. Preparing and submitting the request involves a significant amount of legal work, resulting in a higher transaction cost; and a several-hundred-dollar fee must be paid to the IRS. Second, submitting a request takes time—both to prepare the request and for the IRS to rule. Third, if the IRS's ruling is unfavorable and the transaction has already been closed, there is a risk that attention will be drawn to an issue that may otherwise have gone unnoticed.

a.   When to Consider an IRS Private Letter Ruling

When weighing the downside factors of asking the IRS for a private letter ruling (discussed in the previous section) against the increased certainty, a request should be considered if

- The lessor will not go ahead without a ruling.
- There is considerable doubt as to the lease's true lease status or other tax issues.
- The deal's overall costs are substantial enough to sustain the added costs.
- The lessee has time to wait for the ruling to be issued before closing the deal.

2.   *Proceeding Without a Ruling*

If a ruling is not practical for one or more of the reasons above, the next safest approach is to structure the lease financing so that it complies with the IRS's *Guidelines.* As mentioned earlier, the *Guidelines* tell taxpayers what minimal criteria a transaction must meet to obtain an advance ruling on a leveraged leasing deal. But they do not establish as a matter of law whether a transaction will or will not qualify as a true lease. In addition, the IRS does not promise that compliance with the *Guidelines* will guarantee favorable treatment on audit. As a practical matter, however, it is highly unlikely that a transaction meeting *Guidelines* requirements would have IRS audit problems. Compliance with the *Guidelines* can provide good assurance to parties to a purported leveraged lease transaction that the arrangement will in fact qualify as a true lease.

It should be kept in mind that although following the *Guidelines* does not guarantee true lease treatment, failure to comply precisely with each *Guidelines* provision does not necessarily doom a lease. *Reasons:* (1) The *Guidelines* constitute the IRS's position on advance rulings only; they do not necessarily reflect its view of the law, so a slight variation may not raise a problem on audit. (2) If the transaction goes to court, the *Guidelines* will carry less weight; under *Frank Lyon,* the court will look at all the facts and circumstances, and it may well find that, on balance, a true lease exists.

▶ **Observations:**

- As the equipment leasing industry and its advisors have gained experience working with the *Guidelines* rules, an increasing number of transactions have been put together that do not fully comply with them. For example, some lessors may make less than a 20% equity investment, or they may grant fixed-price purchase options, something that would violate the favorable *Guidelines* ruling requirements, as discussed in the following material. Generally, however, certain *Guidelines* requirements are never deviated from; in particular, the anticipated residual value test and the remaining useful life requirement, which are also discussed later on in this chapter.
- There is another reason the leasing industry and its advisors have increasingly varied from the *Guidelines*—competition. Because the leasing market

has matured, and due to the economic downturn of the late 1980s and early 1990s, too many lessors with too much money are chasing too few lease deals. To win business, let alone survive, lessors have chosen to become more tax-aggressive—taking chances that they may have not otherwise chosen to take.

When a ruling will not be sought, an advisable course of action is to obtain a written opinion from experienced lease tax counsel that the arrangement will have the desired lease treatment, particularly in situations where there will be variation from the *Guidelines*. While this increases costs, it may provide some beneficial support if a transaction is audited—or when defending an IRS litigation challenge.

C. The *Guidelines*

As briefly mentioned above, the following revenue procedures comprise the *Guidelines:*

- *Revenue Procedure 75-21* [1975-1 CB 715] generally sets out conditions that must be met for there to be an advance ruling on a leveraged lease.
- *Revenue Procedure 75-28* [1975-1 CB 752] sets out information and representations required to be furnished by taxpayers in a leveraged leasing transaction ruling request.
- *Revenue Procedure 76-30* [1976-2 CB 647] supplements Revenue Procedure 75–21 on issues of limited use property.
- *Revenue Procedure 79-48* [1979-2 CB 529] supplements Revenue Procedure 75-21 on improvements to leased property.

Keep in mind that the *Guidelines* are expressly designed to tell taxpayers what they must do to obtain an advance ruling—and that following the rules, even where no ruling is sought, is advisable to help ensure true lease treatment. It should also be noted that although the *Guidelines* apply only to leveraged leases, the parties to a nonleveraged transaction should consider those portions of the *Guidelines* that do not apply to the transaction debt aspects.

In addition to following the *Guidelines*, prospective lessors and lessees will want to comply with Revenue Ruling 55-540 [1955-2 CB 39], explained below, which gives some general guidance on all types of leasing transactions, leveraged and nonleveraged.

▶ **Observation:**   When deviating from the *Guidelines*, syndicators must be careful in structuring a lease financing, even though each party initially states that a private ruling will not be required. Invariably, once the parties, particularly the equity investors, hear all about the theoretical risks from their lawyers, they get nervous and frequently ask for a favorable opinion from tax counsel as to the true lease nature. In many situations, when there is a *Guidelines* variance, counsel is reluctant to give an opinion because of the uncertainty as to the variance's effect.

Coming at the last minute, this can lead to a serious roadblock to completing the deal.

When a private ruling is not involved, the *Guidelines* rules are sometimes stretched to keep all the parties satisfied. For example, a company may not be willing to lease equipment unless there is a low fixed-price purchase option. Although prohibited under the rules, a prospective lessor may grant such a right just to win the transaction.

At first glance, the *Guidelines* rules do not appear complex, but do not be deceived. In structuring a particular transaction, take care not to violate the rules inadvertently—not a simple task. The best protection against a violation is a thorough understanding of the principal *Guidelines* concepts. Toward this end, let's examine the various *Guidelines* aspects.

1.   The Lessor Must Make and Maintain a Minimum Investment

Under the *Guidelines*, the lessor must initially make an unconditional equity investment in the equipment equal to at least 20% of its cost. This can be done in a number of ways: with cash, with other consideration, or by personally assuming the obligation to buy the equipment. Typically, the lessor makes a cash payment from its own funds. The 20% equity investment is referred to as the "minimum investment."

The IRS requires the unconditional nature of the initial investment to prevent the lessor from arranging to receive, either from the lessee or certain lessee-related parties, all or any part of its equity back once the equipment is put into service. This is in keeping with the IRS's position that if a lessor wants to be treated as an equipment owner for tax purposes, and thus be entitled to claim the tax benefits, there must be an ownership risk.

When a lessor intends to meet the minimum equity test by personally assuming the obligation to purchase the equipment, its net worth must be sufficient to make the assumption meaningful.

▶ **Observation:**   It is generally felt that the 20% equity investment requirement is higher than is actually necessary to survive an IRS true lease challenge. In the pre-*Guidelines* era, the IRS would issue a favorable true lease ruling even when the equity investment was as low as 15% of equipment cost. Many leveraged lease transactions are structured today with less than a 20% equity investment when a favorable private letter ruling will not be sought.

The lessor must also maintain this 20% "minimum investment" in the equipment during the lease term. The test for determining whether the minimum investment rule has been met during the term is complicated; follow it carefully. The test will be met if the excess of (1) the cumulative payments that the lessee is obligated to pay over (2) the cumulative disbursements that the lessor is obligated to pay as a result of the equipment ownership is never greater than the sum of (a) any excess of the initial equity investment over 20% of the equipment cost and (b) the cumulative pro rata portion of the transaction's projected profit, not considering tax benefits. Simply, this means that the excess of the amounts coming in to the lessor over the amounts going out must never be more than the sum of any equity investment amount greater than 20% of equipment cost and the pro rata portion of the anticipated profit. The tax benefits accruing from ownership cannot be considered as profit in the computation.

▶ **Recommended Computation:**   In Revenue Procedure 75-28, the IRS provides a mechanical formula to establish the 20% investment during the lease term. It may be useful to run the following test on a computer and retain it for audit purposes.

Verify that throughout the lease term the items designated as (1), (2), (3), and (4) below comply with the formula "(1) − (2) never exceeds (3) + (4)."

1. The projected cumulative payments required to be paid by the lessee to or for the lessor.
2. The projected cumulative disbursements required to be paid by or for the lessor in connection with the ownership of the property, excluding the lessor's initial equity investment, but including any direct costs to finance the equity investment.
3. The excess of lessor's initial equity investment over 20% of the cost of the property.
4. A cumulative pro rata portion of the projected profits from the transaction (exclusive of tax benefits). Profit for this purpose is the excess of the sum of (a) the amounts required to be paid by the lessee to or for the lessor over the lease term plus (b) the value of the residual investment referred to in section 4(1)(C) of Revenue Procedure 75-21, over the aggregate disbursements required to be paid by or for the lessor in connection with the ownership of the property, including the lessor's initial equity investment and any direct costs to finance the equity investment.

Also, the minimum investment test must be met at the end of the lease term. It consists of two basic parts:

- The lessor must show that the leased equipment's estimated fair market residual value is equal to at least 20% of its original cost.
- The lessor must show that a reasonable estimate of the equipment's useful life at the end of the lease term is the longer of one year or 20% of the equipment's originally estimated useful life.

Illustrative Example—*At-Risk Residual Test:*   Company A wants to lease a $10,000 steel shipping container from Company B for an 11-year lease term. The container has an estimated useful life of 12 years and an estimated fair market value at the end of 11 years of $2,300. Will the end-of-the-lease-term "at risk" investment test be met?

The estimated fair market residual value test has been met. That is, the $2,300 residual meets the first test (20% of $10,000 = $2,000, the minimum).

The useful life test has not been met. Twenty percent of 12 years is 2.4 years. When the lease term is over there will only be one year of useful life left, and the second test says the remaining useful life must be the longer of either one year or, in our example, 2.4 years.

In making the fair market residual value determination, no weight can be given to any inflationary increases or deflationary decreases during the lease term—the determination must be made as to future value based on current dollars. Also, the estimated residual amount must be reduced by any anticipated costs that may be incurred by the lessor in removing and reacquiring the property at the end of the lease term.

▶ **Observation:**   There is an express exception to the *Guidelines* rule requiring the lessor to take into account anticipated removal and redelivery costs in determining whether the estimated residual value test is met: The lessor generally need not account for such cost when the lessee is obligated under the lease to pay for the removal and redelivery costs. This leads to an implied exception that if the lessor could realize the equipment's residual value without equipment removal by the original lessee, another lessee, the lessor, or a purchaser, then these estimated removal costs also would not have to be taken into account in determining whether the estimated residual test has been met.

These calculations cannot be made without first figuring out what the "lease term" will be for a particular transaction. The lease term is not merely the "primary term" designated by the lease document. By definition, the "term" must include all renewal and extension periods other than those that are at fair market rental value and are at the lessee's option. For example, the lessor would have to include any period for which it could require the lessee to continue to lease the equipment even though the lease period would be at fair market rental value. This rule prevents a lessor from avoiding its "residual risk" through a forced renewal of the lease, which would in effect run until the lessor had no residual value risk. This again reinforces the *Guidelines* intent that if an equipment owner wants to be a "lessor" it must incur real ownership risks.

2.   The Transaction Must Produce a Profit

The *Guidelines* provide that the lessor must make a profit on the transaction. At first, this statement seems ridiculous. What businessperson would be involved in a situation in which a profit was not to be made? None, so what is the IRS getting at? Simply, that the lessor must make money on the deal aside from the return generated by the tax benefits. In other words, the lessor must be able to show that the lease transaction makes economic sense without considering the tax benefits. The IRS wants to make sure that lease deals are not merely tax-avoidance devices.

How does a lessor know whether the profit requirement has been met? By meeting the following *Guidelines* test: The total rent and other amounts that the lessee is obligated to pay over the lease term, when added to the equipment's estimated residual value, has to be greater than the amount of money that the lessor is obligated to pay out for the equipment, such as debt service and equity investment, including any related direct equity financing costs. Simply, the lessor must anticipate having money left over at the end of the lease term after adding in the estimated residual value, repaying any transaction debt (the money it took out of its own pocket to acquire the equipment) and any other direct equity investment financing costs.

▶ **Observation:** Under the *Guidelines*, the profit test would be met even if the profit is as little as $1.

▶ **Recommended Computation:** Run the following profit test calculation from Revenue Procedure 75-28:

Demonstrate that the items identified as (1), (2), and (3) below will solve the formula "(1) + (2) exceed (3)."

(1) The projected aggregate payments required to be paid by the lessee to or for the lessor over the lease term
(2) The value of the residual investment described in Section 4(1)(C) of Revenue Procedure 75-21
(3) The projected sum of the aggregate disbursements required to be paid by or for the lessor in connection with the ownership of the property, including the lessor's initial equity investment, and any direct costs to finance the equity investment

Illustrative Example—*The Profit Test:* Company B has leased a new $100,000 barge to Company A under the following facts:

Lease term:	10 years
Barge residual value:	$20,000
Equity investment:	$20,000
Debt principal:	$80,000
Debt interest rate:	10%
Loan term:	10 years
Total aggregate rentals:	$125,000
Legal fees:	$5,000
Miscellaneous fees:	$1,000

For simplicity, assume that the debt repayments are based on an average outstanding principal of $40,000 over the 10-year period. Based on the above, the deal evolves as follows:

Total debt interest due:	$40,000
Total principal payment:	$80,000
Total fees ($5,000 + $1,000):	$6,000

Does the lessor pass the IRS profit test? The formula is

Aggregate rentals + residual value must exceed cash out.

Aggregate rentals + residual = $125,000 + $20,000 = $145,000

Equity investment + debt service + fees = cash out = $20,000 + $80,000 +
$40,000 + $6,000 = $146,000

The lessor fails the test.
The net result: The rents must be increased to pass the test.

Not only must a lessor anticipate a profit, it must also demonstrate that the transaction will produce a positive cash flow that is "reasonable" in amount. That is, the aggregate rents and other required lessee payments must comfortably exceed the aggregate outflows, basically the debt service and the direct equity financing costs.

▶ **Observations:**

- Although the *Guidelines* do not spell out what will be a reasonable cash flow amount, historically the IRS has ruled favorably when the cash flow amount is in the range of 2 to 4% of the equity investment per annum—computed on a simple interest basis.
- The *Guidelines* do not explicitly state that the positive cash flow must be on an even basis over the lease term; however, it is generally considered prudent to avoid situations in which the positive cash flow only exists for one or two lease periods.

▶ **Recommended Computation:**   Run the following positive cash flow test calculation from Revenue Procedure 75-28.
   Demonstrate that the lessor will have a projected positive cash flow from the lease transaction. This analysis must contain the following information to show that the items identified as (1) and (2) will solve the formula "(1) exceeds (2) by a reasonable minimum amount."

(1) The projected aggregate payments required to be paid by the lessee to or for the lessor over the lease term
(2) The projected aggregate disbursements required to be paid by or for the lessor in connection with the ownership of the property, excluding the lessor's initial equity investment, but including any direct costs to finance the equity investment

3. *No Lessee Investment*

Generally, the lessee cannot invest in the equipment by providing funds necessary to buy, add to, modify, or improve the equipment. There are several exceptions.

The lessee may make "severable improvements," additions or improvements that can easily be removed without causing material damage, so long as they are not necessary for the equipment's intended use, and the lessor does not have the right to buy them at below market price.

The lessee generally cannot make nonseverable improvements, those that cannot readily be removed by the lessee without causing material damage. However, the lessee can make nonseverable improvements if it (1) is not required to complete the property for the lessee's intended use, (2) does not constitute a lessee or lessee-related party equity investment (as, for example, if the lessor is required to buy the improvement), and (3) does not cause the property to become limited-use property (property of use only to the lessee). Also, the lessee can be permitted or required to make nonseverable improvements provided they are necessary to comply with health, safety, or environmental standards which are required by governmental law or regulation (including industry standards which have government recognition) or do not substantially increase the original property's productivity or capacity (essentially more than 25% of original performance, or, if so, do not cost when added to other noncompliance leasehold improvement costs in excess of 10% of the original cost, adjusted for inflation). The rules governing severable and nonseverable improvements are extensive, and an in-depth explanation is beyond the scope of this chapter. The reader can refer to Revenue Procedure 79-48 for a full explanation.

Also, ordinary maintenance and repairs that the lessee must make at its expense are not deemed "additions or improvements" and are thus excluded from the rule. The problem with this exception is that the *Guidelines* do not set up any parameters for determining what is considered "ordinary maintenance and repairs." If the IRS successfully challenges any expenses as not "ordinary," there may be a risk that the true lease nature will be lost.

Under the same basic concept, the lessee cannot pay for any equipment cost overruns. Usually this becomes a problem only when equipment with a long construction period is involved. In many of these situations, the purchase contracts have price escalation clauses. Some prospective lessors committing to lease such equipment before completion limit their cost exposure by specifying they will not pay for equipment if it exceeds a certain amount. If a lessor has this type of "cap," a prospective lessee runs the risk of having to negotiate a new lease deal at the last minute or buy the equipment.

4. The Lessee Cannot Be a Lender

Before the IRS issued Revenue Procedure 75-21, some lessees and parties related to them loaned money to the lessor to be used toward buying the equipment. For example, a prospective lessee may want to lease equipment manufactured by its parent company. The parent company would offer to sell the equipment to the lessor on a favorable installment basis. The payment delay would "pump up" a lessor's time value yield over a nondelayed payment, and at least part of the benefit would be reflected in a more attractive rental rate.

Under the *Guidelines*, the lessee and members of the lessee group are specifically prohibited from lending funds to the lessor to assist in the equipment financing. Thus, direct loans and other credit-extending techniques similar to the one described in the previous paragraph will transgress the *Guidelines* and prevent the issuance of a favorable private ruling on the transaction.

5. Certain Guarantees Cannot Be Used

The lessee and certain lessee-associated parties, such as its parent company or sister subsidiary, cannot guarantee any equipment debt. For example, a lessee's parent company cannot guarantee the repayment of a leveraged lease third-party loan. In most cases this will not be a great loss; however, it was a handy technique for lessors to use, for example, when third-party nonrecourse lenders wanted added security.

The *Guidelines* permit lessee-related parties to guarantee certain conventional obligations found in a net lease, such as rent, maintenance, or insurance premium obligations. This takes some of the sting out of the debt guarantee prohibition.

6. Lessee Purchase Options Must Be at Fair Market Value

To ensure that the lessee is not the equipment owner, the *Guidelines* prohibit any arrangement granting a lessee or lessee-related party the option to buy the leased equipment at a price below its fair market value. The lessee may have a purchase option only if the price is no less than the equipment's fair market value at the time of purchase under the option.

That rule eliminates all fixed-price purchase options, including so-called nominal purchase options. A typical nominal purchase right is one in which the lessee can buy the equipment at the end of the lease term for $1. In the past, some lessors had used this option to induce a prospective lessee to take the deal by claiming that lessees could have the best of both worlds: a rental deduction during the lease term and, in effect, an equipment purchase credit for the rent paid.

▶ **Observation:** Although the IRS will refuse to issue a favorable true lease ruling when a transaction contains a fixed-price purchase option, many tax advisors feel that by following pre-*Guidelines* case law (which upheld as true lease transactions those that contain fixed-price purchase options that were not so low that it was "reasonably certain" the lessee would exercise such option), the transaction would be entitled to true lease treatment. Fixed-price purchase options are particularly attractive to companies that are aware certain equipment will have a "high residual" at the end of the term. With a fair market value purchase option, they run the risk that their cost to buy will be substantial in relation to the original price. This would, in turn, relatively increase their effective leasing cost. Therefore, the lower the option's exercise price, the less the overall cost.

Illustrative Example—*The Purchase Cost Is Critical:*   Company A wants to lease a barge from Company B. The facts are as follows:

Original barge cost:	$100,000
Estimated residual value:	$20,000

If the lessee, Company A, had an option to buy the barge at the lease term's end for $20,000, its cost for leasing could be easily determined in advance. The rents and the purchase price are known. Assume instead that the lessee was granted only a fair market value purchase option under the *Guidelines*. If, at the end of the lease term, the barge was actually worth $50,000 because of the current demand, the lessee would have to pay out an additional $30,000—thus increasing the overall cost.

The above example is not unrealistic. There are many cases in which items, such as barges or private aircraft, have a market value equal to or greater than the original cost after years of use. Leasing that equipment, therefore, can be expensive if the lessee wants to buy it at the end of the term and must pay the fair market value.

7. Lessor Cannot Have Right to Require Sale

A lessor is specifically prohibited from having any initial right to require "any party" to buy the leased equipment for any reason, except when there are nonconformities with written supply, construction, or manufacture specifications. The lessor's investment in the equipment would, therefore, be said to be subject to the "risks of the market."

Thus, a lessor cannot have the right—called a "put"—to force an equipment sale at a predetermined price at the lease term's end to, for example, the lessee, a manufacturer, or a dealer. What does this mean for a lessor concerned about whether certain equipment will have any residual value? Simply, that a zero residual value may have to be assumed in calculating the rent to ensure that the transaction's economic return will be maintained. Were "puts" permitted, a lessor could base its investment return analysis on an anticipated residual value equal to the "put." As a result, a lessee could then be charged a relatively lower rent amount during the lease term on potentially poor residual value equipment. If the equipment could be sold at the end of the lease for an amount equal to, or greater than, the "put" amount, the lessee would have had a rent savings because the lessor would not need to force the lessee to buy the equipment to get its required economic return.

The right of a lessor to abandon the property is considered to be a right to require a purchase and, therefore, is also prohibited.

There is, however, some leeway. The *Guidelines* provide that after the equipment goes on lease the IRS may, depending on the particular facts and circumstances, permit an arrangement in which the lessor could require someone to buy the equipment.

▶ **A Word of Caution:** Parties can be tempted to try to get around this rule by entering into a side agreement before the lease is closed, giving the lessor a sale right. After the equipment is placed in service, the side agreement is to be submitted to the IRS for approval as a proposed arrangement, without mention that it had been agreed to during the prohibited period. This is dangerous and clearly not recommended. Private ruling letters are granted strictly on the basis of the facts submitted in the ruling request, and if the facts actually vary from those as presented, the IRS may not adhere to the tax treatment stated.

8.   *Uneven Rent Programs Must Meet Certain Tests*

"Step rentals," such as "low-high" or "high-low" rent structures, had been a valuable lessor marketing tool. Particularly attractive to lessees were rents that started low and increased during the lease's term, for a variety of reasons, including showing higher profits in early years, anticipating inflation, or increasing cash flow.

The *Guidelines* ask a taxpayer submitting a ruling request to submit certain information on any rent payment variations during the lease term. It should be noted, however, that under the *Guidelines,* uneven rent payments will not impact the IRS's ruling on whether the lease is a true lease. Rather, under the *Guidelines,* uneven rents can result in a portion of the uneven rent being treated as prepaid or deferred rent.

The *Guidelines* set out two safe harbor tests, so that if the rent payments satisfy either test there will be no issue as to prepaid or deferred rent. If the lease fails to meet either test, then the ruling request must also contain a request for a determination of whether any portion of the uneven rent payments will be deemed by the IRS as prepaid or deferred rent.

a.   Ten Percent Variation Test

Under the first test, rent payments come within the safe harbor if the rent for each year does not vary more than 10% above or below the average annual rent payable over the lease term. The average annual rent is computed by dividing the aggregate rent payable over the entire lease term by the number of years in the term. As a practical matter, this does not permit a lessor to offer anything significant when compared to some of the pre-*Guidelines* uneven rent programs.

> **Illustrative Example**—*Uneven Rent Test:*   Company A wants to lease a fuel truck for 10 years for a start-up operation, but anticipates that its cash flow will allow only a $1,000 annual rent expense for the first 3 years. Company B, the prospective lessor, proposes the following rent program:

Lease term:	10 years
Annual rent for years 1–3:	$1,000
Annual rent for years 4–10:	$2,000

> Company A finds the rent to be within its cash flow projections. Is there a deferred rent issue?
> Let's examine the numbers. The rule says the rent for each year cannot be above or below 10% of the average annual rent. The average annual rent is computed by dividing the total of the 10-year rents (3 × $1,000 + 7 × $2,000 = $17,000) by the number of years in the lease.

Annual average rent = $17,000/10 = $1,700

Because 10% of $1,700 is $170, the rent per year cannot be above $1,870 ($1,700 + $170) or below $1,530 ($1,700 − $170). Therefore, this rent program does not meet the test, and the issue of deferred rent must be addressed.

b. Initial Period Test

The second safe harbor is designed to permit, to some degree, rental payments that fluctuate during the lease term. Lease payments satisfy that test if, during at least the initial two-thirds of the lease term, the yearly rent is not more than 10% higher or lower than the average annual rent for such selected initial portion, and the remaining individual yearly rent is not greater than the highest annual rent payable during the initial portion and not less than one-half of the initial term average yearly rent. There is somewhat more flexibility in using this alternative, but it is still limited.

Illustrative Example—*Initial Period Test:* Assume the following rent program:

Lease term:	9 years
Annual rent for years 1–3:	$1,000
Annual rent for years 4–6:	$1,200
Annual rent for years 7–9:	$600

Will this rent structure pass the IRS alternative test?

First the average rent must be computed for the initial two-thirds of the lease term as follows:

$$Average\ rent = \frac{(3 \times \$1,000 + 3 \times \$1,200)}{6\ years} = \$1,100$$

The yearly rent cannot be greater than $1,210 ($1,100 + 10% × $1,100) or less than $990 ($1,100 − 10% × $1,100). The test is met for the initial two-thirds of the lease.

What about years seven through nine? The annual rent ($600) cannot be greater than the highest rent payable during the initial two-thirds of the lease term ($1,200) and less than one-half of the initial term average annual rent (½ × $1,100 = $550). This program just meets the test, so the IRS under the *Guidelines* would not object to the steps as presented.

▶ **Tax Law Observation:** Section 467, added by the 1984 Deficit Reduction Act, may require certain lessors and lessees to accrue uneven lease rental income and deductions in a level manner. Section 467 applies to an equipment lease totaling over $250,000 in rental payments under which either (1) at least one amount is allocable to the use of property during a calendar year or (2) there are increases in the amount of rent to be paid over the lease term. Accrual will not be required if the lease payments satisfy a presumptive tax-avoidance test. Parties to a leasing transaction should review Section 467 if considering an uneven rent structure.

9. Limited Use Property

Limited use property is property not expected to be useful to or usable by the lessor except for purposes of continued leasing or transfer to the lessee or a member of the lessee group. The IRS says this means that, at the lease term's end, there will probably be no potential lessees or buyers other than the lessee or members of the lessee group. As a result, the lessor will probably sell or rent the property to the lessee or a member of the lessee group, so that, in effect, the lessee will receive the equipment's ownership benefits for substantially its entire useful life. To obtain a favorable ruling, it is necessary to establish that it is commercially feasible for a party, not the lessee or a member of the lessee group, to lease or buy the property from the lessor—demonstrating that it is not limited-use property.

D. Ruling Request Submission Requirements

In submitting a ruling request, the taxpayer must present the information the *Guidelines* requires in the manner prescribed by Revenue Procedure 75-28, as modified by Revenue Procedure 79-48. Generally, all the parties to the transaction, including the lessor and the lessee, must join in the ruling request. The request must contain a summary of the surrounding facts. The request must be accompanied by certain relevant documents, such as the lease, or, in the case of a brokered transaction, any economic analysis, prospectus, or other document used to induce the lessor to invest.

The request must include detailed information covering, for example:

- The type and quality of the leased equipment
- Whether the equipment is new, reconstructed, used, or rebuilt
- When, how, and where the equipment will be, or was, first placed in service or use
- Whether the equipment will be permanently or temporarily attached to land, buildings, or other property
- The flow of funds among the parties

The request must disclose the lease term, and any renewals or extensions, and any purchase and sale options. This includes any right the lessor has to force a purchase or to abandon the equipment, and any intention to give this right in the future.

It must be disclosed if the lessee, or any related party, must pay for any cost overruns or will invest in the equipment, by, for example, contributing to its cost or paying for an improvement, modification, or addition. The request must also identify any unrelated parties who will provide funds.

Whether or not the profit and positive cash flow tests have been satisfied, information covering any lessee-related guarantees and any uneven rent structure must be presented. An economic analysis has to be submitted showing that the minimum "at risk" investment rules will be satisfied. A detailed description of the debt and the repayment terms; any lease provisions relating to indemnities, termination, obsolescence, casualty, or insurance; and the party who is to claim any investment credit must be set out. The request must include representations that the property is not limited-use property. The parties must submit an expert's opinion on the equipment's residual value, setting out the manner in which the conclusion was determined, any removal or delivery costs at the end of the lease term, and the useful life of the equipment remaining after the end of the term.

E.   The Foundation Tax Rules

Two decades before issuing the *Guidelines,* the IRS issued Revenue Ruling 55-540 [1955-2 CB 39] setting out the factors that it considers in deciding whether a leasing transaction is really a conditional sale for tax purposes. Unlike the *Guidelines,* Revenue Ruling 55-540 sets out the IRS audit position rather than dealing with what is required to obtain a ruling. However, the ruling is much less useful than the *Guidelines* because it is less precise. But, by checking its tests, you will help ensure a leasing transaction's viability. In that ruling, the IRS stated generally that whether an agreement, which in form is a lease, is in substance a conditional sales contract depends upon the intent of the parties as evidenced by the provisions of the agreement, read in the light of the facts and circumstances existing at the time the agreement was executed.

In addition, it provided that in "ascertaining such intent no single test, or any special combination of tests, is absolutely determinative," no "general rule, applicable to all cases can be laid down," and that each "case must be decided in the light of its particular facts." The IRS then went on to state that an intent that would cause an arrangement to be treated as a sale instead of a lease for tax purposes is found if one or more of the following factors exist:

- Portions of the periodic payments are specifically made applicable to an equity interest to be acquired by the lessee.
- The lessee will acquire title to the property under lease on the payment of a stated amount of "rentals" that the lessee under the contract must make.
- The total amount that the lessee must pay for a relatively short period of use constitutes an inordinately large proportion of the total sum required to acquire title.
- The agreed "rental" payments materially exceed the current fair rental value.
- The property may be acquired by the lessee under a purchase option at a price that is nominal in relation to the property's value at the time the option may be exercised (determined at the time the agreement was entered into) or which is relatively small when compared to the total payments that the lessee must make.
- Some portion of the periodic payments is specifically designated as interest or is otherwise readily recognizable as the equivalent of interest.

▶ **Observation:**   Revenue Ruling 55-540 provides guidelines for determining whether a conditional sale contract exists. The assumption is that everyone is on safe ground if a conditional sales contract does not exist and the parties structured the transaction as a tax lease. If the transaction is structurally complex, experienced tax leasing counsel may be necessary to get adequate assurances.

F.   Potential Penalties

Not only do the parties risk losing their tax benefits if a transaction fails to qualify as a true lease, they also run the risk of incurring penalties. A 5% negligence penalty is possible if the parties fail to exercise reasonable care. In addition, in several tax court cases, the Section 6659 overvaluation penalty has been imposed on lessors where the court found that there was no reasonable expectation that the lessor could make an economic profit apart from tax benefits—from the leasing transaction. The Section 6659 penalty is 30% of the amount of the understatement attributable to the overvaluation (here, the equipment's basis). Applying only to individuals (including partnerships) and closely held or personal service corporations, Section 6659 is not applicable to all lessors, but is a potential risk in certain leasing transactions.

G.   A Quick "True" Lease Checklist

The following checklist can be used as a guide to determine whether a lease transaction's basic features comply with the *Guidelines'* requirements. If any answer is "No," there may be a problem.

	Yes	No
1. Has the lessor made an initial equity investment equal to at least 20% of equipment cost?	☐	☐
2. Is the initial equity investment unconditional in nature?	☐	☐
3. Will the lessor's minimum investment remain equal to at least 20% of equipment cost during the lease term?	☐	☐
4. Is the estimated residual value of the equipment at least equal to 20% of the equipment's original cost?	☐	☐
5. Will the useful life of the equipment remaining at the end of the lease term be equal to the longer of one year or 20% of the originally estimated useful life?	☐	☐
6. If there is a lessee purchase option, is it at fair market value as of the time of exercise?	☐	☐
7. Is the lessor without any rights to force a sale of the equipment to any party?	☐	☐
8. Is the lessor without any specific right to abandon the equipment?	☐	☐
9. Has the lessor furnished all the equipment cost other than any third-party debt?	☐	☐

	Yes	No
10. Will the lessor have to bear the cost of any permanent equipment improvement, modification, or addition?	☐	☐
11. If the lessee pays for a severable improvement, could the equipment be used for its intended use without it?	☐	☐
12. If the lessee pays for a severable improvement, can the lessor buy it only at a price at least equal to its fair market value?	☐	☐
13. If the lessee pays for a nonseverable improvement, could the equipment be used for its intended use without the improvement?	☐	☐
14. If the lessee pays for a nonseverable improvement, will someone other than the lessee be able to use the equipment?	☐	☐
15. Does every nonseverable improvement that is paid for by the lessee not constitute a lessee investment?	☐	☐
16. Will the lessor pay for any equipment cost overruns?	☐	☐
17. Are all the equipment loans from lenders unrelated to the lessee?	☐	☐
18. Is the transaction devoid of any indebtedness guarantees by the lessee or related parties?	☐	☐
19. Will the lessor make a profit on the lease without considering the tax benefits?	☐	☐
20. Will the transaction generate a positive cash flow for the lessor?	☐	☐
21. Will the equipment have a use at the end of the lease term to someone other than to the lessee?	☐	☐
22. Have the required backup information and material been submitted with the request for ruling?	☐	☐

Chapter 9

Advantages and Risks of Leveraged Leasing Decisions

A.   What Is the Concept of Leveraged Leasing?

The leveraged lease can be one of the most complex and sophisticated vehicles for financing capital equipment in today's financial marketplace. The individuals and firms in the leveraged leasing industry are aggressive and creative. As a result, the environment is one of innovation and intense competition.

Is the concept of a leveraged lease complex? Not really. It is simply a lease transaction in which the lessor puts in only a portion, usually 20% to 40%, of the funds necessary to buy the equipment and a third-party lender supplies the remainder. Because the benefits available to the lessor are generally based on the entire equipment cost, the lessor's investment is said to be "leveraged" with third-party debt.

Generally, the third-party loan is on a nonrecourse-to-the-lessor basis and ranges from 60% to 80% of the equipment's cost. The nonrecourse nature means the lender can only look to the lessee, the stream of rental payments that have been assigned to it, and the equipment for repayment. The lessor has no repayment responsibility even if the lessee defaults and the loan becomes uncollectible. The fact that a nonrecourse lender cannot look to the lessor for the loan repayment if there is a problem is not as bad as it seems for two reasons:

- The lender will not make a nonrecourse loan unless the lessee is considered creditworthy.
- The lender's rights to any proceeds coming from a sale or re-release of the equipment come ahead of any of the lessor's rights in the equipment and lease.

The lessor's equity investment is subordinated to the loan repayment obligation. For example, if a lender only contributed 70% of the funds necessary, the subordination arrangement would put it in an over-collateralized loan position, which would decrease its lending risk.

Although the third-party loan is usually made on a nonrecourse basis, this is not always so. If the lessee's financial condition is weak, a lender may only be willing to make a recourse loan. Under this type of loan the lender can look to, or has recourse against, the lessor for repayment if it cannot be satisfied through the lessee or the equipment. The lessor still, however, has the economic advantage of a leveraged investment.

Although the concept of leveraging a lease investment is simple, the mechanics of putting one together are often complex. Leveraged lease transactions, particularly ones involving major dollar commitments, frequently involve many parties brought together through intricate arrangements. The "lessor" is typically a group of investors joined together by a partnership or trust structure. The partnership or trust is the legal owner, or "titleholder," of the equipment. The "lender" is often a group of lenders usually acting through a trust arrangement. This is further complicated by the fact that each participant will be represented by counsel with varying views. As a result, the job of organizing, drafting, and negotiating the necessary documents is generally very difficult.

▶ **Observation:** Because the expenses involved in documenting a leveraged lease can be substantial, transactions involving less than $2 million worth of equipment can be economically difficult to structure as a leveraged lease. However, if documentation fees (such as counsel fees) can be kept within reason, smaller equipment amounts can be financed in this manner. In many cases, a prospective lessor or underwriter has an in-house legal staff with the ability to originate and negotiate the required documents. If so, this will help keep costs down.

Generally, leveraged lease financings are arranged for prospective lessees by companies or individuals who specialize in structuring and negotiating these types of leases. These individuals and firms are referred to as "lease underwriters." Essentially, their function is to structure the lease economics, find the lessor-investors, and provide the necessary expertise to ensure that the transaction will get done. In a limited number of situations, they also find the debt participants. They do not generally participate as an investor in the equipment. Because the vast majority of leveraged leases are brought about with the assistance of lease underwriters, lease underwriting has become synonymous with leveraged leasing.

The premise on which lease underwriting services are provided by an underwriter (that is, on a "best efforts" or "firm" basis) varies significantly. It is, therefore, worthwhile at this stage to explore the two types of underwriter offers: "best efforts" and "firm commitment" underwriting arrangements.

1. A "Best Efforts" Underwriting Arrangement Can Be Risky

Lease underwriting transactions are frequently bid on a "best efforts" basis. This type of bid is an offer by the underwriter to do the best it can to put a transaction together under the terms set out in its proposal letter. There are no guarantees of performance. As a result, a prospective lessee accepting the offer may not know for some time whether it has the financing.

In practice, a best efforts underwriting is not as risky as it appears. Most reputable underwriters have a good feel for the market when bidding on this basis and usually can deliver what they propose. Thus, there is a good chance they will be able to get "firm commitments" from one or more prospective lessor-investors to participate on the basis offered.

► Recommendations:

- A prospective lessee must always keep in mind that a best efforts under-writing proposal gives no guarantee the transaction can be completed un-der the terms proposed. Thus, the prospective lessee must give careful consideration to the experience and reputation of an underwriter propos-ing on this basis before awarding a transaction to it. An inability to perform as presented can result in the loss of valuable time.
- When there is adequate equipment delivery lead time, a prospective lessee may be inclined to award a transaction to an unknown underwriter who has submitted an unusually low bid. However, there is a risk that must be considered. If the transaction is so underpriced that it cannot be sold in the "equity" market, it may meet resistance when it is reoffered on more attractive investor terms. This can happen merely because it has been seen, or "shopped," too much. It is an unfortunate fact that when an investor is presented with a transaction that it knows has been shopped, it may refuse to consider it even if the terms are favorable. Therefore a prospective lessee should not be too eager to accept a "low ball" best efforts bid unless it has taken a hard look at the underwriter's ability to perform.
- Best efforts underwriters sometimes submit proposals that are substan-tially below the market. At times this happens by mistake. For example, transactions may have been priced in good faith based on acceptable inves-tor market yields, but by the time the award is made the market has moved upward. At other times, an underwriter may intentionally underprice a transaction to make sure of winning it. If it cannot be placed as proposed, the underwriter will go back and attempt to get the prospective lessee to agree to a higher rental rate. With its competitors no longer involved, the underwriter may be in a good position to do this. A prospective lessee with near-term deliveries must be particularly careful in recognizing this possibility. Otherwise, it may have little choice but to be pushed into a less favorable deal.
- A prospective lessee can control the risk of nonperformance under a best efforts proposal by putting a time limit on the award, for example, by requiring the underwriter to come up with, or "circle," interested parties within one week following the award and securing formal commitments by the second week.
- It is not unheard of for a prospective lessee to make a time limit award to an unusually low bidding or unknown underwriter without telling the remaining bidders. The purpose is to try to keep them around just in case

the underwriter cannot perform. This can be unfair to an underwriter who, in good faith, is continuing to spend time and money on the transaction in the hope of winning it. Doing this can also hurt a prospective lessee in the long run. *Reason:* It is likely that the other underwriters will find out that this happened. Once the word gets around that a company does business in this manner, reputable underwriters may refuse to participate in future biddings. Even if they do participate, they may quote rates that have not been as finely tuned as possible. *Reason:* They will not spend the time or money necessary in situations in which they may not be treated fairly. Thus, this tactic is not recommended because a prospective lessee may not see the best possible market rates as a result.

2. A "Firm Commitment" Underwriting Arrangement Is Often the Best

From a prospective lessee's viewpoint, a "firm commitment" underwriting proposal is generally the preferred type of offer. When an underwriter has "come in firm" it is guaranteeing to put the proposed lease financing together. Typically, before an underwriter submits this type of proposal, it has solid commitments from lessor-investors to enter into the transaction on the terms presented. However, this is not always the case. The underwriter's firm bid may only represent its willingness to be the lessor if it cannot find a third-party lessor.

► **Recommendations:**

- If an underwriter proposing on a firm basis does not have "committed equity" at the time its proposal is submitted, a prospective lessee may be subject to certain risks. Unless the underwriter is in a strong financial position, its commitment may be worthless if a third-party lessor cannot be found. Thus, a prospective lessee must always investigate whether an underwriter has lined up one or more lessor-investors. If not, the underwriter's financial condition must be reviewed before making the award to determine whether it has the financial ability to stand behind it.
- Underwriters sometimes state that they have firm "equity" even though they have nothing more than a verbal indication from a prospective lessor-investor's contact that it will recommend the transaction to its approving committee. Thus, a prospective lessee must ask to be put in touch with each lessor-investor to confirm its position. Doing this will also ensure that there are no misunderstandings as to the transaction terms.

B. Leveraged Lease Participants Have Unique Characteristics

Generally, a leveraged lease transaction will involve more parties than a nonleveraged one. At a minimum, the participants will include an equity participant (lessor-investor), a debt participant, a lessee, and an equipment supplier. In the event the equity or debt participant acts through a trust arrangement, a trustee will also be a party. Often, these participants have certain unique characteristics.

1. The Equity Participants

An investor in a leveraged lease is referred to as an "equity participant." Generally, more than one investor is involved on the "equity side" of a leveraged lease. These equity participants, or owners, often act together through a trust arrangement. A trust provides partnershiplike tax treatment, while at the same time giving corporatelike liability protection. The equity participants are deemed the beneficial owners of the equipment. Legal title is held by the representative (the trustee) of the trust.

It is possible when more than one lessor-investor is involved for them to act through a partnership arrangement, rather than a trust. Here, the partnership is the lessor. Legal title to the equipment is held in the partnership name.

▶ **Recommendation:**   The actual form of the equipment owning entity—that is, trust or partnership—will depend on the particular needs of each transaction and the participants. Counsel must be used to select the best form for a particular situation.

The typical leveraged lease equity participant is an "institutional investor." For example, banks come within this category. However, because a leveraged lease can be an attractive investment, many "regular" corporations and, in a limited number of situations, wealthy individuals are also potential lessor-investor candidates.

Some prospective leveraged lease investors have their own leasing companies actively looking for lease investment opportunities. But many do not. Those that do not, often referred to as "passive" investors, usually rely exclusively on the lease underwriting community to locate leveraged lease investments for them. Typically, the passive type investor also depends heavily on underwriters for advice on the structure and documentation of these investments.

2. The Lessee

As with any lease transaction, a leveraged lease transaction does not begin to come into existence until an equipment user, the prospective lessee, decides to consider leasing as a way to finance the acquisition of equipment it needs. Thus, the lessee is the key participant in any lease financing.

Because documenting a leveraged lease transaction tends to be expensive, this type of lease usually makes economic sense only for financings involving a significant dollar amount of equipment. As a result, the type of potential lessee is usually a large equipment user who has the financial strength to support the obligations involved.

3. The Debt Participants

A lender in a leveraged lease transaction is generally referred to as a "debt partici-pant." It is common for there to be more than one debt participant involved in a particular lease. When this is the case, they frequently form a trust through which they will act. The document setting out the trust's terms is referred to as the "trust indenture." The amount of money each debt participant intends to loan is transferred to the trust, which in turn lends it to the lessor. The loan made to the lessor is generally nonrecourse in nature. The loan is represented by a note or series of notes payable over the lease term from the rent proceeds the lessor re-ceives.

If properly organized, the lender's trust will receive partnershiplike income tax treatment and corporatelike liability protection. Each participant, as a benefi-cial owner of the trust estate, is treated for income tax purposes as though it made its loan directly to the lessor and will not have a direct exposure to any third-party claim.

Leveraged lease third-party debt is often supplied by banks or insurance companies. However, because a leveraged lease loan is no different from any other loan secured by personal property, generally any lender able and willing to make a secured loan is a potential loan source. There is, however, one limiting factor—the prospective lender's ability to offer competitive market interest rates. The debt interest rate is a critical factor in the rent computation. A leveraged lease rent quotation is usually premised on an assumed debt interest rate. Thus, the lower the interest rate, the more profit a lessor makes, and vice versa. This is so, unless the prospective lessee gets the benefit or bears the risk of interest rate variations. In the latter case the underwriter's proposal will provide that if the debt interest rate comes in other than assumed, the rent will be adjusted upward or downward to appropriately reflect the variance. As a result only the most rate aggressive lenders (such as banks and insurance companies) are usually able to compete, particularly in the better credit transactions.

4. The Underwriter

The lease underwriting business has a relatively low capital entrance require-ment. Because of this there is an overabundance of "packagers" offering lease underwriting services. These packagers run the gamut from individuals op-erating out of telephone booths to investment bankers to specialized lease under-writing firms. Some are well versed in leveraged leasing economics and documentation, and others know little more than the basics. The choice of an underwriter is critical to the success of a transaction. Those who have a solid understanding of the business and who are continually active in the underwriting market are more likely to be able to better structure and ensure leveraged lease financing success.

▶ **Recommendation:** Prospective lessees entertaining leveraged lease pro-posals must make sure before awarding a transaction that the intended underwriter has the necessary qualifications, in both experience and technical knowledge, to do the job.

5. The Equipment Manufacturer

The equipment manufacturer or distributor involved in a leveraged lease transaction usually does nothing more than sell the agreed-on equipment to the lessor at the negotiated price. Once the full price has been paid, its only obligation is to stand behind its product for any warranty period.

In some situations, the vendor's role is not limited to merely selling the equipment to the lessor. It sometimes provides various inducements to a lessor to assist in selling its equipment. For example, it may be willing to guarantee some of the lessee's lease obligations in situations when the lessee's financial condition is weak.

6. The Investor's Representative: The Owner's Trustee

In the event equity participants act through a trust, a trustee will be appointed to be the trust's representative. The trustee is sometimes referred to as the owner's trustee and is usually a commercial bank or trust company.

The owner's trustee is considered the mechanical arm of the trust. *Reason:* The trust arrangement specifically defines the trustee's responsibilities. For example, one of its prescribed duties will be to divide up and disburse the lease funds among the various equity participants under a predetermined formula. As the equity participants' representative, it makes sure their investment is protected by monitoring their rights under the lease.

7. The Lender's Representative: The Indenture Trustee

When a trust arrangement is established for the debt participants, a trustee, referred to as the "indenture trustee," is employed to represent the trust. The trust agreement clearly defines the indenture trustee's duties. For example, the indenture trustee collects the money to be loaned from the debt participants and then turns it over to the lessor. As a part of the loan transaction, the indenture trustee takes an assignment of the lease and a security interest in the equipment as security for the loan repayment. Typically, a commercial bank or trust company is selected to act as the indenture trustee.

C. How Different Is the Leveraged Lease Document?

The format of a typical leveraged lease document is essentially the same as that of any other finance lease. However, the terms and provisions are usually more detailed. *Reason:* The major dollar commitments involved usually dictate that greater attention be paid to each aspect.

What about the collateral, or supplemental, documents? There are typically a greater number of these documents involved in a leveraged lease transaction than in a "straight" lease transaction. For example, in addition to those found in nonleveraged lease situations, such as the lease, opinions of counsel, and board of director resolutions, the leveraged transaction documentation will at a minimum usually include trust agreements, a participation agreement, promissory notes, and a security and loan agreement.

D. Three Advantages to the Lessee in a Leveraged Lease

In certain situations, a leveraged lease transaction offers many benefits for a prospective lessee. In some cases, it may be the only economically viable approach to take.

1. The Rent Can Be More Attractive

As a rule of thumb a competitively bid leveraged lease transaction will provide a lower cost to a lessee than a comparable term nonleveraged lease. Logically, if a company can borrow at a more favorable interest rate than a lessor, it stands to reason that if the lessor pays part of the equipment's cost with a loan based on the lessee's credit it can charge lower rents without sacrificing its economic return. There are, of course, exceptions to this rule, and each situation must be examined on its own. For example, if the dollar amount of equipment financed is small, the documentation expenses involved can offset the economic benefits gained through leveraging.

2. There Is a Better Market for Large Transactions

Major dollar equipment lease financings can generally be arranged more readily by using a leveraged lease structure. This is because a lessor-investor only has to come up with a portion of the required equipment, the remainder being provided by a third-party lender.

Because many investors and lenders are unwilling to make a major dollar investment in one transaction, a number of lessor-investors and lenders must frequently be brought together. By forming investor and lender syndicates, they can keep the dollar exposure for each within desired limits.

Bringing together more than one investor and lender can be beneficial for a lessee. When the investment risk is spread among a greater number of participants, there is a better likelihood that a large dollar lease financing can be done at more reasonable rates. No one party has such a great exposure that it believes it must charge a premium for the risk. The disadvantage is the added paperwork. However, a competent and experienced underwriter will be able to successfully usher everyone through the documentation tangle—a reason why the choice of the underwriter is a critical factor.

▶ **Observation:** There are a small number of prospective lessor-investors willing to act as the sole equity participant in major equipment lease financings. The advantage to using such an investor is that the necessary approvals and potential complications will be kept to a minimum. Generally, however, this type of investor realizes that not many others are willing to take on an entire major transaction and its rent charge will usually be high. Whether the extra rate is worth the reduced risks of a simpler transaction is a matter of judgment. An experienced underwriter should be of great assistance in evaluating the trade-off.

3. The Lessors Can Be More Competitive

The type of lessor interested in pursuing a leveraged lease investment is often most concerned with the available equipment ownership tax benefits. As a result, such a lessor may be willing to be more aggressive on those aspects of a lease transaction that do not impact the lease's tax consequences.

E. Investment Pitfalls and Recommendations for Prospective Lessors

A prospective lessor must consider many factors before deciding whether to enter into a particular lease transaction, leveraged or not. However, these considerations are particularly crucial for leveraged lease investors. *Reason:* The transactions are typically very competitive and the investment economics finely tuned. Thus, a slight mistake or change in the investment assumptions can have a major adverse impact.

For a prospective lessor-investor to evaluate the risks involved, it must know what they are. The following explanation will alert the reader to the fundamental points that must be considered by every lease investor.

1. Equipment Delivery Delays Can Destroy Profits

The date when the equipment is delivered determines when the ownership tax benefits will be available to a lessor. When these benefits are available is a critical factor in a prospective lessor's analysis of its anticipated economic return. An unexpected delivery delay can have a serious negative impact. For example, consider a transaction entered into by a calendar year taxpayer-investor based on the assumption that the equipment will be delivered no later than the end of the current year. A delivery in the following year could jeopardize its contemplated return. *Reason:* The equipment ownership tax benefits would not be available until the next year. If the transaction had been priced in a competitive market, that slippage could easily make the transaction's economics completely unacceptable to the investor.

▶ **Recommendations:**

● A prospective lessor-investor can protect itself against a potential yield deterioration because of equipment delivery delays in two ways. The first is by establishing a commitment cutoff date. That is, setting a point in time after which it will no longer be obligated to buy and lease "undelivered"?

equipment. A second way is to provide for a rent adjustment that preserves the transaction's economics if a certain delivery date is passed.

● From a lessee's viewpoint, either of the lessor delivery delay solutions explained in the above recommendation can create problems. However, the first solution is generally considered the more dangerous. When a delivery cutoff date is imposed, a prospective lessee could end up without a lease financing source for the late equipment. When a rental adjustment is permitted, a lessee may be confronted with an undesirably high rent. In the latter situation, however, it at least knows that lease financing will be available regardless of the delay.

● A prospective lessor should be careful when establishing the rental adjustment criterion to apply to equipment delivered late. For example, if the rental analysis is based on certain yield and after-tax cash flow standards, the prospective lessor should make sure the adjustment provision will permit it to maintain both criteria, because they will not run parallel. In other words, maintaining yield will not necessarily maintain after-tax cash flows, and vice versa.

2. The Lessee's Financial Condition Is Crucial

The financial strength of a prospective lessee is an important lessor consideration in any lease transaction. It should be of prime concern to a passive type lessor-investor with limited equipment knowledge and remarketing capability. A lease default could easily endanger its invested capital and anticipated economic return. Therefore, it is of utmost importance for the prospective lessee's financial standing to be thoroughly reviewed.

3. Changes in Tax Law Can Eliminate Profits

If the tax benefits anticipated by investing in an equipment lease are eliminated or reduced because of a change in tax law, a lessor-investor could be confronted with an extremely unfavorable investment. The possibility of a tax law change is difficult, if not impossible, to predict. However, it is not generally considered an unreasonable risk to assume in certain situations.

In major leveraged leases, lessees are sometimes "forced" to indemnify the lessor against any adverse change in the tax law that causes loss of a tax benefit. The tax indemnification provisions are usually incorporated directly in the lease agreement.

▶ Observations:

● Prospective lessees have become increasingly successful in placing the tax benefit loss risks from changes in law on the lessor. It usually depends on who has the most negotiating strength. A favorite lessee argument is that the burden properly belongs on the lessor. *Reason:* The prospective lessor is better able to assess them through its experience. The argument has some validity as to "regular" leasing companies. However, it may not be true as far as the typical leveraged lease investor is concerned. In its pas-

sive role it may not have the type of exposure necessary to make the appropriate evaluation.

- A prospective lessor-investor can hedge against the change-in-tax-law risk
by having the right to appropriately adjust the rental rate or to exclude
equipment that will be affected and that has not yet been delivered. The
danger to a prospective lessee with these lessor solutions is that it may
have to pay too high a lease rate or may be without financing at the last
minute.

4. Income Variations Can Be Dangerous

A typical leveraged lease transaction may not be economically viable for a lessor-
investor unless it can use all of the available equipment ownership tax benefits in
a timely manner. For example, if the investor had an unexpected net loss for the
year the equipment was placed in service, it would have no taxable income
against which to apply the tax benefits. The inability to use the tax benefits when
anticipated would reduce the transaction's expected time value return. The time
value concept says $1 received today is worth more than $1 received a year from
today because of its earning capability. Thus, a lease investment must be looked
at by a prospective lessor-investor in light of a careful and realistic appraisal of
its present and future earning situations.

5. Tax Rate Variations: Consider the Possibility

How valuable the available tax benefits from owning equipment are to a lessor-
investor depends to a large extent on its overall effective income tax rate. The
greater its effective tax rate the more tax savings it will realize from the tax benefits. Any decrease in its tax rate will reduce the favorable impact of the available
write-offs. Thus, a prospective lessor-investor must consider any potential income
tax rate change in light of the future tax benefits coming from a lease investment.

▶ **Observation:**   A prospective lessor-investor can protect itself against an adverse tax rate change by getting the prospective lessee to agree to indemnify it in
the event this situation occurs. In today's market, however, it is unlikely that any
prospective lessee would agree to provide this type of indemnity.

6. Incorrect Residual Value Assessment: An Easy Trap

Generally, the value of the equipment at the end of a lease, referred to as its
"residual value," can have a dramatic impact on the profitability of the transaction. If a prospective lessor's residual value estimate is too high when it analyzes
a lease investment, its return will be adversely affected. For example, if a prospective investor makes its investment analysis assuming a certain return based on
selling the equipment at the end of the lease for 20% of its original cost, the
transaction's profitability is reduced if the equipment sells for only 5% of its original cost. The overall effect of the diminished value depends on its importance in
the investor's analysis. Very often it is a significant factor.

► **Recommendation:** It is advisable for a prospective lessor-investor to consult an equipment appraiser for assistance in making a reasonable residual value estimate. Remember, however, that an appraiser's opinion as to future value is nothing more than a professional guess. It does not assure the investor of the equipment's future worth. It does, of course, provide a degree of comfort that would otherwise not exist.

7. *An Early Lease Termination Must Be Considered*

A prospective lessor-investor must make sure that a permitted early lease termination will have little, if any, impact on its lease investment economics. For example, consider a 20-year full payout lease that is terminated at the end of 2 years. To begin with, the investor's future lease profits will be cut off. Depending on how the rents have been reported for income purposes, an early termination can cause a "book" loss. For example, if the rent income was reported faster than actually received, the early termination might make it necessary to report as a loss the difference between what was reported on the income statement and what was actually taken in.

If the equipment cannot be favorably re-leased in a timely manner, the lessor may be forced to sell the equipment immediately. An unplanned sale situation can make it difficult for a lessor to realize the best price. This is particularly so if large amounts of equipment scattered all over the country are involved. Having adequate and inexpensive storage space can ease the problem. *Reason:* The lessor may be better able to afford to wait the market out. Lessors sometimes negotiate the right to store it on the lessee's premises free of charge. However, this may not be a good solution if the parties are in an adversary situation. Having to sell equipment early may also create another problem—a recapture of tax benefits claimed. If the tax benefits are an important part of the lessor's yield, a recapture can further destroy the already faltering lease economics.

Incorporating a "termination value" concept into the lease can solve the economic and tax recapture risks of early termination. Essentially, a termination value is an amount a lessee would be obligated to pay to the lessor to help protect its investment and anticipated return.

8. *Casualty Loss: Are There Protections?*

The types of problems confronting a lessor if there is an equipment casualty loss are similar to those that must be addressed if a lease termination occurs, that is, future profits will be unavailable, tax benefit recapture may result, and a "book" loss may have to be reported. However, there is one important difference—the equipment will have little, if any, value. When a casualty loss occurs, therefore, the lessor is left without its collateral protection and must look to the lessee and any insurance proceeds for loss repayment. This is a good reason why prospective lessor-investors must make certain that the lessee is a creditworthy entity and, also, that adequate insurance is secured and maintained.

► **Recommendation:** If a prospective lessee will be obligated to insure the leased equipment, the prospective lessor should require evidence at the time of the lease closing that the appropriate insurance coverage has been secured. Also, arrangements should be made for the insurance company to notify the lessor if the lessee does anything, such as neglecting to pay the premiums, that could cause the policy to lapse. In this way, the lessor will have the opportunity of taking over any lapsed obligations to ensure continued coverage.

Even though the lessee must maintain casualty loss insurance, prospective lessors should also incorporate a "casualty loss value" concept into the lease agreement. Casualty values, sometimes referred to as "stipulated loss values," are calculated in much the same manner as termination values. Their purpose is to protect the lessor's investment position in the event of a casualty loss. Under this concept, the lessee in effect guarantees that the lessor will receive a certain amount of money if there is an equipment casualty. The amount decreases after each rent payment is made to reflect an appropriate recognition of the lessor's decreased financial exposure. It typically will be sufficient to repay the lessor's outstanding investment and any remaining equipment loan obligations. Also, it will provide the lessor with its profit, at least to the date of the loss. Typically, the lessee is given a credit for any insurance money received as a result of the loss against the amount owed. In effect, the lessee becomes an insurer of the lessor's investment and profit.

9. *The Economic Analysis: A Critical Aspect*

When a lease underwriter presents a lease investment to a prospective lessor-investor, it generally submits an economic analysis showing the return the investor can expect. If this method of analysis is incorrect or unrealistic, a prospective investor can end up with a disastrous investment. It is not uncommon, for example, for an underwriter to incorporate a sinking fund arrangement in its analysis calculations. The sinking fund simply improves the investor's economics by assuming that cash available over the lease term will earn a certain amount of interest. If, for some reason, the interest rate assumption is too high, the return analysis will be misleading. Thus, a prospective investor must always verify any economic presentation on which it intends to base its investment decision.

▶ **Recommendation:**   If a prospective lessor-investor cannot independently analyze the resulting economics of investing in a lease submitted by an underwriter, it should bring in an independent expert to review the presentation.

10. *A Long-Term Commitment Can Present a Problem*

Frequently, an equipment lease agreement is entered into well before the equipment is actually delivered. This is done for a number of reasons. From a lessor's viewpoint, the faster the lease is "signed up," the less risk there will be that the prospective lessee will change its mind. Prospective lessees are generally interested in proceeding as quickly as possible in order to avoid last minute documentation problems. If a lease agreement is signed well in advance of the equipment delivery date, an unexpected decision by the lessee not to lease the equipment when it arrives will result in an alternative investment opportunity loss for the lessor during the commitment period—particularly if the lease required that the lessor hold a substantial amount of money available. To avoid this risk, prospective lessors frequently require prospective lessees to agree to pay commitment fees or nonutilization fees. These fees guarantee that the lessor will be compensated for holding funds available.

11. *Documentation Expenses Can Ruin a Lease Investment*

Expenses, such as legal fees, involved in documenting a lease transaction can be substantial. Depending on the transaction's complexity, it is not unheard of for the expenses to run into the hundreds of thousands of dollars. A $30,000 expense for a $3 million lease investment may be acceptable; a $500,000 expense will probably not be. If an investor must pay these expenses, a substantial bill could ruin its investment economics. Thus, it is essential for a prospective lease investor to know who is responsible for the various charges and what the estimated amounts will be. Of particular concern will be who is responsible for the expenses if the transaction falls apart before the lease is signed.

► **Recommendations:**

- In an underwritten leveraged lease transaction, the responsibility for the various documentation expenses is frequently outlined in the underwriter's proposal letter. In many cases, the underwriter will offer to pay most of the expenses. However, it is an area of negotiation between the parties. A prospective investor must make sure it has not inadvertently assumed any expense responsibility that has not been considered. The more the expense burden can be shifted to someone else, the less the risk the economic integrity of the investment will be endangered.
- Frequently, a lease underwriter will place the burden for expenses incurred in a collapsed lease transaction on the prospective lessee. It is recommended, however, that a prospective lessee at least require a sharing of the expenses with any other party contributing to the failure.

F. A Checklist for the Leveraged Lease Investor

Before making a commitment to invest in a leveraged lease, a prospective lessor-investor must consider the following points:

If the equipment will not be put on lease at the time the lease commitment is signed, does it matter when the equipment actually delivers? If so,

- ☐ Does the lease agreement provide for a cutoff date beyond which the lessor will not be obligated to buy and lease the equipment?
- ☐ If there is not an equipment delivery cutoff date, does the lease permit the lessor to appropriately adjust the rents if its economics are affected?

☐   Can the lessee substitute equipment if specific equipment delivers late or
      never arrives? If so, are there controls on the type that will be acceptable?

Has the prospective lessee's financial condition been thoroughly reviewed?

*If any credit support for the lessee's lease obligations will be provided, has
the financial condition of the supporting party been carefully reviewed?*

*Has tax counsel been consulted as to any near-term possibility of the tax
laws changing so as to affect the anticipated equipment ownership tax
benefits?*

*In the event there is a tax law change affecting the equipment ownership
tax benefits, will the lessee have to indemnify the lessor for any resulting
adverse effect?*

*Can the entire future tax benefits generated by a lease investment be used?
That is, will the lessor's taxable income be sufficient to cover the available
write-offs?*

*Has tax counsel been consulted as to any future federal income tax rate
changes? If there is a change adversely affecting the leased equipment, who
must bear the burden?*

*Is the residual value of the equipment an important factor in the lessor's
economic analysis? If so,*

☐   Has it been properly assessed?
☐   Has a qualified equipment appraiser been consulted?

*Will the lessor's economics be protected if there is an early lease
termination?*

☐   If it results from a lease default?
☐   If it results from a permitted termination?

*If a termination value concept has been incorporated to protect a lessor's
investment position, have the values been verified?*

*Will the lessor's investment position be protected if there is an equipment
casualty loss?*

☐   If a stipulated loss value (also referred to as casualty loss value) concept has
      been incorporated in the lease, has each value been verified?

Will an underwriter's economic analysis of a proposed lease investment be relied on? If so,

☐ Has it been independently checked?
☐ Are all the investment criteria assumptions, such as sinking fund interest rate, realistic from the prospective lessor's standpoint?

Must the prospective lessor make a long-term commitment to buy and lease equipment? If so, will the lessee be able to decide at the last minute not to lease the equipment without a penalty? If not, has a proper commitment fee or nonutilization fee been incorporated?

Have the expenses for documenting the lease and the responsibility for payment been clearly defined?

☐ If the transaction actually goes through?
☐ If the transaction collapses before the lease documents are signed?

Chapter 10

Financial Analysis of Leases

A. Overview

As described in Chapter 1, although there are a variety of factors to be considered when a prospective lessee or lessor decides whether to enter into an equipment lease, the lease's financial consequences are always important, and often decisive.

Thus, a prospective lessee should not choose to lease before making a financial comparison with other available methods of financing the equipment's acquisition. The extent of the analysis will, of course, depend on how significant the commitment will be. Similarly, a prospective lessor should not commit to a lease until it has been reviewed for investment soundness.

This chapter explains the financial concepts involved in the analysis of a finance lease, from the viewpoint of both a prospective lessee and a prospective lessor. Although it does not explore every possible method of financial lease analysis, the explanation provides the reader with a concise foundation in lessee and lessor financial lease analysis.

B. The Importance of Cash Flow and Timing for a Lessee

In making a financial assessment of whether to lease or to buy equipment, a prospective lessee must take into account the varying cash flows, and their timing, for each alternative. Stated simply, how much are the cash inflows and outflows, and when do they occur? The timing of the cash inflows and outflows is critical because of the principle—referred to as the "time value" of money—that money received earlier is worth more than money later received.

The following example illustrates in simple terms how taking cash flow and its timing into account alters the result of an analysis:

> **Illustrative Example**—*Cash Flow and Time Value:*   An equipment user
> is considering two options: leasing equipment over a seven-year pe-

riod with an annual rent of $990 payable at the beginning of each year; and buying the equipment using a seven-year loan with $1,000 annual payments due at each year's end. By choosing to lease, the company would pay out $990 one year earlier than the $1,000 loan payment it would be required to pay. If the company could earn, for example, 6% a year on its available funds after taxes, giving up the $990 in advance would result in a "loss" of $59.40 (6% × $990 = $59.40) the first year. In this case, the advance payment could be said to cost $1,049.40 ($990 + $59.40 = $1,049.40). Putting other considerations aside, the $1,000 loan payment would have been less expensive. If the company were able to earn only 1% a year after taxes, paying the $990 would result in only a $9.90 "loss" (1% × $990 = $9.90). That is, the effective cost of paying the $990 would have been $999.90, instead of $1,049.40. In the latter case, the $1,000 loan payment could be said to be more expensive.

C. The Prospective Lessee's Analysis

Once a company has decided that certain equipment is needed, it must determine how to finance the acquisition of that equipment. The following discussion will address three alternatives:

1. The user leases the equipment (the leasing alternative).
2. The user draws on its general funds to buy the equipment (the purchase alternative).
3. The user takes out a specific loan to buy the equipment (the financing alternative).

This section will compare these three financial alternatives by using a common method for taking cash flows and their timing into account, sometimes referred to as the discounted cash flow—or "present value"—analysis method. The first step will be to compute the periodic costs and tax savings for each alternative. The next step will be to factor in the timing of those cash flows so there is a basis for comparison by calculating the present value of each alternative's cash flows. To compute the present value of a series of future cash flows, an interest rate—referred to as the "discount rate"—must be selected to discount the flows back to their present worth. The result will be the present value cost of the alternatives.

Because getting to these results involves many computations, the analysis below will center around one hypothetical equipment acquisition situation.

▶ **Note:**   The financial analysis computations from which the examples in this chapter were developed were done on SuperTRUMP, a lease analysis computer software program, by Ivory Consulting Corporation, Orinda, California. The information from the computer analysis results was at times summarized by the author to aid in the explanation of the concepts described in the textual material.

1.   A Typical Equipment User's Financial Alternatives

White Industries wants to acquire a new computer and can use all available tax benefits. White is considering three financing alternatives—the lease alternative, the purchase alternative, and the financing alternative. Additional facts include (assumed for ease of illustration without regard to whether any applicable tax or other rules will be satisfied) the following:

General Data

Computer Cost	$1 million
Depreciable period	5 years
Residual value	$0
ITC	0%
White Industries income tax rate	35%
White Industries tax year	Calendar year
Delivery date	January 1, 1997
Depreciation method	MACRS (half-year, DB/SL 200%)

Proposed Financial Lease

Lease term	7 years
Rental payments	$200,000, payable in 7 annual payments in arrears
Lease simple interest rate	9.1961%
Commencement date	January 1, 1997

Proposed Bank Loan

Loan amount	$1 million, repayable in 7 equal annual payments of $205,405.50 in arrears
Loan term	7 years
Long-term interest rate	10.0%
Commencement date	January 1, 1997

2.   The Cost of the Leasing Alternative

The first step is to compute the after-tax cost of the various alternatives. Table 10-1 sets out the costs for the leasing alternative.

Table 10-1 is computed as follows:

- The rental payments are the annual payments the lessee must make. These begin in 1998 because the rent is payable in arrears.
- The tax savings from rent deductions represents the federal income tax savings White Industries, as an accrual basis taxpayer, would realize from the rent deductions, computed at White Industries' assumed 35% bracket.

Table 10-1. Leasing alternative costs.

Year Ending	Rental Payments	Tax Savings From Rent Deductions	After-Tax Cost	Cumulative After-Tax Cost
Dec. 30, 1997	$ 0	$ 70,000	$(70,000)	$(70,000)
Dec. 30, 1998	200,000	70,000	130,000	60,000
Dec. 30, 1999	200,000	70,000	130,000	190,000
Dec. 30, 2000	200,000	70,000	130,000	320,000
Dec. 30, 2001	200,000	70,000	130,000	450,000
Dec. 30, 2002	200,000	70,000	130,000	580,000
Dec. 30, 2003	200,000	70,000	130,000	710,000
Dec. 30, 2004	200,000	0	200,000	910,000
TOTAL	$1,400,000	$490,000	$910,000	n/a

- The after-tax cost is derived by subtracting the tax savings from the rent deductions from the rental payments.
- The cumulative after-tax cost represents the transaction's total after-tax cost as of each year-end.

The result is a total after-tax cost of $910,000 if White Industries leases the computer.

3.   *The Cost of the Purchase Alternative*

The next step is to compute the after-tax cost of an outright purchase using internal funds. The annual depreciation expense indicated in Table 10-2 is the amount White Industries, as the computer owner, would be entitled to deduct under MACRS over a five-year period. The other columns are computed as in the leasing example (Table 10-1):

Table 10-2. After-tax cost of an outright purchase using internal funds.

Year Ending	Equity	Annual Depreciation Expense	Tax Savings	After-Tax Cost	Cumulative After-Tax Cost
Dec. 30, 1997	$1,000,000	$200,000	$ 70,000	$930,000	$930,000
Dec. 30, 1998	0	320,000	112,000	(112,000)	818,000
Dec. 30, 1999	0	192,000	67,200	(67,200)	750,800
Dec. 30, 2000	0	115,200	40,320	(40,320)	710,480
Dec. 30, 2001	0	115,200	40,320	(40,320)	670,160
Dec. 30, 2002	0	57,600	20,160	(20,160)	650,000
TOTAL	$1,000,000	$1,000,000	$350,000	$650,000	n/a

4. Comparing Cash Flows

Thus, at this point in the analysis, the purchase alternative seems substantially less expensive than the lease alternative since its total after-tax cost is only $650,000, compared with $910,000 for leasing. However, this ignores the leasing cash flow advantage because, as shown in Table 10-3, the total cost of the lease is less until the seventh year.

Table 10-3. Cash flow comparison.

Year	Lease Cumulative After-Tax Cost	Purchase Cumulative After-Tax Cost	Lease Cash Advantage
1997	$(70,000)	$930,000	$1,000,000
1998	60,000	818,000	758,000
1999	190,000	750,000	560,000
2000	320,000	710,000	390,000
2001	450,000	670,000	220,000
2002	580,000	650,000	70,000
2003	710,000	650,000	(60,000)
2004	910,000	650,000	(260,000)

It is obvious that leasing does conserve money in the early years, and those available funds could be put to use elsewhere. The resulting earnings on those funds would offset the disparity in total cost between the two alternatives. Thus, it cannot be concluded that leasing is more expensive until the present value of each alternative's cash flow is compared.

To calculate the present value of the leasing and buying cash flows, White Industries must discount both alternatives' cash flows to their present worth. Choosing a 10% annual discount rate and assuming White Industries pays its estimated taxes on April 15, June 15, September 15, and December 15 of each year, the after-tax cash flows for the leasing and purchase alternatives are shown in Table 10-4.

The discounted cash flow analysis clearly reverses the outcome. The leasing alternative's present worth is $611,253.72, while the purchase alternative's is $720,947.55. Based on this analysis, leasing the computer would be less expensive than buying it with internal funds.

5. The Financing Alternative

The next step is to calculate the financing alternative's cash flow in the same manner. The computation is the same as the purchase alternative (Table 10-2) with the additional factors being the payment of the 10% interest and the tax savings on deducting the interest. The after-tax cost calculations are shown in Table 10-5.

The present worth calculation, again using a 10% discount rate, results (again assuming estimated federal income tax payments are made on April 15, June 15, September 15, and December 15 of each tax year) are shown in Table 10-6.

Table 10-4. Present value comparison.

	Lease		Purchase	
Year	After-Tax Cost	Present Value	After-Tax Cost	Present Value
Jan. 1, 1997	$ 0.00	$ 0.00	$1,000,000.00	$1,000,000.00
Apr. 15, 1997	(17,500.00)	(17,008.64)	(17,500.00)	(17,008.64)
Jun. 15, 1997	(17,500.00)	(16,729.81)	(17,500.00)	(16,729.81)
Sep. 15, 1997	(17,500.00)	(16,321.77)	(17,500.00)	(16,321.77)
Dec. 15, 1997	(17,500.00)	(15,923.67)	(17,500.00)	(15,923.67)
	$ 70,000.00	$ 65,983.89	$ 930,000.00	$ 934,016.11
Jan. 1, 1998	$200,000.00	$181,179.00	$ 0.00	$ 0.00
Apr. 15, 1998	(17,500.00)	(15,408.09)	(28,000.00)	(24,852.95)
Jun. 15, 1998	(17,500.00)	(15,166.50)	(28,000.00)	(24,245.80)
Sep. 15, 1998	(17,500.00)	(14,785.85)	(28,000.00)	(23,657.37)
Dec. 15, 1998	(17,500.00)	(14,425.22)	(28,000.00)	(23,080.38)
	$130,000.00	$121,404.92	$ 112,000.00	$95,639.47
Jan. 1, 1999	$ 200,000.00	$164,130.23	$ 0.00	$ 0.00
Apr. 15, 1999	(17,500.00)	(13,958.16)	(16,800.00)	(13,399.83)
Jun. 15, 1999	(17,500.00)	(13,729.34)	(16,800.00)	(13,180.16)
Sep. 15, 1999	(17,500.00)	(13,394.47)	(16,800.00)	(12,858.70)
Dec. 15, 1999	(17,500.00)	(13,067.78)	(16,800.00)	(12,545.07)
	$130,000.00	$109,980.48	$ 67,200.00	$ 51,983.76
Jan. 1, 2000	$200,000.00	$148,885.24	$ 0.00	$ 0.00
Apr. 15, 2000	(17,500.00)	(12,644.67)	(10,080.00)	(7,283.33)
Jun. 15, 2000	(17,500.00)	(12,437.38)	(10,080.00)	(7,163.93)
Sep. 15, 2000	(17,500.00)	(12,134.03)	(10,080.00)	(8,989.20)
Dec. 15, 2000	(17,500.00)	(11,838.08)	(10,080.00)	(8,818.737)
	$ 130,000.00	$ 99,631.08	$ 40,320.00	$ 28,255.19
Jan. 1, 2001	$200,000.00	$134,693.66	$ 0.00	$ 0.00
Apr. 15, 2001	(17,500.00)	(11,454.78)	(10,080.00)	(6,597.95)
Jun. 15, 2001	(17,500.00)	(11,287.00)	(10,080.00)	(6,459.79)
Sep. 15, 2001	(17,500.00)	(10,992.19)	(10,080.00)	(6,331.50)
Dec. 15, 2001	(17,500.00)	(10,724.09)	(10,080.00)	(6,177.08)
	$130,000.00	$ 90,255.60	$ 40,320.00	$ 25,598.32
Jan. 1, 2002	$200,000.00	$122,018.71	$ 0.00	$ 0.00
Apr. 15, 2002	(17,500.00)	(10,376.86)	(5,040.00)	(2,988.54)
Jun. 15, 2002	(17,500.00)	(10,208.75)	(5,040.00)	(2,939.54)
Sep. 15, 2002	(17,500.00)	(9,957.80)	(5,040.00)	(2,867.85)
Dec. 15, 2002	(17,500.00)	(9,714.93)	(5,040.00)	(2,797.90)
	$130,000.00	$ 81,762.37	$ 20,160.00	$ 11,593.83

Continues

Table 10-4. Continued.

Year	Lease After-Tax Cost	Lease Present Value	Purchase After-Tax Cost	Purchase Present Value
Jan. 1, 2003	$200,000.00	$110,536.50	$ 0.00	$ 0.00
Apr. 15, 2003	(17,500.00)	(9,400.38)	0.00	0.00
Jun. 15, 2003	(17,500.00)	(9,246.27)	0.00	0.00
Sep. 15, 2003	(17,500.00)	(9,020.75)	0.00	0.00
Dec. 15, 2003	(17,500.00)	(8,800.74)	0.00	0.00
	$130,000.00	$ 74,068.36	$ 0.00	$ 0.00
Jan. 1, 2004	$200,000.00	$100,134.79	$ 0.00	$ 0.00
	200,000.00	100,134.79	0.00	0.00
TOTAL	$910,000.00)	$611,253.72	$ 650,000.00	$ 720,947.55

6. Cash Flow Comparisons

As Table 10-6 shows, the financing alternative results in a present value cost of ($589,599.23), the least expensive of the three alternatives. This result is not intended to mean that financing with borrowed funds is always the best alternative, because the specific result was based on the assumed facts. Rather, it is intended to show how dramatically the present value cash flow analysis alters the result. The financing alternative, with the highest cumulative cost, results in the lowest present worth cost, while the purchase alternative, with the lowest cumulative cost, results in the highest present worth cost.

D.   The Lessor's Lease Investment Analysis

The prospective lessor, in making a financial analysis, wants to know how much the return will be on the leased equipment. The concepts of cash flow and present value also play an important part in the lessor's analysis.

This section will analyze two types of leases, the nonleveraged lease—where the lessor uses its own funds entirely to buy the equipment—and the leveraged lease—where the lessor borrows to pay for a portion of the equipment cost.

1. Nonleveraged Lease

As explained earlier, in a nonleveraged lease, the lessor supplies all the money necessary to buy the equipment from its own funds. Whether this type of investment will make economic sense depends on how profitable the transaction will be to the lessor. Thus, determining the profit—commonly referred to as the "rate of return" (usually computed on an after-tax basis)—is a threshold issue in any financial lease investment evaluation.

Traditionally, an after-tax lessor's rate of return has been defined as the inter-

Table 10-5. Present value of financing alternative's cash flow.

Year Ending	Debt Payments	Year-End Principal Balance Outstanding	10.0% Interest on Principal	Tax Savings (Depreciation and Interest)	Net After-Tax Cost
Dec. 30, 1997	$ 0.00	$1,000,000.00	$100,000.00	$105,000.00	$(105,000.00)
Dec. 30, 1998	205,405.50	894,594.50	89,459.45	143,310.81	62,094.69
Dec. 30, 1999	205,405.50	778,645.45	77,846.85	94,452.70	110,952.80
Dec. 30, 2000	205,405.50	651,107.80	65,110.78	63,108.77	142,296.73
Dec. 30, 2001	205,405.50	510,813.08	51,081.31	58,198.46	147,207.04
Dec. 30, 2002	205,405.50	356,488.88	35,648.89	32,637.11	172,768.39
Dec. 30, 2003	205,405.50	186,732.27	18,673.23	6,535.63	198,869.87
Dec. 30, 2004	205,405.50	0.00	0.00	0.00	205,405.02
TOTAL	$1,437,838.50	$0.00	$437,838.50	$503,243.47	$934,595.02

Table 10-6. Present worth calculation.

	Lease		Financing	
Year	After-Tax Cost	Present Value	After-Tax Cost	Present Value
Jan. 1, 1997	$ 0.00	$ 0.00	$ 0.00	$ 0.00
Apr. 15, 1997	(17,500.00)	(17,008.64)	(26,250.00)	(25,512.96)
Jun. 15, 1997	(17,500.00)	(16,729.81)	(26,250.00)	(25,094.71)
Sep. 15, 1997	(17,500.00)	(16,321.77)	(26,250.00)	(24,482.65)
Dec. 15, 1997	(17,500.00)	(15,923.67)	(26,250.00)	(23,885.51)
	$(70,000.00)	$(65,983.89)	$(105,000.00)	$(98,975.83)
Jan. 1, 1998	$200,000.00	$181,179.59	$205,405.50	186,076.43
Apr. 15, 1998	(17,500.00)	(15,408.09)	(35,827.70)	(31,544.94)
Jun. 15, 1998	(17,500.00)	(15,155.50)	(35,827.70)	(31,027.81)
Sep. 15, 1998	(17,500.00)	(14,785.85)	(35,827.70)	(30,271.04)
Dec. 15, 1998	(17,500.00)	(14,425.22)	(35,827.70)	(29,532.72)
	$130,000.00	$121,404.92	$ 62,094.69	$ 63,699.91
Jan. 1, 1999	$200,000.00	$164,130.23	$205,405.50	$168,566.26
Apr. 15, 1999	(17,500.00)	(13,958.16)	(23,613.17)	(18,834.08)
Jun. 15, 1999	(17,500.00)	(13,729.34)	(23,613.17)	(18,525.33)
Sep. 15, 1999	(17,500.00)	(13,394.47)	(23,613.17)	(18,073.49)
Dec. 15, 1999	(17,500.00)	(13,067.78)	(23,613.17)	(17,632.67)
	$130,000.00	$109,980.48	$110,952.80	$ 95,500.68
Jan. 1, 2000	$200,000.00	$148,685.24	$205,405.50	$152,703.83
Apr. 15, 2000	(17,500.000)	(12,644.67)	(15,777.19)	(11,399.85)
Jun. 15, 2000	(17,500.00)	(12,437.38)	(15,777.19)	(11,212.97)
Sep. 15, 2000	(17,500.00)	(12,134.03)	(15,777.19)	(10,939.48)
Dec. 15, 2000	(17,500.00)	(11,838.08)	(15,777.19)	(10,672.66)
	$130,000.00	$99,631.08	$142,296.73	$108,478.87
Jan. 1, 2001	$200,000.00	$134,693.66	$205,405.50	$138,334.09
Apr. 15, 2001	(17,500.00)	(11,454.78)	(14,549.61)	(9,523.58)
Jun. 15, 2001	(17,500.00)	(11,267.00)	(14,549.61)	(9,367.45)
Sep. 15, 2001	(17,500.00)	(10,992.19)	(14,549.61)	(9,138.98)
Dec. 15, 2001	(17,500.00)	(10,724.09)	(14,549.61)	(8,916.08)
	$130,000.00	$ 90,255.60	$147,207.04	$101,388.00
Jan. 1, 2002	$200,000.00	$122,018.71	$205,405.00	$125,316.57
Apr. 15, 2002	(17,500.00)	(10,376.86)	(8,159.28)	(4,838.15)
Jun. 15, 2002	(17,500.00)	(10,206.75)	(8,159.28)	(4,758.84)
Sep. 15, 2002	(17,500.00)	(9,957.80)	(8,159.28)	(4,642.77)
Dec. 15, 2002	(17,500.00)	(9,714.93)	(8,159.28)	(4,529.53)
	$130,000.00	$81,762.37	$172,768.39	$106,547.27

Continues

Table 10-6. Continued.

Year	Lease		Financing	
	After-Tax Cost	Present Value	After-Tax Cost	Present Value
Jan. 1, 2003	$200,000.00	$110,536.50	$205,405.50	$113,524.03
Apr. 15, 2003	(17,500.00)	(9,400.38)	(1,633.91)	(877.68)
Jun. 15, 2003	(17,500.00)	(9,246.27)	(1,633.91)	(863.29)
Sep. 15, 2003	(17,500.00)	(9,020.75)	(1,633.91)	(842.23)
Dec. 15, 2003	(17,500.00)	(8,800.74)	(1,633.91)	(821.69)
	$130,000.00	$ 74,068.36	$198,869.87	$110,119.14
Jan. 1, 2004	$200,000.00	$100,134.79	$205,405.50	$102,841.18
	$200,000.00	$100,134.79	$205,405.50	$102,841.18
TOTAL	$910,000.00	$611,253.72	$934,595.02	$589,599.23

est rate—sometimes referred to as the discount rate—that will discount a lease's after-tax cash flows back to a value equal to the lessor's initial cash outlay. Looking at it another way, it is the rate that, when applied to the original cash investment, will produce the future cash flow amounts generated by the lease.

To explain the investor rate of return analysis approach, we will work through a hypothetical nonleveraged lease example, assuming the following facts:

Equipment Data

Cost	$1 million
Depreciable life	5 years
Residual value	$0
Delivery date	January 1, 1997
Lease commencement date	January 1, 1997
Description	Computer

Lease Investment Data

Lease term	7 years
Rental payments	7 annual payments in arrears, each equal to $200,000
ITC	0%
Investor income tax rate	35%
Depreciation method	MACRS (Half-Year, DB/SL 200)

Based on these facts and the assumption that the lessor is an accrual basis taxpayer, Table 10-7 sets out the lessor's cash flow and federal income reports.

Table 10-7. Lessor's cash flow and federal income reports.

Year Ending	Rent Income	Annual Depreciation	Federal Taxable Income	Total Taxes Paid	Equity	Pre-Tax Cash Flow	After-Tax Cash Flow
Dec. 30, 1997	$ 0.00	$200,000.00	$ 0.00	$ 0.00	$1,000,000.00	$(1,000,000.00)	$(1,000,000.00)
Dec. 30, 1998	200,000.00	320,000.00	(120,000.00)	(42,000.00)	0.00	200,000.00	242,000.00
Dec. 30, 1999	200,000.00	192,000.00	8,000.00	2,800.00	0.00	200,000.00	197,200.00
Dec. 30, 2000	200,000.00	115,200.00	84,800.00	29,680.00	0.00	200,000.00	170,320.00
Dec. 30, 2001	200,000.00	115,200.00	84,800.00	29,680.00	0.00	200,000.00	170,320.00
Dec. 30, 2002	200,000.00	57,600.00	142,400.00	49,840.00	0.00	200,000.00	150,160.00
Dec. 30, 2003	200,000.00	0.00	200,000.00	70,000.00	0.00	200,000.00	130,000.00
Dec. 30, 2004	200,000.00	0.00	0.00	0.00	0.00	200,000.00	200,000.00
TOTAL	$1,400,000.00	$1,000,000.00	$400,000.00	$140,000.00	$1,000,000.00	$400,000.00	$260,000.00

The columns in Table 10-7 are computed as follows:

- Annual depreciation represents the amount of the annual MACRS deduction available to the lessor on the computer as five-year recovery property and applying the half-year convention.
- The federal taxable income is the result of subtracting the annual depreciation deduction from the rent income. The lessor is an accrual basis taxpayer, so the rent income is accrued for the year ending December 30, 1997, for federal income tax purposes, resulting in no federal taxable income for this year ($200,000 rent income − $200,000 depreciation expense = 0), and there would be no federal tax accrued rent income for the year ending December 30, 2004.
- The total taxes paid represents the dollar savings or cost on the income or loss in the federal taxable income column based on a 35% income tax rate. Where the figure is negative, the lessor reduces his overall tax liability by that amount.
- The after-tax cash flow results from adjusting the pre-tax cash flow by the amount of the taxes paid or saved. Thus, where the total taxes paid figure is negative, this amount is added to the pre-tax cash flow; where the total taxes paid figure is positive, this amount is subtracted from the pre-tax cash flow.

Once the after-tax cash flows have been calculated, the after-tax rate of return—often referred to as the after-tax yield—can be found by finding the interest rate that will discount the after-tax cash flows back to the cost of the computer, $1 million. Here, the lessor will receive an after-tax yield equal to 9.1961%.

2. A Lessor's Leveraged Lease Analysis

While the prospective lessor's goal in analyzing a leveraged lease is the same as with a nonleveraged lease, the addition of the loan makes the analysis much more complex. As a result, the investment analysis is frequently done on a computer.

▶ **Recommendation:** Prospective lessees should consider using a computer software analysis program developed for lessors to estimate a proposing lessor's yield on a transaction. Such a program will also enable prospective lessees to compute other lease-related information. For example, stipulated loss values are based on the lessor's anticipated return, and so a program will enable lessees to verify those values reasonably. Unless this is done, there is no way to know if they have been properly computed. Even though, a prospective lessee will typically not have access to a lessor's computer yield analysis input information and, thus, a simulated lessor "run" may not be exact, a fair approximation can be obtained that will be helpful in negotiations.

To show the lessor's analysis in a leveraged lease, this section will use an illustrative example. Because a computer run is often used, the example's as-

Table 10-8. Summary report.

SUMMARY REPORT

Lessee .... White Industries
Lessor .... Gold Leasing Corporation
Prepared Nov-02-1995 12:32 by .... R. Contino
Parameter filename .... text book: lease, leveraged
Parameter path .... c:\ivory\prms\

=========== CASH FLOWS ===========

asset cost	1,000,000.00	100.000000
loan(s)	800,000.00	80.000000
equity	200,000.00	20.000000
rent	1,400,000.00	140.000000
total cash in	1,400,000.00	140.000000
equity	200,000.00	20.000000
principal	800,000.00	80.000000
interest	350,270.80	35.027080
total cash out	1,350,270.80	135.027080
pre-tax cash flow	49,729.20	4.972920
taxes paid	17,405.22	1.740522
after-tax cash flow	32,323.98	3.232398

=========== STATISTICS ===========

Composite Tax Rate 35.0000
IRS Tests .... PASSED

	pre-tax		after-tax	
	effective	nominal	effective	nominal
MISF (per)	12.8902	12.4202	8.3787	8.0731
MISF (mon)	12.8961	12.4256	8.3825	8.0767
IRR PTCF (per)	6.0421	5.8810	3.9274	3.8226

present value at 10.0000% of Rent
on Jan-01-97 .... 97.368376   973,683.76

payback from Jan-01-97 .... 3 yrs 0 mos 0 days
average-life of loan: borrowing .... 4.3784 years

implicit interest rate 9.1961
effective   cost   (without residual) 9.1961
                     (with residual) 9.1961
implicit   cost   (without residual) 9.1961
                     (with residual) 9.1961

=========== Asset(s) ===========

#	cost	delivery	funding	residual	res. date	description
1	1,000,000.00	Jan-01-97	Jan-01-97	0.0000	Jan-01-04	

=========== Depreciation ===========

#		start date	basis	method	term	salv	convention
1	Fed	Jan-01-97	100.0000	DB/SL 200	5.000	0.000	Half-yr

=========== Rent(s) ===========

#	commencement date			# P/Y	advance / arrears		method	amount	% of cost
	commencement date	Jan-01-97							
1	total payments 1,400,000.00			7 Ann	Jan-01-97 → Jan-01-04		Var.Amt	200,000.00	20.000000

=========== Loan(s) ===========

#		# P/Y	advance / arrears		rate	method	amount	% of cost
1	amount 800,000.00			Jan-01-97		Funding	-800,000.00	-80.000000
		7 Ann	Jan-01-97 → Jan-01-04		10.0000	Var.Amt	164,324.40	16.432440

=========== Taxes/Lessor ===========

sinking fund rate (AT) 0.0000
                                              month fiscal year ends .... Dec
---------- Federal ----------
tax calculation method .... Accrual
tax estimation method .... Level

start date	rate		thru	paid	percent
Jan-01-97	35.0000		Mar	Apr	25.0000
			Jun	Jun	25.0000
			Sep	Sep	25.0000
			Dec	Dec	25.0000

sumed facts and analysis, shown in Table 10-8, are set out in the manner of a computer run that is typical of one that a prospective lessor would receive.

The preceding reports present the transaction facts:

- The summary report cash flows section shows the equipment's total cost is $1 million ("asset cost"). The funds to buy the equipment will come from a $200,000 equity investment ("equity") representing 20% of the total cost, and an $800,000 third-party loan ("loan(s)"). This section also sets out other relevant information, such as pre-tax and after-tax cash flows.

Table 10-9. Federal tax statement.

FEDERAL TAX STATEMENT

Lessee .... White Industries
Lessor .... Gold Leasing Corporation
Prepared Nov-02-1995 12:48 by .... R. Contino
Parameter filename .... text book: lease, leveraged
Parameter path .... c:\ivory\prms\

period ending	revenue	interest paid	deprec -iation	taxable income	federal tax DUE	federal tax PAID
Dec-30-97	200,000.00	80,000.00	200,000.00	-80,000.00	-28,000.00	-28,000.00
Dec-30-98	200,000.00	71,567.56	320,000.00	-191,567.56	-67,048.65	-67,048.65
Dec-30-99	200,000.00	62,291.88	192,000.00	-54,291.88	-19,002.16	-19,002.16
Dec-30-00	200,000.00	52,088.62	115,200.00	32,711.38	11,448.98	11,448.98
Dec-30-01	200,000.00	40,865.05	115,200.00	43,934.95	15,377.23	15,377.23
Dec-30-02	200,000.00	28,519.11	57,600.00	113,880.89	39,858.31	39,858.31
Dec-30-03	200,000.00	14,938.58	0.00	185,061.42	64,771.50	64,771.50
TOTAL	1,400,000.00	350,270.80	1,000,000.00	49,729.20	17,405.22	17,405.22

- The summary statistics section lists various investment return information, on a pre-tax and an after-tax basis. It indicates the method of lease analysis used as the multiple investment sinking fund, or MISF method. The implicit lease interest rate is 9.1961% ("implicit interest rate").
- The summary report asset(s) section specifies the equipment delivery date as January 1, 1997 ("delivery"), and that a $0 residual value ("residual") was assumed.
- The summary report depreciation section shows that depreciation was assumed to begin on January 1, 1997 ("start date"), and that the asset will be depreciated over a period of five years ("term"). It also shows that the method of depreciation was a 200% declining-balance method with a switch to the straight-line method ("method"). A half-year depreciation convention was assumed ("convention").
- The summary report rent(s) section provides the fundamental lease structure information. The lease will begin on January 1, 1997 ("commencement date"). The rent is due annually ("P/Y") and is payable in seven installments ("#") of $200,000.00 each ("amount"). The annual rent as a percentage of equipment cost is also listed ("% of cost").
- The summary report loan(s) section describes the assumed third-party loan. The principal amount of the loan is $800,000 ("amount"), and the annual loan interest rate is 10% ("rate"). The analysis further anticipates that the loan funding date is January 1, 1997 ("start date"), and that the loan is payable in seven installments ("#"). The final payment is due January 1, 2004.

The next component in the prospective lessor's analysis is the federal tax consequences of the proposed transaction. A lessor's lease investment presentation will typically include a tax analysis in the form of Table 10-9.

The following shows the steps involved in determining the tax consequences:

- The "revenue" column shows when the lessor must include the rent payments as income. Although the rent is payable annually in arrears, the taxpayer is an accrual basis taxpayer and must report for federal income tax purposes the rent income for the year 1997.
- The "interest paid" column shows how much interest may be claimed for federal income tax purposes and when it may be claimed. Although the interest is payable in arrears, the taxpayer is an accrual basis taxpayer and will accrue the interest deduction for the year 1997.
- The "depreciation" column shows how much and when the prospective lessor may take the depreciation deduction. Since the equipment will be placed in service in 1997, the lessor is entitled to a $200,000 deduction for 1997. In the year 2003, the depreciation expense is $0 because the asset has been fully depreciated through 2002.
- The amounts in the "taxable income" column are computed by subtracting interest and depreciation deductions from the rent revenue.
- The "federal tax due" column shows the amount of tax savings or additional tax payable for each year of the lease. It assumes that the prospective lessor is in the 35% tax bracket. During the first three years, the transaction will reduce the lessor's overall tax liability; after that it crosses over and no longer produces a loss because the depreciation and interest deductions are less than the rental income.

Another frequently included part of an investor presentation is a cash flow report. Table 10-10 presents the lease's cash flow on an annual basis.

The after-tax cash flows are arrived at as follows:

- The "rent & income & residual" column shows the total amount of income received each year.
- The "equity & fees & expenses" column reflects the lessor's initial $200,000 investment in 1997.
- The "debt service" column shows the annual amount of the payment on the third-party loan.
- The "pre-tax cash flow" column reflects the cumulative rent inflow, offset by the equity and loan payment outflows. In 1997, the lessor received no rent payment and made no loan payment, so the only amount in that column is the initial $200,000 equity payment.
- The "taxes paid" column lists the lessor's federal income taxes that will be due.
- The "after tax cash flow" column is the result of adjusting the pre-tax cash flow by the taxes paid. Where the amount in the "taxes paid" column is negative (in the first three years), it is added to the pre-tax cash flow because the tax savings are an inflow of cash that year. Where the taxes paid amount is positive, this amount is subtracted from the pre-tax cash flow.

After the after-tax cash flows are determined, the investment yields are computed in the same manner as they were in the nonleveraged lease example.

Table 10-10. Cash flow report.

CASH FLOW REPORT

```
Lessee ....................................................... White Industries
Lessor ..................................................... Gold Leasing Corporation
Prepared Nov-02-1995 12:44 by .............................................. R. Contino
Parameter filename ......................................... text book: lease, leveraged
Parameter path ................................................. c:\ivory\prms\
```

date	rent & income & residual	equity & fees & expenses	debt service	pre-tax cash flow	taxes paid	after tax cash flow	cumulative after tax cash flow
Jan-01-97	0.00	200,000.00	0.00	-200,000.00	0.00	-200,000.00	-200,000.00
Apr-15-97	0.00	0.00	0.00	0.00	-7,000.00	7,000.00	-193,000.00
Jun-15-97	0.00	0.00	0.00	0.00	-7,000.00	7,000.00	-186,000.00
Sep-15-97	0.00	0.00	0.00	0.00	-7,000.00	7,000.00	-179,000.00
Dec-15-97	0.00	0.00	0.00	0.00	-7,000.00	7,000.00	-172,000.00
	0.00	200,000.00	0.00	-200,000.00	-28,000.00	-172,000.00	
Jan-01-98	200,000.00	0.00	164,324.40	35,675.60	0.00	35,675.60	-136,324.40
Apr-15-98	0.00	0.00	0.00	0.00	-16,762.16	16,762.16	-119,562.24
Jun-15-98	0.00	0.00	0.00	0.00	-16,762.16	16,762.16	-102,800.08
Sep-15-98	0.00	0.00	0.00	0.00	-16,762.16	16,762.16	-86,037.92
Dec-15-98	0.00	0.00	0.00	0.00	-16,762.16	16,762.16	-69,275.75
	200,000.00	0.00	164,324.40	35,675.60	-67,048.65	102,724.25	
Jan-01-99	200,000.00	0.00	164,324.40	35,675.60	0.00	35,675.60	-33,600.15
Apr-15-99	0.00	0.00	0.00	0.00	-4,750.54	4,750.54	-28,849.61
Jun-15-99	0.00	0.00	0.00	0.00	-4,750.54	4,750.54	-24,099.08
Sep-15-99	0.00	0.00	0.00	0.00	-4,750.54	4,750.54	-19,348.54
Dec-15-99	0.00	0.00	0.00	0.00	-4,750.54	4,750.54	-14,598.00
	200,000.00	0.00	164,324.40	35,675.60	-19,002.16	54,677.76	
Jan-01-00	200,000.00	0.00	164,324.40	35,675.60	0.00	35,675.60	21,077.60
Apr-15-00	0.00	0.00	0.00	0.00	2,862.25	-2,862.25	18,215.36
Jun-15-00	0.00	0.00	0.00	0.00	2,862.25	-2,862.25	15,353.11
Sep-15-00	0.00	0.00	0.00	0.00	2,862.25	-2,862.25	12,490.87
Dec-15-00	0.00	0.00	0.00	0.00	2,862.25	-2,862.25	9,628.62
	200,000.00	0.00	164,324.40	35,675.60	11,448.98	24,226.62	
Jan-01-01	200,000.00	0.00	164,324.40	35,675.60	0.00	35,675.60	45,304.22
Apr-15-01	0.00	0.00	0.00	0.00	3,844.31	-3,844.31	41,459.91
Jun-15-01	0.00	0.00	0.00	0.00	3,844.31	-3,844.31	37,615.60
Sep-15-01	0.00	0.00	0.00	0.00	3,844.31	-3,844.31	33,771.30
Dec-15-01	0.00	0.00	0.00	0.00	3,844.31	-3,844.31	29,926.99
	200,000.00	0.00	164,324.40	35,675.60	15,377.23	20,298.37	
Jan-01-02	200,000.00	0.00	164,324.40	35,675.60	0.00	35,675.60	65,602.59
Apr-15-02	0.00	0.00	0.00	0.00	9,964.58	-9,964.58	55,638.01
Jun-15-02	0.00	0.00	0.00	0.00	9,964.58	-9,964.58	45,673.43
Sep-15-02	0.00	0.00	0.00	0.00	9,964.58	-9,964.58	35,708.85
Dec-15-02	0.00	0.00	0.00	0.00	9,964.58	-9,964.58	25,744.28
	200,000.00	0.00	164,324.40	35,675.60	39,858.31	-4,182.71	
Jan-01-03	200,000.00	0.00	164,324.40	35,675.60	0.00	35,675.60	61,419.88
Apr-15-03	0.00	0.00	0.00	0.00	16,192.87	-16,192.87	45,227.00
Jun-15-03	0.00	0.00	0.00	0.00	16,192.87	-16,192.87	29,034.13
Sep-15-03	0.00	0.00	0.00	0.00	16,192.87	-16,192.87	12,841.25
Dec-15-03	0.00	0.00	0.00	0.00	16,192.87	-16,192.87	-3,351.62
	200,000.00	0.00	164,324.40	35,675.60	64,771.50	-29,095.90	
Jan-01-04	200,000.00	0.00	164,324.40	35,675.60	0.00	35,675.60	32,323.98
	200,000.00	0.00	164,324.40	35,675.60	0.00	35,675.60	
T O T A L	1,400,000.00	200,000.00	1,150,270.80	49,729.20	17,405.22	32,323.98	

E.   Conclusion

The key to a proper lessee lease-versus-purchase analysis, or a lessor's investment return analysis, is determining the various cash inflows and outflows on a present value basis. Because of the complexity in making these determinations, and the risk of human computation error, it is always advisable to use one of the many computer programs available today for this purpose.

Chapter 11

Understanding the Lease Accounting Rules

A. Background

During the early years of the equipment leasing business, the accounting profession devoted considerable time and effort to discussing how leases should be accounted for, both from the standpoint of the lessor and the lessee. There were many inconsistencies and substantive disagreements. Finally, in 1973, the subject of accounting for leases was addressed by the accounting profession's standard-setting body, the Financial Accounting Standards Board (FASB), with the firm intent of resolving the many problems. After issuing several exposure drafts and considering a multitude of letters of comments, position papers, and oral presentations from interested parties, it adopted, in November 1976, the Statement of Financial Accounting Standards No. 13—Accounting for Leases. Commonly referred to as FAS No. 13, the rules promulgated therein established the standards to be followed by lessors and lessees in accounting for and reporting lease transactions. However, the problems were not over. Since FAS No. 13 was issued, the FASB has been called on to address a wide variety of issues raised by these financial accounting and reporting guidelines. As a result, various amendments and interpretations have been put out in an effort to clarify or handle many of the guidelines' complex issues.

The lease accounting rules generally apply to lease transactions and certain lease revisions that were entered into on or after January 1, 1977. For calendar or fiscal years beginning after 1980, however, the rules generally had to be retroactively applied to all leases reported.

▶ **Observation:**   Keep in mind that FAS No. 13 is saying that a lease that transfers substantially all of an asset's ownership benefits and risks to the lessee must be treated by the lessee in the same way an asset bought with borrowed money is treated (capital lease treatment). The lessor must account for the lease as a sale or a financing. All other types of leases should be treated as the rental of property (operating lease treatment).

Because of the scope and detail of the lease accounting rules and because the intent of this chapter is to provide the reader with an awareness of the most relevant concepts, every aspect of the rules will not be explained. However, the material will point out and explain in general terms the fundamental issues that have an impact on the everyday decisions involved in leasing equipment.

B. Lease Classifications for a Lessee Vary Significantly: A Careful Analysis Is Essential

Under FAS No. 13, a lessee must account for and report a lease in its financial statements as either a "capital" lease or an "operating" lease, depending on how the transaction is structured. The way the two types of leases are treated varies significantly. In certain cases, it may not be advisable for a company to lease equipment because of the accounting treatment impact.

The criteria for determining whether a lease from the lessee's viewpoint must be classified as capital lease or an operating lease have been well defined in FAS No. 13. At its inception, a lease must be treated as a capital lease if it meets one or more of the following criteria:

- The lease arrangement provides for a transfer of the property's ownership to the lessee by the end of the lease term.
- There is a bargain purchase option in the lease. A bargain purchase option is basically one in which the lessee has a right to buy the property for a price that is so far below its anticipated fair value at the time it can be exercised that it is likely the lessee will elect to buy the property.
- The term of the lease is for a period equal to or greater than 75% of the property's estimated economic useful life.
- The present value of the "minimum lease payments" at the lease inception (excluding any executory costs included in the payments, such as insurance, maintenance, and taxes that the lessor will pay, and any profits on those costs) is equal to or greater than 90% of the excess of the fair value of the leased property (determined at the beginning of the lease) over any investment tax credit (ITC) claimed and expected to be realized by the lessor. The present value computation is calculated by discounting the payments at the lower of the lessor's implicit lease interest rate or the interest rate the lessee would have to pay for a loan running the length of the lease term (the lessee's "incremental borrowing rate"). If it is not practicable for the lessee to learn the lessor's implicit lease rate of interest, the lessee must use its borrowing rate to make the present value computation. FAS No. 13 defines "minimum lease payments" as those payments that the lessee must make or can be required to make. This includes minimum rent payments, residual value guarantees, and payments for failure to renew or extend the lease.

If the lease does not meet any of the above criteria, it is classified as an "operating lease."

Illustrative Example—*The Present Value Test:*   Company Able is considering leasing a new truck from Company Baker. Will the present value test for capital lease classification be met? Here are the facts:

Noncancelable lease term:	5 years
Monthly rent (in arrears):	$180
Fair market value (FMV) at lease inception:	$10,000
Executory costs:	To be paid by Company Able
ITC:	0%
Company Able's borrowing rate:	10%
Company Baker's implicit lease rate:	Company Able unable to determine

In this example, the minimum lease payments are the rental payments. The present value of the monthly rental payments computed by discounting the future rent payment stream by 10% per annum is equal to $8,472. Ninety percent of the truck's FMV at the beginning of the lease is $9,000. Because the present value of the rental stream is less than $9,000, the present value test for capital lease classification is not met.

C. The Accounting Requirements Have an Impact on a Lessee

The way a lessee must account for a lease in its financial statements depends on the lease's classification, that is, whether it falls within the capital or operating lease category. If a lease is classified as a capital lease, the lessee must record it both as an asset and an obligation at an amount equal to the present value (at the beginning of the lease term) of the minimum lease payments during the lease term. Executory costs included in the payments, such as insurance, maintenance, and taxes that the lessor must pay, and any profit on these costs, must be excluded before making the present value computation. (If the lessee is unable to determine the executory costs included in the payments, the lessee must estimate such executory costs and exclude such estimated amount prior to making the present value determination.) If the minimum lease payment present value amount turns out to be greater than the property's "fair value" (generally the property's purchase cost) determined at the beginning of the lease, then the fair value is to be recorded.

The lease payment present value calculation is to be made in the same manner as it is when determining whether a lease meets the present value criteria for capital lease classification. In other words, the payment stream is to be discounted at the lower of the lessee's incremental borrowing rate for a loan of a similar term or the lessor's implicit lease interest rate. If it is not practicable for the lessee to learn the lessor's implicit interest rate, the incremental borrowing rate must be used.

A lessee must write off (amortize) a capital lease under certain specific rules. Which rule must be followed depends on which of the four capital lease classification criteria is met. If the lease meets the first or second criterion (that is, if the ownership of the property is transferred to the lessee at the end of the lease term or the lessee has a bargain purchase option), the lessee must write it off in a manner consistent with its usual depreciation practice for the assets that it owns. If the lease does not meet either of these two criteria, the lessee must amortize the property over a period equal to the lease term and in a manner consistent with its normal depreciation practice down to a value it expects the property to be worth at the end of the lease.

A lessee must account for a lease categorized as an operating lease in a different manner from one that is classified as a capital lease. Generally, the rental payments will be charged to expense as they become due on a straight-line basis, whether they are in fact payable on a straight-line basis. However, there is an exception to the straight-line reporting rule: If another systematic and rational time pattern method for reflecting the property's use benefit is more representative, that method must be used in reporting the rent expense.

▶ **Recommendation:** The difference in reporting impact between a capital lease and an operating lease is significant. If a prospective lessee does not want a lease obligation to appear as a long-term liability, it must make sure that it will be classified as an operating lease. If it cannot be so treated and there are no other compelling reasons to lease, the possibility of buying the asset must be carefully considered in view of the effect on the lessee's financial picture.

D. The Lease Classification Categories for a Lessor Are Extensive

From the standpoint of lessor accounting, FAS No. 13 provides that all leases must be categorized as either sales-type leases, direct financing leases, leveraged leases, or operating leases. Each category has certain attributes that the lessor must carefully take into account when making the classification determination. A lease will be classified as a sales-type lease if *all* the following four tests are met:

1. The lease gives rise to a dealer's or manufacturer's profit or loss to the lessor.
2. One or more of the lessee criteria for capital lease classification are met.
3. The minimum lease payment collectibility is reasonably predictable.
4. There are no important uncertainties as to the amount of any unreimbursable costs that the lessor has not yet incurred.

A dealer's or manufacturer's profit or loss will exist if the fair value of the leased equipment at the beginning of the lease is greater, or less, as the case may be, than the lessor's cost, or carrying amount if different from the cost. This test is usually met when an equipment manufacturer or dealer leases instead of sells its equipment to a lessee. In this case, the fair value of the equipment will typically be greater than its cost or carrying amount.

▶ **Observation:** There are situations under FAS No. 13 when a lessor could accrue a dealer's or manufacturer's type of profit or loss without actually being a dealer or manufacturer. The lease accounting rules provide that a sales-type lease can exist if the equipment's fair value at the lease inception is greater, or less, than the lessor's cost or carrying amount, if this amount is different from the cost.

The criteria for determining whether a lease will be classified as a direct financing lease is much easier to understand once the governing rules for a sales-type lease and a lessee capital lease have been mastered. Very simply, a lease will be a direct financing lease if *all* of the following five tests are satisfied at its inception:

1. One or more of the criteria for lessee capital lease classification have been met.
2. The lease does not fall within the category of leveraged lease.
3. The lease does not give a dealer's or manufacturer's profit or loss to the lessor.
4. The collectibility of the minimum lease payments is reasonably predictable.
5. There are no important uncertainties as to the amount of any unreimbursable costs that the lessor has yet to incur under the lease.

Ascertaining whether a lease will be categorized as a leveraged lease is more complex than determining whether it is a sales-type lease or a direct financing lease. Basically, if a lease is a direct financing lease and meets *all* of the following five criteria, it will be considered a leveraged lease:

1. No less than three participants, a lessee, a lessor, and a long-term lender, are involved.
2. The long-term debt is nonrecourse as to the lessor's general credit.
3. The principal amount of the long-term debt will substantially leverage the lessor's investment.
4. The lessor's net investment goes down in the early lease years after it has been computed and goes up in the later lease years before it is entirely eliminated. (The term "net investment" is explained in the following section.)
5. Any available ITC that the lessor retains is accounted for as one of the lease cash flow components.

The definition of an operating lease is straightforward. It is simply a lease that does not qualify as a direct financing lease, a sales-type lease, or a leveraged lease.

E. The Lessor's Accounting Requirements Are Complex

FAS No. 13 carefully details how lessors must account for sales-type, direct financing, leveraged, and operating leases. The rules are complex and a lessor must make sure they are clearly understood before committing to a lease transaction to avoid an undesirable accounting treatment.

1.   For a Sales-Type Lease

If a lease fits within the sales-type lease category, a lessor must determine its gross investment in the lease. The lessor's gross investment is the sum of the lease rents and other minimum lease payments and the equipment's unguaranteed residual value that will accrue to the lessor's benefit. The minimum lease payment sum must be the computed net of any executory costs included in the payments that the lessor must pay, such as insurance, maintenance, and taxes, and any profit on such costs.

The lessor must record the lease's unearned income. Unearned income is the difference between the lessor's gross investment and the sum of the present values of the minimum lease payments, adjusted for certain executory costs and any profits on such costs, and the equipment's unguaranteed residual value that will accrue to the lessor's benefit. The present value computations are to be made using the lessor's implicit lease interest rate as the disccunt rate. Generally, the lease's unearned income must be amortized to income over the lease term in such a manner so as to produce a constant periodic rate of return on the lessor's net investment in the lease. Net investment is the difference between the gross investment and the unearned income. The accounting rules require that the lessor's net investment in a lease be treated in the same way as other current or noncurrent assets in a classified balance sheet.

The equipment's sale price, defined as the present value of the minimum lease payments, net of certain executory costs, and any profits on those costs, must also be computed and recorded. The equipment's cost (or carrying amount if different), increased by any initial negotiation and consummation expenses (referred to as "initial direct costs"), such as legal fees, and reduced by the present value of the lessor's unguaranteed residual value, must be charged against income for the same period. The present value computation is to be made using a discount rate equal to the lessor's implicit lease interest rate.

The leased equipment's residual value is given special attention. The rules require a lessor to review the estimated value used in the required computations on an annual basis. If the value experiences a permanent decline, the reporting criteria must be adjusted accordingly. On the other hand, if there has been an increase in the expected residual value, then no adjustments are permitted.

2.   For a Direct Financing Lease

A lessor must account for a direct financing lease in somewhat the same manner as a sales-type lease. As with a sales-type lease, a lessor must determine its gross investment in the lease. Gross investment is defined in the same way as it is for a sales-type lease. Unearned income, defined for a direct financing lease as simply the difference between the lessor's gross investment and the equipment's cost, must be recorded. In the event the carrying amount of the equipment is different from its cost, the carrying amount must instead be used in making this computation.

The lessor's net investment in the lease is recorded and is to be classified in the same way as other current or noncurrent assets in a classified balance sheet. Net investment is defined as the gross investment, plus any amortized initial direct costs minus the unearned income.

The rules require the unearned income and the initial direct costs of putting a lease transaction together, such as commissions or legal fees, to be amortized to income over the lease term in such a way as to show a constant periodic return rate on the lessor's net investment. However, other methods of income recognition may be used if the results produced do not differ materially from those obtained by using this suggested method.

The equipment's estimated residual value must be reviewed annually. If a permanent decrease in the value estimate has occurred, the computations incorporating the value must be adjusted accordingly. No adjustments are allowed to reflect an increase in the value estimate.

3. For an Operating Lease

If a lease is deemed to be an operating lease, the accounting treatment is somewhat simpler for a lessor than if the lease is a sales-type or direct financing lease. Equipment subject to such a lease must be recorded on the lessor's balance sheet in or near the "property, plant, and equipment" category. Also, the equipment must be depreciated under the lessor's usual depreciation policy. The investment in the equipment must be shown to be reduced by the accumulated depreciation.

The rent received under an operating lease is handled in a straightforward manner. It is reported as income when and as due and is taken in on a straight-line basis, regardless of how the rent is actually to be paid. However, there is an exception to this reporting method: If any other systematic method for reporting the rent income would more accurately reflect the time pattern reduction in the property's use benefit, then that method must be used.

In general, any initial direct costs incurred by the lessor in connection with putting the transaction together cannot be treated as they are in a direct financing lease situation. They must be deferred and allocated over the term of the lease in proportion to how the rent income is recognized. However, these costs may be expensed when incurred if the effect would not be materially different from what it would be under the deferred treatment.

4. For a Leveraged Lease

The lessor's investment in a leveraged lease must be stated net of the transaction's nonrecourse debt. The lessor's investment at any point in time is determined by computing (1) the rents receivable, minus the portion going to pay the debt service on the nonrecourse debt; (2) a receivable for any ITC amount to be realized; (3) the equipment's estimated residual value; and (4) the transaction's unearned and deferred income. The unearned and deferred income at any point is defined as the sum of the lease's estimated remaining and unallocated pretax income or loss, adjusted by subtracting any initial direct costs, and any ITC that has not yet been allocated to income over the lease term.

The lessor must also determine the rate of return on its net investment during the years that it is positive. When applied to the net investment during the years it is positive, the rate of return is defined as the rate that will distribute the net income to these years. The lessor's net investment in a leveraged lease is simply the lessor's investment reduced by the deferred taxes arising from the difference between the lessor's pretax accounting income and taxable income.

As with a sales-type lease and a direct financing lease, the lessor must review the estimated residual value of the equipment each year and adjust it downward if it appears that the estimated amount was excessive and that it has undergone a permanent reduction over that originally estimated. If an adjustment is necessary, certain other recalculations are necessary using the new residual assumption. No upward adjustment is permitted if there has been an estimated increase in the residual value.

F. Certain Accounting Rules Govern Sale-Leaseback Situations

Because many leases arise through sale-leaseback transactions, it is worthwhile mentioning the governing lease accounting rules. A "sale-leaseback" is defined as a transaction in which an owner sells equipment to a third party and leases it back. The buyer will then be the lessor and the original owner will become the lessee.

From the lessee's viewpoint, the lease accounting rules are the same as in any lease situation. That is, if the lease would otherwise have to be classified as a capital lease, it will still be considered as a capital lease. If it qualifies as an operating lease, it will still be accounted for as an operating lease. However, the reporting of the profit or loss from the equipment's sale is specially treated. If the lease is a capital lease, the seller-lessee must defer any profit or loss resulting from the sale to the lessor-buyer and amortize it in proportion to the amortization of the leased equipment. If the lease is classified as an operating lease, generally any profit or loss must be amortized in proportion to the rents charged to expense over the term of the lease.

If the lease would qualify for a lessee as a capital lease, the collectibility of the minimum lease payments is reasonably predictable, and if there are no important uncertainties as to the amount of any unreimbursable costs that the lessor has yet to incur under the lease, the transaction must be treated by the lessor as a purchase and a direct financing lease. If it does not, it must be accounted for as a purchase and an operating lease.

G. A Lease Classification Checklist for Lessees

The lessee can use the following checklist as a general guideline in classifying its leases for accounting and reporting purposes:

If a lease meets one or more of the following criteria, has it been classified as a capital lease?

☐   Does the lease transfer the equipment's ownership to the lessee by the end of the lease?

☐ Does the lessee have the right to buy the leased equipment at a price well below its value at the time the right can be exercised?

☐ Does the lease run for a term that is equal to or greater than 75% of the equipment's estimated economic useful life?

☐ Is the present value of the rent and other minimum lease payments, net of certain executory costs and the profits on such costs, equal to or greater than 90% of the equipment's fair value at the lease inception, minus any investment tax credit to be retained by the lessor?

If it is practicable for the lessee to learn the implicit lease rate computed by the lessor and it is lower than the lessee's incremental borrowing rate, has the present value test been computed using this rate?

☐ If it is not lower, has the value been calculated using the lessee's incremental borrowing rate?

*If a lease does not meet **any** of the tests above, has it been classified as an operating lease?*

H. A Lease Classification Checklist for Lessors

The lessor can use the following checklist as a general guideline in classifying its leases for accounting and reporting purposes. [It should be noted that if a lease does not qualify as a sales-type lease, a direct financing lease, or a leveraged lease, in accordance with the following applicable guidelines, it must be classified as an operating lease. In addition, if the lease arises out of a sale-leaseback transaction, it must, as mentioned in Section F of this chapter, also comply with certain sale-leaseback governing rules.]

A lease must be classified as a sales-type lease if it meets all of the following:

☐ The lessor incurs a manufacturer's or dealer's type of profit or loss.

☐ The lease meets at least one of the following criteria:

1. The lease transfers the equipment's ownership to the lessee by the end of the lease.
2. The lessee has the right to buy the leased equipment at a price well below its expected fair value at the time the right can be exercised.
3. The lease runs for a term that is equal to or greater than 75% of the equipment's estimated economic useful life.
4. The present value of the rent and other minimum lease payments, net of certain executory costs and the profits on such costs, is equal to or greater than 90% of the equipment's fair value as of the lease inception, minus any ITC to be retained by the lessor.

☐ The collectibility of the rent and other minimum lease payments is reasonably predictable.

☐ There are no important uncertainties concerning the lessor's yet-to-be-incurred unreimbursable costs.

A lease (other than a leveraged lease) must be classified as a direct financing lease if it meets all of the following:

☐ The lessor does not incur a manufacturer's or dealer's type of profit or loss.
☐ The lease meets at least one of the following criteria:

  1. The lease transfers the equipment's ownership to the lessee by the end of the lease.
  2. The lessee has the right to buy the leased equipment at a price well below its expected fair value at the time the right can be exercised.
  3. The lease runs for a term that is equal to or greater than 75% of the equipment's estimated economic useful life.
  4. The present value of the rent and other minimum lease payments, net of certain executory costs and the profits on such costs, is equal to or greater than 90% of the equipment's fair value as of the lease inception, minus any ITC to be retained by the lessor.

☐ The collectibility of the rent and other minimum lease payments is reasonably predictable.
☐ There are no important uncertainties concerning the lessor's yet-to-be incurred unreimbursable costs.

A lease must be classified as a leveraged lease if all of the following criteria are met:

☐ The lease qualifies as a direct financing lease.
☐ The lease involves at least three parties—a lessee, a long-term lender, and a lessor.
☐ The long-term debt financing is nonrecourse to the general credit of the lessor.
☐ The amount of long-term debt will substantially leverage the lessor's invested funds.
☐ The lessor's "net investment," once it is made, goes down in the early lease years and rises during the later lease years before it is eliminated.
☐ Any available ITC that the lessor retains is accounted for as one of the lease cash flow components.

I. Summary of Accounting Lease Classifications

Table 11-1 summarizes in simple terms the prominent aspects of each accounting lease classification for lessees and lessors. Only the most salient have been listed. The reader is referred to the earlier text of this chapter for the details of each lease classification.

Table 11-1. Key characteristics of lessee/lessor lease classifications.

Lessee/Lessor	*Key Characteristics*
Lessee Lease Classifications	
Capital lease	A lease that runs for 75% or more of an asset's useful life, automatically transfers ownership at the lease end, has a bargain purchase option, or whose rents present value to 90% or more of the asset's fair value, adjusted for any ITC.
	It is treated as a purchase in the lessee's financial statements, the lease recorded as both an asset and an obligation. Most long-term, full payout leases fall into this classification
Operating lease	Any lease not falling within the capital lease classification. Generally, it is the most desirable lease classification for lessee financial reporting purposes. The rent payments are charged to expense as they become due.
Lessor Lease Classifications	
Sales-type lease	A lease that gives rise to a dealer's or manufacturer's profit or loss. In certain situations, even a lessor, not a dealer or manufacturer, may have to report a lease as a sales-type lease.
Direct financing lease	A lease that does not fall within the leveraged lease classification and that does not give rise to a dealer's or manufacturer's profit or loss must be classified as a direct financing lease.
Leveraged lease	A direct financing lease in which there is a third-party nonrecourse lender.
Operating lease	Any lease that is not classified as either a sales-type lease, a direct financing lease, or a leveraged lease.

Chapter 12

The Business of Leasing Equipment

A. Overview

The leasing business in the United States is mature, and competition is intense. There are still many attractive profit opportunities, but you must approach the business knowledgeably and carefully. If you do not, mistakes are inevitable and devastating losses are likely. This has been attested to over and over during the past decade by the many nonbank and bank-affiliated leasing company problems, closings, sell-offs, and bankruptcies. A quick review of a typical problem operation invariably shows a variety of historically repetitive and obvious mistakes. Mistakes that frequently went unnoticed for years—ones often resulting from top management's lack of streetwise business expertise, short-sighted attempts to maintain near-term profits, or desire to increase profit-based bonuses. So if you are considering entering the leasing business or want to expand or improve the profitability of an existing leasing operation, a solid understanding of the basic business strategies successful leasing companies use today to survive and make money is essential. That is what this chapter is about.

The threshold question is why would an individual or company set up a leasing operation? There are a number of basic reasons: (1) to use available equipment ownership tax benefits to offset or defer tax liabilities from unrelated revenue sources—tax shelter; (2) to earn financing profits—the difference between the cost of purchasing and leasing equipment and lease revenues; and (3) to assist in marketing products sold by an affiliate of the leasing company. For example, a manufacturer or vendor of telephone systems may establish a captive (in-house) leasing operation to facilitate the sale of its equipment. Having readily available and attractive product financing, particularly when competitors do not, can cinch the product sale. Paying $200 a month rather than $10,000 up front for needed equipment makes the customer's purchase leap of faith much easier.

▶ **Observation:** To ensure your chances of success in today's competitive equipment leasing environment, you must have a value-added marketing strategy—one, for example, that fills a niche not already crowded with other lessors.

If you can identify such a niche, the opportunity for growth can be great and the business prospects exciting.

B. Key Profit Strategies

Aside from financing profits, equipment leasing offers a leasing company a number of additional benefits. Here are the key ones.

1. *Valuable Assets Purchased With Someone Else's Money*

How would you react if a wealthy neighbor asked you to lease her an $80,000 BMW? Assume you could borrow the entire purchase price from your local bank at a rate that gave you a $200 monthly profit. And assume the loan could be based solely upon your neighbor's credit, having no impact on your future borrowing capabilities. Further, if your neighbor defaulted on her lease payments for any reason, you would not be responsible for paying off any remaining loan balance. Assume also that the lease would be for four years, the rents would pay off the entire bank loan, and, when the lease ended, your neighbor would have to return the car to you in excellent condition. The result: At the end of four years, you would own a cream-puff BMW free and clear to do with as you wished: sell it, re-lease it, or simply use it as your personal car. Sound good? Most people would agree that it does. That's the business of equipment leasing.

You might think it impossible to get a bank to loan you money to invest without holding you responsible for its repayment. But so-called nonrecourse equipment loans, discussed in Chapter 9, are available because banks and other lenders will loan money on the strength of a strong lease contract, generally without checking the creditworthiness of the owner-lessor. As you now know from Chapter 3, the lease must contain a hell-or-high-water clause that obligates the lessee to keep sending in the rent payments no matter what happens, even if the lessor-owner fails to live up to his lease obligations to the lessee or the equipment is destroyed or otherwise unavailable for use. So if you have a hell-or-high-water lease with a good credit lessee, nonrecourse equipment loans are available. The most interesting aspect of nonrecourse loans is that, in effect, they provide the lessor-owner with an unlimited borrowing capacity.

If this sounds attractive, consider going a step further. What if nine more wealthy neighbors approached you at the very same time to have you lease them BMWs under the same terms—for four-year terms and providing you with a $200 per month profit on each car? Your profit would be $2,000 a month and you would own ten BMWs at the end of their respective four-year lease terms, all free and clear. Not a bad return for a no-money-down investment.

That's one basic strategy of the leasing business—getting creditworthy companies to pay for and maintain assets that can be sold or re-leased at a profit, all the time making a profit while waiting for their return. Once the lease deals are put together, all the leasing company has to do is to remember to send out the rent bills and to deposit the payment checks when they come in. And if you, as a lessor, don't want to do that, you can sell the lease packages off at a profit equal, or close, to what you would have earned if you had been a patient businessperson.

2. Windfall Profits: A Possibility

Now using the prior section example, let us assume that at the end of the four-year lease each BMW is worth 50% of original cost. In addition to a $200 monthly profit, selling each car at the end of its lease would bring in $40,000 in end-of-lease, or residual, revenues.

The *residual value revenue expectations,* what assets are expected to be worth at the end of their lease periods, are an important part of today's leasing business. It's not unusual for equipment residual values to range from 10% to 100% of the equipment's original cost—and sometimes even higher. The residual values, of course, depend on the type of asset, its return condition, inflation, and market demand. For example, in the mid-to late 1980s, some 10-year-old river barges would have sold for prices in excess of their original purchase price.

In the early days of the leasing business, when competition was not intense and financing spread profits were high, an asset's expected worth at the end of its lease term was almost irrelevant. When the typical lease was over, a lessor had made all the money it needed from the lease transaction, even if the asset had to be junked. But many quickly augmented their profit objectives when word got around that a few aircraft lessors had made lotterylike windfall profits from selling off their end-of-lease aircraft. Some aircraft sales values after a 10- to 15-year lease approached, or exceeded, original cost. Add to that the fact that these aircraft lessors had, through lease term rents, all but a minimal amount (often between 10% and 15% of original cost) of their invested principal repaid, and made a tidy profit, and you had some very happy aircraft lessors. As you might expect, other leasing companies soon caught on to the aircraft residual "end game" and began to stay alert for high residual return possibilities in other types of equipment as well. The residual end game became so profitable that some lessors even adopted a strategy of acquiring multimillions of dollars of high residual value potential equipment solely for the end-of-lease sale or re-lease profits. They cut their lease term profits to the bare minimum necessary to win business, with rents often covering little more than basic transaction and overhead costs, anticipating profits when the equipment came off lease. Some leasing companies became so aggressive that they wrote leases that produced a loss during the lease term, counting on the fact that once through the initial start-up phase, the cash flow squeeze was over and yearly residual profits would provide solid bottom-line returns. Heavy reliance on residual profits is still a primary objective in leasing today, particularly in "big ticket" lease transactions.

There is risk, however, in placing primary emphasis on residual profit expectations. Lessors that do run the risk that if there is no market demand for it or if it becomes technologically obsolete, the equipment won't be worth much more than scrap value. If rents just pay overhead, the potential for loss is great, particularly if unexpected costs are incurred. And if residual revenue expectations are not met, there is little or no economic return for the effort. Some aircraft lessors, for instance, encountering a market demand lull in the 1980s, had to store equipment and wait years for better sale or re-leasing opportunities. Equipment and industry diversification can reduce this type of risk.

3. The Repeat Business Customer Annuity

Developing an extensive customer lease portfolio should be a strategic business objective of every leasing company. Qualified prospects are valuable; customers that lease, often lease again—at times forgetting about getting competitive bids. Noncompetitive bid situations assure lessors of solid returns.

With qualified leasing customer contacts, a leasing company can readily originate new business with little expense—often a simple letter offering lease financing, with a follow-up telephone call, is enough to identify upcoming leasing opportunities. And doing business with a good-paying existing customer has far less credit risk than dealing with an unknown customer. Clearly, there is no substitute for firsthand payment experience. All the credit-due diligence in the world may not uncover credit potholes—for example, financial statements and discussions with trade references and lenders rarely always tell the whole credit story.

a. The Low Rate Strategy of Buying Repeat Customers

There is no doubt that approaching leasing customers that you have already done business with makes the lease financing sale much easier. If rapport and trust have been established through earlier transactions, many of the marketing barriers are removed. So it may make sense when approaching prospects that regularly lease equipment to make your first deal very attractive—even at times to consider making a deal offer at less than break-even rates if necessary to win business, thereby making an investment in a potentially profitable long-term customer relationship. Satisfied lessees often give incumbent lessors exclusive deals from time to time, deals which can often provide better-than-market lease rates for the lessor.

b. The Master Lease Strategy of Tying Up Repeat Customers

When dealing with new customers, putting a master lease agreement in place with them will pay dividends. Doing so cuts the financing costs for all parties. As explained in Chapter 3, a master lease is a two-part document—the boilerplate portion contains the basic lease terms and conditions, which will remain the same from deal to deal, and an attachment, often called a schedule, which is a short (often one to two pages in length) document which permits future business to be simply added by specifically incorporating the new equipment under the term of the master, or boilerplate, document portion. Having only to negotiate a one or two page document for lease deals allows future financings to be handled with minimal effort and expense on both sides. Lessors with master leases in place are given an edge over competitors not having ones in place because of the ease of documentation, in many situations getting the last opportunity to win by matching the lowest bidder. In some cases, they are awarded deals

even when they are not the lowest rate simply because documentation is easy
and documentation costs are less.

C. Making Money in the Leasing Business

There are many ways to profit in a lease transaction. To succeed, and sometimes
even survive, in the highly competitive business of equipment leasing, a leasing
company must take advantage of every possible profit opportunity. The obvious
areas for leasing profits are

- Interest charges
- Tax benefits
- Equipment sales or re-leases

And, for the less experienced lessor, the less obvious ones are

- Interim rent
- Prepayment penalties
- Casualty occurrences
- Insurance cost markups
- Upgrade financing
- Documentation fees
- Filing fees
- Maintenance charges
- Repair costs
- Excess use charges
- Equity placement fees
- Leveraging a lease investment with third-party debt
- Commitment fees
- Nonutilization fees
- Remarketing fees
- Late payment charges
- Collection telephone charges
- Deal rewrite fees
- Equipment redelivery charges

The profit opportunity areas available to a leasing company may vary depending on the type of transaction, the level of credit risk involved, the dollar
size of the lease transaction, and the business practices of its competition. For
example, in the case of multimillion dollar leases of typically high residual value
equipment, a substantial portion of lease profits come from the equipment ownership tax benefits and the end-of-lease equipment sale, or re-lease, proceeds. In
small ticket transactions, such as $10,000 to $50,000 leases, the lessor expects little
or no profit from end-of-lease sales. Instead it looks to its lease interest rate
spread—the difference between its cost of funds and the interest rate implicit in
the lease—and documentation and deal review charges.

The following discussion of lease profit areas has been taken primarily from earlier material throughout this book and summarily provided below to enable the reader interested in looking at involvement in equipment leasing to have all key aspects pulled together for review.

1. The Basic Lease Profit Areas

The principal lease transaction profit areas are interest charges, equipment tax benefits, and residual earnings. Not maximizing any one can significantly reduce the potential for transaction profits.

a. Interest Charges

The obvious way to make money in an equipment lease is through financing profits. Financing profit, sometimes referred to as financing spread, is the difference between a leasing company's cost of money and the lease interest rate charged. The higher the interest rate charged, the greater the financing profit.

> **Illustrative Example**—*Financing Profit:* Assume a lessor borrows money at a 9% per annum interest rate and charges a lease interest rate of 11%. Its financing spread is 2% per annum. By increasing the lease interest rate to 12%, its financing profit increases to 3%.

▶ **Lease Marketing Tip:** Prospective lessees, particularly small ticket lessees, are often more sensitive to their monthly rent cash outflow than to the lease interest charged. So offering a longer lease term (for example, stretching out the period of lease payments from three years to five years) can maintain, or increase, solid financing profits and provide an acceptable rent payment dollar amount for the lessee. For example, assume that a lessor's cost of money is 9% per annum, and that its desired financing spread is 3% per annum. Assume also that the equipment involved will have a zero end-of-lease value. In this case, the monthly in arrears payment on a three-year lease of a $400,000 lathe would be $13,286. If the prospective lessee finds the $13,286 monthly payment too high, stretching the lease term to five years at the same lease interest rate (9% + 3% = 12%) would drop the monthly lease payment to $8,897. Stretching out the lease term provides an opportunity to build in higher financing profits in a lease, while still keeping periodic cash flow payments relatively lower. For example, increasing the lease interest rate charge to 15% over the same five-year term would result in a monthly lease rent of $9,516.

Market competition, reasonableness, and sometimes state usury laws limit how much financing spread a lessor can build into its lease rate. Typically, the smaller the lease dollar size, the higher the lease interest rate charged. For example, interest rates on $5,000 to $50,000 equipment transactions generally range from 12.5% to 24% per annum. As transactions approach $100,000 and over, simple interest rates are generally in the 10.5% to 13.5% range. Once the deal size hits $1,000,000, rates can run 2% to 4% below the lessee's equivalent long-term borrowing rate. In the latter case, for example, a $4,000,000, 12-year aircraft lease for a lessee that borrows long-term money at 11% per annum could run anywhere from 7% to 9% per annum.

► **Observations:**

- A lower lease rate in larger equipment transactions is not as bad as it may appear because greater absolute dollar profits are available. For example, a profit of 2% on a $1,000,000 lease is $20,000, whereas it is $200 on a $10,000 lease.
- The competitive nature of the multimillion dollar lease transaction market often forces lessors to price their lease rates with little or no financing spread profit, making them look to other transaction aspects, such as tax benefits and equipment residual proceeds, to offset minimal, or nonexistent, cash flow.

► **Recommendation:** Although leasing companies are not generally regulated by federal or state laws, times are changing. Before setting what may be a high lease interest rate, have your lawyer check the governing state laws. A few states have enacted, or are considering implementing, rules which protect lessees. For example, unconscionable profit laws, referred to as usury laws, originally designed to protect individuals, have been extended in Texas to corporations in installment sale-type financing. Included are low fixed price purchase option leases. If your lease runs afoul of state law, a lessee may be able to cancel the lease agreement and walk away without penalty. If you discover after entering into a lease that you have inadvertently charged a lease rate higher than governing law permits, it is always a good idea to approach the lessee with an offer to reduce it, using a plausible business excuse, such as you have decided to make a financing rate adjustment to certain preferred customers.

b. Equipment Tax Benefits

The tax aspects of equipment leasing are explained in detail in Chapters 5, 6, and 7. Very often, particularly in multimillion dollar equipment leases, the tax benefits available to a lessor are a critical component in computing anticipated transaction profits. In fact, good credit companies considering the multimillion dollar lease transactions typically demand that lease rates reflect, and therefore pass through to a lessee in the form of relatively lower rent charges, at least a portion of the transaction tax benefits. Determining how to take into account the transaction tax benefits is very complex—and, fortunately today, there are many lessor profit (sometimes referred to as "yield") analysis software programs that make the job much easier. The reader is referred to Chapter 10 for a discussion of the lessor yield analysis approach.

As explained in earlier chapters, by leasing equipment a lessor, as equipment owner, has the right to claim equipment ownership tax benefits, such as depreciation and any available investment tax credits. In addition, in the case of leveraged lease transactions, there are certain other tax write-offs, such as the interest charges on the long-term equipment loans. On the other hand, a lessee typically cannot claim any equipment ownership tax benefits, but is entitled to deduct the rent payments as a business expense.

▶ **Observation:** By taking into account equipment-related tax benefits, a lessor is able to offer lower rents while maintaining its profit objectives. For example, a lessor who typically offers an annual lease rate of 10% could reduce the lease interest rate to 8% without reducing the economic return by incorporating depreciation benefits into the rent pricing.

c. Residual Earnings

In pricing a lease transaction (setting the lease rents), an ideal lessor objective is to have sufficient lease term rents to return its entire equity investment, repay any equipment loans, and provide a solid profit, with any end-of-lease sale or release (often referred to simply as "residual") earnings simply as windfall profits. In other words, the objective is to set the lessee lease rents using a zero equipment residual assumption. In small ticket equipment transactions this is typically possible; however, largely due to market competition, this is not typically possible in multimillion dollar equipment lease transactions.

2. Additional Areas of Potential Lease Profit

A leasing company can earn significant profits from less obvious transaction aspects, such as interim rent, prepayment penalties, casualty occurrences, insurance cost markups, upgrade financing costs, documentation fees, filing fees, maintenance charges, repair costs, excess use charges, equity placement fees, leveraged leasing investment, debt costs and placement fees, commitment fees, nonutilization fees, remarketing fees, late payment charges, collection telephone call charges, deal rewrite charges, and equipment redelivery charges. Paying attention to each potential profit area can produce attractive additional economic returns.

a. Interim Rent

One way many lessors build in extra profit dollars is to provide for interim rent. Sometimes called pre-commencement or stub period rent, it is rent that is payable for a period running from the start of the lease to the beginning of its primary, or main, term. For example, a seven-year lease transaction might provide for the primary term to begin on the first day of the month. If the equipment is not delivered and accepted under the lease contract on the first of a month, there will be an interim rent period. If equipment was delivered, for instance, on January 7, the seven-year period would begin February 1, with an interim term running from January 7 through January 31. If the lease rents are computed on the basis of the primary term rents, the stub period rent is a windfall profit.

b. Prepayment Penalties

A typical net finance lease may not be canceled for any reason—thus guaranteeing the lease profits, subject of course to a rent payment default. However, some prospective lessees want the right to terminate a lease early if the equipment becomes obsolete or surplus to their needs. This request can be an opportunity for profit. Generally, when a right to terminate a lease early is granted, it is permitted only upon payment of an amount equal to a predetermined termination value. Ensuring the amount that a lessee must pay upon any lease termination not only makes a lessor economically whole, but also has a premium built in, for example, 5% of equipment cost, and the benefit of the original bargain can be preserved—with a profit.

Generally, when an early lease termination right is granted, the lessor incorporates a termination payment schedule into the lease. Each applicable termination payment is expressed as a percentage of the equipment's cost for each rent payment period in which a termination could be exercised. Payment of the appropriate termination value amount on any permitted rent date allows the lessee to terminate a lease as of that time. For example, a monthly lease might provide for a termination payment of 85% of equipment cost when the sixth rent payment is made, 83% of equipment cost when the seventh rent payment is made, and so on.

Properly structured, payment of a lease termination value will return the entire remaining equipment investment, with its anticipated profits at least to the date of termination, provide funds to pay off any equipment purchase loans, and add an additional profit, the exercise penalty.

c. Casualty Occurrences

An equipment casualty occurrence brings a lease to its end. In the same manner as a lessee-elected early lease termination, provision must be made for the protection of a lessor's investment and profit, at least until the date of the casualty occurrence.

Typically, leases contain casualty loss provisions requiring that the lessee pay a predetermined casualty value payment. These payments are usually prescribed by formula in a lease provision or in a casualty payment schedule. Like termination payments, they are designed to make a lessor economically whole, including payment for loss of anticipated residual profits. For example, in the event of an equipment casualty occurrence during a specified rent payment period, a monthly lease might provide for the payment of a casualty value amount equal to 98% of equipment cost anytime during the second rent payment period, 96% of equipment cost anytime during the third rent payment period, and so on.

In structuring equipment casualty payment obligations, the lessor can build in a reasonable profit to compensate for the loss of a long-term investment opportunity. When casualty payments are expressed as a percentage of equipment cost in a casualty payment schedule, one way to do this is to increase rock-bottom casualty loss payments by a small percentage, for example, 2% of equipment, added on each specified casualty value percentage.

d. Insurance Cost Markups

Equipment insurance is a must in any equipment lease, and, generally, the lessee is required to provide the coverage through its insurance carrier. Although care must be taken by a lessor not to run afoul of any insurance regulations, providing the insurance and passing the cost on to the lessee with a markup can create another lease profit opportunity. For example, a lessor might charge $14 a year for a $2,000 casualty insurance policy costing $8 a year, making a $6 profit. On a $20,000,000 equipment portfolio, this means $60,000 annually. A lessor with insurance volume purchasing power can offer equipment lease insurance at a markup, while still providing rates equal to or lower than that available to most lessees.

There is another added benefit to a lessor providing the insurance coverage; doing so eliminates the need to administratively track compliance with the insurance coverage requirement of a lessee.

e. Upgrade Financing Costs

Equipment upgrades, when a lessee adds to or modifies existing leased equipment, can provide an opportunity for leasing profit. If the upgrade is not readily removable or has no stand-alone value, generally the existing lessor is the only one willing or able to finance it. In these situations, the lessee has two choices: to purchase the upgrade with its own funds or to agree to whatever lease rate the lessor offers. In many situations, if the upgrade is deemed, under the terms of the lease, to become the property of the lessor because, for example, it becomes an integral part of the leased equipment and cannot be removed without damage to the existing equipment, paying a higher financing cost may still be cheaper than purchasing an upgrade which automatically becomes the lessor's property.

f. Documentation and Filing Fees

Many lessees, particularly those leasing small ticket items of equipment such as fax machines and small telephone systems, will pay transaction processing, documentation preparation, and security interest filing fees with little or no objection. Small lease transaction documentation fees generally run from $50 to $200 per transaction. Security interest filing fees, such as state Uniform Commercial Code filing fees, are generally nominal, ranging from $15 to $25. The more fees a lessee pays, the less a lessor's profit erosion.

g. Equipment Maintenance and Repair Charges

Requiring a lessee to pay for all normal equipment upkeep, such as maintenance and repair charges, protects a lessor's investment by ensuring that the lessor's profit is not eroded by unexpected maintenance and repair costs. A lessor able to shift the full cost burden of equipment maintenance and repair to a lessee in effect creates profit by eliminating resale or re-lease rehabilitation expenses when the lease term ends. In a typical finance lease arrangement, the lessee assumes all equipment upkeep expense. In other types of equipment leases it is a matter of negotiation.

Lessors willing—and able—to provide equipment maintenance and repair service, even in connection with a finance lease, can create an opportunity for additional profit. Many computer vendors, for example, offer these types of services and have created substantial collateral lease revenues.

Very strict equipment maintenance and return provisions are another way to help ensure the highest potential profits. Provisions that require the lessee to return equipment in good operating condition ensure that end-of-lease equipment sale or re-lease values are the highest possible.

h.   Excess Use Charges

The better the condition leased equipment is in when it is returned, the greater the potential for the highest possible end-of-lease sale or re-lease profits. One way to ensure the best possible return condition is to put use restrictions on the equipment, which, if exceeded, call for penalty charges payable at the end of the lease. Automobile lessors typically have annual mileage limitations, which, if exceeded, require the lessee to pay additional rental charges to make up for potentially reduced end-of-lease sale or re-lease value. Leased aircraft are also often subject to use restrictions. Excess use charges can produce extraordinary profits.

i.   Equity Placement Fees

A lessor able to sell a portion, or all, of its equity investment in a lease to another equity investor can earn a fee for providing the investment opportunity. To ensure this option is available, a lease agreement must explicitly permit the sale of some or all of the lessor's interest in the equipment and the lease without consent by the lessee.

j.   Leveraging a Lease Investment With Third-Party Debt

At times, leasing companies borrow a portion of the funds necessary to purchase the equipment from a third-party lender in transactions referred to as leveraged leases. By properly leveraging a lease investment with third-party debt, a lessor can increase its economic return. The key to doing this is to ensure that the lease agreement explicitly permits the assignment of the lessor's interest in the equipment and the lease to a third-party lender without consent by the lessee.

k.   Commitment and Nonutilization Fees

Commitment and nonutilization fees are another area for leasing profits. Lessors frequently ask lessees to pay a commitment or nonutilization fee if the equipment is to be delivered in the future.

Commitment fees, nonrefundable in nature, are designed to compensate a lessor for holding funds available. These fees help reduce the risk of lessor yield deterioration through adverse changes in its borrowing cost. Commitment fees are typically imposed when equipment deliveries are more than six months away, but many lessors ask for them when deliveries are not that far off. A fee of this nature must be paid up front and can range anywhere from 0.5% to 2% of equipment cost.

In effect, nonutilization fees are a penalty for not using the lease funds that a lessor held available for future delivered equipment. This type of fee can be less onerous because it is payable only if the equipment is not leased and because it is due when the commitment period is over. For example, a lessor may require that the lessee pay a fee equal to 2% of the available funds unused at the end of, for example, five months. If all committed funds are used, the lessee owes nothing.

l.   Remarketing Fees

Equipment remarketing fees are a way for equipment lessors to increase lease profits. For example, a lease may require that the lessee pay a predetermined fee to the lessor if the lessee elects to terminate a lease early or at the end of the lease in connection with the lessor's remarketing (the sale or re-lease) of the equipment. These fees are in addition to any other charges which may be payable, such as termination penalties or costs to repair equipment to the condition required under the lease agreement.

m.   Late Payment Charges

Leases should always incorporate lessee late payment charges. For example, if rent is not paid when due, there should be a penalty added to the late payment. Lessees often tolerate penalties in excess of the actual time value of money cost. In fact, some late payment penalties are as high as 5% to 10% of the rent charge.

n.   Collection Telephone Charges

Although not strictly a profit opportunity, by requiring a lessee to pay for any cost of ensuring timely lease payments, many lessors, particularly small ticket lessors, require lessees to pay telephone charges on collection calls. Anything that reduces overheard is indirectly a lessor profit item.

o.   Deal Rewrites

A lessee requiring a change in the structure of a lease, referred to as a deal rewrite, may agree to pay a deal rewrite fee for the privilege, for example, of having its lease extended. This can provide substantial profits, particularly in small lease transactions.

p.   Redelivery Charges

Equipment redelivery charges are another area of profit opportunity. It is not unusual for a lessee to agree to return the leased equipment at the end of the lease to a designated return point, free of charge to the lessor. And it is not unusual for a lessor selling or re-leasing the equipment to a third party to obtain a delivery fee from the third party from the lessee's location of use. Some lessors get lessees to agree to pay for all such shipment charges regardless of where in the world the equipment is designated to be shipped by the lessor, and then get the purchaser, or new lessee, to pay a delivery charge as well.

D. Considerations for Setting Up a Leasing Operation

Starting a leasing company is an involved process, and a detailed explanation is beyond the scope of this book. However, if you are considering establishing an equipment leasing activity, the following overview will assist you in determining threshold considerations. In making such a threshold assessment, you should take into account all the aspects of leasing that have been discussed earlier in this book, such as the financial, tax, legal, accounting, and business considerations. In addition, you must think about the actual mechanics of starting and running a successful leasing operation, including the day-to-day administrative aspects of running a leasing business, obtaining adequate funding for lease transactions, marketing your financing, credit evaluation, documentation processing, state sales and use tax compliance, equipment appraisal and repossession, handling rent delinquencies, and working with outside counsel in the event a lawsuit is necessary.

The following discussion is a brief overview of the primary start-up and operational considerations necessary for the start-up and day-to-day functioning of a leasing operation. Because of the many individual company variables, it is not possible to address all of the many aspects that a particular company should consider.

1. There Must Be a Solid Competitive Reason for Being in the Leasing Business

In determining whether to start a leasing company in today's competitive environment, a company or individual should have a reason to start a leasing company that goes beyond the mere desire to get into the equipment leasing business because it sounds interesting or profitable. And that means that unless you have something unique to offer, such as filling a financing niche that has not been fully addressed by other leasing companies or your company has a vast appetite for the tax shelter offered by the depreciation benefits of owning equipment, the road to success can be very difficult. On the other hand, the story can be different if you or your company has a valued-added reason for entering the equipment leasing business, for example, your company is an equipment manufacturer or vendor looking to make leasing available for your customers. In addition, if you have significant contacts with equipment vendors who do not have effective financing in their marketing package, entering the leasing business may have competitive merit without offering something unique. For companies or banks already in the financial service business, entering the leasing market using the existing customer base can also make sense even though the financing programs are not market unique.

In a nutshell, before you jump into the leasing business, make sure that you have defined your market—and that there is a niche to be filled or you have a value-added benefit to offer in the traditional market.

2. Are Competitive Interest Rate Loans Available?

Clearly, you must have access to adequate funds at competitive interest rates if you plan to competitively enter the leasing business. Unless you or your company has readily available internal funds, getting the necessary debt and equity funds to purchase equipment for lease may not be easy. Interest rate aggressive equipment lease lenders, such as banks, often require a business track record of as much as two years in the leasing business before they are willing to make loans available. Or they will require other justifications why taking the time to enter into loan arrangements will be worthwhile, such as your company's being an equipment vendor with a solid sales and business history.

3. Will Market-Dictated Leasing Profits Be Acceptable?

You must evaluate the lease rates offered by any lessor competition you may encounter. Competition over recent years in the leasing business has forced lease rates down. You may find that your acceptable profit level for lease transactions may not be competitively possible. For example, in the big ticket leasing market, many leasing companies are accepting after-tax investment yields in the 5% to 6% range. If that is the market you intend to enter, you may not find the economic returns necessary to attract business worthwhile.

4. Residual Assessment Can Determine Profit

In many transactions, except, generally, small ticket leases, what you expect the equipment will be worth at the end of the lease term, the estimated residual value, will be an important ingredient in determining your profit expectations. In highly competitive transactions, you may be forced to make high equipment residual estimates in pricing your lease rents to win transactions. If that is unacceptable, you must find a market area that will fit your residual comfort level.

▶ **Observation:**   If you are willing to play the residual end game, it is always a good idea to get expert equipment appraisal assistance.

5. Prospective Lessee Credit Evaluations Are Critical

A critical element to survival in the leasing business is having the ability to properly assess the credit risk of entering into long-term leases with prospective lessees. Therefore, if your company doesn't have the internal ability to assess the credit risk of a lease investment, it must acquire the expertise. And you should keep in mind that the credit approach for leasing to small business is dramatically different from leasing equipment to Fortune 1000 companies. Someone able to effectively evaluate the creditworthiness of a Fortune 1000 company may be totally unable to make an effective credit evaluation of a small business for lease business purposes.

▶ **Observation:**   In order to be competitive in most leasing markets, your company must be able to make credit assessments quickly—that generally means in a matter of days, not weeks.

a.   A Basic Credit Primer

As mentioned above, a prospective lessee's creditworthiness is the most important consideration in the lessor's decision to provide financing. If the prospective lessee's credit is weak, financial support from the vendor or other third party may be the only way for a prospective lessee to secure desired equipment financing.

A discussion of how to evaluate the creditworthiness of a prospective lessee is beyond the scope of this book. In addition, what may create a credit problem to one lessor may not create a credit problem for another lessor. For example, leasing companies with in-depth equipment and remarketing expertise may be more willing to overlook the typical credit concerns of a leasing company without this expertise.

Notwithstanding the fact that credit evaluation is beyond the scope of this book, it will be helpful to go over some basic considerations. In reviewing a prospective company's credit strength, there are many factors brought into consideration, including assets and liabilities, cash flows, years in business, management strength, market presence, and the dollar size of the requested financing.

Large publicly held companies, particularly the Fortune 1000 companies, are often easiest to evaluate because there is ample and reliable evaluation information available from readily available audited financial statements that have been prepared by recognized accounting firms and from publicly available material on file with the Securities and Exchange Commission. In many cases, these companies have been "rated" for investment purposes by investment rating services, such as Moody's and Standard & Poor's rating services. In addition, valuable credit information can be obtained from companies such as Dun & Bradstreet. Certainly, you will want access to these reports as an equipment lessor.

To give you an idea of the various aspects of the credit evaluation process, let us take a look at the criteria used in a simple credit evaluation—that for a small business prospective lessee. These "credits" are some of the hardest to evaluate.

The criteria actually used by a small ticket lessor whose equipment lease transactions range from $5,000 to $250,000 might be as follows:

- *Minimum time in business.* The applicant must have a minimum verifiable time in business of two years. Three years is required in the case of applications over $25,000 and four years in the case of applications over $100,000.
- *Existing banking relationship.* The applicant must have a business bank relationship of at least two years, and the bank account must show a minimum low-four-figure average balance. In the case of transactions exceeding $25,000, the minimum average account balance must be in the low five

figures. There cannot be any overdrafts or check returns for insufficien[t] funds.

- *Trade references.* The applicant must provide three significant trade refer- ences, and each relationship must go back at least six months. COD trade references will not be acceptable.
- *Good personal credit.* Personal credit reports must be forthcoming that con- tain no derogatory information.
- *Financial statements.* Financial statements must be supplied for transactions exceeding $25,000. Current assets must exceed current liabilities, and, for transactions in excess of $50,000, a minimum equity of $75,000 must be present.

6. Leasing Business Risks

As with any other business activity, there are unique business risks in equipment leasing that you must consider. The reader is referred to Chapter 9 for a discus- sion of investment risk in leveraged lease transactions. The risks are similar in non-leveraged lease transactions. In addition to these risks, you must be prepared to deal with prospective lessee fraud, something that exists, yet something that can be minimized with a careful credit and business analysis of each prospective lessee. An experienced leasing credit person will be invaluable in preventing a credit fraud.

7. Administrative Issues

Whether you intend to enter the leasing business as a lease broker or a principal lessor, you must establish the necessary administrative mechanics to carry out all aspects of your leasing operation. It includes credit review processing, document processing and review, security interest filings, tracking and payment of state sales and use taxes, rent invoicing, ongoing marketing of existing customers for new business, new prospect marketing, collection, accounting, equipment repos- session, and lawsuit initiation and monitoring. There is a variety of computer software available today that can facilitate many of the tracking and processing activities, such as lessor rent pricing and invoicing.

8. Legal, Tax, and Accounting Implications

Every lease transaction contains tax and accounting implications for the leasing company which can vary depending on changes in the business aspects of the lease transaction. For example, offering a $1 purchase option at the end of a lease term changes the lease from a true lease for income tax purposes, in which the lessor is entitled to claim equipment depreciation and any available investment tax credits, to a conditional sale, in which the "lessor" is deemed to be an equip- ment lender and thereby not entitled to the equipment ownership tax benefits.

The characterization of your lease investments for accounting purposes can affect your financial statements. Your accountant must be brought into your early consideration discussions to assist you in understanding the financial reporting

·ires will have on your existing business or in financial
ʰolders or investors.

ɔf legal considerations in addition to the documentation
ɔn. For example, you will have to consider qualifying to do
ᵥarious states in which you intend to do lease business; otherwise,
...ᵤm, the courts in the states where you did not so qualify will not be
...ɪe to you in the event you need to sue a defaulting lessee. And the various
...ᵗe laws must be checked to determine what statutory language, if any, must be
included in your lease agreement. Your lawyer will be instrumental in bringing
the legal considerations into focus for your particular business.

9. Lease Documentation

The strength of your leasing documentation can make a major business difference
in your early success and in your ability to collect from a defaulting lessee. For
example, if you intend to assign your lease as security for equipment loans, the
lease agreement must contain effective assignment clauses, as well as other effective provisions. If the lessee defaults, you will have trouble collecting remaining
rents due unless your lease agreement has a hell-or-high-water provision. The
reader is referred to Chapter 3 for a discussion of lessor assignment and hell-or-
high-water provisions.

Putting a good lease agreement together may take some time and require an
investment for an attorney's advice. Investing thousands or even millions of dollars using a lease you've copied form another lessor can be penny-wise and
pound-foolish.

E. Leasing Offers Equipment Vendors a Marketing Edge

Ask any product-marketing person and you will be told that the easier it is for a
customer to financially acquire a new product, the easier it is for the prospective
customer to make an acquisition decision—and the shorter the sale cycle. The
shorter the sale cycle, the less chance of losing an equipment sale to a competitor.

Studies show that 9 out of 10 companies now lease equipment. So if you have
lease financing available at the time you make a product sales presentation, your
chances of making the sale are increased. The real question then for a product
vendor is how to set up the most effective customer financing program—and a
key aspect of that decision is whether it should work with a third-party lessor or
set up its own captive leasing operation.

1. What Are Internal Business Capabilities?

A product vendor's first step in setting up an effective customer equipment
financing program is to take into account its equipment leasing management,
operational and financial capabilities, as well as its leasing operation interests.

Depending on the answer, the product vendor will pursue establishing its own equipment financing activity, possibly setting up a captive leasing company or entering into a relationship with one or more independent leasing companies, something that will be discussed below. Once that decision is made, the next step is to design a customer financing program that will be responsive to prospective customer financing requirements. For example, the credit considerations in approaching small business customer equipment financings will be considerably different from those in approaching Fortune 1000 business customers. Deciding in advance to handle the various requirements is a critical element is maximizing the benefits of offering customer equipment financing. Nothing is more damaging to product marketing than having to go back to a prospective customer, after offering equipment financing, and stating that the company does not meet the financing requirements of, for example, your third-party lessor—particularly when the reason for the turndown was something to which another type of lessor would not have objected.

2. Is It Better to Have a Third-Party Lessor or an In-House Financing Setup?

As a general rule, having an in-house financing capability, such as a captive leasing company, is the best choice for obvious reasons—you control the financing decision and the lease documentation. In addition, an in-house leasing capability is the right choice if you want to have any assurance that the most effective type of financing program possible—one tailored to fit your particular type of customer's needs—is in place. However, as a general rule, for equipment vendors without financial and operational expertise, good leasing company management, and available competitive funding, the better choice is often to set up an equipment leasing program for prospective customers using outside lessors.

Whether a product vendor's decision is to set up its own internal financing capability or to use outside leasing companies to service the customer's financing needs, for the financing program to work effectively, the funding must be reliable and readily available to every type of prospective vendor customer conceivable. This is a particularly important consideration when working with a third-party leasing company. Merely providing a prospective equipment customer with the name of an equipment leasing company to talk to is not enough; and relying solely on the leasing company to properly put together the equipment financing has its risks. In such a situation, a product vendor must have substantial input into and understanding of the credit decisions and documentation processing.

▶ **Observation:** If the decision is to rely on third-party leasing companies to satisfy equipment sales financing needs, one critical point must be kept in mind: If the success of the equipment sales effort depends heavily on customer product financing, a product vendor cannot rely on just one outside funding relationship. There have been many situations in which both bank-affiliated and nonbank leasing companies have closed their funding doors without warning and, at times, with indifference to customer commitments.

3. *Overall Financing Program Objectives Must Be Established*

The overall objectives for an effective equipment financing program are obvious, yet time and time again they are frequently forgotten in the rush to put business on the books. For example, everyone agrees that maintaining good customer relations is essential, yet many equipment vendors overlook the fact that once a third-party leasing company is involved customer relations may be out of their control. One major U.S. leasing company was well known for aggressively and effectively establishing relationships with equipment vendors. And their customer service/administration department was equally well known for aggressively, and inadvertently, damaging customer relationships through inattention and indifference.

Here are the overall guidelines to follow if you are considering establishing an equipment financing program. A vendor equipment financing program must do the following:

- Preserve good customer relations at all times
- Allow the product vendor to control its customer relationships
- Avoid the whims of individual financing sources
- Give the impression of financing continuity
- Be totally reliable under all circumstances

In order to achieve your financing objectives, you will want to

- *Consider establishing your own financing company.* Although setting up a financing subsidiary may be difficult, doing this properly can go a long way to providing a significant competitive marketing advantage. This can be done in many ways. For example, if you feel you do not have financial resources or management available to run a leasing operation or would prefer not to operate a financing company, explore other similar alternatives in which you can maximize control, such as setting up a financing joint venture with an experienced lessor.
- *Establish multiple funding relationships if you decide to work with third-party lessors.* If establishing your own financing company is not feasible or desirable and you are going to set up a third-party leasing program for your customers, establish relationships with more than one lessor. Relying on one lessor to service all potential customers needs is unrealistic for many reasons. One lessor's credit standards may not be broad enough to fit your prospective customer profile, something you may not discover until you run into a problem which cannot be anticipated, or lessor business changes may put an end to your customer program virtually overnight. Historically, for example, some bank-affiliated and nonbank leasing companies have closed their funding doors without warning and, at times, with indifference to customer commitments. So establishing multiple funding relationships is essential, and working with at least three lease financing companies is recommended.

In establishing third-party lessor funding relationships, here are some tips:

1. *Control the document process.* To ensure that every transaction that can get done actually gets done, make sure you control the deal documentation, which means
   - *Develop uniform lease documentation.* Developing one set of lease documents generally acceptable to all funding sources is an important marketing step. If a deal is turned down by one lessor, documents do not have to be resigned to use another funding source, saving time and possible embarrassment.
   - *Handle Documents.* Handling the lease application and documentation process is important. This ensures problems will be properly addressed in a timely manner. For example, your salesperson should prepare the lease application and documents, submit them to the leasing company, and monitor the transaction weekly, or, if necessary, every several days.

2. *Be wary of funding commitments.* Even if you have what appears to be a written commitment to fund customers that meet certain financial and business standards from a third-party leasing company, you may have no assurance of funding reliability. These commitments are typically filled with qualifications, properly so from the lessor's viewpoint, and are rarely legally enforceable.

3. *Avoid providing financial guarantees.* Be careful about providing financing guarantees for customer leases requested by third-party lessors. It is not unusual, for example, for a leasing company to suggest that if your company would guarantee all your customer leases, deals would always get done. Financial guarantees can adversely affect a product vendor's general growth requirement borrowing capabilities. Worse yet, many lease guarantees permit collection from the guarantor without having first exhausted all remedies against the lessee.

4. *Investigate prospective third-party lessor backgrounds thoroughly.* The financial backgrounds, years in business, and deal track records of every third-party leasing company you consider must be investigated thoroughly. Not doing so can create avoidable risks. For example, many leasing companies simply do not have the funds available to properly service a vendor's repeated financing needs. An investigation can prevent unfortunate surprises.

5. *Use lease brokers cautiously.* Lease brokers have no control over whether a deal will be approved or funded. They often send financing packages out to multiple sources hoping someone will approve it. In small transactions some brokers spend more time sending financing offerings to sources than preparing a good financing package. Improper packaging alone can result in a turndown, something that increases the difficulty of finding future funding.

6. *If using lease brokers, watch out for fees.* Lease brokers often charge a high fee for their services. In large transactions they generally are worth the fee; in small transactions high fees are generally unwarranted. When

questioned about a high fee, brokers often state that the lessor pays the fee so you should not be concerned. The fact is that a lessor needs a minimum deal profit and the fee is something it pays based upon the rent level. The higher the fee, the less competitive the lease financing. Brokers establish a rent level that permits the largest possible fee.

7. *Be skeptical about dealing with lease investment funds.* Lease investment funds promoted by investment bankers and lessors surface from time to time. They are public or private limited investment partnerships that raise money for investment in equipment leases. Historically, many have had problems as a result of poor management or improper structuring. And when problems arise the funding is cut off. So if you decide to work with an investment fund, do not rely on it exclusively for customer funding.

8. *When working with third-party lessors, conduct preliminary funding reviews.* When using third-party leasing companies to provide customer financing, an equipment vendor should conduct its own preliminary "lease acceptability review" before submitting a transaction to the prospective leasing company to head off problems. Very often issues that could result in a turndown can be addressed to facilitate an approval before the application is submitted. Once a prospective customer is turned down by one leasing company, it is more difficult to get a funding approval from another lessor. The reason may be illogical, but it is a fact of business life—credit managers at times turn down business they might otherwise have accepted merely because they are afraid another credit manager spotted a problem they could not find.

In summary, there is a customer financing program structure that can work for every equipment vendor, but care must be taken to guarantee that the best possible program is put together. A vendor that works within the financial market realities has the greatest chance of arranging an attractive and reliable financing program.

F. Conclusion

Entering the equipment leasing business has benefits, but only if your company has a market value-added reason for being in the leasing business. If your company has such a reason, take the time to carefully evaluate all aspects of leasing as it may affect your potential operations.

Chapter 13

Equipment Leasing in International Markets

A.   Overview

The subject of international leasing is complex, and a complete analysis is beyond the scope of this book. However, if you are part of the leasing business you should understand the basic issues. If you believe leasing equipment internationally may be a worthwhile business pursuit, then an understanding of key considerations will put the issues that you or your company may have to address into a quick business perspective and assist you in assessing whether the subject merits further investigation.

You may have heard that there are many exciting opportunities in the international leasing market. That is true—but only for entrants who are financially well-qualified and sophisticated in lease transactions, as you will realize when reading this chapter.

B.   A Complex Market of Growth

There has been a dramatic growth in recent years in the demand for leasing equipment overseas, not only in the industrialized countries, but also in the industrially developing economies, such as China, Korea, and India. This demand has provided unprecedented and major leasing opportunities for U.S. lessors. But there are many business hurdles to overcome—and risks to address—in what is commonly referred to as "cross-border" leasing.

International leasing brings with it complex tax, accounting, and legal issues—and more. For example, an international lessor must address

- Business considerations unique to the particular country in which the lease transaction is done, such as restricted availability of local courts for lease enforcement procedures
- Foreign currency exchange risks
- Possible equipment export issues

Accordingly, the lessors best able to take full advantage of the rising equipment financing needs abroad are those with strong financial capabilities and support resources, such as large multinational equipment financing companies with networks of affiliated leasing companies in various international markets.

▶ **Tips:**   Equipment leasing associations exist in many foreign countries, such as the Leasing Associates of Singapore. If you are interested in exploring international leasing in particular markets, these associations can assist you in identifying local leasing companies to work with, for example, for transaction referrals. They also can provide invaluable advice about local business and legal issues that will impact your company, as well as any lease transactions that you do in their country.

The *World Leasing Yearbook,* published by Hawkins Publishers, Ltd., Coggeshall, Essex, England, is an excellent source of leasing company information—it provides a list of well over 5,500 lessors operating in over 70 countries. It also provides a handy summary of the leasing business in many foreign countries.

C.   The Foreign Lessee Demand

For a foreign lessee, leasing from a U.S. lessor generally has the same type of traditional lease advantages that a U.S. lessee could expect. A discussion of these traditional lessee leasing advantages is in Chapter 1. However, there may be additional advantages. In many countries, local circumstances can add substantially to the attractiveness of leasing from an international lessor. For example:

- If available local funding is expensive, or capital is unavailable or in short supply, the ability to obtain a cross-border lease can be the deciding factor in whether or not to acquire new equipment.
- There are times when a foreign country's lenders are unwilling to provide medium- or long-term financing because of economic instability, but international lessors are willing to do so, because
  1. They want additional business.
  2. Their lease investments are more risk diversified—with relatively little local investment concentration in the country in question.

Make no mistake, the prospective foreign lessee's decision to enter into a cross-border lease is still primarily a cost decision—there generally must be a clear cost advantage over other financing alternatives. In addition, the lease terms and conditions may have to be better than those available locally.

D.   Advantages for Lessors Leasing Internationally

The United States domestic market, as discussed in Chapter 12, is highly competitive, and currently there is more lessor money available than there are lease deals to do. As a result, some U.S. lessors, in an effort to develop new sources of business, have moved aggressively into the international leasing market for opportunities, finding a particularly high demand for equipment financing in the economically emerging countries, such as China. International leasing interests U.S. lessors for another significant reason: There are possibilities for increased economic lease returns through the use of

- Subsidized export financing
- Tax benefits not available to a local foreign financing company

In fact, in some cases, cross-border leases enable lessees and lessors to avail themselves of tax advantages that exist in more than one country—through so-called double dip lease transactions. These added tax benefits can either make lease pricing more aggressive or increase a lessor's economic return.

▶ **Observation:** Although there may be relatively more opportunities for equipment leasing abroad than in the United States, it is still a competitive market, with large multinational finance companies having a substantial foothold in virtually every significant foreign market.

For U.S. equipment manufacturers and vendors looking for increased export business, the ability to lease internationally has marketing advantages. Being able to provide leasing to prospective customers in foreign countries may facilitate foreign equipment sales.

▶ **Recommendation:** Equipment manufacturers not familiar with the business of international equipment leasing should work with multinational third-party leasing companies, at least in the beginning stages of international leasing. This is the easiest and most cost-effective way to gain the necessary financing knowledge and experience, and to avoid the many pitfalls associated with foreign market leasing.

E. Risks of Operating in Foreign Markets

There are a number of risks that a U.S. lessor faces in cross-border leasing that are not present in domestic leasing. The political risk is the most obvious one, and has wide-ranging ramifications for an international lessor. For instance, if foreign relations fall apart between the United States and the country where the equipment or parties are located, there could be a variety of serious problems, including an inability to collect rent and repossess equipment. In addition, if a lessee pays rent in a foreign currency, there could be a transaction profit deterioration if an adverse change in the currency exchange rate occurs.

Even if political relations remain stable with the country in which the foreign lessee is located, there are risks, such as

- The long-term nature of the typical equipment lease, which can subject a lessor to undue currency exchange fluctuation risks.

▶ **Tip:**   There are methods to hedge against the currency fluctuation risk. Investment bankers can often provide guidance in how to handle this risk.

- Certain foreign economies are well known for volatile interest rate and economic fluctuations, which may adversely affect the lease transaction.
- Assessing the creditworthiness of a prospective lessee is more difficult, with a possibility of making a credit decision mistake, because company financial statements and presentations may be quite different from that of U.S. companies.
- The business risks are greater than leasing in the U.S. market, if for no other reason than the leased equipment is in a distant land.
- Leasing-related laws in the international environment are constantly changing.
- Foreign laws, or judicial systems, may make it difficult to repossess equipment from a defaulting lessee.
- The expenses involved in putting together an international lease are typically higher than that of a comparable U.S. lease transaction, and thus the potential for financial loss is increased if the transaction falls apart during the negotiation stage.
- The language barrier, even with local counsel involved, can create basic misunderstandings that may not be discovered until there is a problem.
- An inadvertent violation of local social customs may result in interpersonnel disharmony and mistrust—and eventual business problems.

Properly evaluating these risks takes considerable work, and experienced assistance is critical in determining the extent to which they exist and how to best handle them.

1. Country Risk Management

Commonly referred to as the "country risk," international lessors must contend with the possibility that events, totally or partially within the control of the foreign lessee's government, such as war, the government's expropriation of the leased asset, the cancellation of the lessor's export or import license, or the interference with the lessor's ability to repossess equipment in the case of a lessee default, will result in the loss of some or all of the lease investment.

In certain situations, the country risk can be successfully managed. If the leased equipment will be imported into the lessee's country, some form of guarantee or insurance program may be available though a governmental agency. For example, many governments set up an agency to assist in or support the export of products manufactured in their country. The Export-Import Bank of the United States is one such agency set up by the U.S. government to support the exporting of U.S. products. Eximbank, as it is generally referred to, both directly and through its agent the Foreign Credit Insurance Association (FCIA) offers a number of product export support programs that, for example, can reduce the political and commercial risks that product exporters, lenders, or lessors may be exposed to in a foreign locale. The support programs can in effect provide guarantees against loss from specified political and commercial risks and carry the full faith and credit of the government of the United States.

▶ **Recommendation:** Contact the Export-Import Bank of the United States' Washington, D.C., office and the Foreign Credit Insurance Association's New York City office for information on what support programs they offer and how they work, including to whom they are available and what they cover.

Very briefly, you can generally expect to find in Eximbank and FCIA program offerings that

- Guarantees of, or insurance for, equipment residual values are not available.
- Insurance against the expropriation of leased or financed equipment is available.
- New and used equipment can be covered.
- Programs are available for both United States and non-United States lessors if the equipment under lease is manufactured in the United States.
- Guarantees are available for up to 100% of the principal portion of lease payments and a certain portion of the interest portion of such lease payments.
- Protection against currency fluctuation risk is not available.
- In certain situations, the lessee may be required to make a 15% advance payment to the lessor when the equipment is delivered.
- Program coverage is available for specified short-term leases, as well as long-term leases.
- The following risks are generally covered:
  1. Political risks, such as war, insurrection, and equipment requisition
  2. The risk of lease nonpayment due to a lessee lease payment default or insolvency
  3. The inability to repossess equipment following a lease default due to acts of a local government

F. Local Law Considerations

Leasing companies entering a particular foreign market must assess the local law implications for the types of lease transactions they intend to participate in. For example, lessors must determine

- What local laws and regulations will govern their leasing operation, including what periodic filing requirements may be necessary
- What penalties may be imposed for failure to comply with local laws and regulations

In the United States, there is little regulation, and therefore penalties are non-existent or of minor concern. In many foreign countries, however, the situation can be dramatically different. In some countries penalties can result in

- An inability to use the country's court system
- A change in a lease transaction's taxation
- Fines
- Imprisonment

Some local laws are quite extensive in their regulation of lease transactions, even going as far as dictating the actual terms and conditions of cross-border lease agreements, including how much interest can be charged, how long or how short the lease term can be, and the required or permitted lease payment grace periods.

An important legal consideration that cannot be overlooked for obvious reasons is the creditor rights laws: the rules that govern what a lessor must do to protect and enforce its rights in the lease collateral under a country's local law. To assess these issues, you will have to be thoroughly versed in the applicable bankruptcy or similar creditor rights laws.

▶ **Recommendation:** There is only one way to adequately protect yourself from local law problems: For each transaction, hire competent local counsel for each jurisdiction in which the equipment and transaction parties are located.

And finally, as part of your local law due diligence, you must also check to see if any treaties exist with the country you intend to do business in that can affect tax or other aspects of the lease transaction.

G. The International Lease Documents

The international lease documentation used by U.S. lessors is often based on the documentation used in sophisticated United States-style leveraged leases. (For basic provisions in a lease, the reader is referred to the lease documentation discussion in Chapters 3 and 4.) However, it should go without saying, the lease documentation must incorporate provisions and protections necessary for doing business in a foreign locale.

There is only way to competently approach proper lease document drafting—you must enlist the aid of competent and experienced international U.S. leasing counsel and foreign local counsel. In any event, at a bare minimum, you will want to be particularly careful that

- You have a noncancelable, or "hell-or-high-water," lease, one in which the lessee is specifically required to make all the rental payments due under the lease without abatement, reduction, or setoff.
- You have not inadvertently relinquished legal title to the asset under lease. This may require a careful review of applicable laws to ensure that you, as

lessor, have good title at the start of the lease, and that you have adequate protection against the potential claims by any lessee creditor or other third-party during the lease term.

- The manner in which rent payments are made, including the currency of payment, fits your currency exchange requirements. That means, for example, inserting provisions that detail what happens if there is a currency exchange rate fluctuation or if the lessee is not permitted by law to make the lease payments as prescribed by the lease agreement.

- You have considered more stringent maintenance and repair duties and lease reporting requirements. (Travel costs and distance may make it prohibitive to conduct on-site reviews and inspections.) For example, it is often advisable to include in the lease an expanded maintenance provision that incorporates in detail the maintenance standards suggested by the equipment manufacturer.

- There is no necessity for setting up a maintenance reserve account to cover, for example, repairs that the lessee fails to perform or performs inadequately.

- Comprehensive tax indemnification provisions that cover all expected tax advantages have been incorporated. Typically, the tax aspects of a cross-border lease are crucial to the economic viability of the lease transaction, and are very complex. In addition there is the ever-present possibility that the applicable tax laws may change to the detriment of a lessor after the lease is signed. Accordingly, these tax indemnification provisions must spell out in great detail all lessor tax benefits anticipated and the obligations of the lessee in the event that some or all of these benefits are lost or otherwise unavailable.

- Whether any applicable commercial laws governing the sale of goods create any implied equipment or other warranties that run to the lessee from you as lessor merely because you are the equipment titleholder. In the United States, a lessor is generally able to effectively avoid any such implied warranties by using disclaimer language prescribed by the Uniform Commercial Code laws.

- The method of dealing with any required withholding taxes under local law, such as a requirement that 15% of each rental payment be withheld and remitted to the local taxing authority, is addressed and handled properly. Typically, any required withholding tax payments are the responsibility of the lessor, and the lessee is deemed to be the government's agent for their collection and payment. If the lessee fails to make these payments, the government will go after the lessor to collect. In this case, without a specific provision in the lease agreement for this, the lessor may have no recourse for reimbursement against the lessee. Therefore, it is essential for a lease provision to spell out that payment for any such withholding taxes is the lessee's responsibility, exactly how much the lessee must pay, when payment must be made, and to whom it is to be made.

- The representation and warranties specific to your particular lease transaction have been obtained, such as proper equipment import or governmental authorizations. For example, if proper governmental authorizations have not been obtained and the lease contained a representation that they had been obtained, or if none were necessary, a lessor has the power to move quickly to minimize the potential for loss from potential adverse government actions by calling a lease default and repossessing the equipment.

- The remedies available in the event of a lease default are adequate, and not overreaching. The area of lease default is one that requires careful attention. As a general rule, at a minimum, the lessor's default remedies should conform with any specific remedies available to a lessor under the applicable foreign law. In addition, care must be taken that any additional ones do not run afoul of accepted rules of fairness; otherwise these remedies or possibly the lessor's entire rights against the lessee may be subject to attack under the local laws by the lessee's counsel for being, for example, unconscionable or against public policy.
- Casualty and third-party insurance provisions provide what you need. Clearly, this is a critical aspect of an equipment lease, and an insurance company thoroughly familiar with insurance coverage available in the foreign locale must be consulted.
- There are effective lessor lease assignment rights. Local law must be checked to ensure that there are no assignment restrictions, and also to determine whether or not any type of assignment could result in the obligation to pay a transfer or registration fee or tax.
- There are necessary assignment restrictions on the lessee. As lessor, you do not want the lease to end up in the hands of someone who could jeopardize your lease security or rights.
- You have considered incorporating an arbitration provision to settle disputes and avoid being tied up in local courts. Although an arbitration requirement may not be enforceable under a particular local law if a lessee chooses not to go along with it, having one is recommended. Arbitration is generally a less costly and faster procedure than litigation.
- You have designated which country's law will govern the lease transaction. However, care must be taken to ensure that any choice of law will be enforceable under local law.

H.   The Uniform International Lease Rules

In an attempt to address the many complex issues surrounding equipment leasing in the international market, and in support of the growing interest in this form of financing in various nations, the International Institute for the Unification of Private Law, formerly an affiliate of the League of Nations but now an independent international organization located in Rome, Italy, formed a study group in 1977 consisting of legal and financial experts to review international leasing and put together a set of uniform rules that would eliminate many uncertainties. The study group's efforts were ultimately adopted in a unanimous vote by the representatives of 55 nations gathered in Ottawa, Canada, in May 1988 as a comprehensive set of international leasing rules. The promulgated rules were subject to ratification by all represented nations. The final text of these rules is as follows:

UNIDROIT CONVENTION ON
INTERNATIONAL FINANCIAL LEASING

(Ottawa, 28 May 1988)

THE STATES PARTIES TO THIS CONVENTION,

RECOGNIZING the importance of removing certain legal impediments to the international financial leasing of equipment, while maintaining a fair balance of interests between the different parties to the transaction,

AWARE of the need to make international financial leasing more available,

CONSCIOUS of the fact that the rules of law governing the traditional contract of hire need to be adapted to the distinctive triangular relationship created by the financial leasing transaction,

RECOGNIZING therefore the desirability of formulating certain uniform rules relating primarily to the civil and commercial law aspects of international financial leasing,

HAVE AGREED as follows:

CHAPTER I—SPHERE OF APPLICATION AND
GENERAL PROVISIONS

Article 1

1. This Convention governs a financial leasing transaction as described in paragraph 2 in which one party (the lessor),
    (a) on the specifications of another party (the lessee), enters into an agreement (the supply agreement) with a third party (the supplier) under which the lessor acquires plant, capital goods or other equipment (the equipment) on terms approved by the lessee so far as they concern its interests, and
    (b) enters into an agreement (the leasing agreement) with the lessee, granting to the lessee the right to use the equipment in return for the payment of rentals.
2. The financial leasing transaction referred to in the previous paragraph is a transaction which includes the following characteristics:
    (a) the lessee specifies the equipment and selects the supplier without relying primarily on the skill and judgment of the lessor;
    (b) the equipment is acquired by the lessor in connection with a leasing agreement which, to the knowledge of the supplier, either has been made or is to be made between the lessor and the lessee; and
    (c) the rentals payable under the leasing agreement are calculated so as to take into account in particular the amortization of the whole or a substantial part of the cost of the equipment.
3. This Convention applies whether or not the lessee has or subsequently acquires the option to buy the equipment or to hold it on lease for a further period, and whether or not for a nominal price or rental.

4.   This Convention applies to financial leasing transactions in relation to all equipment save that which is to be used primarily for the lessee's personal, family or household purposes.

Article 2

In the case of one or more sub-leasing transactions involving the same equipment, this Convention applies to each transaction which is a financial leasing transaction and is otherwise subject to this Convention as if the person from whom the first lessor (as defined in paragraph 1 of the previous article) acquired the equipment were the supplier and as if the agreement under which the equipment was so acquired were the supply agreement.

Article 3

1.   This Convention applies when the lessor and the lessee have their places of business in different States and:
     (a)   those States and the State in which the supplier has its place of business are Contracting States; or
     (b)   both the supply agreement and the leasing agreement are governed by the law of a Contracting State.
2.   A reference in this Convention to a party's place of business shall, if it has more than one place of business, mean the place of business which has the closest relationship to the relevant agreement and its performance, having regard to the circumstances known to or contemplated by the parties at any time before or at the conclusion of that agreement.

Article 4

1.   The provisions of this Convention shall not cease to apply merely because the equipment has become a fixture to or incorporated in land.
2.   Any question whether or not the equipment has become a fixture to or incorporated in land, and if so the effect on the rights inter se of the lessor and a person having real rights in the land, shall be determined by the law of the State where the land is situated.

Article 5

1.   The application of this Convention may be excluded only if each of the parties to the supply agreement and each of the parties to the leasing agreement agree to exclude it.
2.   Where the application of this Convention has not been excluded in accordance with the previous paragraph, the parties may, in their relations with each other, derogate from or vary the effect of any of its provisions except as stated in Articles 8 (3) and 13 (3)(b) and (4).

Article 6

1.   In the interpretation of this Convention, regard is to be had to its object and purpose as set forth in the preamble, to its international character and to the need to promote uniformity in its application and the observance of good faith in international trade.

2. Questions concerning matters governed by this Convention which are not expressly settled in it are to be settled in conformity with the general principles on which it is based or, in the absence of such principles, in conformity with the law applicable by virtue of the rules of private international law.

CHAPTER II—RIGHTS AND DUTIES OF THE PARTIES

Article 7

1. (a) The lessor's real rights in the equipment shall be valid against the lessee's trustee in bankruptcy and creditors, including creditors who have obtained an attachment or execution.
   (b) For the purposes of this paragraph "trustee in bankruptcy" includes a liquidator, administrator or other person appointed to administer the lessee's estate for the benefit of the general body of creditors.

2. Where by the applicable law the lessor's real rights in the equipment are valid against a person referred to in the previous paragraph only on compliance with rules as to public notice, those rights shall be valid against that person only if there has been compliance with such rules.

3. For the purposes of the previous paragraph the applicable law is the law of the State which, at the time when a person referred to in paragraph 1 becomes entitled to invoke the rules referred to in the previous paragraph, is:
   (a) in the case of a registered ship, the State in which it is registered in the name of the owner (for the purposes of this sub-paragraph a bareboat charterer is deemed not to be the owner);
   (b) in the case of an aircraft which is registered pursuant to the Convention on International Civil Aviation done at Chicago on 7 December 1944, the State in which it is so registered;
   (c) in the case of other equipment of a kind normally moved from one State to another, including an aircraft engine, the State in which the lessee has its principal place of business;
   (d) in the case of all other equipment, the State in which the equipment is situated.

4. Paragraph 2 shall not affect the provisions of any other treaty under which the lessor's real rights in the equipment are required to be recognized.

5. This article shall not affect the priority of any creditor having:
   (a) a consensual or non-consensual lien or security interest in the equipment arising otherwise than by virtue of an attachment or execution, or
   (b) any right of arrest, detention or disposition conferred specifically in relation to ships or aircraft under the law applicable by virtue of the rules of private international law.

Article 8

1. (a) Except as otherwise provided by this Convention or stated in the leasing agreement, the lessor shall not incur any liability to the lessee in respect of the equipment save to the extent that the lessee has suffered loss as the result of its reliance on the lessor's skill and judgment and of the lessor's intervention in the selection of the supplier or the specifications of the equipment.

(b) The lessor shall not, in its capacity of lessor, be liable to third parties for death, personal injury or damage to property caused by the equipment.

(c) The above provisions of this paragraph shall not govern any liability of the lessor in any other capacity, for example as owner.

2. The lessor warrants that the lessee's quiet possession will not be disturbed by a person who has a superior title or right, or who claims a superior title or right and acts under the authority of a court, where such title, right or claim is not derived from an act or omission of the lessee.

3. The parties may not derogate from or vary the effect of the provisions of the previous paragraph in so far as the superior title, right or claim is derived from an intentional or grossly negligent act or omission of the lessor.

4. The provisions of paragraphs 2 and 3 shall not affect any broader warranty of quiet possession by the lessor which is mandatory under the law applicable by virtue of the rules of private international law.

Article 9

1. The lessee shall take proper care of the equipment, use it in a reasonable manner and keep it in the condition in which it was delivered, subject to fair wear and tear and to any modification of the equipment agreed by the parties.

2. When the leasing agreement comes to an end the lessee, unless exercising a right to buy the equipment or to hold the equipment on lease for a further period, shall return the equipment to the lessor in the condition specified in the previous paragraph.

Article 10

1. The duties of the supplier under the supply agreement shall also be owed to the lessee as if it were a party to that agreement and as if the equipment were to be supplied directly to the lessee. However, the supplier shall not be liable to both the lessor and the lessee in respect of the same damage.

2. Nothing in this article shall entitle the lessee to terminate or rescind the supply agreement without the consent of the lessor.

Article 11

The lessee's rights derived from the supply agreement under this Convention shall not be affected by a variation of any term of the supply agreement previously approved by the lessee unless it consented to that variation.

Article 12

1. Where the equipment is not delivered or is delivered late or fails to conform to the supply agreement:
    (a) the lessee has the right as against the lessor to reject the equipment or to terminate the leasing agreement; and
    (b) the lessor has the right to remedy its failure to tender equipment in conformity with the supply agreement as if the lessee had agreed to buy the equipment from the lessor under the same terms as those of the supply agreement.

2. A right conferred by the previous paragraph shall be exercisable in the same manner and shall be lost in the same circumstances as if the lessee had agreed

to buy the equipment from the lessor under the same terms as those of the supply agreement.

3. The lessee shall be entitled to withhold rentals payable under the leasing agreement until the lessor has remedied its failure to tender equipment in conformity with the supply agreement or the lessee has lost the right to reject the equipment.

4. Where the lessee has exercised a right to terminate the leasing agreement, the lessee shall be entitled to recover any rentals and other sums paid in advance, less a reasonable sum for any benefit the lessee has derived from the equipment.

5. The lessee shall have no other claim against the lessor for non-delivery, delay in delivery or delivery of non-conforming equipment except to the extent to which this results from the act or omission of the lessor.

6. Nothing in this article shall affect the lessee's rights against the supplier under Article 10.

Article 13

1. In the event of default by the lessee, the lessor may recover accrued unpaid rentals, together with interest and damages.

2. Where the lessee's default is substantial, then subject to paragraph 5 the lessor may also require accelerated payment of the value of the future rentals, where the leasing agreement so provides, or may terminate the leasing agreement and after such termination:
   (a) recover possession of the equipment; and
   (b) recover such damages as will place the lessor in the position in which it would have been had the lessee performed the leasing agreement in accordance with its terms.

3. (a) The leasing agreement may provide for the manner in which the damages recoverable under paragraph 2(b) are to be computed.
   (b) Such provision shall be enforceable between the parties unless it would result in damages substantially in excess of those provided for under paragraph 2(b). The parties may not derogate from or vary the effect of the provisions of the present sub-paragraph.

4. Where the lessor has terminated the leasing agreement, it shall not be entitled to enforce a term of that agreement providing for acceleration of payment of future rentals, but the value of such rentals may be taken into account in computing damages under paragraphs 2(b) and 3. The parties may not derogate from or vary the effect of the provisions of the present paragraph.

5. The lessor shall not be entitled to exercise its right of acceleration or its right of termination under paragraph 2 unless it has by notice given the lessee a reasonable opportunity of remedying the default so far as the same may be remedied.

6. The lessor shall not be entitled to recover damages to the extent that it has failed to take all reasonable steps to mitigate its loss.

Article 14

1. The lessor may transfer or otherwise deal with all or any of its rights in the equipment or under the leasing agreement. Such a transfer shall not relieve

the lessor of any of its duties under the leasing agreement or alter either the nature of the leasing agreement or its legal treatment as provided in this Convention.

2. The lessee may transfer the right to the use of the equipment or any other rights under the leasing agreement only with the consent of the lessor and subject to the rights of third parties.

CHAPTER III—FINAL PROVISIONS

Article 15

1. This Convention is open for signature at the concluding meeting of the Diplomatic Conference for the Adoption of the Draft Unidroit Conventions on International Factoring and International Financial Leasing and will remain open for signature by all States at Ottawa until 31 December 1990.
2. This Convention is subject to ratification, acceptance or approval by States which have signed it.
3. This Convention is open for accession by all States which are not signatory States as from the date it is open for signature.
4. Ratification, acceptance, approval or accession is effected by the deposit of a formal instrument to that effect with the depository.

Article 16

1. This Convention enters into force on the first day of the month following the expiration of six months after the date of deposit of the third instrument of ratification, acceptance, approval or accession.
2. For each State that ratifies, accepts, approves, or accedes to this Convention after the deposit of the third instrument of ratification, acceptance, approval or accession, this Convention enters into force in respect of that State on the first day of the month following the expiration of six months after the date of the deposit of its instrument of ratification, acceptance, approval or accession.

Article 17

This Convention does not prevail over any treaty which has already been or may be entered into; in particular it shall not affect any liability imposed on any person by existing or future treaties.

Article 18

1. If a Contracting State has two or more territorial units in which different systems of law are applicable in relation to the matters dealt with in this Convention, it may, at the time of signature, ratification, acceptance, approval or accession, declare that this Convention is to extend to all its territorial units or only to one or more of them, and may substitute its declaration by another declaration at any time.
2. These declarations are to be notified to the depository and are to state expressly the territorial units to which the Convention extends.
3. If by virtue of a declaration under this article, this Convention extends to one or more but not all of the territorial units of a Contracting State, and if the

place of business of a party is located in that State, this place of business, for the purposes of this Convention, is considered not to be in a Contracting State, unless it is in a territorial unit to which the Convention extends.

4. If a Contracting State makes no declaration under paragraph 1, the Convention is to extend to all territorial units of that State.

Article 19

1. Two or more Contracting States which have the same or closely related legal rules on matters governed by this Convention may at any time declare that the Convention is not to apply where the supplier, the lessor and the lessee have their places of business in those States. Such declarations may be made jointly or by reciprocal unilateral declarations.

2. A Contracting State which has the same or closely related legal rules on matters governed by this Convention as one or more non-Contracting States may at any time declare that the Convention is not to apply where the supplier, the lessor and the lessee have their places of business in those States.

3. If a State which is the object of a declaration under the previous paragraph subsequently becomes a Contracting State, the declaration made will, as from the date on which the Convention enters into force in respect of the new Contracting State, have the effect of a declaration made under paragraph 1, provided that the new Contracting State joins in such declaration or makes a reciprocal unilateral declaration.

Article 20

A Contracting State may declare at the time of signature, ratification, acceptance, approval or accession that it will substitute its domestic law for Article 8(3) if its domestic law does not permit the lessor to exclude its liability for its default or negligence.

Article 21

1. Declarations made under this Convention at the time of signature are subject to confirmation upon ratification, acceptance or approval.

2. Declarations and confirmations of declarations are to be in writing and to be formally notified to the depository.

3. A declaration takes effect simultaneously with the entry into force of this Convention in respect of the State concerned. However, a declaration of which the depository receives formal notification after such entry into force takes effect on the first day of the month following the expiration of six months after the date of its receipt by the depository. Reciprocal unilateral declarations under Article 19 take effect on the first day of the month following the expiration of six months after the receipt of the latest declaration by the depository.

4. Any State which makes a declaration under this Convention may withdraw it at any time by a formal notification in writing addressed to the depository. Such withdrawal is to take effect on the first day of the month following the expiration of six months after the date of the receipt of the notification by the depository.

5. A withdrawal of a declaration made under Article 19 renders inoperative in relation to the withdrawing State, as from the date on which the withdrawal takes effect, any joint or reciprocal unilateral declaration made by another State under that article.

Article 22

No reservations are permitted except those expressly authorized in this Convention.

Article 23

This Convention applies to a financial leasing transaction when the leasing agreement and the supply agreement are both concluded on or after the date on which the Convention enters into force in respect of the Contracting States referred to in Article 3(l)(a), or of the Contracting State or States referred to in paragraph 1(b) of that article.

Article 24

1. This Convention may be denounced by any Contracting State at any time after the date on which it enters into force for that State.
2. Denunciation is effected by the deposit of an instrument to that effect with the depository.
3. A denunciation takes effect on the first day of the month following the expiration of six months after the deposit of the instrument of denunciation with the depository. Where a longer period for the denunciation to take effect is specified in the instrument of denunciation it takes effect upon the expiration of such longer period after its deposit with the depository.

Article 25

1. This Convention shall be deposited with the Government of Canada.
2. The Government of Canada shall:
    (a) inform all States which have signed or acceded to this Convention and the President of the International Institute for the Unification of Private Law (Unidroit) of:
        (i)   each new signature or deposit of an instrument of ratification, acceptance, approval or accession, together with the date thereof;
        (ii) each declaration made under Articles 18, 19 and 20;
        (iii) the withdrawal of any declaration made under Article 21(4);
        (iv) the date of entry into force of this Convention;
        (v)   the deposit of an instrument of denunciation of this Convention together with the date of its deposit and the date on which it takes effect;
    (b) transmit certified true copies of this Convention to all signatory States, to all States acceding to the Convention and to the President of the International Institute for the Unification of Private Law (Unidroit).

IN WITNESS WHEREOF the undersigned plenipotentiaries, being duly authorized by their respective Governments, have signed this Convention.

DONE at Ottawa, this twenty-eighth day of May, one thousand nine hundred and eighty-eight, in a single original, of which the English and French texts are equally authentic.

I. Conclusion

There is no doubt that in an expanding global economy cross-border leasing will continue to expand, and that the job of putting together a cross-border lease will become easier as transaction experience is gained. However, leasing equipment internationally is extremely complex and should not be approached without competent advice.

Chapter 14

Equipment Lease Terminology: The Definitions

When entering into a leasing transaction, you may encounter unfamiliar terms that have developed along with the leasing industry. This chapter defines terms according to their industry usage.

accelerated cost recovery system (ACRS). The method prescribed by the Internal Revenue Code that an equipment owner must use in computing depreciation deductions on most equipment placed in service after 1980 and before 1987. Under ACRS, the owner writes off the equipment's cost over a 3-year, 5-year, 10-year, or 15-year period, depending on the recovery period designated for the equipment type.

acceptance certificate. A document in which a lessee acknowledges that certain specified equipment is acceptable for lease. Generally used in transactions where the parties enter into the lease document well in advance of the equipment's delivery date, it serves to notify the lessor that the equipment has been delivered, inspected, and accepted for lease as of a specified date. The typical form requires the lessee to list certain pertinent information, including the equipment manufacturer, purchase price, serial number, and location.

acceptance supplement. The same as an acceptance certificate.

advance rental. Any payment in the form of rent made before the start of the lease term. The term is also sometimes used to describe a rental payment arrangement in which the lessee pays all rentals, on a per period basis, at the start of each rental payment period. For example, a quarterly, in advance rental program requires the lessee to pay one-fourth of the annual rental at the start of each consecutive three-month period during the lease term.

alternative minimum tax (AMT). A system for taxing individuals and corporations that, in effect, prevents a taxpayer from otherwise reducing its tax below a formulated level. If the tax liability calculated under the AMT rules is greater than the taxpayer's regular tax, the excess amount has to be paid along with the regular tax. The AMT is basically an attempt to dampen a taxpayer's typical motivation to reduce excessively its tax liability.

anti-churning. A concept under the federal tax laws that prevents a taxpayer from taking advantage of more favorable equipment depreciation tax benefits through equipment transaction manipulations that violate the spirit of the tax laws.

asset depreciation range (ADR) indemnity. A type of tax indemnification given by the lessee to the lessor relating to leased equipment depreciated under the asset depreciation range system method. The lessee, in effect, guarantees the lessor against loss of or inability to claim anticipated ADR tax benefits under certain conditions.

asset depreciation range (ADR) system. A method prescribed by the Internal Revenue Code that could be used in computing depreciation deductions for certain assets placed in service after 1970 and before 1981. ADR provides a range of useful lives for specified assets that serve as the period over which the asset is depreciated. The lives listed are generally shorter than the period over which an asset may be depreciated under the "facts and circumstances" method of depreciation.

balloon payment. Commonly found in mortgage financings, a balloon payment is a final payment that is larger than the periodic term payments. Usually it results because the debt has not been fully amortized during the repayment period. For example, a one-year financing arrangement providing for interest-only monthly payments during the year, with the principal plus the last interest payment due on the final payment date, is said to have a "balloon payment" or simply a "balloon" due at the end of the term.

bareboat charter party. A net financial lease relating to vessels. Also sometimes referred to simply as a "bareboat charter." See **net lease.**

base lease term. The primary period of time that the lessee is entitled to use the leased equipment, without regard to any interim or renewal lease terms. The base lease term of a five-year lease is five years.

base rental. The rental that the lessee must pay during the base, sometimes called primary, lease term.

beneficial interest holder. Refers to a beneficial, as opposed to legal (title), owner. For example, when a trust has been created by the equity participants to act as the lessor, the equity participants are deemed the beneficial interest holders. They hold interests in the trust that has title to the equipment.

bond. An instrument that represents a long-term debt obligation. The debt instruments, sometimes referred to as loan certificates, issued in a leveraged lease transaction are referred to as bonds or notes.

book reporting. The reporting of income or loss for financial as opposed to tax purposes on the financial records of a corporation or other reporting entity.

book residual value. An estimate of the equipment's residual value that a lessor uses, or "books," to calculate his economic return on a lease transaction.

broker. A person or entity who, for compensation, arranges lease transactions for another's account. A broker is also referred to as a syndicator or underwriter.

call. The right a lessee may have to buy specified leased equipment for a predetermined fixed price, usually expressed as a percentage of the original cost. If provided, such an option commonly does not become exercisable until the end of the lease term, and it lapses if the lessee fails to give the lessor timely notice of its intention to exercise this option. For example, a lessee may have a right to buy equipment at the end of the lease term for 30% of original cost, notice of intention to exercise the option to be given not less than 90 days before the lease term's end.

capital lease. Under the guidelines set out in FASB 13 by the Financial Accounting Standards Board, a lessee must classify certain long-term leases as capital leases for accounting and reporting purposes. Capital leases are accounted for in a manner that reflects the long-term repayment obligation of such leases.

cash flow. In a lease transaction, the amount of cash a lease generates for a lessor.

casualty value. A predetermined amount of money that a lessee guarantees the lessor will receive in the event of an equipment casualty loss during the lease term. Generally expressed as a percentage of original cost, the value varies according to the point in time during the lease term that the loss occurs. It is also referred to as a "stipulated loss value."

certificate of delivery and acceptance. The same as acceptance certificate.

charter party. A document that provides for the lease (charter) of a vessel or vessels. While the format is basically the same as any other lease, there are certain additions and modifications reflecting the requirements dictated by a vessel transaction.

charterer. The lessee of a vessel.

chattel mortgage. A mortgage relating to personal property. Thus, a mortgage on equipment is a chattel mortgage.

collateral. Assets used as security for the repayment of a debt obligation. In a typical leveraged lease, the collateral is the leased equipment.

commencement date. The date the base, or primary, lease term begins.

commission agreement. An agreement between a lease broker and a prospective equity participant providing for the payment of a fee to the broker for services in arranging a lease transaction.

commitment fee. Compensation paid to a lender in return for an agreement to make a future loan or to a lessor for its commitment to lease equipment to a lessee in the future.

conditional sales agreement. A contract, also referred to as a CSA, that provides for the time financing of asset purchases. The seller retains title to the asset until the buyer fulfills all specified conditions, such as installment payments. At that time, title automatically vests in the buyer.

cost of money. Commonly, the cost that a lessor incurs to borrow money. This includes the interest rate and any additional costs related to such borrowing, such as fees or compensating balances. In pricing a lease transaction, a lessor factors this cost into the computation.

cost-to-customer. The simple interest rate on a lease transaction.

DDB/SYD/SLM. A technique of switching methods of depreciation to maximize early depreciation write-offs used on property not covered by ACRS or MACRS. Depreciation deductions are initially computed using the double-declining balance (DDB) method with an appropriately timed change to the sum-of-the-years-digits (SYD) method followed by another appropriately timed change to the straight-line method (SLM).

debt participant. A long-term lender in a leveraged lease transaction. Frequently, those transactions have more than one debt participant.

debt service. The aggregate periodic repayment amount, including principal and interest, due on a loan.

default. In a lease transaction, when a party breaches certain material lease obligations.

deficiency guarantee. A guarantee given to a lessor by a third party, such as an equipment vendor or manufacturer, to induce a lessor to enter into a lease that it would not otherwise enter into usually because the prospective lessee may be a poor credit risk, or the future value of equipment may be highly speculative. For example, a deficiency guarantor may agree to pay the lessor for any shortfall below a designated amount, say 20% of original cost, incurred when the equipment is sold at the end of the lease.

Deficit Reduction Act (DRA). The 1984 Deficit Reduction Act, a federal income tax act.

delivery and acceptance certificate. The same as an acceptance certificate.

depreciation indemnity. A tax indemnification given by a lessee against the lessor's loss of anticipated depreciation tax benefits on leased equipment.

direct financing lease. A classification for a particular type of lease prescribed under the lease accounting guidelines set out by the FASB in FASB 13, applicable to lessors. Those guidelines tell lessors how to report direct financing leases for accounting purposes.

discounted cash flow analysis. The process of determining the present value of future cash flows.

Economic Recovery Tax Act (ERTA). The 1981 Economic Recovery Tax Act, a federal income tax act.

equipment certificate of acceptance. The same as an acceptance certificate.

equity participant. The equity investor in a leveraged lease. Frequently, a leveraged lease transaction has more than one equity participant, who jointly own and lease the equipment. An equity participant is also sometimes referred to as an "owner participant."

event of default. An event that provides the basis for the declaration of a default. For example, the nonpayment of rent under a lease agreement is typically prescribed as an event of default that gives the lessor the right to declare the lease in default and to pursue permitted remedies, such as terminating the lease and reclaiming the equipment.

facts and circumstances depreciation. A method of determining the depreciable life of an asset, generally usable on assets placed in service before 1981. Under the facts and circumstances method, the useful life determination is based on the owner's experience with similar property, giving due consideration to current and anticipated future conditions, such as wear and tear; normal progress of the art; economic changes, inventions, and current developments within the industry and the taxpayer's trade or business; and climatic and other relevant local conditions that can affect the taxpayer's repair, renewal, and replacement program.

fair market purchase value. An asset's value as determined in the open market in an arm's length transaction (one in which there is a willing buyer and a willing seller, under no compulsion to act) under normal selling conditions. It is also referred to simply as the "fair market value."

fair market rental value. The rental rate that an asset would command in the open market in an arm's length transaction (one in which there is a willing lessee and a willing lessor, under no compulsion to act) under normal renting conditions. It is also referred to simply as the "fair rental value."

FASB. The Financial Accounting Standards Board, the accounting profession's guideline-setting authority.

FASB Statement No. 13, Accounting for Leases. FAS No. 13 sets out the standards for financial lease accounting for lessors and lessees. FAS 13 was initially issued by the FASB, Stamford, Connecticut, in November 1976.

finance lease. (1) The same as a full payout lease. (2) A statutory lease category that would have permitted leases that otherwise would not have qualified as true leases for tax purposes to be so treated. Although enacted by TEFRA in 1982, the finance lease's effective date was postponed, and it was repealed by the 1986 TRA before ever having gone into effect, with limited exceptions.

financing agreement. An agreement commonly entered into by the principal parties to a leveraged lease before equipment delivery. The agreement identifies each party's obligation to the transaction and any conditions that must be satisfied before the obligations are fixed. Typically, it will involve the debt and equity participants, their representatives, and the lessee. It is also referred to as a "participation agreement."

floating rental rate. A form of periodic rental payments that change or "float" upward and downward over a lease's term with changes in a specified interest rate. Frequently, a designated bank's prime rate is the measuring interest rate.

full payout lease. A form of lease that will provide the lessor with a cash flow generally sufficient to return his equipment investment; pay the principal, interest, and other financing costs on related debt; cover his related sales and administration expenses; and generate a profit. The cash flow is determined from the rental payments, the ownership tax benefits, and the equipment residual value. The lessee typically has the right to use the leased equipment for most of its actual useful life.

gross income tax. A tax imposed by a state or local taxing authority on gross income generated from sources within its jurisdiction. The tax is deductible by the taxpayer for federal income tax purposes.

grossing up. A concept that reimbursement for a monetary loss will include sufficient additional monies so that the after-tax amount will equal the loss. The recipient is said to be made whole for his loss because the amount paid must take into account any taxes he will have to pay as a result of the receipt of the payments from the payor.

guaranteed residual value. An arrangement in which, for example, a broker or equipment manufacturer guarantees that a lessor will receive not less than a certain amount for specified equipment when it is disposed of at the end of the lease term. It is also sometimes referred to simply as a "guaranteed residual."

guideline lease. A leveraged lease that meets with the IRS's lease guidelines such as set out in Revenue Procedures 75-21, 75-28, 76-30, and 79-48. While the guidelines specifically address only private ruling requests, generally a guideline lease should qualify as a true lease for federal income tax purposes.

half-year convention. A concept under the income tax rules for depreciating equipment under which all equipment placed in service during a tax year is treated as having been placed in service at the midpoint of that year, regardless of when during the year it was in fact placed in service.

hell-or-high-water clause. A lease provision that commits a lessee to pay the rent unconditionally. The lessee waives any right that exists or may arise to withhold any rent from the lessor or any assignee of the lessor for any reason whatsoever, including any setoff, counterclaim, recoupment, or defense.

high-low rental. A rental structure in which the rent payments are reduced from a higher to a lower rate at a prescribed point in the lease term.

implicit lease rate. The annual interest rate that, when applied to the lease rental payments, will discount those payments to an amount equal to the cost of the equipment leased.

indemnity agreement. A contract in which one party commits to insure another party against anticipated and specified losses.

indenture. In a leveraged lease transaction, an agreement entered into by an owner trustee (the lessor's representative) and an indenture trustee (the lender's representative) in which the owner trustee grants a lien on the leased equipment, the lease rents, and other lessor contract rights as security for repayment of the outstanding equipment loan. It is also referred to as an indenture trust.

indenture trustee. The representative of the lenders where, in a leveraged lease transaction, the debt is provided through a trust arrangement. As the lender's representative, the indenture trustee may, for example, have to file and maintain a security interest in the leased equipment, receive rentals from the lessee, pay out the proper amounts to the lenders and the lessor, and take certain action to protect the outstanding loan in the event of a loan default.

installment sale. A sale in which the purchase price is paid in an agreed-upon number of installment payments over an agreed-upon period of time. Typically, title to what is sold does not transfer to the purchaser until, and only when, the last installment has been paid.

institutional investors. Institutions that invest in lease transactions. They can be, for example, insurance companies, pension funds, banks, and trusts.

insured value. The same as casualty value.

interim lease rental. The equipment rental due for the interim lease term. Typically, for each day during the interim lease term, a lessee must pay as interim lease rent an amount equal to the daily equivalent of the primary lease term rent. In a leveraged lease transaction, the lease sometimes instead permits the lessee to pay an amount equal to the daily equivalent of the long-term debt interest.

interim lease term. The lease term period between the lessee's acceptance of the equipment for lease and the beginning of the primary, or base, lease term.

investment tax credit (ITC). A credit allowed against federal income tax liability that can be claimed by a taxpayer for certain "section 38 property" acquired and placed in service by a taxpayer during a tax year. ITC may also be available for certain property under applicable state income tax laws. Under the federal tax laws, ITC is generally not available for property placed in service after 1985.

ITC indemnity. A type of indemnification in which the lessee commits to reimburse the lessor for any financial loss incurred through the loss of, or inability to claim, any or all of the anticipated ITC. If the lessor has "passed through" the ITC to the lessee, the lessor may have to give the indemnity.

ITC "pass-through." An election made by the lessor to treat, for ITC purposes, the lessee as the owner of the leased equipment. After the election, a lessee can claim the ITC on the equipment covered by the election.

layoff. The sale by a lessor of his interest in the lease agreement, including the ownership of the leased equipment and the right to receive the rent payments.

lease agreement. A contract in which an equipment owner, the lessor, transfers the equipment's use, subject to the specified terms and conditions, to another, the lessee, for a prescribed period of time and rental rate.

lease line. A present commitment by a lessor to lease specified equipment to be delivered in the future. A lease line can cover a variety of types of equipment, at varying rental rates and lease terms. It is also referred to as a lease line of credit.

lease underwriting. The process in which a lease broker arranges a lease transaction for the account of third parties, a prospective lessor and a prospective lessee. This can be on a best efforts basis or on a firm commitment basis. In a best efforts underwriting the broker only offers to attempt diligently to arrange the financing on certain proposed terms. In a firm commitment underwriting the broker in effect guarantees to arrange the financing as proposed.

lessee. The user of equipment that is the subject of a lease agreement.

lessor. The owner of equipment that is the subject of a lease agreement.

level payments. Payments that are the same for each payment period during the payment term. Frequently, rent and debt service payments are paid in level payments over the payment period.

leveraged lease. A lease in which a portion, generally 60% to 80% of the equipment acquisition cost, is borrowed from a bank or other lending institution, with the lessor paying the balance. The debt is commonly on a nonrecourse basis, and the rental payments are usually sufficient to cover the loan debt service.

limited use property. Leased property that will be economically usable only by the lessee, or a member of the lessee group, at the lease term's end because, for example, of its immobility or unique aspects. The IRS will not rule that a lease is a true lease where the leased equipment is limited use property.

loan certificate. A certificate that evidences a debt obligation.

loan participant. A debt participant.

low-high rental. A rental structure in which the rent payments are increased from a lower to a higher rate at a prescribed point in the lease term.

management agreement. A contract in which one party agrees to manage a lease transaction during its term, including, for example, rental payment processing and equipment disposal.

management fee. A fee that a lease transaction manager receives for services performed under a management agreement.

master lease agreement. A lease agreement designed to permit future equipment not contemplated when the lease is executed to be added to the lease later. The document is set up in two parts. The main body contains the general, or boilerplate provisions, such as the maintenance and indemnification provisions. An annex, or schedule, contains the type of items that usually vary with a transaction, such as rental rates and options.

mid-quarter convention. A concept under the income tax rules for depreciating equipment in which all equipment placed in service during a quarter of a tax year is treated as placed in service at the midpoint of such quarter, regardless of when it was in fact placed in service during the quarter.

modified accelerated cost recovery system (MACRS). A method prescribed for depreciating assets that was introduced by the 1986 TRA. It applies to most equipment placed in service after 1986.

mortgage. An arrangement whereby a lender (mortgagee) acquires a lien on property owned by a taxpayer (mortgagor) as security for the loan repayment. Once the debt obligation has been fully satisfied, the mortgage lien is terminated.

negative spread. The amount by which a value is below a certain prescribed amount. Generally, in a leveraged lease, a negative spread is the amount by which the transaction's simple interest rate is below the leveraged debt interest rate.

net lease. A lease arrangement in which the lessee is responsible for paying all costs, such as maintenance, certain taxes, and insurance, related to using the leased equipment in addition to the rental payments. Typically, finance leases are net leases.

non-payout lease. A lease arrangement that does not, over the primary term of the lease, generate enough cash flow to return substantially all the lessor's investment, debt financing costs, and sales and administration expenses.

nonrecourse debt financing. A loan as to which the lender agrees to look solely to the lessee, the lease rents, and the leased equipment for the loan's repayment. As security for the loan repayment, the lender receives an assignment of the lessor's rights under the lease agreement and a grant of a first lien on the equipment. Although the lessor has no obligation to repay the debt in the event of a lessee default, his equity investment in the equipment is usually subordinated to the lender's rights.

nonutilization fee. A fee that a lessor may impose in return for its present commitment to buy and lease specified equipment in the future. The fee is generally expressed as a percentage of the aggregate unused portion of the initial dollar commitment, for example, 1% of the unused balance of a $1 million lease line of credit. Thus, if all the commitment is used, no fee is payable.

operating lease. A form of lease arrangement in which the lessor generally commits to provide certain additional equipment-related services, other than the straight financing, such as maintenance, repairs, or technical advice. Generally, operating leases are non-payout in nature. The term also refers to a lease classification under FASB 13.

option. A contractual right that can be exercised under the granting terms. For example, a fair market value purchase option in a lease is the right to buy the equipment covered by it for its fair market value.

packager. A person or entity who arranges a lease transaction for third parties. Also referred to as an underwriter, syndicator, or sometimes, a broker.

participation agreement. The same as a financing agreement.

payout lease. The same as a full payout lease.

personal property. The same as Section 38 property. Equipment is considered personal property, but real estate is not so considered.

portfolio lease. The term commonly refers to a lease that is entered into by a "professional" lessor for its own account and investment.

present value. The term refers to the present worth of a future stream of payments calculated by discounting the future payments at a desired interest rate.

primary lease term. The same as base lease term.

private letter ruling. A written opinion that the IRS issues in response to a taxpayer's request. The letter sets out the IRS's position on the tax treatment of a proposed transaction. In leveraged lease transactions, for the IRS to issue a favorable private letter ruling, the request must comply with the IRS Guidelines.

progress payments. Payments that may be required by an equipment manufacturer or builder during the construction period toward the purchase price. Frequently required for costly equipment with a long construction period, the payments are designed to lessen the manufacturer's or builder's need to tie up his own funds during construction.

purchase option. The right to buy agreed-on equipment at the times and the amounts specified in the option. Frequently, these options are only exercisable at the end of the primary lease term, although they sometimes can be exercised during the primary lease term or at the end of any renewal term.

put. A right that a lessor may have to sell specified leased equipment to the lessee at a fixed price at the end of the initial lease term. It is usually imposed to protect the lessor's residual value assumption.

recourse debt financing. A loan under which the lender may look to the general credit of the lessor, in addition to the lessee and the equipment, for repayment of any outstanding loan obligation. The lender is said to have a "recourse" against the lessor.

recovery property. Property that can be depreciated under ACRS.

renewal option. An option frequently given to a lessee to renew the lease term for a specified rental and time period.

residual sharing. A compensation technique sometimes used by syndicators for arranging a lease transaction. Under this, the equity participants must pay a predetermined percentage of what the equipment is sold for at the end of the lease. For example, a syndicator may get 50% of any amount realized exceeding 20% of the equipment's original cost on sale.

residual value. The value of leased equipment at the end of the lease term.

right of first refusal. The right of the lessee to buy the leased equipment, or renew the lease, at the end of the lease term, for any amount equal to that offered by an unaffiliated third party.

safe harbor lease. A statutory lease category enacted as part of ERTA that permitted a lease to qualify as a true lease for federal income tax purposes although it would not otherwise ordinarily qualify. It was repealed by the 1984 DRA, with limited exceptions. Under a safe harbor lease, an equipment owner could essentially sell the ownership tax benefits without giving up other ownership rights.

sale-leaseback. An arrangement in which an equipment buyer buys equipment for the purpose of leasing it back to the seller.

sales tax. A tax imposed on selling equipment, similar to any other sales tax on property sold.

sales-type lease. A classification for a particular type of lease prescribed under the lease accounting guidelines that the FASB set out in FASB 13, applicable to lessors.

salvage value. The amount, estimated for federal income tax purposes, that an asset is expected to be worth at the end of its useful life.

section 38 property. Tangible personal property and certain other tangible property, as defined by Internal Revenue Code Section 38.

security agreement. An agreement that evidences an assignment by the lessor to the lender, as security for the equipment loan, of the lessor's rights under the lease agreement and a granting of a security interest in the leased equipment.

sinking fund. A fund frequently established in leveraged lease transactions by the lessor to accumulate funds to pay for future taxes.

sinking fund rate. The interest rate that a sinking fund is deemed to earn on accumulated funds.

special purpose equipment. The same as limited use property.

spread. The difference between two values. In lease transactions, the term is generally used to describe the difference between the lease interest rate and the interest rate on the debt.

stipulated loss value. The same as casualty value.

sublease. The re-lease by a lessee of equipment that is on lease to the lessee.

take or pay contract. An agreement in which one party commits to buy an agreed-on quantity of goods or material from another at a predetermined price. If the goods or material are not bought, the party making the purchase commitment must pay the party an amount of money equal to the cost of goods or materials it had committed to buy. For example, a public utility can agree to buy 100 tons of coal annually from a mining company, and if it does not buy this amount in any year it will pay an amount of money equal to its sale price.

tax benefit transfer lease (TBT). The same as a safe harbor lease.

tax lease. The same as a true lease.

Tax Equity and Fiscal Responsibility Act (TEFRA). The 1982 Tax Equity and Fiscal Responsibility Act, a federal income tax act.

Tax Reform Act (TRA). The 1986 Tax Reform Act, a federal income tax act.

termination option. An option entitling a lessee to terminate the lease during the lease term for a predetermined value, called the termination value, if the equipment becomes obsolete or surplus to the lessee's needs. The lessor usually requires the lessee to sell the equipment to an unaffiliated third party, and the lessee must pay the lessor any amount by which the sale proceeds are less than the termination value. Typically, any excess sale proceeds go to the lessor.

termination value. The amount that the lessee must pay the lessor if he exercises a termination option. Typically, the termination value is set as of each rental payment period and is generally expressed as a percentage of equipment cost. For example, the lessee may be permitted to terminate the lease at the end of the third year of a seven-year lease for an amount equal to 60% of cost.

time sale. An installment sale.

total earnings. The amount by which the aggregate rentals due the lessor over the entire lease term exceed the total equipment costs, including equity investment and debt financing costs. This concept does not consider the time value of money.

TRAC lease. A lease of motor vehicles or trailers that contains what is referred to as a terminal rental adjustment clause (TRAC). The clause permits or requires the rent amount to be adjusted based on the proceeds the lessor receives from the sale of the leased equipment. TRAC leases qualify as true leases.

Where to Call for a Refund

We're here to help you...
24 hours a day, wherever you travel.

Just call our Refund Service Center for the area/country from which you are dialing.

Help is also available from the nearest American Express Travel Service Office.

In		Call
North/South America		
U.S., Canada, Antigua, Bahamas, Barbados, Bermuda, Dominican Rep., Puerto Rico, U.S. Virgin Islands	Toll free	1-800-221-7282
Anguilla, BR Virgin Isl, Venezuela, Costa Rica, Montserrat, St. Kitts & Nevis, Turks & Caicos, Cayman Isl, Chile, Grenada, Panama	Toll free	1-800-828-0366
Argentina collect	Buenos Aires	(1) 312-0900
Brazil collect	and São Paulo	(011) 256-5573
		(011) 545-5018
Mexico	Toll free	1-800-221-7282
Other countries	USA collect	(1) 801-964-6665
Africa and Middle East		
Africa	England collect	(44) 1273-571-600
Middle East	Bahrain	(973) 256-834
Israel	Tel Aviv	17744-08694

In	Call	
Australia/South Pacific		
All countries	Sydney collect	61-2-886-0689
Europe		
Belgium	Toll free	0800-12112
France	Toll free	05-908600
Holland	Toll free	06022-0100
Italy	Toll free	1678-72000
Spain	Toll free	900-99-4426
Switzerland*	Toll free	155-0100
United Kingdom	Toll free	0800-521313
Germany	Toll free	013-085-3100
Other countries	England collect	(44) 1273-571-600
Asia		
Singapore, Malaysia, Burma, Brunei	Singapore collect	65-738-3383
India	New Delhi collect	(011) 687-5930
Japan	Toll free	0120-030-130
Korea	Seoul collect	(02) 739-0060
Pakistan		9221-263-0260
Thailand	Bangkok collect	66-227-30022
Other countries	Hong Kong collect	852-885-9331

Refer to your local directory for additional American Express® Travelers Cheque refund numbers or call our U.S. office collect, 801-964-6665.
Carry this form separately from your Travelers Cheques.
*A local charge will be incurred for this number.

REV. 12/96

Cheque Register

Record the full serial number of your first Cheque:

_____

List the last three digits of each Cheque's serial number and, as used, record the date spent.

Number	Date Spent	Number	Date Spent
1		6	
2		7	
3		8	
4		9	
5		10	

Keep this form and your copy of the Purchase Record separately from your Cheques. Having these records will help speed your refund if your Cheques are lost or stolen. See refund information on reverse side.

Keep unused Cheques for your next vacation or business trip—or as emergency money for unexpected situations.

We appreciate your comments

Because we care about our customers and the quality of our service, we'd like to hear from you.
If you have any comments or require additional assistance, please call our toll-free number or write to:
Carl Lehmann/President, American Express
Travelers Cheque Group, 4315 South 2700 West,
Salt Lake City, Utah 84184-3400.

transition rules. Statutory rules enacted when there is a change in the tax laws. The transition rules allow certain transactions to be exempted from the law change. For example, transition rules permitted ITC to be claimed on certain equipment placed in service after 1985.

true lease. An arrangement that qualifies for lease treatment for federal income tax purposes. Under a true lease, the lessee may deduct rental payments and the lessor may claim the tax benefits accruing to an equipment owner.

trust. An arrangement in which property is held by one party for the benefit of another. It is frequently used in leveraged lease transactions.

trust certificate. A trust document issued on behalf of a trust to evidence the beneficial ownership in the trust estate.

trustee. The person or entity appointed, or designated, to carry out a trust's terms. In leveraged lease transactions, the trustee is generally a bank or trust company.

trustee fees. Fees payable to a trustee as compensation for services performed.

trustor. An individual or entity who causes the creation of a trust and for whose benefit it is established.

unleveraged lease. A lease in which the lessor puts up 100% of the equipment's acquisition cost from its own funds.

use tax. A tax imposed upon the use, storage, or consumption of tangible personal property within a taxing jurisdiction. For example, in most states a lessor purchasing equipment has the option of paying an up-front sales tax equal to a specified percentage of the equipment's purchase price or a use tax equal to a specified percentage of lease rents under the equipment's lease.

useful life. Commonly, the economic usable life of an asset.

vendor. A seller of property. Commonly, the manufacturer or distributor of equipment.

vendor program. A program in which an equipment lessor provides a lease financing service to customers of an equipment manufacturer.

Appendixes:
Sample Documents

The following sample equipment lease documents have been included in these appendixes:

The documents are reproduced merely as guidelines to give you an idea of the various format approaches. They should not be used without expert guidance.

Depreciation tables are reproduced beginning at page 315.

Request for Lease Quotation

THE MIDEASTERN RAILWAY CORPORATION

Lessee:	The Mideastern Railway Corporation.
Equipment:	Model 6 RD-10, 23,000 hp. diesel locomotives (est. unit cost-$525,000), manufactured by Arcane Locomotive Corp.
Estimated Total Cost:	$3,150,000
Equipment Delivery:	February, 19×8-Two units. March, 19×8-Two units. April, 19×8-Two units.
Equity Contribution & Commitment:	Not less than 20% of cost. The equity investor(s) must agree to buy equipment with a maximum equipment cost up to $3.5 million.
Interest Rate Assumptions:	7 3/4%, 8%, 8 1/4%.
Agent for Debt Placement:	Samon & Smith Co.
Attorney for Long-Term Agreement of Lenders:	Carr, Swift & Moore, subject to the long-term lenders.
Structuring of the Transaction:	15-year net finance leveraged lease with semiannual, in arrears, level payments. Any other proposal format will be considered provided a bid as requested has been submitted.
	The lessee must have three two-year fair market rental renewal options. A fair market purchase option at the end of the initial term and each renewal term should also be provided. The lessee will give a letter stating that, in its opinion, the locomotives will have a useful life exceeding 18 years and a residual value equal to 20% of the original cost at the end of 15 years.
Delivery Cutoff Date:	The cutoff date for the equipment deliveries will be July 1, 19X8. All equipment not delivered before this date will be excluded from the transaction unless the lessor and the lessee agree to extend such date.
Expenses:	All expenses of the transaction, including rating fees and the investment banking fees, will be borne by the lessor.
Security:	The lessee's lease obligations will be unconditionally guaranteed by The Eastern Railway Company. The Mideastern Railway Company is a wholly owned subsidiary of The Eastern Railway Company.
	The long-term debt will be secured by an assignment of the lease. An agent bank will be selected by The Eastern Railway Company and Samon & Smith Co. after the long-term debt is placed. The long-term debt will be noncallable except for casualty occurrences.

Indemnification: Preference will be given to bids with minimum indemnifica-
                          tion. All indemnification requirements must be precisely
                          stated in the proposal.

Interim Rentals: All quotations must assume not more than three equity clos-
                          ing dates and provide interim rents from such dates to July
                          1, 19×8, the beginning of the primary lease term. Interim
                          rentals will be equal to the daily equivalent of the long-term
                          debt interest rate.

Casualty Values: All bidders must provide a schedule of casualty values, ex-
                          pressed as a percentage of original cost, both for the primary
                          lease term and any extensions thereafter. The method of cal-
                          culating the casualty values must also be supplied.

Insurance: The equipment will be self-insured.

Please mail us your proposal in writing postmarked no later than April 15, 19×7. Your
proposal must be on a "firm" basis, and at the time of submission you must be prepared
to identify the investor source(s) so that they may be contacted immediately by telephone
for verification in the event you are the successful bidder.

Nonunderwriting Proposal Letter

December 5, 19×8

Secour Corporation
800 Second Avenue
New York, New York 10017

Attention: Mr. R. Babcox
                      President

Gentlemen:

Able Leasing Corporation ("ALC") offers to purchase and lease to Secour Corporation ("Secour") an item of newly manufactured computer equipment on the following terms and conditions:

1. Equipment Description:	The equipment will consist of one (1) new computer, model no. EA-1, manufactured by IXT Computer Corp.
2. Equipment Cost:	Approximately $1 million.
3. Delivery and Payment:	Delivery of the Equipment is anticipated on January 1, 19×9, but in no event shall be later than March 1, 19×9. ALC shall pay for the Equipment on delivery and acceptance.
4. Lease Term:	Eight years, beginning on delivery and acceptance of the Equipment.
5. Rental Program:	Secour shall remit 32 consecutive, level, quarterly payments, in advance, each equal to 4.4000% of Equipment Cost.
6. Options:	At the conclusion of the Lease Term, Secour may (with at least 120 days' prior written notice)
	A. Buy the Equipment for an amount equal to its then fair market value.
	B. Renew the lease with respect to the Equipment for its then fair rental value.
7. Tax Benefits:	The rent is calculated based on the assumption that ALC will be entitled to
	A. Five-year MACRS depreciation on the full Equipment Cost, 200% declining-balance switching to straight-line, and
	B. A corporate income tax rate equal to 35%
8. Fixed Expenses:	This is a net financial lease proposal and all fixed expenses, such as insurance maintenance and personal property taxes, shall be for the account of Secour.

9. Conditions Precedent: This offer is subject to the approval of the Board of Directors of ALC and to the execution of lease documentation mutually acceptable to Secour and ALC.

If the foregoing is satisfactory to you, please indicate your acceptance of this offer by signing the duplicate copy of this letter in the space provided therefor and returning it directly to the undersigned.

This offer expires as of the close of business on December 19, 19×8.

Very truly yours,

ABLE LEASING CORPORATION

By _____

Vice President

Accepted and Agreed to on this

_____ day of _____ , 19×8

SECOUR CORPORATION

By: _____

Its: _____

Underwriting Proposal Letter

July 8, 19×8

White Airline Corporation
200 Park Avenue
New York, New York 10017

Attention: R. Rosset
           Assistant Treasurer

Gentlemen:

Able Leasing Corporation ("ALC"), on behalf of its nominees, proposes to use its best efforts to arrange a lease for one new Martin RC–75 aircraft for use by White Airline Corporation under the following terms and conditions:

Lessee:	The Lessee shall be White Airline Corporation.
Lessor:	The Lessor will be a commercial bank or trust company acting as owner trustee ("Owner Trustee") pursuant to one or more owners' trusts (the "Trust") for the benefit of one or more commercial banks or other corporate investors (the "Owner Participant"). The Trust shall acquire the Equipment and lease it to the Lessee.
Equipment:	One new Martin RC-75 aircraft.
Cost:	For purposes of this proposal, a total cost of $28 million, plus or minus 5% has been assumed.
Delivery Date:	Delivery of the Equipment is anticipated as of November 1, 19×8; however, shall be no later than December 30, 19×8.
Interim Lease Term:	The interim lease term shall extend from the Delivery Date until the Commencement Date. For the purposes of this proposal the Commencement Date is assumed to be January 1, 19×9.
Interim Rent:	The Lessee shall pay interim rent equal to interest-only on the total cost of the Equipment at an interest rate equal to the Long-Term Debt Interest Rate.
Primary Lease Term:	The primary lease term shall be 20 years from the Commencement Date.
Primary Rent:	From the Commencement Date, the Lessee shall make 40 consecutive, level, semiannual payments, in arrears, each equal to 4.400% of Cost.
Debt Financing:	An investment banker acceptable to ALC and the Lessee shall arrange for the private placement of secured notes or similar instruments ("Indebtedness") to be issued by the Lessor for a principal amount equal to 80% of total Equipment Cost to certain institutional investors ("Lenders"), who may be repre-

sented by an indenture trustee or agent bank ("Agent"). This proposal assumes that the Indebtedness shall be amortized in semiannual payments of principal and interest at an 8% per annum interest rate ("Long-Term Debt Interest Rate"), payable in arrears over the term of the lease. In the event that the Long-Term Debt Interest Rate varies from that assumed, the rent shall be adjusted, upward or downward, so that the Owner Participant's after-tax yield and after-tax cash flows will be maintained. The Indebtedness shall be secured by an assignment of the lease and a security interest in the Equipment but otherwise shall be without recourse to the Owner Participant and the Lessor.

Insurance: The Lessee may self-insure the Equipment.

Purchase & Renewal: At the end of the Primary Lease Term, the Lessee Options may (with 180 days' written notice prior to the end of the term)

1. renew the lease on the Equipment for its then fair rental value for one five-year period.

2. buy the Equipment for an equivalent price and under similar conditions as rendered by a third party approached by the Lessor and agreed to by the Lessor prior to sale to that third party.

If the Lessee does not elect to exercise any of the above options, the Lessee shall return the Equipment to the Lessor at the end of the term at a mutually agreeable location.

Termination Option: At any time during the Primary Lease Term, on or after 10 years from the Commencement Date, the Lessee may (with 180 days' prior written notice) terminate the lease in the event the Equipment becomes obsolete or surplus to its needs, on paying a mutually agreed on termination value.

Fixed Expenses: This is a net financial lease proposal, with all fixed expenses, such as maintenance, insurance, taxes (other than net income taxes), for the account of the Lessee.

Expenses of Transaction: ALC shall pay all transaction expenses, including

1. fees and disbursements of special counsel for the Agent and the Lenders;

2. acceptance and annual fees and expenses of the Agent;

3. fees and disbursements of special counsel for the Owner Trustee and the Trustor;

4. acceptance and annual fees and expenses of the Owner Trustee;

5. fees and disbursements in connection with obtaining a ruling from the Internal Revenue Service;

6. expenses of documentation, including printing and reproduction; and

7. fees and disbursements in connection with the private placement of the Indebtedness.

If the transaction is not consummated for any reason, the Lessee shall pay all of the above fees and expenses.

Nonutilization Fee: Once ALC has obtained equity investor commitments satisfactory to the Lessee, the Lessee shall be liable to ALC for a non-utlilization fee equal to 0.5% of the Equipment Cost in the event it does not lease the Equipment in accordance with intent of this proposal.

Commitment Fee: A commitment fee of 0.5% per annum shall be paid by the Lessee to the equity investors on the outstanding equity investor commitment. The fee shall accrue as of the date investor commitments satisfactory to White Airline Corporation have been obtained, shall run up to the Commencement Date, and shall be payable quarterly, in arrears.

Tax Assumptions:

A. The Rent is calculated based on the assumptions that

1. the organization created by the Trust will be treated as a partnership for Federal income tax purposes;

2. the Lessor will be entitled to seven-year MACRS depreciation on 100% of the Equipment Cost, 200% declining-balance switching to straight-line;

3. the Lessor will be entitled to deduct interest on the Indebtedness under Section 163 of the 1986 Internal Revenue Code;

4. the Lessor will be entitled to amortize the transaction expenses over the Interim and Primary Lease Terms using a straight-line method;

5. the effective Federal income tax rate of the Owner Participant is 35%; and

6. the Lessor will not recognize any income from the transaction other than from Lessee rental, termination value, stipulated loss value, and indemnity payments payable to the Lessor.

B. The Lessee shall provide necessary representation relating to the estimated economic life and residual value of the Equipment.

Tax Ruling: The Lessor plans to obtain an Internal Revenue Service ruling with respect to the tax assumptions stated above. The Lessee shall agree to indemnify for the tax assumptions above. Such indemnity shall remain in effect until a favorable ruling has been obtained.

If the foregoing proposal is satisfactory to you, please indicate your acceptance by signing the duplicate copy of this letter in the space provided therefor, and returning it directly to the undersigned.

This offer expires at the close of business on October 28, 19×8 and is subject to the approval of the Owner Participant's Board of Directors and mutually satisfactory lease documentation.

Very truly yours,

ABLE LEASING CORPORATION

By: _____
         Vice President

Accepted and Agreed to on this
_____ day of _____, 19×8.
WHITE AIRLINE CORPORATION

By: _____

Its: _____

Form of Net Finance Lease When the Lessor Is Not Also the Vendor

═══════════════════════════════════

MASTER LEASE

of

COMPUTER EQUIPMENT

dated as of _____, 19 _____

between

[   ]

Lessor

and

[   ]

Lessee

═══════════════════════════════════

Author's note: The following lease form can be used as a basic guide in drafting a Master Lease for any type of equipment, but do so only with the advice of legal counsel. It is an actual Lessee Master Lease written for one of my clients, and contains an approach that fits its particular business and legal needs in large ticket lease transactions of computer equipment.

Master Lease of Computer Equipment

TABLE OF CONTENTS

MASTER LEASE OF COMPUTER EQUIPMENT, dated as of _____, 19 _____, between _____, a _____ corporation, with a principal place of business located at _____ (the "Lessor," such term to include, to the extent permitted hereunder, its successors and assigns), and _____, a _____ corporation, with a principal place of business located at _____ (the "Lessee," such term to include, to the extent permitted hereunder, its successors and assigns).

SECTION 1. *DEFINITIONS*

The following terms shall have the respective meanings set forth below for all purposes of this Lease.

1.1 "Acceptance Date" as to each Item of Equipment shall mean the date on which Lessee determines that such Item of Equipment is acceptable for lease pursuant to the terms and conditions of this Lease, as specified by Lessee in the applicable Certificate of Acceptance.

1.2 "Appraiser" shall mean a qualified independent computer equipment appraiser selected in accordance with the provisions of Section 14 of this Lease.

1.3 "Basic Lease Commencement Date" as to each Unit shall mean the date on which the Primary Term shall begin, as specified in the applicable Equipment Schedule.

1.4 "Basic Lease Rate Factor" as to each Unit shall mean the percentage rental set forth in the applicable Equipment Schedule.

1.5 "Basic Rent" as to each Unit shall mean the rent due and payable on each Rent Date during the Primary Term, as specified in the applicable Equipment Schedule.

1.6 "Business Day" shall mean a calendar day, excluding Saturdays, Sundays, and all days on which banking institutions in [insert jurisdiction(s) of Lessee's and/or Lessor's principal place(s) of business] shall be closed.

1.7 "Casualty Occurrence" shall have the meaning set forth in Section 9 of this Lease.

1.8 "Casualty Value" as to each Unit shall be the amount calculated in accordance with the Casualty Value provisions of the applicable Equipment Schedule.

1.9 "Certificate of Acceptance" shall mean a certificate substantially in the form attached as Annex A to the form of Equipment Schedule attached hereto as Exhibit A.

1.10 "Code" shall mean the United States Internal Revenue Code of 1986, as amended and in effect from time to time [if appropriate, insert other relevant governing tax law].

1.11 "Cutoff Date" as to each Item of Equipment shall mean the date specified in the applicable Equipment Schedule after which Lessor shall not be obligated to purchase and lease such Item of Equipment to Lessee in accordance with the terms and conditions of this Lease.

1.12 "Discount Rate" shall mean the per annum interest charge (calculated on the basis of a 360-day year and 30-day month) specified in the applicable Equipment Schedule.

1.13 "Equipment Schedule" shall mean each schedule, substantially in the form of Exhibit A attached hereto, which shall refer to this Lease and which shall become a part hereof as executed from time to time by the parties hereto, covering one or more Items of Equipment that may be leased by Lessee from Lessor hereunder.

1.14 "Event of Default" shall mean any of the events specified in Section 13.1 of this Lease.

1.15 "Fair Market Rental" shall mean the rental value of a Unit determined in accordance with the provisions of Section 14 of this Lease.

1.16 "Fair Market Value" shall mean the sale value of a Unit determined in accordance with the provisions of Section 14 of this Lease.

1.17 "Impositions" shall have the meaning set forth in Section 7.1 of this Lease.

1.18 "Interim Rent" as to each Unit shall mean the rent payable with respect to any Interim Term, as specified in the applicable Equipment Schedule.

1.19 "Interim Term" as to each Unit shall mean the period of time, if any, commencing on the Acceptance Date and ending on the day immediately preceding the Basic Lease Commencement Date.

1.20 "Item of Equipment" shall mean an item of electronic data processing equipment described in an Equipment Schedule. When an "Item of Equipment" becomes subject to this Lease it is thereafter for all purposes of this Lease referred to and defined as a "Unit."

1.21 "Invoice Purchase Price" as to each Unit shall mean the aggregate amount payable by the Lessor to Manufacturer for such Unit, as specified in one or more Manufacturer's invoices for such Unit.

1.22 "Lease" shall mean this Master Lease of Computer Equipment between Lessor and Lessee, including without limitation all Equipment Schedules and all exhibits to this Lease and to all Equipment Schedules. The words "herein," "hereof," "hereunder," and other words of similar import used in this Lease refer to this Lease as a whole and not to any particular Section, Subsection, or other portion of this Lease.

1.23 "Lessor's Cost" as to each Unit shall mean the Invoice Purchase Price plus additional costs and expenses that are assumed and subsequently paid by Lessor pursuant to the applicable Equipment Schedule.

1.24 "Lessor's Lien" shall have the meaning set forth in Section 15.3 of this Lease.

1.25 "Lien" shall have the meaning set forth in Section 15.3 of this Lease.

1.26 "Loss Payment Date" as to a Unit suffering a Casualty Occurrence shall mean the date on which Lessee shall be obligated to pay Lessor the Casualty Value in accordance with provisions of Section 9.1 of this Lease.

1.27 "Manufacturer" as to each Unit shall mean the manufacturer or vendor thereof specified by Lessee in the applicable Equipment Schedule.

1.28 "Overdue Rate" shall mean the per annum interest charge (calculated on the basis of a 360-day year and 30-day month) pursuant to Section 18 as specified in the applicable Equipment Schedule.

1.29 "Primary Term" as to each Unit shall mean that period of time commencing on, and including, the Basic Lease Commencement Date and ending that period of time thereafter, as designated in the applicable Equipment Schedule, unless earlier terminated pursuant to the provisions of this Lease.

1.30 "Purchase Documents" shall mean those documents relating to the purchase of a Unit or Units by Lessor from Manufacturer.

1.31 "Purchase Right" as to each Unit shall have the meaning specified in Section 16.1 of this Lease.

1.32 "Renewal Rent" as to each Unit shall mean the rent due and payable on each Rent Date during a Renewal Term, as specified in the applicable Equipment Schedule.

1.33 "Renewal Right" as to each Unit shall have the meaning specified in Section 16.2 of this Lease.

1.34 "Renewal Term" as to each Unit shall mean that aggregate period of time following the end of the Primary Term for which this Lease is extended.

1.35 "Rent" as to each Unit shall mean and include Basic Rent and any Interim Rent and Renewal Rent payable, or to become payable, by Lessee to Lessor.

1.36 "Rent Date" as to each Unit shall mean each date during the Term on which Rent is due and payable, as specified in the applicable Equipment Schedule.

1.37 "Term" as to each Unit shall mean the Primary Term and any Interim Term and Renewal Term.

1.38 "Termination Right" as to each Unit shall have the meaning specified in Section 16.3 of this Lease.

1.39 "Termination Value" as to each Unit shall be the amount calculated in accordance with the Termination Value provisions of the applicable Equipment Schedule.

1.40 "Unit" shall mean an Item of Equipment, and any modifications thereof, or improvements or additions thereto, which is leased by Lessor to Lessee pursuant to the terms and provisions of this Lease.

1.41 "Upgrade Right" shall have all the meaning specified in Section 16.4 of this Lease.

SECTION 2. *EQUIPMENT ACQUISITION AND ACCEPTANCE*

2.1 *Lease Commitment.* In consideration of the Rent to be paid by Lessee and the other covenants contained in this Lease to be kept and performed by Lessee, Lessor hereby agrees to lease to Lessee each Item of Equipment described in each Equipment Schedule in accordance with the terms and conditions of this Lease.

2.2 *Lessor Payment.* Lessor shall purchase each Unit from Manufacturer solely for its own investment and account as a principal and not as a broker and promptly pay to Manufacturer the full Invoice Purchase Price for each Unit. In no event shall Lessor make such payment later than the earlier of the due date specified by Manufacturer or thirty (30) days after the Acceptance Date. Lessor shall, immediately upon making such payment, deliver to Lessee reasonably satisfactory evidence of such payment. If the full Invoice Purchase Price for any such Unit is not so paid to Manufacturer as provided in this Section 2.2, Lessee shall have the absolute right, in its discretion, (a) to make such payment to Manufacturer whereupon all of Lessor's rights in, and title to, such Unit shall automatically vest in Lessee and (b) to withhold any Rent and/or (c) terminate this Lease as to such Unit. In addition to paying the Invoice Purchase Price for each Unit, Lessor shall also pay, no later than the due date, such other costs and expenses as to a Unit as specified as part of the Lessor's Cost for such Unit in the applicable Equipment Schedule.

2.3 *Cutoff Date.* Lessor shall have no obligation to purchase and lease any Item of Equipment hereunder which has not been accepted by Lessee in accordance with the provisions of Section 2.5 on or before the Cutoff Date.

2.4 *Installation Location.* Each Unit shall be installed at the address set forth in the applicable Equipment Schedule. Lessee may, without Lessor's consent, move any such Unit from such address, or any relocated address, to any other address in the United States of America, provided Lessee has notified Lessor in writing at least thirty (30) days prior to effecting any change of location.

2.5 *Lessee Acceptance.* Lessee shall acknowledge its acceptance of each Item of Equipment for lease hereunder by executing and delivering to Lessor a Certificate of Acceptance as to each such Item of Equipment, whereupon each such Item of Equipment shall become subject to this Lease as of the Acceptance Date.

SECTION 3. *LEASE TERM*

3.1 *Term of Lease.* The Term of each Unit shall be as specified in the applicable Equipment Schedule.

3.2 *Lease Termination.* This Lease shall not be terminated by Lessor or Lessee with respect to any Unit for any reason whatsoever, except as expressly provided herein.

SECTION 4. *NET LEASE*

This Lease is a net lease and Lessee, subject to the provisions of Section 2.2, shall not be entitled to any abatement or reduction of Rent, or set-off against Rent, including without limitation abatements, reductions, or set-offs due or alleged to be due by reason of any past, present, or future claims of Lessee against Lessor under this Lease. Notwithstanding the foregoing, however, nothing shall preclude Lessee from otherwise enforcing any and all other rights it may have against Lessor under this Lease or otherwise.

SECTION 5. *RENT AND USAGE*

5.1 *Rent Payment.* Lessee agrees to pay Lessor Rent for each Unit in accordance with the provisions of this Lease. The Rent for each Unit shall be paid on each Rent Date in the amount set forth in the applicable Equipment Schedule. In accordance with Section 23.1 hereof, if any date on which a Rent payment is due is not a Business Day, the Rent payment otherwise payable on such date shall be payable on the next succeeding Business Day.

5.2 *Unlimited Usage.* Lessor agrees that there shall be no limit on the number of hours for which any Unit may be used.

SECTION 6. *IDENTIFICATION MARKS*

Lessee, at its own cost and expense, will cause each Unit to be legibly and permanently marked, in a reasonably prominent location, with the following legend evidencing the fact that such Unit is owned by Lessor and subject to this Lease:

> "[Name and Address of Lessor],
> Owner, Lessor."

Lessee shall, upon at least thirty (30) Business Days' prior written notice from Lessor, make such changes and/or additions in such markings specified by Lessor as may be required by law in order to protect Lessor's ownership of such Unit and the rights of Lessor under this Lease. Lessee will promptly replace or cause to be replaced any such markings that are removed, defaced, or destroyed.

SECTION 7. *GENERAL TAX INDEMNIFICATION*

7.1 *General Tax Indemnity.* All Rent and other payments required to be made by Lessee hereunder shall be net of any deductions, charges, costs, expenses, and Impositions with respect to collection or otherwise. Lessee agrees to pay, on written demand by Lessor specifying such Impositions in reasonable detail, any and all Impositions and shall keep and save harmless and indemnify Lessor from and against all such Impositions. "Impositions" shall mean the amount of any local, state, federal, or foreign taxes of any nature whatsoever, assessments, license fees, governmental charges, duties, fines, interest charges, or penalties with respect to any Unit or any part thereof, or with respect to the purchase, ownership, delivery, leasing, possession, use, or operation thereof. The term "Impositions" shall not include (a) federal, state, local, and foreign tax on, or measured by, the net income of Lessor; (b) any tax based on, or measured by, gross income or gross receipts of Lessor as a substitute for and not in addition to taxes based on net income of Lessor; (c) any tax imposed by Section 531 [Accumulated Earnings Tax] or Section 541 [Personal Holding Company Tax] of the Code; (d) taxes, fees, or other charges included in Lessor's Cost; (e) the aggregate of all franchise taxes or other similar taxes up to the amount in the aggregate of any such taxes which would be payable to the states and cities in which Lessor maintains or has maintained places of, or otherwise does, business during the Term of this Lease, except any such tax which is in substitution for or relieves Lessee from the payment of taxes which it would otherwise be obligated to pay or reimburse Lessor for as herein provided; (f) any fines or penalties that are imposed as a result of (A) the misconduct or negligence of Lessor or (B) a failure by Lessor to take reasonable action or to furnish reasonable cooperation to Lessee as a result of which Lessee is unable to diligently fulfill its obligations under this Section 7; (g) any claim made against Lessor for any Imposition that Lessee is obligated to pay hereunder with respect to which Lessor has not notified Lessee in writing pursuant to Section 7.2; (h) any tax imposed on the purchase of a Unit or Units from Manufacturer; and (i) any sales or use tax imposed upon (A) the voluntary transfer or other disposition by Lessor, or any assignee of Lessor, of all or any of the Units, or (B) another obtaining any interest in a Unit by, through or under Lessor. In this regard it is understood that any transfer or disposition (A) that occurs in the Lessor's exercise of the remedies provided in Section 13.2 after an Event of Default has occurred and while the same is continuing or (B) of a unit which has suffered a Casualty Occurrence, shall not be deemed to be a voluntary transfer or disposition.

7.2 *Claim Notification.* If a claim is made against Lessor for any Imposition that Lessee is obligated to pay hereunder, Lessor shall promptly notify Lessee in writing.

7.3 *Right to Contest.* Lessee shall be under no obligation to pay any imposition so long as Lessee is contesting such Imposition in good faith. Lessor hereby agrees to fully cooperate with Lessee, including providing any information Lessee shall request, in connection with any such contest. So long as Lessee is so contesting such Imposition and no final, unreviewable judgment adverse to Lessee has been entered by a court of competent jurisdiction, Lessee shall not be in default hereunder with respect to the nonpayment of any such Imposition.

7.4 *Lessor Payment Reimbursement.* If any Imposition shall have been charged or levied against Lessor directly and paid by Lessor, Lessee shall reimburse Lessor on presentation of reasonably satisfactory evidence of payment; provided, however, Lessor has obtained Lessee's prior written approval for the payment thereof, which approval shall not be unreasonably withheld.

7.5 *Lessor Refund Reimbursement.* If Lessee has reimbursed Lessor for any Imposition pursuant to this Section 7 (or if Lessee has made a payment to the appropriate taxing authority for an Imposition which it is required to pay hereunder), Lessee may take such steps (in the name of Lessee or in the name of Lessor) as are necessary or appropriate to seek a refund of such Imposition, and Lessor shall fully cooperate with Lessee in seeking such refund. In the event of a refund of any Imposition for which Lessor has received a payment from Lessee, the amount of such refund shall be immediately paid over to or retained by Lessee, as appropriate.

SECTION 8. *GENERAL INDEMNIFICATION*

8.1 *Conflict.* The provisions of this Section 8 are in addition to, and not in limitation of, the provisions of Section 7 hereof; provided, however, that in the event of a conflict between the provisions of this Section 8 and the provisions of Section 7, the provisions of Section 7 shall be controlling.

8.2 *General Indemnity.* Lessee hereby agrees to assume liability for, and does hereby agreed to indemnify, protect, save, and keep Lessor harmless from and against any and all liabilities, obligations, losses, damages, penalties, claims, actions, suits, costs, expenses, or disbursements arising out of Lessee's actions that may be imposed on, incurred by, or asserted against Lessor relating to or arising out this Lease or the manufacture, purchase, acceptance, rejection, return, lease, ownership, possession, use, condition, operation, or sale of each Unit or any accident in connection therewith. Lessor hereby expressly authorizes Lessee to contest, and agrees to cooperate fully with Lessee in contesting, in the name of Lessee or Lessor as Lessee shall deem appropriate for the benefit of Lessee, any such liability, obligation, penalty, or claim asserted against either Lessee or Lessor. Lessee shall not be required to indemnify Lessor except as specifically set forth in the preceding sentence, including without limitation as to (a) loss or liability in respect of any Unit arising from any act or event which occurs after such Unit has been returned to Lessor pursuant to the provisions of this Lease; (b) loss or liability resulting from the breach of any covenant, representation or warranty made by Lessor in this Lease or in any document relating to the transactions contemplated by this Lease; (c) loss or liability resulting from the negligence or misconduct of Lessor (including acts by employees, agents or other representatives of Lessor); (d) any legal or accounting fees or other expense incurred by Lessor in connection with this Lease and the other documents referred to herein and any amendments or other modifications or additions to this Lease or such other documents; (e) any brokerage fees or similar fees or commissions incurred by Lessor in connection with any transactions contemplated hereby; or (f) any liability, obligation, penalty, or claim indemnified against herein so long as the validity or amount thereof is being contested by Lessee in good faith.

SECTION 9. *PAYMENT FOR CASUALTY OCCURRENCE*

9.1 *Casualty Occurrence.* In the event that any Unit becomes damaged or otherwise inoperable so as to preclude its use for the purpose intended by Lessee, as determined by Lessee in good faith, or in the event any Unit is lost or stolen or is permanently returned by Lessee to Manufacturer pursuant to the Purchase Documents [Author's Note: This relates to when a Unit is permitted to be returned to the manufacturer because it is defective or otherwise fails to meet requirements set forth in the Purchase Documents], or for ninety (90) consecutive days or more is taken or requisitioned by condemnation or otherwise in such a manner as to result in Lessee's loss of possession or use, excluding any permitted sublease (any such occurrence being hereinafter referred to as a "Casualty Occurrence") during the Term of this Lease, Lessee shall promptly so notify Lessor. On the Rent Date next succeeding a Casualty Occurrence (the "Loss Payment Date"), Lessee shall pay to Lessor an amount equal to the Casualty Value of such Unit applicable on the date of such Casualty Occurrence. [*Author's Note:* Casualty Value payments vary in arrangement—each situation must be looked at independently.] Upon, but not prior to, the time when such payment is made by Lessee as to any Unit, Lessee's obligation to pay Rent for such Unit, including without limitation any Rent that would be attributable to any Rent payment period subsequent to the Loss Payment Date, shall cease and the Term of this Lease as to such Unit shall automatically terminate. Lessor hereby appoints Lessee as its sole agent to dispose of any Unit or any part thereof suffering a Casualty Occurrence in the best manner and at the best price obtainable, as determined by Lessee in its sole discretion, on an "as is, where is" basis. If Lessee shall have so paid the Casualty Value to Lessor, unless an Event of Default shall have occurred and be continuing, Lessee shall be entitled to the proceeds of such sale up to an amount equal to the sum of the Casualty Value of such Unit plus all costs, expenses, and damages incurred by Lessee in connection with such Casualty Occurrence and the disposition of such Unit. Lessor shall be entitled to any excess. In the case of the taking or requisition of any Unit by any governmental authority, any payments received from such governmental authority as compensation for such taking or requisition shall, if Lessee has therefore paid the Casualty Value, be immediately paid over to or retained by Lessee, as appropriate, up to an amount equal to the sum of the Casualty Value of such Unit plus all costs, expenses, and damages incurred by Lessee in connection with such Casualty Occurrence, and Lessor shall be entitled to any excess. Lessor shall have no duty to Lessee to pursue any claim against any governmental authority but Lessee may at its own cost and expense pursue the same on its own behalf and on behalf of Lessor, and Lessor shall cooperate fully in Lessee's pursuit of such claim.

9.2 *Manufacturer Returned Unit.* As to each Unit returned to Manufacturer in the manner described in the first sentence of Section 9.1, Lessee shall be entitled to immediately receive and retain all amounts paid or payable to Lessor by Manufacturer with respect to the return of such Unit, up to the Casualty Value paid by Lessee hereunder plus all cost, expenses, and damages incurred by Lessee in connection therewith. Any excess shall immediately be paid over to or retained by Lessor, as appropriate.

9.3. *Return After Requisition.* In the event of the taking or requisition for use by any governmental authority of any Unit during the Term of this Lease as to such Unit, unless such taking or requisition shall constitute a Casualty Occurrence, all of Lessee's obligations under this Lease with respect to such Unit shall continue to the same extent as if such taking or requisition had not occurred, except that if such Unit is returned by such governmental authority to Lessee at any time after the end of the Term of this Lease as to such Unit, anything to the contrary contained in this Lease notwithstanding, Lessee shall only be required to promptly return such Unit to Lessor upon such return by such governmental authority, rather than at the end of the Term of this Lease as to such Unit. All payments received by Lessor or Lessee from any governmental authority for the use during the Term of this Lease of such Unit as provided in this Section 9.3 shall be immediately paid over to or retained by Lessee, as appropriate, unless an Event of Default shall have occurred and be continuing, in which case the amount otherwise payable to Lessee may be retained by Lessor and applied to discharge the liabilities of Lessee under Section 13.

SECTION 10. *INSURANCE*

10.1 *Insurance Maintenance.* Lessee will, at all times during the Term of this Lease as to each Unit prior to the return of such Unit to Lessor in accordance with Section 17 of this Lease, at its own expense, cause to be carried and maintained with insurers of recognized responsibility (a) property and casualty insurance for such Unit and (b) public liability insurance against claims for personal injury, death, or property damage resulting from the ownership, possession, maintenance, use or operation of such Unit, in both cases in at least such amounts and against such risks as are customarily insured against by Lessee on similar equipment; provided, however, that in no event shall (a) the amount of such property and casualty insurance be less than the Casualty Value of such Unit from time to time (except that Lessee may self-insure in an amount up to _____) and (b) the amount of such public liability insurance be less than [$ _____] as to any one occurrence. The benefits under such insurance shall be payable to Lessor and Lessee, as their respective interests may appear. Any policy of insurance carried in accordance with this Section 10 shall (a) require thirty (30) days prior written notice to Lessor of a material change or cancellation or nonrenewal; (b) name Lessor as additional insured, as its interest may appear, and provide that all provisions of such policy, except the limits of liability, will operate in the same manner as if there were a separate policy governing such additional insured; and (c) provide that, as to Lessor's interest, such insurance shall not be invalidated by reason of any breach of representation or violation of warranty made by Lessee to the insurer in connection with obtaining such policy of insurance or maintaining the same in full force and effect. Lessee shall deliver to Lessor together with each Certificate of Acceptance a copy of each such policy (or a certificate of insurance relating thereto) with respect to each Unit covered by such Certificate of Acceptance.

10.2 *Insurance Proceeds.* Any insurance proceeds resulting from insurance carried by Lessee or condemnation payments received by Lessor for each Unit suffering a Casualty Occurrence shall be deducted from the amounts payable by Lessee for a Casualty Occurrence pursuant to Section 9. If Lessor shall receive any such insurance proceeds or condemnation payments after Lessee shall have made payment to Section 9 without deduction for such insurance proceeds or such condemnation payments, Lessee shall immediately pay such insurance proceeds or condemnation payments to Lessee, up to the sum of the Casualty Value amount paid by Lessee plus all costs, expenses, and damages incurred by Lessee in connection with the disposition of each Unit suffering a Casualty Occurrence, unless an Event of Default shall have occurred and be continuing, in which case the amount otherwise payable to Lessee may be retained by Lessor and applied to discharge the liabilities of Lessee under Section 13. The balance of such insurance proceeds or condemnation payments shall be retained by Lessor. All property damage insurance proceeds received by Lessor or Lessee with respect to a damaged Unit not suffering a Casualty Occurrence shall be applied toward the payment, when due, of the cost of repairing such Unit. Any condemnation payments received with respect to a Unit not suffering a Casualty Occurrence shall be the property of Lessee unless an Event of Default shall have occurred and be continuing, in which case the amount otherwise payable to Lessee shall be paid to or retained by Lessor, as appropriate, and applied to discharge the liabilities of Lessee under Section 13.

SECTION 11. *INSPECTION*

Lessor shall have the right during the Term of this Lease upon not less than ten (10) Business Days' prior written notice to Lessee to inspect any Unit for the purpose of confirming its existence, condition, and proper maintenance, at mutually agreeable times during Lessee's regular business hours. Notwithstanding the foregoing, Lessor may not inspect any Units if it would unreasonably interfere with Lessee's business operations, violate any applicable governmental security laws, regulations rules, or violate the reasonable security regulations or procedures of Lessee.

SECTION 12. *DISCLAIMER OF WARRANTIES; COMPLIANCE WITH LAWS AND RULES; MAINTENANCE; ADDITIONS*

12.1 *Warranty Disclaimer.* LESSOR MAKES NO WARRANTY OR REPRESENTATION, EITHER EXPRESS OR IMPLIED, AS TO THE DESIGN OR CONDITION, OR QUALITY OF THE MATERIAL, EQUIPMENT OR WORKMANSHIP OF THE UNITS LEASED HEREUNDER, AND LESSOR MAKES NO WARRANTY OF MERCHANTABILITY OR FITNESS OF THE UNITS FOR ANY PARTICULAR PURPOSE [*Author's Note*: This warranty disclaimer should be given to a lessor only when the lessor is not also the vendor], it being agreed that all such risks, as between Lessor and Lessee, are to be borne by Lessee; but Lessor hereby assigns and transfers to Lessee, and hereby irrevocably appoints and constitutes Lessee as its agent and attorney-in-fact to assert and enforce from time to time as Lessee shall deem appropriate, in the name of and for the account of Lessor and/or Lessee, as their respective interests may appear, at Lessee's sole cost and expense, whatever claims and rights Lessor may have as owner of each Unit against Manufacturer (or any subcontractor or supplier of Manufacturer) under the Purchase Documents or otherwise. Lessor agrees to cooperate fully at Lessee's request in Lessee's pursuit of any such claims or rights. If for any reason Lessee is prevented from asserting such claims or rights in the name of and for the account of Lessor and/or Lessee, as their respective interests may appear, Lessor will, at Lessee's expense, promptly upon Lessee's request enforce such claims or rights as directed from time to time by Lessee.

12.2 *Compliance With Laws.* Lessee agrees to use its best efforts to comply in all material respects with all applicable laws (including without limitation laws with respect to Lessee's use, maintenance, and operation of each Unit) of each jurisdiction in which a Unit is located; provided, however, Lessee shall not be required to comply with any such law so long as Lessee is, in good faith, contesting the validity or application of any such law. Lessor agrees to cooperate fully at Lessee's request in Lessee's contest of any such law or its applicability.

12.3 *Maintenance.* Lessee shall pay all costs, expenses, fees, and charges (other than those included in Lessor's Cost) incurred in connection with Lessee's use and operation of the Units. Subject to the provisions of Section 9, Lessee, at its own cost and expense, shall maintain, repair, and service, or cause to be maintained, repaired, and serviced, each Unit so as to keep it in the same operating condition and repair as it was when it first became subject to this Lease, ordinary wear and tear for the use intended by Lessee excepted, and within a reasonable period of time shall replace all parts of any Unit that may have become worn out, stolen, confiscated, destroyed, or otherwise rendered permanently unfit for use with appropriate replacement parts, which shall be free and clear from all Liens, other than any Lessor's Lien. Upon replacement, title to the replacement parts shall automatically be vested in Lessee.

12.4 *Maintenance Agreement.* Lessee shall, upon expiration of the Manufacturer's warranty period applicable to each Unit, enter into and maintain in force for the longest possible period obtainable by Lessee during the Term of this Lease as to such Unit a maintenance agreement (the "Maintenance Agreement") with Manufacturer or with another qualified party covering at least the prime shift maintenance of such Unit; provided, however, if Lessee is unable to obtain Maintenance Agreement reasonably satisfactory to it as to any Unit, Lessee shall have the right to maintain such Unit itself. Charges under the Maintenance Agreement and all other maintenance and service charges, including installation and dismantling charges, shall be borne by Lessee.

12.5 *Additions.* Lessee may, at its option and at its own cost and expense, make additions, modifications, and improvements to any Unit provided such additions, modifications, and improvements are readily removable without causing material damage to such Unit. All such additions, modifications, and improvements shall remain the property of Lessee and shall be removed by Lessee before such Unit is returned to Lessor. Lessee shall repair all damage to any such Unit resulting from such installation and removal. Lessee shall not, without the prior written consent of Lessor, which consent shall not be unreasonably withheld, alter any Unit, or affix or install any accessories or devices on any Unit, if the same shall materially impair the function or use of such Unit. Except to the extent otherwise provided in the first sentence of this Section 12.5, any and all other additions or modifications and improvements to any Lien (except for any Lessor's Lien) shall immediately be vested in Lessor, any and all warranties of Manufacturer with respect thereto shall thereupon automatically be assigned to Lessee, and Lessor shall cooperate fully with Lessee in their enforcement to the same extent and on the same basis as provided in Section 12.1

SECTION 13. *EVENTS OF DEFAULT AND REMEDIES*

13.1 *Events of Default.* During the Term of this Lease the occurrence of any of the following events shall constitute an "Event of Default:"

(a) Nonpayment of all or any part of the Rent provided for in Section 5 (except as otherwise expressly provided in Section 2.2), if such nonpayment shall continue for ten (10) Business Days after Lessee's receipt from Lessor of written notice of such nonpayment;

(b) Lessee shall make or permit any unauthorized assignment or transfer of this Lease or any interest herein or any unauthorized transfer of the right to possession of any Unit;

(c) Lessee shall fail or refuse to comply with any other covenant, agreement, term, or provision of this Lease required to be kept or performed by Lessee or to make reasonable provision for such compliance within thirty (30) days after Lessee's receipt from Lessor of a written demand for the performance thereof, which demand shall specify in reasonable detail the nonperformance;

(d) Any proceedings shall be commenced by or against Lessee for any relief under any bankruptcy or insolvency law, or any law relating to the relief of debtors, readjustment of indebtedness, reorganization, arrangement, composition, or extension, and, unless such proceedings shall have been dismissed, nullified, stayed, or otherwise rendered ineffective (but then only so long as such stay shall continue in force or such ineffectiveness shall continue), all of the obligations of Lessee hereunder shall not have been and shall not continue to be duly assumed in writing, pursuant to a court order or decree, by a trustee or trustees or receiver or receivers appointed (whether or not subject to ratification) for Lessee or its property in connection with any such proceedings in such manner that such obligations shall have the same status as obligations incurred by such trustee or trustees or receiver or receivers, within thirty (30) days after such appointment, if any, or thirty (30) days after such proceedings shall have been commenced, whichever is earlier, or Lessee shall make a general assignment for the benefit of creditors or shall admit in writing its inability to pay its debts generally as they become due;

(e) any representation or warranty made by Lessee in this Lease, or in any certificate or other document delivered by Lessee pursuant hereto, shall be incorrect in any material respect as of the date made and shall remain uncorrected for a period of thirty (30) days after receipt by Lessee of written notice from Lessor specifying in reasonable detail the incorrect representation or warranty.

13.2 *Remedies.* Upon the occurrence of an Event of Default, and so long as such Event of Default shall be continuing, Lessor may, at its option, declare this Lease to be in default and may exercise in its sole discretion any one or more of the following remedies:

   (a) proceed by appropriate court action or actions, either at law or in equity, to enforce performance by Lessee of the applicable covenants of this Lease or to recover damages for the breach thereof; or

   (b) by notice in writing to Lessee terminate this Lease with respect to any or all of the Units, whereupon all rights of Lessee to the possession and use of such Unit or units shall absolutely cease and terminate as though this Lease had never been made, but Lessee shall remain liable as hereinafter provided; and thereupon Lessor may, by its agent or agents, enter upon the premises of Lessee or any other premises where any of such Units may be located and take possession of all or any of such Units and thenceforth hold, possess, operate, sell, lease, and enjoy such Unit or Units free from any right of Lessee to use such Unit or Units for any purpose whatsoever and without any duty to account to Lessee for any action or inaction or for any proceeds arising therefrom, but Lessor shall, nevertheless, have a right to recover from Lessee any and all amounts that under the provisions of this Lease and any applicable Equipment Schedule may then be due or which may have accrued to the date of such termination (computing the Rent for any number of days less than a full Rent payment period by multiplying the Rent for such full Rent payment period by a fraction the numerator of which is such number of days and the denominator of which is the total number of days in the full Rent payment period) and also to recover from Lessee (i) as damages for loss of the bargain and not as a penalty, whichever of the following sums, with respect to each such Unit, Lessor, in its sole discretion, shall specify by written notice to Lessee: (a) an amount equal to the excess, if any, computed as of the Rent Date immediately succeeding the date of the Event of Default, of the Casualty Value for such Unit over the present value of the Fair Market Rental of such Unit for the remainder of the Term of this Lease following such Rent Date, such present value to be computed in each case using the Discount Rate specified in the applicable Equipment Schedule [*Author's Note*: This is for an "in advance" rental structure]; or (b) an amount equal to the excess, if any, computed as of the Rent Date immediately succeeding the date of the Event of Default, of the Casualty Value for such Unit over the Fair Market Value of such Unit [Author's Note: This is for an "in advance" rental structure]; and any reasonable costs and expenses (including legal and accounting fees) incurred in connection with the recovery, repair, repainting, return, and re-marketing of such Unit or other exercise of Lessor's remedies hereunder.

The remedies in this Lease provided in favor of Lessor shall not be deemed exclusive, but shall be cumulative and shall be in addition to all other remedies existing in its favor at law or in equity.

Lessor shall use its best efforts to mitigate any damages suffered by it. IN NO EVENT SHALL LESSEE BE LIABLE FOR ANY INDIRECT, SPECIAL, OR CONSEQUENTIAL DAMAGES OF ANY KIND UNDER THE LEASE.

SECTION 14. *FAIR MARKET VALUE AND FAIR MARKET RENTAL*

"Fair Market Value" and "Fair Market Rental," as to each Unit for all purposes in connection with this Lease, shall have the respective meanings and shall be determined in accordance with the procedure set forth in this Section 14. Fair Market Value and Fair Market Rental shall be determined on the basis of, and be equal in amount to, the value which would obtain in an arm's-length transaction between an informed and willing buyer-user (or lessee, if determining Fair Market Rental), other than a lessee currently in possession or a used equipment dealer, under no compulsion to buy (or lease), and an informed and willing seller (or lessor, if determining Fair Market Rental) under no compulsion to sell (or lease), and, in such determination, costs of removal from the location of current use shall not be a deduction from such value.

In the event that a determination of Fair Market Value or Fair Market Rental of a Unit shall be made under any provision of this Lease, the party requesting the determination shall deliver a written notice to the other party so indicating and appointing an Appraiser selected by the requesting party to determine the Fair Market Value or Fair Market Rental. Within fifteen (15) days after the receipt of such written notice the party receiving such notice shall deliver to the requesting party a written notice appointing an Appraiser of its selection to make such determination. The two Appraisers appointed in such written notices shall meet promptly to determine the Fair Market Value or Fair Market Rental of such Unit as of the applicable date. If within thirty (30) days after the initial written notice the two Appraisers so appointed by Lessor and Lessee shall be unable to agree upon the Fair Market Value or the Fair Market Rental of such Unit, whichever is applicable, such Appraisers shall within five (5) days thereafter appoint a third Appraiser. The decision of the three Appraisers so appointed shall be given within a period of ten (10) days after the appointment of such third Appraiser. Any decision in which any two Appraisers so appointed and acting hereunder concur shall in all cases be binding and conclusive upon Lessor and Lessee. The fees and expenses of the Appraisers shall be borne equally by Lessee and Lessor, unless the Lease shall have been terminated pursuant to Section 13 hereof, in which case Lessee shall pay all such fees and expenses.

SECTION 15. *ASSIGNMENT, POSSESSION, LIENS, SUBLEASE, AND MERGER*

15.1 *Lessor Assignment.* Lessor agrees that it will not assign all or any portion of its rights under, or interests in, this Lease or any of the Units unless such assignment is made pursuant to a security agreement relating to any borrowing by Lessor from one or more institutional lenders. Notwithstanding the foregoing, Lessor agrees that it will not make any such assignment to any entities listed on an Annex to any Equipment Schedule. Lessor agrees that if such a security interest in any Unit is granted, the security agreement covering such Unit shall expressly provide that the rights and interests of Lessee in and to such Unit as provided in this Lease shall remain paramount so long as no Event of Default shall have occurred and be continuing. Lessor shall give Lessee prompt written notice of any such assignment by Lessor. All the rights of Lessor hereunder (including without limitation the right to receive Rent payable under this Lease) shall inure to the benefit of Lessor's permitted assigns to the extent of such assignment. Any payment of Rent or other payment by Lessee to such assignee shall be full satisfaction of Lessee's obligation to make such payment under this Lease and Lessor hereby indemnifies Lessee against any damages, claims, costs, or expenses incurred by Lessee in connection therewith, but Lessee shall be under no obligation to make any payment to any such assignee until Lessor shall give Lessee written notice to make such payment to such assignee. Notwithstanding anything to the contrary herein, any permitted assignee of Lessor can declare an Event of Default hereunder only with respect to one or more Units subject to such assignee's security interest.

15.2 *Lessee Possession and Assignment.* So long as an Event of Default under this Lease shall not have occurred and be continuing, Lessee shall be entitled to the quiet enjoyment and peaceful possession and use of the Units in accordance with and subject to all the terms and conditions of this Lease, but without the prior written consent of Lessor, which consent shall not be unreasonably withheld, Lessee shall not, except as otherwise permitted herein, lease, assign, or transfer its leasehold interest in any or all of the Units.

15.3 *Liens.* Except as otherwise provided herein, Lessee, at its own expense, shall promptly pay or discharge any and all sums claimed by, or liabilities in favor of, any person that, if unpaid, would become a mortgage, lien, charge, security interest, or other encumbrance (any of the foregoing being herein referred to as a "Lien"), other than a Lien by, through or under Lessor on or with respect to any Unit, including any accession thereto, or the interest of Lessor or Lessee therein, which shall include without limitation any Lien resulting from a breach of Lessor's covenant in Section 2.2 or resulting from claims against Lessor not related to the ownership or leasing of any Unit (any of the foregoing being herein referred to as a "Lessor's Lien"), and shall promptly discharge any such Lien that arises. Lessee shall not be required to pay or discharge any such Lien so long as the validity thereof is being contested in good faith. The existence of any Lessor's Lien or any Lien for taxes, assessments, or governmental charges, or levies (in each case so long as not due and delinquent), or inchoate materialmen's, mechanics', workmen's, repairmen's, employees' or other like Liens arising in the ordinary course of business and in each case not delinquent shall not constitute a breach of this covenant.

15.4 *Lessee Sublease.* So long as no Event of Default under this Lease shall have occurred and be continuing, Lessee shall be entitled without Lessor's consent to sublease any or all of the Units, or any part thereof, to, or permit their use by, any person or entity, including without limitation any subsidiary, affiliate or parent corporation of Lessee, incorporated in the United States of America or any state thereof, but in all cases only upon and subject to all the terms and conditions of this Lease. No such sublease or other assignment of use by Lessee shall relieve Lessee of its obligations hereunder.

15.5 *Merger or Consolidation.* Notwithstanding anything herein to the contrary, Lessee may assign or transfer this Lease and its leasehold interest in the Units to any corporation incorporated under the laws of any state of the United States of America into or with which Lessee shall have merged or consolidated or which shall have acquired all or substantially all of the property of Lessee, provided that such assignee or transferee will not, upon the effectiveness of such merger, consolidation, or acquisition and the assignment or transfer of this Lease to it, be in default under any provision of this Lease.

SECTION 16. *LESSEE RIGHTS*

16.1 *Purchase Right.* Lessee shall have the right to purchase any Unit as provided in the applicable Equipment Schedule.

16.2 *Renewal Right.* Lessee shall have the right to renew this Lease as to any Unit as provided in the applicable Equipment Schedule.

16.3 *Termination Right.* Lessee shall have the right to terminate this Lease as to any Unit as provided in the applicable Equipment Schedule.

16.4 *Upgrade Right.* Lessee shall have the right to upgrade any Unit as provided in the applicable Equipment Schedule.

SECTION 17. *RETURN OF EQUIPMENT*

As soon as practicable on or after the expiration of the Term of this Lease as to each Unit, Lessee shall prepare the Unit for return to Lessor and deliver possession of such Unit to

Lessor at the location of such Unit on the final day of the Term of this Lease. The Units shall be returned in the condition in which they are required to be maintained by Lessee under Section 12.3.

SECTION 18. *INTEREST ON OVERDUE PAYMENTS*

Anything herein to the contrary notwithstanding, any nonpayment of Rent or any other payment obligation with respect to any Unit after the due date shall result in the obligation on the part of Lessee promptly to pay with respect to such Unit, to the extent legally enforceable, interest on such Rent or other payment obligation for the period of time during which it is overdue at the Overdue Rate as specified in the applicable Equipment Schedule, or such lesser amount as may be legally enforceable.

SECTION 19. *CONFIDENTIAL INFORMATION*

Lessor agrees that it will not, without first obtaining Lessee's written consent, disclose to any person, firm, or enterprise, or use for its benefit, any information not generally available to the public relating to Lessee's business, including without limitation any pricing methods, processes, financial data, lists, apparatus, statistics, program, research, development, or related information concerning past, present, or future business activities of Lessee.

SECTION 20. *ADVERTISING OR PUBLICITY*

Neither Lessor nor Lessee shall use the name of the other in publicity releases or advertising without securing the prior written consent of the other.

SECTION 21. *REPRESENTATIONS AND WARRANTIES*

Each of Lessor and Lessee represents and warrants to the other that

(a) It is a corporation duly organized, validly existing, and in good standing under the laws of the jurisdiction of its incorporation. It has full power and authority to carry on its business presently conducted, to own or hold under lease its properties, and to enter into and perform its obligations under this Lease; and it is duly qualified to do business as a foreign corporation and is in good standing in each jurisdiction in which the location of any Unit requires such qualification.

(b) Its execution, delivery, and performance of this Lease have been duly authorized by all necessary corporate action on its part, do not contravene its corporate charter or by-laws or any law, governmental rule, or regulation, or any order, writ, injunction, decree, judgment, award, determination, direction, or demand (collectively "Order") of which it is aware binding on it or its properties, and do not and will not contravene the provisions of, or constitute a default under, or result in the creation of any Lien upon any Unit under, any material indenture, mortgage, contract, or other instrument to which it is a party or by which it or its property is bound.

(c) No consent or approval of, giving notice to, registration with, or taking of any other action by, any [state/province—as appropriate], federal or other governmental commission, agency, or regulatory authority is required for the performance by it of the transactions contemplated by this Lease, or if any such approval, registration, or giving of notice is required it has been obtained, so registered, or given, as the case may be.

(d) This Lease has been duly entered into and delivered by it and constitutes a legal, valid, and binding agreement of it enforceable against it in accordance with its terms, except as limited by (i) any bankruptcy, insolvency, reorganization, or other similar laws of general application affecting the enforcement of creditors' or lessors' rights generally, (ii) emergency powers lawfully conferred upon any governmental agency, and (iii) laws or judicial decisions limiting the right to specific performance or other equitable remedies.

(e) To the best of its knowledge there are no actions, suits, or proceedings pending or threatened against or affecting it or any of its property in any court or before any arbitrator or before or by any federal, state, municipal or other governmental department, commission, board, bureau, agency, or instrumentality, domestic or foreign (collectively "Governmental Body"), except actions, suits, or proceedings of the character normally incident to the kind of business conducted by it as to which any adverse determination in excess of any accruals to reflect potential liability would not materially adversely affect its business, assets, operations, or condition, financial or otherwise, taken as a whole, or materially adversely affect its ability to perform its obligations under this Lease, and it is not in material default with respect to any material Order of any court, arbitrator, or Governmental Body.

(f) As to Lessee only, its consolidated balance sheet as of _____, and its related consolidated statements of income, retained earnings and changes in financial position for the two years then ended, heretofore delivered to Lessor, fairly present its consolidated financial position as of such date and its consolidated results of operations and consolidated changes in financial position for the two years then ended, all in conformity with generally accepted accounting principles consistently applied during the periods. Since the date of such balance sheet there has not been any material adverse change in its business, assets, liabilities, results of operations, or condition, financial or otherwise.

(g) It is not a party to any agreement or instrument or subject to any charter or other corporate restriction that, so far as it is now aware, materially adversely affects or will, so far as it can now foresee, materially adversely affect, its business, operations, or properties or its ability to perform its obligations under this Lease.

(h) To the best of its knowledge it has filed all required tax returns in all jurisdictions in which such returns were required to be filed and has paid, or made provision for, all material taxes shown to be due and payable on such returns and all other material taxes and assessments that are payable by it, except for any taxes and assessments of which the amount, applicability, or validity is currently being contested in good faith and as to which any adverse determination in excess of any accruals to reflect potential liability would not materially adversely affect its ability to perform its obligations under this Lease.

SECTION 22. *FINANCIAL INFORMATION*

During the term of this Lease, Lessee agrees to provide Lessor with its consolidated quarterly and annual financial statements promptly as they become available and such other financial information as may be provided to Lessee's shareholders from time to time.

SECTION 23. *PAYMENTS*

23.1 *Postponement of Payment Date.* If any date on which a Rent or other payment is due and payable is not a Business Day, the payment otherwise payable on such date shall be due and payable on the next succeeding Business Day.

23.2 *Payment Address.* All Rent and other payments required to be made by Lessee to Lessor shall be made to Lessor at the address of Lessor set forth in Section 24 or at such other address as may be specified in writing by Lessor at least thirty (30) Business Days prior to the date such notice is intended to become effective.

23.3 *Method of Payment.* All Rent and other payments under this Lease shall be made in lawful money of the United States of America.

SECTION 24. *NOTICES*

Any notice or document or payment to be delivered hereunder to any of the persons designated below, except as otherwise expressly provided herein, shall be deemed to have been properly delivered if delivered personally or deposited with the United States Postal Service, registered or certified mail, return receipt requested, postage prepaid, to the following respective addresses:

If to Lessor: _____

_____

Attn: _____

If to Lessee _____

_____

Attn: _____

or such other address as may be furnished from time to time by any of the parties hereto upon at least thirty (30) days prior written notice.

SECTION 25. *STATEMENT OF LEASE*

It is expressly understood and agreed by and between the parties hereto that this instrument constitutes a lease of the Units, and nothing herein shall be construed as conveying to Lessee any right, title, or interest in the Units except as a lessee only. Neither the execution nor the filing of any financing statement with respect to any of the Units or the execution or filing of any financing statement with respect to this Lease or the recording hereof shall in any manner imply that the relationship between Lessor and Lessee is anything other than that of lessor and lessee. Any such filing of financing statements or recordation of this Lease is solely to protect the interests of Lessor and Lessee in the event of any unwarranted assertions by any person not a party to this Lease transaction.

SECTION 26. *SEVERABILITY, EFFECT, AND INTERPRETATION OF LEASE*

26.1 *Severability.* Any provision of this Lease that is prohibited or unenforceable by any applicable law of any jurisdiction shall as to such jurisdiction be ineffective to the extent of such prohibition or unenforceability without invalidating the remaining provisions hereof, and any such prohibition or unenforceability in any jurisdiction shall not invalidate or render unenforceable such provision in any other jurisdiction.

26.2 *Complete Statement of Rights.* This Lease exclusively and completely states the rights of Lessor and Lessee with respect to the leasing of the Units and supersedes all other agreements, oral or written, with respect thereto.

26.3 *Section Headings.* All Section headings are inserted for convenience only and shall not affect any construction or interpretation of this Lease.

SECTION 27. *LAW GOVERNING*

The terms and provisions of this Lease and all rights and obligations hereunder shall be governed in all respects by the laws of [_____].

SECTION 28. *FURTHER ASSURANCES*

Each of Lessor and Lessee agrees that at any time and from time to time, after the execution and delivery of this Lease, it shall, upon request of the other party, promptly execute and deliver such further documents and do such further acts and things the requesting party may reasonably request in order fully to effectuate the purposes of this Lease.

SECTION 29. *MODIFICATION, WAIVER, AND CONSENT*

Any modification or waiver of any provision of this Lease, or any consent to any departure by Lessee or Lessor, as the case may be, therefrom, shall not be effective in any event unless the same is in writing and signed by the party to be charged, and then such modification, waiver, or consent shall be effective only in the specific instance and for the specific purpose given.

SECTION 30. *BINDING EFFECT*

This Lease shall be binding upon and shall inure to the benefit of the respective successors and permitted assigns of Lessee and Lessor.

(continues on next page)

SECTION 31. *EXECUTION IN COUNTERPARTS*

This Lease may be executed in any number of counterparts, each of which shall constitute an original and which taken together shall constitute one and the same Lease.

IN WITNESS WHEREOF, the parties, pursuant to due authority, have caused this Lease to be signed in their respective names by duly authorized officers or representatives as of the date first above written.

_____

as Lessor

By: _____

Title: _____

_____

as Lessee

By: _____

Title: _____

EXHIBIT A
Equipment Schedule

Equipment Schedule No. _____ ("Schedule")

Dated as of _____, 19_____

to Master Lease of Computer Equipment ("Lease")

Dated as of _____, 19_____

between

_____ ("Lessor")

and

_____ ("Lessee")

1. *EQUIPMENT DESCRIPTION*

					Estimated Invoice Purchase Price	
Quantity	*Manufacturer*	*Model*	*New/Used*	*Description*	*Per Unit*	*Aggregate*

TOTAL ESTIMATED INVOICE PURCHASE PRICE _____

2. *BASIC LEASE COMMENCEMENT DATE*
   The Basic Lease Commencement Date for each Unit shall commence on [insert relevant time—such as the 1st day of the month immediately following the Unit's Acceptance Date if the Acceptance Date does not fall on the 1st day of a month].

3. *CUTOFF DATE*
   Lessor shall be obligated to purchase and lease each Item of Equipment specified in Section 1 of this Schedule to Lessee provided such Item of Equipment has been accepted by Lessee for lease in accordance with the provisions of Section 2.5 of the Lease on or before _____, 19_____.

4. *DISCOUNT RATE*
   The Discount Rate applicable to each Unit shall be equal to an interest charge of _____ % per annum.

5. *LESSOR'S COST*
   The Lessor's Cost for each Item of Equipment subject to this Schedule shall be an amount equal to the Invoice Purchase Price for such Item of Equipment plus all sales taxes in connection with the purchase from Manufacturer of such Item of Equipment, transportation charges in connection with the delivery of such Item of Equipment from the Manufacturer to Lessee, and [insert other relevant charges which are to be included].

6. *OVERDUE RATE*
The Overdue Rate for each Unit shall be equal to an interest charge of _____% per annum.

7. *RENT DATE*
The Rent Date as to each Unit shall be the _____ day of each _____ during the Primary Term and the _____ day of each _____ during any Renewal Term.

8. *UNIT LOCATION*
Each Unit shall be located at Lessee's place of business at _____.

9. *LESSOR COMMITMENT*
Lessor shall be obligated to purchase and lease Items of Equipment pursuant to the terms of the Lease and this Schedule with an aggregate Lessor's Cost of not less than $ _____.

10. *LEASE TERM*
(a) The Primary Term for each Unit shall commence on the Basic Lease Commencement Date of such Unit and shall end on the anniversary date thereof that number of years indicated below opposite the relevant Unit thereafter.

Unit Description   *Primary Term in Years*

(b) The Renewal Term for each Unit shall be as specified in Section 13 of this Schedule.

11. *UNIT RENT*
(a) The Interim Rent for each Unit as to any Interim Term shall be payable on the Basic Lease Commencement Date of such Unit and shall be an amount equal to the Basic Rent multiplied by a fraction, the numerator of which is that number of days in the Interim Term and the denominator of which is that number of days in a Primary Term Rent payment period.

(b) The Basic Rent shall be an amount equal to the product of the Basic Lease Rate Factor indicated below for the relevant Unit times the Lessor's Cost of such Unit.

Unit Description   *Basic Lease Rate Factor*
                                                As a % of Lessor's Cost

(c) The Renewal Rent for each Unit shall be payable on each Rent Date during the Renewal Term in the amounts specified in Section 13 of this Schedule.

12. *CASUALTY VALUE*
The Casualty Value of each Unit shall be that percentage of the Lessor's Cost for such Unit as specified on Annex B attached hereto opposite the Rent Date through which Lessee has paid Rent.

13. *PURCHASE AND RENEWAL RIGHT*

Provided that the Lease has not been terminated earlier and no Event of Default has occurred and is continuing not earlier than one hundred eighty (180) days and not later than ninety (90) days before the end of the Primary Term or each year of any Renewal Term of each Unit, Lessee may deliver to Lessor a written notice (a) tentatively electing either to purchase such Unit at the end of the Primary Term or each year of any Renewal Term for an amount equal to the Fair Market Value of such Unit at the end of such Term, or to extend the Term of this Lease at the end of the Primary Term or each year of any Renewal Term as to such Unit on a year-to-year basis (but such aggregate Renewal Term shall not exceed _____ years) at the Fair Market Rental at the end of such Term; and (b) appointing an Appraiser selected by Lessee to determine the Fair Market Value or the Fair Market Rental thereof, whichever is applicable, in accordance with the provisions of Section 14 of the Lease. If no such written notice is delivered by Lessee to Lessor within such period, Lessee shall be deemed to have waived any right to purchase or extend the Term with respect to such Unit. At any time within the fifteen (15) day period following the determination of Fair Market Value or Fair Market Rental, as appropriate, of such Unit, Lessee may deliver to Lessor a further written notice finally electing to purchase or extend the Term with respect to such Unit. If no such further notice is delivered by Lessee to Lessor within such fifteen (15) day period, Lessee shall be deemed to have waived any right to purchase or extend the Term with respect to such Unit. At the end of the Term, if Lessee has finally elected to purchase such Unit, Lessee shall purchase from Lessor, and Lessor shall sell to Lessee, such Unit for a cash consideration equal to the Fair Market Value of such Unit, and Lessor shall transfer title to such Unit to Lessee without recourse or warranty, except that Lessor shall represent and warrant that it owns such Unit free and clear of any Lessor's Lien.

14. *EARLY TERMINATION RIGHT*

(a) Provided an Event of Default shall not have occurred and be continuing, Lessee shall have the right at its option at any time on not less than ninety (90) days' prior written notice to Lessor to terminate the Lease with respect to any or all of the Units on the _____ Primary Term Rent Date or any Primary Term Rent Date thereafter for any one or more such Units (hereinafter called the "Termination Date"), provided that Lessee shall have made a good faith determination that such Unit or Units are obsolete or surplus to Lessee's requirements. During the period from the giving of such notice until the Termination Date Lessee, as agent for Lessor, shall use its best efforts to obtain bids for the purchase of such Unit or Units by a person other than Lessee or an affiliate of Lessee. Lessee shall promptly certify in writing to Lessor the amount and terms of each bid received by Lessee and the name and address of the party submitting such bid. Subject to Lessor's right to retain such Unit or Units as provided in Subsection (b) below, on the Termination Date Lessor shall sell such Unit or Units for cash to the bidder or bidders who shall have submitted the highest bid for each such Unit prior to such date and shall transfer title to such Unit or Units to such purchaser or purchasers without recourse or warranty, except that Lessor shall represent and warrant that it owns such Unit or Units free and clear of any Lessor's Lien. The total sale price realized upon such sale shall be retained by Lessor and, in addition, on the Termination Date, Lessee shall pay to Lessor the amount, if any, by which the Termination Value of such Unit or Units as provided in Subsection (d) below, computed as of the Termination Date, exceeds the proceeds of such sale, whereupon the Lease shall terminate as to such Unit or Units except as herein otherwise expressly provided. Subject to the provisions of Subsection (c) below, in the event no bids are received by Lessee, Lessee shall pay to Lessor the Termination Value of such Unit or Units, computed as of the Termination Date, and deliver such Unit or Units to the

Lessor in accordance with the provisions of Section 17 of the Lease, whereupon the Lease shall terminate as to such Unit or Units, except as herein otherwise expressly provided.

(b) Notwithstanding the provisions of Subsection (a) above but subject to the provisions of Subsection (c) below, Lessor shall have the right at any time up to and including thirty (30) days prior to the Termination Date, within its sole discretion, to elect not to sell such Unit or Units to any prospective purchaser obtained by Lessee ("Third Party Purchaser"). In the event Lessor elects not to sell such Unit or Units to the Third Party Purchaser, Lessee shall return such Unit or Units to Lessor in accordance with the provisions of Section 17 of the Lease, and Lessor thereupon may retain such Unit or Units for its own account without further obligation under the Lease. If no sale shall have occurred on or as of the Termination Date because the Third Party Purchaser fails to consummate a proposed sale and Lessor shall not have requested the return of such Unit or Units pursuant hereto, the Lease shall continue in full force and effect as to such Unit or Units. In the event of any such sale or the return of such Unit or Units to Lessor pursuant hereto, and provided no Event of Default has occurred and is continuing, all obligations of Lessee to pay Rent and otherwise with respect to such Unit or Units for any period subsequent to the Termination Date shall cease.

(c) If the Termination Value exceeds the highest bidder or in the event no bids are received by Lessee, or if Lessor should exercise its election under Subsection (b) above, Lessee may, at its option, upon written notice given to Lessor not less than fifteen (15) days prior to the Termination Date, elect to (i) rescind and cancel Lessee's notice of termination with respect to any one or more of such Units, whereupon the Lease shall not terminate with respect to such Unit or Units pursuant to this Section 14 but shall continue in full force and effect as though no notice of termination had been given by Lessee with respect to such Unit or Units, or (ii) pay Lessor the applicable Termination Value with respect to any one or more of such Units, whereupon Lessor shall transfer title to such Unit or Units to Lessee without recourse or warranty, except that Lessor shall represent and warrant that it owns such Unit or Units free and clear of any Lessor's Lien. In the event Lessee fails to pay Lessor an amount of money equal to the applicable Termination Value on the Termination Date, the Lease as to such Unit or Units shall continue in full force and effect.

(d) The Termination Value of any Unit shall be that percentage described on Annex C attached hereto of Lessor's Cost set forth opposite the Rent Date through which the Lessee has paid Rent.

15. *UPGRADE RIGHT*
   [*Author's Note:* This must be negotiated on a case-by-case basis. There is no one standard form.]

16. *REPRESENTATIONS AND WARRANTIES*
   Each of Lessor and Lessee represents and warrants to the other that:

   (a) Its representations and warranties contained in Section 21 of the Lease are true and accurate on and as of the date of this Schedule as though made on and as of such date.

   (b) It is not in default under any of the terms, covenants, agreements, or other provisions of the Lease.

   (c) Simultaneously with the execution and delivery hereof it has delivered to the other its Incumbency Certificate, Certified Resolutions, and Opinion of Counsel substantially in the respective forms of Annexes D, E, and F attached hereto, with such changes as the receiving party shall reasonably request.

17. *TERM DEFINITIONS*

The terms used in this Schedule, where not defined in this Schedule to the contrary, shall have the same meanings as defined in the Lease.

_____

as Lessor

By: _____

Title: _____

_____

as Lessee

By: _____

Title: _____

ANNEX A

Certificate of Acceptance

Date _____

Certificate of Acceptance No. _____
to Equipment Schedule No. _____ ("Schedule")
dated as of _____, 19_____
to Master Lease of Computer Equipment ("Lease")
dated as of _____, 19_____
_____ ("Lessor")
and
_____ ("Lessee")

    Lessee hereby confirms that the Acceptance Date of the Unit or Units described in Exhibit A attached hereto shall be the date of this Certificate.

    Lessee confirms that (a) such Unit or Units have been examined by duly appointed and authorized representatives of Lessee, (b) such Unit or Units have been duly accepted by Lessee as Units for Leasing under the Lease, (c) such Unit or Units have become subject to and governed by the terms of the Lease, and (d) Lessee has become obligated to pay to Lessor the Rent provided for in the Lease and the Schedule with respect to such Unit or Units.

    The terms used herein shall have the respective meanings given to such terms in the Lease.

_____

as Lessee

By: _____

Title: _____

ANNEX B

Casualty Values

After Rent Date No.   *Percentage of Per Unit Cost*

ANNEX C

Termination Values

<u>*After Rent Date No.*</u>   <u>*Percentage of Lessor's Cost*</u>

ANNEX D

Incumbency Certificate

This Certificate is delivered by the undersigned pursuant to the Master Lease of Computer Equipment (the "Lease") dated as of _____ between _____ (the "Lessor") and _____ (the "Lessee"):

The undersigned hereby certifies that the following persons are on the date hereof, and have been at all times since _____, duly elected or appointed, qualified and acting officers of the undersigned holding the offices set forth opposite their respective names below and that the signatures set forth opposite their respective names and offices below are their genuine signatures:

Name	*Title*	*Signature*
		_____
		_____
		_____
		_____

By: _____

Title: _____

ANNEX E

Certified Resolutions

The undersigned, being the _____ of _____ a _____ corporation (" _____ "), does hereby certify that the following is a true and correct copy of certain resolutions duly adopted by the _____ of _____ on _____, 19 _____, and that such resolutions have not been modified or rescinded and remain in full force and effect on the date hereof:

"RESOLVED, that the proposed Master Lease of Computer Equipment (the "Lease"), including the proposed Equipment Schedule attached as Annex A thereto (the "Schedule"), between _____ as _____ and this Corporation as _____, in the form of the draft of _____, 19 _____ filed with the records of this Corporation, be, and it hereby is, approved in all respects; and further

RESOLVED, that the officers of this Corporation be, and each and any of them hereby is, authorized and empowered, in the name and on behalf of this Corporation, to execute and deliver the Lease and any Schedule substantially in the form approved in the preceding resolution, together with such changes therein as such officers or any of them, in conjunction with counsel to this Corporation, shall from time to time in their discretion deem necessary or desirable and shall approve, such approval to be conclusively evidenced by their execution and delivery thereof, and to enforce all rights and perform all obligations of this Corporation thereunder; provided, however, that without further action by this Board of Directors the aggregate cost of equipment to become subject to the Lease and all Schedules shall not exceed \$_____; and further

RESOLVED, that the officers of this Corporation be, and each and any of them hereby is, authorized and empowered, in the name and on behalf of this Corporation, to execute, deliver, file, and record any and all such further agreements, undertakings, instruments, certificates, letters, and documents, and to perform any and all such further actions, as such officers or any of them, in conjunction with counsel to this Corporation, shall from time to time in their discretion deem necessary or desirable to fully effectuate the Lease and the purposes of the foregoing resolutions."

IN WITNESS WHEREOF, the undersigned has made and executed this Certificate as of this _____ day of _____, 19 _____.

                                        _____

                                        By: _____

                                        Title: _____

ANNEX F

Opinion of Counsel

———————————————, 19———

Gentlemen:

As counsel to ————————— (" ————————— ") I have examined the Master Lease of Computer Equipment dated as of ——————, 19—— (the "Lease"), between ————————— and ————————— and Equipment Schedule No. ————————— to the Lease dated of even date herewith, such other documents and corporate records, and such questions of law as I have deemed relevant for purposes of the opinions expressed below. The terms used herein have the same meanings as defined in the Lease. Based on such examination, I am of the opinion that:

1. ————————— is a corporation duly organized, validly existing and in good standing under the laws of the —————————; has full power and authority to carry on its business as presently conducted, to own or hold under lease its properties and to enter into and perform its obligations under the Lease; and is duly qualified to do business as a foreign corporation and is in good standing in each jurisdiction in which the location of any (Unit) requires such qualification.

2. The execution, delivery, and performance by ————————— of the Lease have been duly authorized by all necessary corporate action on the part of —————————, do not materially contravene any law, governmental rule, regulation, or Order binding on ————————— or its properties or the corporate charter or By-laws of —————————, and to the best of my knowledge do not contravene the provisions of, or constitute a material default under, or result in the creation of any Lien upon the (Units) under, any material indenture, mortgage, contract, or other instrument to which ————————— is a party or by which ————————— or its property is bound.

3. No consent or approval of, giving of notice to, registration with or taking of any other action by any state, federal or other governmental commission, agency or regulatory authority is required for the performance by ————————— of the transactions contemplated by the Lease; or, if any such action is required, it has been obtained, performed or registered.

4. The Lease has been duly entered into and delivered by —————————, and constitutes a legal, valid and binding agreement of ————————— enforceable against ————————— in accordance with its terms, except as limited by (a) bankruptcy, insolvency, reorganization, or other similar laws of general application affecting the enforcement of creditors' or lessors' rights (b) emergency powers lawfully conferred upon any governmental agency, and (c) laws or judicial decisions limiting the right to specific performance or other equitable remedies, and the Lease creates a valid leasehold interest in the (Units).

5. To the best of my knowledge there are no actions, suits or proceedings pending or threatened before any court, administrative agency, arbitrator or Governmental Body which would, if determined adversely to —————————, have a material adverse effect on the business, assets, operations or condition, financial or otherwise, of —————————, or materially adversely affect the ability of ————————— to perform its obligations under the Lease; and to the best of my knowledge

_____ is not in material default with respect to any material Order of any court, arbitrator or Governmental Body.

6. No recorded Lien other than the Lease of any nature whatsoever which now covers or affects, or which will hereafter cover or affect, any property (or interests therein) of _____ now attaches or hereafter will attach to any of the (Units,) or materially adversely affects or will affect _____ right, title and interest in or to any of the (Units.)

                                        Very truly yours,

                                        _____

ANNEX G

Prohibited Lender Assignees

MACRS Depreciation Tables

Reproduced below, from Revenue Procedure 87-57 [1987-2 CB 687], as amplified and clarified by Rev. Proc. 89-15 [1989-1 CB 816], are those tables that set out the annual deduction rates under the Modified Accelerated Cost Recovery System (MACRS) for equipment. (Tables pertaining only to real property are omitted.) Tables 1–5 set out rates under the general MACRS system; Tables 8–12 provide rates under the MACRS Alternative Depreciation System; and Tables 14–18 set out rates when the Alternative Minimum Tax applies.

Table 1.   General Depreciation System
           Applicable Depreciation Method: 200 or 150 Percent
           Declining Balance Switching to Straight Line
           Applicable Recovery Periods: 3, 5, 7, 10, 15, 20 years
           Applicable Convention: Half-year

If the Recovery Year is:	and the Recovery Period is:					
	3-year	5-year	7-year	10-year	15-year	20-year
	the Depreciation Rate is:					
1	33.33	20.00	14.29	10.00	5.00	3.750
2	44.45	32.00	24.49	18.00	9.50	7.219
3	14.81	19.20	17.49	14.40	8.55	6.677
4	7.41	11.52	12.49	11.52	7.70	6.177
5		11.52	8.93	9.22	6.93	5.713
6		5.76	8.92	7.37	6.23	5.285
7			8.93	6.55	5.90	4.888
8			4.46	6.55	5.90	4.522
9				6.56	5.91	4.462
10				6.55	5.90	4.461
11				3.28	5.91	4.462
12					5.90	4.461
13					5.91	4.462
14					5.90	4.461
15					5.91	4.462
16					2.95	4.461
17						4.462
18						4.461
19						4.462
20						4.461
21						2.231

Table 2.   General Depreciation System
           Applicable Depreciation Method: 200 or 150 Percent
           Declining Balance Switching to Straight Line
           Applicable Recovery Periods: 3, 5, 7, 10, 15, 20 years
           Applicable Convention: Mid-quarter (property placed in
           service in first quarter)

If the Recovery Year is:	3-year	and the Recovery Period is:				
		5-year	7-year	10-year	15-year	20-year
		the Depreciation Rate is:				
1	58.33	35.00	25.00	17.50	8.75	6.563
2	27.78	26.00	21.43	16.50	9.13	7.000
3	12.35	15.60	15.31	13.20	8.21	6.482
4	1.54	11.01	10.93	10.56	7.39	5.996
5		11.01	8.75	8.45	6.65	5.546
6		1.38	8.74	6.76	5.99	5.130
7			8.75	6.55	5.90	4.746
8			1.09	6.55	5.91	4.459
9				6.56	5.90	4.459
10				6.55	5.91	4.459
11				0.82	5.90	4.459
12					5.91	4.460
13					5.90	4.459
14					5.91	4.460
15					5.90	4.459
16					0.74	4.460
17						4.459
18						4.460
19						4.459
20						4.460
21						0.557

Table 3. General Depreciation System
          Applicable Depreciation Method: 200 or 150 Percent
          Declining Balance Switching to Straight Line
          Applicable Recovery Periods: 3, 5, 7, 10, 15, 20 years
          Applicable Convention: Mid-quarter (property placed in
          service in second quarter)

If the Recovery Year is:	3-year	and the Recovery Period is				
		5-year	7-year	10-year	15-year	20-year
		the Depreciation Rate is:				
1	41.67	25.00	17.85	12.50	6.25	4.688
2	38.89	30.00	23.47	17.50	9.38	7.148
3	14.14	18.00	16.76	14.00	8.44	6.612
4	5.30	11.37	11.97	11.20	7.59	6.116
5		11.37	8.87	8.96	6.83	5.658
6		4.26	8.87	7.17	6.15	5.233
7			8.87	6.55	5.91	4.841
8			3.33	6.55	5.90	4.478
9				6.56	5.91	4.463
10				6.55	5.90	4.463
11				2.46	5.91	4.463
12					5.90	4.463
13					5.91	4.463
14					5.90	4.463
15					5.91	4.462
16					2.21	4.463
17						4.462
18						4.463
19						4.462
20						4.463
21						1.673

Table 4.   General Depreciation System
           Applicable Depreciation Method: 200 or 150 Percent
           Declining Balance Switching to Straight Line
           Applicable Recovery Periods: 3, 5, 7, 10, 15, 20 years
           Applicable Convention: Mid-quarter (property placed in
           service in third quarter)

If the Recovery Year is:	3-year	and the Recovery Period is: 5-year	7-year	10-year	15-year	20-year
		the Depreciation Rate is:				
1	25.00	15.00	10.71	7.50	3.75	2.813
2	50.00	34.00	25.51	18.50	9.63	7.289
3	16.67	20.40	18.22	14.80	8.66	6.742
4	8.33	12.24	13.02	11.84	7.80	6.237
5		11.30	9.30	9.47	7.02	5.769
6		7.06	8.85	7.58	6.31	5.336
7			8.86	6.55	5.90	4.936
8			5.53	6.55	5.90	4.566
9				6.56	5.91	4.460
10				6.55	5.90	4.460
11				4.10	5.91	4.460
12					5.90	4.460
13					5.91	4.461
14					5.90	4.460
15					5.91	4.461
16					3.69	4.460
17						4.461
18						4.460
19						4.461
20						4.460
21						2.788

Table 5   General Depreciation System
           Applicable Depreciation Method: 200 or 150 Percent
           Declining Balance Switching to Straight Line
           Applicable Recovery Periods: 3, 5, 7, 10, 15, 20 years
           Applicable Convention: Mid-quarter (property placed in
           service in fourth quarter)

| If the Recovery Year is: | 3-year | and the Recovery Period is: | | | | |
| | | 5-year | 7-year | 10-year | 15-year | 20-year |
		the Depreciation Rate is:				
1	8.33	5.00	3.57	2.50	1.25	0.938
2	61.11	38.00	27.55	19.50	9.88	7.430
3	20.37	22.80	19.68	15.60	8.89	6.872
4	10.19	13.68	14.06	12.48	8.00	6.357
5		10.94	10.04	9.98	7.20	5.880
6		9.58	8.73	7.99	6.48	5.439
7			8.73	6.55	5.90	5.031
8			7.64	6.55	5.90	4.654
9				6.56	5.90	4.458
10				6.55	5.91	4.458
11				5.74	5.90	4.458
12					5.91	4.458
13					5.90	4.458
14					5.91	4.458
15					5.90	4.458
16					5.17	4.458
17						4.458
18						4.459
19						4.458
20						4.459
21						3.901

TABLE 8 General and Alternative Depreciation Systems
Applicable Depreciation Method: Straight Line
Applicable Recovery Periods: 2.5 – 50 years
Applicable Convention: Half-year

and the Recovery Period is:

If the Recovery Year is:	2.5	3.0	3.5	4.0	4.5	5.0	5.5	6.0	6.5	7.0	7.5	8.0	8.5	9.0	9.5
					the Depreciation Rate is:										
1	20.00	16.67	14.29	12.50	11.11	10.00	9.09	8.33	7.69	7.14	6.67	6.25	5.88	5.56	5.26
2	40.00	33.33	28.57	25.00	22.22	20.00	18.18	16.67	15.39	14.29	13.33	12.50	11.77	11.11	10.53
3	40.00	33.33	28.57	25.00	22.22	20.00	18.18	16.67	15.38	14.29	13.33	12.50	11.76	11.11	10.53
4		16.67	28.57	25.00	22.23	20.00	18.18	16.67	15.39	14.28	13.33	12.50	11.77	11.11	10.53
5				12.50	22.22	20.00	18.19	16.66	15.38	14.29	13.34	12.50	11.76	11.11	10.52
6						10.00	18.18	16.67	15.39	14.28	13.33	12.50	11.77	11.11	10.52
7								8.33	15.38	14.29	13.34	12.50	11.77	11.11	10.52
8										7.14	13.33	12.50	11.76	11.11	10.53
9												6.25	11.76	11.11	10.52
10														5.56	10.53

and the Recovery Period is:

If the Recovery Year is:	10.0	10.5	11.0	11.5	12.0	12.5	13.0	13.5	14.0	14.5	15.0	15.5	16.0	16.5	17.0
					the Depreciation Rate is:										
1	5.00	4.76	4.55	4.35	4.17	4.00	3.85	3.70	3.57	3.45	3.33	3.23	3.13	3.03	2.94
2	10.00	9.52	9.09	8.70	8.33	8.00	7.69	7.41	7.14	6.90	6.67	6.45	6.25	6.06	5.88
3	10.00	9.52	9.09	8.69	8.33	8.00	7.69	7.41	7.14	6.90	6.67	6.45	6.25	6.06	5.88
4	10.00	9.53	9.09	8.70	8.33	8.00	7.69	7.41	7.14	6.90	6.67	6.45	6.25	6.06	5.88
5	10.00	9.52	9.09	8.69	8.33	8.00	7.69	7.41	7.14	6.90	6.67	6.45	6.25	6.06	5.88
6	10.00	9.52	9.09	8.70	8.34	8.00	7.69	7.41	7.14	6.89	6.67	6.45	6.25	6.06	5.88
7	10.00	9.52	9.09	8.69	8.33	8.00	7.69	7.41	7.15	6.90	6.67	6.45	6.25	6.06	5.88
8	10.00	9.53	9.09	8.70	8.34	8.00	7.69	7.41	7.14	6.89	6.67	6.45	6.25	6.06	5.88
9	10.00	9.52	9.09	8.69	8.33	8.00	7.69	7.41	7.15	6.90	6.66	6.45	6.25	6.06	5.88
10	10.00	9.53	9.09	8.69	8.34	8.00	7.69	7.41	7.14	6.89	6.67	6.45	6.25	6.06	5.89
11	5.00	9.52	9.09	8.70	8.33	8.00	7.70	7.40	7.15	6.90	6.66	6.45	6.25	6.06	5.88
12			4.55	8.69	8.34	8.00	7.69	7.41	7.14	6.89	6.67	6.45	6.25	6.06	5.89
13					4.17	8.00	7.70	7.40	7.15	6.90	6.66	6.46	6.25	6.06	5.88
14						4.00	7.69	7.41	7.14	6.89	6.67	6.45	6.25	6.06	5.89
15							3.85	7.40	7.15	6.90	6.66	6.46	6.25	6.06	5.88
16									3.57	6.90	6.67	6.46	6.25	6.06	5.89
17											3.33		3.12	6.07	5.88
18															2.94

and the Recovery Period is:

the Depreciation Rate is:

If the Recovery Year is:	17.5	18.0	18.5	19.0	19.5	20.0	20.5	21.0	21.5	22.0	22.5	23.0	23.5	24.0	24.5
1	2.86	2.78	2.70	2.63	2.56	2.500	2.439	2.381	2.326	2.273	2.222	2.174	2.128	2.083	2.041
2	5.71	5.56	5.41	5.26	5.13	5.000	4.878	4.762	4.651	4.545	4.444	4.348	4.255	4.167	4.082
3	5.71	5.56	5.41	5.26	5.13	5.000	4.878	4.762	4.651	4.545	4.445	4.348	4.255	4.167	4.082
4	5.72	5.55	5.40	5.26	5.13	5.000	4.878	4.762	4.651	4.546	4.444	4.348	4.255	4.167	4.082
5	5.71	5.56	5.41	5.26	5.13	5.000	4.878	4.762	4.651	4.545	4.445	4.348	4.255	4.167	4.082
6	5.72	5.55	5.40	5.26	5.13	5.000	4.878	4.762	4.651	4.546	4.444	4.348	4.255	4.167	4.082
7	5.71	5.56	5.41	5.26	5.13	5.000	4.878	4.762	4.651	4.545	4.445	4.348	4.255	4.167	4.082
8	5.72	5.55	5.40	5.27	5.13	5.000	4.878	4.762	4.651	4.546	4.444	4.348	4.255	4.167	4.082
9	5.71	5.56	5.41	5.26	5.13	5.000	4.878	4.762	4.651	4.545	4.445	4.348	4.255	4.167	4.081
10	5.72	5.55	5.40	5.27	5.13	5.000	4.878	4.762	4.651	4.546	4.444	4.348	4.256	4.166	4.082
11	5.71	5.56	5.41	5.26	5.13	5.000	4.878	4.762	4.651	4.545	4.445	4.348	4.255	4.167	4.081
12	5.72	5.55	5.40	5.27	5.13	5.000	4.878	4.762	4.651	4.546	4.444	4.348	4.256	4.166	4.082
13	5.71	5.56	5.41	5.26	5.13	5.000	4.878	4.762	4.651	4.545	4.445	4.348	4.256	4.167	4.081
14	5.72	5.55	5.40	5.27	5.13	5.000	4.878	4.762	4.651	4.546	4.444	4.348	4.255	4.166	4.082
15	5.71	5.56	5.41	5.26	5.13	5.000	4.878	4.762	4.651	4.545	4.445	4.348	4.256	4.167	4.082
16	5.72	5.55	5.40	5.27	5.12	5.000	4.878	4.762	4.651	4.546	4.444	4.348	4.255	4.166	4.081
17	5.71	5.56	5.41	5.26	5.13	5.000	4.878	4.762	4.652	4.545	4.445	4.347	4.256	4.167	4.082
18	5.72	5.55	5.40	5.27	5.12	5.000	4.878	4.762	4.651	4.546	4.444	4.348	4.256	4.166	4.081
19	5.71	2.78		5.26	5.13	5.000	4.879	4.761	4.652	4.545	4.445	4.347	4.255	4.167	4.082
20				2.63	5.13	5.000	4.878	4.762	4.651	4.546	4.444	4.348	4.256	4.166	4.081
21					5.12	2.500	4.878	4.761	4.652	4.545	4.445	4.347	4.255	4.166	4.082
22								2.381	4.651	4.546	4.444	4.348	4.256	4.166	4.081
23										2.273	4.444	4.348	4.255	4.167	4.082
24												2.174	4.256	4.166	4.081
25													4.255	2.083	4.081

and the Recovery Period is:

the Depreciation Rate is:

If the Recovery Year is:	25.0	25.5	26.0	26.5	27.0	27.5	28.0	28.5	29.0	29.5	30.0	30.5	31.0	31.5	32.0
1	2.000	1.961	1.923	1.887	1.852	1.818	1.786	1.754	1.724	1.695	1.667	1.639	1.613	1.587	1.563
2	4.000	3.922	3.846	3.774	3.704	3.636	3.571	3.509	3.448	3.390	3.333	3.279	3.226	3.175	3.125
3	4.000	3.922	3.846	3.774	3.704	3.636	3.571	3.509	3.448	3.390	3.333	3.279	3.226	3.175	3.125
4	4.000	3.922	3.846	3.774	3.704	3.636	3.571	3.509	3.448	3.390	3.333	3.279	3.226	3.175	3.125
5	4.000	3.922	3.846	3.774	3.704	3.636	3.571	3.509	3.448	3.390	3.333	3.279	3.226	3.175	3.125
6	4.000	3.921	3.846	3.773	3.704	3.636	3.571	3.509	3.448	3.390	3.333	3.279	3.226	3.175	3.125
7	4.000	3.922	3.846	3.774	3.704	3.636	3.572	3.509	3.448	3.390	3.333	3.279	3.226	3.175	3.125
8	4.000	3.921	3.846	3.773	3.704	3.637	3.571	3.509	3.448	3.390	3.333	3.279	3.226	3.175	3.125
9	4.000	3.922	3.846	3.773	3.704	3.636	3.572	3.509	3.448	3.390	3.333	3.279	3.226	3.175	3.125
10	4.000	3.921	3.846	3.774	3.704	3.636	3.571	3.509	3.448	3.390	3.333	3.279	3.226	3.174	3.125
11	4.000	3.922	3.846	3.773	3.704	3.637	3.572	3.509	3.448	3.390	3.333	3.279	3.226	3.175	3.125
12	4.000	3.921	3.846	3.774	3.704	3.636	3.571	3.509	3.448	3.390	3.333	3.279	3.226	3.174	3.125
13	4.000	3.922	3.846	3.773	3.703	3.637	3.572	3.509	3.449	3.390	3.334	3.278	3.226	3.175	3.125
14	4.000	3.921	3.846	3.773	3.703	3.636	3.571	3.509	3.448	3.390	3.333	3.279	3.226	3.174	3.125
15	4.000	3.922	3.846	3.774	3.704	3.637	3.572	3.509	3.449	3.390	3.334	3.278	3.226	3.175	3.125
16	4.000	3.921	3.846	3.773	3.703	3.636	3.571	3.509	3.448	3.390	3.333	3.279	3.226	3.174	3.125
17	4.000	3.922	3.846	3.773	3.704	3.637	3.572	3.508	3.449	3.390	3.334	3.278	3.226	3.175	3.125
18	4.000	3.921	3.846	3.774	3.703	3.636	3.571	3.509	3.448	3.390	3.333	3.279	3.226	3.174	3.125
19	4.000	3.922	3.846	3.773	3.704	3.637	3.572	3.508	3.449	3.390	3.334	3.278	3.226	3.175	3.125
20	4.000	3.921	3.846	3.774	3.703	3.636	3.571	3.509	3.448	3.390	3.333	3.279	3.226	3.174	3.125
21	4.000	3.922	3.846	3.773	3.704	3.637	3.572	3.508	3.449	3.389	3.334	3.278	3.226	3.175	3.125
22	4.000	3.921	3.847	3.774	3.703	3.636	3.571	3.509	3.448	3.390	3.333	3.279	3.225	3.174	3.125
23	4.000	3.922	3.846	3.773	3.704	3.637	3.572	3.508	3.449	3.389	3.334	3.278	3.226	3.175	3.125
24	4.000	3.921	3.847	3.774	3.703	3.636	3.571	3.509	3.448	3.390	3.333	3.279	3.225	3.174	3.125
25	4.000	3.922	3.846	3.773	3.704	3.637	3.572	3.508	3.449	3.389	3.334	3.278	3.226	3.175	3.125
26	2.000	3.921	3.847	3.774	3.703	3.636	3.571	3.509	3.448	3.390	3.333	3.279	3.225	3.174	3.125
27			1.923	3.774	3.704	3.637	3.572	3.508	3.449	3.389	3.334	3.278	3.226	3.175	3.125
28				1.852	3.636	3.571	3.509	3.448	3.390	3.333	3.279	3.225	3.174	3.125	
29						1.786	3.509	3.449	3.389	3.334	3.279	3.226	3.175	3.125	
30								1.724	3.390	3.333	3.278	3.225	3.174	3.125	
31										1.667	3.279	3.226	3.175	3.125	
32												1.613	3.174	3.125	
33															1.562

and the Recovery Period is:

the Depreciation Rate is:

If the Recovery Year is:	39.5	39.0	38.5	38.0	37.5	37.0	36.5	36.0	35.5	35.0	34.5	34.0	33.5	33.0	32.5
1	1.266	1.282	1.299	1.316	1.333	1.351	1.370	1.389	1.408	1.429	1.449	1.471	1.493	1.515	1.538
2	2.532	2.564	2.597	2.632	2.667	2.703	2.740	2.778	2.817	2.857	2.899	2.941	2.985	3.030	3.077
3	2.532	2.564	2.597	2.632	2.667	2.703	2.740	2.778	2.817	2.857	2.899	2.941	2.985	3.030	3.077
4	2.532	2.564	2.597	2.632	2.667	2.703	2.740	2.778	2.817	2.857	2.899	2.941	2.985	3.030	3.077
5	2.532	2.564	2.597	2.632	2.667	2.703	2.740	2.778	2.817	2.857	2.899	2.941	2.985	3.030	3.077
6	2.532	2.564	2.597	2.631	2.667	2.703	2.740	2.778	2.817	2.857	2.899	2.941	2.985	3.030	3.077
7	2.532	2.564	2.597	2.631	2.667	2.703	2.740	2.778	2.817	2.857	2.898	2.941	2.985	3.030	3.077
8	2.532	2.564	2.597	2.632	2.667	2.703	2.740	2.778	2.817	2.857	2.899	2.941	2.985	3.030	3.077
9	2.532	2.564	2.597	2.631	2.667	2.703	2.740	2.778	2.817	2.857	2.898	2.941	2.985	3.030	3.077
10	2.532	2.564	2.598	2.632	2.667	2.703	2.740	2.778	2.817	2.857	2.899	2.941	2.985	3.030	3.077
11	2.532	2.564	2.597	2.631	2.667	2.703	2.740	2.778	2.817	2.857	2.898	2.941	2.985	3.030	3.077
12	2.532	2.564	2.598	2.632	2.666	2.703	2.740	2.778	2.817	2.857	2.899	2.941	2.985	3.030	3.077
13	2.532	2.564	2.597	2.631	2.667	2.703	2.740	2.778	2.817	2.857	2.898	2.941	2.985	3.031	3.077
14	2.531	2.564	2.598	2.632	2.666	2.703	2.740	2.778	2.817	2.857	2.899	2.941	2.985	3.031	3.077
15	2.532	2.564	2.597	2.631	2.667	2.703	2.740	2.778	2.817	2.857	2.898	2.941	2.985	3.030	3.077
16	2.531	2.564	2.598	2.632	2.666	2.703	2.739	2.778	2.817	2.857	2.899	2.941	2.985	3.031	3.077
17	2.532	2.564	2.597	2.631	2.667	2.703	2.740	2.778	2.817	2.857	2.898	2.941	2.985	3.030	3.077
18	2.531	2.564	2.598	2.632	2.666	2.702	2.739	2.778	2.817	2.857	2.899	2.941	2.985	3.031	3.077
19	2.532	2.564	2.597	2.631	2.667	2.703	2.740	2.778	2.817	2.857	2.898	2.941	2.985	3.031	3.077
20	2.531	2.564	2.598	2.632	2.666	2.702	2.739	2.778	2.817	2.857	2.899	2.941	2.985	3.031	3.077
21	2.531	2.564	2.597	2.631	2.667	2.703	2.740	2.778	2.817	2.857	2.898	2.941	2.985	3.030	3.077
22	2.531	2.564	2.598	2.632	2.666	2.702	2.739	2.777	2.817	2.857	2.899	2.941	2.985	3.031	3.077
23	2.531	2.564	2.597	2.631	2.667	2.703	2.740	2.778	2.817	2.857	2.898	2.942	2.985	3.030	3.077
24	2.531	2.564	2.598	2.632	2.666	2.702	2.739	2.777	2.817	2.857	2.899	2.941	2.985	3.031	3.077
25	2.532	2.564	2.597	2.631	2.667	2.703	2.740	2.778	2.817	2.857	2.898	2.941	2.985	3.030	3.077
26	2.531	2.564	2.598	2.632	2.666	2.702	2.739	2.777	2.817	2.857	2.899	2.942	2.985	3.031	3.077
27	2.532	2.564	2.597	2.631	2.667	2.703	2.740	2.778	2.817	2.858	2.898	2.941	2.985	3.030	3.077
28	2.531	2.564	2.598	2.632	2.666	2.702	2.739	2.777	2.817	2.857	2.899	2.942	2.985	3.031	3.077
29	2.532	2.564	2.597	2.631	2.667	2.703	2.740	2.778	2.817	2.857	2.898	2.941	2.985	3.030	3.077
30	2.531	2.564	2.598	2.632	2.666	2.702	2.739	2.777	2.817	2.858	2.899	2.941	2.986	3.031	3.077
31	2.532	2.564	2.597	2.631	2.667	2.703	2.740	2.778	2.817	2.857	2.898	2.942	2.985	3.030	3.076
32	2.531	2.564	2.598	2.632	2.666	2.702	2.739	2.777	2.817	2.858	2.899	2.941	2.986	3.031	3.077
33	2.531	2.565	2.597	2.631	2.667	2.703	2.740	2.778	2.817	2.857	2.898	2.942	2.985	3.030	3.076
34	2.532	2.564	2.598	2.632	2.666	2.702	2.739	2.777	2.816	2.858	2.899	2.941	2.985	1.515	
35	2.531	2.564	2.597	2.631	2.667	2.702	2.740	2.777	2.817	2.857	2.899	1.471			
36	2.531	2.565	2.598	2.632	2.666	2.702	2.739	2.778	2.816	1.429					
37	2.531	2.565	2.597	2.631	2.667	2.703	2.739	1.389							
38	2.532	2.564	2.598	2.632	2.666	1.351									
39	2.531	2.565	2.597	1.316											
40	2.531	1.282													

and the Recovery Period is:

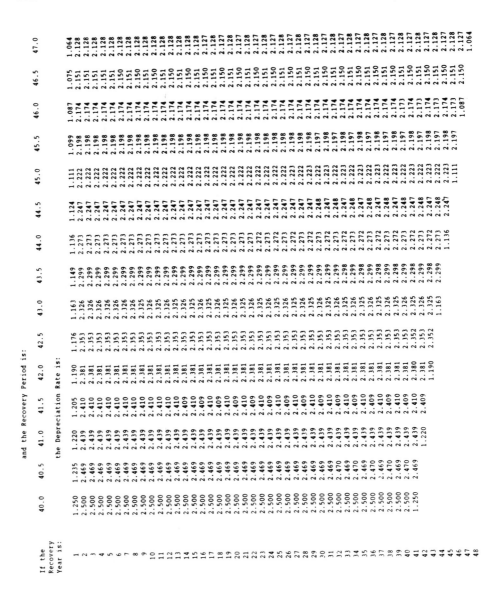

If the Recovery Year is:	40.0	40.5	41.0	41.5	42.0	42.5	43.0	43.5	44.0	44.5	45.0	45.5	46.0	46.5	47.0
					the Depreciation Rate is:										
1	1.250	1.235	1.220	1.205	1.190	1.176	1.163	1.149	1.136	1.124	1.111	1.099	1.087	1.075	1.064
2	2.500	2.469	2.439	2.410	2.381	2.353	2.326	2.299	2.273	2.247	2.222	2.198	2.174	2.151	2.128
3	2.500	2.469	2.439	2.410	2.381	2.353	2.326	2.299	2.273	2.247	2.222	2.198	2.174	2.151	2.128
4	2.500	2.469	2.439	2.410	2.381	2.353	2.326	2.299	2.273	2.247	2.222	2.198	2.174	2.151	2.128
5	2.500	2.469	2.439	2.410	2.381	2.353	2.326	2.299	2.273	2.247	2.222	2.198	2.174	2.151	2.128
6	2.500	2.469	2.439	2.410	2.381	2.353	2.326	2.299	2.273	2.247	2.222	2.198	2.174	2.150	2.128
7	2.500	2.469	2.439	2.410	2.381	2.353	2.326	2.299	2.273	2.247	2.222	2.198	2.174	2.151	2.128
8	2.500	2.469	2.439	2.410	2.381	2.353	2.326	2.299	2.273	2.247	2.222	2.198	2.174	2.150	2.128
9	2.500	2.469	2.439	2.410	2.381	2.353	2.326	2.299	2.273	2.247	2.222	2.198	2.174	2.151	2.128
10	2.500	2.469	2.439	2.410	2.381	2.353	2.326	2.299	2.273	2.247	2.222	2.198	2.174	2.150	2.128
11	2.500	2.469	2.439	2.410	2.381	2.353	2.326	2.299	2.273	2.247	2.222	2.198	2.174	2.151	2.128
12	2.500	2.469	2.439	2.410	2.381	2.353	2.326	2.299	2.273	2.247	2.222	2.198	2.174	2.150	2.128
13	2.500	2.469	2.439	2.410	2.381	2.353	2.325	2.299	2.273	2.247	2.222	2.198	2.174	2.151	2.128
14	2.500	2.469	2.439	2.409	2.381	2.353	2.326	2.299	2.273	2.247	2.222	2.198	2.174	2.150	2.128
15	2.500	2.469	2.439	2.410	2.381	2.353	2.325	2.299	2.273	2.247	2.222	2.198	2.174	2.151	2.127
16	2.500	2.469	2.439	2.409	2.381	2.353	2.326	2.299	2.273	2.247	2.222	2.198	2.174	2.150	2.128
17	2.500	2.469	2.439	2.410	2.381	2.353	2.325	2.299	2.273	2.247	2.222	2.198	2.174	2.151	2.127
18	2.500	2.469	2.439	2.409	2.381	2.353	2.326	2.299	2.273	2.247	2.222	2.198	2.174	2.150	2.128
19	2.500	2.469	2.439	2.410	2.381	2.353	2.325	2.299	2.273	2.247	2.222	2.198	2.174	2.151	2.127
20	2.500	2.469	2.439	2.409	2.381	2.353	2.326	2.299	2.273	2.247	2.222	2.198	2.174	2.150	2.128
21	2.500	2.469	2.439	2.410	2.381	2.353	2.325	2.299	2.273	2.247	2.222	2.198	2.174	2.151	2.127
22	2.500	2.469	2.439	2.409	2.381	2.353	2.326	2.299	2.273	2.247	2.222	2.198	2.174	2.150	2.128
23	2.500	2.469	2.439	2.410	2.381	2.353	2.325	2.299	2.273	2.247	2.222	2.198	2.174	2.151	2.127
24	2.500	2.469	2.439	2.409	2.381	2.353	2.326	2.299	2.273	2.247	2.222	2.198	2.174	2.150	2.128
25	2.500	2.469	2.439	2.410	2.381	2.353	2.325	2.299	2.273	2.247	2.222	2.198	2.174	2.151	2.127
26	2.500	2.469	2.439	2.409	2.381	2.353	2.326	2.299	2.273	2.247	2.222	2.198	2.174	2.150	2.128
27	2.500	2.469	2.439	2.410	2.381	2.353	2.325	2.299	2.273	2.247	2.222	2.198	2.174	2.151	2.127
28	2.500	2.469	2.439	2.409	2.381	2.353	2.326	2.299	2.273	2.247	2.222	2.198	2.174	2.150	2.128
29	2.500	2.469	2.439	2.410	2.381	2.353	2.325	2.299	2.273	2.247	2.222	2.197	2.174	2.151	2.127
30	2.500	2.469	2.439	2.409	2.381	2.353	2.326	2.299	2.272	2.247	2.222	2.198	2.174	2.150	2.128
31	2.500	2.469	2.439	2.410	2.381	2.353	2.325	2.299	2.273	2.247	2.223	2.197	2.174	2.151	2.127
32	2.500	2.470	2.439	2.409	2.381	2.353	2.326	2.299	2.272	2.248	2.223	2.198	2.174	2.150	2.128
33	2.500	2.469	2.439	2.410	2.381	2.353	2.325	2.299	2.273	2.247	2.223	2.197	2.174	2.151	2.128
34	2.500	2.469	2.439	2.409	2.381	2.353	2.326	2.298	2.272	2.248	2.223	2.198	2.174	2.150	2.127
35	2.500	2.470	2.439	2.410	2.381	2.353	2.325	2.299	2.273	2.247	2.222	2.197	2.174	2.151	2.128
36	2.500	2.469	2.439	2.409	2.381	2.353	2.326	2.298	2.272	2.248	2.223	2.198	2.174	2.150	2.127
37	2.500	2.469	2.439	2.410	2.381	2.353	2.325	2.299	2.273	2.247	2.222	2.197	2.174	2.151	2.128
38	2.500	2.470	2.439	2.409	2.381	2.353	2.326	2.298	2.272	2.248	2.223	2.198	2.174	2.150	2.127
39	2.500	2.469	2.439	2.410	2.381	2.353	2.325	2.299	2.273	2.247	2.222	2.197	2.173	2.151	2.128
40	2.500	2.470	2.439	2.409	2.381	2.353	2.326	2.298	2.272	2.248	2.223	2.198	2.174	2.150	2.127
41	1.250	2.469	2.439	2.410	2.380	2.353	2.325	2.299	2.273	2.247	2.222	2.197	2.173	2.151	2.128
42		2.469	1.220	2.409	2.381	2.352	2.326	2.298	2.272	2.248	2.223	2.198	2.174	2.150	2.127
43				2.409	1.190	2.353	2.325	2.299	2.273	2.247	2.222	2.197	2.173	2.151	2.128
44						1.176	2.326	2.298	2.272	2.248	2.223	2.198	2.174	2.150	2.127
45							1.163	2.299	2.273	2.247	2.222	2.197	2.173	2.151	2.128
46									1.136	2.248	2.223	2.198	2.174	2.150	2.127
47											1.111	2.198	2.173	2.151	2.128
48												2.197		2.150	1.064

and the Recovery Period is:

If the Recovery Year is:	47.5	48.0	48.5	49.0	49.5	50.0
			the Depreciation Rate is:			
1	1.053	1.042	1.031	1.020	1.010	1.000
2	2.105	2.083	2.062	2.041	2.020	2.000
3	2.105	2.083	2.062	2.041	2.020	2.000
4	2.105	2.083	2.062	2.041	2.020	2.000
5	2.105	2.083	2.062	2.041	2.020	2.000
6	2.105	2.083	2.062	2.041	2.020	2.000
7	2.105	2.083	2.062	2.041	2.020	2.000
8	2.105	2.083	2.062	2.041	2.020	2.000
9	2.105	2.083	2.062	2.041	2.020	2.000
10	2.105	2.083	2.062	2.041	2.020	2.000
11	2.105	2.083	2.062	2.041	2.020	2.000
12	2.105	2.083	2.062	2.041	2.020	2.000
13	2.105	2.083	2.062	2.041	2.020	2.000
14	2.105	2.083	2.062	2.041	2.020	2.000
15	2.105	2.083	2.062	2.041	2.020	2.000
16	2.105	2.083	2.062	2.041	2.020	2.000
17	2.105	2.083	2.062	2.041	2.020	2.000
18	2.105	2.083	2.062	2.041	2.020	2.000
19	2.105	2.083	2.062	2.041	2.020	2.000
20	2.105	2.083	2.062	2.041	2.020	2.000
21	2.105	2.084	2.062	2.041	2.020	2.000
22	2.105	2.083	2.062	2.041	2.020	2.000
23	2.105	2.084	2.062	2.041	2.020	2.000
24	2.105	2.083	2.062	2.041	2.020	2.000
25	2.105	2.084	2.062	2.041	2.020	2.000
26	2.106	2.083	2.062	2.041	2.020	2.000

and the Recovery Period is:

If the Recovery Year is:	47.5	48.0	48.5	49.0	49.5	50.0
			the Depreciation Rate is:			
27	2.105	2.084	2.062	2.041	2.020	2.000
28	2.106	2.083	2.062	2.041	2.020	2.000
29	2.105	2.084	2.062	2.041	2.020	2.000
30	2.106	2.083	2.062	2.041	2.020	2.000
31	2.105	2.084	2.062	2.041	2.021	2.000
32	2.106	2.083	2.062	2.041	2.020	2.000
33	2.105	2.084	2.062	2.041	2.020	2.000
34	2.106	2.083	2.062	2.040	2.021	2.000
35	2.105	2.084	2.062	2.041	2.020	2.000
36	2.106	2.083	2.062	2.040	2.021	2.000
37	2.105	2.084	2.061	2.041	2.020	2.000
38	2.106	2.083	2.062	2.040	2.021	2.000
39	2.105	2.084	2.061	2.041	2.020	2.000
40	2.106	2.083	2.062	2.040	2.021	2.000
41	2.105	2.084	2.061	2.041	2.020	2.000
42	2.106	2.083	2.062	2.040	2.021	2.000
43	2.105	2.084	2.061	2.041	2.020	2.000
44	2.106	2.083	2.062	2.040	2.020	2.000
45	2.105	2.084	2.061	2.041	2.021	2.000
46	2.106	2.083	2.062	2.040	2.020	2.000
47	2.105	2.084	2.061	2.041	2.021	2.000
48	2.106	2.083	2.062	2.040	2.020	2.000
49	2.105	2.084	2.062	2.041	2.021	2.000
50	2.106	2.083	2.062	2.040	2.020	2.000
51		1.042	2.061	1.020	2.020	1.000

TABLE 9

General and Alternative Depreciation Systems
Applicable Depreciation Method: Straight Line
Applicable Recovery Periods: 2.5 – 50 years
Applicable Convention: Mid-quarter (property placed in service in first quarter)

and the Recovery Period is:

the Depreciation Rate is:

If the Recovery Year is:	2.5	3.0	3.5	4.0	4.5	5.0	5.5	6.0	6.5	7.0	7.5	8.0	8.5	9.0	9.5
1	35.00	29.17	25.00	21.88	19.44	17.50	15.91	14.58	13.46	12.50	11.67	10.94	10.29	9.72	9.21
2	40.00	33.33	28.57	25.00	22.22	20.00	18.18	16.67	15.38	14.29	13.33	12.50	11.77	11.11	10.53
3	25.00	33.33	28.57	25.00	22.22	20.00	18.18	16.67	15.39	14.28	13.33	12.50	11.76	11.11	10.53
4		4.17	17.86	25.00	22.23	20.00	18.18	16.67	15.38	14.29	13.33	12.50	11.77	11.11	10.53
5				3.12	13.89	20.00	18.18	16.66	15.39	14.29	13.34	12.50	11.76	11.11	10.52
6						2.50	11.37	16.67	15.38	14.28	13.33	12.50	11.77	11.11	10.53
7								2.08	9.62	14.29	13.34	12.50	11.76	11.11	10.52
8										1.79	8.33	12.50	11.77	11.11	10.53
9												1.56	7.35	11.11	10.53
10														1.39	6.58

and the Recovery Period is:

the Depreciation Rate is:

If the Recovery Year is:	10.0	10.5	11.0	11.5	12.0	12.5	13.0	13.5	14.0	14.5	15.0	15.5	16.0	16.5	17.0
1	8.75	8.33	7.95	7.61	7.29	7.00	6.73	6.48	6.25	6.03	5.83	5.65	5.47	5.30	5.15
2	10.00	9.52	9.09	8.70	8.33	8.00	7.69	7.41	7.14	6.90	6.67	6.45	6.25	6.06	5.88
3	10.00	9.52	9.09	8.70	8.33	8.00	7.69	7.41	7.14	6.90	6.67	6.45	6.25	6.06	5.88
4	10.00	9.53	9.09	8.69	8.33	8.00	7.69	7.41	7.14	6.90	6.67	6.45	6.25	6.06	5.88
5	10.00	9.52	9.09	8.70	8.34	8.00	7.69	7.41	7.14	6.90	6.67	6.45	6.25	6.06	5.88
6	10.00	9.53	9.09	8.69	8.33	8.00	7.69	7.41	7.14	6.90	6.66	6.45	6.25	6.06	5.88
7	10.00	9.52	9.09	8.70	8.34	8.00	7.69	7.41	7.14	6.89	6.67	6.45	6.25	6.06	5.88
8	10.00	9.53	9.09	8.69	8.33	8.00	7.69	7.41	7.15	6.90	6.66	6.45	6.25	6.06	5.88
9	10.00	9.52	9.09	8.70	8.34	8.00	7.70	7.40	7.14	6.89	6.67	6.45	6.25	6.06	5.89
10	10.00	9.53	9.09	8.69	8.33	8.00	7.69	7.41	7.15	6.90	6.66	6.45	6.25	6.06	5.88
11	1.25	5.95	9.10	8.70	8.34	8.00	7.70	7.40	7.14	6.89	6.67	6.45	6.25	6.06	5.88
12			1.14	5.43	8.33	8.00	7.69	7.41	7.15	6.90	6.66	6.45	6.25	6.06	5.89
13					1.04	5.00	7.70	7.40	7.14	6.89	6.67	6.45	6.25	6.06	5.88
14							0.96	4.63	7.15	6.90	6.66	6.46	6.25	6.06	5.89
15									0.89	4.31	6.67	6.46	6.25	6.06	5.88
16											0.83	4.03	6.25	6.07	5.89
17													0.78	3.79	5.88
18															0.74

and the Recovery Period is:

the Depreciation Rate is:

If the Recovery Year is:	17.5	18.0	18.5	19.0	19.5	20.0	20.5	21.0	21.5	22.0	22.5	23.0	23.5	24.0	24.5
1	5.00	4.86	4.73	4.61	4.49	4.375	4.268	4.167	4.070	3.977	3.889	3.804	3.723	3.646	3.571
2	5.71	5.56	5.41	5.26	5.13	5.000	4.878	4.762	4.651	4.545	4.444	4.348	4.255	4.167	4.082
3	5.71	5.56	5.41	5.26	5.13	5.000	4.878	4.762	4.651	4.545	4.444	4.348	4.255	4.167	4.082
4	5.71	5.55	5.40	5.26	5.13	5.000	4.878	4.762	4.651	4.546	4.444	4.348	4.255	4.167	4.082
5	5.72	5.56	5.41	5.26	5.13	5.000	4.878	4.762	4.651	4.545	4.445	4.348	4.255	4.167	4.082
6	5.71	5.55	5.40	5.26	5.13	5.000	4.878	4.762	4.651	4.546	4.444	4.348	4.255	4.167	4.082
7	5.72	5.56	5.41	5.26	5.13	5.000	4.878	4.762	4.651	4.546	4.445	4.348	4.255	4.167	4.082
8	5.71	5.55	5.40	5.26	5.13	5.000	4.878	4.762	4.651	4.545	4.444	4.348	4.255	4.167	4.082
9	5.71	5.56	5.41	5.27	5.13	5.000	4.878	4.762	4.651	4.546	4.445	4.348	4.256	4.167	4.082
10	5.72	5.55	5.40	5.26	5.13	5.000	4.878	4.762	4.651	4.545	4.444	4.348	4.255	4.166	4.082
11	5.71	5.56	5.41	5.27	5.13	5.000	4.878	4.762	4.651	4.546	4.445	4.348	4.256	4.167	4.081
12	5.72	5.55	5.40	5.26	5.13	5.000	4.878	4.762	4.651	4.545	4.444	4.348	4.255	4.166	4.082
13	5.71	5.56	5.41	5.27	5.13	5.000	4.878	4.762	4.651	4.546	4.445	4.348	4.256	4.167	4.081
14	5.72	5.55	5.40	5.26	5.13	5.000	4.878	4.762	4.651	4.545	4.444	4.348	4.255	4.166	4.082
15	5.71	5.56	5.41	5.27	5.12	5.000	4.878	4.762	4.651	4.546	4.445	4.348	4.256	4.167	4.081
16	5.72	5.55	5.40	5.26	5.13	5.000	4.878	4.762	4.651	4.545	4.444	4.348	4.255	4.166	4.082
17	5.71	5.56	5.41	5.27	5.12	5.000	4.878	4.762	4.652	4.546	4.445	4.348	4.256	4.167	4.081
18	5.72	5.55	5.40	5.26	5.13	5.000	4.878	4.761	4.651	4.545	4.444	4.348	4.255	4.166	4.082
19	3.57	5.56	5.40	5.26	5.13	5.000	4.878	4.762	4.652	4.546	4.445	4.347	4.256	4.167	4.081
20		0.69	3.38	0.66	3.20	5.000	4.879	4.761	4.651	4.545	4.444	4.348	4.255	4.166	4.082
21						0.625	3.049	4.762	4.652	4.546	4.445	4.347	4.256	4.167	4.081
22								0.595	4.652	4.545	4.444	4.348	4.255	4.166	4.082
23									2.907	4.546	4.445	4.347	4.256	4.167	4.081
24										0.568	4.444	4.348	4.255	4.166	4.082
25											2.778	0.543	2.660	0.521	4.081
26															2.551

and the Recovery Period is:

the Depreciation Rate is:

If the Recovery Year is:	25.0	25.5	26.0	26.5	27.0	27.5	28.0	28.5	29.0	29.5	30.0	30.5	31.0	31.5	32.0
1	3.500	3.431	3.365	3.302	3.241	3.182	3.125	3.070	3.017	2.966	2.917	2.869	2.823	2.778	2.734
2	4.000	3.922	3.846	3.774	3.704	3.636	3.571	3.509	3.448	3.390	3.333	3.279	3.226	3.175	3.125
3	4.000	3.922	3.846	3.774	3.704	3.636	3.571	3.509	3.448	3.390	3.333	3.279	3.226	3.175	3.125
4	4.000	3.922	3.846	3.774	3.704	3.636	3.571	3.509	3.448	3.390	3.333	3.279	3.226	3.175	3.125
5	4.000	3.922	3.846	3.774	3.704	3.636	3.572	3.509	3.448	3.390	3.333	3.279	3.226	3.175	3.125
6	4.000	3.922	3.846	3.773	3.704	3.636	3.571	3.509	3.448	3.390	3.333	3.279	3.226	3.175	3.125
7	4.000	3.921	3.846	3.774	3.704	3.636	3.572	3.509	3.448	3.390	3.333	3.279	3.226	3.174	3.125
8	4.000	3.922	3.846	3.773	3.704	3.636	3.571	3.509	3.448	3.390	3.333	3.279	3.226	3.175	3.125
9	4.000	3.922	3.846	3.774	3.704	3.637	3.572	3.509	3.448	3.390	3.333	3.279	3.226	3.174	3.125
10	4.000	3.921	3.846	3.773	3.704	3.636	3.571	3.509	3.448	3.390	3.333	3.279	3.226	3.175	3.125
11	4.000	3.921	3.846	3.773	3.704	3.636	3.572	3.509	3.448	3.390	3.333	3.279	3.226	3.174	3.125
12	4.000	3.922	3.846	3.774	3.704	3.637	3.571	3.509	3.448	3.390	3.333	3.279	3.226	3.175	3.125
13	4.000	3.921	3.846	3.773	3.703	3.636	3.572	3.509	3.448	3.390	3.334	3.278	3.226	3.174	3.125
14	4.000	3.922	3.846	3.774	3.704	3.637	3.571	3.509	3.448	3.390	3.333	3.279	3.226	3.175	3.125
15	4.000	3.921	3.846	3.774	3.703	3.636	3.572	3.509	3.449	3.390	3.334	3.278	3.226	3.174	3.125
16	4.000	3.922	3.846	3.774	3.704	3.637	3.571	3.509	3.449	3.390	3.333	3.279	3.226	3.175	3.125
17	4.000	3.921	3.846	3.773	3.703	3.636	3.572	3.509	3.448	3.390	3.334	3.278	3.226	3.174	3.125
18	4.000	3.922	3.846	3.774	3.704	3.637	3.571	3.508	3.449	3.390	3.333	3.279	3.226	3.175	3.125
19	4.000	3.921	3.847	3.773	3.703	3.636	3.572	3.509	3.448	3.390	3.334	3.278	3.226	3.174	3.125
20	4.000	3.922	3.846	3.774	3.704	3.637	3.571	3.508	3.449	3.390	3.333	3.279	3.225	3.175	3.125
21	4.000	3.921	3.847	3.773	3.703	3.636	3.572	3.509	3.448	3.390	3.334	3.278	3.226	3.174	3.125
22	4.000	3.922	3.846	3.774	3.704	3.637	3.571	3.508	3.449	3.389	3.333	3.279	3.225	3.175	3.125
23	4.000	3.921	3.847	3.773	3.703	3.636	3.572	3.509	3.448	3.390	3.334	3.278	3.226	3.174	3.125
24	4.000	3.922	3.846	3.774	3.704	3.637	3.571	3.508	3.449	3.389	3.333	3.279	3.225	3.175	3.125
25	4.000	3.921	3.847	3.774	3.703	3.636	3.572	3.509	3.448	3.390	3.334	3.278	3.226	3.174	3.125
26	0.500	2.451	3.846	3.774	3.704	3.637	3.571	3.508	3.449	3.389	3.333	3.279	3.225	3.175	3.125
27			0.481	3.774	3.703	3.636	3.572	3.509	3.449	3.390	3.334	3.278	3.226	3.174	3.125
28				2.358	0.463	2.273	0.446	3.508	3.448	3.389	3.333	3.279	3.225	3.175	3.125
29								2.193	0.431	3.390	3.334	3.278	3.226	3.174	3.125
30										2.118	3.333	3.279	3.225	3.175	3.125
31											0.417	2.049	3.226	3.174	3.125
32													0.403	3.175	3.125
33														1.984	0.391

and the Recovery Period is:

If the Recovery Year is:	32.5	33.0	33.5	34.0	34.5	35.0	35.5	36.0	36.5	37.0	37.5	38.0	38.5	39.0	39.5
	the Depreciation Rate is:														
1	2.692	2.652	2.612	2.574	2.536	2.500	2.465	2.431	2.397	2.365	2.333	2.303	2.273	2.244	2.215
2	3.077	3.030	2.985	2.941	2.899	2.857	2.817	2.778	2.740	2.703	2.667	2.632	2.597	2.564	2.532
3	3.077	3.030	2.985	2.941	2.899	2.857	2.817	2.778	2.740	2.703	2.667	2.632	2.597	2.564	2.532
4	3.077	3.030	2.985	2.941	2.899	2.857	2.817	2.778	2.740	2.703	2.667	2.632	2.597	2.564	2.532
5	3.077	3.030	2.985	2.941	2.899	2.857	2.817	2.778	2.740	2.703	2.667	2.632	2.597	2.564	2.532
6	3.077	3.030	2.985	2.941	2.899	2.857	2.817	2.778	2.740	2.703	2.667	2.632	2.597	2.564	2.532
7	3.077	3.030	2.985	2.941	2.898	2.857	2.817	2.778	2.740	2.703	2.667	2.632	2.597	2.564	2.532
8	3.077	3.030	2.985	2.941	2.899	2.857	2.817	2.778	2.740	2.703	2.667	2.632	2.597	2.564	2.532
9	3.077	3.030	2.985	2.941	2.899	2.857	2.817	2.778	2.740	2.703	2.667	2.631	2.598	2.564	2.532
10	3.077	3.030	2.985	2.941	2.898	2.857	2.817	2.778	2.740	2.703	2.667	2.632	2.597	2.564	2.532
11	3.077	3.030	2.985	2.941	2.899	2.857	2.817	2.778	2.740	2.703	2.667	2.631	2.598	2.564	2.532
12	3.077	3.030	2.985	2.941	2.898	2.857	2.817	2.778	2.740	2.703	2.667	2.631	2.597	2.564	2.532
13	3.077	3.030	2.985	2.941	2.899	2.857	2.817	2.778	2.740	2.703	2.667	2.632	2.598	2.564	2.532
14	3.077	3.030	2.985	2.941	2.899	2.857	2.817	2.778	2.740	2.703	2.667	2.631	2.597	2.564	2.531
15	3.077	3.030	2.985	2.941	2.898	2.857	2.817	2.778	2.740	2.703	2.666	2.632	2.598	2.564	2.532
16	3.077	3.031	2.985	2.941	2.898	2.857	2.817	2.778	2.740	2.703	2.667	2.632	2.597	2.564	2.532
17	3.077	3.030	2.985	2.941	2.899	2.857	2.817	2.778	2.740	2.703	2.666	2.631	2.598	2.564	2.531
18	3.077	3.031	2.985	2.941	2.898	2.857	2.817	2.778	2.740	2.703	2.667	2.632	2.597	2.564	2.532
19	3.077	3.030	2.985	2.941	2.899	2.857	2.817	2.778	2.739	2.702	2.667	2.632	2.598	2.564	2.532
20	3.077	3.031	2.985	2.941	2.898	2.857	2.817	2.778	2.740	2.703	2.667	2.631	2.597	2.564	2.531
21	3.077	3.030	2.985	2.941	2.899	2.857	2.817	2.777	2.740	2.703	2.666	2.632	2.598	2.564	2.532
22	3.077	3.031	2.985	2.941	2.898	2.857	2.817	2.778	2.739	2.702	2.667	2.631	2.597	2.564	2.531
23	3.077	3.030	2.985	2.941	2.899	2.857	2.817	2.777	2.740	2.703	2.666	2.632	2.598	2.564	2.531
24	3.077	3.031	2.985	2.941	2.898	2.857	2.817	2.778	2.739	2.702	2.667	2.631	2.597	2.564	2.532
25	3.077	3.030	2.985	2.942	2.899	2.857	2.817	2.777	2.740	2.703	2.666	2.632	2.598	2.564	2.531
26	3.077	3.031	2.985	2.941	2.898	2.858	2.817	2.778	2.739	2.702	2.667	2.631	2.597	2.564	2.532
27	3.077	3.030	2.985	2.942	2.899	2.857	2.817	2.777	2.740	2.703	2.666	2.632	2.598	2.564	2.531
28	3.077	3.031	2.985	2.941	2.898	2.858	2.817	2.778	2.739	2.702	2.667	2.631	2.597	2.564	2.532
29	3.077	3.030	2.986	2.942	2.899	2.857	2.817	2.777	2.740	2.703	2.666	2.632	2.598	2.564	2.531
30	3.076	3.031	2.985	2.941	2.898	2.858	2.817	2.778	2.739	2.702	2.667	2.631	2.597	2.564	2.532
31	3.077	3.030	2.986	2.942	2.899	2.857	2.816	2.777	2.740	2.702	2.666	2.631	2.598	2.564	2.531
32	3.076	3.031	2.985	2.941	2.898	2.858	2.817	2.778	2.739	2.703	2.667	2.632	2.597	2.564	2.532
33	1.923	3.030	2.986	2.942	2.899	2.857	2.816	2.777	2.740	2.702	2.666	2.631	2.598	2.564	2.531
34		0.379	2.985	2.941	2.898	2.858	2.817	2.778	2.739	2.702	2.667	2.632	2.597	2.564	2.531
35			1.866	2.941	2.899	2.857	2.816	2.777	2.740	2.703	2.666	2.632	2.598	2.564	2.532
36				0.368	2.898	2.858	2.817	2.778	2.739	2.702	2.667	2.631	2.597	2.564	2.532
37					1.812	0.357	1.760	2.778	2.740	2.703	2.666	2.632	2.598	2.565	2.531
38								0.347	1.712	2.702	2.667	2.631	2.597	2.564	2.532
39										0.338	2.666	2.631	2.598	2.564	2.531
40											1.667	0.329	1.623	0.321	1.582

and the Recovery Period is:

the Depreciation Rate is:

If the Recovery Year is:	40.0	40.5	41.0	41.5	42.0	42.5	43.0	43.5	44.0	44.5	45.0	45.5	46.0	46.5	47.0
1	2.188	2.160	2.134	2.108	2.083	2.059	2.035	2.011	1.989	1.966	1.944	1.923	1.902	1.882	1.862
2	2.500	2.469	2.439	2.410	2.381	2.353	2.326	2.299	2.273	2.247	2.222	2.198	2.174	2.151	2.128
3	2.500	2.469	2.439	2.410	2.381	2.353	2.326	2.299	2.273	2.247	2.222	2.198	2.174	2.151	2.128
4	2.500	2.469	2.439	2.410	2.381	2.353	2.326	2.299	2.273	2.247	2.222	2.198	2.174	2.151	2.128
5	2.500	2.469	2.439	2.410	2.381	2.353	2.326	2.299	2.273	2.247	2.222	2.198	2.174	2.150	2.128
6	2.500	2.469	2.439	2.410	2.381	2.353	2.326	2.299	2.273	2.247	2.222	2.198	2.174	2.151	2.128
7	2.500	2.469	2.439	2.410	2.381	2.353	2.326	2.299	2.273	2.247	2.222	2.198	2.174	2.151	2.128
8	2.500	2.469	2.439	2.410	2.381	2.353	2.326	2.299	2.273	2.247	2.222	2.198	2.174	2.150	2.128
9	2.500	2.469	2.439	2.410	2.381	2.353	2.326	2.299	2.273	2.247	2.222	2.198	2.174	2.151	2.128
10	2.500	2.469	2.439	2.410	2.381	2.353	2.326	2.299	2.273	2.247	2.222	2.198	2.174	2.151	2.128
11	2.500	2.469	2.439	2.410	2.381	2.353	2.326	2.299	2.273	2.247	2.222	2.198	2.174	2.151	2.128
12	2.500	2.469	2.439	2.410	2.381	2.353	2.326	2.299	2.273	2.247	2.222	2.198	2.174	2.150	2.128
13	2.500	2.469	2.439	2.410	2.381	2.353	2.326	2.299	2.273	2.247	2.222	2.198	2.174	2.151	2.128
14	2.500	2.469	2.439	2.410	2.381	2.353	2.326	2.299	2.273	2.247	2.222	2.198	2.174	2.151	2.128
15	2.500	2.469	2.439	2.409	2.381	2.353	2.326	2.299	2.273	2.247	2.222	2.198	2.174	2.150	2.128
16	2.500	2.469	2.439	2.410	2.381	2.353	2.326	2.299	2.273	2.247	2.222	2.198	2.174	2.151	2.127
17	2.500	2.469	2.439	2.409	2.381	2.353	2.325	2.299	2.273	2.247	2.222	2.198	2.174	2.151	2.127
18	2.500	2.469	2.439	2.410	2.381	2.353	2.326	2.299	2.273	2.247	2.222	2.198	2.174	2.150	2.128
19	2.500	2.469	2.439	2.409	2.381	2.353	2.325	2.299	2.273	2.247	2.222	2.198	2.174	2.151	2.128
20	2.500	2.469	2.439	2.410	2.381	2.353	2.326	2.299	2.273	2.247	2.222	2.198	2.174	2.151	2.128
21	2.500	2.469	2.439	2.410	2.381	2.353	2.325	2.299	2.273	2.247	2.222	2.198	2.174	2.150	2.127
22	2.500	2.469	2.439	2.410	2.381	2.353	2.326	2.299	2.273	2.247	2.222	2.198	2.174	2.151	2.127
23	2.500	2.469	2.439	2.410	2.381	2.353	2.325	2.298	2.272	2.247	2.222	2.198	2.174	2.151	2.128
24	2.500	2.469	2.439	2.409	2.381	2.353	2.326	2.299	2.273	2.247	2.222	2.198	2.174	2.150	2.128
25	2.500	2.469	2.439	2.410	2.381	2.353	2.325	2.299	2.272	2.247	2.222	2.198	2.174	2.151	2.128
26	2.500	2.469	2.439	2.410	2.381	2.353	2.326	2.299	2.273	2.247	2.223	2.198	2.174	2.151	2.127
27	2.500	2.469	2.439	2.409	2.381	2.353	2.325	2.299	2.272	2.247	2.222	2.198	2.174	2.150	2.127
28	2.500	2.469	2.439	2.410	2.381	2.353	2.326	2.299	2.273	2.247	2.223	2.198	2.174	2.151	2.128
29	2.500	2.469	2.439	2.409	2.381	2.353	2.325	2.299	2.272	2.248	2.222	2.198	2.174	2.151	2.128
30	2.500	2.470	2.439	2.410	2.381	2.353	2.326	2.299	2.273	2.247	2.223	2.197	2.174	2.150	2.128
31	2.500	2.469	2.439	2.409	2.381	2.353	2.325	2.299	2.272	2.248	2.222	2.198	2.174	2.151	2.127
32	2.500	2.469	2.439	2.410	2.381	2.353	2.326	2.299	2.273	2.247	2.223	2.197	2.174	2.151	2.128
33	2.500	2.469	2.439	2.409	2.381	2.353	2.325	2.298	2.272	2.248	2.222	2.198	2.174	2.150	2.127
34	2.500	2.470	2.439	2.410	2.381	2.353	2.326	2.299	2.273	2.247	2.223	2.197	2.174	2.151	2.128
35	2.500	2.469	2.439	2.409	2.381	2.353	2.325	2.298	2.272	2.248	2.222	2.198	2.174	2.150	2.127
36	2.500	2.470	2.439	2.410	2.381	2.353	2.326	2.299	2.273	2.247	2.222	2.197	2.174	2.151	2.128
37	2.500	2.469	2.439	2.409	2.381	2.353	2.325	2.298	2.273	2.248	2.223	2.198	2.174	2.150	2.127
38	2.500	2.469	2.439	2.410	2.381	2.353	2.326	2.299	2.272	2.247	2.222	2.197	2.174	2.151	2.128
39	2.500	2.469	2.439	2.409	2.381	2.353	2.326	2.299	2.273	2.248	2.222	2.198	2.174	2.150	2.128
40	2.500	2.470	2.440	2.410	2.380	2.353	2.326	2.298	2.272	2.247	2.223	2.197	2.173	2.151	2.127
41	0.312	1.543	2.439	2.409	2.381	2.352	2.326	2.298	2.273	2.248	2.222	2.198	2.174	2.150	2.128
42			0.305	1.506	2.380	2.353	2.325	2.299	2.273	2.247	2.222	2.197	2.173	2.151	2.127
43					0.298	1.470	2.326	2.298	2.272	2.248	2.223	2.198	2.174	2.150	2.128
44							0.291	1.437	2.273	2.247	2.222	2.197	2.173	2.151	2.127
45									0.284	1.405	2.222	2.198	2.174	2.150	2.128
46											0.278	1.373	2.173	2.151	2.127
47													0.272	1.344	2.128
48															0.266

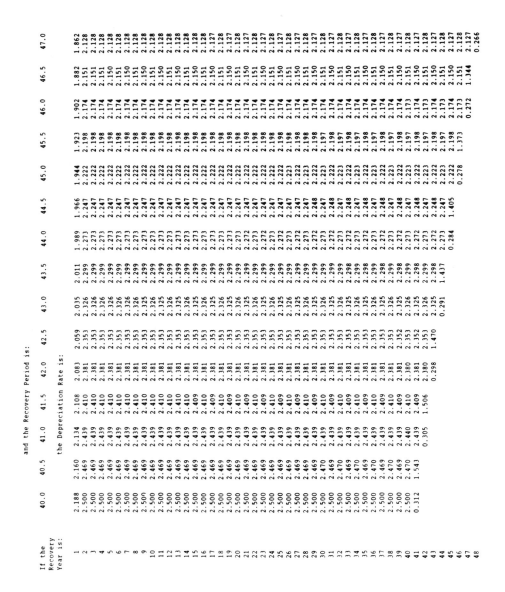

and the Recovery Period is:

the Depreciation Rate is:

If the Recovery Year is:	47.5	48.0	48.5	49.0	49.5	50.0
1	1.842	1.823	1.804	1.786	1.768	1.750
2	2.105	2.083	2.062	2.041	2.020	2.000
3	2.105	2.083	2.062	2.041	2.020	2.000
4	2.105	2.083	2.062	2.041	2.020	2.000
5	2.105	2.083	2.062	2.041	2.020	2.000
6	2.105	2.083	2.062	2.041	2.020	2.000
7	2.105	2.083	2.062	2.041	2.020	2.000
8	2.105	2.083	2.062	2.041	2.020	2.000
9	2.105	2.083	2.062	2.041	2.020	2.000
10	2.105	2.083	2.062	2.041	2.020	2.000
11	2.105	2.083	2.062	2.041	2.020	2.000
12	2.105	2.083	2.062	2.041	2.020	2.000
13	2.105	2.083	2.062	2.041	2.020	2.000
14	2.105	2.083	2.062	2.041	2.020	2.000
15	2.105	2.083	2.062	2.041	2.020	2.000
16	2.105	2.083	2.062	2.041	2.020	2.000
17	2.105	2.083	2.062	2.041	2.020	2.000
18	2.105	2.083	2.062	2.041	2.020	2.000
19	2.105	2.083	2.062	2.041	2.020	2.000
20	2.105	2.084	2.062	2.041	2.020	2.000
21	2.105	2.083	2.062	2.041	2.020	2.000
22	2.105	2.084	2.062	2.041	2.020	2.000
23	2.105	2.083	2.062	2.041	2.020	2.000
24	2.106	2.084	2.062	2.041	2.020	2.000
25	2.105	2.083	2.062	2.041	2.020	2.000
26	2.106	2.084	2.062	2.041	2.020	2.000

and the Recovery Period is:

the Depreciation Rate is:

If the Recovery Year is:	47.5	48.0	48.5	49.0	49.5	50.0
27	2.105	2.083	2.062	2.041	2.020	2.000
28	2.106	2.084	2.062	2.041	2.020	2.000
29	2.105	2.083	2.062	2.041	2.020	2.000
30	2.106	2.084	2.062	2.041	2.020	2.000
31	2.105	2.083	2.062	2.041	2.020	2.000
32	2.106	2.084	2.062	2.040	2.021	2.000
33	2.105	2.083	2.062	2.041	2.020	2.000
34	2.106	2.084	2.062	2.040	2.021	2.000
35	2.105	2.083	2.062	2.041	2.020	2.000
36	2.106	2.084	2.062	2.040	2.021	2.000
37	2.105	2.083	2.061	2.041	2.020	2.000
38	2.106	2.084	2.062	2.040	2.021	2.000
39	2.105	2.083	2.061	2.041	2.020	2.000
40	2.106	2.084	2.062	2.040	2.021	2.000
41	2.105	2.083	2.061	2.041	2.020	2.000
42	2.106	2.084	2.062	2.040	2.021	2.000
43	2.105	2.083	2.061	2.041	2.020	2.000
44	2.106	2.084	2.062	2.040	2.020	2.000
45	2.105	2.083	2.061	2.041	2.021	2.000
46	2.106	2.084	2.062	2.040	2.020	2.000
47	2.105	2.083	2.061	2.041	2.021	2.000
48	1.316	2.084	2.062	2.040	2.020	2.000
49		0.260	1.288	2.041	2.021	2.000
50				0.255	2.020	2.000
51					1.263	0.250

TABLE 10

General and Alternative Depreciation Systems
Applicable Depreciation Method: Straight Line
Applicable Recovery Periods: 2.5 - 50 years
Applicable Convention: Mid-quarter (property placed in service in second quarter)

and the Recovery Period is:

the Depreciation Rate is:

If the Recovery Year is:	2.5	3.0	3.5	4.0	4.5	5.0	5.5	6.0	6.5	7.0	7.5	8.0	8.5	9.0	9.5
1	25.00	20.83	17.86	15.63	13.89	12.50	11.36	10.42	9.62	8.93	8.33	7.81	7.35	6.94	6.58
2	40.00	33.33	28.57	25.00	22.22	20.00	18.18	16.67	15.38	14.29	13.33	12.50	11.77	11.11	10.53
3	35.00	33.34	28.57	25.00	22.22	20.00	18.18	16.67	15.38	14.28	13.33	12.50	11.76	11.11	10.53
4		12.50	25.00	25.00	22.22	20.00	18.18	16.66	15.39	14.29	13.34	12.50	11.77	11.11	10.53
5				9.37	19.45	20.00	18.19	16.66	15.38	14.28	13.33	12.50	11.77	11.11	10.52
6						7.50	15.91	16.67	15.39	14.29	13.34	12.50	11.76	11.11	10.53
7								6.25	13.46	14.28	13.33	12.50	11.77	11.11	10.52
8										5.36	11.67	12.50	11.76	11.11	10.53
9												4.69	10.29	11.12	10.52
10														4.17	9.21

and the Recovery Period is:

the Depreciation Rate is:

If the Recovery Year is:	10.0	10.5	11.0	11.5	12.0	12.5	13.0	13.5	14.0	14.5	15.0	15.5	16.0	16.5	17.0
1	6.25	5.95	5.68	5.43	5.21	5.00	4.81	4.63	4.46	4.31	4.17	4.03	3.91	3.79	3.68
2	10.00	9.52	9.09	8.70	8.33	8.00	7.69	7.41	7.14	6.90	6.67	6.45	6.25	6.06	5.88
3	10.00	9.52	9.09	8.70	8.33	8.00	7.69	7.41	7.14	6.90	6.67	6.45	6.25	6.06	5.88
4	10.00	9.53	9.09	8.69	8.33	8.00	7.69	7.41	7.14	6.90	6.67	6.45	6.25	6.06	5.88
5	10.00	9.52	9.09	8.70	8.33	8.00	7.69	7.41	7.14	6.90	6.67	6.45	6.25	6.06	5.88
6	10.00	9.53	9.09	8.69	8.34	8.00	7.69	7.41	7.14	6.90	6.66	6.45	6.25	6.06	5.88
7	10.00	9.52	9.09	8.70	8.33	8.00	7.69	7.41	7.15	6.89	6.67	6.45	6.25	6.06	5.88
8	10.00	9.53	9.09	8.69	8.34	8.00	7.69	7.40	7.14	6.90	6.66	6.45	6.25	6.06	5.88
9	10.00	9.52	9.09	8.69	8.33	8.00	7.69	7.41	7.15	6.89	6.67	6.45	6.25	6.06	5.88
10	10.00	9.53	9.09	8.70	8.34	8.00	7.69	7.40	7.14	6.90	6.66	6.45	6.25	6.06	5.88
11	3.75	8.33	9.10	8.69	8.33	8.00	7.70	7.41	7.15	6.89	6.67	6.45	6.25	6.06	5.88
12			3.41	7.61	8.34	8.00	7.69	7.40	7.14	6.90	6.66	6.45	6.25	6.06	5.89
13					3.13	7.00	7.69	7.41	7.15	6.89	6.67	6.45	6.25	6.06	5.88
14							2.89	6.48	7.14	6.90	6.66	6.45	6.25	6.06	5.88
15									2.68	6.03	6.67	6.46	6.25	6.06	5.89
16											2.50	5.65	6.25	6.06	5.88
17													2.34	5.31	5.89
18															2.21

and the Recovery Period is:

the Depreciation Rate is:

If the Recovery Year is:	17.5	18.0	18.5	19.0	19.5	20.0	20.5	21.0	21.5	22.0	22.5	23.0	23.5	24.0	24.5
1	3.57	3.47	3.38	3.29	3.21	3.125	3.049	2.976	2.907	2.841	2.778	2.717	2.660	2.604	2.551
2	5.71	5.56	5.41	5.26	5.13	5.000	4.878	4.762	4.651	4.545	4.444	4.348	4.255	4.167	4.082
3	5.71	5.56	5.41	5.26	5.13	5.000	4.878	4.762	4.651	4.545	4.444	4.348	4.255	4.167	4.082
4	5.71	5.56	5.40	5.26	5.13	5.000	4.878	4.762	4.651	4.546	4.444	4.348	4.255	4.167	4.082
5	5.72	5.55	5.41	5.26	5.13	5.000	4.878	4.762	4.651	4.546	4.445	4.348	4.255	4.167	4.082
6	5.71	5.56	5.40	5.26	5.13	5.000	4.878	4.762	4.651	4.545	4.444	4.348	4.255	4.167	4.082
7	5.72	5.55	5.41	5.26	5.13	5.000	4.878	4.762	4.651	4.545	4.444	4.348	4.255	4.167	4.082
8	5.71	5.56	5.41	5.27	5.13	5.000	4.878	4.762	4.651	4.546	4.444	4.348	4.255	4.167	4.082
9	5.72	5.55	5.41	5.26	5.13	5.000	4.878	4.762	4.651	4.545	4.445	4.348	4.255	4.167	4.082
10	5.71	5.56	5.40	5.27	5.13	5.000	4.878	4.762	4.651	4.546	4.444	4.348	4.255	4.167	4.081
11	5.72	5.55	5.41	5.26	5.13	5.000	4.878	4.762	4.651	4.546	4.445	4.348	4.255	4.166	4.082
12	5.71	5.56	5.40	5.27	5.13	5.000	4.878	4.762	4.651	4.545	4.444	4.348	4.256	4.167	4.081
13	5.72	5.55	5.41	5.26	5.12	5.000	4.878	4.762	4.651	4.545	4.445	4.348	4.255	4.166	4.082
14	5.71	5.56	5.40	5.27	5.13	5.000	4.878	4.762	4.651	4.546	4.444	4.348	4.256	4.167	4.081
15	5.72	5.55	5.41	5.26	5.12	5.000	4.878	4.762	4.651	4.546	4.445	4.348	4.255	4.166	4.082
16	5.71	5.56	5.40	5.27	5.13	5.000	4.878	4.762	4.651	4.545	4.444	4.348	4.256	4.167	4.081
17	5.72	5.55	5.41	5.26	5.12	5.000	4.878	4.762	4.652	4.546	4.445	4.347	4.255	4.166	4.082
18	5.00	5.56	5.40	5.26	5.13	5.000	4.878	4.762	4.651	4.545	4.444	4.348	4.256	4.167	4.081
19		2.08	4.73	5.27	5.13	5.000	4.878	4.762	4.652	4.546	4.445	4.347	4.255	4.166	4.082
20				1.97	4.48	5.000	4.878	4.761	4.651	4.545	4.444	4.348	4.256	4.167	4.081
21						1.875	4.878	4.762	4.652	4.546	4.445	4.347	4.255	4.166	4.082
22							4.269	4.761	4.651	4.545	4.444	4.348	4.256	4.167	4.081
23								1.786	4.652	4.546	3.889	4.347	4.255	4.166	4.082
24									4.070	4.545		1.630	3.724	4.167	4.081
25										1.705				1.562	3.571

and the Recovery Period is:

the Depreciation Rate is:

If the Recovery Year is:	25.0	25.5	26.0	26.5	27.0	27.5	28.0	28.5	29.0	29.5	30.0	30.5	31.0	31.5	32.0
1	2.500	2.451	2.404	2.358	2.315	2.273	2.232	2.193	2.155	2.119	2.083	2.049	2.016	1.984	1.953
2	4.000	3.922	3.846	3.774	3.704	3.636	3.571	3.509	3.448	3.390	3.333	3.279	3.226	3.175	3.125
3	4.000	3.922	3.846	3.774	3.704	3.636	3.571	3.509	3.448	3.390	3.333	3.279	3.226	3.175	3.125
4	4.000	3.922	3.846	3.774	3.704	3.636	3.571	3.509	3.448	3.390	3.333	3.279	3.226	3.175	3.125
5	4.000	3.922	3.846	3.774	3.704	3.636	3.572	3.509	3.448	3.390	3.333	3.279	3.226	3.175	3.125
6	4.000	3.921	3.846	3.774	3.704	3.636	3.571	3.509	3.448	3.390	3.333	3.279	3.226	3.174	3.125
7	4.000	3.922	3.846	3.774	3.704	3.636	3.572	3.509	3.448	3.390	3.333	3.279	3.226	3.175	3.125
8	4.000	3.921	3.846	3.773	3.704	3.636	3.571	3.509	3.448	3.390	3.333	3.279	3.226	3.174	3.125
9	4.000	3.922	3.846	3.774	3.704	3.637	3.572	3.509	3.448	3.390	3.333	3.279	3.226	3.175	3.125
10	4.000	3.921	3.846	3.773	3.704	3.636	3.571	3.509	3.448	3.390	3.333	3.279	3.226	3.174	3.125
11	4.000	3.922	3.846	3.774	3.704	3.636	3.572	3.509	3.448	3.390	3.333	3.279	3.226	3.175	3.125
12	4.000	3.921	3.846	3.773	3.704	3.637	3.571	3.509	3.448	3.390	3.333	3.279	3.226	3.174	3.125
13	4.000	3.922	3.846	3.774	3.703	3.636	3.572	3.509	3.448	3.390	3.334	3.279	3.226	3.175	3.125
14	4.000	3.921	3.846	3.773	3.704	3.637	3.571	3.509	3.448	3.390	3.333	3.279	3.226	3.174	3.125
15	4.000	3.922	3.846	3.774	3.703	3.636	3.572	3.509	3.449	3.390	3.334	3.279	3.226	3.175	3.125
16	4.000	3.921	3.846	3.773	3.703	3.637	3.571	3.509	3.448	3.390	3.333	3.279	3.226	3.174	3.125
17	4.000	3.922	3.846	3.773	3.704	3.636	3.572	3.509	3.449	3.390	3.334	3.278	3.226	3.175	3.125
18	4.000	3.921	3.846	3.774	3.703	3.637	3.571	3.508	3.448	3.390	3.333	3.279	3.226	3.174	3.125
19	4.000	3.922	3.846	3.773	3.704	3.636	3.572	3.509	3.449	3.390	3.334	3.278	3.226	3.175	3.125
20	4.000	3.921	3.846	3.774	3.703	3.637	3.571	3.508	3.448	3.390	3.333	3.279	3.226	3.174	3.125
21	4.000	3.922	3.846	3.773	3.704	3.636	3.572	3.509	3.448	3.390	3.334	3.278	3.225	3.175	3.125
22	4.000	3.921	3.847	3.773	3.703	3.637	3.571	3.508	3.449	3.389	3.333	3.279	3.226	3.174	3.125
23	4.000	3.922	3.847	3.774	3.703	3.636	3.572	3.509	3.448	3.390	3.333	3.278	3.225	3.175	3.125
24	4.000	3.921	3.846	3.773	3.704	3.637	3.571	3.508	3.449	3.389	3.334	3.279	3.226	3.174	3.125
25	4.000	3.922	3.847	3.774	3.703	3.636	3.572	3.509	3.448	3.390	3.333	3.278	3.225	3.175	3.125
26	1.500	3.431	3.847	3.773	3.703	3.637	3.571	3.508	3.448	3.389	3.334	3.279	3.226	3.174	3.125
27			1.442	3.302	3.703	3.636	3.572	3.509	3.449	3.389	3.333	3.278	3.225	3.175	3.125
28					1.389	3.182	3.571	3.508	3.448	3.390	3.334	3.279	3.226	3.174	3.125
29							1.339	3.070	3.449	3.389	3.333	3.278	3.225	3.175	3.125
30									1.293	2.966	3.334	3.279	3.226	3.174	3.125
31											1.250	2.869	3.225	3.175	3.125
32													1.210	2.778	3.125
33															1.172

and the Recovery Period is:

the Depreciation Rate is:

If the Recovery Year is:	32.5	33.0	33.5	34.0	34.5	35.0	35.5	36.0	36.5	37.0	37.5	38.0	38.5	39.0	39.5
1	1.923	1.894	1.866	1.838	1.812	1.786	1.761	1.736	1.712	1.689	1.667	1.645	1.623	1.603	1.582
2	3.077	3.030	2.985	2.941	2.899	2.857	2.817	2.778	2.740	2.703	2.667	2.632	2.597	2.564	2.532
3	3.077	3.030	2.985	2.941	2.899	2.857	2.817	2.778	2.740	2.703	2.667	2.632	2.597	2.564	2.532
4	3.077	3.030	2.985	2.941	2.899	2.857	2.817	2.778	2.740	2.703	2.667	2.632	2.597	2.564	2.532
5	3.077	3.030	2.985	2.941	2.899	2.857	2.817	2.778	2.740	2.703	2.667	2.632	2.597	2.564	2.532
6	3.077	3.030	2.985	2.941	2.899	2.857	2.817	2.778	2.740	2.703	2.667	2.632	2.597	2.564	2.532
7	3.077	3.030	2.985	2.941	2.899	2.857	2.817	2.778	2.740	2.703	2.667	2.632	2.597	2.564	2.532
8	3.077	3.030	2.985	2.941	2.899	2.857	2.817	2.778	2.740	2.703	2.667	2.632	2.597	2.564	2.532
9	3.077	3.030	2.985	2.941	2.899	2.857	2.817	2.778	2.740	2.703	2.667	2.632	2.597	2.564	2.532
10	3.077	3.030	2.985	2.941	2.899	2.857	2.817	2.778	2.740	2.703	2.667	2.632	2.598	2.564	2.532
11	3.077	3.030	2.985	2.941	2.899	2.857	2.817	2.778	2.740	2.703	2.667	2.631	2.597	2.564	2.532
12	3.077	3.030	2.985	2.941	2.899	2.857	2.817	2.778	2.740	2.703	2.667	2.632	2.598	2.564	2.532
13	3.077	3.030	2.985	2.941	2.899	2.857	2.817	2.778	2.740	2.703	2.667	2.631	2.597	2.564	2.532
14	3.077	3.031	2.985	2.941	2.899	2.857	2.817	2.778	2.740	2.703	2.666	2.631	2.598	2.564	2.531
15	3.077	3.030	2.985	2.941	2.898	2.857	2.817	2.778	2.740	2.703	2.667	2.632	2.597	2.564	2.532
16	3.077	3.031	2.985	2.941	2.899	2.857	2.817	2.778	2.740	2.703	2.666	2.631	2.598	2.564	2.531
17	3.077	3.030	2.985	2.941	2.898	2.857	2.817	2.778	2.740	2.703	2.667	2.632	2.597	2.564	2.532
18	3.077	3.031	2.985	2.941	2.899	2.857	2.817	2.778	2.740	2.702	2.666	2.631	2.598	2.564	2.531
19	3.077	3.030	2.985	2.941	2.898	2.857	2.817	2.778	2.739	2.703	2.667	2.632	2.597	2.564	2.532
20	3.077	3.031	2.985	2.941	2.899	2.857	2.817	2.778	2.740	2.702	2.666	2.631	2.598	2.564	2.531
21	3.077	3.030	2.985	2.941	2.898	2.857	2.817	2.778	2.739	2.703	2.667	2.632	2.597	2.564	2.532
22	3.077	3.031	2.985	2.941	2.899	2.857	2.817	2.777	2.740	2.702	2.666	2.631	2.598	2.564	2.531
23	3.077	3.030	2.985	2.941	2.898	2.857	2.817	2.778	2.739	2.703	2.667	2.632	2.597	2.564	2.532
24	3.077	3.031	2.985	2.941	2.899	2.857	2.817	2.778	2.740	2.702	2.666	2.632	2.598	2.564	2.531
25	3.077	3.030	2.985	2.941	2.898	2.857	2.817	2.777	2.739	2.703	2.667	2.631	2.597	2.564	2.532
26	3.077	3.031	2.985	2.942	2.899	2.857	2.817	2.778	2.740	2.702	2.666	2.632	2.598	2.564	2.531
27	3.077	3.030	2.985	2.941	2.898	2.857	2.817	2.778	2.739	2.703	2.667	2.631	2.597	2.564	2.532
28	3.077	3.031	2.985	2.942	2.899	2.857	2.817	2.777	2.740	2.702	2.666	2.632	2.598	2.564	2.531
29	3.077	3.030	2.985	2.941	2.898	2.858	2.817	2.778	2.739	2.703	2.667	2.631	2.597	2.564	2.532
30	3.076	3.031	2.985	2.942	2.899	2.857	2.817	2.778	2.740	2.702	2.666	2.632	2.598	2.564	2.531
31	3.077	3.030	2.985	2.941	2.898	2.857	2.816	2.777	2.739	2.703	2.667	2.631	2.597	2.564	2.531
32	3.076	3.031	2.985	2.942	2.899	2.858	2.816	2.778	2.740	2.702	2.666	2.632	2.598	2.564	2.532
33	2.692	3.030	2.986	2.941	2.898	2.857	2.817	2.777	2.739	2.703	2.667	2.631	2.598	2.564	2.531
34		1.136	2.612	2.942	2.899	2.858	2.816	2.778	2.740	2.703	2.667	2.632	2.597	2.564	2.532
35				1.103	2.536	2.857	2.817	2.777	2.739	2.702	2.666	2.631	2.598	2.565	2.532
36						1.072	2.464	2.778	2.740	2.703	2.667	2.632	2.597	2.564	2.531
37								1.042	2.397	2.702	2.666	2.631	2.598	2.564	2.531
38										1.013	2.333	2.632	2.597	2.565	2.532
39												0.987	2.273	2.564	2.531
40														0.962	2.215

and the Recovery Period is:

the Depreciation Rate is:

If the Recovery Year is:	40.0	40.5	41.0	41.5	42.0	42.5	43.0	43.5	44.0	44.5	45.0	45.5	46.0	46.5	47.0
1	1.563	1.543	1.524	1.506	1.488	1.471	1.453	1.437	1.420	1.404	1.389	1.374	1.359	1.344	1.330
2	2.500	2.469	2.439	2.410	2.381	2.353	2.326	2.299	2.273	2.247	2.222	2.198	2.174	2.151	2.128
3	2.500	2.469	2.439	2.410	2.381	2.353	2.326	2.299	2.273	2.247	2.222	2.198	2.174	2.151	2.128
4	2.500	2.469	2.439	2.410	2.381	2.353	2.326	2.299	2.273	2.247	2.222	2.198	2.174	2.151	2.128
5	2.500	2.469	2.439	2.410	2.381	2.353	2.326	2.299	2.273	2.247	2.222	2.198	2.174	2.150	2.128
6	2.500	2.469	2.439	2.410	2.381	2.353	2.326	2.299	2.273	2.247	2.222	2.198	2.174	2.151	2.128
7	2.500	2.469	2.439	2.410	2.381	2.353	2.326	2.299	2.273	2.247	2.222	2.198	2.174	2.150	2.128
8	2.500	2.469	2.439	2.410	2.381	2.353	2.326	2.299	2.273	2.247	2.222	2.198	2.174	2.151	2.128
9	2.500	2.469	2.439	2.410	2.381	2.353	2.326	2.299	2.273	2.247	2.222	2.198	2.174	2.150	2.128
10	2.500	2.469	2.439	2.410	2.381	2.353	2.326	2.299	2.273	2.247	2.222	2.198	2.174	2.151	2.128
11	2.500	2.469	2.439	2.410	2.381	2.353	2.325	2.299	2.273	2.247	2.222	2.198	2.174	2.151	2.128
12	2.500	2.469	2.439	2.410	2.381	2.353	2.326	2.299	2.273	2.247	2.222	2.198	2.174	2.150	2.128
13	2.500	2.469	2.439	2.410	2.381	2.353	2.325	2.299	2.273	2.247	2.222	2.198	2.174	2.151	2.128
14	2.500	2.469	2.439	2.410	2.381	2.353	2.325	2.299	2.273	2.247	2.222	2.198	2.174	2.150	2.128
15	2.500	2.469	2.439	2.409	2.381	2.353	2.326	2.299	2.273	2.247	2.222	2.198	2.174	2.150	2.128
16	2.500	2.469	2.439	2.410	2.381	2.353	2.325	2.299	2.273	2.247	2.222	2.198	2.174	2.151	2.127
17	2.500	2.469	2.439	2.410	2.381	2.353	2.326	2.299	2.273	2.247	2.222	2.198	2.174	2.151	2.128
18	2.500	2.469	2.439	2.409	2.381	2.353	2.325	2.299	2.273	2.247	2.222	2.198	2.174	2.151	2.127
19	2.500	2.469	2.439	2.410	2.381	2.353	2.326	2.299	2.273	2.247	2.222	2.198	2.174	2.150	2.127
20	2.500	2.469	2.439	2.409	2.381	2.353	2.325	2.299	2.273	2.247	2.222	2.198	2.174	2.151	2.127
21	2.500	2.469	2.439	2.410	2.381	2.353	2.326	2.299	2.273	2.247	2.222	2.198	2.174	2.150	2.128
22	2.500	2.469	2.439	2.409	2.381	2.353	2.325	2.299	2.273	2.247	2.222	2.198	2.174	2.151	2.128
23	2.500	2.469	2.439	2.410	2.381	2.353	2.325	2.299	2.273	2.247	2.222	2.198	2.174	2.150	2.128
24	2.500	2.469	2.439	2.409	2.381	2.353	2.325	2.299	2.273	2.247	2.222	2.198	2.174	2.151	2.128
25	2.500	2.469	2.439	2.410	2.381	2.353	2.326	2.299	2.273	2.247	2.222	2.198	2.174	2.151	2.127
26	2.500	2.469	2.439	2.409	2.381	2.353	2.325	2.299	2.273	2.247	2.222	2.198	2.174	2.151	2.128
27	2.500	2.469	2.439	2.410	2.381	2.353	2.326	2.299	2.273	2.247	2.222	2.198	2.174	2.151	2.127
28	2.500	2.469	2.439	2.409	2.381	2.353	2.325	2.299	2.272	2.247	2.223	2.198	2.174	2.151	2.127
29	2.500	2.469	2.439	2.410	2.381	2.353	2.326	2.299	2.273	2.248	2.223	2.198	2.174	2.151	2.128
30	2.500	2.469	2.439	2.409	2.381	2.353	2.325	2.299	2.272	2.247	2.222	2.198	2.174	2.150	2.128
31	2.500	2.469	2.439	2.410	2.381	2.353	2.325	2.299	2.273	2.248	2.223	2.197	2.174	2.151	2.127
32	2.500	2.469	2.439	2.409	2.381	2.353	2.326	2.299	2.272	2.247	2.222	2.198	2.174	2.150	2.128
33	2.500	2.469	2.439	2.410	2.381	2.353	2.325	2.298	2.273	2.248	2.223	2.197	2.174	2.151	2.128
34	2.500	2.470	2.439	2.410	2.381	2.353	2.326	2.299	2.273	2.247	2.223	2.198	2.174	2.150	2.128
35	2.500	2.469	2.439	2.409	2.381	2.353	2.325	2.298	2.273	2.248	2.223	2.197	2.174	2.150	2.127
36	2.500	2.470	2.439	2.410	2.381	2.353	2.325	2.298	2.272	2.247	2.222	2.198	2.174	2.150	2.128
37	2.500	2.469	2.439	2.409	2.381	2.353	2.326	2.299	2.273	2.248	2.223	2.197	2.174	2.151	2.127
38	2.500	2.469	2.439	2.410	2.381	2.353	2.325	2.298	2.273	2.247	2.222	2.198	2.173	2.151	2.128
39	2.500	2.469	2.439	2.409	2.381	2.353	2.326	2.299	2.273	2.248	2.223	2.197	2.174	2.150	2.127
40	2.500	2.470	2.439	2.410	2.380	2.352	2.325	2.298	2.273	2.247	2.222	2.198	2.173	2.150	2.128
41	0.937	2.469	2.439	2.409	2.381	2.353	2.326	2.299	2.272	2.248	2.223	2.198	2.174	2.151	2.128
42		2.161	2.439	2.410	2.381	2.352	2.325	2.298	2.273	2.247	2.222	2.197	2.173	2.150	2.127
43			0.915	2.410	2.380	2.353	2.326	2.299	2.272	2.248	2.223	2.198	2.174	2.151	2.128
44				2.108	0.893	2.353	2.325	2.298	2.273	2.247	2.222	2.198	2.174	2.151	2.127
45						2.058	0.872	2.299	2.273	2.248	2.222	2.197	2.173	2.150	2.128
46								2.011	0.852	2.247	2.223	2.198	2.174	2.150	2.127
47										1.967	0.833	2.197	2.174	2.150	2.127
48												1.923	0.815	1.882	0.798

and the Recovery Period is:

the Depreciation Rate is:

If the Recovery Year is:	47.5	48.0	48.5	49.0	49.5	50.0
1	1.316	1.302	1.289	1.276	1.263	1.250
2	2.105	2.083	2.062	2.041	2.020	2.000
3	2.105	2.083	2.062	2.041	2.020	2.000
4	2.105	2.083	2.062	2.041	2.020	2.000
5	2.105	2.083	2.062	2.041	2.020	2.000
6	2.105	2.083	2.062	2.041	2.020	2.000
7	2.105	2.083	2.062	2.041	2.020	2.000
8	2.105	2.083	2.062	2.041	2.020	2.000
9	2.105	2.083	2.062	2.041	2.020	2.000
10	2.105	2.083	2.062	2.041	2.020	2.000
11	2.105	2.083	2.062	2.041	2.020	2.000
12	2.105	2.083	2.062	2.041	2.020	2.000
13	2.105	2.083	2.062	2.041	2.020	2.000
14	2.105	2.083	2.062	2.041	2.020	2.000
15	2.105	2.083	2.062	2.041	2.020	2.000
16	2.105	2.083	2.062	2.041	2.020	2.000
17	2.105	2.083	2.062	2.041	2.020	2.000
18	2.105	2.084	2.062	2.041	2.020	2.000
19	2.105	2.083	2.062	2.041	2.020	2.000
20	2.105	2.084	2.062	2.041	2.020	2.000
21	2.105	2.083	2.062	2.041	2.020	2.000
22	2.105	2.084	2.062	2.041	2.020	2.000
23	2.105	2.083	2.062	2.041	2.020	2.000
24	2.105	2.084	2.062	2.041	2.020	2.000
25	2.106	2.083	2.062	2.041	2.020	2.000
26	2.105	2.084	2.062	2.041	2.020	2.000

and the Recovery Period is:

the Depreciation Rate is:

If the Recovery Year is:	47.5	48.0	48.5	49.0	49.5	50.0
27	2.106	2.083	2.062	2.041	2.020	2.000
28	2.105	2.084	2.062	2.041	2.020	2.000
29	2.106	2.083	2.062	2.041	2.020	2.000
30	2.105	2.084	2.062	2.041	2.020	2.000
31	2.106	2.083	2.062	2.041	2.021	2.000
32	2.105	2.084	2.062	2.040	2.020	2.000
33	2.106	2.083	2.062	2.041	2.021	2.000
34	2.105	2.084	2.062	2.040	2.020	2.000
35	2.106	2.083	2.062	2.041	2.021	2.000
36	2.105	2.084	2.061	2.040	2.020	2.000
37	2.106	2.083	2.062	2.041	2.021	2.000
38	2.105	2.084	2.061	2.040	2.020	2.000
39	2.106	2.083	2.062	2.041	2.021	2.000
40	2.105	2.084	2.061	2.040	2.020	2.000
41	2.106	2.083	2.062	2.041	2.021	2.000
42	2.105	2.084	2.061	2.040	2.020	2.000
43	2.106	2.083	2.062	2.041	2.021	2.000
44	2.105	2.084	2.061	2.040	2.020	2.000
45	2.106	2.083	2.062	2.041	2.021	2.000
46	2.105	2.084	2.061	2.040	2.020	2.000
47	2.106	2.083	2.062	2.041	2.021	2.000
48	2.105	2.083	2.062	2.041	2.020	2.000
49	1.842	2.084	2.062	2.040	2.021	2.000
50		0.781	2.061	2.041	2.020	2.000
51			1.804	0.765	1.768	0.750

TABLE 11   General and Alternative Depreciation Systems
Applicable Depreciation Method: Straight Line
Applicable Recovery Periods: 2.5 - 50 years
Applicable Convention: Mid-quarter (property placed in service in third quarter)

and the Recovery Period is:

the Depreciation Rate is:

If the Recovery Year is:	2.5	3.0	3.5	4.0	4.5	5.0	5.5	6.0	6.5	7.0	7.5	8.0	8.5	9.0	9.5
1	15.00	12.50	10.71	9.38	8.33	7.50	6.82	6.25	5.77	5.36	5.00	4.69	4.41	4.17	3.95
2	40.00	33.33	28.57	25.00	22.22	20.00	18.18	16.67	15.38	14.29	13.33	12.50	11.76	11.11	10.53
3	40.00	33.34	28.57	25.00	22.22	20.00	18.18	16.66	15.39	14.28	13.33	12.50	11.77	11.11	10.53
4	5.00	20.83	28.58	25.00	22.23	20.00	18.18	16.67	15.38	14.29	13.33	12.50	11.76	11.11	10.52
5			3.57	15.62	22.22	20.00	18.18	16.66	15.39	14.28	13.34	12.50	11.77	11.11	10.53
6					2.78	12.50	18.18	16.67	15.38	14.29	13.33	12.50	11.76	11.11	10.52
7							18.19	16.66	15.39	14.28	13.34	12.50	11.77	11.11	10.53
8							2.27	10.42	1.92	14.28	13.33	12.50	11.76	11.11	10.52
9										8.93	1.67	7.81	11.77	11.11	10.53
10													1.47	6.95	10.52
11															1.32

and the Recovery Period is:

the Depreciation Rate is:

If the Recovery Year is:	10.0	10.5	11.0	11.5	12.0	12.5	13.0	13.5	14.0	14.5	15.0	15.5	16.0	16.5	17.0
1	3.75	3.57	3.41	3.26	3.13	3.00	2.88	2.78	2.68	2.59	2.50	2.42	2.34	2.27	2.21
2	10.00	9.52	9.09	8.70	8.33	8.00	7.69	7.41	7.14	6.90	6.67	6.45	6.25	6.06	5.88
3	10.00	9.52	9.09	8.70	8.33	8.00	7.69	7.41	7.14	6.90	6.67	6.45	6.25	6.06	5.88
4	10.00	9.52	9.09	8.70	8.33	8.00	7.69	7.41	7.14	6.90	6.67	6.45	6.25	6.06	5.88
5	10.00	9.53	9.09	8.69	8.33	8.00	7.69	7.41	7.14	6.89	6.67	6.45	6.25	6.06	5.88
6	10.00	9.52	9.09	8.70	8.33	8.00	7.69	7.41	7.14	6.90	6.66	6.45	6.25	6.06	5.88
7	10.00	9.53	9.09	8.69	8.34	8.00	7.69	7.41	7.14	6.89	6.67	6.45	6.25	6.06	5.88
8	10.00	9.52	9.09	8.70	8.33	8.00	7.69	7.40	7.14	6.90	6.66	6.45	6.25	6.06	5.88
9	10.00	9.53	9.09	8.70	8.34	8.00	7.70	7.41	7.15	6.90	6.67	6.45	6.25	6.06	5.88
10	10.00	9.52	9.09	8.69	8.33	8.00	7.69	7.40	7.14	6.89	6.66	6.45	6.25	6.06	5.88
11	6.25	9.53	9.10	8.70	8.34	8.00	7.70	7.41	7.15	6.90	6.67	6.45	6.25	6.06	5.89
12		1.19	5.68	8.69	8.33	8.00	7.69	7.40	7.14	6.89	6.66	6.46	6.25	6.06	5.88
13				1.09	5.21	8.00	7.70	7.41	7.15	6.90	6.67	6.45	6.25	6.06	5.88
14						1.00	4.81	7.40	7.14	6.89	6.66	6.46	6.25	6.06	5.89
15								0.93	4.47	6.90	6.66	6.45	6.25	6.06	5.88
16										0.86	4.17	6.45	6.25	6.06	5.89
17												0.81	3.91	6.07	5.88
18														0.76	3.68

and the Recovery Period is:

If the Recovery Year is: the Depreciation Rate is:

Recovery Year	17.5	18.0	18.5	19.0	19.5	20.0	20.5	21.0	21.5	22.0	22.5	23.0	23.5	24.0	24.5
1	2.14	2.08	2.03	1.97	1.92	1.875	1.829	1.786	1.744	1.705	1.667	1.630	1.596	1.563	1.531
2	5.71	5.56	5.41	5.26	5.13	5.000	4.878	4.762	4.651	4.545	4.444	4.348	4.255	4.167	4.082
3	5.71	5.56	5.40	5.26	5.13	5.000	4.878	4.762	4.651	4.545	4.444	4.348	4.255	4.167	4.082
4	5.72	5.55	5.41	5.26	5.13	5.000	4.878	4.762	4.651	4.546	4.444	4.348	4.255	4.167	4.082
5	5.71	5.56	5.40	5.26	5.13	5.000	4.878	4.762	4.651	4.545	4.445	4.348	4.255	4.167	4.082
6	5.71	5.55	5.40	5.26	5.13	5.000	4.878	4.762	4.651	4.546	4.444	4.348	4.255	4.167	4.082
7	5.72	5.56	5.41	5.26	5.13	5.000	4.878	4.762	4.651	4.545	4.445	4.348	4.255	4.167	4.082
8	5.71	5.55	5.40	5.27	5.13	5.000	4.878	4.762	4.651	4.546	4.444	4.348	4.256	4.167	4.082
9	5.72	5.56	5.41	5.26	5.13	5.000	4.878	4.762	4.651	4.545	4.445	4.348	4.255	4.166	4.081
10	5.71	5.55	5.40	5.27	5.13	5.000	4.878	4.762	4.651	4.546	4.444	4.348	4.256	4.167	4.082
11	5.72	5.56	5.41	5.26	5.13	5.000	4.878	4.762	4.651	4.545	4.445	4.348	4.255	4.166	4.081
12	5.71	5.55	5.40	5.27	5.13	5.000	4.878	4.762	4.651	4.546	4.444	4.348	4.256	4.167	4.082
13	5.72	5.56	5.41	5.26	5.12	5.000	4.878	4.762	4.652	4.545	4.445	4.348	4.255	4.166	4.082
14	5.71	5.55	5.40	5.27	5.13	5.000	4.878	4.762	4.651	4.546	4.444	4.348	4.256	4.167	4.082
15	5.72	5.56	5.40	5.26	5.12	5.000	4.878	4.762	4.652	4.545	4.445	4.348	4.255	4.166	4.081
16	5.71	5.55	5.41	5.27	5.13	5.000	4.878	4.762	4.651	4.546	4.444	4.347	4.256	4.167	4.082
17	5.72	5.56	5.40	5.26	5.12	5.000	4.878	4.762	4.652	4.545	4.445	4.348	4.255	4.166	4.081
18	5.71	5.55	5.40	5.27	5.13	5.000	4.878	4.762	4.651	4.546	4.444	4.347	4.256	4.167	4.082
19	0.71	3.47	5.41	5.26	5.13	5.000	4.878	4.762	4.652	4.545	4.445	4.348	4.255	4.166	4.081
20			0.68	3.29	5.13	5.000	4.878	4.761	4.651	4.546	4.444	4.347	4.256	4.167	4.082
21					0.64	3.125	4.879	4.762	4.652	4.545	4.445	4.348	4.255	4.166	4.081
22							0.610	2.976	4.651	4.546	4.444	4.347	4.256	4.167	4.082
23									0.581	2.841	4.445	4.348	4.255	4.166	4.081
24											0.556	2.717	4.256	4.167	4.082
25													0.532	2.604	4.081
26															0.510

and the Recovery Period is:

the Depreciation Rate is:

If the Recovery Year is:	25.0	25.5	26.0	26.5	27.0	27.5	28.0	28.5	29.0	29.5	30.0	30.5	31.0	31.5	32.0
1	1.500	1.471	1.442	1.415	1.389	1.364	1.339	1.316	1.293	1.271	1.250	1.230	1.210	1.190	1.172
2	4.000	3.922	3.846	3.774	3.704	3.636	3.571	3.509	3.448	3.390	3.333	3.279	3.226	3.175	3.125
3	4.000	3.922	3.846	3.774	3.704	3.636	3.571	3.509	3.448	3.390	3.333	3.279	3.226	3.175	3.125
4	4.000	3.922	3.846	3.774	3.704	3.636	3.571	3.509	3.448	3.390	3.333	3.279	3.226	3.175	3.125
5	4.000	3.921	3.846	3.774	3.704	3.636	3.571	3.509	3.448	3.390	3.333	3.279	3.226	3.175	3.125
6	4.000	3.922	3.846	3.774	3.704	3.636	3.572	3.509	3.448	3.390	3.333	3.279	3.226	3.175	3.125
7	4.000	3.921	3.846	3.773	3.704	3.636	3.571	3.509	3.448	3.390	3.333	3.279	3.226	3.175	3.125
8	4.000	3.922	3.846	3.774	3.704	3.636	3.572	3.509	3.448	3.390	3.333	3.279	3.226	3.175	3.125
9	4.000	3.921	3.846	3.773	3.704	3.636	3.571	3.509	3.448	3.390	3.333	3.279	3.226	3.175	3.125
10	4.000	3.922	3.846	3.774	3.704	3.636	3.572	3.509	3.448	3.390	3.333	3.279	3.226	3.175	3.125
11	4.000	3.921	3.846	3.773	3.704	3.637	3.571	3.509	3.448	3.390	3.333	3.279	3.226	3.174	3.125
12	4.000	3.922	3.846	3.774	3.704	3.636	3.572	3.509	3.448	3.390	3.333	3.279	3.226	3.175	3.125
13	4.000	3.921	3.846	3.773	3.703	3.637	3.571	3.509	3.448	3.390	3.333	3.278	3.226	3.174	3.125
14	4.000	3.922	3.846	3.774	3.704	3.636	3.572	3.509	3.448	3.390	3.334	3.279	3.226	3.175	3.125
15	4.000	3.921	3.846	3.773	3.703	3.637	3.571	3.509	3.449	3.390	3.333	3.278	3.226	3.174	3.125
16	4.000	3.922	3.846	3.774	3.704	3.636	3.572	3.509	3.448	3.390	3.334	3.279	3.226	3.175	3.125
17	4.000	3.921	3.846	3.773	3.703	3.637	3.571	3.508	3.449	3.390	3.333	3.278	3.226	3.174	3.125
18	4.000	3.922	3.846	3.774	3.704	3.636	3.572	3.509	3.448	3.390	3.333	3.279	3.226	3.175	3.125
19	4.000	3.921	3.846	3.773	3.703	3.637	3.571	3.508	3.449	3.390	3.333	3.278	3.226	3.174	3.125
20	4.000	3.922	3.846	3.774	3.704	3.636	3.572	3.509	3.448	3.390	3.334	3.279	3.226	3.175	3.125
21	4.000	3.921	3.846	3.773	3.703	3.637	3.571	3.508	3.449	3.390	3.333	3.278	3.226	3.174	3.125
22	4.000	3.922	3.846	3.774	3.704	3.636	3.572	3.509	3.448	3.390	3.334	3.279	3.226	3.175	3.125
23	4.000	3.921	3.847	3.773	3.703	3.637	3.571	3.508	3.449	3.390	3.333	3.278	3.226	3.174	3.125
24	4.000	3.922	3.846	3.774	3.703	3.636	3.572	3.509	3.448	3.389	3.334	3.279	3.225	3.175	3.125
25	4.000	3.921	3.847	3.773	3.704	3.637	3.571	3.508	3.449	3.390	3.333	3.278	3.226	3.174	3.125
26	2.500	3.922	3.846	3.774	3.703	3.636	3.572	3.509	3.448	3.389	3.334	3.279	3.225	3.175	3.125
27		0.490	3.847	3.773	3.704	3.637	3.571	3.508	3.449	3.390	3.333	3.278	3.226	3.174	3.125
28			2.404	3.773	2.315	3.636	3.572	3.509	3.448	3.389	3.334	3.279	3.225	3.175	3.125
29				0.472		0.455	2.232	3.508	3.449	3.390	3.333	3.278	3.226	3.174	3.125
30								0.439	2.155	3.389	3.334	3.279	3.225	3.175	3.125
31										0.424	2.083	3.278	3.226	3.174	3.125
32												0.410	3.225	3.174	3.125
33													2.016	0.397	1.953

and the Recovery Period is:

the Depreciation Rate is:

If the Recovery Year is:	32.5	33.0	33.5	34.0	34.5	35.0	35.5	36.0	36.5	37.0	37.5	38.0	38.5	39.0	39.5
1	1.154	1.136	1.119	1.103	1.087	1.071	1.056	1.042	1.027	1.014	1.000	0.987	0.974	0.962	0.949
2	3.077	3.030	2.985	2.941	2.899	2.857	2.817	2.778	2.740	2.703	2.667	2.632	2.597	2.564	2.532
3	3.077	3.030	2.985	2.941	2.899	2.857	2.817	2.778	2.740	2.703	2.667	2.632	2.597	2.564	2.532
4	3.077	3.030	2.985	2.941	2.899	2.857	2.817	2.778	2.740	2.703	2.667	2.632	2.597	2.564	2.532
5	3.077	3.030	2.985	2.941	2.899	2.857	2.817	2.778	2.740	2.703	2.667	2.632	2.597	2.564	2.532
6	3.077	3.030	2.985	2.941	2.899	2.857	2.817	2.778	2.740	2.703	2.667	2.632	2.597	2.564	2.532
7	3.077	3.030	2.985	2.941	2.899	2.857	2.817	2.778	2.740	2.703	2.667	2.631	2.597	2.564	2.532
8	3.077	3.030	2.985	2.941	2.898	2.857	2.817	2.778	2.740	2.703	2.667	2.632	2.597	2.564	2.532
9	3.077	3.030	2.985	2.941	2.899	2.857	2.817	2.778	2.740	2.703	2.667	2.631	2.597	2.564	2.531
10	3.077	3.030	2.985	2.941	2.899	2.857	2.817	2.778	2.740	2.703	2.667	2.632	2.598	2.564	2.532
11	3.077	3.030	2.985	2.941	2.899	2.857	2.817	2.778	2.740	2.703	2.667	2.631	2.597	2.564	2.532
12	3.077	3.030	2.985	2.941	2.898	2.857	2.817	2.778	2.740	2.703	2.667	2.632	2.598	2.564	2.532
13	3.077	3.031	2.985	2.941	2.899	2.857	2.817	2.778	2.740	2.703	2.667	2.631	2.597	2.564	2.531
14	3.077	3.030	2.985	2.941	2.898	2.857	2.817	2.778	2.740	2.703	2.666	2.632	2.598	2.564	2.532
15	3.077	3.031	2.985	2.941	2.899	2.857	2.817	2.778	2.740	2.703	2.667	2.632	2.597	2.564	2.531
16	3.077	3.030	2.985	2.941	2.898	2.857	2.817	2.778	2.740	2.702	2.666	2.631	2.597	2.564	2.532
17	3.077	3.030	2.985	2.941	2.899	2.857	2.817	2.778	2.740	2.703	2.667	2.632	2.598	2.564	2.532
18	3.077	3.031	2.985	2.941	2.898	2.857	2.817	2.778	2.740	2.703	2.666	2.631	2.597	2.564	2.531
19	3.077	3.030	2.985	2.941	2.899	2.857	2.817	2.778	2.740	2.702	2.667	2.632	2.598	2.564	2.532
20	3.077	3.031	2.985	2.941	2.898	2.857	2.817	2.778	2.740	2.703	2.667	2.631	2.597	2.564	2.531
21	3.077	3.030	2.985	2.941	2.899	2.857	2.817	2.778	2.740	2.702	2.666	2.632	2.598	2.564	2.532
22	3.077	3.031	2.985	2.941	2.898	2.857	2.817	2.777	2.740	2.703	2.667	2.631	2.597	2.564	2.532
23	3.077	3.030	2.985	2.941	2.899	2.857	2.817	2.778	2.739	2.703	2.666	2.632	2.598	2.564	2.531
24	3.077	3.031	2.985	2.941	2.898	2.857	2.817	2.777	2.740	2.702	2.667	2.631	2.597	2.564	2.532
25	3.077	3.030	2.985	2.942	2.899	2.857	2.817	2.778	2.739	2.703	2.666	2.632	2.598	2.564	2.531
26	3.077	3.031	2.985	2.941	2.898	2.858	2.817	2.777	2.740	2.702	2.667	2.631	2.597	2.564	2.532
27	3.077	3.030	2.985	2.942	2.899	2.857	2.817	2.778	2.739	2.703	2.666	2.632	2.598	2.564	2.531
28	3.077	3.031	2.985	2.941	2.898	2.858	2.817	2.777	2.740	2.702	2.667	2.631	2.597	2.564	2.532
29	3.076	3.030	2.985	2.942	2.899	2.857	2.817	2.778	2.739	2.703	2.666	2.632	2.598	2.564	2.531
30	3.077	3.031	2.986	2.941	2.898	2.858	2.817	2.777	2.740	2.702	2.667	2.631	2.597	2.564	2.532
31	3.076	3.030	2.985	2.942	2.899	2.857	2.816	2.778	2.739	2.703	2.666	2.632	2.598	2.564	2.531
32	3.077	3.031	2.986	2.941	2.898	2.858	2.817	2.777	2.740	2.702	2.666	2.631	2.597	2.564	2.532
33	3.076	3.030	2.985	2.942	2.899	2.857	2.816	2.778	2.739	2.702	2.667	2.632	2.598	2.564	2.531
34	0.385	1.894	2.986	2.941	2.898	2.858	2.817	2.777	2.740	2.703	2.666	2.631	2.597	2.564	2.532
35			0.373	1.838	2.899	2.857	2.816	2.777	2.739	2.702	2.667	2.632	2.598	2.565	2.531
36					0.362	1.786	2.817	2.778	2.740	2.703	2.666	2.631	2.597	2.564	2.532
37							0.352	1.736	2.740	2.702	2.667	2.632	2.598	2.565	2.531
38									0.342	1.689	2.666	2.631	2.597	2.564	2.532
39											0.333	1.645	2.598	2.565	2.531
40													0.325	1.603	2.532
41															0.316

and the Recovery Period is:

the Depreciation Rate is:

If the Recovery Year is:	40.0	40.5	41.0	41.5	42.0	42.5	43.0	43.5	44.0	44.5	45.0	45.5	46.0	46.5	47.0
1	0.938	0.926	0.915	0.904	0.893	0.882	0.872	0.862	0.852	0.843	0.833	0.824	0.815	0.806	0.798
2	2.500	2.469	2.439	2.410	2.381	2.353	2.326	2.299	2.273	2.247	2.222	2.198	2.174	2.151	2.128
3	2.500	2.469	2.439	2.410	2.381	2.353	2.326	2.299	2.273	2.247	2.222	2.198	2.174	2.151	2.128
4	2.500	2.469	2.439	2.410	2.381	2.353	2.326	2.299	2.273	2.247	2.222	2.198	2.174	2.151	2.128
5	2.500	2.469	2.439	2.410	2.381	2.353	2.326	2.299	2.273	2.247	2.222	2.198	2.174	2.151	2.128
6	2.500	2.469	2.439	2.410	2.381	2.353	2.326	2.299	2.273	2.247	2.222	2.198	2.174	2.151	2.128
7	2.500	2.469	2.439	2.410	2.381	2.353	2.326	2.299	2.273	2.247	2.222	2.198	2.174	2.151	2.128
8	2.500	2.469	2.439	2.410	2.381	2.353	2.326	2.299	2.273	2.247	2.222	2.198	2.174	2.150	2.128
9	2.500	2.469	2.439	2.410	2.381	2.353	2.326	2.299	2.273	2.247	2.222	2.198	2.174	2.151	2.128
10	2.500	2.469	2.439	2.410	2.381	2.353	2.326	2.299	2.273	2.247	2.222	2.198	2.174	2.150	2.128
11	2.500	2.469	2.439	2.410	2.381	2.353	2.326	2.299	2.273	2.247	2.222	2.198	2.174	2.151	2.128
12	2.500	2.469	2.439	2.410	2.381	2.353	2.326	2.299	2.273	2.247	2.222	2.198	2.174	2.150	2.128
13	2.500	2.469	2.439	2.410	2.381	2.353	2.325	2.299	2.273	2.247	2.222	2.198	2.174	2.151	2.127
14	2.500	2.469	2.439	2.410	2.381	2.353	2.326	2.299	2.273	2.247	2.222	2.198	2.174	2.150	2.128
15	2.500	2.469	2.439	2.409	2.381	2.353	2.325	2.299	2.273	2.247	2.222	2.198	2.174	2.151	2.128
16	2.500	2.469	2.439	2.410	2.381	2.353	2.326	2.299	2.273	2.247	2.222	2.198	2.174	2.150	2.128
17	2.500	2.469	2.439	2.409	2.381	2.353	2.325	2.299	2.273	2.247	2.222	2.198	2.174	2.151	2.127
18	2.500	2.469	2.439	2.410	2.381	2.353	2.326	2.299	2.273	2.247	2.222	2.198	2.174	2.150	2.128
19	2.500	2.469	2.439	2.409	2.381	2.353	2.325	2.299	2.273	2.247	2.222	2.198	2.174	2.151	2.127
20	2.500	2.469	2.439	2.409	2.381	2.353	2.326	2.299	2.273	2.247	2.222	2.198	2.174	2.150	2.128
21	2.500	2.469	2.439	2.410	2.381	2.353	2.325	2.299	2.273	2.247	2.222	2.198	2.174	2.151	2.128
22	2.500	2.469	2.439	2.409	2.381	2.353	2.326	2.299	2.273	2.247	2.222	2.198	2.174	2.150	2.127
23	2.500	2.469	2.439	2.410	2.381	2.353	2.325	2.299	2.273	2.247	2.222	2.198	2.174	2.151	2.128
24	2.500	2.469	2.439	2.409	2.381	2.353	2.326	2.299	2.273	2.247	2.222	2.198	2.174	2.150	2.128
25	2.500	2.469	2.439	2.410	2.381	2.353	2.325	2.299	2.273	2.247	2.222	2.198	2.174	2.151	2.127
26	2.500	2.469	2.439	2.409	2.381	2.353	2.326	2.299	2.273	2.247	2.222	2.198	2.174	2.151	2.128
27	2.500	2.469	2.439	2.410	2.381	2.353	2.325	2.299	2.272	2.247	2.222	2.198	2.174	2.150	2.127
28	2.500	2.469	2.439	2.409	2.381	2.353	2.326	2.299	2.273	2.247	2.222	2.198	2.174	2.151	2.128
29	2.500	2.469	2.439	2.410	2.381	2.353	2.325	2.299	2.272	2.247	2.222	2.198	2.174	2.150	2.128
30	2.500	2.469	2.439	2.409	2.381	2.353	2.326	2.299	2.273	2.248	2.222	2.198	2.174	2.151	2.127
31	2.500	2.469	2.439	2.410	2.381	2.353	2.325	2.299	2.272	2.247	2.223	2.198	2.174	2.150	2.128
32	2.500	2.469	2.439	2.409	2.381	2.353	2.326	2.298	2.273	2.248	2.222	2.198	2.174	2.151	2.128
33	2.500	2.469	2.439	2.410	2.381	2.353	2.325	2.299	2.272	2.247	2.223	2.197	2.174	2.150	2.127
34	2.500	2.469	2.439	2.410	2.381	2.353	2.326	2.298	2.273	2.248	2.222	2.198	2.174	2.151	2.128
35	2.500	2.469	2.439	2.409	2.381	2.353	2.325	2.299	2.272	2.247	2.223	2.197	2.173	2.150	2.128
36	2.500	2.469	2.439	2.410	2.381	2.353	2.326	2.298	2.273	2.248	2.222	2.198	2.173	2.151	2.127
37	2.500	2.470	2.439	2.409	2.381	2.353	2.325	2.299	2.272	2.247	2.223	2.197	2.174	2.150	2.128
38	2.500	2.469	2.439	2.410	2.381	2.353	2.326	2.298	2.273	2.248	2.222	2.198	2.174	2.151	2.128
39	2.500	2.470	2.439	2.409	2.381	2.353	2.325	2.299	2.272	2.247	2.223	2.197	2.173	2.150	2.127
40	2.500	2.469	2.439	2.410	2.380	2.353	2.326	2.298	2.273	2.248	2.222	2.198	2.174	2.151	2.128
41	1.562	2.470	2.439	2.409	2.381	2.353	2.325	2.299	2.272	2.247	2.223	2.197	2.173	2.150	2.128
42		0.309	2.439	2.410	2.380	2.352	2.326	2.298	2.273	2.248	2.222	2.198	2.174	2.151	2.127
43			1.525	2.409	1.488	2.353	2.326	2.299	2.272	2.247	2.223	2.197	2.174	2.150	2.128
44				0.301		0.294	1.453	2.298	2.273	2.248	2.222	2.198	2.174	2.151	2.128
45								0.287	1.420	2.247	2.223	2.197	2.173	2.150	2.127
46										0.281	1.389	2.198	2.173	2.151	2.128
47												0.275	1.358	2.150	2.128
48														0.269	1.330

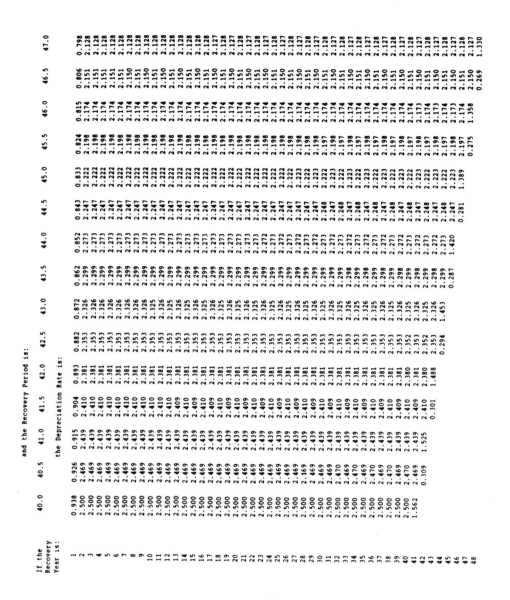

and the Recovery Period is:

the Depreciation Rate is:

If the Recovery Year is:	47.5	48.0	48.5	49.0	49.5	50.0
1	0.789	0.781	0.773	0.765	0.758	0.750
2	2.105	2.083	2.062	2.041	2.020	2.000
3	2.105	2.083	2.062	2.041	2.020	2.000
4	2.105	2.083	2.062	2.041	2.020	2.000
5	2.105	2.083	2.062	2.041	2.020	2.000
6	2.105	2.083	2.062	2.041	2.020	2.000
7	2.105	2.083	2.062	2.041	2.020	2.000
8	2.105	2.083	2.062	2.041	2.020	2.000
9	2.105	2.083	2.062	2.041	2.020	2.000
10	2.105	2.083	2.062	2.041	2.020	2.000
11	2.105	2.083	2.062	2.041	2.020	2.000
12	2.105	2.083	2.062	2.041	2.020	2.000
13	2.105	2.083	2.062	2.041	2.020	2.000
14	2.105	2.083	2.062	2.041	2.020	2.000
15	2.105	2.083	2.062	2.041	2.020	2.000
16	2.105	2.083	2.062	2.041	2.020	2.000
17	2.105	2.083	2.062	2.041	2.020	2.000
18	2.105	2.084	2.062	2.041	2.020	2.000
19	2.105	2.083	2.062	2.041	2.020	2.000
20	2.105	2.084	2.062	2.041	2.020	2.000
21	2.105	2.083	2.062	2.041	2.020	2.000
22	2.105	2.084	2.062	2.041	2.020	2.000
23	2.105	2.083	2.062	2.041	2.020	2.000
24	2.106	2.084	2.062	2.041	2.020	2.000
25	2.105	2.083	2.062	2.041	2.020	2.000
26	2.106	2.084	2.062	2.041	2.020	2.000

and the Recovery Period is:

the Depreciation Rate is:

If the Recovery Year is:	47.5	48.0	48.5	49.0	49.5	50.0
27	2.105	2.083	2.062	2.041	2.020	2.000
28	2.106	2.084	2.062	2.041	2.020	2.000
29	2.105	2.083	2.062	2.041	2.020	2.000
30	2.106	2.084	2.062	2.041	2.020	2.000
31	2.105	2.083	2.062	2.041	2.020	2.000
32	2.106	2.084	2.062	2.041	2.020	2.000
33	2.105	2.083	2.062	2.041	2.020	2.000
34	2.106	2.084	2.062	2.040	2.021	2.000
35	2.105	2.083	2.062	2.041	2.021	2.000
36	2.106	2.084	2.062	2.040	2.020	2.000
37	2.105	2.083	2.061	2.041	2.021	2.000
38	2.106	2.084	2.062	2.040	2.020	2.000
39	2.105	2.083	2.061	2.041	2.021	2.000
40	2.106	2.084	2.062	2.040	2.020	2.000
41	2.105	2.083	2.061	2.041	2.021	2.000
42	2.106	2.084	2.062	2.040	2.020	2.000
43	2.105	2.083	2.061	2.041	2.021	2.000
44	2.106	2.084	2.062	2.040	2.020	2.000
45	2.105	2.083	2.061	2.041	2.021	2.000
46	2.106	2.084	2.062	2.040	2.020	2.000
47	2.105	2.083	2.061	2.041	2.021	2.000
48	2.106	2.084	2.062	2.040	2.020	2.000
49	2.105	2.083	2.061	2.041	2.021	2.000
50	2.106	2.083	2.062	2.040	2.020	2.000
51	0.263	1.302	0.258	1.275	0.253	1.250

TABLE 12

General and Alternative Depreciation Systems
Applicable Depreciation Method: Straight Line
Applicable Recovery Periods: 2.5 - 50 years
Applicable Convention: Mid-quarter (property placed in service in fourth quarter)

and the Recovery Period is:

the Depreciation Rate is:

If the Recovery Year is:	2.5	3.0	3.5	4.0	4.5	5.0	5.5	6.0	6.5	7.0	7.5	8.0	8.5	9.0	9.5
1	5.00	4.17	3.57	3.13	2.78	2.50	2.27	2.08	1.92	1.79	1.67	1.56	1.47	1.39	1.32
2	40.00	33.33	28.57	25.00	22.22	20.00	18.18	16.67	15.39	14.29	13.33	12.50	11.76	11.11	10.53
3	40.00	33.33	28.57	25.00	22.22	20.00	18.18	16.67	15.39	14.28	13.33	12.50	11.77	11.11	10.53
4	15.00	29.17	28.57	25.00	22.22	20.00	18.18	16.67	15.38	14.29	13.33	12.50	11.76	11.11	10.52
5		10.72	21.87	22.23	20.00	18.19	16.66	15.39	14.28	13.33	12.50	11.77	11.11	10.53	
6				8.33	17.50	18.18	16.67	15.38	14.29	13.33	12.50	11.77	11.11	10.53	
7						6.82	14.58	15.38	14.28	13.34	12.50	11.76	11.11	10.52	
8								5.77	12.50	13.34	12.50	11.77	11.11	10.53	
9										5.00	10.94	11.76	11.11	10.52	
10												4.41	9.73	10.53	
11														10.52	

and the Recovery Period is:

the Depreciation Rate is:

If the Recovery Year is:	10.0	10.5	11.0	11.5	12.0	12.5	13.0	13.5	14.0	14.5	15.0	15.5	16.0	16.5	17.0
1	1.25	1.19	1.14	1.09	1.04	1.00	0.96	0.93	0.89	0.86	0.83	0.81	0.78	0.76	0.74
2	10.00	9.52	9.09	8.70	8.33	8.00	7.69	7.41	7.14	6.90	6.67	6.45	6.25	6.06	5.88
3	10.00	9.52	9.09	8.69	8.33	8.00	7.69	7.41	7.14	6.90	6.67	6.45	6.25	6.06	5.88
4	10.00	9.52	9.09	8.70	8.33	8.00	7.69	7.41	7.14	6.90	6.67	6.45	6.25	6.06	5.88
5	10.00	9.52	9.09	8.69	8.34	8.00	7.69	7.41	7.14	6.90	6.67	6.45	6.25	6.06	5.88
6	10.00	9.52	9.09	8.70	8.33	8.00	7.69	7.41	7.14	6.90	6.67	6.45	6.25	6.06	5.88
7	10.00	9.52	9.09	8.70	8.33	8.00	7.69	7.40	7.14	6.90	6.66	6.45	6.25	6.06	5.88
8	10.00	9.53	9.09	8.69	8.34	8.00	7.69	7.41	7.15	6.89	6.67	6.45	6.25	6.06	5.88
9	10.00	9.52	9.09	8.70	8.33	8.00	7.70	7.40	7.15	6.90	6.66	6.45	6.25	6.06	5.88
10	10.00	9.53	9.09	8.69	8.34	8.00	7.69	7.41	7.14	6.89	6.67	6.45	6.25	6.06	5.88
11	8.75	9.52	9.09	8.70	8.33	8.00	7.70	7.40	7.15	6.89	6.66	6.45	6.25	6.06	5.89
12		3.57	7.96	8.70	8.34	8.00	7.70	7.41	7.14	6.89	6.67	6.45	6.25	6.06	5.88
13				3.26	7.29	8.00	7.70	7.40	7.14	6.90	6.67	6.45	6.25	6.06	5.89
14						3.00	6.73	7.41	7.15	6.89	6.66	6.45	6.25	6.06	5.88
15								2.78	6.25	6.89	6.67	6.46	6.25	6.06	5.89
16										2.59	5.83	6.46	6.25	6.06	5.89
17												2.42	5.47	6.07	5.88
18														2.27	5.15

and the Recovery Period is:

the Depreciation Rate is:

If the Recovery Year is:	17.5	18.0	18.5	19.0	19.5	20.0	20.5	21.0	21.5	22.0	22.5	23.0	23.5	24.0	24.5
1	0.71	0.69	0.68	0.66	0.64	0.625	0.610	0.595	0.581	0.568	0.556	0.543	0.532	0.521	0.510
2	5.71	5.56	5.41	5.26	5.13	5.000	4.878	4.762	4.651	4.545	4.444	4.348	4.255	4.167	4.082
3	5.71	5.56	5.40	5.26	5.13	5.000	4.878	4.762	4.651	4.545	4.444	4.348	4.255	4.167	4.082
4	5.72	5.56	5.41	5.26	5.13	5.000	4.878	4.762	4.651	4.546	4.444	4.348	4.255	4.167	4.082
5	5.71	5.56	5.41	5.26	5.13	5.000	4.878	4.762	4.651	4.545	4.445	4.348	4.255	4.167	4.082
6	5.72	5.55	5.40	5.26	5.13	5.000	4.878	4.762	4.651	4.546	4.444	4.348	4.255	4.167	4.082
7	5.71	5.56	5.41	5.26	5.13	5.000	4.878	4.762	4.651	4.545	4.445	4.348	4.255	4.167	4.082
8	5.72	5.55	5.40	5.26	5.13	5.000	4.878	4.762	4.651	4.546	4.444	4.348	4.255	4.167	4.082
9	5.71	5.56	5.41	5.27	5.13	5.000	4.878	4.762	4.651	4.545	4.445	4.348	4.255	4.167	4.081
10	5.72	5.55	5.40	5.26	5.13	5.000	4.878	4.762	4.651	4.546	4.444	4.348	4.255	4.166	4.082
11	5.71	5.56	5.41	5.27	5.13	5.000	4.878	4.762	4.651	4.545	4.445	4.348	4.256	4.167	4.082
12	5.72	5.55	5.40	5.26	5.13	5.000	4.878	4.762	4.651	4.546	4.444	4.348	4.255	4.166	4.081
13	5.71	5.56	5.41	5.27	5.13	5.000	4.878	4.762	4.651	4.545	4.445	4.348	4.256	4.167	4.082
14	5.72	5.55	5.41	5.27	5.13	5.000	4.878	4.762	4.652	4.546	4.444	4.348	4.255	4.166	4.081
15	5.71	5.56	5.40	5.26	5.12	5.000	4.878	4.762	4.651	4.545	4.445	4.348	4.256	4.167	4.082
16	5.72	5.55	5.41	5.27	5.13	5.000	4.878	4.762	4.651	4.546	4.444	4.348	4.255	4.166	4.082
17	5.71	5.56	5.40	5.26	5.12	5.000	4.878	4.762	4.652	4.545	4.445	4.348	4.256	4.167	4.082
18	5.72	5.55	5.41	5.27	5.13	5.000	4.878	4.762	4.651	4.546	4.444	4.348	4.255	4.166	4.081
19	5.71	5.56	5.40	5.26	5.12	5.000	4.878	4.761	4.652	4.545	4.445	4.347	4.256	4.167	4.082
20	5.72	5.55	5.41	5.26	5.13	5.000	4.879	4.762	4.651	4.546	4.444	4.348	4.255	4.166	4.081
21	2.14	5.56	5.40	4.61	1.92	4.375	1.829	4.762	4.652	4.545	4.445	4.347	4.256	4.167	4.082
22		4.86	2.03					4.166	4.651	4.546	4.444	4.348	4.255	4.166	4.082
23									1.744	3.977	4.445	3.804	4.256	4.167	4.082
24											1.667		4.255	4.166	4.081
25													1.596	3.646	4.081
26															1.531

and the Recovery Period is:

the Depreciation Rate is:

If the Recovery Year is:	25.0	25.5	26.0	26.5	27.0	27.5	28.0	28.5	29.0	29.5	30.0	30.5	31.0	31.5	32.0
1	0.500	0.490	0.481	0.472	0.463	0.455	0.446	0.439	0.431	0.424	0.417	0.410	0.403	0.397	0.391
2	4.000	3.922	3.846	3.774	3.704	3.636	3.571	3.509	3.448	3.390	3.333	3.279	3.226	3.175	3.125
3	4.000	3.922	3.846	3.774	3.704	3.636	3.571	3.509	3.448	3.390	3.333	3.279	3.226	3.175	3.125
4	4.000	3.922	3.846	3.774	3.704	3.636	3.571	3.509	3.448	3.390	3.333	3.279	3.226	3.175	3.125
5	4.000	3.922	3.846	3.773	3.704	3.636	3.571	3.509	3.448	3.390	3.333	3.279	3.226	3.175	3.125
6	4.000	3.921	3.846	3.774	3.704	3.636	3.572	3.509	3.448	3.390	3.333	3.279	3.226	3.175	3.125
7	4.000	3.922	3.846	3.774	3.704	3.636	3.571	3.509	3.448	3.390	3.333	3.279	3.226	3.175	3.125
8	4.000	3.921	3.846	3.773	3.704	3.636	3.572	3.509	3.448	3.390	3.333	3.279	3.226	3.175	3.125
9	4.000	3.922	3.846	3.774	3.704	3.636	3.571	3.509	3.448	3.390	3.333	3.279	3.226	3.175	3.125
10	4.000	3.921	3.846	3.773	3.704	3.636	3.572	3.509	3.448	3.390	3.333	3.279	3.226	3.175	3.125
11	4.000	3.922	3.846	3.774	3.704	3.637	3.571	3.509	3.448	3.390	3.333	3.279	3.226	3.174	3.125
12	4.000	3.921	3.846	3.773	3.704	3.636	3.572	3.509	3.448	3.390	3.333	3.279	3.226	3.175	3.125
13	4.000	3.922	3.846	3.774	3.704	3.637	3.571	3.509	3.448	3.390	3.334	3.279	3.226	3.174	3.125
14	4.000	3.921	3.846	3.773	3.703	3.636	3.572	3.509	3.449	3.390	3.333	3.279	3.226	3.175	3.125
15	4.000	3.922	3.846	3.774	3.704	3.637	3.571	3.509	3.448	3.390	3.334	3.279	3.226	3.174	3.125
16	4.000	3.921	3.846	3.773	3.703	3.636	3.572	3.509	3.449	3.390	3.333	3.278	3.226	3.175	3.125
17	4.000	3.922	3.847	3.774	3.704	3.637	3.571	3.508	3.448	3.390	3.334	3.279	3.226	3.174	3.125
18	4.000	3.921	3.846	3.773	3.703	3.636	3.572	3.509	3.449	3.390	3.333	3.278	3.226	3.175	3.125
19	4.000	3.922	3.846	3.774	3.703	3.637	3.571	3.508	3.448	3.390	3.334	3.279	3.226	3.174	3.125
20	4.000	3.921	3.846	3.773	3.704	3.636	3.572	3.509	3.448	3.390	3.333	3.279	3.226	3.175	3.125
21	4.000	3.922	3.847	3.774	3.703	3.637	3.571	3.508	3.449	3.390	3.334	3.278	3.226	3.174	3.125
22	4.000	3.921	3.846	3.773	3.704	3.636	3.572	3.509	3.448	3.389	3.333	3.279	3.226	3.175	3.125
23	4.000	3.922	3.847	3.774	3.703	3.637	3.571	3.508	3.449	3.390	3.334	3.278	3.226	3.174	3.125
24	4.000	3.921	3.846	3.773	3.704	3.636	3.572	3.509	3.448	3.389	3.333	3.279	3.226	3.175	3.125
25	4.000	3.922	3.847	3.774	3.703	3.637	3.571	3.508	3.449	3.390	3.334	3.278	3.225	3.174	3.125
26	3.500	3.921	3.846	3.773	3.704	3.636	3.572	3.509	3.448	3.390.	3.333	3.279	3.226	3.175	3.125
27		1.471	3.366	3.774	3.703	3.637	3.571	3.508	3.449	3.389	3.334	3.278	3.225	3.174	3.125
28				1.415	3.241	3.636	3.572	3.509	3.448	3.390	3.333	3.279	3.226	3.175	3.125
29						1.364	3.571	3.508	3.449	3.389	3.334	3.278	3.225	3.174	3.125
30							3.125	3.508	3.448	3.390	3.333	3.279	3.226	3.175	3.125
31								1.316	3.449	1.271	2.917	3.278	3.225	3.174	3.125
32									3.017			1.229	3.226	3.175	3.125
33													2.822	1.190	2.734

and the Recovery Period is:

the Depreciation Rate is:

If the Recovery Year is:	32.5	33.0	33.5	34.0	34.5	35.0	35.5	36.0	36.5	37.0	37.5	38.0	38.5	39.0	39.5
1	0.385	0.379	0.373	0.368	0.362	0.357	0.352	0.347	0.342	0.338	0.333	0.329	0.325	0.321	0.316
2	3.077	3.030	2.985	2.941	2.899	2.857	2.817	2.778	2.740	2.703	2.667	2.632	2.597	2.564	2.532
3	3.077	3.030	2.985	2.941	2.899	2.857	2.817	2.778	2.740	2.703	2.667	2.632	2.597	2.564	2.532
4	3.077	3.030	2.985	2.941	2.899	2.857	2.817	2.778	2.740	2.703	2.667	2.632	2.597	2.564	2.532
5	3.077	3.030	2.985	2.941	2.899	2.857	2.817	2.778	2.740	2.703	2.667	2.632	2.597	2.564	2.532
6	3.077	3.030	2.985	2.941	2.899	2.857	2.817	2.778	2.740	2.703	2.667	2.632	2.597	2.564	2.532
7	3.077	3.030	2.985	2.941	2.898	2.857	2.817	2.778	2.740	2.703	2.667	2.631	2.597	2.564	2.532
8	3.077	3.030	2.985	2.941	2.899	2.857	2.817	2.778	2.740	2.703	2.667	2.632	2.597	2.564	2.532
9	3.077	3.030	2.985	2.941	2.899	2.857	2.817	2.778	2.740	2.703	2.667	2.631	2.597	2.564	2.532
10	3.077	3.030	2.985	2.941	2.899	2.857	2.817	2.778	2.740	2.703	2.667	2.632	2.597	2.564	2.532
11	3.077	3.030	2.985	2.941	2.898	2.857	2.817	2.778	2.740	2.703	2.667	2.632	2.598	2.564	2.532
12	3.077	3.030	2.985	2.941	2.899	2.857	2.817	2.778	2.740	2.703	2.667	2.631	2.597	2.564	2.531
13	3.077	3.030	2.985	2.941	2.898	2.857	2.817	2.778	2.740	2.703	2.667	2.632	2.598	2.564	2.532
14	3.077	3.030	2.985	2.941	2.899	2.857	2.817	2.778	2.740	2.703	2.667	2.632	2.597	2.564	2.532
15	3.077	3.030	2.985	2.941	2.898	2.857	2.817	2.778	2.740	2.703	2.667	2.631	2.598	2.564	2.531
16	3.077	3.031	2.985	2.941	2.899	2.857	2.817	2.778	2.740	2.703	2.666	2.632	2.597	2.564	2.532
17	3.077	3.030	2.985	2.941	2.898	2.857	2.817	2.778	2.740	2.703	2.667	2.631	2.598	2.564	2.532
18	3.077	3.031	2.985	2.941	2.899	2.857	2.817	2.778	2.740	2.703	2.666	2.632	2.598	2.564	2.531
19	3.077	3.030	2.985	2.941	2.898	2.857	2.817	2.778	2.739	2.703	2.667	2.632	2.597	2.564	2.532
20	3.077	3.031	2.985	2.941	2.899	2.857	2.817	2.778	2.740	2.702	2.666	2.631	2.598	2.564	2.531
21	3.077	3.030	2.985	2.941	2.898	2.857	2.817	2.778	2.739	2.703	2.667	2.632	2.597	2.564	2.532
22	3.077	3.031	2.985	2.941	2.899	2.857	2.817	2.778	2.740	2.702	2.666	2.631	2.598	2.564	2.531
23	3.077	3.030	2.985	2.942	2.898	2.857	2.817	2.777	2.739	2.702	2.667	2.632	2.597	2.564	2.532
24	3.077	3.031	2.985	2.941	2.898	2.857	2.817	2.778	2.740	2.703	2.666	2.631	2.598	2.564	2.531
25	3.077	3.030	2.985	2.941	2.899	2.857	2.817	2.778	2.739	2.702	2.667	2.632	2.597	2.564	2.532
26	3.077	3.031	2.985	2.942	2.899	2.857	2.817	2.777	2.740	2.703	2.666	2.631	2.598	2.564	2.531
27	3.077	3.030	2.985	2.941	2.898	2.858	2.817	2.778	2.739	2.702	2.667	2.632	2.597	2.564	2.532
28	3.077	3.031	2.985	2.941	2.899	2.857	2.817	2.777	2.740	2.703	2.666	2.631	2.598	2.564	2.531
29	3.076	3.030	2.985	2.941	2.898	2.857	2.817	2.778	2.739	2.702	2.666	2.632	2.597	2.564	2.532
30	3.077	3.031	2.985	2.942	2.899	2.858	2.817	2.777	2.740	2.703	2.667	2.631	2.598	2.564	2.531
31	3.076	3.030	2.985	2.941	2.898	2.857	2.816	2.778	2.739	2.702	2.666	2.632	2.597	2.564	2.532
32	3.077	3.031	2.985	2.942	2.899	2.858	2.817	2.777	2.740	2.703	2.667	2.631	2.598	2.564	2.531
33	3.076	3.030	2.986	2.941	2.898	2.857	2.816	2.778	2.739	2.702	2.666	2.632	2.597	2.565	2.532
34	1.154	3.030	2.985	2.942	2.899	2.858	2.817	2.777	2.740	2.702	2.666	2.631	2.598	2.564	2.531
35		2.652	1.120	2.574	2.898	2.857	2.816	2.778	2.739	2.703	2.667	2.632	2.597	2.565	2.531
36					1.087	2.500	2.817	2.778	2.740	2.702	2.666	2.631	2.598	2.564	2.532
37							1.056	2.430	2.739	2.703	2.667	2.632	2.597	2.564	2.532
38									1.027	2.365	2.666	2.631	2.598	2.564	2.531
39											1.000	2.303	2.598	2.564	2.532
40													0.974	2.244	2.531
41															0.949

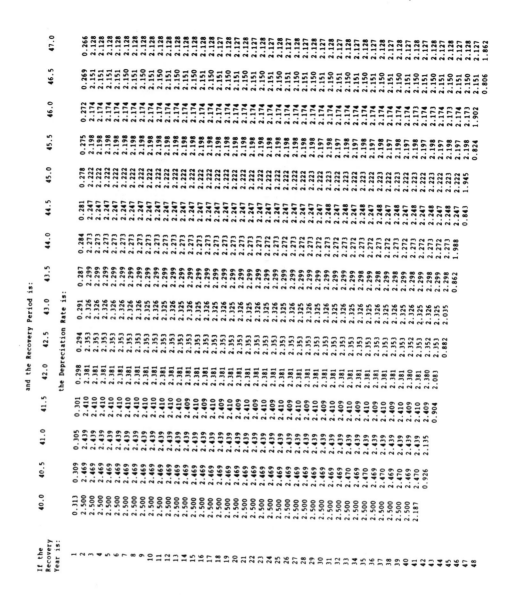

and the Recovery Period is:

the Depreciation Rate is:

If the Recovery Year is:	40.0	40.5	41.0	41.5	42.0	42.5	43.0	43.5	44.0	44.5	45.0	45.5	46.0	46.5	47.0
1	0.313	0.309	0.305	0.301	0.298	0.294	0.291	0.287	0.284	0.281	0.278	0.275	0.272	0.269	0.266
2	2.500	2.469	2.439	2.410	2.381	2.353	2.326	2.299	2.273	2.247	2.222	2.198	2.174	2.151	2.128
3	2.500	2.469	2.439	2.410	2.381	2.353	2.326	2.299	2.273	2.247	2.222	2.198	2.174	2.151	2.128
4	2.500	2.469	2.439	2.410	2.381	2.353	2.326	2.299	2.273	2.247	2.222	2.198	2.174	2.151	2.128
5	2.500	2.469	2.439	2.410	2.381	2.353	2.326	2.299	2.273	2.247	2.222	2.198	2.174	2.150	2.128
6	2.500	2.469	2.439	2.410	2.381	2.353	2.326	2.299	2.273	2.247	2.222	2.198	2.174	2.150	2.128
7	2.500	2.469	2.439	2.410	2.381	2.353	2.326	2.299	2.273	2.247	2.222	2.198	2.174	2.151	2.128
8	2.500	2.469	2.439	2.410	2.381	2.353	2.326	2.299	2.273	2.247	2.222	2.198	2.174	2.151	2.128
9	2.500	2.469	2.439	2.410	2.381	2.353	2.326	2.299	2.273	2.247	2.222	2.198	2.174	2.151	2.128
10	2.500	2.469	2.439	2.410	2.381	2.353	2.326	2.299	2.273	2.247	2.222	2.198	2.174	2.150	2.128
11	2.500	2.469	2.439	2.410	2.381	2.353	2.326	2.299	2.273	2.247	2.222	2.198	2.174	2.150	2.128
12	2.500	2.469	2.439	2.410	2.381	2.353	2.326	2.299	2.273	2.247	2.222	2.198	2.174	2.151	2.128
13	2.500	2.469	2.439	2.410	2.381	2.353	2.326	2.299	2.273	2.247	2.222	2.198	2.174	2.150	2.128
14	2.500	2.469	2.439	2.410	2.381	2.353	2.326	2.299	2.273	2.247	2.222	2.198	2.174	2.151	2.128
15	2.500	2.469	2.439	2.409	2.381	2.353	2.326	2.299	2.273	2.247	2.222	2.198	2.174	2.150	2.128
16	2.500	2.469	2.439	2.410	2.381	2.353	2.326	2.299	2.273	2.247	2.222	2.198	2.174	2.151	2.128
17	2.500	2.469	2.439	2.410	2.381	2.353	2.325	2.299	2.273	2.247	2.222	2.198	2.174	2.150	2.127
18	2.500	2.469	2.439	2.409	2.381	2.353	2.325	2.299	2.273	2.247	2.222	2.198	2.174	2.150	2.128
19	2.500	2.469	2.439	2.410	2.381	2.353	2.326	2.299	2.273	2.247	2.222	2.198	2.174	2.151	2.128
20	2.500	2.469	2.439	2.410	2.381	2.353	2.325	2.299	2.273	2.247	2.222	2.198	2.174	2.150	2.128
21	2.500	2.469	2.439	2.409	2.381	2.353	2.325	2.299	2.273	2.247	2.222	2.198	2.174	2.151	2.128
22	2.500	2.469	2.439	2.410	2.381	2.353	2.326	2.299	2.273	2.247	2.222	2.198	2.174	2.151	2.128
23	2.500	2.469	2.439	2.410	2.381	2.353	2.325	2.299	2.272	2.247	2.222	2.198	2.174	2.150	2.127
24	2.500	2.469	2.439	2.409	2.381	2.353	2.326	2.299	2.273	2.247	2.222	2.198	2.174	2.151	2.128
25	2.500	2.469	2.439	2.410	2.381	2.353	2.325	2.299	2.273	2.247	2.222	2.198	2.174	2.151	2.128
26	2.500	2.469	2.439	2.410	2.381	2.353	2.325	2.299	2.272	2.247	2.222	2.198	2.174	2.150	2.127
27	2.500	2.469	2.439	2.410	2.381	2.353	2.326	2.299	2.273	2.247	2.222	2.198	2.174	2.150	2.128
28	2.500	2.469	2.439	2.409	2.381	2.353	2.326	2.299	2.273	2.247	2.223	2.198	2.174	2.151	2.128
29	2.500	2.469	2.439	2.410	2.381	2.353	2.326	2.299	2.273	2.247	2.222	2.198	2.174	2.151	2.127
30	2.500	2.469	2.439	2.409	2.381	2.353	2.325	2.299	2.273	2.248	2.223	2.198	2.174	2.150	2.128
31	2.500	2.469	2.439	2.410	2.381	2.353	2.326	2.299	2.272	2.247	2.222	2.198	2.174	2.150	2.127
32	2.500	2.469	2.439	2.410	2.381	2.353	2.325	2.299	2.272	2.247	2.223	2.197	2.174	2.150	2.127
33	2.500	2.470	2.439	2.409	2.381	2.353	2.326	2.299	2.273	2.248	2.222	2.197	2.174	2.151	2.128
34	2.500	2.469	2.439	2.410	2.381	2.353	2.325	2.298	2.272	2.248	2.223	2.198	2.174	2.151	2.127
35	2.500	2.469	2.439	2.410	2.381	2.353	2.326	2.299	2.273	2.247	2.223	2.198	2.174	2.150	2.128
36	2.500	2.469	2.439	2.409	2.381	2.353	2.325	2.298	2.272	2.247	2.222	2.197	2.174	2.151	2.128
37	2.500	2.470	2.439	2.410	2.381	2.353	2.326	2.298	2.273	2.248	2.223	2.198	2.174	2.150	2.127
38	2.500	2.469	2.439	2.410	2.381	2.352	2.326	2.299	2.272	2.247	2.222	2.198	2.174	2.150	2.128
39	2.500	2.470	2.439	2.410	2.381	2.353	2.326	2.298	2.273	2.248	2.222	2.197	2.174	2.150	2.127
40	2.500	2.469	2.439	2.410	2.380	2.353	2.326	2.299	2.272	2.247	2.223	2.198	2.173	2.150	2.128
41	2.500	2.470	2.439	2.410	2.381	2.353	2.325	2.298	2.273	2.248	2.222	2.197	2.174	2.150	2.127
42	2.187	2.470	2.439	2.410	2.381	2.352	2.326	2.299	2.272	2.247	2.223	2.198	2.173	2.151	2.128
43		0.926	2.135	2.409	2.380	2.353	2.326	2.299	2.273	2.248	2.222	2.197	2.174	2.150	2.127
44				0.904	2.083	2.353	2.035	2.298	2.272	2.247	2.223	2.198	2.173	2.151	2.128
45						0.882		0.862	1.988	2.248	2.222	2.197	2.174	2.150	2.127
46										0.843	1.945	2.198	2.173	2.150	2.128
47												0.824	1.902	2.151	2.128
48														0.806	1.862

and the Recovery Period is:

If the Recovery Year is:	47.5	48.0	48.5	49.0	49.5	50.0
	the Depreciation Rate is:					
1	0.263	0.260	0.258	0.255	0.253	0.250
2	2.105	2.083	2.062	2.041	2.020	2.000
3	2.105	2.083	2.062	2.041	2.020	2.000
4	2.105	2.083	2.062	2.041	2.020	2.000
5	2.105	2.083	2.062	2.041	2.020	2.000
6	2.105	2.083	2.062	2.041	2.020	2.000
7	2.105	2.083	2.062	2.041	2.020	2.000
8	2.105	2.083	2.062	2.041	2.020	2.000
9	2.105	2.083	2.062	2.041	2.020	2.000
10	2.105	2.083	2.062	2.041	2.020	2.000
11	2.105	2.083	2.062	2.041	2.020	2.000
12	2.105	2.083	2.062	2.041	2.020	2.000
13	2.105	2.083	2.062	2.041	2.020	2.000
14	2.105	2.083	2.062	2.041	2.020	2.000
15	2.105	2.083	2.062	2.041	2.020	2.000
16	2.105	2.083	2.062	2.041	2.020	2.000
17	2.105	2.083	2.062	2.041	2.020	2.000
18	2.105	2.084	2.062	2.041	2.020	2.000
19	2.105	2.083	2.062	2.041	2.020	2.000
20	2.105	2.084	2.062	2.041	2.020	2.000
21	2.105	2.083	2.062	2.041	2.020	2.000
22	2.105	2.084	2.062	2.041	2.020	2.000
23	2.105	2.083	2.062	2.041	2.020	2.000
24	2.105	2.084	2.062	2.041	2.020	2.000
25	2.106	2.083	2.062	2.041	2.020	2.000
26	2.105	2.084	2.062	2.041	2.020	2.000
27	2.106	2.083	2.062	2.041	2.020	2.000
28	2.105	2.084	2.062	2.041	2.020	2.000
29	2.106	2.083	2.062	2.041	2.020	2.000
30	2.105	2.084	2.062	2.041	2.020	2.000
31	2.106	2.083	2.062	2.041	2.020	2.000
32	2.105	2.084	2.062	2.041	2.020	2.000
33	2.106	2.083	2.062	2.041	2.020	2.000
34	2.105	2.084	2.062	2.040	2.021	2.000
35	2.106	2.083	2.062	2.041	2.021	2.000
36	2.105	2.084	2.061	2.040	2.021	2.000
37	2.106	2.083	2.062	2.041	2.020	2.000
38	2.105	2.084	2.061	2.040	2.021	2.000
39	2.106	2.083	2.062	2.041	2.020	2.000
40	2.105	2.084	2.061	2.040	2.021	2.000
41	2.106	2.083	2.062	2.041	2.020	2.000
42	2.105	2.084	2.061	2.040	2.021	2.000
43	2.106	2.083	2.062	2.041	2.020	2.000
44	2.105	2.084	2.061	2.040	2.020	2.000
45	2.106	2.083	2.062	2.041	2.021	2.000
46	2.105	2.084	2.061	2.040	2.020	2.000
47	2.106	2.083	2.062	2.041	2.021	2.000
48	2.105	2.084	2.061	2.040	2.020	2.000
49	0.790	1.823	2.062	2.041	2.020	2.000
50			0.773	1.785	2.021	2.000
51					0.758	1.750

TABLE 14   Alternative Minimum Tax (see section 7 of this revenue procedure)
Applicable Depreciation Method: 150 Percent Declining Balance
Switching to Straight Line
Applicable Recovery Periods: 2.5 - 50 years
Applicable Convention: Half-year

and the Recovery Period is:

If the Recovery Year is:	2.5	3.0	3.5	4.0	4.5	5.0	5.5	6.0	6.5	7.0	7.5	8.0	8.5	9.0	9.5
						the Depreciation Rate is:									
1	30.00	25.00	21.43	18.75	16.67	15.00	13.64	12.50	11.54	10.71	10.00	9.38	8.82	8.33	7.89
2	42.00	37.50	33.67	30.47	27.78	25.50	23.55	21.88	20.41	19.13	18.00	16.99	16.09	15.28	14.54
3	28.00	25.00	22.45	20.31	18.52	17.85	17.13	16.41	15.70	15.03	14.40	13.81	13.25	12.73	12.25
4		12.50	22.45	20.31	18.52	16.66	15.23	14.06	13.09	12.25	11.52	11.22	10.91	10.61	10.31
5				10.16	18.51	16.66	15.23	14.06	13.09	12.25	11.52	10.80	10.19	9.65	9.17
6						8.33	15.22	14.06	13.09	12.25	11.52	10.80	10.19	9.64	9.17
7								7.03	13.08	12.25	11.52	10.80	10.18	9.65	9.17
8										6.13	11.52	10.80	10.19	9.64	9.17
9												5.40	10.18	9.65	9.17
10														4.82	9.16

and the Recovery Period is:

If the Recovery Year is:	10.0	10.5	11.0	11.5	12.0	12.5	13.0	13.5	14.0	14.5	15.0	15.5	16.0	16.5	17.0
						the Depreciation Rate is:									
1	7.50	7.14	6.82	6.52	6.25	6.00	5.77	5.56	5.36	5.17	5.00	4.84	4.69	4.55	4.41
2	13.88	13.27	12.71	12.19	11.72	11.28	10.87	10.49	10.14	9.81	9.50	9.21	8.94	8.68	8.43
3	11.79	11.37	10.97	10.60	10.25	9.93	9.62	9.33	9.05	8.80	8.55	8.32	8.10	7.89	7.69
4	10.02	9.75	9.48	9.22	8.97	8.73	8.51	8.29	8.08	7.88	7.70	7.51	7.34	7.17	7.01
5	8.74	8.35	8.18	8.02	7.85	7.69	7.53	7.37	7.22	7.07	6.93	6.79	6.65	6.52	6.39
6	8.74	8.35	7.98	7.64	7.33	7.05	6.79	6.55	6.44	6.34	6.23	6.13	6.03	5.93	5.83
7	8.74	8.35	7.98	7.64	7.33	7.05	6.79	6.55	6.32	6.10	5.90	5.72	5.55	5.39	5.32
8	8.74	8.35	7.97	7.63	7.33	7.05	6.79	6.55	6.32	6.10	5.90	5.72	5.55	5.39	5.23
9	8.74	8.36	7.98	7.64	7.33	7.04	6.79	6.55	6.32	6.10	5.91	5.72	5.55	5.39	5.23
10	8.74	8.35	7.97	7.63	7.33	7.05	6.79	6.55	6.32	6.10	5.90	5.72	5.55	5.39	5.23
11	4.37	8.36	7.98	7.64	7.32	7.04	6.79	6.55	6.32	6.11	5.91	5.72	5.54	5.38	5.23
12			3.99	7.63	7.33	7.05	6.78	6.55	6.32	6.10	5.90	5.72	5.55	5.39	5.23
13					3.66	7.04	6.79	6.56	6.32	6.11	5.91	5.72	5.55	5.39	5.23
14							3.39	6.55	6.31	6.11	5.91	5.72	5.54	5.38	5.23
15									3.16	6.10	5.90	5.72	5.55	5.39	5.23
16											2.95	5.72	5.55	5.39	5.23
17													2.77	5.38	5.23
18															2.62

and the Recovery Period is:

the Depreciation Rate is:

If the Recovery Year is:	24.5	24.0	23.5	23.0	22.5	22.0	21.5	21.0	20.5	20.0	19.5	19.0	18.5	18.0	17.5
1	3.061	3.125	3.191	3.261	3.333	3.409	3.488	3.571	3.659	3.750	3.85	3.95	4.05	4.17	4.29
2	5.935	6.055	6.179	6.309	6.444	6.586	6.733	6.888	7.049	7.219	7.40	7.58	7.78	7.99	8.20
3	5.572	5.676	5.785	5.898	6.015	6.137	6.264	6.396	6.534	6.677	6.83	6.98	7.15	7.32	7.50
4	5.231	5.322	5.416	5.513	5.614	5.718	5.827	5.939	6.055	6.177	6.30	6.43	6.57	6.71	6.86
5	4.910	4.989	5.070	5.153	5.240	5.328	5.420	5.515	5.612	5.713	5.82	5.93	6.04	6.15	6.27
6	4.610	4.677	4.746	4.817	4.890	4.965	5.042	5.121	5.202	5.285	5.37	5.46	5.55	5.64	5.73
7	4.327	4.385	4.443	4.503	4.564	4.627	4.690	4.755	4.821	4.888	4.96	5.03	5.10	5.17	5.24
8	4.062	4.111	4.160	4.210	4.260	4.311	4.363	4.415	4.468	4.522	4.57	4.69	4.81	4.94	5.08
9	3.814	3.854	3.894	3.935	3.976	4.063	4.155	4.252	4.354	4.462	4.58	4.69	4.81	4.94	5.08
10	3.655	3.729	3.808	3.890	3.976	4.063	4.155	4.252	4.354	4.461	4.57	4.69	4.81	4.94	5.08
11	3.655	3.729	3.808	3.890	3.976	4.063	4.155	4.252	4.354	4.462	4.58	4.69	4.81	4.94	5.08
12	3.655	3.730	3.808	3.890	3.976	4.063	4.155	4.252	4.354	4.461	4.57	4.69	4.81	4.95	5.08
13	3.655	3.729	3.808	3.890	3.976	4.064	4.155	4.252	4.354	4.462	4.58	4.69	4.82	4.94	5.09
14	3.655	3.730	3.808	3.890	3.976	4.063	4.155	4.252	4.354	4.461	4.57	4.69	4.81	4.95	5.08
15	3.655	3.729	3.808	3.890	3.976	4.064	4.155	4.252	4.354	4.462	4.58	4.69	4.82	4.94	5.09
16	3.655	3.730	3.808	3.890	3.976	4.063	4.155	4.252	4.354	4.461	4.57	4.69	4.81	4.95	5.08
17	3.655	3.730	3.808	3.889	3.976	4.064	4.155	4.252	4.354	4.462	4.58	4.69	4.82	4.94	5.09
18	3.655	3.729	3.807	3.890	3.976	4.063	4.155	4.252	4.354	4.461	4.57	4.69	4.81	4.95	5.08
19	3.655	3.730	3.808	3.889	3.976	4.064	4.156	4.251	4.353	4.462	4.58	4.70	4.82	2.47	
20	3.655	3.729	3.807	3.890	3.976	4.063	4.155	4.252	4.354	4.461	4.57	4.69			
21	3.655	3.730	3.808	3.889	3.976	4.064	4.156	4.251	4.353	2.231		2.35			
22	3.655	3.730	3.807	3.890	3.976	4.063	4.155	2.126							
23	3.654	3.729	3.808	3.889	3.976	2.032	4.156								
24	3.655	3.730	3.807	3.890											
25	3.654	1.865		1.945											

and the Recovery Period is:

the Depreciation Rate is:

If the Recovery Year is:	25.0	25.5	26.0	26.5	27.0	27.5	28.0	28.5	29.0	29.5	30.0	30.5	31.0	31.5	32.0
1	3.000	2.941	2.885	2.830	2.778	2.727	2.679	2.632	2.586	2.542	2.500	2.459	2.419	2.381	2.344
2	5.820	5.709	5.603	5.500	5.401	5.306	5.214	5.125	5.039	4.955	4.875	4.797	4.722	4.649	4.578
3	5.471	5.374	5.280	5.189	5.101	5.016	4.934	4.855	4.778	4.704	4.631	4.561	4.493	4.427	4.363
4	5.143	5.057	4.975	4.895	4.818	4.743	4.670	4.599	4.531	4.464	4.400	4.337	4.276	4.216	4.159
5	4.834	4.760	4.688	4.618	4.550	4.484	4.420	4.357	4.297	4.237	4.180	4.124	4.069	4.016	3.964
6	4.544	4.480	4.417	4.357	4.297	4.239	4.183	4.128	4.074	4.022	3.971	3.921	3.872	3.824	3.778
7	4.271	4.216	4.163	4.110	4.059	4.008	3.959	3.911	3.864	3.817	3.772	3.728	3.685	3.642	3.601
8	4.015	3.968	3.922	3.877	3.833	3.790	3.747	3.705	3.664	3.623	3.584	3.545	3.506	3.469	3.432
9	3.774	3.735	3.696	3.658	3.620	3.583	3.546	3.510	3.474	3.439	3.404	3.370	3.337	3.304	3.271
10	3.584	3.515	3.483	3.451	3.419	3.387	3.356	3.325	3.294	3.264	3.234	3.204	3.175	3.146	3.118
11	3.583	3.515	3.448	3.383	3.321	3.262	3.205	3.150	3.124	3.098	3.072	3.047	3.022	2.996	2.971
12	3.584	3.515	3.448	3.383	3.321	3.262	3.205	3.150	3.096	3.044	2.994	2.945	2.899	2.854	2.832
13	3.583	3.515	3.448	3.383	3.321	3.262	3.205	3.150	3.096	3.044	2.994	2.945	2.899	2.854	2.809
14	3.584	3.515	3.448	3.383	3.321	3.262	3.205	3.150	3.096	3.044	2.994	2.945	2.899	2.854	2.809
15	3.583	3.515	3.448	3.383	3.321	3.262	3.205	3.150	3.096	3.044	2.994	2.945	2.899	2.854	2.809
16	3.584	3.515	3.448	3.383	3.322	3.262	3.205	3.150	3.096	3.044	2.994	2.945	2.899	2.854	2.809
17	3.583	3.515	3.448	3.383	3.321	3.262	3.205	3.150	3.096	3.044	2.994	2.945	2.899	2.854	2.809
18	3.584	3.516	3.448	3.383	3.322	3.262	3.205	3.150	3.096	3.044	2.994	2.946	2.899	2.854	2.809
19	3.583	3.515	3.448	3.383	3.321	3.262	3.205	3.150	3.096	3.044	2.994	2.945	2.899	2.854	2.809
20	3.584	3.516	3.447	3.384	3.322	3.262	3.205	3.150	3.096	3.044	2.993	2.946	2.899	2.854	2.809
21	3.583	3.515	3.448	3.383	3.321	3.262	3.205	3.150	3.096	3.044	2.994	2.945	2.899	2.854	2.809
22	3.584	3.516	3.447	3.384	3.322	3.262	3.205	3.150	3.096	3.044	2.993	2.946	2.898	2.854	2.809
23	3.583	3.515	3.448	3.383	3.321	3.262	3.205	3.150	3.096	3.044	2.994	2.945	2.899	2.854	2.809
24	3.584	3.516	3.447	3.384	3.322	3.262	3.205	3.151	3.096	3.044	2.993	2.946	2.898	2.854	2.809
25	3.583	3.515	3.448	3.383	3.321	3.262	3.205	3.150	3.096	3.044	2.994	2.945	2.899	2.854	2.810
26	1.792	3.516	3.447	3.384	3.322	3.262	3.205	3.151	3.096	3.044	2.993	2.946	2.898	2.854	2.809
27			1.724	3.383	3.321	3.262	3.205	3.151	3.096	3.044	2.994	2.945	2.899	2.853	2.810
28					1.661	1.263	1.602	3.150	3.096	3.044	2.993	2.946	2.898	2.854	2.809
29									3.095	3.044	2.994	2.945	2.899	2.853	2.809
30									1.548	3.043	2.993	2.946	2.898	2.854	2.810
31											1.497	2.945	2.899	2.853	2.809
32													1.449	2.854	2.810
33														2.853	1.405

and the Recovery Period is:

the Depreciation Rate is:

If the Recovery Year is:	32.5	33.0	33.5	34.0	34.5	35.0	35.5	36.0	36.5	37.0	37.5	38.0	38.5	39.0	39.5
1	2.308	2.273	2.239	2.206	2.174	2.143	2.113	2.083	2.055	2.027	2.000	1.974	1.948	1.923	1.899
2	4.509	4.442	4.377	4.314	4.253	4.194	4.136	4.080	4.025	3.972	3.920	3.869	3.820	3.772	3.725
3	4.301	4.240	4.181	4.124	4.068	4.014	3.961	3.910	3.860	3.811	3.763	3.717	3.671	3.627	3.584
4	4.102	4.048	3.994	3.942	3.892	3.842	3.794	3.747	3.701	3.656	3.613	3.570	3.528	3.488	3.448
5	3.913	3.864	3.815	3.768	3.722	3.677	3.634	3.591	3.549	3.508	3.468	3.429	3.391	3.353	3.317
6	3.732	3.688	3.645	3.602	3.560	3.520	3.480	3.441	3.403	3.366	3.329	3.294	3.259	3.225	3.191
7	3.560	3.520	3.481	3.443	3.406	3.369	3.333	3.298	3.263	3.229	3.196	3.164	3.132	3.100	3.070
8	3.396	3.360	3.325	3.291	3.258	3.225	3.192	3.160	3.129	3.099	3.068	3.039	3.010	2.981	2.953
9	3.239	3.208	3.177	3.146	3.116	3.086	3.057	3.029	3.001	2.973	2.946	2.919	2.893	2.867	2.841
10	3.090	3.062	3.034	3.007	2.980	2.954	2.928	2.903	2.877	2.852	2.828	2.804	2.780	2.756	2.733
11	2.947	2.923	2.898	2.875	2.851	2.828	2.804	2.782	2.759	2.737	2.715	2.693	2.671	2.650	2.629
12	2.811	2.790	2.769	2.748	2.727	2.706	2.686	2.666	2.646	2.626	2.606	2.587	2.567	2.548	2.529
13	2.766	2.725	2.685	2.646	2.608	2.590	2.572	2.555	2.537	2.519	2.502	2.485	2.467	2.450	2.433
14	2.766	2.725	2.685	2.646	2.608	2.571	2.535	2.500	2.466	2.434	2.402	2.386	2.371	2.356	2.341
15	2.766	2.725	2.685	2.646	2.608	2.571	2.535	2.500	2.466	2.434	2.402	2.370	2.340	2.310	2.281
16	2.766	2.725	2.685	2.646	2.608	2.571	2.535	2.500	2.466	2.434	2.402	2.370	2.340	2.310	2.281
17	2.766	2.725	2.685	2.646	2.608	2.571	2.535	2.500	2.467	2.434	2.402	2.370	2.340	2.310	2.281
18	2.766	2.725	2.685	2.646	2.609	2.571	2.535	2.500	2.466	2.434	2.402	2.370	2.340	2.310	2.281
19	2.766	2.725	2.685	2.646	2.608	2.571	2.535	2.500	2.467	2.434	2.402	2.370	2.340	2.310	2.281
20	2.766	2.725	2.685	2.646	2.609	2.571	2.535	2.500	2.466	2.434	2.402	2.370	2.340	2.310	2.281
21	2.766	2.725	2.685	2.646	2.608	2.571	2.535	2.500	2.467	2.434	2.402	2.370	2.340	2.310	2.281
22	2.766	2.725	2.685	2.646	2.609	2.571	2.535	2.500	2.466	2.434	2.402	2.370	2.340	2.310	2.281
23	2.766	2.725	2.685	2.646	2.608	2.571	2.535	2.500	2.467	2.434	2.402	2.370	2.340	2.310	2.281
24	2.767	2.724	2.684	2.646	2.609	2.571	2.535	2.500	2.466	2.433	2.402	2.370	2.340	2.310	2.281
25	2.766	2.725	2.685	2.646	2.608	2.571	2.535	2.500	2.467	2.434	2.402	2.370	2.339	2.310	2.281
26	2.767	2.724	2.684	2.646	2.609	2.571	2.535	2.500	2.466	2.433	2.402	2.370	2.340	2.310	2.281
27	2.766	2.725	2.685	2.646	2.608	2.572	2.536	2.500	2.467	2.434	2.402	2.370	2.339	2.310	2.281
28	2.767	2.724	2.684	2.646	2.609	2.571	2.535	2.501	2.466	2.433	2.402	2.370	2.340	2.310	2.281
29	2.766	2.725	2.685	2.646	2.608	2.572	2.536	2.500	2.467	2.434	2.402	2.370	2.339	2.310	2.281
30	2.767	2.724	2.684	2.646	2.609	2.571	2.535	2.501	2.466	2.433	2.402	2.371	2.340	2.310	2.281
31	2.766	2.725	2.685	2.646	2.608	2.572	2.536	2.500	2.467	2.434	2.401	2.370	2.339	2.310	2.281
32	2.767	2.724	2.684	2.646	2.609	2.571	2.535	2.501	2.466	2.433	2.402	2.371	2.340	2.310	2.281
33	2.766	2.725	2.685	2.646	2.608	2.572	2.536	2.500	2.467	2.434	2.401	2.370	2.339	2.310	2.281
34		1.362	2.684	2.645	2.609	2.571	2.535	2.501	2.466	2.433	2.402	2.371	2.340	2.310	2.281
35				1.323	2.608	2.572	2.536	2.500	2.467	2.434	2.401	2.370	2.339	2.310	2.281
36						1.286	2.535	2.501	2.466	2.433	2.402	2.371	2.340	2.310	2.281
37								1.250	2.467	2.434	2.401	2.370	2.339	2.310	2.281
38										1.217	2.402	2.371	2.340	2.310	2.281
39												1.185	2.339	2.310	2.282
40														1.155	2.281

and the Recovery Period is:

the Depreciation Rate is:

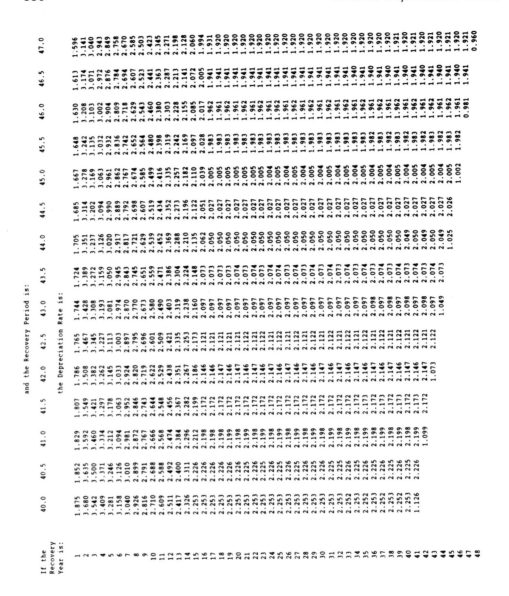

If the Recovery Year is:	40.0	40.5	41.0	41.5	42.0	42.5	43.0	43.5	44.0	44.5	45.0	45.5	46.0	46.5	47.0
1	1.875	1.852	1.829	1.807	1.786	1.765	1.744	1.724	1.705	1.685	1.667	1.648	1.630	1.613	1.596
2	3.680	3.635	3.592	3.549	3.508	3.467	3.428	3.389	3.351	3.314	3.278	3.242	3.208	3.174	3.141
3	3.542	3.500	3.460	3.421	3.382	3.345	3.308	3.272	3.237	3.202	3.169	3.135	3.103	3.071	3.040
4	3.409	3.371	3.334	3.297	3.262	3.227	3.193	3.159	3.126	3.094	3.063	3.032	3.002	2.972	2.943
5	3.281	3.246	3.212	3.178	3.145	3.113	3.081	3.050	3.020	2.990	2.961	2.932	2.904	2.876	2.849
6	3.158	3.126	3.094	3.063	3.033	3.003	2.974	2.945	2.917	2.889	2.862	2.836	2.809	2.784	2.758
7	3.040	3.010	2.981	2.952	2.924	2.897	2.870	2.843	2.817	2.792	2.767	2.742	2.718	2.694	2.670
8	2.926	2.899	2.872	2.846	2.820	2.795	2.770	2.745	2.721	2.698	2.674	2.652	2.629	2.607	2.585
9	2.816	2.791	2.767	2.743	2.719	2.696	2.673	2.651	2.629	2.607	2.585	2.564	2.543	2.523	2.503
10	2.710	2.688	2.666	2.644	2.622	2.601	2.580	2.559	2.539	2.519	2.499	2.480	2.460	2.441	2.423
11	2.609	2.588	2.568	2.548	2.529	2.509	2.490	2.471	2.452	2.434	2.416	2.398	2.380	2.363	2.345
12	2.511	2.492	2.474	2.456	2.438	2.421	2.403	2.386	2.369	2.352	2.335	2.319	2.303	2.287	2.271
13	2.417	2.400	2.384	2.367	2.351	2.335	2.319	2.304	2.288	2.273	2.257	2.242	2.228	2.213	2.198
14	2.326	2.311	2.296	2.282	2.267	2.253	2.238	2.224	2.210	2.196	2.182	2.169	2.155	2.141	2.128
15	2.253	2.226	2.212	2.199	2.186	2.173	2.160	2.148	2.135	2.122	2.110	2.097	2.085	2.072	2.060
16	2.253	2.226	2.198	2.172	2.146	2.121	2.097	2.073	2.062	2.051	2.039	2.028	2.017	2.005	1.994
17	2.253	2.226	2.198	2.172	2.146	2.121	2.097	2.073	2.050	2.027	2.005	1.983	1.962	1.941	1.931
18	2.253	2.226	2.198	2.172	2.146	2.121	2.097	2.073	2.050	2.027	2.005	1.983	1.961	1.941	1.920
19	2.253	2.226	2.199	2.172	2.146	2.121	2.097	2.073	2.050	2.027	2.005	1.983	1.962	1.941	1.920
20	2.253	2.225	2.198	2.172	2.147	2.121	2.097	2.074	2.050	2.027	2.005	1.983	1.962	1.941	1.920
21	2.253	2.225	2.199	2.172	2.146	2.121	2.097	2.073	2.050	2.027	2.005	1.983	1.962	1.941	1.920
22	2.253	2.226	2.198	2.172	2.147	2.121	2.097	2.073	2.050	2.027	2.005	1.983	1.961	1.941	1.920
23	2.253	2.225	2.199	2.172	2.146	2.122	2.097	2.074	2.050	2.027	2.005	1.983	1.961	1.941	1.920
24	2.253	2.226	2.198	2.172	2.147	2.121	2.097	2.073	2.050	2.027	2.005	1.983	1.961	1.941	1.920
25	2.253	2.226	2.199	2.172	2.146	2.121	2.097	2.074	2.050	2.027	2.004	1.983	1.961	1.941	1.920
26	2.253	2.225	2.198	2.172	2.147	2.121	2.097	2.073	2.050	2.027	2.004	1.983	1.961	1.941	1.920
27	2.253	2.226	2.199	2.172	2.146	2.121	2.097	2.073	2.050	2.027	2.005	1.983	1.962	1.941	1.920
28	2.253	2.225	2.198	2.172	2.147	2.122	2.097	2.073	2.050	2.027	2.005	1.983	1.961	1.941	1.920
29	2.253	2.226	2.199	2.172	2.146	2.121	2.097	2.074	2.050	2.027	2.004	1.983	1.961	1.941	1.920
30	2.253	2.225	2.199	2.172	2.146	2.121	2.097	2.073	2.050	2.027	2.004	1.983	1.962	1.941	1.920
31	2.253	2.226	2.198	2.172	2.147	2.121	2.097	2.074	2.050	2.027	2.005	1.983	1.961	1.941	1.920
32	2.253	2.225	2.199	2.172	2.146	2.122	2.097	2.073	2.050	2.027	2.005	1.983	1.962	1.941	1.920
33	2.253	2.225	2.198	2.172	2.147	2.121	2.097	2.073	2.050	2.027	2.004	1.983	1.961	1.941	1.920
34	2.252	2.226	2.199	2.172	2.146	2.122	2.097	2.074	2.050	2.027	2.005	1.983	1.961	1.941	1.920
35	2.253	2.225	2.198	2.172	2.147	2.121	2.098	2.073	2.050	2.027	2.005	1.983	1.961	1.941	1.920
36	2.252	2.226	2.199	2.172	2.146	2.121	2.097	2.074	2.050	2.027	2.004	1.983	1.962	1.941	1.920
37	2.252	2.225	2.199	2.172	2.147	2.122	2.098	2.073	2.050	2.027	2.005	1.982	1.961	1.940	1.920
38	2.253	2.225	2.198	2.173	2.146	2.121	2.097	2.074	2.050	2.027	2.004	1.982	1.961	1.941	1.920
39	2.252	2.226	2.199	2.172	2.147	2.122	2.098	2.073	2.050	2.027	2.004	1.983	1.962	1.940	1.921
40	2.253	2.225	2.198	2.173	2.146	2.121	2.097	2.073	2.050	2.027	2.005	1.982	1.961	1.941	1.920
41	1.126	2.226	2.199	2.172	2.147	2.122	2.098	2.074	2.049	2.027	2.004	1.983	1.962	1.940	1.921
42		2.225	1.099	2.173	2.146	2.121	2.097	2.073	2.050	2.027	2.005	1.982	1.962	1.941	1.921
43				2.172	1.073	2.122	2.097	2.074	2.049	2.027	2.005	1.982	1.961	1.940	1.920
44						2.122	1.049	2.073	2.050	2.027	2.004	1.983	1.961	1.940	1.920
45								2.073	1.025	2.027	2.004	1.982	1.961	1.940	1.920
46										2.026	1.002	1.983	1.961	1.941	1.920
47												1.982	0.981	1.941	1.920
48														1.941	0.960

and the Recovery Period is:
the Depreciation Rate is:

If the Recovery Year is:	47.5	48.0	48.5	49.0	49.5	50.0
1	1.579	1.563	1.546	1.531	1.515	1.500
2	3.108	3.076	3.045	3.014	2.984	2.955
3	3.010	2.980	2.951	2.922	2.894	2.866
4	2.915	2.887	2.860	2.833	2.806	2.780
5	2.823	2.797	2.771	2.746	2.721	2.697
6	2.734	2.709	2.685	2.662	2.639	2.616
7	2.647	2.625	2.602	2.580	2.559	2.538
8	2.564	2.543	2.522	2.501	2.481	2.461
9	2.483	2.463	2.444	2.425	2.406	2.388
10	2.404	2.386	2.368	2.351	2.333	2.316
11	2.328	2.312	2.295	2.279	2.262	2.246
12	2.255	2.239	2.224	2.209	2.194	2.179
13	2.184	2.169	2.155	2.141	2.127	2.114
14	2.115	2.102	2.089	2.076	2.063	2.050
15	2.048	2.036	2.024	2.012	2.000	1.989
16	1.983	1.972	1.961	1.951	1.940	1.929
17	1.921	1.911	1.901	1.891	1.881	1.871
18	1.900	1.880	1.861	1.842	1.824	1.815
19	1.900	1.880	1.861	1.842	1.824	1.806
20	1.900	1.880	1.861	1.842	1.824	1.806
21	1.900	1.880	1.861	1.842	1.824	1.806
22	1.900	1.880	1.861	1.842	1.824	1.806
23	1.900	1.880	1.861	1.842	1.824	1.806
24	1.900	1.880	1.861	1.842	1.824	1.806
25	1.900	1.880	1.861	1.842	1.824	1.806
26	1.900	1.880	1.861	1.842	1.824	1.806

and the Recovery Period is:
the Depreciation Rate is:

If the Recovery Year is:	47.5	48.0	48.5	49.0	49.5	50.0
27	1.900	1.880	1.861	1.842	1.824	1.806
28	1.900	1.880	1.861	1.842	1.824	1.806
29	1.900	1.880	1.861	1.843	1.824	1.806
30	1.900	1.881	1.861	1.842	1.824	1.806
31	1.900	1.880	1.861	1.842	1.824	1.806
32	1.900	1.881	1.861	1.842	1.824	1.806
33	1.900	1.880	1.861	1.843	1.824	1.806
34	1.900	1.881	1.861	1.842	1.824	1.806
35	1.900	1.880	1.861	1.843	1.824	1.806
36	1.900	1.881	1.861	1.842	1.824	1.806
37	1.900	1.880	1.861	1.843	1.824	1.806
38	1.900	1.881	1.861	1.842	1.824	1.806
39	1.900	1.880	1.861	1.843	1.824	1.806
40	1.900	1.881	1.861	1.842	1.824	1.806
41	1.900	1.880	1.861	1.843	1.824	1.806
42	1.900	1.881	1.862	1.842	1.824	1.806
43	1.900	1.880	1.861	1.843	1.824	1.805
44	1.900	1.881	1.862	1.842	1.824	1.806
45	1.900	1.880	1.861	1.843	1.824	1.805
46	1.900	1.881	1.862	1.842	1.825	1.805
47	1.900	1.880	1.861	1.843	1.824	1.806
48	1.900	1.881	1.862	1.842	1.825	1.805
49	1.900	1.880	1.861	1.843	1.824	1.805
50	1.899	1.880	1.862	0.921	1.825	1.806
51		0.940	1.861		1.824	0.903

TABLE 15

Alternative Minimum Tax (see section 7 of this revenue procedure)
Applicable Depreciation Method: 150 Percent Declining Balance
Switching to Straight Line
Applicable Recovery Periods: 2.5 - 50 years
Applicable Convention: Mid-quarter (property placed in service in first quarter)

and the Recovery Period is:

the Depreciation Rate is:

If the Recovery Year is:	2.5	3.0	3.5	4.0	4.5	5.0	5.5	6.0	6.5	7.0	7.5	8.0	8.5	9.0	9.5
1	52.50	43.75	37.50	32.81	29.17	26.25	23.86	21.88	20.19	18.75	17.50	16.41	15.44	14.58	13.82
2	29.23	28.13	26.79	25.20	23.61	22.13	20.77	19.53	18.42	17.41	16.50	15.67	14.92	14.24	13.61
3	18.27	25.00	21.98	19.76	17.99	16.52	15.27	14.65	14.17	13.68	13.20	12.74	12.29	11.86	11.46
4		3.12	13.73	19.76	17.99	16.52	15.28	14.06	13.03	12.16	11.42	10.77	10.20	9.89	9.65
5				2.47	11.24	16.52	15.27	14.06	13.03	12.16	11.42	10.77	10.19	9.64	9.15
6						2.06	9.55	14.06	13.02	12.16	11.41	10.76	10.20	9.65	9.15
7								1.76	8.14	12.16	11.42	10.77	10.19	9.64	9.15
8										1.52	7.13	10.76	10.20	9.65	9.15
9												1.35	6.37	9.64	9.14
10														1.21	5.72

and the Recovery Period is:

the Depreciation Rate is:

If the Recovery Year is:	10.0	10.5	11.0	11.5	12.0	12.5	13.0	13.5	14.0	14.5	15.0	15.5	16.0	16.5	17.0
1	13.13	12.50	11.93	11.41	10.94	10.50	10.10	9.72	9.38	9.05	8.75	8.47	8.20	7.95	7.72
2	13.03	12.50	12.01	11.56	11.13	10.74	10.37	10.03	9.71	9.41	9.13	8.86	8.61	8.37	8.14
3	11.08	10.71	10.37	10.05	9.74	9.45	9.18	8.92	8.67	8.44	8.21	8.00	7.80	7.61	7.42
4	9.41	9.18	8.96	8.74	8.52	8.32	8.12	7.93	7.74	7.56	7.39	7.23	7.07	6.92	6.77
5	8.71	8.32	7.96	7.64	7.46	7.32	7.18	7.04	6.91	6.78	6.65	6.53	6.41	6.29	6.17
6	8.71	8.32	7.96	7.64	7.33	7.04	6.77	6.53	6.31	6.10	5.99	5.89	5.80	5.71	5.63
7	8.71	8.32	7.96	7.64	7.33	7.04	6.78	6.54	6.31	6.11	5.90	5.72	5.54	5.38	5.23
8	8.71	8.32	7.96	7.64	7.33	7.04	6.77	6.53	6.31	6.10	5.91	5.72	5.54	5.38	5.23
9	8.71	8.32	7.96	7.64	7.33	7.04	6.78	6.54	6.31	6.11	5.90	5.71	5.54	5.38	5.23
10	8.71	8.31	7.97	7.63	7.32	7.04	6.77	6.53	6.31	6.10	5.91	5.72	5.54	5.38	5.23
11	1.09	5.20	7.96	7.64	7.33	7.04	6.78	6.54	6.31	6.11	5.90	5.71	5.55	5.38	5.22
12			1.00	4.77	7.32	7.03	6.77	6.53	6.32	6.11	5.90	5.72	5.54	5.38	5.23
13					0.92	4.40	6.78	6.54	6.31	6.10	5.91	5.71	5.55	5.38	5.22
14							0.85	4.08	6.31	6.11	5.90	5.72	5.54	5.37	5.23
15									0.79	3.82	5.91	5.71	5.55	5.38	5.22
16											0.74	3.57	5.54	5.38	5.23
17													0.69	3.36	5.22
18															0.65

and the Recovery Period is:

the Depreciation Rate is:

If the Recovery Year is:	17.5	18.0	18.5	19.0	19.5	20.0	20.5	21.0	21.5	22.0	22.5	23.0	23.5	24.0	24.5
1	7.50	7.29	7.09	6.91	6.73	6.563	6.402	6.250	6.105	5.966	5.833	5.707	5.585	5.469	5.357
2	7.93	7.73	7.53	7.35	7.17	7.008	6.849	6.696	6.551	6.411	6.278	6.150	6.026	5.908	5.794
3	7.25	7.08	6.92	6.77	6.62	6.482	6.347	6.218	6.094	5.974	5.859	5.748	5.642	5.539	5.440
4	6.63	6.49	6.36	6.23	6.11	5.996	5.883	5.774	5.669	5.567	5.469	5.374	5.282	5.193	5.107
5	6.06	5.95	5.85	5.74	5.64	5.546	5.453	5.362	5.273	5.187	5.104	5.023	4.945	4.868	4.794
6	5.54	5.45	5.37	5.29	5.21	5.130	5.054	4.979	4.905	4.834	4.764	4.696	4.629	4.564	4.500
7	5.08	5.00	4.94	4.87	4.81	4.746	4.684	4.623	4.563	4.504	4.446	4.389	4.333	4.279	4.225
8	5.08	4.94	4.81	4.69	4.57	4.459	4.354	4.293	4.245	4.197	4.150	4.103	4.057	4.011	3.966
9	5.08	4.94	4.81	4.69	4.57	4.459	4.354	4.252	4.154	4.061	3.972	3.888	3.808	3.761	3.723
10	5.08	4.95	4.81	4.69	4.57	4.459	4.354	4.252	4.154	4.061	3.973	3.888	3.808	3.729	3.654
11	5.08	4.94	4.81	4.69	4.57	4.459	4.354	4.252	4.154	4.061	3.972	3.888	3.808	3.729	3.654
12	5.09	4.95	4.81	4.69	4.57	4.460	4.354	4.252	4.154	4.061	3.973	3.888	3.808	3.730	3.654
13	5.08	4.94	4.81	4.69	4.57	4.459	4.355	4.252	4.154	4.061	3.972	3.888	3.808	3.729	3.654
14	5.09	4.95	4.82	4.68	4.57	4.460	4.354	4.252	4.154	4.061	3.973	3.888	3.808	3.730	3.654
15	5.08	4.94	4.81	4.69	4.57	4.459	4.355	4.252	4.154	4.061	3.972	3.888	3.808	3.729	3.654
16	5.09	4.95	4.81	4.69	4.57	4.460	4.354	4.252	4.154	4.061	3.973	3.889	3.808	3.730	3.654
17	5.08	4.94	4.82	4.68	4.57	4.459	4.355	4.252	4.153	4.061	3.972	3.888	3.808	3.729	3.654
18	3.18	4.94	4.81	4.69	4.57	4.460	4.354	4.251	4.154	4.061	3.973	3.889	3.808	3.730	3.654
19		0.62	3.01	4.68	4.58	4.459	4.355	4.252	4.153	4.061	3.972	3.888	3.808	3.729	3.654
20				0.59	4.57	4.460	4.354	4.251	4.154	4.060	3.973	3.889	3.808	3.730	3.654
21					2.86	0.557	2.722	4.252	4.153	4.061	3.972	3.888	3.808	3.729	3.654
22								0.531	2.596	4.060	3.973	3.889	3.809	3.730	3.654
23										0.508	2.483	3.888	3.809	3.729	3.654
24												0.486	2.380	3.730	3.654
25														0.466	2.284

and the Recovery Period is:

the Depreciation Rate is:

If the Recovery Year is:	25.0	25.5	26.0	26.5	27.0	27.5	28.0	28.5	29.0	29.5	30.0	30.5	31.0	31.5	32.0
1	5.250	5.147	5.048	4.953	4.861	4.773	4.688	4.605	4.526	4.449	4.375	4.303	4.234	4.167	4.102
2	5.685	5.580	5.478	5.380	5.286	5.194	5.106	5.021	4.938	4.859	4.781	4.706	4.634	4.563	4.495
3	5.344	5.251	5.162	5.075	4.992	4.911	4.832	4.757	4.683	4.611	4.542	4.475	4.410	4.346	4.285
4	5.023	4.942	4.864	4.788	4.714	4.643	4.574	4.506	4.441	4.377	4.315	4.255	4.196	4.139	4.084
5	4.722	4.652	4.584	4.517	4.453	4.390	4.329	4.269	4.211	4.154	4.099	4.046	3.993	3.942	3.892
6	4.439	4.378	4.319	4.262	4.205	4.150	4.097	4.044	3.993	3.943	3.894	3.847	3.800	3.754	3.710
7	4.172	4.121	4.070	4.020	3.972	3.924	3.877	3.831	3.787	3.743	3.700	3.657	3.616	3.576	3.536
8	3.922	3.878	3.835	3.793	3.751	3.710	3.669	3.630	3.591	3.552	3.515	3.478	3.441	3.405	3.370
9	3.687	3.650	3.614	3.578	3.543	3.508	3.473	3.439	3.405	3.372	3.339	3.307	3.275	3.243	3.212
10	3.582	3.513	3.447	3.383	3.346	3.316	3.287	3.258	3.229	3.200	3.172	3.144	3.116	3.089	3.062
11	3.582	3.513	3.447	3.384	3.321	3.261	3.204	3.148	3.095	3.044	3.013	2.989	2.965	2.942	2.918
12	3.582	3.513	3.447	3.383	3.321	3.261	3.204	3.148	3.095	3.044	2.994	2.945	2.898	2.853	2.809
13	3.582	3.513	3.447	3.384	3.321	3.261	3.204	3.149	3.095	3.044	2.994	2.945	2.898	2.853	2.809
14	3.582	3.513	3.447	3.383	3.321	3.261	3.204	3.148	3.095	3.044	2.994	2.945	2.898	2.853	2.809
15	3.582	3.513	3.447	3.384	3.321	3.261	3.204	3.149	3.095	3.044	2.994	2.945	2.898	2.852	2.809
16	3.582	3.513	3.447	3.383	3.321	3.261	3.204	3.148	3.095	3.044	2.994	2.945	2.898	2.853	2.809
17	3.582	3.513	3.447	3.384	3.321	3.262	3.204	3.149	3.095	3.044	2.994	2.945	2.898	2.852	2.809
18	3.582	3.513	3.447	3.383	3.321	3.261	3.204	3.148	3.095	3.044	2.994	2.945	2.898	2.853	2.809
19	3.581	3.513	3.447	3.384	3.321	3.262	3.204	3.149	3.095	3.044	2.994	2.945	2.898	2.852	2.809
20	3.582	3.513	3.447	3.383	3.321	3.261	3.204	3.148	3.095	3.044	2.994	2.945	2.898	2.853	2.809
21	3.581	3.513	3.447	3.384	3.322	3.262	3.203	3.149	3.095	3.044	2.993	2.945	2.898	2.852	2.808
22	3.582	3.512	3.446	3.383	3.321	3.261	3.204	3.148	3.096	3.044	2.994	2.945	2.898	2.853	2.809
23	3.581	3.513	3.447	3.384	3.322	3.262	3.203	3.149	3.095	3.044	2.993	2.945	2.898	2.852	2.808
24	3.581	3.512	3.446	3.383	3.321	3.261	3.204	3.148	3.096	3.044	2.994	2.945	2.898	2.852	2.808
25	3.582	3.513	3.447	3.384	3.322	3.262	3.203	3.149	3.095	3.044	2.993	2.945	2.898	2.852	2.809
26	0.448	2.195	3.446	3.383	3.321	3.261	3.204	3.148	3.096	3.044	2.994	2.944	2.898	2.853	2.808
27			0.431	2.115	3.322	3.262	3.203	3.149	3.095	3.044	2.993	2.945	2.898	2.852	2.809
28					0.415	2.038	3.204	3.148	3.096	3.045	2.994	2.944	2.897	2.853	2.808
29							0.400	1.968	3.095	3.044	2.993	2.945	2.898	2.852	2.809
30									0.387	1.903	2.994	2.944	2.897	2.853	2.809
31											0.374	1.840	2.898	2.852	2.808
32													0.362	2.852	2.809
33														1.783	0.351

and the Recovery Period is:

the Depreciation Rate is:

If the Recovery Year is:	32.5	33.0	33.5	34.0	34.5	35.0	35.5	36.0	36.5	37.0	37.5	38.0	38.5	39.0	39.5
1	4.038	3.977	3.918	3.860	3.804	3.750	3.697	3.646	3.596	3.547	3.500	3.454	3.409	3.365	3.323
2	4.429	4.365	4.302	4.241	4.182	4.125	4.069	4.015	3.962	3.910	3.860	3.811	3.763	3.717	3.671
3	4.225	4.166	4.110	4.054	4.001	3.948	3.897	3.847	3.799	3.752	3.706	3.661	3.617	3.574	3.532
4	4.030	3.977	3.926	3.876	3.827	3.779	3.733	3.687	3.643	3.600	3.557	3.516	3.476	3.436	3.398
5	3.844	3.796	3.750	3.705	3.660	3.617	3.575	3.534	3.493	3.454	3.415	3.377	3.340	3.304	3.269
6	3.666	3.624	3.582	3.541	3.501	3.462	3.424	3.386	3.350	3.314	3.278	3.244	3.210	3.177	3.145
7	3.497	3.459	3.421	3.375	3.343	3.312	3.281	3.245	3.212	3.179	3.147	3.116	3.085	3.055	3.025
8	3.336	3.302	3.268	3.235	3.203	3.172	3.141	3.110	3.080	3.050	3.021	2.993	2.965	2.937	2.910
9	3.182	3.152	3.122	3.093	3.064	3.036	3.008	2.980	2.953	2.927	2.901	2.875	2.849	2.824	2.800
10	3.035	3.008	2.982	2.956	2.931	2.906	2.881	2.856	2.832	2.808	2.785	2.761	2.738	2.716	2.693
11	2.895	2.872	2.849	2.826	2.803	2.781	2.759	2.737	2.716	2.694	2.673	2.652	2.632	2.611	2.591
12	2.766	2.741	2.721	2.701	2.682	2.662	2.642	2.623	2.604	2.585	2.566	2.548	2.529	2.511	2.493
13	2.766	2.725	2.684	2.645	2.607	2.571	2.535	2.514	2.497	2.480	2.464	2.447	2.431	2.414	2.398
14	2.766	2.725	2.684	2.645	2.607	2.571	2.535	2.500	2.466	2.433	2.401	2.370	2.340	2.322	2.307
15	2.766	2.725	2.684	2.645	2.608	2.571	2.535	2.500	2.466	2.433	2.401	2.370	2.340	2.310	2.281
16	2.766	2.725	2.684	2.645	2.607	2.571	2.535	2.500	2.466	2.433	2.401	2.370	2.340	2.310	2.281
17	2.766	2.725	2.684	2.645	2.608	2.571	2.535	2.500	2.466	2.433	2.401	2.370	2.340	2.310	2.281
18	2.766	2.725	2.684	2.645	2.607	2.571	2.535	2.500	2.466	2.433	2.401	2.370	2.340	2.310	2.281
19	2.766	2.725	2.685	2.645	2.608	2.571	2.535	2.500	2.466	2.433	2.401	2.370	2.340	2.310	2.281
20	2.767	2.725	2.684	2.645	2.607	2.571	2.535	2.500	2.466	2.433	2.401	2.370	2.340	2.310	2.281
21	2.766	2.725	2.684	2.645	2.608	2.571	2.535	2.500	2.466	2.433	2.401	2.370	2.340	2.310	2.281
22	2.767	2.725	2.685	2.645	2.608	2.571	2.535	2.500	2.466	2.433	2.401	2.370	2.340	2.310	2.281
23	2.766	2.725	2.684	2.645	2.607	2.571	2.536	2.501	2.466	2.433	2.401	2.370	2.340	2.310	2.281
24	2.767	2.724	2.685	2.646	2.608	2.570	2.535	2.500	2.466	2.433	2.401	2.370	2.339	2.310	2.281
25	2.767	2.725	2.684	2.645	2.607	2.571	2.536	2.501	2.466	2.433	2.401	2.370	2.340	2.310	2.281
26	2.766	2.724	2.685	2.646	2.608	2.570	2.535	2.500	2.466	2.433	2.401	2.370	2.339	2.310	2.281
27	2.767	2.725	2.684	2.645	2.607	2.571	2.536	2.501	2.466	2.433	2.401	2.370	2.340	2.310	2.281
28	2.767	2.724	2.685	2.646	2.608	2.570	2.535	2.500	2.466	2.433	2.401	2.370	2.339	2.310	2.281
29	2.766	2.724	2.684	2.645	2.607	2.571	2.536	2.501	2.466	2.433	2.401	2.370	2.340	2.310	2.281
30	2.767	2.725	2.685	2.645	2.608	2.570	2.535	2.500	2.467	2.434	2.401	2.370	2.339	2.310	2.280
31	2.766	2.724	2.684	2.646	2.607	2.571	2.536	2.501	2.466	2.433	2.401	2.370	2.340	2.310	2.281
32	2.767	2.725	2.685	2.645	2.608	2.570	2.535	2.500	2.467	2.433	2.401	2.370	2.339	2.310	2.281
33	1.729	2.724	2.684	2.646	2.607	2.571	2.536	2.501	2.466	2.434	2.402	2.370	2.340	2.310	2.281
34		0.341	1.678	2.645	2.608	2.570	2.535	2.500	2.467	2.433	2.401	2.370	2.339	2.310	2.281
35				0.331	1.630	2.571	2.536	2.501	2.466	2.434	2.401	2.370	2.340	2.310	2.280
36						0.321	1.585	2.500	2.467	2.433	2.401	2.370	2.339	2.310	2.281
37								0.313	1.542	2.434	2.401	2.370	2.340	2.310	2.281
38										0.304	1.501	2.370	2.339	2.310	2.280
39												0.296	1.462	2.309	2.281
40														0.289	1.425

and the Recovery Period is:

the Depreciation Rate is:

If the Recovery Year is:	40.0	40.5	41.0	41.5	42.0	42.5	43.0	43.5	44.0	44.5	45.0	45.5	46.0	46.5	47.0
1	3.281	3.241	3.201	3.163	3.125	3.088	3.052	3.017	2.983	2.949	2.917	2.885	2.853	2.823	2.793
2	3.627	3.584	3.541	3.500	3.460	3.420	3.382	3.344	3.307	3.271	3.236	3.202	3.168	3.135	3.102
3	3.491	3.451	3.412	3.374	3.336	3.300	3.264	3.229	3.195	3.161	3.128	3.096	3.065	3.034	3.003
4	3.360	3.323	3.287	3.252	3.217	3.183	3.150	3.118	3.086	3.055	3.024	2.994	2.965	2.936	2.908
5	3.234	3.200	3.167	3.134	3.102	3.071	3.040	3.010	2.981	2.952	2.923	2.895	2.868	2.841	2.815
6	3.113	3.082	3.051	3.021	2.991	2.963	2.934	2.906	2.879	2.852	2.826	2.800	2.774	2.749	2.725
7	2.996	2.967	2.939	2.912	2.885	2.858	2.832	2.806	2.781	2.756	2.732	2.708	2.684	2.661	2.638
8	2.884	2.857	2.832	2.806	2.782	2.757	2.733	2.709	2.686	2.663	2.640	2.618	2.596	2.575	2.554
9	2.776	2.752	2.728	2.705	2.682	2.660	2.638	2.616	2.594	2.573	2.552	2.532	2.512	2.492	2.472
10	2.671	2.650	2.628	2.607	2.586	2.566	2.546	2.526	2.506	2.487	2.467	2.448	2.430	2.411	2.393
11	2.571	2.552	2.532	2.513	2.494	2.475	2.457	2.439	2.421	2.403	2.385	2.368	2.351	2.334	2.317
12	2.475	2.457	2.440	2.422	2.405	2.388	2.371	2.354	2.338	2.322	2.306	2.290	2.274	2.258	2.243
13	2.382	2.366	2.350	2.335	2.319	2.304	2.288	2.273	2.258	2.243	2.229	2.214	2.200	2.186	2.171
14	2.293	2.278	2.264	2.250	2.236	2.222	2.209	2.195	2.181	2.168	2.154	2.141	2.128	2.115	2.102
15	2.252	2.225	2.198	2.172	2.156	2.144	2.132	2.119	2.107	2.095	2.083	2.071	2.059	2.047	2.035
16	2.252	2.225	2.198	2.172	2.147	2.121	2.097	2.073	2.050	2.027	2.013	2.002	1.992	1.981	1.970
17	2.253	2.225	2.198	2.172	2.146	2.121	2.097	2.073	2.050	2.027	2.005	1.983	1.961	1.940	1.920
18	2.252	2.225	2.198	2.172	2.147	2.121	2.097	2.073	2.050	2.027	2.005	1.983	1.961	1.940	1.920
19	2.253	2.225	2.198	2.172	2.146	2.121	2.097	2.073	2.050	2.027	2.005	1.983	1.961	1.940	1.920
20	2.252	2.225	2.198	2.172	2.147	2.121	2.097	2.073	2.050	2.027	2.005	1.983	1.961	1.940	1.920
21	2.253	2.225	2.198	2.172	2.146	2.121	2.097	2.073	2.050	2.027	2.005	1.983	1.961	1.940	1.920
22	2.252	2.225	2.198	2.172	2.147	2.121	2.097	2.073	2.050	2.027	2.005	1.983	1.961	1.940	1.920
23	2.253	2.225	2.198	2.172	2.146	2.121	2.097	2.073	2.050	2.027	2.005	1.983	1.961	1.940	1.920
24	2.252	2.225	2.198	2.172	2.147	2.121	2.097	2.073	2.050	2.027	2.005	1.983	1.961	1.940	1.920
25	2.253	2.225	2.198	2.172	2.146	2.121	2.097	2.073	2.050	2.027	2.005	1.983	1.961	1.940	1.920
26	2.252	2.225	2.198	2.172	2.147	2.122	2.097	2.073	2.050	2.027	2.005	1.983	1.961	1.940	1.920
27	2.253	2.225	2.198	2.172	2.146	2.121	2.097	2.073	2.049	2.027	2.004	1.982	1.961	1.940	1.920
28	2.252	2.225	2.199	2.172	2.147	2.122	2.097	2.073	2.050	2.027	2.005	1.983	1.961	1.940	1.920
29	2.253	2.225	2.198	2.172	2.146	2.121	2.097	2.073	2.049	2.027	2.004	1.982	1.961	1.940	1.920
30	2.252	2.225	2.199	2.172	2.147	2.122	2.097	2.073	2.050	2.027	2.005	1.983	1.961	1.941	1.920
31	2.253	2.225	2.198	2.172	2.146	2.121	2.097	2.073	2.049	2.027	2.004	1.982	1.961	1.940	1.920
32	2.252	2.225	2.199	2.172	2.147	2.122	2.096	2.073	2.050	2.027	2.004	1.982	1.962	1.941	1.920
33	2.253	2.225	2.198	2.172	2.146	2.121	2.097	2.073	2.049	2.027	2.004	1.982	1.961	1.940	1.920
34	2.252	2.225	2.199	2.173	2.147	2.122	2.096	2.073	2.050	2.027	2.004	1.982	1.962	1.941	1.920
35	2.253	2.225	2.198	2.172	2.146	2.121	2.097	2.073	2.049	2.027	2.005	1.983	1.961	1.940	1.920
36	2.252	2.225	2.199	2.172	2.147	2.122	2.096	2.073	2.050	2.027	2.004	1.982	1.962	1.941	1.920
37	2.253	2.225	2.198	2.173	2.146	2.121	2.097	2.073	2.049	2.027	2.005	1.983	1.961	1.940	1.920
38	2.252	2.225	2.199	2.172	2.147	2.122	2.096	2.073	2.050	2.027	2.004	1.982	1.962	1.941	1.920
39	2.253	2.225	2.198	2.173	2.146	2.121	2.097	2.073	2.049	2.027	2.005	1.983	1.961	1.940	1.920
40	2.252	2.225	2.199	2.172	2.147	2.122	2.096	2.073	2.050	2.027	2.004	1.982	1.962	1.941	1.920
41	0.282	1.390	2.198	2.172	2.146	2.121	2.097	2.073	2.049	2.027	2.005	1.983	1.961	1.940	1.920
42			0.275	1.358	2.147	2.122	2.096	2.073	2.050	2.027	2.004	1.982	1.962	1.941	1.920
43					0.268	1.326	2.097	2.073	2.049	2.027	2.005	1.983	1.961	1.940	1.920
44							0.262	1.295	2.050	2.027	2.004	1.982	1.962	1.941	1.920
45									0.256	1.267	2.005	1.983	1.961	1.940	1.920
46											0.251	1.239	1.962	1.941	1.920
47													0.245	1.213	1.920
48															0.240

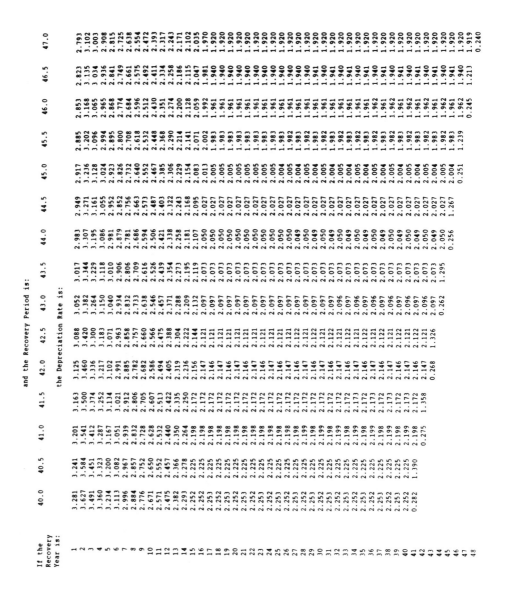

If the Recovery Year is: / and the Recovery Period is: / the Depreciation Rate is:

If the Recovery Year is:	47.5	48.0	48.5	49.0	49.5	50.0
1	2.763	2.734	2.706	2.679	2.652	2.625
2	3.071	3.040	3.009	2.979	2.950	2.921
3	2.974	2.945	2.916	2.888	2.861	2.834
4	2.880	2.853	2.826	2.800	2.774	2.749
5	2.789	2.763	2.738	2.714	2.690	2.666
6	2.701	2.677	2.654	2.631	2.608	2.586
7	2.615	2.593	2.572	2.550	2.529	2.509
8	2.533	2.512	2.492	2.472	2.453	2.433
9	2.453	2.434	2.415	2.397	2.378	2.360
10	2.375	2.358	2.340	2.323	2.306	2.290
11	2.300	2.284	2.268	2.252	2.236	2.221
12	2.228	2.213	2.198	2.183	2.169	2.154
13	2.157	2.144	2.130	2.116	2.103	2.090
14	2.089	2.077	2.064	2.052	2.039	2.027
15	2.023	2.012	2.000	1.989	1.977	1.966
16	1.959	1.949	1.938	1.928	1.917	1.907
17	1.900	1.888	1.878	1.869	1.859	1.850
18	1.900	1.880	1.861	1.842	1.824	1.806
19	1.900	1.880	1.861	1.842	1.824	1.806
20	1.900	1.880	1.861	1.842	1.824	1.806
21	1.900	1.880	1.861	1.842	1.824	1.806
22	1.900	1.880	1.861	1.842	1.824	1.806
23	1.900	1.880	1.861	1.842	1.824	1.806
24	1.900	1.880	1.861	1.842	1.824	1.806
25	1.900	1.880	1.861	1.842	1.824	1.806
26	1.900	1.880	1.861	1.842	1.824	1.806

If the Recovery Year is: / and the Recovery Period is: / the Depreciation Rate is:

If the Recovery Year is:	47.5	48.0	48.5	49.0	49.5	50.0
27	1.900	1.880	1.861	1.842	1.824	1.806
28	1.900	1.880	1.861	1.842	1.824	1.805
29	1.900	1.880	1.861	1.842	1.824	1.806
30	1.900	1.880	1.861	1.842	1.824	1.805
31	1.900	1.881	1.861	1.842	1.824	1.806
32	1.900	1.880	1.861	1.842	1.824	1.806
33	1.900	1.881	1.861	1.842	1.823	1.805
34	1.900	1.880	1.861	1.842	1.824	1.806
35	1.900	1.881	1.861	1.842	1.823	1.805
36	1.900	1.880	1.861	1.842	1.824	1.806
37	1.900	1.881	1.861	1.842	1.823	1.805
38	1.900	1.881	1.861	1.842	1.824	1.806
39	1.900	1.880	1.861	1.842	1.823	1.805
40	1.900	1.881	1.861	1.842	1.824	1.806
41	1.900	1.880	1.861	1.842	1.823	1.805
42	1.900	1.881	1.861	1.842	1.824	1.806
43	1.900	1.880	1.861	1.843	1.823	1.805
44	1.901	1.881	1.861	1.843	1.824	1.806
45	1.900	1.880	1.861	1.843	1.823	1.805
46	1.901	1.881	1.862	1.842	1.824	1.806
47	1.900	1.880	1.861	1.843	1.823	1.805
48	1.900	1.881	1.862	1.842	1.824	1.806
49	1.188	0.235	1.861	1.843	1.823	1.806
50			1.163	0.230	1.824	1.806
51					1.140	0.226

TABLE 16

Alternative Minimum Tax (see section 7 of this revenue procedure)
Applicable Depreciation Method: 150 Percent Declining Balance Switching to Straight Line
Applicable Recovery Periods: 2.5 - 50 years
Applicable Convention: Mid-quarter (property placed in service in second quarter)

and the Recovery Period is:

If the Recovery Year is:	2.5	3.0	3.5	4.0	4.5	5.0	5.5	6.0	6.5	7.0	7.5	8.0	8.5	9.0	9.5
	the Depreciation Rate is:														
1	37.50	31.25	26.79	23.44	20.83	18.75	17.05	15.63	14.42	13.39	12.50	11.72	11.03	10.42	9.87
2	37.50	34.38	31.38	28.71	26.39	24.38	22.62	21.09	19.75	18.56	17.50	16.55	15.70	14.93	14.23
3	25.00	25.00	22.31	20.15	18.36	17.06	16.45	15.82	15.19	14.58	14.00	13.45	12.93	12.44	11.98
4		9.37	19.52	20.15	18.36	16.76	15.26	14.06	13.07	12.22	11.49	10.93	10.65	10.37	10.09
5				7.55	16.06	16.76	15.26	14.06	13.07	12.22	11.49	10.82	10.19	9.64	9.16
6						6.29	13.36	14.07	13.07	12.22	11.49	10.82	10.19	9.65	9.16
7								5.27	11.43	12.23	11.48	10.83	10.19	9.64	9.16
8										4.58	10.05	10.82	10.20	9.65	9.17
9												4.06	8.92	9.64	9.16
10														3.62	8.02

and the Recovery Period is:

If the Recovery Year is:	10.0	10.5	11.0	11.5	12.0	12.5	13.0	13.5	14.0	14.5	15.0	15.5	16.0	16.5	17.0
	the Depreciation Rate is:														
1	9.38	8.93	8.52	8.15	7.81	7.50	7.21	6.94	6.70	6.47	6.25	6.05	5.86	5.68	5.51
2	13.59	13.01	12.47	11.98	11.52	11.10	10.71	10.34	10.00	9.68	9.38	9.09	8.83	8.57	8.34
3	11.55	11.15	10.77	10.42	10.08	9.77	9.47	9.19	8.92	8.67	8.44	8.21	8.00	7.80	7.60
4	9.82	9.56	9.31	9.06	8.82	8.60	8.38	8.17	7.97	7.78	7.59	7.42	7.25	7.09	6.93
5	8.73	8.34	8.04	7.88	7.72	7.56	7.41	7.26	7.12	6.97	6.83	6.70	6.57	6.44	6.32
6	8.73	8.34	7.98	7.64	7.33	7.04	6.78	6.55	6.35	6.25	6.15	6.05	5.95	5.86	5.76
7	8.73	8.34	7.98	7.64	7.33	7.05	6.79	6.55	6.32	6.10	5.91	5.72	5.55	5.38	5.25
8	8.73	8.34	7.98	7.64	7.33	7.04	6.78	6.54	6.32	6.11	5.90	5.72	5.55	5.39	5.23
9	8.73	8.34	7.98	7.64	7.33	7.05	6.79	6.55	6.32	6.10	5.91	5.72	5.54	5.38	5.23
10	8.73	8.35	7.98	7.63	7.33	7.04	6.78	6.54	6.32	6.11	5.90	5.72	5.55	5.39	5.23
11	3.28	7.30	7.99	7.64	7.33	7.05	6.79	6.55	6.32	6.10	5.91	5.72	5.54	5.38	5.23
12			2.99	6.68	7.32	7.04	6.78	6.54	6.32	6.11	5.90	5.72	5.55	5.39	5.24
13					2.75	6.16	6.79	6.55	6.32	6.10	5.90	5.72	5.54	5.38	5.23
14							2.54	5.73	6.33	6.11	5.91	5.72	5.55	5.39	5.24
15									2.37	5.34	5.91	5.72	5.54	5.38	5.23
16											2.21	5.00	5.55	5.39	5.24
17													2.08	4.71	5.23
18															1.96

and the Recovery Period is:

the Depreciation Rate is:

If the Recovery Year is:	17.5	18.0	18.5	19.0	19.5	20.0	20.5	21.0	21.5	22.0	22.5	23.0	23.5	24.0	24.5
1	5.36	5.21	5.07	4.93	4.81	4.688	4.573	4.464	4.360	4.261	4.167	4.076	3.989	3.906	3.827
2	8.11	7.90	7.70	7.51	7.32	7.148	6.982	6.824	6.673	6.528	6.389	6.256	6.128	6.006	5.888
3	7.42	7.24	7.07	6.91	6.76	6.612	6.472	6.337	6.207	6.083	5.963	5.848	5.737	5.631	5.528
4	6.78	6.64	6.50	6.37	6.24	6.116	5.998	5.884	5.774	5.668	5.565	5.467	5.371	5.279	5.189
5	6.20	6.08	5.97	5.86	5.76	5.658	5.559	5.464	5.371	5.281	5.194	5.110	5.028	4.949	4.872
6	5.67	5.58	5.49	5.40	5.32	5.233	5.152	5.073	4.996	4.921	4.848	4.777	4.707	4.639	4.573
7	5.18	5.11	5.04	4.98	4.91	4.841	4.775	4.711	4.648	4.586	4.525	4.465	4.407	4.349	4.293
8	5.08	4.94	4.81	4.69	4.57	4.478	4.426	4.375	4.324	4.273	4.223	4.174	4.126	4.078	4.030
9	5.08	4.94	4.81	4.69	4.57	4.463	4.354	4.252	4.155	4.063	3.975	3.902	3.862	3.823	3.784
10	5.08	4.95	4.81	4.69	4.57	4.463	4.354	4.252	4.155	4.063	3.975	3.890	3.808	3.729	3.655
11	5.08	4.94	4.81	4.69	4.57	4.463	4.354	4.252	4.155	4.062	3.975	3.890	3.808	3.729	3.655
12	5.09	4.94	4.82	4.69	4.58	4.463	4.354	4.252	4.155	4.063	3.975	3.890	3.808	3.730	3.654
13	5.08	4.95	4.81	4.69	4.57	4.463	4.355	4.252	4.155	4.062	3.975	3.891	3.808	3.729	3.655
14	5.09	4.94	4.82	4.69	4.58	4.462	4.354	4.252	4.155	4.063	3.975	3.890	3.808	3.730	3.654
15	5.08	4.95	4.81	4.69	4.57	4.463	4.355	4.252	4.155	4.062	3.975	3.890	3.808	3.729	3.655
16	5.09	4.94	4.82	4.69	4.58	4.462	4.354	4.252	4.154	4.063	3.975	3.891	3.808	3.730	3.654
17	5.08	4.95	4.81	4.69	4.57	4.463	4.355	4.252	4.155	4.062	3.975	3.890	3.808	3.729	3.655
18	4.45	4.95	4.82	4.69	4.58	4.462	4.354	4.251	4.154	4.063	3.975	3.891	3.808	3.730	3.654
19		1.85	4.21	4.69	4.57	4.463	4.355	4.252	4.155	4.062	3.974	3.890	3.808	3.729	3.655
20				1.76	4.00	4.463	4.354	4.251	4.154	4.063	3.975	3.891	3.808	3.730	3.654
21						1.673	3.810	4.252	4.155	4.062	3.974	3.890	3.808	3.729	3.655
22								1.594	3.635	4.063	3.975	3.891	3.808	3.730	3.654
23										1.523	3.478	3.890	3.809	3.729	3.655
24												1.459	3.332	3.730	3.654
25														1.399	3.198

and the Recovery Period is:

the Depreciation Rate is:

If the Recovery Year is:	25.0	25.5	26.0	26.5	27.0	27.5	28.0	28.5	29.0	29.5	30.0	30.5	31.0	31.5	32.0
1	3.750	3.676	3.606	3.538	3.472	3.409	3.348	3.289	3.233	3.178	3.125	3.074	3.024	2.976	2.930
2	5.775	5.666	5.561	5.460	5.363	5.269	5.178	5.090	5.005	4.923	4.844	4.767	4.692	4.620	4.550
3	5.429	5.333	5.240	5.151	5.065	4.981	4.900	4.822	4.746	4.673	4.602	4.532	4.465	4.400	4.337
4	5.103	5.019	4.938	4.859	4.783	4.710	4.638	4.568	4.501	4.435	4.371	4.310	4.249	4.191	4.134
5	4.797	4.724	4.653	4.584	4.518	4.453	4.389	4.328	4.268	4.210	4.153	4.098	4.044	3.991	3.940
6	4.509	4.446	4.385	4.325	4.267	4.210	4.154	4.100	4.047	3.996	3.945	3.896	3.848	3.801	3.755
7	4.238	4.184	4.132	4.080	4.030	3.980	3.932	3.884	3.838	3.792	3.748	3.704	3.662	3.620	3.579
8	3.984	3.938	3.893	3.849	3.806	3.763	3.721	3.680	3.639	3.600	3.561	3.522	3.485	3.448	3.411
9	3.745	3.707	3.669	3.631	3.594	3.558	3.522	3.486	3.451	3.417	3.383	3.349	3.316	3.283	3.251
10	3.583	3.514	3.457	3.426	3.395	3.364	3.333	3.303	3.273	3.243	3.213	3.184	3.156	3.127	3.099
11	3.583	3.515	3.448	3.384	3.321	3.262	3.205	3.150	3.103	3.078	3.053	3.028	3.003	2.978	2.954
12	3.583	3.514	3.448	3.383	3.321	3.262	3.205	3.150	3.096	3.044	2.994	2.945	2.898	2.853	2.815
13	3.583	3.515	3.448	3.384	3.321	3.262	3.205	3.150	3.096	3.044	2.994	2.945	2.898	2.853	2.810
14	3.583	3.514	3.448	3.383	3.321	3.262	3.205	3.150	3.096	3.044	2.994	2.945	2.899	2.853	2.810
15	3.583	3.515	3.448	3.384	3.321	3.262	3.205	3.150	3.096	3.044	2.994	2.945	2.898	2.853	2.810
16	3.583	3.515	3.448	3.383	3.321	3.262	3.204	3.150	3.096	3.044	2.994	2.945	2.899	2.854	2.809
17	3.583	3.514	3.448	3.384	3.321	3.262	3.205	3.150	3.097	3.044	2.994	2.945	2.898	2.853	2.810
18	3.583	3.515	3.448	3.383	3.321	3.262	3.204	3.149	3.096	3.044	2.993	2.945	2.899	2.854	2.809
19	3.583	3.514	3.449	3.384	3.321	3.261	3.205	3.150	3.097	3.044	2.994	2.945	2.898	2.853	2.810
20	3.583	3.515	3.448	3.383	3.322	3.262	3.204	3.149	3.096	3.044	2.993	2.945	2.899	2.854	2.809
21	3.583	3.514	3.449	3.384	3.321	3.261	3.205	3.150	3.097	3.044	2.994	2.945	2.898	2.853	2.810
22	3.583	3.514	3.448	3.383	3.322	3.262	3.204	3.149	3.096	3.044	2.993	2.945	2.899	2.854	2.809
23	3.583	3.515	3.449	3.384	3.321	3.261	3.205	3.150	3.097	3.044	2.994	2.945	2.898	2.853	2.810
24	3.582	3.515	3.448	3.383	3.322	3.262	3.204	3.149	3.096	3.044	2.993	2.946	2.899	2.854	2.809
25	3.583	3.514	3.438	3.384	3.321	3.261	3.205	3.150	3.097	3.044	2.994	2.945	2.898	2.853	2.810
26	1.343	3.075	3.449	3.383	3.322	3.262	3.204	3.149	3.096	3.044	2.993	2.945	2.899	2.854	2.809
27			1.293	2.961	3.321	3.261	3.205	3.150	3.097	3.044	2.994	2.945	2.898	2.854	2.810
28					1.246	2.854	3.204	3.149	3.096	3.044	2.993	2.945	2.899	2.854	2.809
29							1.202	2.756	3.097	3.044	2.994	2.945	2.898	2.854	2.810
30									1.161	2.663	2.993	2.946	2.899	2.853	2.809
31											1.123	2.577	2.898	2.854	2.810
32													1.087	2.497	2.809
33															1.054

and the Recovery Period is:

the Depreciation Rate is:

If the Recovery Year is:	32.5	33.0	33.5	34.0	34.5	35.0	35.5	36.0	36.5	37.0	37.5	38.0	38.5	39.0	39.5
1	2.885	2.841	2.799	2.757	2.717	2.679	2.641	2.604	2.568	2.534	2.500	2.467	2.435	2.404	2.373
2	4.482	4.416	4.352	4.290	4.230	4.171	4.114	4.058	4.004	3.951	3.900	3.850	3.801	3.754	3.707
3	4.275	4.216	4.157	4.101	4.046	3.992	3.940	3.889	3.840	3.791	3.744	3.698	3.653	3.609	3.567
4	4.078	4.024	3.971	3.920	3.870	3.821	3.773	3.727	3.682	3.637	3.594	3.552	3.511	3.471	3.431
5	3.890	3.841	3.793	3.747	3.702	3.657	3.614	3.572	3.530	3.490	3.450	3.412	3.374	3.337	3.301
6	3.710	3.666	3.624	3.582	3.541	3.501	3.461	3.423	3.385	3.349	3.312	3.277	3.243	3.209	3.175
7	3.539	3.500	3.461	3.424	3.387	3.351	3.315	3.280	3.246	3.213	3.180	3.148	3.116	3.085	3.055
8	3.376	3.341	3.306	3.273	3.239	3.207	3.175	3.144	3.113	3.083	3.053	3.024	2.995	2.967	2.939
9	3.220	3.189	3.158	3.128	3.099	3.069	3.041	3.013	2.985	2.958	2.931	2.904	2.878	2.852	2.827
10	3.071	3.044	3.017	2.990	2.964	2.938	2.912	2.887	2.862	2.838	2.813	2.790	2.766	2.743	2.720
11	2.930	2.906	2.882	2.858	2.835	2.812	2.789	2.767	2.745	2.723	2.701	2.679	2.658	2.637	2.617
12	2.794	2.773	2.753	2.732	2.712	2.692	2.671	2.651	2.632	2.612	2.593	2.574	2.555	2.536	2.517
13	2.766	2.725	2.685	2.646	2.608	2.576	2.559	2.541	2.524	2.506	2.489	2.472	2.455	2.438	2.422
14	2.766	2.725	2.685	2.646	2.608	2.571	2.535	2.500	2.466	2.433	2.402	2.374	2.359	2.345	2.330
15	2.767	2.725	2.685	2.646	2.608	2.571	2.535	2.500	2.466	2.433	2.402	2.370	2.340	2.310	2.281
16	2.766	2.725	2.685	2.646	2.608	2.571	2.535	2.500	2.466	2.433	2.402	2.370	2.340	2.310	2.281
17	2.767	2.725	2.685	2.646	2.608	2.571	2.535	2.500	2.466	2.433	2.402	2.370	2.340	2.310	2.281
18	2.766	2.725	2.685	2.646	2.608	2.571	2.535	2.500	2.466	2.434	2.402	2.370	2.340	2.310	2.281
19	2.767	2.725	2.685	2.646	2.608	2.571	2.535	2.500	2.466	2.433	2.402	2.370	2.340	2.310	2.281
20	2.766	2.725	2.685	2.646	2.608	2.571	2.535	2.500	2.466	2.434	2.401	2.371	2.340	2.310	2.281
21	2.767	2.725	2.685	2.646	2.608	2.571	2.535	2.500	2.467	2.433	2.402	2.371	2.340	2.310	2.281
22	2.766	2.725	2.684	2.646	2.608	2.571	2.535	2.500	2.466	2.434	2.401	2.370	2.340	2.310	2.281
23	2.767	2.725	2.685	2.646	2.608	2.571	2.535	2.500	2.467	2.433	2.402	2.371	2.340	2.310	2.281
24	2.766	2.725	2.685	2.645	2.608	2.571	2.535	2.500	2.466	2.434	2.401	2.370	2.340	2.310	2.281
25	2.767	2.725	2.684	2.646	2.608	2.572	2.536	2.501	2.467	2.433	2.402	2.371	2.340	2.310	2.281
26	2.766	2.724	2.685	2.646	2.608	2.571	2.535	2.500	2.466	2.434	2.401	2.370	2.340	2.310	2.281
27	2.767	2.725	2.684	2.645	2.608	2.572	2.536	2.501	2.467	2.433	2.402	2.371	2.339	2.310	2.281
28	2.766	2.725	2.685	2.646	2.608	2.571	2.535	2.500	2.466	2.434	2.401	2.370	2.340	2.310	2.281
29	2.767	2.724	2.684	2.646	2.608	2.572	2.536	2.500	2.467	2.433	2.402	2.371	2.339	2.310	2.281
30	2.766	2.725	2.685	2.645	2.608	2.571	2.535	2.501	2.466	2.434	2.401	2.370	2.340	2.310	2.281
31	2.767	2.724	2.684	2.646	2.608	2.572	2.536	2.500	2.467	2.433	2.402	2.371	2.339	2.310	2.281
32	2.766	2.725	2.685	2.646	2.608	2.571	2.535	2.501	2.466	2.434	2.401	2.370	2.340	2.310	2.281
33	2.767	2.724	2.684	2.645	2.608	2.572	2.536	2.500	2.467	2.433	2.402	2.371	2.339	2.310	2.281
34	2.421	2.725	2.685	2.646	2.608	2.571	2.535	2.501	2.466	2.434	2.401	2.370	2.340	2.310	2.281
35		2.724	2.684	2.646	2.282	2.572	2.536	2.500	2.467	2.433	2.402	2.371	2.339	2.309	2.281
36		2.725	2.685	2.645		2.571	2.535	2.501	2.466	2.434	2.401	2.370	2.340	2.310	2.281
37		2.724	2.684	2.646		2.572	2.536	2.500	2.158	2.433	2.402	2.371	2.339	2.309	2.281
38		1.022	2.685	2.645		2.571	2.535	2.501		2.434	2.101	2.370	2.340	2.310	2.280
39			2.349	2.646		2.572	2.536	2.500		0.913		0.889	2.047	2.309	2.281
40				0.992		0.964	2.219	2.501						0.866	1.995

and the Recovery Period is:

the Depreciation Rate is:

If the Recovery Year is:	40.0	40.5	41.0	41.5	42.0	42.5	43.0	43.5	44.0	44.5	45.0	45.5	46.0	46.5	47.0
1	2.344	2.315	2.287	2.259	2.232	2.206	2.180	2.155	2.131	2.107	2.083	2.060	2.038	2.016	1.995
2	3.662	3.618	3.575	3.533	3.492	3.452	3.412	3.374	3.336	3.300	3.264	3.229	3.194	3.161	3.128
3	3.525	3.484	3.444	3.405	3.367	3.330	3.293	3.258	3.223	3.189	3.155	3.122	3.090	3.059	3.028
4	3.393	3.355	3.318	3.282	3.247	3.212	3.178	3.145	3.113	3.081	3.050	3.019	2.990	2.960	2.931
5	3.265	3.231	3.197	3.163	3.131	3.099	3.068	3.037	3.007	2.977	2.948	2.920	2.892	2.865	2.838
6	3.143	3.111	3.080	3.049	3.019	2.989	2.961	2.932	2.904	2.877	2.850	2.824	2.798	2.772	2.747
7	3.025	2.996	2.967	2.939	2.911	2.884	2.857	2.831	2.805	2.780	2.755	2.731	2.706	2.683	2.660
8	2.912	2.885	2.858	2.833	2.807	2.782	2.758	2.733	2.710	2.686	2.663	2.640	2.618	2.596	2.575
9	2.802	2.778	2.754	2.730	2.707	2.684	2.661	2.639	2.617	2.596	2.574	2.553	2.533	2.513	2.492
10	2.697	2.675	2.653	2.632	2.610	2.589	2.569	2.548	2.528	2.508	2.489	2.469	2.450	2.431	2.413
11	2.596	2.576	2.556	2.536	2.517	2.498	2.479	2.460	2.442	2.424	2.406	2.388	2.370	2.353	2.336
12	2.499	2.481	2.463	2.445	2.427	2.410	2.392	2.375	2.359	2.342	2.325	2.309	2.293	2.277	2.261
13	2.405	2.389	2.372	2.356	2.340	2.325	2.309	2.294	2.278	2.263	2.248	2.233	2.218	2.204	2.189
14	2.315	2.300	2.286	2.271	2.257	2.243	2.228	2.214	2.200	2.187	2.173	2.159	2.146	2.133	2.119
15	2.253	2.225	2.202	2.189	2.176	2.163	2.151	2.138	2.125	2.113	2.101	2.088	2.076	2.064	2.052
16	2.253	2.225	2.199	2.172	2.147	2.121	2.097	2.073	2.053	2.042	2.031	2.019	2.008	1.997	1.986
17	2.253	2.225	2.199	2.172	2.146	2.121	2.097	2.073	2.050	2.027	2.005	1.983	1.961	1.941	1.923
18	2.253	2.225	2.199	2.172	2.147	2.121	2.097	2.073	2.050	2.027	2.005	1.983	1.961	1.941	1.920
19	2.253	2.225	2.199	2.172	2.146	2.121	2.097	2.073	2.050	2.027	2.005	1.983	1.961	1.941	1.920
20	2.253	2.225	2.199	2.172	2.146	2.121	2.097	2.073	2.050	2.027	2.005	1.983	1.962	1.941	1.920
21	2.253	2.225	2.199	2.172	2.147	2.121	2.097	2.073	2.050	2.027	2.005	1.983	1.961	1.941	1.920
22	2.253	2.225	2.199	2.172	2.146	2.122	2.097	2.073	2.050	2.027	2.005	1.983	1.962	1.941	1.920
23	2.253	2.225	2.199	2.172	2.146	2.121	2.097	2.073	2.050	2.027	2.005	1.983	1.961	1.941	1.920
24	2.253	2.225	2.198	2.172	2.146	2.122	2.097	2.073	2.050	2.027	2.004	1.983	1.962	1.941	1.920
25	2.253	2.225	2.199	2.172	2.147	2.122	2.097	2.073	2.050	2.027	2.005	1.983	1.961	1.941	1.920
26	2.253	2.226	2.198	2.172	2.146	2.121	2.097	2.073	2.050	2.027	2.004	1.983	1.962	1.941	1.920
27	2.253	2.225	2.199	2.172	2.147	2.121	2.097	2.073	2.050	2.027	2.005	1.983	1.961	1.941	1.920
28	2.253	2.225	2.198	2.172	2.146	2.122	2.097	2.073	2.050	2.027	2.004	1.983	1.962	1.941	1.920
29	2.253	2.225	2.199	2.172	2.147	2.121	2.097	2.073	2.050	2.027	2.005	1.983	1.961	1.941	1.920
30	2.252	2.226	2.198	2.172	2.146	2.122	2.097	2.074	2.050	2.027	2.004	1.983	1.962	1.940	1.920
31	2.253	2.225	2.199	2.172	2.147	2.122	2.097	2.073	2.050	2.027	2.005	1.983	1.961	1.941	1.920
32	2.252	2.226	2.198	2.173	2.146	2.122	2.097	2.074	2.050	2.027	2.004	1.983	1.962	1.940	1.920
33	2.253	2.225	2.199	2.172	2.146	2.121	2.097	2.073	2.050	2.027	2.005	1.983	1.961	1.941	1.920
34	2.252	2.226	2.198	2.173	2.147	2.122	2.097	2.074	2.050	2.027	2.004	1.983	1.962	1.940	1.920
35	2.253	2.225	2.199	2.172	2.146	2.121	2.097	2.073	2.050	2.027	2.005	1.983	1.961	1.941	1.920
36	2.252	2.226	2.198	2.173	2.146	2.122	2.097	2.074	2.050	2.027	2.004	1.982	1.962	1.940	1.920
37	2.253	2.226	2.198	2.172	2.147	2.121	2.097	2.073	2.050	2.027	2.005	1.983	1.961	1.941	1.920
38	2.252	2.226	2.199	2.172	2.146	2.122	2.097	2.074	2.050	2.027	2.004	1.982	1.962	1.940	1.920
39	2.253	2.225	2.198	2.172	2.147	2.121	2.097	2.073	2.050	2.027	2.005	1.983	1.961	1.941	1.921
40	2.252	2.226	2.199	2.172	2.146	2.122	2.097	2.074	2.050	2.027	2.004	1.982	1.962	1.940	1.920
41	0.845	1.947	2.199	2.173	2.147	2.121	2.097	2.073	2.050	2.026	2.005	1.983	1.961	1.941	1.920
42			0.824	1.901	2.146	2.122	2.097	2.074	2.050	2.027	2.004	1.982	1.962	1.940	1.921
43					0.805	1.856	2.098	2.073	2.050	2.027	2.005	1.983	1.961	1.941	1.920
44							0.787	1.814	2.050	2.027	2.004	1.983	1.962	1.941	1.920
45									0.769	1.773	2.005	1.982	1.961	1.941	1.921
46											0.752	1.735	1.962	1.940	1.920
47													0.736	1.698	1.920
48															0.720

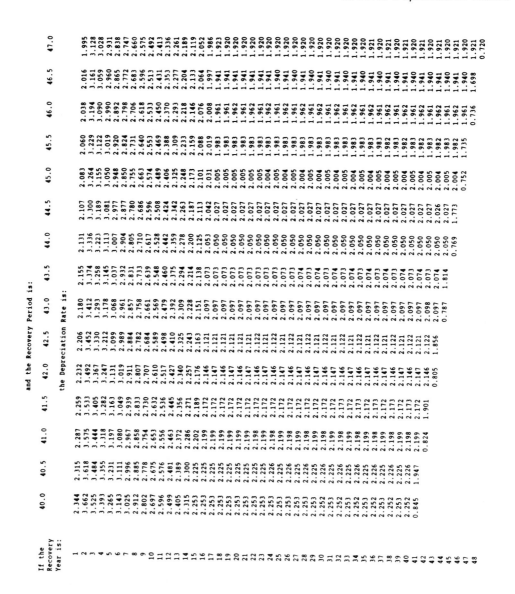

and the Recovery Period is:

the Depreciation Rate is:

If the Recovery Year is:	47.5	48.0	48.5	49.0	49.5	50.0
1	1.974	1.953	1.933	1.913	1.894	1.875
2	3.096	3.064	3.033	3.003	2.973	2.944
3	2.998	2.968	2.939	2.911	2.883	2.855
4	2.903	2.875	2.848	2.822	2.795	2.770
5	2.811	2.786	2.760	2.735	2.711	2.687
6	2.723	2.699	2.675	2.652	2.629	2.606
7	2.637	2.614	2.592	2.570	2.549	2.528
8	2.553	2.533	2.512	2.492	2.472	2.452
9	2.473	2.453	2.434	2.415	2.397	2.378
10	2.395	2.377	2.359	2.341	2.324	2.307
11	2.319	2.302	2.286	2.270	2.254	2.238
12	2.246	2.230	2.215	2.200	2.185	2.171
13	2.175	2.161	2.147	2.133	2.119	2.106
14	2.106	2.093	2.080	2.068	2.055	2.042
15	2.040	2.028	2.016	2.004	1.993	1.981
16	1.975	1.964	1.954	1.943	1.932	1.922
17	1.913	1.903	1.893	1.884	1.874	1.864
18	1.900	1.880	1.861	1.842	1.824	1.808
19	1.900	1.880	1.861	1.842	1.824	1.806
20	1.900	1.880	1.861	1.842	1.824	1.806
21	1.900	1.880	1.861	1.842	1.824	1.806
22	1.900	1.880	1.861	1.842	1.824	1.806
23	1.900	1.880	1.861	1.842	1.824	1.806
24	1.900	1.880	1.861	1.842	1.824	1.806
25	1.900	1.880	1.861	1.842	1.824	1.806
26	1.900	1.881	1.861	1.842	1.824	1.806
27	1.900	1.880	1.861	1.842	1.824	1.806
28	1.900	1.881	1.861	1.842	1.824	1.806
29	1.900	1.880	1.861	1.842	1.824	1.806
30	1.900	1.881	1.861	1.842	1.824	1.806
31	1.900	1.880	1.861	1.843	1.824	1.806
32	1.900	1.881	1.861	1.842	1.824	1.806
33	1.900	1.880	1.861	1.843	1.824	1.806
34	1.900	1.881	1.861	1.842	1.824	1.806
35	1.900	1.880	1.861	1.843	1.824	1.806
36	1.900	1.881	1.861	1.842	1.824	1.806
37	1.900	1.880	1.861	1.843	1.824	1.806
38	1.900	1.881	1.861	1.842	1.824	1.806
39	1.900	1.880	1.861	1.843	1.824	1.806
40	1.900	1.881	1.861	1.842	1.824	1.806
41	1.900	1.880	1.861	1.843	1.824	1.806
42	1.900	1.881	1.862	1.843	1.824	1.806
43	1.900	1.880	1.861	1.842	1.824	1.806
44	1.900	1.881	1.862	1.843	1.824	1.806
45	1.900	1.880	1.861	1.842	1.823	1.805
46	1.900	1.881	1.862	1.843	1.824	1.806
47	1.900	1.880	1.861	1.842	1.823	1.805
48	1.900	1.881	1.862	1.843	1.824	1.806
49	1.900	1.880	1.861	1.842	1.823	1.805
50	1.900	1.881	1.861	1.842	1.823	1.805
51	1.663	0.705	1.629	0.691	1.596	0.677

TABLE 17

Alternative Minimum Tax (see section 7 of this
revenue procedure)
Applicable Depreciation Method: 150 Percent Declining Balance
Switching to Straight Line
Applicable Recovery Periods: 2.5 - 50 years
Applicable Convention: Mid-quarter (property placed
in service in third quarter)

and the Recovery Period is:

the Depreciation Rate is:

If the Recovery Year is:	2.5	3.0	3.5	4.0	4.5	5.0	5.5	6.0	6.5	7.0	7.5	8.0	8.5	9.0	9.5
1	22.50	18.75	16.07	14.06	12.50	11.25	10.23	9.38	8.65	8.04	7.50	7.03	6.62	6.25	5.92
2	46.50	40.63	35.97	32.23	29.17	26.63	24.48	22.66	21.08	19.71	18.50	17.43	16.48	15.63	14.85
3	27.56	25.00	22.57	20.46	19.44	18.64	17.81	16.99	16.22	15.48	14.80	14.16	13.57	13.02	12.51
4	3.44	15.62	22.57	20.46	18.30	16.56	15.19	14.06	13.10	12.28	11.84	11.51	11.18	10.85	10.53
5			2.82	12.79	18.30	16.57	15.20	14.06	13.11	12.27	11.48	10.78	10.18	9.65	9.64
6					2.29	10.35	15.19	14.06	13.10	12.28	11.48	10.78	10.17	9.64	9.17
7							1.90	8.79	13.10	12.28	11.48	10.78	10.18	9.64	9.18
8									1.64	7.67	11.48	10.79	10.17	9.65	9.17
9											1.44	6.74	10.18	9.64	9.18
10													1.27	6.03	9.17
11															1.15

and the Recovery Period is:

the Depreciation Rate is:

If the Recovery Year is:	10.0	10.5	11.0	11.5	12.0	12.5	13.0	13.5	14.0	14.5	15.0	15.5	16.0	16.5	17.0
1	5.63	5.36	5.11	4.89	4.69	4.50	4.33	4.17	4.02	3.88	3.75	3.63	3.52	3.41	3.31
2	14.16	13.52	12.94	12.41	11.91	11.46	11.04	10.65	10.28	9.94	9.63	9.33	9.05	8.78	8.53
3	12.03	11.59	11.18	10.79	10.43	10.08	9.77	9.46	9.18	8.92	8.66	8.42	8.20	7.98	7.78
4	10.23	9.93	9.65	9.38	9.12	8.88	8.64	8.41	8.20	7.99	7.80	7.61	7.43	7.26	7.09
5	8.75	8.51	8.33	8.16	7.98	7.81	7.64	7.48	7.32	7.17	7.02	6.87	6.73	6.60	6.47
6	8.75	8.34	7.97	7.63	7.33	7.05	6.79	6.65	6.54	6.42	6.31	6.21	6.10	6.00	5.90
7	8.74	8.34	7.97	7.63	7.33	7.05	6.79	6.55	6.31	6.10	5.90	5.72	5.55	5.45	5.38
8	8.75	8.34	7.97	7.63	7.33	7.05	6.79	6.54	6.31	6.10	5.90	5.72	5.55	5.38	5.23
9	8.74	8.34	7.97	7.63	7.33	7.05	6.79	6.55	6.32	6.10	5.91	5.72	5.55	5.38	5.23
10	8.75	8.35	7.97	7.63	7.32	7.05	6.79	6.54	6.31	6.10	5.90	5.72	5.55	5.38	5.23
11	5.47	8.35	7.96	7.63	7.33	7.05	6.79	6.55	6.32	6.11	5.91	5.72	5.55	5.39	5.23
12		1.04	4.98	7.64	7.32	7.05	6.79	6.54	6.31	6.10	5.90	5.72	5.55	5.38	5.22
13				0.95	4.58	7.04	6.80	6.55	6.32	6.11	5.91	5.72	5.55	5.39	5.23
14						0.88	4.25	6.54	6.31	6.10	5.90	5.73	5.55	5.39	5.23
15								0.82	3.95	6.11	5.91	5.72	5.55	5.38	5.22
16										0.76	3.69	5.73	5.55	5.39	5.23
17												0.72	3.47	5.38	5.22
18														0.67	3.27

and the Recovery Period is:

the Depreciation Rate is:

If the Recovery Year is:	17.5	18.0	18.5	19.0	19.5	20.0	20.5	21.0	21.5	22.0	22.5	23.0	23.5	24.0	24.5
1	3.21	3.13	3.04	2.96	2.88	2.813	2.744	2.679	2.616	2.557	2.500	2.446	2.394	2.344	2.296
2	8.30	8.07	7.86	7.66	7.47	7.289	7.116	6.952	6.794	6.644	6.500	6.362	6.230	6.104	5.982
3	7.58	7.40	7.22	7.06	6.90	6.742	6.596	6.455	6.320	6.191	6.067	5.947	5.833	5.722	5.616
4	6.94	6.78	6.64	6.50	6.37	6.237	6.113	5.994	5.879	5.769	5.662	5.559	5.460	5.364	5.272
5	6.34	6.22	6.10	5.99	5.88	5.769	5.666	5.566	5.469	5.375	5.285	5.197	5.112	5.029	4.949
6	5.80	5.70	5.61	5.51	5.42	5.336	5.251	5.168	5.088	5.009	4.932	4.858	4.785	4.715	4.646
7	5.30	5.23	5.15	5.08	5.01	4.936	4.867	4.799	4.733	4.667	4.604	4.541	4.480	4.420	4.362
8	5.08	4.94	4.81	4.69	4.62	4.566	4.511	4.456	4.402	4.349	4.297	4.245	4.194	4.144	4.095
9	5.08	4.94	4.82	4.69	4.57	4.460	4.353	4.252	4.156	4.064	4.010	3.968	3.926	3.885	3.844
10	5.08	4.94	4.81	4.69	4.57	4.460	4.353	4.252	4.156	4.064	3.975	3.889	3.807	3.729	3.655
11	5.08	4.94	4.82	4.69	4.57	4.460	4.353	4.252	4.156	4.064	3.975	3.889	3.807	3.730	3.655
12	5.08	4.94	4.82	4.69	4.57	4.461	4.353	4.252	4.156	4.064	3.975	3.889	3.807	3.729	3.655
13	5.08	4.95	4.81	4.69	4.58	4.460	4.353	4.252	4.156	4.064	3.975	3.889	3.807	3.730	3.655
14	5.08	4.94	4.82	4.69	4.57	4.461	4.353	4.252	4.155	4.064	3.975	3.889	3.807	3.729	3.655
15	5.08	4.94	4.81	4.70	4.58	4.460	4.353	4.252	4.156	4.064	3.975	3.889	3.808	3.730	3.655
16	5.08	4.95	4.82	4.69	4.57	4.461	4.354	4.252	4.155	4.064	3.975	3.889	3.807	3.729	3.655
17	5.09	4.94	4.81	4.70	4.58	4.460	4.353	4.252	4.156	4.064	3.974	3.889	3.808	3.730	3.655
18	5.08	4.95	4.82	4.69	4.57	4.461	4.354	4.251	4.155	4.065	3.975	3.889	3.807	3.729	3.655
19	0.64	3.09	4.81	4.70	4.58	4.460	4.353	4.252	4.156	4.064	3.974	3.889	3.808	3.730	3.655
20			4.82	2.93	0.57	2.788	4.354	4.251	4.155	4.065	3.975	3.889	3.807	3.729	3.655
21			0.60				0.544	4.252	4.156	4.064	3.974	3.889	3.808	3.730	3.655
22								2.657	0.519	4.065	3.975	3.889	3.807	3.729	3.655
23										2.540	0.497	3.889	3.808	3.730	3.655
24												2.431	3.807	3.729	3.655
25													0.476	3.730	3.656
26														2.331	3.655
27															0.457

and the Recovery Period is:

the Depreciation Rate is:

If the Recovery Year is:	25.0	25.5	26.0	26.5	27.0	27.5	28.0	28.5	29.0	29.5	30.0	30.5	31.0	31.5	32.0
1	2.250	2.206	2.163	2.123	2.083	2.045	2.009	1.974	1.940	1.907	1.875	1.844	1.815	1.786	1.758
2	5.865	5.753	5.644	5.540	5.440	5.343	5.250	5.159	5.072	4.988	4.906	4.827	4.751	4.677	4.605
3	5.513	5.414	5.319	5.227	5.138	5.052	4.968	4.888	4.810	4.734	4.661	4.590	4.521	4.454	4.389
4	5.182	5.096	5.012	4.931	4.852	4.776	4.702	4.630	4.561	4.493	4.428	4.364	4.302	4.242	4.184
5	4.871	4.796	4.723	4.652	4.583	4.515	4.450	4.387	4.325	4.265	4.207	4.150	4.094	4.040	3.987
6	4.579	4.514	4.450	4.388	4.328	4.269	4.212	4.156	4.101	4.048	3.996	3.945	3.896	3.848	3.800
7	4.304	4.248	4.194	4.140	4.088	4.036	3.986	3.937	3.889	3.842	3.796	3.751	3.707	3.664	3.622
8	4.046	3.998	3.952	3.906	3.860	3.816	3.773	3.730	3.688	3.647	3.607	3.567	3.528	3.490	3.453
9	3.803	3.763	3.724	3.685	3.646	3.608	3.571	3.534	3.497	3.461	3.426	3.392	3.357	3.324	3.291
10	3.584	3.542	3.509	3.476	3.443	3.411	3.379	3.348	3.316	3.286	3.255	3.225	3.195	3.165	3.136
11	3.584	3.514	3.447	3.383	3.321	3.262	3.205	3.171	3.145	3.118	3.092	3.066	3.040	3.015	2.989
12	3.584	3.514	3.447	3.383	3.321	3.262	3.205	3.150	3.096	3.044	2.994	2.946	2.899	2.871	2.849
13	3.584	3.514	3.447	3.383	3.321	3.262	3.205	3.150	3.096	3.044	2.994	2.946	2.899	2.853	2.809
14	3.584	3.514	3.447	3.383	3.321	3.262	3.205	3.150	3.096	3.044	2.994	2.945	2.899	2.853	2.809
15	3.584	3.514	3.447	3.383	3.321	3.262	3.205	3.149	3.096	3.044	2.994	2.946	2.899	2.853	2.809
16	3.584	3.515	3.447	3.383	3.322	3.262	3.206	3.150	3.096	3.044	2.994	2.945	2.899	2.853	2.809
17	3.584	3.514	3.447	3.383	3.321	3.262	3.205	3.149	3.095	3.044	2.994	2.946	2.899	2.853	2.809
18	3.584	3.515	3.447	3.383	3.322	3.262	3.206	3.150	3.096	3.044	2.994	2.945	2.899	2.853	2.809
19	3.584	3.514	3.447	3.383	3.321	3.263	3.205	3.149	3.095	3.044	2.994	2.946	2.899	2.853	2.809
20	3.584	3.515	3.447	3.383	3.322	3.262	3.206	3.150	3.096	3.044	2.993	2.945	2.899	2.853	2.809
21	3.585	3.514	3.448	3.383	3.321	3.263	3.205	3.149	3.095	3.043	2.994	2.946	2.899	2.854	2.809
22	3.584	3.515	3.447	3.383	3.322	3.262	3.206	3.150	3.096	3.044	2.993	2.945	2.899	2.853	2.809
23	3.584	3.514	3.448	3.383	3.321	3.263	3.205	3.149	3.095	3.043	2.994	2.946	2.899	2.854	2.809
24	3.584	3.515	3.447	3.382	3.322	3.262	3.206	3.150	3.096	3.044	2.993	2.946	2.899	2.853	2.809
25	3.585	3.514	3.448	3.383	3.321	3.263	3.205	3.149	3.095	3.043	2.994	2.946	2.900	2.854	2.810
26	2.240	3.515	3.447	3.383	3.322	3.262	3.206	3.150	3.096	3.044	2.993	2.945	2.899	2.853	2.809
27		0.439	2.155	3.383	3.321	3.263	3.205	3.149	3.095	3.043	2.994	2.946	2.899	2.854	2.809
28				0.423	2.076	3.262	3.206	3.150	3.096	3.044	2.993	2.945	2.899	2.853	2.809
29						0.408	2.003	3.149	3.095	3.043	2.994	2.946	2.899	2.854	2.809
30								0.394	1.935	3.044	2.993	2.946	2.900	2.854	2.809
31										0.380	1.871	2.945	2.899	2.854	2.809
32												0.368	1.812	2.853	2.810
33														0.357	1.756

and the Recovery Period is:

the Depreciation Rate is:

If the Recovery Year is:	32.5	33.0	33.5	34.0	34.5	35.0	35.5	36.0	36.5	37.0	37.5	38.0	38.5	39.0	39.5
1	1.731	1.705	1.679	1.654	1.630	1.607	1.585	1.563	1.541	1.520	1.500	1.480	1.461	1.442	1.424
2	4.535	4.468	4.402	4.339	4.277	4.217	4.158	4.102	4.046	3.992	3.940	3.889	3.839	3.791	3.743
3	4.326	4.265	4.205	4.147	4.091	4.036	3.983	3.931	3.880	3.831	3.782	3.735	3.690	3.645	3.601
4	4.127	4.071	4.017	3.964	3.913	3.863	3.814	3.767	3.721	3.675	3.631	3.588	3.546	3.505	3.465
5	3.936	3.886	3.837	3.790	3.743	3.698	3.653	3.610	3.568	3.526	3.486	3.446	3.408	3.370	3.333
6	3.754	3.709	3.665	3.622	3.580	3.539	3.499	3.459	3.421	3.383	3.346	3.310	3.275	3.240	3.206
7	3.581	3.541	3.501	3.463	3.425	3.387	3.351	3.315	3.280	3.246	3.213	3.180	3.147	3.116	3.085
8	3.416	3.380	3.345	3.310	3.276	3.242	3.209	3.177	3.146	3.115	3.084	3.054	3.025	2.996	2.967
9	3.258	3.226	3.195	3.164	3.133	3.103	3.074	3.045	3.016	2.988	2.961	2.934	2.907	2.881	2.855
10	3.108	3.080	3.052	3.024	2.997	2.970	2.944	2.918	2.892	2.867	2.842	2.818	2.794	2.770	2.746
11	2.964	2.940	2.915	2.891	2.867	2.843	2.820	2.796	2.774	2.751	2.729	2.707	2.685	2.663	2.642
12	2.828	2.806	2.784	2.763	2.742	2.721	2.700	2.680	2.660	2.639	2.619	2.600	2.580	2.561	2.542
13	2.766	2.725	2.685	2.646	2.623	2.605	2.586	2.568	2.550	2.532	2.515	2.497	2.480	2.462	2.445
14	2.766	2.725	2.685	2.646	2.608	2.571	2.535	2.500	2.467	2.434	2.414	2.399	2.383	2.368	2.352
15	2.766	2.725	2.685	2.646	2.608	2.571	2.535	2.500	2.466	2.434	2.402	2.370	2.340	2.310	2.281
16	2.766	2.725	2.685	2.646	2.608	2.571	2.535	2.500	2.467	2.434	2.402	2.370	2.339	2.310	2.281
17	2.766	2.725	2.685	2.646	2.608	2.571	2.535	2.500	2.467	2.434	2.402	2.370	2.340	2.310	2.281
18	2.766	2.725	2.685	2.646	2.608	2.571	2.535	2.500	2.466	2.434	2.402	2.370	2.339	2.310	2.281
19	2.766	2.725	2.685	2.646	2.608	2.571	2.535	2.500	2.467	2.434	2.401	2.370	2.340	2.310	2.281
20	2.766	2.725	2.685	2.646	2.608	2.571	2.535	2.500	2.466	2.434	2.402	2.370	2.339	2.310	2.281
21	2.766	2.725	2.685	2.646	2.608	2.571	2.535	2.500	2.467	2.434	2.401	2.370	2.340	2.310	2.281
22	2.766	2.725	2.685	2.646	2.608	2.571	2.535	2.500	2.466	2.434	2.402	2.370	2.339	2.310	2.281
23	2.766	2.725	2.685	2.646	2.608	2.571	2.535	2.500	2.467	2.434	2.401	2.370	2.340	2.310	2.281
24	2.766	2.725	2.685	2.646	2.608	2.571	2.535	2.500	2.466	2.434	2.402	2.370	2.339	2.310	2.281
25	2.766	2.724	2.685	2.646	2.608	2.571	2.535	2.500	2.467	2.434	2.401	2.370	2.340	2.310	2.281
26	2.767	2.725	2.685	2.646	2.608	2.571	2.535	2.501	2.466	2.434	2.402	2.370	2.339	2.310	2.281
27	2.766	2.724	2.685	2.646	2.608	2.571	2.535	2.500	2.467	2.434	2.401	2.370	2.340	2.310	2.281
28	2.766	2.725	2.685	2.646	2.608	2.571	2.535	2.501	2.466	2.434	2.402	2.370	2.339	2.310	2.281
29	2.766	2.724	2.685	2.646	2.608	2.571	2.535	2.500	2.467	2.434	2.401	2.370	2.340	2.310	2.281
30	2.767	2.725	2.684	2.646	2.608	2.571	2.535	2.500	2.466	2.434	2.402	2.370	2.339	2.310	2.281
31	2.766	2.724	2.685	2.646	2.608	2.571	2.535	2.501	2.467	2.434	2.401	2.370	2.340	2.310	2.281
32	2.767	2.725	2.684	2.647	2.608	2.571	2.535	2.500	2.466	2.434	2.402	2.370	2.339	2.310	2.281
33	2.766	2.724	2.685	2.646	2.608	2.571	2.536	2.500	2.467	2.434	2.401	2.370	2.340	2.310	2.281
34	0.346	1.703	2.684	2.647	2.608	2.571	2.535	2.501	2.466	2.434	2.402	2.370	2.339	2.310	2.281
35			0.336	1.654	2.609	2.571	2.536	2.500	2.467	2.434	2.401	2.370	2.340	2.310	2.281
36					0.326	1.607	2.535	2.501	2.466	2.434	2.402	2.370	2.339	2.310	2.282
37							0.317	1.563	2.467	2.433	2.402	2.371	2.340	2.309	2.282
38									0.308	1.521	2.401	2.370	2.340	2.310	2.281
39											0.300	1.482	2.339	2.309	2.282
40													2.340	2.310	2.282
41													0.292	1.443	0.285

and the Recovery Period is:

the Depreciation Rate is:

If the Recovery Year is:	40.0	40.5	41.0	41.5	42.0	42.5	43.0	43.5	44.0	44.5	45.0	45.5	46.0	46.5	47.0
1	1.406	1.389	1.372	1.355	1.339	1.324	1.308	1.293	1.278	1.264	1.250	1.236	1.223	1.210	1.197
2	3.697	3.652	3.608	3.565	3.524	3.483	3.443	3.404	3.366	3.328	3.292	3.256	3.221	3.187	3.153
3	3.559	3.517	3.476	3.437	3.398	3.360	3.323	3.286	3.251	3.216	3.182	3.149	3.116	3.084	3.053
4	3.425	3.387	3.349	3.312	3.276	3.241	3.207	3.173	3.140	3.108	3.076	3.045	3.014	2.984	2.955
5	3.297	3.261	3.227	3.193	3.159	3.127	3.095	3.064	3.033	3.003	2.973	2.944	2.916	2.888	2.861
6	3.173	3.141	3.109	3.077	3.047	3.016	2.987	2.958	2.929	2.902	2.874	2.847	2.821	2.795	2.770
7	3.054	3.024	2.995	2.966	2.938	2.910	2.883	2.856	2.830	2.804	2.778	2.754	2.729	2.705	2.681
8	2.940	2.912	2.885	2.859	2.833	2.807	2.782	2.757	2.733	2.709	2.686	2.663	2.640	2.618	2.596
9	2.829	2.804	2.780	2.756	2.732	2.708	2.685	2.662	2.640	2.618	2.596	2.575	2.554	2.533	2.513
10	2.723	2.700	2.678	2.656	2.634	2.613	2.591	2.571	2.550	2.530	2.510	2.490	2.471	2.451	2.433
11	2.621	2.600	2.580	2.560	2.540	2.520	2.501	2.482	2.463	2.444	2.426	2.408	2.390	2.372	2.355
12	2.523	2.504	2.486	2.467	2.449	2.431	2.414	2.396	2.379	2.362	2.345	2.329	2.312	2.296	2.280
13	2.428	2.411	2.395	2.378	2.362	2.346	2.330	2.314	2.298	2.282	2.267	2.252	2.237	2.222	2.207
14	2.337	2.322	2.307	2.292	2.277	2.263	2.248	2.234	2.220	2.206	2.192	2.178	2.164	2.150	2.137
15	2.253	2.236	2.223	2.209	2.196	2.183	2.170	2.157	2.144	2.131	2.118	2.106	2.093	2.081	2.068
16	2.253	2.225	2.198	2.172	2.146	2.122	2.097	2.083	2.071	2.059	2.048	2.036	2.025	2.014	2.002
17	2.253	2.225	2.198	2.172	2.146	2.122	2.097	2.073	2.050	2.027	2.005	1.983	1.962	1.949	1.938
18	2.253	2.225	2.198	2.172	2.147	2.121	2.097	2.073	2.050	2.027	2.005	1.983	1.962	1.941	1.920
19	2.253	2.225	2.198	2.172	2.146	2.122	2.097	2.073	2.050	2.027	2.005	1.983	1.962	1.941	1.920
20	2.253	2.226	2.198	2.172	2.147	2.122	2.097	2.073	2.050	2.027	2.005	1.983	1.962	1.941	1.920
21	2.253	2.225	2.198	2.172	2.146	2.121	2.097	2.073	2.050	2.027	2.005	1.983	1.962	1.941	1.920
22	2.253	2.226	2.198	2.172	2.147	2.122	2.097	2.073	2.050	2.027	2.005	1.983	1.961	1.941	1.920
23	2.253	2.225	2.198	2.172	2.146	2.121	2.097	2.073	2.050	2.027	2.005	1.983	1.962	1.941	1.920
24	2.253	2.226	2.198	2.172	2.147	2.122	2.097	2.073	2.050	2.027	2.005	1.983	1.961	1.941	1.920
25	2.253	2.225	2.198	2.172	2.146	2.121	2.097	2.073	2.050	2.027	2.005	1.983	1.962	1.941	1.920
26	2.253	2.226	2.198	2.172	2.147	2.122	2.097	2.073	2.050	2.027	2.005	1.983	1.961	1.941	1.920
27	2.253	2.225	2.198	2.172	2.146	2.121	2.097	2.073	2.050	2.027	2.004	1.983	1.962	1.940	1.920
28	2.253	2.225	2.198	2.172	2.147	2.122	2.097	2.073	2.050	2.027	2.004	1.983	1.961	1.940	1.920
29	2.253	2.226	2.199	2.172	2.146	2.121	2.097	2.073	2.050	2.027	2.004	1.983	1.962	1.941	1.920
30	2.253	2.225	2.198	2.172	2.147	2.121	2.097	2.073	2.050	2.027	2.005	1.983	1.961	1.940	1.920
31	2.253	2.226	2.198	2.172	2.146	2.122	2.097	2.073	2.050	2.027	2.005	1.983	1.962	1.941	1.920
32	2.253	2.225	2.199	2.172	2.147	2.121	2.097	2.074	2.050	2.027	2.004	1.983	1.961	1.940	1.920
33	2.253	2.226	2.198	2.172	2.146	2.122	2.097	2.073	2.050	2.027	2.004	1.982	1.962	1.941	1.920
34	2.253	2.226	2.199	2.172	2.147	2.121	2.098	2.074	2.050	2.027	2.005	1.983	1.961	1.940	1.920
35	2.253	2.225	2.198	2.172	2.146	2.122	2.097	2.073	2.049	2.027	2.004	1.983	1.962	1.941	1.920
36	2.253	2.226	2.199	2.172	2.147	2.121	2.098	2.074	2.050	2.027	2.004	1.982	1.961	1.940	1.920
37	2.253	2.225	2.198	2.172	2.146	2.122	2.097	2.073	2.049	2.027	2.004	1.983	1.962	1.941	1.920
38	2.253	2.225	2.198	2.172	2.147	2.121	2.098	2.074	2.050	2.027	2.004	1.983	1.961	1.940	1.920
39	2.253	2.225	2.198	2.172	2.146	2.122	2.097	2.073	2.049	2.027	2.005	1.982	1.962	1.941	1.920
40	2.254	2.226	2.199	2.172	2.147	2.121	2.098	2.074	2.050	2.027	2.004	1.983	1.961	1.940	1.920
41	1.408	2.225	2.198	2.172	2.146	2.122	2.097	2.073	2.049	2.027	2.004	1.983	1.962	1.941	1.920
42		0.278	1.374	2.173	2.147	2.121	2.098	2.074	2.050	2.026	2.005	1.982	1.961	1.941	1.920
43				0.272	1.342	2.122	2.098	2.073	2.049	2.027	2.004	1.983	1.962	1.940	1.920
44						0.265	1.311	2.074	2.050	2.026	2.005	1.982	1.961	1.941	1.920
45								0.259	1.281	2.027	2.004	1.983	1.962	1.940	1.920
46										0.253	1.253	1.982	1.961	1.941	1.921
47												0.248	1.226	1.940	1.920
48														0.243	1.200

and the Recovery Period is:

the Depreciation Rate is:

If the Recovery Year is:	47.5	48.0	48.5	49.0	49.5	50.0
27	1.900	1.880	1.861	1.842	1.824	1.806
28	1.900	1.881	1.861	1.843	1.824	1.806
29	1.900	1.880	1.861	1.842	1.824	1.806
30	1.900	1.881	1.861	1.843	1.824	1.806
31	1.900	1.880	1.861	1.842	1.824	1.806
32	1.900	1.881	1.861	1.843	1.824	1.806
33	1.900	1.880	1.861	1.842	1.824	1.806
34	1.900	1.880	1.861	1.842	1.824	1.806
35	1.900	1.881	1.861	1.843	1.824	1.806
36	1.900	1.880	1.861	1.842	1.824	1.805
37	1.900	1.881	1.861	1.843	1.824	1.806
38	1.900	1.880	1.861	1.842	1.824	1.805
39	1.900	1.881	1.861	1.843	1.824	1.806
40	1.900	1.880	1.861	1.842	1.824	1.806
41	1.900	1.880	1.861	1.842	1.824	1.805
42	1.900	1.881	1.862	1.843	1.824	1.806
43	1.900	1.880	1.861	1.842	1.824	1.805
44	1.900	1.881	1.862	1.843	1.824	1.806
45	1.900	1.880	1.861	1.842	1.824	1.805
46	1.900	1.880	1.862	1.843	1.824	1.806
47	1.899	1.880	1.861	1.842	1.824	1.805
48	1.900	1.881	1.862	1.843	1.824	1.806
49	1.900	1.880	1.861	1.842	1.823	1.805
50	0.237	1.175	1.861	1.843	1.824	1.806
51			0.233	1.152	1.823	1.805
52					0.228	1.128

and the Recovery Period is:

the Depreciation Rate is:

If the Recovery Year is:	47.5	48.0	48.5	49.0	49.5	50.0
1	1.184	1.172	1.160	1.148	1.136	1.125
2	3.121	3.088	3.057	3.026	2.996	2.966
3	3.022	2.992	2.962	2.933	2.905	2.877
4	2.927	2.898	2.871	2.844	2.817	2.791
5	2.834	2.808	2.782	2.757	2.732	2.707
6	2.745	2.720	2.696	2.672	2.649	2.626
7	2.658	2.635	2.613	2.590	2.569	2.547
8	2.574	2.553	2.532	2.511	2.491	2.471
9	2.493	2.473	2.453	2.434	2.415	2.397
10	2.414	2.396	2.378	2.360	2.342	2.325
11	2.338	2.321	2.304	2.288	2.271	2.255
12	2.264	2.248	2.233	2.217	2.202	2.187
13	2.192	2.178	2.164	2.150	2.136	2.122
14	2.123	2.110	2.097	2.084	2.071	2.058
15	2.056	2.044	2.032	2.020	2.008	1.996
16	1.991	1.980	1.969	1.958	1.947	1.937
17	1.928	1.918	1.908	1.898	1.888	1.878
18	1.900	1.880	1.861	1.842	1.831	1.822
19	1.900	1.880	1.861	1.842	1.824	1.806
20	1.900	1.880	1.861	1.842	1.824	1.806
21	1.900	1.880	1.861	1.842	1.824	1.806
22	1.900	1.880	1.861	1.843	1.824	1.806
23	1.900	1.880	1.861	1.842	1.824	1.806
24	1.900	1.880	1.861	1.843	1.824	1.806
25	1.900	1.880	1.861	1.842	1.824	1.806
26	1.900	1.880	1.861	1.843	1.824	1.806

TABLE 18   Alternative Minimum Tax (see section 7 of this revenue procedure)
Applicable Depreciation Method: 150 Percent Declining Balance Switching to Straight Line
Applicable Recovery Periods: 2.5 - 50 years
Applicable Convention: Mid-quarter (property placed in service in fourth quarter)

and the Recovery Period is:

If the Recovery Year is:	2.5	3.0	3.5	4.0	4.5	5.0	5.5	6.0	6.5	7.0	7.5	8.0	8.5	9.0	9.5
	the Depreciation Rate is:														
1	7.50	6.25	5.36	4.69	4.17	3.75	3.41	3.13	2.88	2.68	2.50	2.34	2.21	2.08	1.97
2	55.50	46.88	40.56	35.74	31.94	28.88	26.34	24.22	22.41	20.85	19.50	18.31	17.26	16.32	15.48
3	26.91	25.00	23.18	22.34	21.30	20.21	19.16	18.16	17.24	16.39	15.60	14.88	14.21	13.60	13.03
4	10.09	21.87	22.47	19.86	17.93	16.40	15.14	14.06	13.26	12.87	12.48	12.09	11.70	11.33	10.98
5			8.43	17.37	17.93	16.41	15.14	14.06	13.10	12.18	11.41	10.75	10.16	9.65	9.24
6					6.73	14.35	15.13	14.06	13.10	12.18	11.41	10.74	10.16	9.65	9.17
7							5.68	12.31	13.10	12.19	11.41	10.75	10.16	9.64	9.17
8									4.91	10.66	11.41	10.75	10.16	9.65	9.17
9											4.28	9.40	10.17	9.64	9.17
10													3.81	8.44	9.18
11															3.44

and the Recovery Period is:

If the Recovery Year is:	10.0	10.5	11.0	11.5	12.0	12.5	13.0	13.5	14.0	14.5	15.0	15.5	16.0	16.5	17.0
	the Depreciation Rate is:														
1	1.88	1.79	1.70	1.63	1.56	1.50	1.44	1.39	1.34	1.29	1.25	1.21	1.17	1.14	1.10
2	14.72	14.03	13.40	12.83	12.31	11.82	11.37	10.96	10.57	10.21	9.88	9.56	9.27	8.99	8.73
3	12.51	12.03	11.58	11.16	10.77	10.40	10.06	9.74	9.44	9.16	8.89	8.64	8.40	8.17	7.96
4	10.63	10.31	10.00	9.70	9.42	9.15	8.90	8.66	8.43	8.21	8.00	7.80	7.61	7.43	7.25
5	9.04	8.83	8.63	8.44	8.24	8.06	7.87	7.69	7.52	7.36	7.20	7.04	6.90	6.75	6.61
6	8.72	8.31	7.96	7.63	7.33	7.09	6.96	6.84	6.72	6.60	6.48	6.36	6.25	6.14	6.03
7	8.72	8.32	7.95	7.63	7.33	7.05	6.78	6.53	6.31	6.10	5.90	5.75	5.66	5.58	5.50
8	8.72	8.31	7.96	7.62	7.33	7.05	6.78	6.53	6.31	6.10	5.90	5.72	5.54	5.38	5.22
9	8.72	8.32	7.95	7.63	7.32	7.05	6.78	6.54	6.31	6.10	5.91	5.72	5.54	5.38	5.23
10	8.71	8.31	7.96	7.62	7.33	7.05	6.78	6.53	6.31	6.10	5.90	5.72	5.54	5.38	5.22
11	7.63	8.32	7.95	7.63	7.32	7.05	6.78	6.53	6.30	6.10	5.91	5.72	5.54	5.38	5.23
12		3.12	6.96	7.62	7.33	7.05	6.78	6.54	6.31	6.09	5.90	5.73	5.55	5.38	5.22
13				2.86	6.41	7.04	6.78	6.53	6.30	6.10	5.90	5.72	5.55	5.38	5.23
14						2.64	5.94	6.54	6.31	6.09	5.91	5.72	5.54	5.38	5.23
15								2.45	5.52	6.10	5.90	5.72	5.55	5.38	5.22
16										2.29	5.17	5.72	5.54	5.37	5.23
17												2.15	4.85	5.37	5.23
18														2.02	4.57

and the Recovery Period is:

the Depreciation Rate is:

If the Recovery Year is:	17.5	18.0	18.5	19.0	19.5	20.0	20.5	21.0	21.5	22.0	22.5	23.0	23.5	24.0	24.5
1	1.07	1.04	1.01	0.99	0.96	0.938	0.915	0.893	0.872	0.852	0.833	0.815	0.798	0.781	0.765
2	8.48	8.25	8.03	7.82	7.62	7.430	7.250	7.079	6.916	6.760	6.611	6.469	6.332	6.201	6.076
3	7.75	7.56	7.38	7.20	7.03	6.872	6.720	6.573	6.433	6.299	6.170	6.047	5.928	5.814	5.704
4	7.09	6.93	6.78	6.63	6.49	6.357	6.228	6.104	5.985	5.870	5.759	5.652	5.549	5.450	5.354
5	6.48	6.35	6.23	6.11	5.99	5.880	5.772	5.668	5.567	5.469	5.375	5.284	5.195	5.110	5.027
6	5.93	5.82	5.72	5.63	5.53	5.439	5.350	5.263	5.179	5.097	5.017	4.939	4.864	4.790	4.719
7	5.42	5.34	5.26	5.18	5.11	5.031	4.958	4.887	4.817	4.749	4.682	4.617	4.553	4.491	4.430
8	5.08	4.94	4.83	4.77	4.71	4.654	4.596	4.538	4.481	4.425	4.370	4.316	4.263	4.210	4.159
9	5.08	4.94	4.81	4.69	4.57	4.458	4.352	4.252	4.169	4.124	4.079	4.034	3.991	3.947	3.904
10	5.08	4.95	4.81	4.69	4.57	4.458	4.352	4.252	4.156	4.062	3.972	3.887	3.807	3.730	3.665
11	5.08	4.94	4.82	4.69	4.57	4.458	4.352	4.252	4.156	4.062	3.972	3.888	3.807	3.729	3.655
12	5.08	4.95	4.81	4.69	4.57	4.458	4.352	4.252	4.156	4.062	3.973	3.887	3.807	3.730	3.655
13	5.08	4.94	4.82	4.69	4.57	4.458	4.352	4.252	4.155	4.062	3.972	3.888	3.807	3.729	3.655
14	5.08	4.95	4.81	4.69	4.57	4.458	4.352	4.252	4.156	4.061	3.973	3.887	3.807	3.730	3.655
15	5.08	4.94	4.82	4.69	4.57	4.458	4.352	4.252	4.155	4.062	3.972	3.888	3.806	3.729	3.655
16	5.08	4.95	4.81	4.69	4.57	4.458	4.352	4.252	4.156	4.061	3.973	3.887	3.807	3.730	3.655
17	5.08	4.94	4.82	4.68	4.57	4.458	4.353	4.252	4.155	4.062	3.972	3.888	3.806	3.729	3.655
18	5.08	4.33	4.81	4.69	4.57	4.459	4.352	4.252	4.156	4.061	3.973	3.887	3.807	3.730	3.655
19	1.90		1.81	4.68	4.57	4.458	4.353	4.252	4.155	4.062	3.972	3.888	3.806	3.729	3.655
20				4.10	1.72	4.459	4.352	4.251	4.156	4.061	3.973	3.887	3.807	3.730	3.655
21						3.901	4.353	4.252	4.155	4.062	3.972	3.888	3.806	3.729	3.655
22							1.632	3.720	4.156	4.061	3.973	3.887	3.807	3.730	3.655
23									1.558	3.554	3.972	3.888	3.806	3.729	3.655
24											1.490	3.887	3.807	3.730	3.656
25												3.402	3.806	3.729	3.655
26													1.427	3.263	1.371

and the Recovery Period is:

the Depreciation Rate is:

If the Recovery Year is:	32.0	31.5	31.0	30.5	30.0	29.5	29.0	28.5	28.0	27.5	27.0	26.5	26.0	25.5	25.0
1	0.586	0.595	0.605	0.615	0.625	0.636	0.647	0.658	0.670	0.682	0.694	0.708	0.721	0.735	0.750
2	4.660	4.734	4.809	4.888	4.969	5.052	5.139	5.229	5.321	5.417	5.517	5.620	5.728	5.839	5.955
3	4.442	4.508	4.577	4.647	4.720	4.796	4.873	4.953	5.036	5.122	5.211	5.302	5.397	5.496	5.598
4	4.233	4.293	4.355	4.419	4.484	4.552	4.621	4.693	4.766	4.842	4.921	5.002	5.086	5.172	5.262
5	4.035	4.089	4.145	4.202	4.260	4.320	4.382	4.446	4.511	4.578	4.648	4.719	4.792	4.868	4.946
6	3.846	3.894	3.944	3.995	4.047	4.101	4.155	4.212	4.269	4.329	4.389	4.452	4.516	4.582	4.649
7	3.666	3.709	3.753	3.798	3.845	3.892	3.940	3.990	4.041	4.093	4.146	4.200	4.255	4.312	4.370
8	3.494	3.532	3.572	3.612	3.653	3.694	3.737	3.780	3.824	3.869	3.915	3.962	4.010	4.059	4.108
9	3.330	3.364	3.399	3.434	3.470	3.506	3.543	3.581	3.619	3.658	3.698	3.738	3.779	3.820	3.862
10	3.174	3.204	3.234	3.265	3.296	3.328	3.360	3.393	3.426	3.459	3.492	3.526	3.561	3.595	3.630
11	3.025	3.051	3.078	3.105	3.132	3.159	3.186	3.214	3.242	3.270	3.321	3.383	3.446	3.513	3.582
12	2.883	2.906	2.929	2.952	2.994	3.043	3.095	3.148	3.204	3.262	3.321	3.382	3.446	3.513	3.582
13	2.808	2.853	2.898	2.945	2.994	3.043	3.095	3.148	3.204	3.262	3.321	3.383	3.446	3.513	3.582
14	2.808	2.853	2.898	2.945	2.994	3.043	3.095	3.148	3.204	3.262	3.321	3.382	3.446	3.513	3.582
15	2.808	2.852	2.898	2.945	2.994	3.043	3.095	3.148	3.204	3.262	3.321	3.383	3.446	3.513	3.582
16	2.809	2.853	2.898	2.946	2.994	3.043	3.095	3.148	3.204	3.262	3.321	3.382	3.446	3.513	3.583
17	2.808	2.852	2.898	2.945	2.994	3.043	3.095	3.148	3.204	3.262	3.322	3.383	3.446	3.513	3.582
18	2.809	2.853	2.898	2.946	2.994	3.043	3.095	3.149	3.204	3.262	3.321	3.382	3.446	3.513	3.583
19	2.808	2.852	2.898	2.945	2.993	3.043	3.095	3.148	3.204	3.262	3.322	3.383	3.446	3.513	3.582
20	2.809	2.852	2.898	2.946	2.994	3.044	3.095	3.149	3.204	3.262	3.321	3.382	3.446	3.513	3.583
21	2.808	2.853	2.898	2.945	2.993	3.043	3.095	3.148	3.204	3.263	3.322	3.383	3.447	3.512	3.582
22	2.809	2.852	2.898	2.946	2.994	3.044	3.095	3.149	3.204	3.262	3.321	3.382	3.446	3.513	3.583
23	2.808	2.853	2.898	2.945	2.993	3.043	3.095	3.148	3.205	3.263	3.322	3.383	3.447	3.512	3.582
24	2.809	2.852	2.898	2.946	2.994	3.044	3.095	3.149	3.204	3.263	3.321	3.382	3.446	3.513	3.583
25	2.808	2.853	2.898	2.945	2.993	3.043	3.095	3.148	3.205	3.262	3.322	3.383	3.447	3.512	3.582
26	2.809	2.852	2.898	2.946	2.994	3.044	3.095	3.149	3.204	3.263	3.321	3.382	3.446	3.513	3.135
27	2.808	2.853	2.898	2.945	2.993	3.043	3.095	3.148	3.205	3.263	3.322	3.383	3.016	1.317	
28	2.809	2.852	2.898	2.946	2.994	3.044	3.095	3.149	3.204	1.223	2.906	1.268			
29	2.808	2.853	2.899	2.945	2.993	3.043	3.094	3.148	2.804						
30	2.809	2.852	2.898	2.946	2.994	3.044	2.708	1.181							
31	2.808	2.853	2.899	2.945	2.619	1.141									
32	2.809	2.852	2.536	1.105											
33	2.457	1.070													

and the Recovery Period is:

If the Recovery Year is: / the Depreciation Rate is:

Recovery Year	32.5	33.0	33.5	34.0	34.5	35.0	35.5	36.0	36.5	37.0	37.5	38.0	38.5	39.0	39.5
1	0.577	0.568	0.560	0.551	0.543	0.536	0.528	0.521	0.514	0.507	0.500	0.493	0.487	0.481	0.475
2	4.589	4.520	4.453	4.387	4.324	4.263	4.203	4.145	4.088	4.034	3.980	3.928	3.877	3.828	3.779
3	4.377	4.314	4.253	4.194	4.136	4.080	4.025	3.972	3.920	3.870	3.821	3.773	3.726	3.680	3.636
4	4.175	4.118	4.063	4.009	3.956	3.905	3.855	3.807	3.759	3.713	3.668	3.624	3.581	3.539	3.498
5	3.982	3.931	3.881	3.832	3.784	3.738	3.692	3.648	3.605	3.563	3.521	3.481	3.441	3.403	3.365
6	3.798	3.752	3.707	3.663	3.620	3.578	3.536	3.496	3.457	3.418	3.380	3.343	3.307	3.272	3.237
7	3.623	3.582	3.541	3.501	3.462	3.424	3.387	3.350	3.315	3.280	3.245	3.212	3.178	3.146	3.114
8	3.456	3.419	3.382	3.347	3.312	3.278	3.244	3.211	3.178	3.147	3.115	3.085	3.055	3.025	2.996
9	3.296	3.263	3.231	3.199	3.168	3.137	3.107	3.077	3.048	3.019	2.991	2.963	2.936	2.909	2.882
10	3.144	3.115	3.086	3.058	3.030	3.003	2.976	2.949	2.923	2.897	2.871	2.846	2.821	2.797	2.773
11	2.999	2.974	2.948	2.923	2.898	2.874	2.850	2.826	2.802	2.779	2.756	2.734	2.711	2.689	2.668
12	2.861	2.838	2.816	2.794	2.772	2.751	2.729	2.708	2.687	2.666	2.646	2.626	2.606	2.586	2.566
13	2.766	2.725	2.690	2.671	2.652	2.633	2.614	2.595	2.577	2.558	2.540	2.522	2.504	2.486	2.469
14	2.766	2.725	2.685	2.646	2.608	2.570	2.535	2.500	2.471	2.455	2.439	2.423	2.407	2.391	2.375
15	2.766	2.725	2.685	2.646	2.607	2.571	2.535	2.500	2.467	2.433	2.401	2.370	2.339	2.310	2.285
16	2.766	2.725	2.685	2.645	2.608	2.570	2.535	2.500	2.467	2.433	2.401	2.370	2.339	2.310	2.281
17	2.766	2.725	2.685	2.646	2.607	2.571	2.535	2.500	2.467	2.433	2.401	2.370	2.339	2.310	2.281
18	2.766	2.725	2.685	2.645	2.608	2.570	2.535	2.500	2.467	2.433	2.401	2.370	2.339	2.310	2.281
19	2.766	2.725	2.685	2.646	2.607	2.571	2.535	2.500	2.466	2.433	2.401	2.370	2.340	2.310	2.281
20	2.766	2.725	2.685	2.645	2.608	2.570	2.535	2.500	2.467	2.433	2.401	2.370	2.339	2.310	2.281
21	2.766	2.725	2.685	2.646	2.607	2.571	2.535	2.500	2.466	2.433	2.401	2.370	2.340	2.310	2.281
22	2.766	2.725	2.685	2.645	2.608	2.570	2.535	2.500	2.467	2.433	2.401	2.370	2.339	2.310	2.281
23	2.766	2.725	2.685	2.646	2.607	2.571	2.535	2.500	2.466	2.433	2.401	2.370	2.340	2.310	2.281
24	2.766	2.725	2.685	2.645	2.608	2.570	2.535	2.501	2.467	2.433	2.401	2.370	2.339	2.310	2.281
25	2.766	2.725	2.685	2.646	2.607	2.571	2.535	2.500	2.467	2.433	2.401	2.370	2.340	2.310	2.281
26	2.766	2.725	2.685	2.645	2.608	2.570	2.535	2.501	2.466	2.433	2.401	2.370	2.339	2.310	2.281
27	2.766	2.725	2.685	2.646	2.607	2.571	2.535	2.500	2.467	2.433	2.401	2.370	2.340	2.310	2.281
28	2.766	2.725	2.685	2.645	2.608	2.570	2.535	2.501	2.466	2.434	2.401	2.369	2.340	2.310	2.281
29	2.766	2.724	2.685	2.646	2.607	2.571	2.535	2.500	2.467	2.433	2.401	2.370	2.339	2.310	2.281
30	2.766	2.725	2.685	2.645	2.608	2.570	2.535	2.501	2.466	2.434	2.401	2.369	2.340	2.310	2.281
31	2.766	2.725	2.685	2.646	2.607	2.571	2.535	2.500	2.467	2.433	2.401	2.370	2.339	2.310	2.281
32	2.766	2.724	2.685	2.645	2.608	2.570	2.535	2.501	2.466	2.434	2.401	2.369	2.340	2.310	2.281
33	2.766	2.725	2.684	2.646	2.607	2.571	2.535	2.500	2.467	2.433	2.402	2.370	2.339	2.310	2.281
34	1.037	2.724	2.684	2.645	2.608	2.570	2.535	2.501	2.466	2.434	2.401	2.369	2.340	2.309	2.282
35		2.384	1.007	2.646	2.607	2.571	2.535	2.500	2.467	2.433	2.402	2.370	2.339	2.310	2.281
36				2.315	0.978	2.570	2.535	2.501	2.466	2.434	2.401	2.369	2.340	2.309	2.281
37						2.249	0.950	2.500	2.467	2.433	2.402	2.370	2.339	2.310	2.282
38								2.188	0.925	2.434	2.401	2.369	2.340	2.309	2.281
39										2.129	0.901	2.370	2.339	2.310	2.281
40												2.073	0.877	2.309	2.282
41														2.021	0.856

and the Recovery Period is:

the Depreciation Rate is:

If the Recovery Year is:	47.0	46.5	46.0	45.5	45.0	44.5	44.0	43.5	43.0	42.5	42.0	41.5	41.0	40.5	40.0
1	0.399	0.403	0.408	0.412	0.417	0.421	0.426	0.431	0.436	0.441	0.446	0.452	0.457	0.463	0.469
2	3.179	3.213	3.248	3.283	3.319	3.357	3.395	3.433	3.473	3.514	3.556	3.598	3.642	3.687	3.732
3	3.077	3.109	3.142	3.175	3.209	3.243	3.279	3.315	3.352	3.390	3.429	3.468	3.509	3.550	3.592
4	2.979	3.009	3.039	3.070	3.102	3.134	3.167	3.201	3.235	3.270	3.306	3.343	3.380	3.419	3.458
5	2.884	2.912	2.940	2.969	2.998	3.028	3.059	3.090	3.122	3.155	3.188	3.222	3.257	3.292	3.328
6	2.792	2.818	2.844	2.871	2.898	2.926	2.955	2.984	3.013	3.043	3.074	3.105	3.137	3.170	3.203
7	2.703	2.727	2.751	2.776	2.802	2.828	2.854	2.881	2.908	2.936	2.964	2.993	3.023	3.053	3.083
8	2.617	2.639	2.662	2.685	2.708	2.732	2.757	2.782	2.807	2.832	2.858	2.885	2.912	2.939	2.968
9	2.533	2.554	2.575	2.596	2.618	2.640	2.663	2.686	2.709	2.732	2.756	2.781	2.805	2.831	2.856
10	2.452	2.471	2.491	2.511	2.531	2.551	2.572	2.593	2.614	2.636	2.658	2.680	2.703	2.726	2.749
11	2.374	2.392	2.410	2.428	2.447	2.465	2.484	2.504	2.523	2.543	2.563	2.583	2.604	2.625	2.646
12	2.298	2.315	2.331	2.348	2.365	2.382	2.400	2.417	2.435	2.453	2.472	2.490	2.509	2.528	2.547
13	2.225	2.240	2.255	2.271	2.286	2.302	2.318	2.334	2.350	2.367	2.383	2.400	2.417	2.434	2.451
14	2.154	2.168	2.182	2.196	2.210	2.224	2.239	2.253	2.268	2.283	2.298	2.313	2.328	2.344	2.359
15	2.085	2.098	2.110	2.123	2.136	2.149	2.162	2.176	2.189	2.203	2.216	2.230	2.243	2.257	2.271
16	2.019	2.030	2.042	2.053	2.065	2.077	2.089	2.101	2.113	2.125	2.146	2.172	2.198	2.225	2.253
17	1.954	1.965	1.975	1.986	2.005	2.027	2.050	2.073	2.097	2.122	2.146	2.172	2.198	2.225	2.253
18	1.920	1.940	1.961	1.983	2.005	2.027	2.050	2.073	2.097	2.122	2.147	2.172	2.198	2.225	2.253
19	1.920	1.940	1.961	1.983	2.005	2.027	2.050	2.073	2.097	2.121	2.146	2.172	2.198	2.225	2.253
20	1.920	1.940	1.961	1.983	2.005	2.027	2.050	2.073	2.097	2.122	2.147	2.172	2.198	2.225	2.253
21	1.920	1.940	1.961	1.983	2.005	2.027	2.050	2.073	2.097	2.121	2.146	2.172	2.198	2.225	2.253
22	1.920	1.940	1.961	1.983	2.005	2.027	2.050	2.073	2.097	2.122	2.147	2.172	2.198	2.225	2.253
23	1.920	1.940	1.961	1.983	2.005	2.027	2.049	2.073	2.097	2.121	2.146	2.172	2.198	2.225	2.253
24	1.920	1.940	1.961	1.983	2.005	2.027	2.050	2.073	2.097	2.122	2.147	2.172	2.198	2.225	2.253
25	1.920	1.940	1.961	1.983	2.005	2.027	2.049	2.073	2.097	2.121	2.146	2.172	2.198	2.225	2.253
26	1.920	1.940	1.961	1.983	2.005	2.027	2.050	2.073	2.097	2.122	2.147	2.172	2.198	2.225	2.252
27	1.920	1.940	1.962	1.983	2.005	2.027	2.049	2.073	2.097	2.121	2.146	2.172	2.198	2.225	2.253
28	1.920	1.940	1.961	1.983	2.004	2.027	2.050	2.073	2.097	2.122	2.147	2.172	2.198	2.225	2.252
29	1.920	1.940	1.961	1.983	2.005	2.027	2.049	2.073	2.097	2.121	2.146	2.172	2.198	2.225	2.253
30	1.920	1.941	1.962	1.983	2.004	2.027	2.050	2.073	2.097	2.122	2.147	2.172	2.198	2.225	2.252
31	1.920	1.940	1.961	1.983	2.005	2.027	2.049	2.073	2.097	2.121	2.146	2.172	2.198	2.225	2.253
32	1.920	1.940	1.962	1.983	2.004	2.027	2.050	2.073	2.097	2.122	2.147	2.172	2.198	2.225	2.252
33	1.920	1.940	1.961	1.983	2.005	2.027	2.049	2.073	2.097	2.121	2.146	2.172	2.198	2.225	2.253
34	1.920	1.941	1.962	1.983	2.004	2.027	2.050	2.073	2.097	2.122	2.147	2.172	2.198	2.225	2.252
35	1.920	1.940	1.961	1.983	2.004	2.027	2.049	2.073	2.097	2.121	2.146	2.172	2.198	2.225	2.253
36	1.920	1.941	1.962	1.983	2.005	2.027	2.050	2.073	2.097	2.122	2.147	2.172	2.198	2.225	2.252
37	1.920	1.940	1.961	1.983	2.004	2.027	2.049	2.073	2.097	2.121	2.146	2.172	2.198	2.225	2.253
38	1.920	1.941	1.962	1.983	2.005	2.027	2.050	2.073	2.097	2.122	2.147	2.172	2.198	2.225	2.252
39	1.920	1.940	1.961	1.983	2.004	2.027	2.049	2.073	2.097	2.121	2.146	2.172	2.199	2.224	2.253
40	1.920	1.941	1.962	1.982	2.005	2.027	2.050	2.073	2.097	2.122	2.147	2.172	2.199	2.224	2.252
41	1.920	1.940	1.961	1.983	2.004	2.027	2.049	2.073	2.097	2.121	2.146	2.172	2.198	2.225	1.971
42	1.920	1.941	1.962	1.982	2.005	2.027	2.050	2.073	2.097	2.122	2.147	2.172	1.924	0.834	
43	1.919	1.940	1.961	1.983	2.004	2.027	2.049	2.073	2.097	2.121	1.878	0.814			
44	1.920	1.941	1.962	1.982	2.005	2.027	2.050	2.073	1.834	0.796					
45	1.920	1.940	1.961	1.983	2.004	2.027	1.793	0.777							
46	1.920	1.941	1.962	1.982	1.754	0.760									
47	1.919	1.940	1.716	0.743											
48	1.680	0.728													

and the Recovery Period is:

the Depreciation Rate is:

If the Recovery Year is:	47.5	48.0	48.5	49.0	49.5	50.0
1	0.395	0.391	0.387	0.383	0.379	0.375
2	3.145	3.113	3.081	3.050	3.019	2.989
3	3.046	3.016	2.986	2.956	2.927	2.899
4	2.950	2.921	2.893	2.866	2.839	2.812
5	2.857	2.830	2.804	2.778	2.753	2.728
6	2.767	2.742	2.717	2.693	2.669	2.646
7	2.679	2.656	2.633	2.610	2.588	2.567
8	2.595	2.573	2.552	2.531	2.510	2.490
9	2.513	2.492	2.473	2.453	2.434	2.415
10	2.433	2.415	2.396	2.378	2.360	2.342
11	2.356	2.339	2.322	2.305	2.289	2.272
12	2.282	2.266	2.250	2.235	2.219	2.204
13	2.210	2.195	2.181	2.166	2.152	2.138
14	2.140	2.127	2.113	2.100	2.087	2.074
15	2.073	2.060	2.048	2.036	2.023	2.011
16	2.007	1.996	1.984	1.973	1.962	1.951
17	1.944	1.933	1.923	1.913	1.903	1.893
18	1.900	1.880	1.864	1.854	1.845	1.836
19	1.900	1.880	1.861	1.842	1.824	1.806
20	1.900	1.880	1.861	1.842	1.824	1.806
21	1.900	1.880	1.861	1.842	1.824	1.806
22	1.900	1.880	1.861	1.842	1.824	1.806
23	1.900	1.880	1.861	1.842	1.824	1.806
24	1.900	1.880	1.861	1.842	1.824	1.806
25	1.900	1.880	1.861	1.842	1.824	1.805
26	1.900	1.880	1.861	1.842	1.824	1.805

and the Recovery Period is:

the Depreciation Rate is:

If the Recovery Year is:	47.5	48.0	48.5	49.0	49.5	50.0
27	1.900	1.880	1.861	1.842	1.824	1.806
28	1.900	1.880	1.861	1.842	1.824	1.805
29	1.900	1.880	1.861	1.842	1.824	1.806
30	1.900	1.881	1.861	1.842	1.824	1.805
31	1.900	1.880	1.861	1.842	1.824	1.806
32	1.900	1.881	1.861	1.842	1.824	1.805
33	1.900	1.880	1.861	1.842	1.824	1.806
34	1.900	1.881	1.861	1.842	1.823	1.805
35	1.900	1.880	1.861	1.842	1.824	1.806
36	1.900	1.881	1.861	1.842	1.823	1.805
37	1.900	1.880	1.861	1.842	1.824	1.806
38	1.900	1.880	1.861	1.843	1.823	1.805
39	1.900	1.881	1.861	1.842	1.824	1.806
40	1.900	1.880	1.861	1.843	1.823	1.805
41	1.899	1.880	1.861	1.842	1.824	1.806
42	1.900	1.881	1.861	1.843	1.823	1.805
43	1.899	1.880	1.862	1.842	1.824	1.806
44	1.900	1.881	1.861	1.842	1.823	1.805
45	1.899	1.880	1.862	1.843	1.824	1.806
46	1.900	1.881	1.861	1.842	1.823	1.805
47	1.899	1.880	1.862	1.843	1.824	1.806
48	1.900	1.881	1.861	1.842	1.823	1.805
49	0.712	1.645	1.862	1.843	1.824	1.806
50			0.698	1.612	1.823	1.805
51					0.684	1.580

Index

About the Author

Richard M. Contino is an internationally known equipment financing expert, as well as a practicing attorney, business consultant, and businessman. He is the Managing Partner of Contino + Partners, an equipment lease and business law firm located in White Plains, New York. Prior to entering private practice, Mr. Contino held the positions, over a five-year period, of Marketing Vice President and Eastern Regional Counsel for GATX Leasing Corporation, a major independent equipment lessor and lease underwriter.

Mr. Contino is the author of three equipment lease financing books, two human potential development books, and the finance author of a business handbook. In addition to his books, he has written numerous articles and conducted seminars throughout the United States for many private corporations, business groups, law associations, and other professional organizations on the legal, financial, business, and marketing aspects of equipment leasing.

Mr. Contino received an LL.M. in corporate law from the New York University Graduate School of Law, a Juris Doctor from the University of Maryland School of Law, and a Bachelor of Aeronautical Engineering from Rensselaer Polytechnic Institute. He is a member of the bars of the State of New York, State of Maryland, and District of Columbia. Mr. Contino is also a member of the American Bar Association and is listed in *Who's Who of American Law, Who's Who of Emerging Leaders, Who's Who in the World,* and *The International Who's Who of Contemporary Achievement.*